PENGUIN CLASSICS

THE JOURNALS OF CAPTAIN COOK

JAMES COOK was born in Marton, Yorkshire, in 1728, the son of an agricultural labourer. Apprenticed to a Whitby shipowner, he joined the Navy in 1755, becoming Master in 1757. Cook led three expeditions to the Pacific Ocean. The first, from 1768 to 1771, as Lieutenant in the *Endeavour*; the second, from 1772 to 1775, as Commander in the *Resolution*, accompanied by the *Adventure*; and the last, from 1776 until his death in 1779, as Captain in the *Resolution*, accompanied by the *Discovery*. Cook did more than any other navigator to add to our knowledge of the Pacific and Southern oceans, circumnavigating and charting New Zealand, surveying and claiming the east coast of Australia, exploring the extent of Antarctica, visiting Tahiti and discovering island groups like New Caledonia and Hawaii. He died on 14 February 1779, in Hawaii, after being forced to turn back during his attempt to find a passage around the north coast of America from the Pacific. The inhabitants of the island, while friendly to begin with, killed Cook when he landed to recover a stolen boat.

Cook wrote in great detail about his voyages, to begin with for the eyes of the Admiralty, but then, having been upset by the authorized account published by Dr John Hawkesworth, with a view to his work being read by the public. His first, and only, publication, was *A Voyage Towards the South Pole and Round the World* (1777).

PHILIP EDWARDS has been a professor of English Literature at Trinity College Dublin, Essex University and Liverpool University, and has held visiting posts in the United States, Canada, New Zealand and Japan. He is now in retirement, Emeritus Professor of English at Liverpool University. He is a Fellow of the British Academy. During the Second World War he served with the Royal Navy in both the Indian and Pacific oceans.

He is the author of numerous studies on the literature of voyages, including *Last Voyage: Cavendish, Hudson, Ralegh* (1988) and *The Story of the Voyage: Sea Narratives in Eighteenth-Century England* (1994). He has also written widely on Shakespeare and the literature of his time, including *Shakespeare and the Confines of Art* (1968), *Threshold of a Nation* (1979),

Shakespeare: A Writer's Progress (1986) and *Seamark: The Metaphorical Voyage, Spenser to Milton* (1997). He has edited *Pericles* and *Hamlet*, and Kyd's *Spanish Tragedy*, and co-edited the plays of Massinger.

THE JOURNALS OF
CAPTAIN COOK

*Prepared from the original manuscripts by
J. C. Beaglehole for the Hakluyt Society, 1955–67*

Selected and edited by
PHILIP EDWARDS

PENGUIN BOOKS

PENGUIN BOOKS

Published by the Penguin Group
Penguin Books Ltd, 80 Strand, London WC2R 0RL, England
Penguin Putnam Inc., 375 Hudson Street, New York, New York 10014, USA
Penguin Books Australia Ltd, Ringwood, Victoria, Australia
Penguin Books Canada Ltd, 10 Alcorn Avenue, Toronto, Ontario, Canada M4V 3B2
Penguin Books India (P) Ltd, 11 Community Centre, Panchsheel Park, New Delhi – 110 017, India
Penguin Books (NZ) Ltd, Cnr Rosedale and Airborne Roads, Albany, Auckland, New Zealand
Penguin Books (South Africa) (Pty) Ltd, 24 Sturdee Avenue, Rosebank 2196 South Africa

Penguin Books Ltd, Registered Offices: 80 Strand, London WC2R 0RL, England

www.penguin.com

First published by Hakluyt Society 1955–67, in 4 volumes
Published in Penguin Classics 1999

5

Maps by Nigel Andrews

Set in 10/12.5 pt Monotype Baskerville
Typeset by Rowland Phototypesetting Ltd, Bury St Edmunds, Suffolk
Printed in England by Clays Ltd, St Ives plc

CONTENTS

LIST OF MAPS

GENERAL INTRODUCTION

James Cook led three famous expeditions to the Pacific Ocean: in
the *Endeavour* (as lieutenant) from 1768 to 1771; in the *Resolution* (as
commander), with the *Adventure*, from 1772 to 1775; and in the *Resolution*
again (now captain), this time with the *Discovery*, from 1776 until his
death in Hawaii in 1779. Accounts of these voyages, based on Cook's
journals, were published at the time, soon after the completion of each
voyage, but it was not until halfway through the twentieth century
that the texts of Cook's own manuscripts were made available, in a
monumental edition by John Cawte Beaglehole for the Hakluyt
Society.[1] The journal of the first voyage was published in 1955, that
of the second in 1961, that of the third in 1967. This edition is one of
the finest achievements of twentieth-century scholarship, but, running
to four large volumes, totalling 3,350 pages, and long out of print, the
original is hard to come by and second-hand copies are very expensive.
An American reprint used to be available, and this has now been
replaced by an English reprint (Boydell and Brewer, 1999), which
makes Beaglehole's full text once more accessible. Nevertheless, there
has for a long time been a real need for a shorter version of the full
edition for the general reader, and that is what the present volume,
undertaken by permission of the Hakluyt Society, sets out to meet.
The great plenitude of Beaglehole's edition, surrounding the journals
with magisterial introductions, a wealth of footnotes, appendices and
extracts from the journals of others, cannot be reproduced in this
abridgement, but the text of the journals themselves, reduced to about
one-third of their length, is Beaglehole's text, preserving Cook's own
idiosyncratic spelling and in every line giving the reader a sense of the

great seaman's presence. It is my hope that this shortened version preserves the spirit and the rhythm of Cook's narrative, and, without doubt, compression of the full texts into manageable form has advantages of its own. All omissions are clearly indicated and I have provided short narratives to cover gaps of importance. There is a new introduction to each voyage, and a Postscript in which I give my understanding of events from the point at which Cook's journal breaks off until his death.

Cook gave an enormous amount of time and labour – mostly at sea but also ashore – to writing up the story of his voyages, constantly revising and rewriting, and it was no easy matter for Beaglehole to choose, for each of the voyages, the version of the journal which was best to print. Cook kept his own log of the ship's movements and daily events (separate from the official ship's log) and from this he wrote up what he called on the first voyage the 'remarkable occurrences' – meaning of course things worthy of note, not just out-of-the-way things. On this first voyage Cook was not expecting his account to be published, but he was certainly preparing it with an audience in mind – the Admiralty, to whom he was required to report – and he often rewrote what he had first set down. Even when he had given his clerk his own revised version to copy out fair for their Lordships, he might still continue to make alterations.

What the Admiralty did with their copy of Cook's journal for the first voyage was to hand it – along with the journals of Byron, Wallis and Carteret from earlier expeditions – to Dr John Hawkesworth to prepare an authorized history of recent voyages. Cook did not see Hawkesworth's three volumes, published in 1773, until he was at the Cape of Good Hope in 1775, near to the end of his second voyage. He was deeply upset by the freedom Hawkesworth had taken with his work, altering and omitting what he had written and supplying him with sentiments he had never expressed, and making a prodigious profit into the bargain. Even if the thought that he might be the author of his own story had crossed his mind before, it would seem that from then on he was quite determined that he should be in charge of the authorized account, and, to judge from the extant manuscripts, the amount of writing and rewriting now undertaken by this unlettered

seaman to provide an account of his second voyage satisfying to him
and suitable for the public was extraordinary. Cook won from the
Admiralty the permission to publish, and took his manuscript to Canon
John Douglas to be edited, being careful to explain in the preface that
he had 'not had the advantage of much school education', having
been mostly at sea since his youth.

Cook was at sea again, on his third voyage, before *A Voyage Towards
the South Pole and Round the World*, his first and only publication, appeared
in 1777. He never saw it. What he was writing, however, as the journal
of this third voyage was from the very first intended as a literary,
publishable account of his doings, and it is the worse for it, in terms
of immediacy and vitality. His premature death meant that this journal,
unlike its predecessors, was never revised and rewritten, and this at
least simplified Beaglehole's task of choosing his text.

What Beaglehole was able to present over the years of his labours,
and what this abridged version preserves, is a majestic story of epic
proportions of three expeditions to the Pacific Ocean in converted
Whitby colliers, ranging from the Antarctic Circle to the Arctic Sea,
which negotiated and charted for the first time ever the entire coast
of New Zealand and the eastern coast of Australia, brought into view
innumerable islands not previously known in the west, and provided
far and away the fullest and most intimate account of the life of the
inhabitants of Tahiti, the Tonga islands, New Zealand and elsewhere,
besides bringing back to Europe an unrivalled access of knowledge in
natural history – a sphere in which Cook saw himself as no expert.

The story in these pages is Cook's story, written in his own hand,
stamped with the clumsiness of the 'plain man' he called himself, but
radiating in every line the ambition, determination, control, courage,
seamanship, knowledge and skill which enabled him to carry through
an unrivalled series of explorations in dangerous waters. It is Cook's
story, the story of these voyages as *he* wanted them to be known. He
recorded what he chose to record, and he recorded it as he saw it.
There are very many examples of Cook's careful revision of his
accounts of awkward moments – the best-known being his reworking
of the account of the fatal shooting of 'two or three' Maoris in Poverty
Bay at the time of first contact (9 October 1769). It is important to

emphasize this seemingly obvious point in an edition which does not have the space to fill in gaps and provide contrasting viewpoints from other observers. Beaglehole's full edition provides this corrective view to some extent, though it has to be said that Beaglehole's loyalty to his hero was so intense that he hardly ever saw Cook as biased or unfair or just wrong. Later generations are less reverential, and it does no harm to Cook's great qualities and achievements to recognize that he was human enough to be concerned with his image. If he ever doubted the wisdom of his judgements and decisions it does not appear from his journals. An important study by Sir James Watt published in 1979 showed that in spite of his quite admirable concern for ship hygiene, Cook constantly overemphasized the healthiness of his crews and the effectiveness of his dietary methods to combat scurvy.[2]

Something to remember also in reading these journals is the question of hindsight. Obviously, by the time he was revising his journal or preparing a copy for their lordships in London and whatever other audience he might have in mind, Cook knew what the consequence was of any decision he might have made, and what the outcome was of any crisis confronting him. It is different on the third voyage, of course, but there too it is clear that the journal is looking back, even though over a few days only. It would not appear that Cook ever saw the presence of a double point of view – that of immediate observation and that of subsequent knowledge – as a literary problem. The nature of the journal as he saw it demanded that things were recorded as they happened. If there is reshaping of the record after the event, it is done silently. There is only one little tell-tale sign that when he was writing up the separation of the *Adventure* from the *Resolution* in October 1773, on the second voyage, and his anxiety about her fate, he had actually heard her story and knew that she was safe.

It has been my wish in making this abridgement to try to preserve the wholeness of Cook's daily entries, with their conjunction of routine sailing matters and unusual incidents, rather than present a disconnected string of the more exciting moments. When a day's entry is abbreviated, the omission is noted with four dots (. . . .). More substantial omissions are marked by a row of asterisks.

It will be noted that Beaglehole's text makes frequent use of square brackets, within which letters, a word, a phrase or a bearing are supplied. Beaglehole does not specify in each particular case where the supplied material comes from. Mostly (and particularly in the second voyage) he is providing names or figures from other MSS to fill gaps which Cook had left in his text. But often what Beaglehole is doing is correcting Cook's slips and mistakes. I can't help feeling that many of these 'slips' were not slips at all but just the way Cook wrote and spoke. We should certainly be more cautious these days about insisting on such readings as 'load[ed]', 'bring[ing]', 'dire[c]tly', 'c[h]annel' and 'the best [of] our way'. I have only rarely overruled Beaglehole: to prefer 'leward' to 'le[e]ward', for example, and to preserve the strange 'notwithstand', given as 'notwithstand[ing]'.[3] It is evident that Beaglehole became less eager to interfere with Cook's 'mistakes' in his text of the second and third voyages. On very rare occasions I am responsible for what is supplied within the square brackets, usually to simplify a textual difficulty which has spilled over into Beaglehole's footnotes.

In order to reduce what would otherwise be a very large number of footnotes, I have provided three appendices. Firstly there is a Glossary which offers help with the sailing terms, obsolete words and foreign phrases which Cook has used. Next there is an index of persons, giving brief information about the dramatis personae of the voyages, both the ships' companies and the islanders, as well as the grandees after whom Cook named innumerable capes, bays and islands. The cross-references in this index should help to sort out the confusions which arise from Cook's attempts to transcribe what he understood to be the names of the people he had commerce with in the islands and territories he visited. Finally there is an index of places, where again the cross-references may help to clarify the complications of multiple names. There are names given by Cook, names which Cook wrongly thought were indigenous names (Tanna or Tana is a fine example), correct indigenous names and current modern names. The comparatively few footnotes which are provided generally derive from Beaglehole, but when an opinion or specialist knowledge seems to require an originator I indicate the source as [B] for Beaglehole or [E] for Edwards.

It was not feasible to reproduce the wealth of maps provided by Beaglehole. There were far too many for this compact edition, and the intricate details of the ships' tracks, combined with a lack of distinction between land and sea, often made the maps hard to read. For this edition world maps have been prepared to show in clear outline the progress of each voyage, with more detailed maps of the main centres of interest. When a territory was visited a number of times by Cook, and on different voyages, as were Tahiti, Tonga and New Zealand, only the single map is provided.

NOTES

1. J. C. Beaglehole, CMG, OM (1901–71) was born in Wellington, New Zealand, and studied at Victoria University College before coming to England for his PhD. He eventually became Professor of British Commonwealth History at Victoria University, Wellington. The conclusion of his great labours on Pacific exploration and Cook's journals was his *Life of Captain James Cook*, which was virtually complete at the time he died. It was published in 1974.

2. Sir James Watt, 'Medical Aspects and Consequences of Cook's Voyages', in *Captain James Cook and his Times*, eds. R. Fisher and H. Johnston (1979), 129–57.

3. It is an interesting question whether Cook's constant omission of the final -ed when he is giving the past tense of verbs ending in -d (such as load, intend, proceed) is just carelessness or indicates his speech habits.

THE FIRST VOYAGE
1768–1771

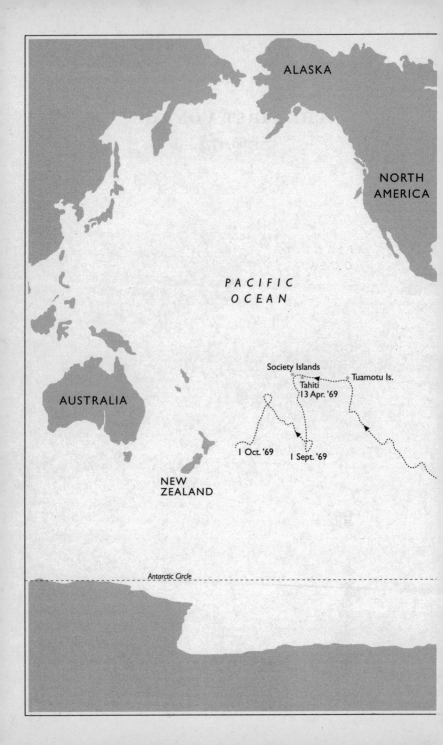

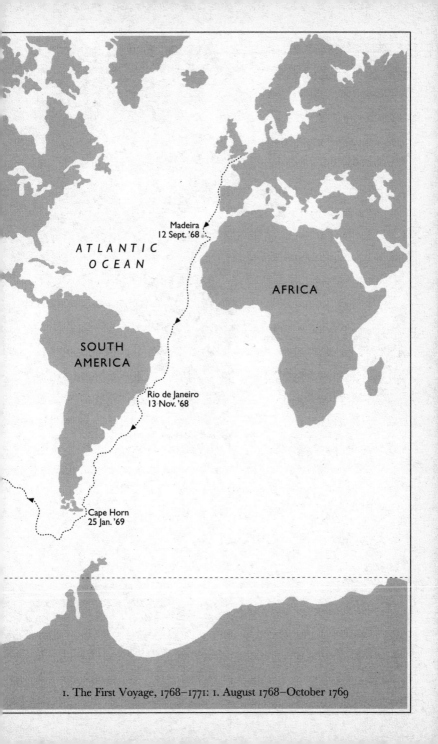

ATLANTIC
OCEAN

AFRICA

SOUTH
AMERICA

Madeira
12 Sept. '68

Rio de Janeiro
13 Nov. '68

Cape Horn
25 Jan. '69

1. The First Voyage, 1768–1771: 1. August 1768–October 1769

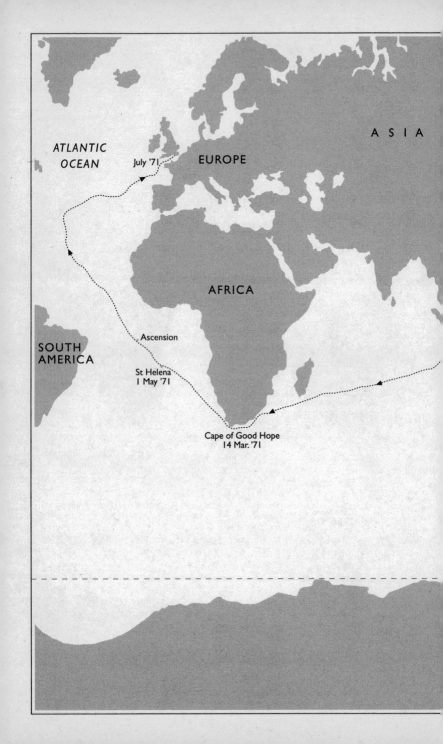

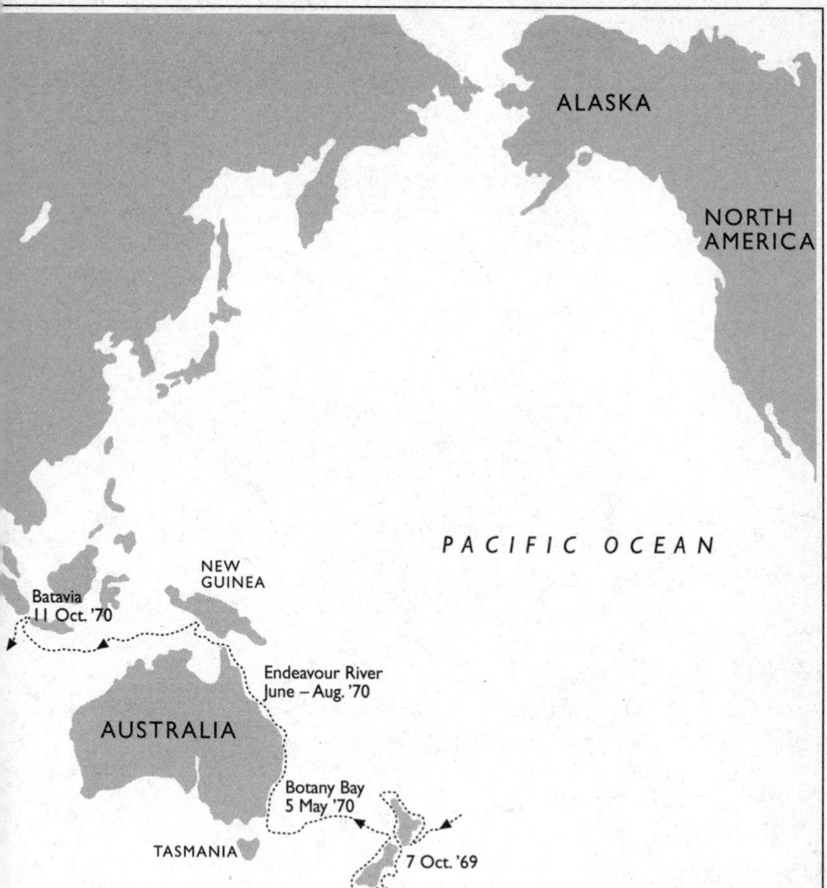

ALASKA

NORTH
AMERICA

PACIFIC OCEAN

NEW
GUINEA

Batavia
11 Oct. '70

Endeavour River
June – Aug. '70

AUSTRALIA

Botany Bay
5 May '70

TASMANIA

7 Oct. '69

NEW
ZEALAND

Antarctic Circle

2. The First Voyage, 1768–1771: 2. October 1769–July 1771

INTRODUCTION

Cook's three voyages, from 1768 to 1780, were the culmination of centuries of European interest in the Pacific. There was much more to be done, of course, by his immediate successors, Vancouver and Flinders, for example, and later generations, but Cook's work opened up vast areas that had only been tentatively probed before and charted them with extraordinary accuracy. After Magellan's daring voyage round South America and across to the Philippines (1519–21), the magnet of Pacific exploration was *Terra Australis Incognita*, the great southern continent supposed to lie between the Cape of Good Hope and the Straits of Magellan. Álvaro de Mendaña, the Spanish voyager, sailed from Callao in Peru in 1567 and reached the Solomon Islands. It was not until 1595 that he went back, with Pedro Fernández de Quirós, found the Marquesas and got as far as the Santa Cruz Islands. Quirós went out from Callao in 1605 with the Portuguese Luiz de Vaez de Torres and believed he had found the continent when they reached Vanuatu (the New Hebrides), which Quirós called 'Austrialia del Espiritu Santo' – managing a compliment to Philip III of Spain who was Archduke of Austria. Quirós and Torres now split: Quirós went north-east to California, while Torres went north-west through the strait named after him, discovering that New Guinea was an island, but failing to see Australia.

The English circumnavigations by Drake (1577–80) and Cavendish (1586–8) were not rich in discoveries. The Dutch merchant Isaac le Maire, with Willem Corneliszoon Schouten, reached the Pacific in 1615 via Cape Horn (which they named) but had no luck with the missing continent before reaching Batavia in 1616. Sailing from there, the Dutch had made several sightings of the coast of Australia, north, west and south, in the early seventeenth century, and Anthony van Diemen, governor-general of the Dutch East Indies from 1631 to 1645, was responsible for a number of expeditions, of which the most important was that of Abel Janszoon Tasman with Frans Jacobszoon Visscher, which left Batavia in August 1642. Tasmania was reached (Van Diemen's Land), then the south island of New Zealand where four men were killed, followed by the Tonga group and Fiji. Much later, another Dutch expedition, under Jacob Roggeveen, left the Netherlands in 1721 in search of the southern continent. Roggeveen went through the Strait of Le Maire and found Easter Island and Samoa before reaching Batavia after a year's voyage.

The English had now come strongly on the scene, with the expeditions of Narborough up the South American coast (1669–71), a mixed assembly of buccaneers, adventurers and privateers, including Dampier, Wafer, Cowley, Ringrose, Woodes Rogers and Shelvocke, followed by the grand naval expedition of 1740–44 under Anson. As far as discoveries go, the most important of these men was the remarkable amateur William Dampier, whose painfully assembled *New Voyage Round the World* (1697) set alight the imagination of eighteenth-century England. On this first voyage Dampier had touched on Australia (New Holland), 'a very large Tract of Land', and had thought the inhabitants 'the miserablest People in the World'. He returned on his second voyage but was only able to make a cursory investigation of the north-western and northern coasts.

The major period of English exploration in the Pacific followed the ending of the Seven Years War with France in 1763. The Earl of Egmont, First Lord of the Admiralty from 1763 until 1766, sent out John Byron in the *Dolphin* in 1764, and on its return from a speedy circumnavigation in 1766, sent the ship out again under Samuel Wallis, with Philip Carteret in the *Swallow* as consort. Wallis and Carteret were separated. Wallis went on to find Tahiti, unknown to Europeans. He named it King George's Island and his five-week visit had an importance for Europeans and Polynesians that is hard to measure. Carteret struggled on alone, and made many important discoveries, including Pitcairn. At this very time the French expedition in *La*

Boudeuse and *L'Étoile* under the great Louis-Antoine de Bougainville was making its way through the Pacific, reaching Tahiti, *la nouvelle Cythère*, hard on Wallis's heels.

However important these voyages were for geographical knowledge and the advancement of science – and Bougainville with his naturalist Commerson were deeply concerned with the advancement of science – all these expeditions by the competing European powers of Spain, France and Britain were undertaken for the control of new territory for commercial exploitation and strategic use. The scientific element was very much to the fore, however, in the next British expedition. The Royal Society, which in the hundred years of its existence had always regarded voyages to distant lands as a vital source of scientific information, was making plans for a voyage to the Pacific to observe the transit of Venus across the sun in 1769. The observations were needed to help establish the distance of the earth from the sun, and it was necessary for observers to be stationed at different points on the earth's surface. The planet had crossed the sun in 1761, but the observations world-wide were unsatisfactory. The phenomenon would not occur again for over a hundred years.

In 1767 the Royal Society recommended Alexander Dalrymple to lead the expedition. He was an energetic and imaginative thirty year old who had spent much time in Madras and was a keen advocate of English commercial expansion, as well as a firm believer in the possibilities of the great southern continent. He was a skilled navigator but had comparatively little experience of command at sea. His idea was that he should command the expedition and that he should have a master to sail the ship. This was Bougainville's position, and the practice was common in England in Tudor times. But the Royal Society knew that it depended on the Royal Navy to transport its observers to the Pacific and the Navy was totally opposed to a divided command. James Cook, thirty-nine years of age, a master in the Navy engaged on the survey of Newfoundland, was proposed by the Navy, and during April and May 1768 it was agreed that he should become leader of the expedition.

Cook was born on 27 October 1728 in the village of Marton-in-Cleveland in Yorkshire. His parents were humble enough, his father being a day labourer who became a farm-foreman at nearby Great Ayton. Cook got an education at the village school, and, after a time as apprentice in a shop in Staithes on the coast, at the age of seventeen became apprentice to the Quaker ship-owner and coal-shipper, John Walker of Whitby. For nine years Cook was engaged in the coal trade from Whitby, sailing in the broad-bottomed or 'cat-built' colliers which were later to become the ships he went round the world in. He was eventually offered his own command, but he made the rather surprising decision to transfer to the Royal Navy in 1755. Being an older, experienced and skilled seaman, he won quick promotion, first as master's mate and then after two years as master. It was in the *Pembroke*, and then the *Northumberland*, engaged in the French war in the St Lawrence, that he built up his formidable reputation as surveyor and chart-maker. He had become a good mathematician and was a skilled navigator, and after the war was engaged in a prolonged naval survey of Newfoundland – including accurate observations of a solar eclipse, and calculations of longitude, which were communicated to the Royal Society and published in *Philosophical Transactions*.

Cook was married in 1762 to Elizabeth Batts, and was the father of two sons and a daughter by the time the question of his appointment to the Pacific expedition arose. That appointment, considering the extraordinary commendations that Cook had received for his skill, competence and reliability, was no surprise. The decision was made, and the invitation accepted, during April 1768, and on 25 May Cook was promoted to the rank of lieutenant, and put in command of His Majesty's Bark, the *Endeavour*. The ship had been bought in March; she was then the *Earl of Pembroke*, a strong Whitby collier nearly four years old, cat-built, with a bluff rounded bow, 106 feet long overall. Much had to be done to the ship at Deptford, 'sheathing' her (adding an outer skin as protection against tropical worm), providing her with guns, overhauling her masts and rigging, and generally fitting her out for a long expedition. The agreed complement, including twelve marines, was eighty-five. Cook's officers were Zachary Hicks, John Gore (who had been round the world in the *Dolphin* with both Byron and Wallis) and Robert Molyneux (master). The master's mates included Richard Pickersgill and Charles Clerke, both of them *Dolphin* men;

Clerke was second lieutenant on Cook's second voyage, and in command of the *Discovery* on the third voyage, moving to the *Resolution* and taking over the expedition on Cook's death. The surgeon was William Brougham Monkhouse, from Penrith in Cumberland; his brother Jonathan was one of the midshipmen. Neither of them reached home, victims of the infamous Batavia fever at the end of the voyage. John Edgcumbe was sergeant of the marines, moving to lieutenant in the second voyage. The carpenter, a man of first importance, was John Satterley, and the cook, popular and competent despite having lost his right hand, was John Thompson.

First among the supernumeraries, and in the eyes of many in England first in the entire expedition, was Joseph Banks, a rich man and a Fellow of the Royal Society although only twenty-five years of age. He had shown his eagerness for the development of natural science at Oxford, and had been in Newfoundland and Labrador collecting plants and insects. He was responsible for bringing Daniel Carl Solander, Swedish pupil of Linnaeus. The assistant naturalist was another Swede, Herman Diedrich Spöring. The astronomer was Charles Green, formerly an assistant of Nevil Maskelyne, the Astronomer Royal. The two artists were Sydney Parkinson and Alexander Buchan, neither of whom survived the voyage.

A matter of first importance was settled when on 20 May Wallis returned in the *Dolphin* with news of the discovery of King George's Island – Tahiti, and thenceforward that was to be the station for observing the transit of Venus. Cook's instructions from the Admiralty fell into two parts. The first related to King George's Island, observing the transit, cultivating friendship with the inhabitants and charting the island. The second, marked secret, instructed him to explore for the southern continent, and 'with the Consent of the Natives to take possession of Convenient Situations in the Country in the Name of the King of Great Britain', or, if the country was uninhabited, to 'take Possession for His Majesty'. If he failed to find the continent he was to make a thorough survey of New Zealand, and to chart and take possession of any hitherto undiscovered islands. The object which he was always to have in view, however, was 'the Discovery of the Southern Continent'.

The *Endeavour* left Plymouth on 26 August 1768. She called at Madeira, for wine, and at Rio de Janeiro, where she was met with a suspicion and a lack of respect that deeply angered Cook. Following his instructions, Cook went into the Pacific via Cape Horn, passed through the Tuamotu Islands and reached Tahiti on 13 April 1769 – seven weeks before the transit was due. The ship was anchored in Matavai Bay and Cook immediately organized the setting up of a fort and erecting the portable observatory containing the instruments provided by the Royal Society. There was some anxiety about the observations when the time came, because a 'dusky shade' round the planet created difficulty over the precise moments of entry and exit. But although there was scepticism in some quarters in England about the value of the results, the observations were accurate and they played their part in the calculations which were eventually made.

Carrying out the second part of his instructions Cook made his way to New Zealand, and his brilliant mapping of the entire coast of the two islands proved conclusively that the country was not the northern tip of the undiscovered and undiscoverable continent. Cook made his own decision to return home via the unknown eastern coast of New Holland, and on 11 June 1770 the ship was trapped within the Great Barrier Reef and holed. Saving the ship, repairing her and getting her outside the reefs again must stand as Cook's greatest feat of seamanship. It is the saddest sequel to his efforts that while the ship was in dock at Batavia (Jakarta), fever broke out, and before the ship reached the Cape of Good Hope thirty men had died. On 13 July 1771, the *Endeavour* anchored in the Downs, off the Kent coast.

The manuscript of the journal used by Beaglehole and reprinted in abridged form here is one of several copies. It is in Cook's own hand, and is (wrote Beaglehole) 'the product of a great deal of writing, drafting and re-drafting, summarizing and expanding, with afterthoughts both of addition and deletion'. Cook clearly had Banks's journal close at hand as he was writing, and he made use of it on a number of occasions. The manuscript is known as the Canberra MS, after its present location.

JOURNAL OF THE
FIRST VOYAGE
1768–1771

REMARKABLE OCCURENCES ON BOARD HIS
MAJESTYS BARK ENDEAVOUR

[1768]

FRIDAY May 27*th* to FRIDAY July 29*th*.[1] Moderate and fair weather, at 11 am hoisted the Pendant and took charge of the Ship agreeable to my Commission of the 25th Instant, She lying in the Bason in Deptford Yard. From this day to the 21st of July we were constantly employed in fitting the Ship takeing on board stores and Provisions &c^a when we saild from Deptford and anchor'd in Gallions reach where we remain'd until the 30th. . . .

SATURDAY July 30*th* to SUNDAY August 7*th*. Wiegh'd from Gallions with the wind at W and made sail down the River, the same day anchor'd at Gravesend, and the next morning wiegh'd from thence and at Noon Anchor'd at the Buoy of the Fairway. On Wednesday 3rd of Augt Anchor'd in the Downs in 9 fathom water, Deal Castle NWBW. On Sunday the 7th I Joined the Ship, discharged the Pilot and the next Day sail'd for Plymouth.

1. NOTE ON THE DATING: the dating of the Journal is according to 'ship time', by which the twenty-four hour day begins twelve hours before the day of civil time, and runs from noon to noon. Cook's p.m. therefore precedes his a.m., and his a.m. alone is identical with civil a.m. Thus his Friday, May 27 (with which the Journal opens) corresponds with civil Thursday, May 26 p.m. and civil Friday, May 27 a.m.; his Saturday begins on civil Friday afternoon; and so on. At Tahiti, as he explains, he abandons this convention for civil time, reverting thereafter to ship time for the rest of the voyage. [B]

*   *   *

SUNDAY 14*th*. Fine breezes at NE and clear weather. At ½ past 8 pm Anchor'd in the entrance of Plym° Sound in 9 fathom water. At 4 am Weigh'd and worked into proper anchoring ground and anchor'd in 6 fathom the Mewstone SE, Mount Batten NNE½E and Draks Island NBW. Dispatched an express to London for M[r] Banks and D[r] Solander to join the ship, their Servants and baggage being already on board.[2]

*   *   *

TUESDAY 16*th*. Winds from SSE to NE. First part Moderate and hazey Middle hard Squalls with rain, the latter Moderate and fair. Received on board a Supply of Bread Beer & Water, a Serj[t] Corp[l] a Drummer and Nine Private Marines as part of the Compliment.

WEDNESDAY 17*th*. *Winds SE to EBS.* Little wind Easterly and hazey weather. Sent some Cordage to the Yard in order to be exchanged for smaller. Several Ship wrights and Joiners from the Yard Employ'd on board refiting the Gentlemens Cabbins and making a Platform over the Tiller &c[a].

*   *   *

FRIDAY 19*th*. Winds from NW to SW. Former part little wind with rain remainder fair weather, AM Read to the Ships Company the articles of War and the Act of Parliament,[3] they likewise were paid two Months Wages in advance. I also told them that they were not to expect any additional pay for the performance of our intended Voyage, they were well satisfied and express'd great chearfullness and readyness to prosecute the Voyage. Received on board another supply of Provisions, Rum etc[a].

*   *   *

FRIDAY 26*th*. *Winds NBW, NW, WBS. Course S 21° E. Distce 23 M[t] Latd in 49°30'. Longd in West from Greenwich 5°52' W. Bearings at Noon Lizard*

2. Banks and Solander joined the ship on the day she sailed, 26 August.
3. The Articles of War were contained within the Act of Parliament which described all laws for the government of His Majesty's ships at sea, relating particularly to conduct, discipline and punishment.

N 21° *W. Dist.* 23 *miles*. First part fresh breeze and Clowdy, remainder little wind and Clear. At 2 pm got under sail and put to sea having on board 94 persons including Officers Seamen Gentlemen and their servants, near 18 months provisions, 10 Carriage guns 12 Swivels with good store of Ammunition and stores of all kinds. At 8 the Dodman point wnw Dist^t 4 or 5 Leagues. At 6 am the Lizard bore wnw½w 5 or 6 Leagues Dist^t. At Noon sounded and had 50 fathoms Grey sand with small stones and broken shells.

*   *   *

[SEPTEMBER 1768]

THURSDAY *1st. Winds Westerly. Course S* 70° *W. Distce* 20 *M. Latd in* 44°56′. *Longd in West from Greenwich* 9°9′ *W. Bearings at Noon Lizd N* 28°15′ *D.* 109 *leagues*. Very hard gales with some heavy showers of rain the most part of these 24 hours which brought us under our two courses, broke one of our Main topmast Puttock plates, Washed over board a small boat belonging to the Boatswain and drown'd between 3 and 4 Doz^n of our Poultry which was worst of all, towards Noon it moderated so that we could bear our Main topsail close reef'd. At Midnight Wore and stood to the Southward.

FRIDAY *2nd. Winds WBN, West, SW, WSW. Course SBW. Distce* 64 *M. Latd in* 43°53′. *Longd in West from Greenwich* 9°26′ *W. Bearings at Noon Lizd NNE D.* 130 *leagues*. Fresh gales and clowdy the most part of these 24 hours. PM got up the spare Mainsail to dry it being wet by the water geting into the sail room, occassiond by the Ship being very leaky in her upper works. At 5 am loosed 2 reefs out of each topsail and saw the land which we judged to be between Cape Finister and Cape Ortegal. At 10 Tacked being about 4 Miles off shore and stood to the NW. Loosed all the reefs out and set topg^t sails. At Noon Cape Ortegal bore EBS distant about 8 Leagues.

*   *   *

MONDAY *12th. Winds NNW. Course S* 40° *W. Distce in miles* 102. *Latd in* 32°43′. *Longd in West from Greenwich* 15°53′. Moderate breeze and fine clear weather. At 6 AM the Island of Porto Santo bore NWBW, Dist^{ce}

9 or 10 Leagues. Hauld the wind to the westward. At Noon the Desertas extending from wsw to swbs, the body of Madiera w¹⁄₂s and Porto Santo nnw¹⁄₂w. Lat^d obser'd 32°43′n.

TUESDAY 13*th. Winds N, Westerly. Moor'd in Fenchal Road, Island of Madeira.* Fresh breeze and clear weather. At 8 pm anchor'd in Fenchal Road in 22 fathom water. Found here His Majestys Ship Rose and several Merchant Vessels. In the morning new birthed the Ship and Moor'd with Stream Anch^r half a Cable on the best bower and a Hawser and a half on the Stream.

WEDNESDAY 14*th. Winds Easterly.* First part fine clear weather, remainder Clowdy with squalls from the land attended with showers of rain. In the night the bend of the Hawsers of the stream Anchor slip'd, owing to the carelesness of the person who made it fast. In the morning hove up the Anchor in the Boat and carried it out to the Southward, in heaving the Anchor out of the Boat Mr Weir Masters mate was carried over board by the Buoy-rope and to the bottom with the anchor. Hove up the anchor by the Ship as soon as possible and found his body intangled in the Buoy-rope. Moor'd the ship with the two Bowers in 22 fathom water, the Loo Rock w and the Brazen head e Saild his Majestys ship Rose. The Boats imploy'd carrying the casks ashore for Wine and the caulkers caulking the Ships sides.

THURSDAY 15*th. Winds NE to SE.* Squalls of Wind from the land with rain the most part of these 24 hours. Rec'd on board fresh Beef and Greens for the Ships Compney and sent on shore all our Casks for wine and Water having a shore boat employ'd for that purpose.

FRIDAY 16*th. Winds Easterly.* The most part fine clear weather. Punished Hen^ry Stephens Seaman and Thos Dunister Marine with 12 lashes each for refusing to take their allowance of fresh Beef. Emp^d taking on board wine and water.

SATURDAY 17*th. Winds Westerly.* Little wind and fine clear weather. Issued to the Whole Ships Company 20 Pounds of Onions per man. Emp^d takeing on board Wine Water &c^a.

SUNDAY 18*th. Winds Southerly, ESE, SW.* D° Weather. PM Ricieved on board 270 pounds of fresh Beef and a Live Bullock charg'd 613 pounds. Compleated our wine and Water having recd of the former 3032 Gall[ns] of the latter 10 Tuns. AM unmoord and prepar'd for sailing.

* * *

TUESDAY 27*th. Wind NE. Course S* 19° *W. Distce in miles* 145. *Latd in* 21°26'. *Longd in West from Greenwich* 20°14'. *Bearings at Noon Do N* 26° *E Dt* 154 *leagues.* The same wind and weather this day as yesterday. Served Wine to the Ships Compney, the Beer being all expended to two cask which I intend to keep some time longer as the whole has proved very good to the Very last cask. At Noon found the ship by observation 10 Miles a head of the Log, which I suppose may be owing to a Current Setting in the same diriction as the trade wind.

WEDNESDAY 28*th. Winds NE, ENE. Course S* 12°30' *W. Distce in miles* 150. *Latd in* 18°59'. *Longd in West from Greenwich* 20°48' *W. Bearings at Noon Peek of Teneriff N* 23°15' *E Dt* 204 *L.* A Fresh trade wind and hazey weather. The Variation of the Compass by the mean of several Azimuths taken this evening 12°46' and in the morning by the same method 12°43' w. This day Log and observed Lat[d] agree which is not reconsilable to yesterday. Exercised the People at small Arms.

* * *

[OCTOBER 1768]

TUESDAY 25*th. Winds SE to SEBE. Course S* 30° *W. Distce in miles* 95. *Latd in* 0°15' *South. Longd in West from Greenwich* 29°30'. *Bearings at Noon Do N* 26° *E Dt* 358 *leagues.*[4] A Gentle breeze and clear weather, with a moist air. Soon after sun Rise found the Variation of the Compass to be 2°24' West being the mean result of sever[l] very good Azimuths, this was just before we crossed the line in Longitude of 29°29' West from Greenwich. We also try'd the Deping Needle belonging to the Royal Society and found the North point to dep 26° below the Horizon, but this instrument cannot be used at sea to any great degree of accuracy on account of the motion of the Ship which hinders the

4. Bearings are now from Bonavista Island, Cape Verde Islands.

Needle from resting; however as the Ship was pretty steady and by means of a swinging table I had made for that purpose we could be certain of the dep to two degrees at most. The observed Lat^d and that by account nearly agrees.

WEDNESDAY 26*th*. *Winds SE to SSE. Course S* 31° *W. Distce in miles* 77. *Latd in* 1°21′ *S. Longd in West from Greenwich* 30°18′. *Bearings at Noon Do N* 25°30′ *E Dt* 385 *leagues*. First part light airs and clowdy weather, the remainder a Moderate breeze and clowdy. After we had got an Observation and it was no longer doubted that we were to the southward of the Line, the Ceremony on this occassion practised by all Nations was not omitted: every one that could not prove upon a Sea Chart that he had before crossed the Line, was either to pay a bottle of Rum or be ducked in the sea, which former case was the fate of by far the greatest part on board, and as several of the Men choose to be ducked and the weather was favourable for that purpose, this ceremony was performed on about 20 or 30 to the no small deversion of the rest.

*   *   *

FRIDAY 28*th*. *Winds SE to SEBE. Course S* 33° *W. Distce in miles* 93. *Latd in* 3°41′. *Longd in West from Greenwich* 32°29′. *Bearings at Noon Do*. Fresh Breeze and fine clear weather. At a little past 1 AM Long^d in by the three following observations (viz.) by the Moon and the * Arietis, 32°27′0″, by the moon and Pollux 32°0′15″, by D° 31°48′32″; the mean of the Whole is 32°5′16″ West from Greenwich, which is 31′ more westerly then the Long^d by account carried on sence the last observation. The two first observation were made and computed by Mr Green and the last by my self. The * Arietis was on one side of the Moon and Pollux on the other. This day at Noon being nearly in the Lat^d of the Island Ferdinand Noronha[5] to the westward of it by some charts and to the Eastward by other, was in expectation of seeing it or some of those shoals that are laid down in most charts between it and the main, but we saw neither one nor a nother. We certainly pass'd to the Eastward of the Island, and as to the shoals I do not think they

5. About 250 miles off the Brazilian coast.

exhist grounding this my opinion on the Journal of some East India Ships I have seen, who were detain some days by contrary winds between this Island and the main and being 5 or Six Ships in compney, doubtless must have seen some of them did they lay as marked in the charts.

*   *   *

[NOVEMBER 1768]

SUNDAY 6th. *Winds NNE, Varble, South. Course S* 55° *W. Distce in miles* 74. *Latd in* 19°3'. *Longd in West from Greenwich* 35°50'. First and latter part Squally with heavy Showers of rain, Middle Moderate and fair. I now determined to put into Rio de Janeiro in preference to any other Port in Brazil or Faulkland Islands, for at this place I knew we could recruit our stock of Provisions, several Articles of which I found we should in time be in want of, and at the same time procure Live Stock and refreshments for the People and from the reception former Ships had met with here I doubted not but we should be well received.

*   *   *

TUESDAY 8th. *Winds NNE, NBW, SSW to SBW. Course S* 50° *W. Distce in miles* 140. *Latd in* 21°16'. *Longd in West from Greenwich* 37°35'. Fresh breeze and Clowdy weather. PM Variation by the mean of 12 Azimuth 5°26' East, and by an Amplitude in the morning 7°52'. At 6 AM saw the Land of Brasil bearing NW½N Dist^{ce} 8 or 10 Leagues; at 8 sounded had 37 fathom Coarse sand broken shells and coral rocks. At 9 brought too and spoke with a fishing Boat who informed us that the land in sight lay to the southward of Santo Espiritu, it appears high and mountainous. . . .

WEDNESDAY 9th. *Winds SSE, SSW, South. Course S* 62°15' *West. Distce in miles* 28 M. *Latd in* 21°29'. First and latter parts hazey with a Moderate breeze. Middle fresh gales with thunder Lightning and rain. At 3 pm Tack'd in 16 fathom, distance from the Shore 5 Leagues, the land extending from the NWBW to NE. At 5 took the 2nd reef in the topsails and got down top g^t yards. Stood to the SE untill midnight then Tacked, soundings from 16 to 55 f^m. At 8 AM Loosed the reefs out of the topsails and got topg^t yards aCross, unstowed the Anchors and bit the Cables. At Noon Lat^d Obser^d 21°29′ s, the land extending from SWBS to NNW, distant 4 Leagues. Soundings from 55 to 10 f^m.

*　　*　　*

SUNDAY 13*th*. *Winds EBN, Calm, SE*. Fore and latter parts a gentle Sea breeze and clear weather, the middle calm. PM standing a long shoar for Rio de Janeiro, observed that the land on the Sea coast is high and mountainous, and the shoar forms some small Bays or Coves wherein are sandy beaches. At 8 shortend sail, the Sug^r Loaf Hill at the west entrance to Rio de Janeiro, NNW dist. 4 or 5 Leagues, at the same time was abreast of two small rocky Islands that lies about 4 Miles from the shore. At 9 am sprung up a light breeze at SE at which time we made sail for the Harbour, and set the Pinnace with a Lieut^t before us up to the City of Rio de Janeiro to acquaint the Vice Roy[6] with the reasons that induced us to put in here; which was to procure Water and other refreshments; and to desire the assistance of a Pilot to bring us into proper anchoring ground. At Noon standing in for the Harbour.

MONDAY 14*th*. Moderate Sea and Land breezes and fine plasant weather. At 5 pm anchor'd in 5 fathom water just above the Isle of Cobras which lies before the City of Rio de Janeiro: a little before we anchor'd the Pinnace ret'd and inform'd me that the Viceroy had thought proper to detain the Officer untill I went a shore. Soon after we anchor'd a boat came on board bringing several of the Viceroys officers who asked ma[n]y questions in respect to the Ship, from whence She came, Cargo, number of men Guns &c^a all of which was answerd to their satisfaction – they told me that it was the custom of this Port to detain the first officer that came from any ship on her first Arrival untill a Boat from the Vice roy had visited her, that my officer would be sent on board as soon as they got a shore, which was accordingly done. About this time a Boat fill'd with soldiers kept rowing about the Ship, which had orders as I afterwards understood,

6. Dom António Rolim de Moura (1709–82).

not to suffer any on
go out of the ship. I
obtain'd leave to purc
but obliged me to em
pretence that it was the
(notwithstanding all I co
into the Boats that broug
it was the Orders of his
despence with, and this ind
I could not have got the sup
me lay to avoide all manne
delay, and at the same time
here to trade as I believe he im
a word about our being bound to   ...nsit
of Venus but look'd upon it only   ,o cover some
other design we must be upon,   ...d form no other Idea of
that Phenomenon (after I had explained it to him) then the North
Star passing thro the South Pole (these were his own words.) He would
not permit the Gentlemen to reside a shore during our stay here, not
permit Mr Banks to go into the Country to gather Plants &c^a but not
the least hint was given me at this time that no one of the Gentlemen
was to come out of the Ship but my self, or that I was to be put under
a guard when I did come; but this I was soon convinced of after I
took my leave of His Excellency and found that an Officer was to
attend upon me where ever I went, which at first the Viceroy pretended
was only meant as a compliment and to order me all the Assistance I
wanted. This day the people were employ'd in unbending the Sails,
in fiting and rigging the spare top-masts in the room of the others,
and getting on Shore empty water casks.

*   *   *

[*In the three weeks spent at Rio cleaning and caulking the ship's timbers, repairing the sails and rigging, and getting aboard water, rum and other supplies, Cook's resentment at the Viceroy's suspicions and restrictions did not lessen. The insistence on a Portuguese guard in each boat that left or returned to the ship particularly vexed him, and he refused to go ashore himself on such a condition. The exchange*

[*the temporary imprisonment of a boat's ... completely. Banks and Solander managed to ... to make expeditions.*]

...RDAY 26*th*. Employ'd geting on board water as ...rs could set up and repair the Casks, seting up the ...aulking the Ship sides.

...Y 27*th*. Bent the sails and cleaned the Ship fore and abaft.

MONDAY 28*th*. Fine pleasent weather, the caulkers having finished the sides paid them with tar. This Day I unexpectedly received an Answer to my last Memorial wherein were only a few week arguements to support his Excellencys suspicions that the Ship did not belong to the King and that my people smugled: this Memorial I answerd.

TUESDAY 29*th*. Employ'd lashing the Cask that were on the upper decks and between decks and making ready for sea.

WEDNESDAY 30*th*. Punished Rob' Anderson Seaman and Willm Judge Marine with twelve lashes each, the former for leaving his duty a Shore and attempting to disert from the Ship, and the latter for useing abusive language to the Officer of the Watch, and John Readon Boatswains Mate with twelve lashes for not doing his duty in punishing the above two Men. Sent a Shore to the Viceroy for a Pilot to carry us to sea, who sent one on board together with a large Boat, which I did not want, but it is the Custom in this Port for the Pilots to have such a boat to attend upon the Ships they Pilot out and for which you must pay 10/- per Day besides the Pilots fees which is Seven pounds four shillings Sterling.

[DECEMBER 1768]

THURSDAY 1*st* DECEMBER. Wind at SE which hinder'd us from sailing as we intended. Recd on board a large quantity of fresh Beef Greens and Yams for the Ships Compney.

FRIDAY 2*nd*. This Morning sent a Packet for the Secretary of the Admiralty, on board the Spanish Packet *Hopp* Don Antonio Monte

Negro y Velasco, commander, containing copies of all the Memorials and letters that have pass'd between the Viceroy and me, and likewise another Packet containing duplicates thereof I left with the Viceroy to be by him forwarded to Lisbon. At 9 weigh'd and came to sea and turn'd down the Bay. Peter Flower seaman fell over board and before any assistance could be given him was drown'd, in his room we got a Portuguse.

* * *

[*The* Endeavour *eventually got clear of Rio de Janeiro on 7 December. Cook headed south-west with little incident, putting the crew on 'watch and watch' (four hours on and four hours off). In early January they were in latitude 48° s about 200 miles off the South American coast.*]

[JANUARY 1769]

WEDNESDAY 4*th. Winds WNW to SWBS. Course S 20° E. Distce in miles 76. Latd in* 48°28'. *Longd in West from Greenwich* 60'51'. First part Gentle breezes and clear, latter fresh gales with heavy squalls of wind and rain which brought us under our Courses and Main Topsail close reef'd. Soon after noon saw the appearence of land to the Eastward, and being in the Lat^d of Peypes Island[7] as its laid down in some Charts, immagined it might be it. Bore down to be certain and at ½ past 2 pm discover'd our mistake and hauld the wind again. At 6 Sounded and had 72 fathom black sand and Mud. Variation 19°45' E^t.

THURSDAY 5*th. Winds SW, NW, & NNE. Course S* 28° *W. Distce in miles* 92 M. *Latd in* 49°49'. *Longd in West from Greenwich* 61°57'. The Fore part fresh gales and clear, the Middle light airs, remainder fresh gales and a little hazey. PM found the Variation to be 20°4' E^t. Soundings 75 and 73 fathom. A great Number of water fowl about the Ship.

FRIDAY 6*th. Winds Wt, Srly. Course S* 8°45' *W. Distce in miles* 92. *Latd in* 51°20'. *Longd in West from Greenwich* 62°19'. Fresh gales, the Air very sharp and cold, frequent showers of Rain and Squalls. Soundings 75

7. 'Pepys Island' was the arbitrary positioning in a 1699 collection of voyages of a sighting reported by Cowley in 1684. Probably Jason Island, in the north-western Falkland Islands.

fathom, saw some Penguins. Gave to each of the People a Fearnought Jacket and a pair of Trowers: after which I never heard one man complain of cold not but the weather was cold enough.

SATURDAY 7*th. Winds Southerly. Course S 62° E. Distce in miles* 14. *Latd in* 51°26'. *Longd in West from Greenwich* 61°59'. First part Strong gales with excessive hard Squales accompney'd with rain, at 9 pm wore and brought too her head to the westward under the Main sail, and reef'd the Fore sail for the first time; the Storm continued with little intermission untill toward Noon when it abated so as we could set the Topsails close reef'd. Saw ma[n]y Penguins and some Seals.

* * *

WEDNESDAY 11*th. Winds Westerly. Course S 30° W. Distce in miles* 100. *Latd in* 54°20'. *Longd in West from Greenwich* 64°35' *pr Logg.* A Steady gentle breeze and clear weather. PM after standing 13 Leagues ssw Sounded and had 64 fathom, gravel and small Stones, standing SWBS a 11 Leagues farther had 46 fathom, the same sort of bottom. At 8 am Saw the Land of Terra del Fuego extending from the West to SEBS, distance off shore between 3 and 4 Leagues, sounded and had 35 fathom small soft slate stones. Variation 23°30' E. In rainging a long the shore to the SE at the distance of 2 or 3 Leagues had 27 and 26 f^m a muddy bottom, saw some of the Natives who made a smook in several places, which must have been done as a signal to us as they did not continue it after we pass'd. By our Longitude we ought not to have been so far to the westward as Staten Land as it is laid down in the Charts, but it appear'd from Subsequent Observations that the Ship had got near a degree of Longitude to the westward of the Log which is 35 Miles in these Latitudes, probably this in part may be owing to a small current seting to the westward occasioned by the westerly Current which comes round Cape Horn and through Strait la Maire and the in draught of the Straits Magellan.

THURSDAY 12*th. Winds N & NNE, Varble, WSW. Latd in* 54°34' *pr Observn.* First part Moderate breeze and clowdy, remainder some times a fresh breeze, some times calm, hazey and rainy weather; at 5 the wind coming to the Northward, oblige'd us to Tack and stand NW ward being then about 5 Miles from the shore and had 23 fathom Sandy bottom, at Midnight Tacked and stood to the Eastward. At Noon the land near the entrance of Strait Le Maire ENE dist^{ce} 7 Leagues, Soundings from 28 to 38 f^m.

FRIDAY 13*th. Winds NEBE, WSW, SW. Bearings at Noon Cape St Diego North 2 Leagues. Plying in Strait Le Maire.* The greatest part of this day little wind and clowdy, at 8 pm Cape St Diego at the west entrance of Strait Le Maire East dist^{ce} about 5 Leagues, kept under an easy sail untill day light at which time we were abreast of Cape St Diego and then put into the Straights, but the tide soon turn'd against us and oblige'd us to haul under the Cape again and wait untill 9 am when it shifted in our favour. Put into the Straits again with a moderate breeze at sw which soon grew boisterous, with very heavy squalls with rain & hail and oblig'd us to close reef our top-sails.

SATURDAY 14*th. Winds SSW & SWBS.* First part Strong gales and very heavy Squalles with Hail and rain, the remainder more moderate but unsettled some times a fresh breeze and Squally and some times little wind. Kept Plying in the Straits untill ½ past 4 pm at which time the Tide had made Strong against us and the wind not abating bore away intending to have hauld under Cape St Diego, but was prevented by the force of the tide which carried us past that Cape with surprising rappidity, at the same time caused a very great sea. . . . At ½ past 7 Tacked and stud to the SE Cape St Diego bearing SBE dist^{ce} 5 Leagues. At 1 am Squally, wore Ship, Staten land extending from North to East. At 4 Moderate weather loose'd a reef out of each topsail, the Cape of Good Success WBS and Cape St Diego NNW being now in the Strait, but the tide turning against us soon carried us out. The Violence of the Tide of Ebb rais'd such a Sea off Cape St Diego that it looked as if it was breaking Voilently on a lidge of rocks and would be taken for such by any who knew not the true cause: when the Ship was in this torrent she frequently Pitched her bowsprit in the Water. By noon we got under the land between Cape St Diego and Cape St Vincent where I thought to have Anchor'd, but found the bottom every where hard and rocky, the depth of water from 30 to 12 fathom. Set the

Master to examine a small Cove which appeared to our View a little to the Eastward of Cape St Vincent.

SUNDAY 15*th*. Moderate breeze at South & SE and Clowdy weather the greatest part of this Day. At 2 pm the Master return'd with an account that there was Anchorage in 4 fathom water and a good bottom close to the Eastward of the first black bluf point which is on the East side of Cape St Vincent, at the very entrance of the Cove we saw from the Ship, (which I named *Vincents Bay*) before this Anchoring ground lay several rocky Ledges cover'd with Sea Weed, on these ledges I was informed was not less than 8 and 9 fathom, but in standing in with the Ship the first we came upon had only 4 fathom upon it. I therefore thought that Anchoring here would be attended with some risk, and that it would be better to endeavour to find some port in the Strait and there compleat our Wood and Water. However I sent a Boat with an officer a Shore to attend on Mr Banks and People who was very desireous of being aShore at any rate, while I kept plying as near the shore as possible with the Ship. At 9 they return'd on board bringing with them several Plants Flowers &c^a most of them unknown in Europe and in that alone consisted their whole Value; they saw none of the Natives but met with several of their old Hutts. Hoisted the Boat in and made sail into the Strats, and at 3 am Anchor'd in 12½ fathom water (the bottom Corral rock,) before a small Cove which we took for Port Maurice and near ½ a Mile from the Shore Cape St Diego ssw and Cape Bartholomew (which is the s point of Staten land) ESE. Port Maurice appeared to afford so little Shelter for Shipping that I did not think it worth while to hoist a Boat out to Examine it. We saw here two of the Natives come down to the Shore who stay'd some time then retired into the woods again. At 10 oClock got under sail wind at SE and Plyed to Windward.

MONDAY 16*th*. A Fresh breeze of wind at South and SW with frequent Showers of Snow and rain. At 2 pm Anchor'd in the Bay of Success, 9 fathom the bottom owse and sand, the south point of the Bay bore SE and the North Point ENE. . . . Hoisted out the Boats and Moor'd with the Stream Anchor, while this was doing I went a Shore accompany'd by Mr Banks and Dr Solander to look for a Watering place and to speak with the Natives who were assembled on the beach at the head of the Bay to the number of 30 or 40; they were so far from being afraid or surprised at our coming amongest them that three of them came on board without the least hesitation. They are something above the Middle size of a dark copper Colour with long black hair, they paint their bodies in Streakes mostly Red and Black, their cloathing consists wholy of a Guanacoes skin or that of a Seal, in the same form as it came from the Animals back, the Women wear a peice of skin over their privey parts but the Men observe no such decency. Their Hutts are made like a behive and open on one side where they have their fire, they are made of small Sticks and cover'd with branches of trees, long grass &cᵃ in such a manner that they are neither proff against wind, Hail, rain, or snow, a sufficient proff that these People must be a very hardy race; they live chiefly on shell fish such as Muscles which they gather from off the rocks along the seashore and this seems to be the work of the Women; their arms are Bows and Arrows neatly made, their arows are bearded some with glass and others with fine flint, several pieces of the former we saw amongst them with other European things such as Rings, Buttons, Cloth, Canvas &cᵃ which I think proves that they must sometimes travel to the Northward, as we know of no ship that hath been in those parts for many years, besides they were not at all surprised at our fire arms on the contrary seem'd to know the use of them by making signs to us to fire at Seals or Birds that might come in the way. They have no boats that we saw, or any thing to go upon the water with. Their number doth not exceed 50 or 60 young and old and there are fewer Women then Men. They are extreeamly fond of any Red thing and seemed to set more Value on Beeds than any thing we could give them: in this consists their whole pride, few either men or Women are without a necklace or string of Beeds made of small Shells or bones about their necks. They would not taste any strong Liquor, neither did they seem fond of our provisions. We could not discover that they had any head or chief, or form of Goverment, neither have they any usefull or neccessary Utentials except it be a Bagg or Basket to gather their Muscels into: in a Word they are perhaps as miserable a set of People as are this day upon Earth. Having found a convenient place on the s side of the

Bay to wood and Water at, we set about that work in the morning, and Mr Banks with a party went into the Country to gather Plants &c^a.

THURSDAY 17*th* Jan^ry.[8] Fresh gales at South, sw, and w, with rain and Snow and of course very cold weather, nothwithstanding we kept geting on board Wood and water, and finished the Survey of the Bay. Mr Banks and his party not returning this Evening as I expected gave me great uneasiness as they were not prepared for staying out the night, however about noon they returned in no very comfortable condition and what was still worse two Blacks servants to Mr Banks had perished in the night with cold;[9] great part of the day they landed was spent before they got through the woods, after which they advanced so far into the Country that they were so far from being able to return that night that it was with much difficulty they got to a place of tolerable shelter where they could make a fire. These two men being intrusted with great part of the Liquor that was for the whole party had made too free with it and stupified themselves to that degree that they either could or would not travel but laid themselves down in a place where there was not the least thing to shelter them from the inclemency of the night. This was about a ¼ of a mile from where the rest took up their quarters and notwithstanding their repeted endeavours they could not get them to move one step farther, and the bad traveling made it impossible for any one to carry them, so that they were oblig'd to leave them and the next morning they were both found dead.

*   *   *

[*Very stormy weather and high surf made the task of getting wood and water difficult, and the small kedge anchor, being used with the longboat, was lost. They set sail out of the bay on 21 January and proceeded towards Cape Horn.*]

WEDNESDAY 25*th* of Jan^ry. Winds from the South to the WNW, the first part fresh gales and squally with some rain, middle little wind with hail and rain, latter fresh gales and hazey with showers of rain. At 8

8. Cook's error. It should be 'Tuesday'.
9. Thomas Richmond and George Dorlton.

pm the Island of Evouts NW dist^t 3 or 4 Miles. Variation p^r morning Amplitude 21° 16′ East. At 8 am the Southermost low point of land seen yesterday boare s 74° w^t and a remarkable Peeked Hill to the southward of it sw and soon after we discoverd that the land which we took yesterday to be apart of the main or an Island, was three Islands which I take to be Hermites, at Noon the south point of the Southermost Island bore NWBW dist^t 3 Leagues, having then 55 fathom Peble stones; this point is pretty high and consists of Peeked craggy rocks and not far from it lay several others high above water; it lies in the Latitude of 55°53′ South and sw 26 Leagues from Strait La Mair, and by some on board thought to be Cape Horn, but I was of another oppinion and with good reason because we saw land to the southward of it about 3 or 4 Leagues. It appeared not unlike an Island with a very high round hummock upon it: this I believe to be Cape Horn for after we had stood to the Southward about 3 Leagues the weather clear'd up for about a ¼ of an hour, which gave us a sight of this land bearing then wsw but we could see no land either to the Southward or westward of it, and therefore conclude that it must be the Cape, but whether it be an Island of it self, a part of the Southermost of Hermites Islands or a part of Terra del Fuego I am not able to determine. However this is of very little concequence to Navigation, I only wished to have been certain whether or no it was the Southermost land on or near to Terra del Fuego, but the thick Foggy weather, and the westerly winds which carried us from the land prevented me from satisfying My curiosity in this point; but from its Latitude and the reasons before given I think it must, and if so it must be Cape Horn and lies in the Latitude of 55°59′ South and Longitude 68°13′ West from the Meridian of Greenwich, beeing the mean result of Several Observ^{ns} of the Sun and Moon made the day after we left the land and which agree'd with those made at Straits Le Maire, allowing for the distance between one place and the other, which I found means very accuratly to determine.[10] . . .

THURSDAY 26*th. Winds SWBW to WNW. Courses S* 15° *W. Distce in miles*

10. Cook had correctly located Cape Horn. It is the southern end of Horn Island, the southernmost of the Hermite group.

63. *Latd in South* 56°57′. *Longd in West of Greenwich* 68°13′. *Bearings at Noon C. Horn North Distant* 58 *miles*. Fresh gales and thick hazey weather with small rain, at 2 pm the weather clearing up a little saw cape Horn bearing wsw Distant about 6 Leagues and from which I take my Departure, it[s] Latitude and Longitude have before been taken notice of.

* * *

SUNDAY 29*th. Winds W, Northerly. Courses SW. Distce sail'd in miles* 79. *Latd in South* 59°0′. *Longd in West of Greenwich* 72°48′. First and latter part fresh gales and squally with flying showers of rain and Hail, the Middle Strong gales with heavy Squalls and showers of rain. At 8 pm took the 2nd reef in the topsails. At 6 am Close reef'd the Fore topsail and took in the Mizon topsail, and at 10 set it again and loosed the reef out of the fore topsail.

* * *

TUESDAY 31*st. Winds WNW, Calm, ESE, SSE. Courses N 71° W. Distce sail'd in miles* 55. *Latd in South* 59°46′. *Longd in West of Greenwich* 75°54′. First part Moderate and Clowdy with some rain, in the night little wind and Calm, towards noon fresh gales and Clowdy. Between 7 and 8 pm being then in the Lat^{d} of 60°10′ which was the fartherest south we was, and in the Longitude of 74°30′, found the Variation of the compass by the mean of 18 Azimuths to be 27°9′ East. At 3 am wind at ESE a Moderate breeze, set the S[t]udding sails, and soon after 2 birds like Penguins was seen by the mate of the watch.

[FEBRUARY 1769]

WEDNESDAY 1*st. Winds SEBE, SSE, E. Courses NWBW. Distce sail'd in miles* 106. *Latd in South* 58°46′. *Longd in West of Greenwich* 78°42′. Former part fresh gales, latter light airs and Clowdy. PM found the Variation by several Azimuth to be 24°53′ East. At Noon sound^{d} but had no ground with 240 fathom of line. Hoisted a small boat out to try if there was any current but found none. The weather was such as to admit Mr Banks to row round the Ship in a Lightermans skiff shooting birds.

* * *

SATURDAY 4*th. Winds Westerly. Courses N* 13° *W. Distce sail'd in miles* 48. *Latd in South* 57°45'. *Longd in West of Greenwich* 82°16'. Fore and middle parts little wind and dark clowdy weather latter fresh gales and clowdy with some rain. PM had a boat out and shott several sorts of Birds, one of which was an Albetross as large as a Goose, whose wings when extended measured 10 feet 2 Inches, this was grey but there are of them all white except the very tip end of their wing; a nother sort in size between an Albestross and a large Gull, of a gray colour with a white spot above their tail about the bredth of ones hand, and several other sorts.

* * *

SUNDAY 12*th. Winds SW & S. Courses N* 48° *W. Distce sail'd in miles* 113. *Latd in South* 49°41'. *Longd in West of Greenwich* 89°36'. First and Middle part fresh gales and clowdy latter little wind clear. Having for some time past generally found the Ship by obser^n to the Northward of the Logg, which is not owing to a current as I at first immagined but to a wrong division of the Log Line being 2½ feet in each knot; but this is now rectified.

MONDAY 13*th. Winds West Norly. Courses N* 75° *W. Distce sail'd in miles* 35. *Latd in South* 49°32'. *Longd in West of Greenwich* 90°37'. The first part of these 24 hours Moderate breezes and clowdy, the remainder fresh gales and clowdy. PM Saw a great many Albetrosses and other Birds about the Ship, some were all white and about the Size of Teal. Took several observations of the Sun and Moon, the result of which gave 90°13' West Longitude from Greenwich. The Variation of the Compass by the Mean of Several Azth 17° East. The Longitude by account is less then that by Obser^n 37' which is about 20 Miles in these high latitudes, and nearly equall to the Error of the Logg Line before mentioned: this near agreement of the two Longitudes proves to a demonstration that we have had no Western current sence we left land.

From the foregoing observations it will appear that we are now advanced about 12° to the westward of the Strait of Magellan and

$3^{1}/_{2}°$ to the northward of it, having been 33 days in doubbling Cape Horn or the land of Terra del Fuego, and arriving into the degree of Latitude and Longitude we are now in without ever being brought once under our close reefe'd Topsails since we left strait la Maire, a circumstance that perhaps never happen'd before to any Ship in those seas so much dreaded for hard gales of wind, insomuch that the doubling of Cape Horn is thought by some to be a mighty thing and others to this Day prefer the Straits of Magellan. As I have never been in those Straits, can only form my judgement on a carefull comparrison of the different Ships Journals that have pass'd them and those that have sail'd round Cape Horn, particularly the Dolphins two last Voyages and this of ours being made at the same Season of the Year when one may reasonably expect the Same winds to prevail. The Dolphin in her last Voyage was 3 Months in geting through the Straits not reckoning the time she lay in Port Famine, and I am firmly perswaded from the winds that we have had, that had we come by that passage we should not yet have been in these Seas; beside the fatiguing of our people the Damage we must have done to our Anchors Cables Sails and Rigging none of which have suffered in our passage round Cape Horn.

From what I have said it will appear that I am no advocate for the Straits of Magellan, but it may be expected that I should say some thing of Strait le Maire through which we pass'd, and this is the more incumbant on me as it was by choise and contrary to the advice given by Mr Walter the ingenious Author of Lord Ansons Voyage who adveiseth all Ships not to go through this Strait but to go to the Eastward of Staten land, and likewise to Stand to the Southward as far as 61° or 62° South before any endeavour is made to get to the westward; with respect to the passing of Strait Le Maire or going round Staten land I look upon of little concequence and either one or the other to be pursue'd according to circumstances: for if you happen to fall in with the land to the westward of the Strait and the winds favourable for going through it certainly must be a peice of folly to loose time in going round Staten land, for by paying a little attention to the directions I have already given no ill concequences can attend; but, on the contrary if you should fall in with the land to the eastward of the Strait or the wind should prove boisterous, or unfavourable, in any of these cases the going to the Eastward of Staten land is the most adviseable. And next, as to the runing into the Latitude of 61° or 62° South before any endeavour is made to get to the westward, is what I think no man will ever do that can avoide it, for it cannot be suppose'd that any one will Stear South mearly to get into a high Latitude when at the same time he can Steer west, for it is not Southing but Westing thats wanting, but this way you cannot steer because the winds blow almost constantly from that quarter, so that you have no other choise but to stand to the Southward close upon a wind, and by keeping upon that Tack you not only make southing but westing also and sometimes not a little when the wind Varies to the northward of west, and the farther you advance to the Southrd the better chance you have of having the winds from that quarter or easterly and likewise of meeting with finer weather, both of which we ourselves experence'd. Prudence will direct every man when in these high Latitudes to make sure of Sufficient westing to double all the lands before he thinks of Standing to the Northward. When the winds was westerly the mountains on Terra del Fuego were generally cover'd with dense clowds, formed as one may reasonably suppose by watery exhalations and by Vapours brought thither by the westerly winds, for from that quarter came frequent showers of Rain Hail and Snow, and after we had left the land and were standing to the Southward with the winds westerly dark dense clowds were continuely forming in the horizon and rose to about 45° where they began to disspate, these was generally attended with showers of rain or hail and Sq^{ls} of wind; but as we advanced to the southward these clowds became less dence, and in ye Lat^d 60°10′ where we got the winds Easterly the weather was more serene and milder, again as we advanced to the northward we had a constant clowded sky & dark gloomy weather, ye whole time exceed^g cold.

* * *

TUESDAY 28*th. Winds West to NW. Courses N* 13° *W. Distce sail'd in miles* 42. *Latd in South* 39°33′30″. *Longd in West of Greenwich* 110°38′. The former part Little wind and fine clear weather, the air full as warm as in the same degree of North Latitude at the correspondent season of the year: the sw swell still keeps up notwithstand the gale hath been over about thirty hours, a proof that there is no land near in that quarter. The remainder part of this Day fresh breezes and clear: at 9 am took three sets of Observations of the Sun and Moon in order to find the Longitude of the Ship.

[MARCH 1769]

WEDNESDAY 1st. *Winds WBS, NW. Courses N 76° W. Distce sail'd in miles 52. Latd in South 38°44′. Longd in West of Greenwich 111°43′. Bearings at Noon C. Horn 60° E Distce 660 Leagues.* First part fresh breeze the remainder moderate breezes and clear weather. The result of the forementioned Observations gives 110°33′ w. Longitude from Greenwich and exactly agrees with the Longitude given by the Log, from Cape Horn: this agreement of the two Longitudes after a Run of 660 Leagues is surpriseing and much more then could be expected, but as it is so, it serves to prove as well as the repeted trials we have made when the weather would permit, that we have had no Current that hath affected the Ship Since we came into these Seas, this must be a great sign that we have been near no land of any extent because near land are generally found Currents: it is well known that on the East side of the Continent in the North sea we meet with Currents above 100 Leagues from the Land, and even in the Middle of the Atlantic Ocean between Africa and America are always found Currents, and I can see no reason why currents should not be found in this Sea Supposing a Continent or lands lay not far west from us as some have immagine'd, and if such land was ever seen we cannot be far from it, as we are now 560 Leagues West of the Coast of Chili.

* * *

[*Cook continued on his north-westerly course, bringing the ship's company from watch and watch to the more relaxed three watches, and fetching up the six waist guns, which had gone down to the hold for the passage round Cape Horn.*]

THURSDAY 23rd. *Winds NBW to WBN. Courses N 13° W. Distce sail'd in miles 49. Latd in South 24°43′. Longd in West of Greenwich 130°8′.* Fresh gales and squally with rain the first part, the remainder fresh gales and clowdy. PM Saw some men of war Birds and Egg Birds and in the Morning saw more Egg Birds and Tropic Birds. The Man of War and Tropic Birds are pretty well known but the Egg Bird (as it is call'd in the Dolphins Journals) require some description to know it by that name. It is a small slender Bird of the Gull kind and all white, and not much unlike the small white Gulls we have in England, only not so big; there are also Birds in Newfoundland call'd Stearings that are of the same shape and Bigness only they are of a Greyish Colour. These Birds were call'd by the Dolphin Egg Birds on account of their being like those known by that name by Salors in the Gulph of Florida. Neither they nor the Men of War Birds are ever reckoned to go very far from land.

FRIDAY 24*th. Winds WNW to NW. Courses NEBN¼E. Distce sail'd in miles* 99. *Latd in South* 23°23'. *Longd in West of Greenwich* 129°2'. Fresh gales and Clowdy, with some rain in the fore part of this day. All the Fore part of these 24 hours the Sea was Smooth but at 12 at night it was more so, and about 3 in the Morning one of the People saw or thought he saw a Log of wood pass the Ship; this made us think we were near some land, but at Day light we saw not the least appearences of any and I did not think my self at liberty to spend time in searching for what I was not sure to find, altho I thought my self not far from those Islands discover'd by Quiros in 1606 and very probable we were not, from the Birds &cᵃ we have seen for these 2 or 3 days past.

SATURDAY 25*th. Winds NWBN to WBN. Courses NE½N. Distce sail'd in miles* 95. *Latd in South* 22°11'. *Longd in West of Greenwich* 127°55'. First part Dark Clowdy weather with rain and a fresh breeze of wind, the remainder fair and Clowdy.

SUNDAY 26*th. Winds NW to W. Longd in West of Greenwich* 127°43'. Squally weather with rain. A 5 pm Saw some Sea Weed pass the Ship, and at 7 Wᵐ Greenslade Marine either by Accident or design went over board and was drownded; the following circumstances makes it appear as tho it was done designedly, he had been Centinal at the Stearage door between 12 and 4 oClock where he had taken part of a Seal Skin put under his charge which was found upon him, the other Marines thought themselves hurt by one of their party commiting a crime of this Nature, and he being a raw young fellow, and as very probable made him resolve upon commiting this rash action; for the Sergant, not being willing that it should pass over unknown to me, was about 7 oClock going to bring him aft to have it inqure^d into when he gave him the Slip between decks and was seen go upon the Fore Castle, and from that time was seen no more. I was niether made acquainted with the Theft or the circumstances attending it untill the Man was gone.

*   *   *

[*The* Endeavour *must have passed close to Pitcairn Island, but the first sighting of land, after 66 days, was in the Tuamotu archipelago, east of the Society Islands.*]

[APRIL 1769]

SATURDAY 1*st. Winds SE to E½N. Courses West. Distce sail'd in miles* 122. *Latd in South* 19°7'. *Longd in West of Greenwich* 133°28'. A Steady fresh Trade and fine weather. Variation per Several Azimuth 2°32' East.

SUNDAY 2*nd. Winds East. Courses N* 86½ W. *Distce sail'd in miles* 118. *Latd in South* 19°0'. *Longd in West of Greenwich* 135°33'. A fresh trade wind and fine pleasent weather. At Noon saw a large flock of Birds, they had brown backs and white bellies, they fly and make a noise like Stearings and are shaped like them only some thing larger. Saw likewise some black sheer waters and several Men of War Birds.

MONDAY 3*rd. Winds East. Courses N* 82°45' *W. Distce sail'd in miles* 110. *Latd in South* 18°46'. *Longd in West of Greenwich* 137°29'. First and latter part a Steady fresh breeze and clowdy, the Middle sometimes Squally with rain at other times little wind. PM saw two Birds like Albatrosses, they were all white except the Tip of their wings and tails.

TUESDAY 4*th. Winds E, EBS. Courses N* 88° *W. Distce sail'd in miles* 114. *Latd in South* 18°42'. *Longd in West of Greenwich* 139°29'. A Steady fresh Trade and clear weather. At ½ past 10 AM saw land bearing South distant 3 or 4 Leagues; hauld up for it and soon found it to be an Island of about 2 Leagues in circuit and of an Oval form with a Lagoon in the Middle for which I named it *Lagoon Island*. The border of land circumscribing this Lagoon is in many places very low and narrow particularly on the South side where it is mostly a beach or Reef of Rocks, it is the same on the North in three places and these disjoins the firm land and makes it appear like so many Islands cover'd with Wood. On the west end of the Island is a large tree which we took for a   tree that looks like a Large Tower – and about the Middle of the Island are two Cocoa-nut trees that appear above all the other wood, which as we approche'd the Island look'd very much like a flag. We approach'd the north side of this Island within a Mile and found no bottom with a 130 fathom of line nor did there appear to be any Anchorage about it. We saw several of the Inhabitants, the Most of them Men and these March'd along the shore abreast of the Ship with long clubs in their hands as tho they ment to oppose our landing, they were all naked except their privy parts and were of a dark Coper colour with long black hair, but upon our leaving the Island some of them were seen to put on a covering and one or two we saw in the skirts of the Wood was cloathd in white, these we supposed to be Women. This Island lies in the Latitude of 18°47' and Long^d 139°28' West from the Meridian of Greenwich. Variation 2°54' East.

*   *   *

[*Continuing a westerly course, they sighted numerous islands, including Osnaburg (Mehetia), the first of the Society Islands, on 10 April.*]

TUESDAY 11*th. Winds Varble. Courses N* 66° *W. Distce sail'd in miles* 54. *Latd in South* 17°38'. *Longd in West of Greenwich* 148°39'. *Bearings at Noon Osnaburg Island E*½*S Distce* 13 *Leagues*. First part little wind and clowdy, the remainder Little wind and very Variable unsettled weather with some rain. PM Took several Observations of the Sun and Moon which gave the Long^d of the Ship to be 148°18' w and differs but little from that given by the Log. At 6 AM Saw *King Georges Island* extending from WBS½S to WBN½N it appear'd very high and Mountainous.

WEDNESDAY 12*th. Winds Do. Courses West. Distce sail'd in miles* 18. *Latd in South* 17°38'. *Longd in West of Greenwich* 148°58'. *Bearings at Noon King*

Georges Island from South to WBN Distce 5 Leagues. Variable light airs all these 24 hours and hot sultry weather. At 5 PM King Georges Island extending from NWBW to SW Distant 6 or 7 Leagues, and at 6 AM it bore from SSW to WBN. Being little wind and calm several of the Natives came off to us in their Canoes, but more to look at us then any thing else we could not prevail with any of them to come on board and some would not come near the Ship.

THURSDAY 13*th. Winds Easterly. At Anchor in Royl Bay Georges Island.*[11] The first part Clowdy and Squally with Showers of rain the remainder Gentle Breezes and clear weather. At 4 PM the NE Point of Royal Bay W½N. Run under an easy Sail all night and had soundings from 22 to 12 f^m 2 or 3 Miles from the Shore. At 5 AM Made Sail for the Bay and at 7 Anchor'd in 13 fathom.

At this time we had but a very few men upon the Sick list and these had but slite complaints, the Ships compney had in general been very healthy owing in a great measure to the Sour krout, Portable Soup and Malt; the two first were serve'd to the People, the one on Beef Days and the other on Banyan Days, Wort was made of the Malt and at the discrition of the Surgeon given to every man that had the least symptoms of Scurvy upon him, by this Means and the care and Vigilance of Mr Munkhous the Surgeon this disease was prevented from geting a footing in the Ship. The Sour Krout the Men at first would not eate untill I put in pratice a Method I never once knew to fail with seamen, and this was to have some of it dress'd every Day for the Cabbin Table, and permitted all the Officers without exception to make use of it and left it to the option of the Men either to take as much as they pleased or none atall; but this pratice was not continued above a week before I found it necessary to put every one on board to an Allowance, for such are the Tempers and disposissions of Seamen in general that whatever you give them out of the Common way, altho it be ever so much for their good yet it will not go down with them and you will hear nothing but murmurings gainest the man that first invented it; but the Moment they see their Superiors set a Value upon

11. Matavai Bay, on the northern coast of Tahiti. Cook now had seven weeks in hand before the transit of Venus.

it, it becomes the finest stuff in the World and the inventer an honest fellow.[12]

REMARKABLE OCCURRENCES AT GEORGES ISLAND

Note. The way of reckoning the Day in Sea Journals is from Noon to Noon, but as the Most material transactions at this Island must happen in the Day time this method will be attended with ilconveniences in inserting the transactions of each Day; for this reason I shall during our stay at this Island but no longer reckon the day according to the civil account, that is to begin and end at midnight.

We had no sooner come to an Anchor in Royal Bay as before Mentioned than a great number of the natives in their Canoes came off to the Ship and brought with them Cocoa-nuts &c^a and these they seem'd to set a great Value upon. Amongst those that came off to the Ship was an elderly Man whose name is *Owhaa*, him the Gentlemen that had been here before in the Dolphin knew and had often spoke of him as one that had been of service to them, this man (together with some others) I took on board, and made much of him thinking that he might on some occasion be of use to us. As our stay at this place was not likly to be very Short, I thought it very necessary that some order Should be Observed in Trafficing with the Natives: that such Merchantdize as we had on board for that purpose might continue to bear a proper value, and not leave it to every ones own particular fancy which could not fail to bring on confution and quarels between us and the Natives, and would infallible lesen the Value of such Articles as we had to Traffic with: in order to prevent this the following Rules were orderd to be observed, viz.

RULES to be observe'd by every person in or belonging to His Majestys Bark the Endevour, for the better establishing a regular and uniform Trade for Provisions &c^a with the Inhabitants of Georges Island.

12. Cook first wrote 'a damn'd honest fellow'.

1st *To endeavour by every fair means to cultivate a friendship with the Natives and to treat them with all imaginable humanity.*

2^d *A proper person or persons will be appointed to trade with the Natives for all manner of Provisions, Fruit, and other productions of the earth; and no officer or Seaman, or other person belonging to the Ship, excepting such as are so appointed, shall Trade or offer to Trade for any sort of Provisions, Fruit, or other productions of the earth unless they have my leave so to do.*

3^d *Every person employ'd a Shore on any duty what soever is strictly to attend to the same, and if by neglect he looseth any of his Arms or woorking tools, or suffers them to be stole, the full Value thereof will be charge'd against his pay according to the Custom of the Navy in such cases, and he shall recive such farther punishment as the nature of the offence may deserve.*

4th *The same penalty will be inflicted on every person who is found to imbezzle, trade or offer to trade with any part of the Ships Stores of what nature soever.*

5th *No Sort of Iron, or any thing that is made of Iron, or any sort of Cloth or other usefull or necessary articles are to be given in exchange for any thing but provisions.*

J. C.

As soon as the Ship was properly secure'd I went on Shore accompanied by Mr Banks and the other gentlemen, with a party of Men under arms, we took along with us Owhaa who conducted us to the place where the Dolphin water'd, and made signs to us as well as we could understand that we might occupy that ground but it happen'd not to be fit for our purpose. No one of the Natives made the least oppossission at our landing but came to us with all imaginable marks of friendship and submission. We afterwards made a circuit through the Woods, and then came on board. We did not find the Inhabitants to be numerous and therefore at first imagined that several of them had fled from their habitations upon our arrival in the Bay but Mr Gore & some others who had been here before observ'd that a very great revolution must have happen'd – not near the number of inhabitants a great number of houses raiz'd, har[d]ly a vestage of some to be seen particularly what was call'd the Queens and not so much as a Hog or Fowl was to be seen – no very agreeable discovery to us whose Ideas of plenty upon our arrival at this Island (from the report of the Dolphin) was carried to the very highest pitch.

FRIDAY Apl. 14*th*. This morning we had a great many Canoes about the Ship, the Most of them came from the westward but brought nothing with them but a few Cocoa-nuts &cᵃ. Two that appear'd to be Chiefs we had on board together with several others for it was a hard matter to keep them out of the Ship as they clime like Munkeys, but it was still harder to keep them from Stealing but every thing that came within their reach, in this they are prodiges expert. I made each of the two Chiefs a present of a Hatchet things that they seem'd mostly to Value. As soon as we had partly got clear of these people, I took two Boats and went to the Westward all the Gentlemen being along with me, my design was to see if there was not a more comm[o]dious Harbour and to try the disposission of the Natives having along with us the two Chiefs above mentioned: the first place we landed at was in Great Canoe Harbour (so call'd by Capᵗ Wallis) here the Natives Flock'd about us in great Numbers and in as friendly a Manner as we could wish, only that they shew'd a great inclination to pick our pockets. We were conducted to a Chief who for distinction sake we call'd *Hercules*,[13] after staying a Short time with him and distributing a few presents about us, we proceeded further and came to a Chief who I shall call *Lycurgus*, this Man entertain'd us with Broil'd fish Bread fruit Cocoa-nuts &cᵃ with great hospitality, and all the time took great care to tell us to take care of our pockets, as a great number of people had crowded about us. Notwithstanding the care we took Dʳ Solander and Dʳ Munkhouse had each of them their pockets pick'd the one of his spy glass and the other of his snuff Box, as soon as Lycurgus was made acquainted with the theift he disperse'd the people in a Moment and the method he made use of was to lay hold of the first thing that came in his way and throw it at them and happy was he or she that could get first out of his way; he seem'd very much concern'd for whàt had happend and by way of recompence offer'd us but every thing that was in his House, but we refuse'd to except of any thing and made signs to him that we only wanted the things again. He had

13. These classical names were supplied by Banks.

already sent people out after them and it was not long before they were return'd. We found the Natives very Numerous where ever we came and from what we could judge seem'd very peaceably inclin'd. About 6 oClock in the evening we return'd on board very well satisfied with our little excursion.

SATURDAY 15*th*. Winds at East during the day, in the night a light breeze off the land, and as I apprehend it be usual here for the Trade wind to blow during great part of the Day from the Eastern board and to have it Calm or light breezes from the land that is Southerly during the night with fair weather, I shall only mention the wind and weather when they deviate from this rule.

This morning several of the Chiefs we had seen yesterday came on board and brought with them Hogs, Bread fruit &c^a for these we gave them Hatchets, Linnen and such things as they Valued. Having not met with yesterday a more convenient situation for every purpose we wanted than the place where we now are, I therefore without delay resolved to pitch upon some spot upon the NE point of the Bay properly situated for observing the Transit of Venus and at the same time under the command of the Ships Guns, and there to throw up a small fort for our defence, accordingly I went a Shore with a party of men accompanie'd by Mr Banks Dr Solander and Mr Green. We took along with us one of Mr Banks Tents, and after we had fix'd upon a place fit for our purpose we set up the Tent and Mark'd out the ground we intended to occupy. By this time a great number of the Natives had got collected together about us, seemingly only to look on as not one of them had any weaphon either offensive or defensive. I would suffer none to come within the lines I had marked out excepting one who appear'd to be a Chief and old Owhaa, to these two men we endeavour'd to explain as well as we could that we wanted that ground to sleep upon such a number of nights and than we should go a way. Whether they understood us or no is uncertain but no one appear'd the least displeased at what we was about. Indeed the ground we had fix'd upon was of no use to them being part of the Sandy beach upon the shore of the Bay and not near to any of their habitations. It being too late in the Day to do any thing more a party with a Petty officer was left to guard the Tent while we with a nother party took a walk into the woods and with us most of the natives. We had but just cross'd the River when Mr Banks shott three Ducks at one shott which surprise'd them so much that the most of them fell down as tho they had been shott likewise. I was in hopes this would have had some good effect but the event did not prove it, for we had not been gone long from the Tent before the natives again began to gather about it and one of them more daring then the rest push'd one of the Centinals down, snatched the Musquet out of his hand and made a push at him and then made off and with him all the rest, emmidiatly upon this the officer order'd the party to fire[14] and the Man who took the Musquet was shott dead before he had got far from the Tent but the Musquet was carried quite off; when this happen'd I and Mr Banks with the other party were about half a Mile off returning out of the woods, upon hearing the fireing of musquets and the natives leaving us at the same time we susspected that some thing was the Matter and hasten'd our march, but before we arrive'd the whole was over and every one of the Natives fled except old Owhaa who stuck by us the whole time, and I beleive from the first either knew or had some suspicion that the People would attempt something at the Tent as he was very much agai[n]st our going into the woods out of sight of this Tent. However he might have other reasons for Mr Hicks being a shore the Day before the natives would not permit him to go into the woods, this made me resolve to go to see whether they mea[n]t to proscribe bounds to us or no. Old Owhaa as I have said before was the only one of the Natives that stay'd by us and by his means we prevail'd on about 20 of them to come to the Tent and their sit down with us and endeavour'd by every means in our power to convence them that the man was kill'd for taking away the Musquet and that we still would be friends with them. At sunset they left us seemingly satisfied and we struck our Tent and went on board.

SUNDAY 16*th*. This Day warped the Ship nearer the Shore and moor'd her in such a Manner as to command all the Shore of the NE part of the Bay, but more particularly the place where we indended to Erect

14. The midshipman in charge was Jonathan Monkhouse.

a Fort. Punished Rich[d] Hutchins Seaman with 12 lashes for disobaying command. Several of the Natives came down to y[e] Shore of the Bay but not one of them came off to the Ship during the whole day; in the evening I went a Shore with only a Boats crew and some of the Gentlemen, the natives gather'd about us to the number of about 30 or 40 and b[r]ought us Cocoa nuts &c[a] and seem'd as friendly as ever.

MONDAY 17*th*. At 2 oClock this Morning departed this Life M[r] Alex Buchan Landscip Draftsman to M[r] Banks, a Gentlemen well skill'd in his profession and one that will be greatly miss'd in the course of this Voyage, he had long been subject to a disorder in his Bowels which had more than once brought him to the Very point of death and was at the same time subject to fits of one of which he was taken on Saturday morning, this brought on his former disorder which put a period to his life. M[r] Banks thought it not so adviseable to Enterr the Body a shore in a place where we was utter strangers to the Customs of the Natives on such Occations, it was therefore set out to Sea and commited to that Element with all the decencey the circumstance of the place would admit of. This morning several Chiefs from the Westward made us a visit, they brought with them Emblems of Peace which are young Plantain Trees, these they put on board the Ship before they would venture themselves; they brought us a present of two Hogs (an Article we find here very scarce) and some bread fruit, for these they had Hatchets and other things. In the afternoon we set up one of the Ships Tents a Shore and M[r] Green and myself stay'd a Shore the night to Observe an Eclipse of Jupiters fi[r]st setilite which we was hinder'd from seeing by clowds.

TUESDAY 18*th*. Clowdy weather with some Showers of rain. This morning took as many people out of the Ship as could possibly be spar'd and set about Erecting a Fort, some were employ'd in troughing up intrenchments while others was cutting faccines Pickets &c[a]. The natives were so far from hindering us that several of them assisted in bring[ing] the Pickets and Faccines out of the woods and seem'd quite unconcern'd at what we were about, the wood we made use on for this occation we purchased of them and we cut no tree down before we had first obtain'd their consent. By this time all the Ships sails were unbent and the Armourers Forge set up to repair the Iron work &c[a] Serve'd Fresh Pork to the Ships Compney to day for the first time, this is like to be a very scarce Article with us but as to Bread fruit Cocoa-nuts and Plantains the Natives supply us with as much as we can distroy.

WEDNESDAY 19*th*. This morning Lycurgus, whose real name is Toobou-ratomita came with his Family from the westward in order from what we could understand to live near us, he brought with him the covering of a house with several other Materials for building one; we intend to requite the conf[i]dence this man seems to put in us by treating him with all imaginable kindness. Got on Shore some empty casks which we place'd in a double row along the bank of the River by way of a breast work on that side.

THURSDAY 20*th*. Wind at SE and Squally with rain; all hands employ'd a Shore, and nothing remarkable excepting that a Hog weighing about 90 pounds was brought along side the Ship for sale, but those who brought it would not part with it for any thing we could offer them but a carpenters broad ax and as this was what we could not part with they carried it away; thus we see those very People who but two years ago perfer'd a spike Nail to an Axe of any sort, have now so far learnt the use of them that they will not part with a Pig of 10 or 12 pounds weight for any thing under a Hatchet and even those of an inferior or small sort are in no great esteem with them, and small Nails such as 10[d] 20[d] or any under 40[d] are of no Value attall; but Beeds particularly white cut glass Beeds are much Value'd by them.

M[r] Banks and D[r] Solander lay ashore tonight for the first time, their Markee's being set up within the walls of the Fort and fit for their riceptoin.

FRIDAY 21*st*. Got the Copper Oven aShore and fix'd it in the Bank of the breast works.

Yesterday as M[r] Green and D[r] Munkhouse were taking a Walk they happen'd to meet with the Body of the Man we had Shot, as the Natives by signs made them fully understand, the manner in which the body was enterr'd being a little extraordinary I went to day with some others to see it. Close by the House wherein he resided when living was built a small Shade, but whether for the purpose or no I cannot say for it was in all respects like some of the Shades or house's they live in. This Shade was about 14 or 16 feet long, 10 or 12 broad and of a proportional height, one end was wholy open the other end [and] the two sides were partly inclosed with a kind of wicker'd work. In this shade lay the Corps upon a Bier or frame of wood with a Matted bottom like a Cot frame use'd at sea, and supported by 4 posts about 5 feet from the Ground, the Body was cover'd with a Mat and over that a white Cloth, along side of the Body lay a wooden Club, one of their weapons of warr. The head of the Corps lay next the close end of the Shad[e], and at this end lay 2 Cocoa-nut Shells such as they some times use to carry water in. At the other end of the Shade was a bunch of Green leaves with some dry'd twigs tied all together and stuck in the ground and a stone lying by them about as big as a Cocoa-nut, near to these lay a young Plantain tree, such as they use as Emblems of Peace, and by it lay a stone Axe; at the open end of the Shade was hung in several Strings a great number of Palm nuts. Without the Shad[e] was Stuck upright in the ground the Stem of a Plantain tree about 5 feet high on the Top of which stud a Cocoa-nut shell full of fresh water, and on the side of the Post hung a small Bag wherein were a few peices of Bread fruit roasted ready for eating, some of the peices were fresh and others stale. The Natives did not seem to like that we should go near the Body and stud at a little distance themselves while we examine'd these matters and appear'd to be please'd when we came away. It certainly was no very agreeable place for it Stunk intollerably and yet it was not above 10 yards from the Huts wherein several of the Living resided. The first day we landed we saw the Skeleton of a human being laying in this manner under a Shade that was just big enough to cover it, and some days after that when some of the gentlemen went with a design to examine it more narrowly it was gone.

It was at this time thought that this manner of entering their Dead was not common to all ranks of people as this was the first we had seen except the Skeleton just mentioned, but various were the opinions concerning the Provisions &c^a laid about the dead; upon the whole it should seem that these people not only beleive in a Supream being but on a futerue state also, and that this must be meant either as an offering to some Deitie, or for the use of the dead in the other world, but this last is not very probable as there appear'd to be no Priest craft in the thing, for what ever provisions were put there, it appear'd very plain to us that there it remaind untill it consum'd away of it self. It is most likely that we shall see more of this before we leave the Island, but if it is a Religious ceremoney we may not be able to understand it, for the Misteries of most Religions are very dark and not easily understud even by those who profess them.

*   *   *

FRIDAY 28*th*. This Morning a great number of the Natives came to us in their Canoes from different parts of the Island several of whome we had not seen before, one of these was the Woman called by the Dolphin the Queen of this Island. She first went to Mr Banks's Tent at the Fort where she was not known till the Master happening to go aShore who knew her and brought her on board with two men and several Women who seem'd to be all of her Family. I made them all some presents or other, but to Obariea, for such is this womans name, I gave several things, in return for which, as soon as I went a Shore with her, she gave me a Hog and several Bunches of Plantains, these she caused to be carried from her Canoe's up to the Fort in a kind of a Procession she and I bringing up the rear. This Woman is about 40 years of Age and like most of the other Women very Masculine. She is head or Chief of her own Family or Tribe but to all appearence hath no authority over the rest of the Inhabitants whatever she might have had when the Dolphin was here. Hercules, whose real name is Tootaha, is to all appearences the Chief man of the Island and hath generally Viseted us twice a Week since we have been here, and came always attended by a number of Canoes and people, and at those times we were sure to have a supply, more or less, of every thing the Island afforded, both from himself and from those that came with him, and it is a Chance thing that we got a Hog at any other time; he was with us at this time and did not appear very well pleased at the Notice we took of Obariea but I soon put him into a good humor by takeing him on board and makeing him some presents.

SATURDAY 29*th*. This Day got the four Guns out of the Hold and mounted 2 of them on the Quarter Deck, and the other 2 in the Fort on the bank of the River. For this day or 2 past about 30 Double Canoes, in which might be between 2 & 300 people, had come into our neighbourhood this made us keep a very good lookout & a strick eye over all their motions.

*   *   *

[MAY 1769]

MONDAY May the 1*st*. This morning Tootaha came on board the Ship and was very desireous of seeing into every Chest and Drawer that was in the Cabbin. I satisfied his curiosity so far as to open most of those that belong'd to me, he saw several things that he took a fancy to and collected them together, but at last he cast his eye upon the Adze I had from Mr Stephens that was made in immitation of one of their Stone Adzes or axes, the moment he lay his hands upon it he of his own accord put away every thing he had got before and ask'd me if I would give him that, which I very readily did and he went away without asking for any one thing more, which I by experence knew was a sure sign that he was well pleased with what he had got.

This day one of the Natives who appear'd to be a Chief dined with us as he had done some days before, but than there were always some Women present and one or a nother of them put the Victuals into his mouth but this day there happen'd to be none to perform that office; when he was helpt to Victuals and desired to eat he sat in the chair like a Stattute without once attempting to put one morsel to his mouth and would certainly have gone without his dinner if one of the Servants had not fed him. We have often found the Women very officious in feeding of us, from which it would seem that it is a Custom upon some occations for them to feed the Chiefs, however this is the only instance of that kind we have seen, or that they could not help themselves as well as any of us.

This afternoon we set up the Observatory and took the Astronomical

Quad^t a shore for the first time, together with some other Instruments. The Fort being no[w] finished and made as Tenable as the Time, Nature and situation of the ground, and materials we had to work upon would admit of. The North and south parts consisted of a Bank of earth 4½ feet high on the inside, and a Ditch without, 10 feet broad and 6 feet deep: on the west side faceing the Bay a Bank of earth 4 feet high and Pallisades upon that, but no ditch the works being at highwater mark: on the East side upon the Bank of the River was place'd a double row of casks: and as this was the weakest side the 2 four pounders were planted there, and the whole was defended besides these 2 guns with 6 Swivels and generally about 45 Men with small arms including the officers and gentlemen who resided aShore. I now thought my self perfectly secure from any thing these people could attempt.

TUESDAY 2*nd*. This morning about 9 oClock when Mr Green and I went to set up the Quad^t it was not to be found, it had never been taken out of the Packing case (which was ab^t 18 Inches square), sence it came from Mr Bird the Maker, and the whole was pretty heavy, so that it was a matter of astonishment to us all how it could be taken away, as a Centinal stood the whole night within 5 yards of the door of the Tent where it was put together with several other Instruments but none of them was missing but this. However it was not long before we got information that one of the natives had taken it away and carried it to the Eastward. Immidiatly a resolution was taken to detain all the large Canoes that were in the Bay, and to seize upon Tootaha and some others of the Principle people and keep them in Custody untill the Quad^t was produce'd, but this last we did not think proper immidiatly to put in execution as we had only Obaria in our power and the detaining of her by force would have alarm'd all the rest. In the meantime Mr Banks (who is always very alert upon all occations wherein the Natives are concern'd) and Mr Green went into the woods to enquire of Toobouratomita which way and where the Quadrant was gone; I very soon was inform'd that these Three were gone to the Eastward in quest of it and some time after I follow'd my self with a small party of Men, but before I went away I gave orders that if

Tootaha came either to the Ship or the Fort he was not to be detain'd, for I found that he had no hand in takeing away the Quadrant and that there was almost a certainty of geting it again. I met Mr Banks and Mr Green about 4 Miles from the Fort returning with the Quadrant, this was about Sunset and we all got back to the Fort about 8 oClock, where I found Tootaha in Custody and a Number of the Natives Crowding about the gate of the Fort. My going into the Woods with a party of arm'd men so alarm'd the Natives that in the evening they began to move off with their effects and a double Canoe puting off from the Bottom of the Bay was observ'd by the Ship and a boat sent after her, in this Canoe happen'd to be Tootaha and as soon as our boat came up with her he and all the people that were in the Canoe jump'd over board, and he only was taken up and brought on board the Ship together with the Canoe, the rest were permited to swim ashore. From the Ship Tootaha was sent to the Fort, where Mr Hicks thought proper to detain him untill I return'd. The scene between Toobouratomita and Tootaha when the former came into the Fort and found the latter in custody, was realy moveing, they wept over each other for some time, as for Tootaha he was so far prepossess'd with the thought that he was to be kill'd that he could not be made sensible to the contrary till he was carried out of the Fort to the people, many of whom express'd their joy by embraceing him; and after all he would not go away untill he had given us two Hoggs notwithstanding we did all in our power to hinder him, for it is very certain that the treatment he had met with from us did not merit such a reward. However we had it in our power to make him a present of equal Value whenever we pleased.

We had now time to consider how the quadrant was Stoln: it is very probable that the man who took it had seen the box brought into the Tent or else had been well inform'd by others and had from that moment resolved to steal it, for about sunset last night a man was seen crawling a long the bank of the River behind the Fort, but on being spoken to he went away; however it is very clear that he was watching for an opportunity to get into the Fort in the dusk of the evening before the centinals were call'd in and while the most of our people, after leaving of work, were diverting themselves with the natives.

However my self and some others were never out of the Fort and I did not stir out of the Tent where the quad^t was till Sun set, then walk'd several times round the Inside of the Fort after which I went into Mr Banks's Markee and order'd the Drumer to beat the Tattoo, in the doing of which he went 3 times round the works yet in one of these Short intervals when either mine or the drumers back [was] turn'd the man found means to carry off the Box for immidiately upon beating the Tattoo every boddy came into the Fort, the centinals call'd and place'd in the inside when it wold have been impossible for him to have done it. Indeed we found it difficult to beleive that a naked Indian frighten'd of f[i]rearms as they are, would have made such an attemp'd at the certain risk of his life.[15]

*   *   *

[*It took time for Tuteha to become reconciled with the English visitors after the incident of the quadrant, but the reconciliation when it came (5 May) was handsome. There was a huge gathering, an exchange of gifts, and a display of public wrestling. Tuteha then provided a feast to be eaten aboard the* Endeavour.]

TUESDAY 9*th*, WEDNESDAY 10*th* and THURSDAY 11*th*. Nothing remarkable happen'd for the three days. Obarea, the Dolphins Queen, made us a Visit for the first time sence the Quadrant was Stolen, she introduce'd her self with a small Pigg for which she had a Hatchet and as soon as She got it she lugg'd out a Broken Ax and several peices of Old Iron, these I believe she must have had from the Dolphin, the Ax she wanted to be mended and Axes made of the Old Iron. I obliged her in the first but excuse'd my self from the latter. Sence the Natives have Seen the Forge at work they have frequently brought pieces of Iron to be made into one sort of Tools or other, which hath generally been done when ever it did not hinder our own work, being willing to oblige them in every thing in my power; these peices of Old Iron the natives must have got from the Dolphin, as we know of no other Ship being here and very probably some from us; for there is no species of theft they will not commit to get this Artic[l]e and I may say the same of the common seamen when in these parts.

15. Minor damage to the quadrant was put right by Spöring.

FRIDAY 12*th*. Clowdy weather with Showers of Rain. This Morning a Man and two young women with some others came to the Fort whome we had not seen before: and as their manner of introduceing themselves was a little uncommon I shall insert it: Mr Banks was as usual at the gate of the Fort trading with the people, when he was told that some Strangers were coming and therefore stood to receive them, the compney had with them about a Doz^n young Plantains Trees and some other small Plants, these they laid down about 20 feet from Mr Banks, the People then made a lane between him and them, when this was done the Man (who appear'd to be only a Servant to the 2 Women) brought the young Plantains Singley, together with some of the other Plants and gave them to Mr Banks, and at the delivery of each pronounce'd a Short sentence, which we understood not, after he had thus dispose'd of all his Plantain trees he took several peices of Cloth and spread them on the ground, one of the Young Women then step'd upon the Cloth and with as much Innocency as one could possibly conceve, expose'd herself intirely naked from the waist downwards, in this manner she turn'd her Self once or twice round, I am not certain which, then step'd of the Cloth and drop'd down her clothes, more Cloth was then spread upon the Former and she again perform'd the same ceremony; the Cloth was then rowled up and given to Mr Banks and the two young women went and embraced him which ended the Ceremoney.

SATURDAY 13*th*. Nothing worthy of note happen'd dureing the day, in the night one of the Natives attempted to get into the Fort by climing over the Walls but being discover'd by the Centinals he made off; the Iron and Iron tools daily in use at the Armourers Forge are temptations that these people cannot possibly withstand.

SUNDAY 14*th*. This day we perform'd divine Service in one of the Tents in the Fort where several of the Natives attended and behaved with great decency the whole time: this day closed with an odd Scene at the Gate of the Fort where a young fellow above 6 feet high lay with a little Girl about 10 or 12 years of age publickly before several of our people and a number of the Natives. What makes me mention this, is because, it appear'd to be done more from Custom than Lewdness, for there were several women present particularly Obarea and several others of the better sort and these were so far from shewing the least disaprobation that they instructed the girl how she should act her part, who young as she was, did not seem to want it.

* * *

SUNDAY 28*th*. Winds Southerly and clear weather. This morning, my self, Mʳ Banks and Dʳ Solander set out in the Pinnace to pay Tootaha a Viset who had moved from Apparra to the sw part of the Islᵈ. What induced us to make him this Viset was a message we had received from him some days ago importing that if we would go to him he would give us several Hogs, we had no great faith in this yet we was resolved to try, and set out accordingly, it was night before we reached the place where he was and as we had left the Boat about half way behind us we were oblige'd to take up our quarters with him for the night. The Chief received us in a very friendly manner and a Pig was order'd to be kill'd & dressed for supper, but we saved his Life for the present thinking it would do us more service in a nother place and we supp'd on fruit and what else we could get: here was along with the Chief Obarea and many more that we knowed, they all seem'd to be travellers like ourselves, for nither the Canoes they had along with them nor the houses where they were were sufficient to contain the one half of them. We were in all Six of us and after supper began to look out for lodgings. Mʳ Banks went to one place Dʳ Solander to a nother, while I and the other three went to a third, we all of us took as much care of the little we had about us as possible knowing very well what sort of people we were among, yet notwithstanding all the care we took before 12 oClock the most of us had lost something or other, for my own part I had my stockings taken from under my head and yet I am certain that I was not a Sleep the whole time, Obarea took charge of Mʳ Banks's things and yet they were stolen from her as she pretended, Tootaha was acquainted with what had happen'd I believe by Obarea her self and both he and her made some stir about it but this was all meer shew and ended in nothing; a little time after this Tootaha came to the Hutt where I and those with me lay and entertain'd us with a consort of Musick, consisting of three Drums four Flutes and singing, this lasted about an hour and then they retire'd; the Musick and singing was so much of a peice that I was very glad when it was over. We stay'd with them till near noon the next day in hopes of geting some of our things again, and likewise some Hogs but we were at last obliged to come away with the one we had save'd out of the fire last night, and a promise from Tootaha that he would come to the Ship in a Day or two with more and bring with him the things that we had lost, a promise that we had no reason to expect he will fulfill. Thus ended our Viset and we got to the Fort late in the evening.

TUESDAY 30th. We are now very buisy in preparing our Instruments &c^a for the Observation and Instructing such Gentlemen in the use of them as I intend to send to other parts to Observe for fear we should fail here.

*   *   *

[JUNE 1769]

THURSDAY 1st June 1769. This day I sent Lieutenant Gore in the Long-boat to York Island[16] with Dr Munkhouse and Mr Sporing (a Gentleman belonging to Mr Banks) to observe the Transit of Venus, Mr Green having furnished them with Instruments for that purpose. Mr Banks and some of the Natives of this Island went along with them.

FRIDAY 2nd of June. Very early this morning Lieut^{nt} Hicks, Mr Clerk, Mr Petersgill and Mr Saunders, went away in the Pinnace to the Eastward, with orders to fix upon some convenient situation on this Island[17] and there to observe the Transit of Venus – they being likewise provided with Instruments for that purpose.

SATURDAY 3rd. This day prov'd as favourable to our purpose as we could wish, not a Clowd was to be seen the whole day and the Air was perfectly clear, so that we had every advantage we could desire in Observing the whole of the passage of the Planet Venus over the

16. Moorea, to the west.
17. The islet Taaupiri.

Suns disk: we very distinctly saw an Atmosphere or dusky shade round the body of the Planet which very much disturbed the times of the Contacts particularly the two internal ones.[18] D[r] Solander observed as well as M[r] Green and my self, and we differ'd from one another in observeing the times of the Contacts much more than could be expected. M[r] Greens Telescope and mine were of the same Mag[n]ify-ing power but that of the D[r] was greater then ours. It was ne[a]rly calm the whole day and the Thermometer expose'd to the Sun about the middle of the Day rose to a degree of heat (119) we have not before met with.

SUNDAY *4th* June. Punished Arch[d] Wolf with two Doz[n] Lashes for theft, having broken into one of the Store rooms and stolen from thence a large quantity of spike Nails, some few of them were found upon him. This evening the gentlemen that were sent to observe the Transit of Venus returnd with success. Those that were sent to York Island were well received by the Natives; that Island appear'd to them not to be very fruitfull.

MONDAY *5th*. Got some of the Bread a Shore out of the Bread room to dry and clean. Yesterday being His Majestys Birth Day we kept it to day, and had several of the Chiefs to dine with us.

TUESDAY *6th*. This Day and for some days past we have been inform'd by several of the Natives that about 10 or 15 Months ago, Two Ships touched at this Island and stay'd 10 days in a Harbour to the Eastward calle'd *Ohidea*,[19] the Commanders name was *Toottera* so at least they call'd him and that one of the Natives call'd *Orette* Brother to the Chief of Ohidea went away with him; they likewise say that these Ship[s] brought the Venerial distemper to this Island where it is now as common as in any part of the world and which the people bear with as little concern as if they had been accustomed to it for ages past.

18. The blur which made precision about the moment of contact difficult put a question mark against the observations, but in the end made no serious difference to their value.
19. This was Bougainville, with *La Boudeuse* and *L'Étoile*, in April 1768. Cook learned about the French expedition when he reached Batavia. Orette (Ereti) was the name of the chief. The brother who went with the French was Ahutoru.

We had not been here many days before some of our people got this disease and as no such thing happen'd to any of the Dolphins people while she was here that I ever heard off, I had reason (notwithstanding the improbability of the thing) to think that we had brought it along with us which gave me no small uneasiness and did all in my power to prevent its progress, but all I could do was to little purpose for I may safely say that I was not assisted by any one person in ye Ship, and was oblige'd to have the most part of the Ships Compney a Shore every day to work upon the Fort and a Strong guard every night and the Women were so very liberal with their favours, or else Nails, Shirts &c^a were temptations that they could not withstand, that this distemper very soon spread it self over the greatest part of the Ships Compney but now I have the satisfaction to find that the Natives all agree that we did not bring it here. However this is little satisfaction to them who must suffer by it in a very great degree and may in time spread it self over all the Islands in the South Seas, to the eternal reproach of those who first brought it among them. I had taken the greatest pains to discover if any of the Ships Company had the disorder upon him for above a month before our arrival here and ordered the Surgeon to examine every man the least suspected who declar'd to me that only one man in the Ship was the least affected with it and his complaint was a carious shin bone; this man has not had connection with one woman in the Island. We have several times seen Iron tools and other articles with these people that we suspected came not from the Dolphin and these they now say they had from these two Ships.

WEDNESDAY 7*th*, THURSDAY 8*th*, FRIDAY 9*th*. These three days we have been employ'd in careening both sides of the Ship and paying them with Pitch and Brimstone, we found her bottom in good order and that the Worm had not got into it.

SATURDAY 10*th*. Winds Variable with very much Rain all Day and last night.

SUNDAY 11*th*. Clowdy with rain last night and this Morning the remainder of the day fair weather. This Day Mr Banks and I took

Toobouratomita on board the Ship and shew'd him the Print contain-ing the Colours worne by the Ships of different Nations and very soon made him understand that we wanted to know which of them was worne by the Ships that were at Ohidea, he at once pitched upon the Spanish Flag and would by no means admit of any other: this together with several Articles we have lately seen amongst these people Such as Jackets Shirts &c^a usually worne by Spanish Seamen, proves beyond doubt that they must have been Ships of that Nation and come from some Port on the Coast of South America.

MONDAY 12*th*. Yesterday complaint was made to me by some of the Natives that Jno Thurman and Jam^s Nicholson Seam^n had taken by force from them several Bows and Arrows and Plated Hair, and the fact being proved upon them they were this Day punish'd with two Doz^n lashes each.

TUESDAY 13*th*. Some Showers of rain last night, but fair weather the most part of the Day. Tootaha whome we have not seen for some time past paid us a Viset to Day, he brought with him a Hog and some Bread fruit for which he was well paid.

WEDNESDAY 14*th*. Between 2 and 4 oClock this Morning one of the Natives Stole out of the Fort an Iron rake made use of for the Oven, it happend to be set up against the wall and by that means was Visible from the outside and had been seen by them in the evening as a Man had been seen lurking about the Fort some hours before the thing was miss'd. I was inform'd by some others of the Natives that he watched an oppertunity when the Centinal back was turn'd and hooked it with a long crooked stick and haled it over the wall; when I came to be inform'd of this theft in the Morning, I resolved to recover it by some means or other and accordingly went and took posession of all the Canoes of any Value I could meet with and brought them into the River behind the Fort to the number of 22, and told the Natives then present (most of them being the owners of the Canoes) that unless the Principal things they had stolen from us were restored, I would burn them every one, not that I ever intend to put this in execution, and yet I was very much displeased with them as they were daily either commiting or attempting to commit one theft or other, when at the same time (contrary to the opinion of every body) I would not suffer them to be fired upon, for this would have been puting it in the power of the Centinals to have fired upon them upon the most sligh[t]est occasions as I had before experienced, and I have a great objection to fireing with powder only amongest people who know not the difference; for by this they would learn to dispise fire arms and think their own arms superior and if ever such an Opinion prevail'd they would certainly attack you the event of which might prove as unfavourable to you as them.

About Noon the rake was restore'd us, when they wanted to have their Canoes again: but now as I had them in my posession I was resolved to try if they would not redeem them by restoring what they had stolen from us before; the principal things which we had lost were the Marine Musquet, a pair of Pistols belonging to Mr Banks, a sword belonging one of the Petty officers and a Water Cask with some other articles not worth mentioning: some said that these things were not in the Island, others that Tootaha had them and those of Tootaha's friends laid the whole to Obarea and I believe the whole was between these two persons.

THURSDAY 15*th*. We have been employ'd for some days past in overhauling all the Sea provisions, and stowing such as we found in a state of decay to hand in order to be first expended but having the people divided between the Ship and the Shore this work as well as the refiting the Ship goes but slowly on.

FRIDAY 16*th* and SATURDAY 17*th*. Variable winds with Showers of rain and Clowdy weather.

SUNDAY 18*th*. Variable winds and clear weather. This night we observe'd the Moon totally eclipse'd.

MONDAY 19*th*. Punished James Tunley with 12 lashes for takeing Rum out of the Cask on the quarter deck.

TUESDAY 20*th*. Got the Powder a Shore to air all of which we found in a bad condition and the Gunner inform's me that it was very little

better when it came first on board. Last night Obarea made us a Viset
who we have not seen for some time: we were told of her coming and
that she would bring with her some of the Stolen things, which we
gave credit to because we knew several of them were in her posession,
but we were surprised to find this woman put her self wholy in our
power and not bring with her one article of what we had lost. The
excuse she made was that her gallant, a Man that used to be along
with her, did steal them and she had beat him and turn'd him away;
but she was so sensible of her own guilt that she was ready to drop
down through fear – and yet she had resolution enough to insist upon
sleeping in Mr Bank's Tent all night and was with diffucculty prevaild
upon to go to her Canoe altho no one took the least notice of her. In
the Morning she brought her Canoe with every thing she had to the
Gate of the Fort, after which we could not help admireing her for her
Courage and the confidence she seem'd to place in us and thought
that we could do no less than to receive her into favour and accept
the presents she had brought us which Consisted of a Hog a Dog
Some Bread fruit & Plantains. We refused to except of the Dog as
being an animal we had no use for, at which she seem'd a little
surprised and told us that it was very good eating and we very soon
had an opportunity to find that it was so, for Mr Banks having bought
a basket of fruit in which happend to be the thigh of a Dog ready
dress'd, of this several of us taisted and found that it was meat not to
be dispise'd and therefore took Obarea's dog and had him immidiatly
dress'd by some of the Natives in the following manner. They first
made a hole in the ground about a foot deep in which they made a
fire and heated some small Stones, while this was doing the Dog was
Strangle'd and the hair got off by laying him frequently upon the fire,
and as clean as if it had been scalded off with hot water, his intrails
were taken out and the whole washed clean, and as soon as the stones
and hole was sufficiently heated, the fire was put out, and part of the
Stones were left in the bottom of the hole, upon these stones were laid
Green leaves and upon them the Dog together with the entrails. These
were likwise cover'd with leaves and over them hot stones, and then
the whole was close cover'd with mould: after he had laid here about
4 hours, the Oven (for so I must call it) was open'd and the Dog taken

out whole and well done, and it was the opinion of every one who taisted of it that they Never eat sweeter meat, we therefore resolved for the future not to despise Dogs flesh. It is in this manner that the Natives dress, or Bake all their Victuals that require it, Flesh, Fish and fruit.

I now gave over all thought of recovering any of the things the natives had stolen from us and therefore intend to give them up their Canoes when ever they apply for them.

WEDNESDAY 21*st*. Emp^d drying the Powder geting on board Wood, Water &c^a. Confin'd Robt Anderson seaman for refuseing to obey the orders of the Mate when at work in the hold. This morning a Chief whose name is Oamo, and one we had not seen before, came to the Fort, there came with him a Boy about 7 years of Age and a young Woman about 18 or 20; at the time of their Coming Obarea and several others were in the Fort, they went out to meet them, having first uncover'd their heads and bodies as low as their waists and the same thing was done by all those that were on the out side of the Fort; as we looked upon this as a ceremonial Respect and had not seen it paid to any one before we thought that this Oamo must be some extraordinary person, and wonder'd to see so little notice taken of him after the Ceremony was over. The young Woman that came along with him Could not be prevaild upon to come into the Fort and the Boy was carried upon a Mans Back, altho he was as able to walk as the Man who carried him. This lead us to inquire who they were and we was inform'd that the Boy was Heir apparent to the Sovereignty of the Island and the young woman was his sister and as such the respect was paid them,[20] which was due to no one else except the *Arreedehi* which was not Tootaha from what we could learn, but some other person who we had not seen, or like to do, for they say that he is no friend of ours and therefore will not come near us. The young Boy above mention'd is Son to Oamo by Obarea, but Oamo and Obarea did not at this time live together as man and wife he not being able to endure with her troublesome disposission. I mention this

20. The boy was Temarii, or Teriirere, the *arii rahi* or *nui* (chieftain of the highest rank) of the Papara region. The young woman was his intended bride.

because it shews that separation in the Marrige state is not unknown to this people.

THURSDAY 22nd. This morning I released Robt Anderson from confinement at the intercession of the Master and a promise of behaving better for the futher.

FRIDAY 23rd. This morning Manuel Ferrara Seaman a Portugese was missing, and I had some reason to think that he was gone with an intent to stay here. It was not long before I was inform'd that he was at Apparra with Tootaha, the man who gave us this information was one of Tootahas Servants, he was offer'd a Hatchet if he would go to Apparra and bring him to us. This was no doubt the very thing he came for, for he immidiately set out and return'd with the man in the evening; the man in his own difence said, that as he was going to the boat in order to go on board last night, he was taken away by force by 3 men, put into a Canoe and carried to Apparra; upon enquiry I found it to be so and that Tootaha wold have kept him had he not been perswaided to the Contrary or perhaps he thought the ax of more value then the man.

*   *   *

[*For six days, 26 June–1 July, Cook and Banks made a circuit of the island, on foot where possible, otherwise being rowed in the pinnace. They were impressed by the sacred sites, or* marae, *which Cook described in detail, particularly the great marae at Mahaiatea, in the south-west, a stepped pyramid of stone and coral built by Amo and Purea in 1766–8.*]

[JULY 1769]

Upon my return to the Ship I found that the Provisions had been all examin'd & the Water got on b^d amounting to 65 Tuns, I now determin'd to get every thing off from the Shore & leave the Place as soon as Possible, the geting the several Articles on board & Scraping & Paying the Ships Sides took us up the whole of the following week without anything remarkable happening until

SUNDAY 9th. When sometime in the Middle Watch Clement Webb &

Sam¹ Gibson both Marines & young Men found means to get away from the Fort (which was now no hard matter to do) & in the morning were not to be found, as it was known to every body that all hands were to go on board on the monday morning & that the ship would sail in a day or 2, there was reason to think that these 2 Men intended to stay behind, However I was willing to wait one day to see if they would return before I took any steps to find them.

MONDAY 10*th*. The 2 Marines not returning this morning I began to enquire after them & was inform'd by some of the Natives that they were gone to the Mountains & that they had got each of them a Wife & would not return, but at the same time no one would give us any Certain intelligence where they were, upon which a resolution was taken to seize upon as many of the Chiefs as we could, this was thought to be the readiest method to induce the other natives to produce the two men. We had in our Custody Obarea, Toobouratomita, and two other Chiefs but as I know'd that Tootaha would have more weight with the Natives then all these put together, I dispatch'd Lieut¹ Hicks away in the Pinnace to the place where Tootaha was to endeavour to decoy him into the boat and bring him on board which Mʳ Hicks perform'd without the least disturbance. We had no sooner taken the other Chiefs into Custody in Mʳ Banks's Tent than they became as desireous of having the men brought back as they were before of keeping them, and only desire'd that one of our people might be sent with some of theirs for them; accordingly I sent a Petty Officer²¹ and the Corporal of Marines with three or four of their people not doubting but what they would return with the two Men in the evening, but, they not coming so soon as I expected I took all the Chiefs on board the Ship for greater safety. About 9 oClock in the evening Web the Marine was brought in by some of the Natives and sent on board, he inform'd me that the Petty officer & the Corporal that had been sent in quest of them were disarm'd and seiz'd upon by the Natives and that Gibson was with them. Immidiatly upon geting this information I dispatch'd Mʳ Hicks away in the Long boat with a Strong party of men to resque them but before he went, Tootaha and the other Chiefs

21. The midshipman Monkhouse.

was made to understand that they must send some of their people with Mr Hicks to shew him the place where our men were, and at the same time to send orders for their immidiate releasement for if any harm came to these men they, the Chiefs, would suffer for it, and I believe at this time they wished as much to see the Men return in safty as I did, for the guides conducted Mr Hicks to the place before daylight and he recover'd the men without the least opposission and return'd with them about 7 oClock in the Morning of

TUESDAY 11*th*. I then told the Chiefs that there remaind nothing more to be done to regain their liberty but to deliver up the Arms the people had taken from the petty Officer and Corporal and these were brought on board in less then half an hour and then I sent them all a Shore, they made but a short stay with our people there before they went away and most of the Natives with them but they first wanted to have given us four Hogs, these we refus'd to accept as they would take no thing for them. Thus we are likly to leave these people in disgust with our behaviour towards them, owing wholy to the folly of two of our own people for it doth not appear that the natives had any hand in inticeing them away and therefore were not the first agressors, however it is very certain that had we not taken this step we never should have recover'd them.

The Petty officer whom I sent in quest of the deserters told me that the Natives would give him no intellingence where they were nor those that went along with him, but on the contrary grew very troblesome and as they were returning in the evening they were suddenly Siezed upon by a number of arm'd men that had hid themselves in the woods for that purpose; this was after Tootaha had been seized upon by us so that they did this by way of retaliation in order to recover their Chief, but this method did not meet with the approbation of them all, a great many condem'd these proceedings and were for having them set at liberty, while others were for keeping them untill Tootaha was relase'd. The desputes went so far that they came from words to blowes and our people were several times very near being set at liberty but at last the party for keeping them prevail'd; but as they had still some freinds no insult was offer'd them; a little while after they brought Web and Gibson the two deserters to them as prisoners likwise but at last they agree'd that Web should be sent to inform us where the others were.

When I came to examine these two men touching the reasons that induce'd them to go away, it appear'd that an acquentence they had contracted with two Girls and to whome they had stron[g]ly attache'd themselves was the sole reason of their attempting to Stay behind.

Yesterday we weigh'd the small bower Anchor the Stock of which was so much eaten by the worms as to break in heaving up and to day we hove up the best bower and found the Stock in the very same Condition. This day we got every thing off from the shore and to night every body lays on board.

WEDNESDAY 12*th*. The Carpenters Emp^d Stocking the Anchors and the Seamen in geting the Ship ready for sea; this morning we found the Staves of the Cask the Natives stole from us some time ago laying at the watering place, but they had been sencible enough to keep the Iron Hoops and only return what to them was of no use.

THURSDAY 13*th*. Winds Easterly a light breeze. This morning we was viseted by Obarea and several others of our acquaintances, a thing we did not expect after what had happend but two days ago; but this was in some measure owing to Mr Banks Dr Solander and my self going to Apparra last night where we so far convinced them of our friendly disposission that several of them were in tears at our comeing away. Between a 11 and 12 oClock we got under sail and took our final leave of this people after a stay of just Three Month, the most part of which time we have been upon good terms with them: some few differences have now and than happen'd, owing partly to the want of rightly understanding one another and partly to their natural thievish disposission which we could not at all times, neither bear with or guard against, but these have been attended with no ill concequences to either side except the first in which one of them was kill'd, and this I was very sorry for because from what had happen'd to them by the Dolphin I thought it would have been no hard matter to have got and kept a footing with them without bloodshed. For some time before we left this Island several of the natives were daily offering themselves to go away with us, and as it was thought that they must be of use to us in our future discoveries, we resolved to bring away one whose name is *Tupia*, a Cheif and a Priest: This man had been with us the most part of the time we had been upon the Island which gave us an oppertunity to know some thing of him: we found him to be a very intelligent person and to know more of the Geography of the Islands situated in these seas, their produce and the religion laws and customs of the inhabitants then any one we had met with and was the likeliest person to answer our purpose; for these reasons and at the request of Mr Banks I received him on board together with a you[n]g boy his servant.

*   *   *

[*Cook now gives a long and detailed 'Description of King Georges Island' or Otaheite, its topography, climate, flora and fauna, the physical characteristics of its people, their customs, religion, political and class system, dwellings, canoes etc. He gives a close account of tattooing, and of the way cloth is made from bark. He is disturbed and perplexed by the sect of* arioi, *who practised infanticide, and whose young women performed 'a very indecent dance'.*]

REMARKABLE OCCURRENCES AT SEA

FRIDAY July 14*th*. Gentle breezes at NE and clear weather. I have before made mention of our departure from Royal Bay on the preceeding fore-noon, and like wise that I had determined to run down to *Haheine* and *Ulietea*[22] before we stood to the southward, but haveing discover'd from the Hills of Georges Island an Island laying to the Northward, we first stood that way to take a nearer View of it (this Island is call'd *Tethuroa*) it lies N½w distant 8 Leagues from point Venus and is a small low uninhabited Island frequented by the people of Georges Island for fish with which it is said to abound. At 6 AM the Westermost part of York Island Bore SE½S and the body of Georges Island E½S.

22. Huahine and Raiatea. The other two islands mentioned are Tetiaroa and Tubuai Manu (or Maïao).

Punished the two Marines, who attempted to desert from us at Georges Island, with 2 Doz^n lashes each and then released them from confinement. At Noon the body of York Island bore EBS^1/2S, Royal Bay s 70°45′ E distant 61 Miles and an Island which we took to be Saunders Island discover'd by Capt. Wallice (call'd by the Natives *Tapoamanau*) bore ssw. Lat^{de} Ob^d 17°9′ South. Saw land bearing NW^1/2W which Tupia calls the Island of *Huaheine*.

SATURDAY 15*th*. Light Airs and Variable between the North and wsw, clear weather. At 6 pm York Island bore SE and Huaheine WNW and at 7 am it bore West. Lat^d observ'd at Noon 16°50′ South. Royal Bay s 37°30′ E Distant 22 leagues.

SUNDAY 16*th*. Winds at South and SSE a gentle breeze with some few showers of rain. At 6 PM the Island of Huaheine w^1/2s Dis^t 7 or 8 Leagues. At 8 AM being close in with the NW part of the Island sounded but had no ground with 80 fathoms, some of the Natives came off to the Ship but they were very shy of coming near untill they discover'd Tupia, but after that they came on board without hesitation, among those who came was the King of the Island whose Name is *Oree* he had not been long on board before he and I exchange'd Names and we afterwards address'd each other accordingly. At Noon the North end of the Island bore SBE^1/2E dis^t half a league Lat^d Obser^d 16°40′ s. Three other Islands in sight viz. *Ulitea*, *Otaha*, and *Bolabola*, so call'd by the Natives.[23]

MONDAY 17*th*. Winds Southerly fine pleasent weather. At 3 PM Anchor'd in a small Harbour on the West side of the Island (call'd by the Native[s] *Owharhe*) in 18 fathom water clear ground and secure from all winds; soon after I went a Shore, accompined by Mr Banks, Dr Solander and Dr Munkhouse, Tupia, the King of the Island and some other of the Natives who had been on board since the morning. The moment we landed Tupia striped him self as low as his waist and disired Mr Munkhouse to do the same, he then sat down before a great number of the natives that were collected together in a large Shade or house, the rest of us by his own desire standing behind; he

23. Raiatea, Tahaa, Bora-bora.

JULY 1769 *Society Islands* 67

then begun a long speach or prayer which lasted near a ¼ of an hour and in the Course of this speach presented to the people two handkerchiefs, a black silk neckcloth, some beads and two very small bunches of feathers, these things he had before provided for this purpose, at the same time two Chiefs spoke on the other side in answer to Tupia as I suppose in behalf of the people and presented us with some young Plantain Plants and two small bunches of feathers. These were by Tupia order'd to be carried on board the Ship, after the Peace was thus concluded and ratified every one was at liberty to go where he pleased and the first thing Tupia did was to go and pay his oblations at one of the Maries. This seem'd to be a common ceremony with this people and I suppose always perform'd upon landing on each others Territories in a peaceable manner; it farther appear'd that the things which Tupia gave away was for the God of this people as they gave us a Hog and some Cocoa-nuts for our God, and thus they have certainly drawn us in to commit sacrilege for the Hog hath already received sentence of death and is to be dissected to morrow.

AM. I set about surveying the Island and Dr Munkhouse with some hands went a shore to trade with the Natives, while the Long-boat was employ'd compleating our water.

TUESDAY 18*th*. Gentle breezes at s and ssw clear weather. The trading party had no success today, the Natives pretend that they have not had time to collect their provisions from the different parts of the Island, but that on the morrow we should have some and as I had not seen so much of the Island as I disired I resolved to stay one day longer to see if any thing was to be got.

WEDNESDAY 19*th*. PM Variable light airs and clear weather, the trading party had better Success to day then yesterday. AM A Gentle breeze at SE. As it was known to the natives that we intended to sail to day, Oree the Chief and several more came on board to take their leave of us, to the chief was given a small plate on which was stamp'd the following Inscription viz. *His Britannick Maj. Ship Endeavour, Lieut*[t] *Cook Commander 16*[th] *July 1769. Huaheine.* This was accompanied with some Medals or Counters of the English coine struck 1761 together with some other presents, all these but more particularly the plate the Chief promised never to part with; this we thought would prove as lasting a Testimony of our having first discover'd this Island as any we could leave behind. After this was done they were dismiss'd and w[e] begun to prepare to leave the place but as that falls out on the following day I shall conclude this with a discription of the Island, which is situated in the Latitude of 16°43′ s and Longitude 150°52′ West from Greenwich and North 58° West distant 31 Leagues from King Georges Island or Otaheite. It is about 7 Leagues in compass and of a Hilly and uneven surface; it hath a safe and commodious Harbour which lies on the west side under the northermost high land and within the north end of the reef which lays along that side of the Island; into this Harbour are two inlets or openings in the reef about 1½ Mile from each other, the southermost is the broadest on the s side of which is a very small sandy Island. This Harbour is called by the natives Ohwarhe.

The produce of this Island is in all respects the same as King Georges Island and the manners and customs of the inhabitants much the same only that they are not addicted to stealing and with respect to Colour they are rather fairer than the natives of Georges Island and the whole more uniformly of one Colour.

*   *   *

[*Cook now sailed to Raiatea, taking possession of it in the same manner, and from that base explored further the group of islands which he then named the Society Islands 'as they lay contiguous to one another'. On 9 August he set out for the south 'in search of the Continent' (pausing at Hita-roa or Rurutu). John Reading, the boastswain's mate, died of drink on the 28th. At the beginning of September, in latitude 40°s, they ran into violent storms, and having found no land Cook turned north and then west. At the beginning of October the presence of birds, seals and seaweed suggested they might be near land. They were in fact approaching the east coast of New Zealand's North Island.*]

[OCTOBER 1769]

SATURDAY 7th. *Winds NE, SE, Varble. Courses N 70° Wt. Distce sail'd* [in] *miles* 41. *Latd in South* 38°57′. *Longd in West* 177°54′. Gentle breezes and settled weather. At 2 PM saw land from the mast head bearing WBN, which we stood directly for, and could but just see it of the deck at sun set. Variation p^r Az. and Amp^d 15°4½′ East. By observations of the Sun and Moon made this afternoon the Longitude of the Ship is 180°55′ w: by the mean of these and subsequent observations the error of the Ships accou[n]t in Long^d from Georges Island is 3°16′, that is the Ship is so much to the Westward of the Long^{de} resulting from the Log which is what is insert'd [in] the columns. At midnight brought too and sounded but had no ground with 170 fath: at day light made sail in for the land. At Noon it bore from sw to NWBN distant 8 Leagues. Latitude Observed 38°57′ s.

SUNDAY 8*th*. Gentle breezes between the ENE and north, clear weather. At 5 PM seeing the opening of a Bay that appear'd to run pretty far inland, hauled our wind and stood in for it, but as soon as night came on we kept plying on and off untill day light when we found our selves to Leeward of the Bay the wind being at north. By noon we fetched in with the sw point, but not being able to weather it we tacked and stood off. We saw in the Bay several Canoes, People upon the shore and some houses in the Country. The land on the Sea-Coast is high with white steep clifts and back inland are very high mountains, the face of the Country is of a hilly surface and appeares to be cloathed with wood and Verdure.

MONDAY 9*th*. Gentle breezes and clear weather. PM stood into the Bay and anchored on the NE side before the entrance of a small river in 10 fathom water a fine sandy bottom; the NE point of the Bay bore EBS½s and the sw point south, distant from the shore half a League. After this I went ashore with a party of men in the Pinnace and yawl accompaned by Mr Banks and Dr Solander, we land[ed] abrest of the Ship and on the east side of the river just mentioned, but seeing some of the natives on the other side of the river whome I was desirous of speaking with and finding that we could not ford the river, I order'd the yawl in to carry us over and the Pinnace to lay at the entrance. In the mean time the Indians made off; however we went as far as their hutts which lay about 2 or 3 hundred yards from the water side leaving four boys to take care of the yawl, which we had no sooner left than four men came out of the woods on the other side the river and would certainly have cut her off, had not the people in the pinnace discover'd them and called to her to drop down the stream which they did being closely pursued by the Indians; the Coxswain of the pinnace who had the charge of the Boats, seeing this fire'd two musquets over their heads, the first made them stop and look round them, but the 2^d they took no notice of upon which a third was fired and killed one of them upon the spot just as he was going to dart his spear at the boat; at this the other three stood motionless for a minute or two, seemingly quite surprised wondering no doubt what it was that had thus killed their commorade: but as soon as they recover'd themselves they made off draging the dead body a little way and then left it. Upon our hearing the report of the Musquets we immidiatly repair'd to the boats and after viewing the dead body we return'd on board. In the morning seeing a good number of the natives at the same place where we saw them last night, I went a shore with the boats man'd and arm'd and landed on the opposite side of the river: Mr Banks Dr Solander and my self at first only landed and went to the side of the river, the natives being got together on the opposite side. We call'd to them in the George Island Language, but they answered us by florishing their weapons over their heads and danceing, as we supposed the war dance; upon this we retired untill the marines were landed which I order'd to be drawn up about two hundred yards behind us. We then went again to the river side having Tupia Mr Green and Dr Munkhouse along with us. Tupia spoke to them in his own language and it was an [a]greeable surprise to us to find that they perfectly understood him. After some little conversation had pass'd one of them swam over to us and after him 20 or 30 more, these last brought their arms with them which the first man did not, we made them every one presents but this did not satisfy them they wanted but every thing we had about us particularly our arms, and made several attempts to snatch them out of our hands. Tupia told us several times as soon as they came over to take care of our selves for they were not our friends, and this we very soon found for one of them snatched Mr Greens Hanger from him and would not give it up, this incourage'd the rest to be more insolent and seeing others comeing over to join them I order'd the man who had taken the hanger to be fired at, which was accordingly done and wounded in such a manner that he died soon after; upon the first fire, which was only two musquets, the others retire'd to a rock which lay nearly in the middle of the river, but upon seeing the man fall they return'd probably to carry him off or his arms, the last of which they accomplished and this we could not prevent unless we had run our Bayonets into them, for upon their returning from off the rock we had discharg'd of our peices which were load[ed] with small shott and wound[d] three more, but these got over the river and where carried off by the others who now thought proper to retire.[24]

Finding that nothing was to be done with the people on this side and the water in the river being salt I embarked with an intent to row round the head of the Bay in search of fresh water, and if possible to surprise some of the natives and to take them on board and by good treatment and presents endeavour to gain their friendship; with this View on

TUESDAY 10*th*. PM I rowed round the head of the Bay but could find no place to land, on account of the great surff which beat every where upon the shore; seeing two boats or Canoes coming in from Sea, I rowed to one of them in order to seize upon the people and came so near before they took notice of us that Tupia called to them to come along side and we would not hurt them, but instead of doing this they endeavoured to get away, upon which I order'd a Musquet to be fire'd over their heads thinking that this would either make them surrender or jump over board, but here I was misstaken for they immidiatly took to thier arms or whatever they had in the boat and began to attack us, this obliged us to fire upon them and unfortunatly either two or three were kill'd, and one wounded, and three jumped over board, these last we took up and brought on board, where they were clothed and treated with all immaginable kindness and to the surprise of every body became at once as cheerful and as merry as if they had

24. In an earlier version of his much rewritten account of this encounter, Cook said that on his order to fire at the man who had stolen Green's hanger (or sword), Banks fired first, with small shot, which had no effect. He then ordered the surgeon, Monkhouse, whose piece was loaded with ball, to fire. When the Maoris rallied, it was Cook himself, with Green and Tupaia, who fired at them with small shot.

been with their own friends; they were all three young, the eldest not above 20 years of age and the youngest about 10 or 12.

I am aware that most humane men who have not experienced things of this nature will cencure my conduct in fireing upon the people in this boat nor do I my self think that the reason I had for seizing upon her will att all justify me, and had I thought that they would have made the least resistance I would not have come near them, but as they did I was not to stand still and suffer either my self or those that were with me to be knocked on the head.[25]

In the morning as I intended to put our three prisioners a shore and stay here the day to see what effect it might have upon the other natives, I sent an Officer aShore with the marines and a party of men to cut wood, and soon after followed my self accompanied by Mr Banks Dr Soland[er] and Tupia, takeing the three natives along with us whome we landed on the west side of the river before mentioned; they were very unwilling to leave us pretending that they should fall into the hands of their enimies who would kill and eat them; however they at last of their own accords left us and hid themselves in some bushes. Soon after this we discover'd several bodies of the Natives marching towards us, upon which we retire'd a Cross the River and join'd the wooders and with us came the three natives we had just parted with, for we could not prevail upon them to go to their own people. We had no sooner got over the river than the others assembled on the other side to the number of 150 or 200 all arm'd. Tupia now began to parly with them and the three we had with us shew'd every thing we had given them, part of which they laid and left upon the body of the man that was killed the day before, these things seemed so far to convince them of our friendly intentions that one man came over to us while all the others set down upon the sand: we every one made this man a present and the three natives that were with us likewise presented him with such things as they had got from us, with which

25. In an earlier version, Cook continued: 'or else retire and let them gone off in triumph and this last they would of Course have attributed to their own bravery and our timorousness.' Banks summed up these events by saying 'thus ended the most disagreeable day my life has yet seen. Black be the mark for it, and heaven send that such may never return to embitter future reflection.'

after a short stay he retired a cross the river. I now thought proper to take every body on board to prevent any more quarrels and with us came the three natives, whome we could not prevail upon to stay behind and this appear'd the more strange as the Man who came over to us was uncle to one of them. After we had return'd on board we saw them carry off the dead man but the one that was kill'd the first evening we landed remaind in the very spot they had left him.

WEDNESDAY 11*th*. In the PM as I intended to sail in the morning we put the three youths ashore seemingly very much against their inclination, but whether this was owing to a desire they had to remain with us or the fear of falling into the hands of their eminies as they pretended I know not; the latter however seem'd to be ill founded for we saw them carried aCross the river in a Catamaran and walk leasurely off with the other natives.

At 6 AM we weigh'd and stood out of the Bay which I have named *Poverty Bay* because it afforded us no one thing we wanted (Lat^{de} 38°42' s. Long^{de} 181°36' w) it is in the form of a Horse shoe and is known by an Isl^d lying close und[er] the NE point, the two points which forms the entrance are high with steep white clifts and lay a league and a half or two leagues from each other NEBE and SWBW. . . .

The shore of this bay from a little within each entrance is a low flat sand but this is only a narrow slip, for the face of the Country appears with a variety of hills and vallies all cloathed with woods and Verdure and to all appearence well inhabeted especialy in the Vallies leading up from the bay where we dayly saw smooks at a great distance in land, and far back in the Country are very high mountains. At Noon the SW Point of Poverty Bay (which I have named *Young Nicks head* after the boy who first saw this land)[26] bore NBW distant 3 or 4 Leagues, being at this time about 3 Miles from the shore and had 25 fathom, the Main land extending from NEBN to South. My intention is to fowlow the direction of the Coast to the Southward as far as the Latitude of 40° or 41° and then to return to the northward in case we meet with nothing to incourage us to proceed farther.

26. Nicholas Young, about twelve years old.

THURSDAY 12*th.* Gentle breezes at NW and north with frequent calms. In the afternoon while we lay becalm'd several Canoes came off to the Ship but kept at a distance untill one who appear'd to come from a different part came off and put along side at once and after her all the rest. The people in this boat had heard of the treatment those had met we had had on board before and therefore came on board without hesitation. They were all kindly treated and very soon enter'd into a traffick with our people for George Island Cloth &c[a] giving in exchange their paddles (having little else to dispose of) and hardly left themselves a Sufficient number to paddle a shore, nay the People in one Canoe after disposing of the Paddles offer'd to sell the Canoe. After a stay of about two hours they went away, but by some means or a nother three were left on board and not one boat would put back to take them in and what was more surprising those on board did not seem attall uneasy with their situation. In the evening a light breeze springing up at NW we steer'd along shore under an easy sail untill midnight, then brought too, soon after it fell calm and continued so untill 8 oClock AM when a breeze sprung up at north with which we stood along shore SSW. At and after sun rise found the Variation to be 14°46' East. About this time two Canoes came off to the ship one of which was prevaild upon to come along side to take in the three people we had had on board all night who now seem'd glad of the oppertunity to get a shore; as the people in the Canoe were a little shy at first it was observed that one arguement those on board made use on to intice the others along side was in telling them that we did not eat men, from which it should seem that these people have such a Custom among them. At the time we made sail we were a breast of the point of land set yesterday at Noon from which the land trends SSW. This point I have named *Cape Table* on account of its shape and figure, it lies 7 Leagues to the Southward of Poverty Bay. . . . At Noon Cape Table bore N 20° East distant 4 Leagues, and a small Island (being the Southermost land in sight) bore South 70° W distant 3 Miles: this Island I have named *Isle of Portland* on account of its very great resemblance to Portland in the English Channell. . . .

We saw a great number of the Natives assembled together on the

Isle of Portland, we likewise saw some on the Main land and several places that were cultivated and laid out in square plantations.

FRIDAY 13*th*. At 1 PM we discoverd land behind or to the Westward of Portland extending to the Southward as far as we could see. In hauling round the south end of Portland we fell into shoal water and broken ground which we however soon got clear of: at this time four Canoes came off to us full of people and kept for some time under our stern threating of us all the while. As I did not know but what I might be obliged to send our boats a head to sound I thought these gentry would be as well out of the way, I order'd a musquet shott to be fired close to one of them, but this they took not the least notice of; a four pounder was then fired a little wide of them, at this they began to shake thier spears and Paddles at us, but notwithstanding this they thought fit to retire. . . .

The land near the shore is of a moderate height with white clifts and sandy beaches – inland are several pretty high mountains and the whole face of the country appears with a very hilly surface and for the most part covered with wood and hath all the appearences of a very pleasent and fertile country.

SATURDAY 14*th*. PM had gentle breezes between the NE and NW. Kept runing down along shore at the distance of two or 3 Miles off, our soundings was from 20 to 13 fathom an even sandy bottom. We saw some canoes or boats in shore and several houses upon the land, but no harbour or convenient watering place, the main thing we were looking for. In the night had little wind and sometimes Calm with dirty rainy weather. AM had Variable light airs next to a Calm and fair weather. In the Morning being not above two Leagues from the SW Cod of the great Bay we have been in for these 2 days past, the Pinnace and Long boat were hoisted out in order to search for fresh water; but just as they were ready to put off we observe'd several Boats full of People coming off from the shore and for that reason I did not think it prudent to send our own from the Ship; the first that came were five in number, in them were between 80 and 90 Men. Every method was tried to gain their friend Ship and several things were thrown over board to them, but all we could do was to no purpose neither would they except of any one thing from us but seem'd fully bent on attacking us; in order to prevent this and our being obliged to fire upon them I order'd a 4 pounder load[ed] with Grape to be fire'd a little wide of them, leting them know at the same time by means of Tupia what we were going to do; this had the desired effect and not one of these would afterwards trust themselves abreast of the Ship. Soon after four more came off, one of these put what arms they had into a nother boat and then came along side so near as to take what things we gave them, and I believe might have been prevaild upon to come on board had not some of the first 5 come up under our stern and begun again to t[h]reaten us at which the people in this one boat seem'd displeased, emmidiatly after this they all went a Shore. At Noon Lat. In per Observation 39°37′ s. Portland bore by our run from it EBN Dist. 14 Leagues, the southermost land in sight and which is the south point of the Bay SEBS, distant 4 or 5 Leagues, and a bluff head lying in the SW Cod of the Bay, SBW 2 or 3 Miles. . . . Inland are a chain of pretty high mountains extending N and S, on the sumets and sides of these mountains were many patches of snow, but between them and the Sea the land is Cloathed with wood.

SUNDAY 15*th*. PM Stood over for the Southermost land or South point of the Bay, having a light breeze at NE, our soundings from 12 to 8 fathom; not reaching this point before dark, we stood off an[d] on all night, having Variable light airs next to a Calm, depth of water from 8 to 7 fathom. Variation 14° 10′ E. At 8 AM being a breast of the SW Point of the Bay, some fishing boats came off to us and sold us some stinking fish, however it was such as the[y] had and we were glad to enter into traffick with them upon any terms. These people behaved at first very well untill a large arm'd boat wherein were 22 Men, came along side. We soon saw that this boat had nothing for traffic, yet as they came boldly along side we gave them two or three peices of Cloth, articles they seem the most fond off; One man in this boat had on him a black skin something like a bear skin which I was desireous of having that I might be a better judge what sort of an Animal the first owner was. I offer'd him for it a peice of Red Cloth which he

seem'd to jump at by emmidiatly puting of the Skin and holding it up
to us, but would not part with it untill he had the Cloth in his possession,
and after that not attall but put of the boat and went away and with
them all the rest, but in a very short time they return'd again and one
of the fishing boat came along side and offer'd us some more fish, the
Indian Boy Tiata, Tupia's servent being over the side, they seized
hold of him, pulld him into the boat and endeavourd to carry him
off, this obliged us to fire upon them which gave the Boy an oppertunity
to jump over board and we brought the Ship too, lower'd a boat into
the Water and took him up unhurt. Two or Three paid for this daring
attempt with the loss of their lives and many more would have suffered
had it [not] been for fear of killing the boy. This affair occation'd my
giveing this point of Land the name of *Cape Kidnappers*: it is remarkable
on account of two white rocks in form of Hay Stacks standing very
near it: on each side of the Cape are tollerable high white steep clifts.
Lat^d 39°43′ s, Longd. 182°24′ w. It lies South w в West distant 13
Leagues from the Isle of Portland, between them is a large Bay wherein
we have been for these 3 Days past; this Bay I have name'd *Hawke's
Bay* in honour of Sr Edward first Lord of the Admiralty; we found in
it from 24 to 8 and 7 fathom every where good Anchoring.

* * *

TUESDAY 17*th*. PM Winds at West a fresh breeze in the night, Variable
light Airs and Calm, AM a gentle breeze between the NW and NE.
Seeing no likelyhood of meeting with a harbour and the face of the
Country Vissibly altering for the worse I thought that the standing
farther to the South would not be attended with any Valuable discovery, but would be loosing of time which might be better employ'd
and with a greater probabillity of Success in examining the Coast to
the Northward; with this View at 1 PM we tacked and stood to the
Northward having the wind at west a fresh breeze, at this time we
could see the land extending SWBS at least 10 or 12 Leagues.

The Bluff head or high point of land we were abreast off at noon,
I have calld *Cape Turnagain* because here we returnd, it lies in the
Latitude of 40°34′ s, Longitude 182°56′ West and 18 Leagues ssw and
ssw½w from Cape Kidnappers.

*   *   *

[*The* Endeavour *headed north again, and off the Isle of Portland a canoe came alongside, and the five men in her came aboard, showing no fear, and 'insisted upon staying with us the whole night'. They were sent ashore near Table Cape, and the ship continued north, passing the original landfall of Young Nick's Head.*]

FRIDAY 20*th*. PM A fresh breeze at SSW, in the night Variable light breezes with rain; AM a fresh breeze at SW. At 3 PM pass'd by a remarkable head Land which I call'd *Gable-end Foreland* on account of the very great reseblence the white clift at the very point hath to the Gable end of a house, it is made still more remarkable by a spire'd rock standing a little distance from it. This head land lies from Cape Table N 24° East distant 12 Leagues, between them the Shore forms a Bay wherein lies Poverty Bay, 4 Leagues from the former and 8 Leagues from the latter. From Gable end Forland the land trends NBE as far as we could see: the land from Poverty Bay to this place is of a moderate but very unequal height distinguished by hills and Vallies that are cover'd with woods. We saw as we run along shore several Villages cultivated lands and some of the Natives, in the evening some Canoes came off to the Ship and one man came on board to whome we gave a few trifles and then sent him away. Stood off and on untill day light then made sail in shore in order to look into two Bays that appear'd to our View about 2 Leagues to the northward of the Foreland; the southermost we could not fetch, but in the other we anchor'd about 11 oClock in 7 fathom water a black sandy bottom; the North point bore NE½N distant 2 Miles and the S point SEBE dist^t 1 Mile and about ¾ of a Mile from the Shore. This Bay is not so much shilterd from the sea as I at first thought it was, but as the Natives many of whome come about us in thier canoes, appear'd to be of a friendly disposission I was willing to try if we could not get a little water on board and to see a little into the nature of the Country before we proceed'd farther to the northward.

SATURDAY 21*st*. We had no sooner come to an Anchor as mentioned above, than preceiving two old men in the Canoes, who from their garbe appear'd to be chiefs, these I invited on board and they came without hesitation. To each I gave about 4 yards of Linnen and a Spike nail, the linnen they were very fond of, but the nails they seem'd to set no Value upon. Tupia explained to them the reasons of our comeing here and that we should neither hurt nor molest them if they did but behave in the same peaceable manner to us, indeed we were under very little apprehension but what they would as they had heard of what happend in Poverty bay.

Between 1 and 2 PM I put off with the Boats man'd and Arm'd in order to land to look for fresh water, having these 2 Men along with us, but the surf runing very high and it begun to blow and rain at the same time, I return'd back to the Ship having first put the 2 Chiefs into one of their Canoes. In the Evening it fell Moderate and we landed and found 2 small streams of fresh water and the natives to all appearences very friendly and peaceable, on which account I resolved to stay one day at least to fill a little water and to give Mr Banks an oppertunity to Collect a little of the produce of the Country. In the Morning Lieut^t Gore went ashore to superintend the watering with a strong party of men, but the geting the Casks off was so very difficult on account of the surff, that it was near noon before one turn came on board.

SUNDAY 22nd. PM Light breezes and Clowdy. About or a little after noon several of the natives came off to the Ship in their Canoes and began to traffic with us, our people giving them Georges Island Cloth for theirs, for they had little else to dispose of. This kind of exchange they seemd at first very fond of and prefer'd the Cloth we had got at the Islands to English Cloth, but it fell in its Value above 500 per cent before night. I had some of them on board and shewed them the Ship with which they were well pleased.

The same friendly disposission was observe'd by those on Shore and upon the whole they behaved as well or better than one could expect, But as the geting the Water from the shore proved so very tedious on account of the surf, I resolved upon leaving this place in the morning and Accordingly at 5 AM we weigh'd and put to Sea. . . .

MONDAY 23rd. PM fresh gales at North and Clowdy weather. At 1 Tacked and stood in shore, at 6 sounded and had 56 fath. a fine sandy bottom, the Bay of Tegadoo bore SW½W distant 4 Leagues. At 8 Tacked in 36 fathom being then about two Leagues from land. Stood off and on all night having gentle breezes. At 8 AM being right before the Bay of Tegadoo and about a League from it, some of the natives came off to us, and inform'd us that in a Bay a little to the south-ward (being the same that we could not fetch the day we put into Tegadoo) was fresh water and easy geting at it, and as the wind was now against us and we got nothing by beating to windward, I thought the time would be better spent in this Bay in geting on board a little water and forming some connections with the natives than by keep-ing the sea. With this View we bore up for it and sent two Boats in Man'd and Arm'd to examine the watering place who returnd about noon and conform'd the acco^t the Natives had given. We then anchord in 11 fathom water a fine sandy bottom – the North point of the Bay NBE and the south point SE and the watering place which was in a small Cove a little within the South p^t of the bay SBE distant 1 Mile.

TUESDAY 24*th*. Winds Westerly and fine weather. This afternoon, as soon as the Ship was moor'd, I went ashore to examine the Watering place, accompan'd by Mr Banks and Dr Solander. I found the water good and the place pretty convenient, and plenty of Wood close to high water mark and the natives to all appearence not only very friendly, but ready to traffic with us for what little they had. Early in the Morning I sent Lieutenant Gore a Shore to superintend the Cuting Wood and filling of Water with a Sufficient number of men for both purposes and all the Marines as a guard; after breakfast I went my self and remain'd there the whole day, but before this Mr Green and I took several observations of the Sun and Moon, the mean result of them gave 180°47′ West Long^d. from the Meridian of Greenwich but as all the obser^{ns} made before exceeded these I have laid down this coast agreeable to the mean of the whole. At Noon I took the Suns Meridian Alt^d with the Astro^l Quad^t and found the Latitude to be 38°22′24″ S.

WEDNESDAY 25*th*. Winds and weather as yesterday. PM set up the Armourer's Forge to repair the Tiller braces, they being broke; by night we had got on board 12 Ton of water and two or three boat loads of wood, and this I looked upon to be a good days work. The natives gave us not the least disturbance, but brought us now and then different sorts of fish, both to the Ship and watering place which we purchased of them with Cloth beeds &c^a.

* * *

SATURDAY 28*th*. Gentle breezes southerly and fine weather. Employ'd Wooding, cuting of Broom stuff and making of Brooms, there being a shrub here very fit for that purpose: and as I intend^d to sail in the morning some hands were employ'd picking of Sellery to take to sea with us, this is found here in great plenty and I have caused it to be boild with Portable Soup and Oatmeal every morning for the Peoples breakfast, and this I design to continue as long as it will last or any is to be got, because I look upon it to be very wholesome and a great Antiscorbutick.

SUNDAY 29*th*. PM Gentle breezes at NE with Thunder and lightning up in the Country, in the night had light airs off the land and very Foggy: in the forenoon had a gentle breeze at NNE and Clear wea^r. At 4 AM Unmoor'd and at 6 Weigh'd and put to sea. At Noon the Bay saild from bore North 63° w distant 4 Leagues.

This Bay is call'd by the Natives *Tolaga*. . . .

During our stay in this Bay we had every day more or less traffic with the Natives, they bringing us fish and now and then a few sweet Potatoes and several trifles which we deem'd curiosities for these we gave them cloth, Beeds nails &c^a. The Cloth we got at King Georges Island and Uliatea they Valued more than any thing we could give them and as every one in the Ship were provided with some of this sort of Cloth, I suffer'd every body to purchase what ever they pleased without limitation, for by this means I knew that the natives would not only sell, but get a good price for every thing they brought; this I thought would induce them to bring to market what ever the Country afforded and I have great reason to think that they did, yet it amounted to no more than what is above mention'd. We saw no four footed Animals either tame or wild or signs of any except Dogs and Ratts and these were very scarce especialy the latter, the flesh of the former they eat and ornament their clothing with their skins as we do ours with furs &c^a. While we lay here I went upon some of the Hills in order to view the Country, but when I came there I could see but very little of it, the sight being interrupted by still higher hills; the tops and ridges of the hills are for the most part barren, at least little grows on them but fern. But, the Vallies and sides of many of the Hills were luxuriously clothed with Woods and Verdure and little Plantations of the Natives lying dispers'd up and down the Country.

We found in the woods Trees of above 20 different sorts, specimens of each I took on board as all of them were unknown to any of us: the tree which we cut for fireing was something like Maple and yielded a whitish Gum, there was another sort of a deep yallow which we imagined might prove usefull in dying. We likewise found one Cabbage tree which we cut down for the sake of the Cabbage. The Country abounds with a great number of Plants and the Woods with as great a Variety of very beautifull Birds, many of them unknown to us. The soil both of the hills and Vallies is light and sandy and very proper for produceing all kinds of Roots but we saw only sweet Potatous and Yamms among them; these they plant in little round hills, and have plantations of them containing several Acres neatly laid out and kept in good order, and many of them are fence'd in with low pailing which can only serve for ornament.

*　　*　　*

[*Cook rounded a cape which, being confident it was 'the Eastermost land on this whole Coast', he named East Cape. Further west they frightened off a flotilla of five warlike canoes with grape-shot, then a round shot. Cook named the place Cape Runaway.*]

[NOVEMBER 1769]

WEDNESDAY November 1st. PM As we stood along shore, (having little wind and Variable) we saw a great deal of Cultivated land laid out in regular inclosures a sure sign that the Country is both fertile and well inhabited; some Canoes came off from the Shore but would not come near the Ship. At 8 brought too 3 Miles from the shore, the land seen yesterday bearing west and which we now saw was an Island bore sw distant 8 Leagues. I have named it *white Island* because as such it always appear'd to us. At 5 AM made sail along shore to the SW having little wind at ESE and Clowdy weather. At 8 saw between 40 and 50 Canoes in shore, several of them came off to the Ship and after being about us some time they venterd along side and sold us some Lobster Mussels and two Conger ells. After these were gone some others came off from a nother place with mussels only and but few of these they thought proper to part with, thinking that they had a right to every thing we handed them into their boats without makeing any return. At last the people in one Canoe took away some linnen that was towing over the side which they would not return for all that we could say to them; upon this I fire'd a Musquet ball thro' the boat, and after that another musquet load[ed] with small shott, neither of which they minded, only pull'd off a little and then shook their paddles at us, at which I fired a third musquet and the ball striking the water pretty near them, they immidiatly apply'd their paddles to a nother use, but after they thought themselves out of reach, they got all together and shook again their paddles at us. I then gave the Ship a yaw and fire'd a four pounder this sent them quite off and we kept on our Course along shore having a light breeze at ESE. At Noon we were in the Latitude of 37°45', White Island bearing N 29° West distant 8 Leagues.

THURSDAY 2nd. Gentle breeze from NW round northerly to ESE and fair weather. At 2 PM saw a pretty high Island bearing west from us and at 5 Saw more Islands and Rocks to the westward of it; hauld our wind in order to go without them but finding that we could not weather them before dark bore up and run between them and the main. At 7 was close under the first Island from whence a large double Canoe full of people came off to us, this was the first double Canoe we had seen in this Country. They stayd about the Ship untill dark then left us, but not before they had thrown a few stones: they told us the name of the Island which was *Mowtohora*, it is but of a small circuit but high and lies 6 Miles from the Main, under the south side is anchorage in 14 fathom water. SWBS from this Island on the main land, seemingly at no great distance from the sea is a high round mountain which I have named *Mount Edgecomb*, it stands in the middle of a large plane which makes it the more conspicuous. Latitude 37°59′ Long^d 183°07′. In standing to the westward we shoalden'd our water from 17 to 10 fathom, and knowing that we were not far from some small Islands, and Rocks that we had seen before dark, after passing of which I intended to have brought too for the night, but now I thought it more prudent to tack and spend the night under the Island Mowtohora where I knowd there was no danger, and it was well we did for in the morning, after we had made sail to the westward we discover'd ahead of us Rocks level with and under water; they lay 1½ League from the Island Mowtohora and about 9 Miles from the Main and NNE from Mount Edgcumbe. We pass'd between these rocks and the Main having from 7 to 10 fathom water. The Double Canoe which we saw last night follow'd us again to day under sail and kept abreast of the Ship near an houre talking to Tupia, but at last they began to pelt us with stones but upon fireing one Musquet they drop'd a stern and left us. At half past 10 pass'd between a low flat Island and the Main the distance from one to the other being 4 Miles, depth of water, 10, 12 and 15 fathom. At Noon the Flat Island bore from NE to E½N distant 5 or 6 Miles, Latitude in per Observation 37°39′s Long^d in 183°30′. The Main land between this and the Island of Mowtohora which is [10] Leagues is of a Moderate height and all a level flat Country pritty clear of wood and full of Plantations and Villages; the Villages are built upon eminences near the Sea, and are fortified on the land side with a Bank and a Ditch, and Pallisaded all round, besides this some of them appear'd to have out works. We have before now observed on several parts of the Coast small Villages inclosed with Pallisades, and Works of this kind built on eminences and ridges of hills, but Tupia hath all along told us that they were Mories or places of Worship, but I rather think that they are places of retreat or Stronghold where they defend themselves againest the Attack of an Enimy as some of them seem'd not ill design'd for that purpose.

*   *   *

SATURDAY 4*th*. The first and Middle parts little wind at ENE and clear weather: the latter had a fresh breeze at NNW and hazey with rain. At 1 PM three Canoes Came off from the Main to the Ship and after parading about a little while they darted two pikes at us, the first was at one of our men as he was going to give them a rope thinking that they were coming on board, but the second they throw'd into the Ship, the fireing of one Musquet sent them away. Each of these Canoes were made out of one large tree and were without any sort of ornament and the people in them were mostly quite naked. At 2 PM saw a large opening or inlet in the land which we bore up for, with an intent to come to an Anchor; at this time had 41 fathom water which gradually decreased to 9 fathom at which time we were 1½ Miles from a high tower'd rock lying near the South p^t of the inlet, the Rock and the northermost of the Court of Aldermen[27] being in one bearing s 61° E. At half past 7 Anchor'd in 7 fathom a little within the south entrance of the Bay or inlet. We were Accompaned in here by several Canoes, who stay'd about the Ship untill dark, and before they went away they were so generous as to tell us that they would come and attack us in the morning, but some of them paid us a Veset in the night, thinking no doubt but what they should find all hands a sleep, but as soon as they found their mistake they went off. My reasons for puting in here were the hopes of discovering a good Harbour and the disire I had of being in some convenient place to observe the Transit of Mercury which happens on the 9th Instant and will be wholy Visible here if the day is clear. If we should be so fortunate as to Obtain this Observation the Longitude of this place and Country will thereby be very accuratly determined.

Between 5 and 6 oClock in the Morning several Canoes came to us from all Parts of the Bay; in them were about 130 or 140 People, to all appearences their first design was to attack us being all compleatly Arm'd in their way; however this they never attempted but after Parading about the Ship near three hours, some times trading with us and at other times tricking of us, they disperse'd but not before we had fired a few Musquets and one great gun, not with any design to hurt any of them, but to shew them what sort of Weapons we had and that we could revenge any insult they offer'd to us. It was observable that they paid but little regard to the Musquets that were fire'd

27. 'A Cluster of small Islands and Rocks', named on 3 November.

notwithstanding one ball was fired thro' one of their Canoes, but what effect the great gun had I know not for this was not fired untill they were going away.

At 10 the weather clearing up a little I went with 2 boats to sound the Bay and to look for a more convenient Anchoring place, the Master being in one boat and I in the other. We pull'd first over to the North shore, where some Canoes came out to meet us, but as we came near them they retired to the Shore and invited us to follow them, but seeing that they were all arm'd I did not think fit to except of their invitation, but after trading with them out of the boat a few minutes, we left them and went towards the head of the [bay]. I observed on a high po[i]nt a fortified Village but I could only see a part of the woorks, and as I intend to see the whole shall say no more about it at this time. After having fix'd upon an Anchoring place not far from where the Ship lay I returnd on board.

SUNDAY 5*th*. Winds at NNW, Hazey weather with rain in the night. At 4 PM wieghd run in nearer the South shore and Anchord in 4½ fathom water a Soft sandy bottom,[28] the south point of the Bay bearing East distant 1 Mile and a River into which the Boats can go at low water SSE distant 1½ Mile.

In the Morning the Natives came off again to the Ship but their behavour was very different to what it was yestermorning and the little traffick we had with them was carried on very fair and friendly. Two came on board the Ship to each I gave a piece of English Cloth and some Spike nails.

After the natives were gone I went with the Pinnace and Long-boat into the River to haule the Sene and sent the Master to sound the Bay and dridge for fish in the yawl. We hauled the Sene in several places in the River but caught only a few Mullet, with which we return'd on board about noon.

* * *

WEDNESDAY 8*th*. PM Fresh breeze at NNW and hazey rainy weather, the remainder a gentle breeze at WSW and Clear weather. AM heel'd

28. Cook Bay, within Mercury Bay.

and scrubed both sides of the Ship and sent a party of men a Shore to Cut wood and fill water. The Natives brought of to the Ship and sold us for small peeces of Cloth as much fish as served all hands, they were of the Mackarel kind and as good as ever was eat.

At Noon I observed the Suns Meridian Zenith distance by the Astromical Quadrant which gave the Latitude 36°47′43″ s, this was in the River beformentioned, that lies within the s entr^ce of ye Bay.

THURSDAY 9*th*. Variable light breezes and clear weather. As soon as it was day light the Natives began to bring off Mackarel and more then we well know'd what to do with, notwithstanding I orderd all they brought to be purchas'd in order to incourage them in this kind of traffick. At 8 Mr Green and I went on shore with our Instruments to Observe the Transit of Mercury which came on at 7^h 20′ 58″ Apparent time and was Observed by Mr Green only. I at this time was taking the Suns Altitude in order to asertain the time. The Egress was observed as followes.

$$h \quad ' \quad ''$$

By Mr Green $\left\{ \begin{array}{l} \text{Internal Contact at } 12 \;\; 8 \;\; 58 \\ \text{External Contact} - 12 \;\; 9 \;\; 55 \end{array} \right\}$ afternoon

By My self $\left\{ \begin{array}{l} \text{Internal Contact at } 12 \;\; 8 \;\; 45 \\ \text{External Contact} - 12 \;\; 9 \;\; 43 \end{array} \right\}$ D°

Latitude observed at Noon 36° 48′28″, the Mean of this and yesterdays observation gives 36° 48′5½″ s, the Latitude of the place of Observation, and the Variation of the Compass was at this time found to be 11°9′ East. While we were making these observations five Canoes came along side of the Ship, two large and three small ones, in one were 47 people but in the others not so many. They were wholy strangers to us and to all appearence they came with a hostal intention, being compleatly arm'd with Pikes, Darts, Stones &c^a however they made no attempt and this was very probable owing to their being inform'd by some other Canoes (who at this time were along side selling fish) what sort of people they had to deal with. At their first coming along side they begun to sell our people some of their Arms and one Man offer'd to sale an Haāhow, that is a square pice of Cloth such as they wear. Lieut^t Gore, who at this time was Commanding officer, sent in to the Canoe a peice of Cloth which the man had agreed to take in exchange for his, but as soon as he had got Mr Gore's Cloth in his posission he would not part with his own, but put off the Canoe from along side and then shook their paddles at the People in the Ship. Upon this Mr Gore fired a Musquet at them and from what I can learn kill'd the man who tooke the Cloth, after this they soon went away. I have here inserted the account of this affair just as I had it from Mr Gore but I must own that it did not meet with my approbation because I thought the punishment a little too severe for the Crime, and we had now been long enough acquainted with these People to know how to chastise trifling faults like this without taking away their lives.

FRIDAY 10*th*. PM Gentle breezes and Varble, the remainder a Strong breeze at ENE and Hazey weather. AM I went with two Boats accompaned by Mr Banks and the other gentlemen into the River which empties it self into the head of this Bay in order to examine it. None of the Natives came off to the Ship this morning which we think is owing to the bad weather.

SATURDAY 11*th*. Fresh gales at ENE and Clowdy hazey weather with rain. Between 7 and 8 oClock PM I returnd on board from out of the River having been about 4 or 5 Miles up it and could have gone much farther had the weather been favourable. I landed on the East side and went up on the hills from whence I saw or at least I thought I saw the head of the River, it here branched into several Channels and form'd a number of very low flat Islands all cover'd with a sort of Mangrove trees and several places of the Shores of both sides of the River were cover'd with the same sort of wood: the sand banks were well store'd with Cockles, and clams and in many places were Rock Oysters. Here is likewise pretty plenty of wild Foul, such as Shags, Ducks, Curlews, and a Black Bird about as big as a Crow, with a long sharp bill of a Colour between Red and yellow. We also saw fish in the River but of what sort I know not. The Country Especialy on the East side is barren and for the most part distitute of wood or any other signs of fertillity but the face of the Country on the other side looked much better and is in many places cover'd with wood. We met with some of the natives and saw several more and smookes a long way inland, but saw not the least sign of cultivation either here or in any part about the Bay, so that the Inhabitents must live wholy on shell and other Fish and Fern roots which they eat by way of bread. In the entrance of this River and for 2 or 3 Miles up it is very safe and commodious Anchoring in 3, 4 and 5 fathom water, and convenient places for laying a Vessel a shore where the Tides rises and falls about 7 feet at full and change.

I could not see whether or no any considerable fresh water stream came out of the Country into this River but there are a number of small Rivulets which come from the adjacent hills. A little with[in] the entrance of the river on the East side is a high point or peninsula juting out into the River on which are the remains of one of thier Fortified towns, the Situation is such that the best Engineer in Europe could not have choose'd a better for a small number of men to defend themselves against a greater, it is strong by nature and made more so by Art. It is only accessible on the land side, and there have been cut a Ditch and a bank raised on the inside, from the top of the bank to the bottom of the ditch was about 22 feet and depth of the ditch on the land side 14 feet; its breadth was in proportion to its depth and the whole seem'd to have been done with great judgement. There had been a row of Pickets on the top of the bank and another on the outside of the ditch, these last had been set deep in the ground and sloaping with their upper ends hanging over the ditch; the whole had been burnt down, so that it is probable that this place has been taken and distroy'd by an Enimy. The people on this side of the Bay seem now to have no houses or fix'd habitations but sleep in the open air, under trees and in small temporary shades, but to all appearence they are better of on the other side but there we have not yet set foot. In the Morning being dirty rainy weather I did not expect any of the Natives off with fish, but thinking that they might have some a shore, I sent a boat with some trade who returnd about noon load[ed] with oysters which they got in the River which is abreast of the Ship, but saw no fish among the natives.

SUNDAY 12th. PM had strong gales at NE and hazey rainy weather, AM a fresh breeze at NW and Clear weather. In the morning got on board a turn of water and after wards sent the Long-boat into the River for Oysters to take to sea with us, and I went with the Pinnace and Yawl accompaned by Mr Banks and Dr Solander, over to the North side of the Bay in order to take a View of the Country and the Fortified Village which stands their; we landed about a Mile from it and were met by the Inhabitants in our way thether who with a great deal of good nature and friendship conducted us into the place and shewed us every thing that was there. . . .

MONDAY 13th. PM Gentle breezes at NW and clear weather. After taking a slight View of the Country and loading both boats with Sellery, which we found in great plenty near the sea beach, we return'd on board about 5 oClock, the Long-boat at the same time returnd out of the River loaded as deep as she could swim with oysters, and now I intended to put to sea in the morning if wind and weather will permit. In the night had the wind at SE with rainy dirty hazey weather which continued all day, so that I could not think of sailing but thought my self very happy in being in a good port. Sam^1 Jones seaman having been confined on Saturday last for refuseing to come upon deck when all hands were called and afterwards refuse'd to comply with the orders of the officer on deck, he was this morning punished with 12 lashes and remited back to confinement.

TUESDAY 14th. Fresh gales Easterly & rainy dirty weather.

WEDNESDAY 15th. In the evening I went in the Pinnace and landed upon one of the Island[s] that lies off the South head of the Bay, with a View to see if I could discover any sunken rocks or other dangers lying before the entrence of the bay as there was a pretty large swell at this time. The Island we landed upon was very small yet there were upon it a Village the Inhabitants of which received us very friendly; this little Village was laid out in small oblong squares and each pallisaded round. The Island afforded no fresh water and was only accessible on one side, from this I concluded that it was not choose for any conveniencey it could afford them but for its natural strength.

At 7 AM weigh'd with a light breeze at West and clear weather, and made sail out of the Bay steering NE for the Northeastermost of a number of Islands lying off the North Point of the Bay, these Islands are of various extent and ly scattered to the NW in a parallel deriction with the Main as far as we could see. I was at first afraid to go within them thinking that there was no safe Passage, but I afterwards thought that we might and I would have attempted it but the wind comeing to the NW prevented it; so that we were obliged to Stand out to sea. At Noon was in the Latitude of 36°46′s. The northermost Island above mentioned bore North distant half a League, the Court of Aldermen SEBS dist^t 6 Leagues and the Bay saild from, which I have named *Mercury Bay* on acco^t of the observ^n be[ing] made there, SWBW distant 6 Miles. . . .

The Country on the SE side of this River and Bay is very barren produceing little but Fern and such other Plants as delight in a poor soil. The land on the NW side is pretty well cover'd with Wood, the soil more fertile and would no doubt produce the necessarys of life was it cultivated. However thus much must be said against it, that it is not near so rich and fertile as the lands we have seen to South-ward, and the same may be said of its Inhabitants who altho pretty numerous are poor to the highest degree when compair'd to others we have seen; they have no plantations but live wholy on Fern roots and fish, their canoes are mean and without ornament, and so are their houses or hutts and in general every thing they have about them. This may be owing to the frequent wars in which they are certainly ingaged, strong proofs of this we have seen, for the people who resided near the place where we wooded and who slept every night in the open air place'd themselves in such a manner when they laid down to sleep as plainly shewed that it was necessary for them to be always upon their guard. They do not own subjection to *Teeratu* the Earee de hi,[29] but say that he would kill them was he to come a mong them. They confirm the custom of eating their enimies so that this is a thing no longer to be doubted. I have before observed that many of the people about this bay had no fix'd habitations and

29. Cook's spelling of *arii rihi*, 'high chief'.

we thought so then, but have sence learnt that they have strong holds or Hippa's as they call them, which they retire to in time of danger.

We found thrown upon the Shore in several places in this Bay quantities of Iron Sand which is brought down out of the Country by almost every little frish water brook, this proves that there must be of that ore not far inland. Neither the Inhabitants of this place or any other where we have been know the use of Iron, or set the least Value upon it, prefering the most trifleing thing we could give them to a nail or any sort of Iron tools. Before we left this Bay we cut out upon one of the trees near the watering place, the Ships Name, date &c^a and after displaying the English Colours I took formal posession of the place in the name of His Majesty.

* * *

[*Cook proceeded up the coast, rounded Cape Colville, and found himself in a large bay. Keeping to the east side, he came to an anchor in the middle of the channel, which he reckoned to be about eleven miles wide, and sent two boats ahead to sound.*]

MONDAY 20*th*. Moderate breeze at SSE and fair weather. At 2 PM the Boats returnd from sounding not haveing found above 3 feet more water then where we now lay; upon this I resolved to go no farther with the Ship, but to examine the head of the Bay in the boats, for as it appeared to run a good way inland I thought this a good opportunity to see a little of the Interior parts of the Country and its produce; Accordingly at Day light in the morning I set out with the Pinnace and Long boat accompaned by Mr Banks, Dr Solander and Tupia. We found the inlet end in a River about 9 Miles above the Ship, into which we enterd with the first of the flood and before we had gone 3 miles up it found the water quite fresh. We saw a number of the natives and landed at one of their Villages the Inhabitants of which received us with open arms; we made but a short stay with them but proceeded up the River untill near Noon, when finding the face of the Country to continue pretty much the same and no alteration in the Course or stream of the River or the least probillity of seeing the end of it, we landed on the West side in order to take a View of the lofty Trees which adorn its banks, being at this time 12 or 14 Miles within the entrance and here the tide of flood run as strong as it doth in the River Thams below bridge.

TUESDAY 21*st*. After land[ing] as above mentioned we had not gone a hundred yards into the Woods before we found a tree that girted 19 feet 8 Inches 6 feet above the Ground, and having a quadrant with me I found its length from the root to the first branch to be 89 feet, it was as streight as an arrow and taper'd but very little in proportion to its length, so that I judged that there was 356 solid feet of timber in this tree clear of the branches. We saw many others of the same sort several of which were taller than the one we measured and all of them very stout;[30] there were likewise many other sorts of very stout timber-trees all of them wholy unknown to any of us. We brought away a few specimans and at 3 oClock we embarqued in order to return on board with the very first of the Ebb, but not before we had named this River the *Thames* on account of its bearing some resemblence to that river in england. In our return down the River the inhabitants of the Village where we landed in going, seeing that we return'd by a nother Channell put off in thier Canoes and met us and trafficked with us in the most friendly manner immagineable untill they had disposed of the few trifles they had. The Tide of Ebb just carried us out of the narrow part of the River into the Sea reach as I may call it, where meeting with the flood and a strong breeze at NNW obliged us to come to a grappling and we did not reach the Ship untill 7 oClock in the AM.

*   *   *

[*Cook continued to explore the Firth of Thames, and then proceeded north up Hauraki Gulf and along the coast, naming Cape Colville, Point Rodney, Bream Head and Bay (after the fish), Hen and Chicken Islands, and Poor Knights Islands (after the well-known pudding). Cape Brett was named in honour of Sir Percy Brett, because of 'a Rock with a hole perced quite thro' it'; the name 'Piercy' 'seemed proper for that of the island'. Contacts with Maoris were frequent but uneasy. One was flogged for stealing the half-hour glass, and visiting canoes were*

30. The *kahikatea* or white pine, *Podocarpus dacrydioides* – now alas! all gone. [B]

twice dispersed with musket and gun shot. Cook anchored in the bay 'of many Islands' west of Cape Brett.]

THURSDAY 30*th*. PM had the winds Westerly with some very heavy showers of rain. We had no sooner come to an Anchor than between 3 and 4 hundred of the Natives Assembled in their Canoes about the Ship, some few were admited on board and to one of the Chiefs I gave a piece of Broad Cloth and distributed a few nails &c^a a Mongest some others of them. Many of these people had been off to the Ship when we were at sea and seem'd to be very sencible of the use of fire arms and in the little trade we had with them they behaved tollerable well, but continued not long before some of them wanted to take away the Buoy and would not desist at the fireing of several Musquets untill one of them was hurt by small shott, after which they withdrew a small distance from the Ship and this was thought a good oppertunity to try what effect a great Gun would have as they had paid so little respect to the Musquets, and accordingly one was fired over their heads, this I beleive would have sent them quite off, if it had not been for Tupia who soon preavaild upon them to return to the Ship, when their behaver was such as gave us no room to susspect that they meant to give us any farther trouble.

After the Ship was moved into deeper water I went with the Pinnace and yawl Man'd and Arm'd and landed upon the Island accompan'd by Mr Banks and Dr Solander. We had scarce landed before all the Canoes left the Ship and landed at different parts of the Island and before we could well look about us we were surrounded by 2 or 3 hundred people, and notwithstanding that they were all arm'd they came upon us in such a confused Stragleing manner that we hardly suspected that the[y] meant us any harm, but in this we were very soon undeceaved for upon our indeavouring to draw a line on the sand between us and them they set up the war dance and immidiatly some of them attempted to seize the two Boats; being disapointed in this they next attempted to break in upon us upon which I fired a Musquet load[ed] with small shott at one of the forwardest of them and Mr Banks and 2 of the men fired immidiatly after; this made them retire back a little; but in less than a minute one of the Chiefs rallied them again, Dr Solander seeing this gave him a peppering with small shott which sent him off and made them retire a second time; they attempted to rally several times after and only seem'd to want some one of resolution to head them; but they were at last intirely dispersed by the Ship fire[ing] a few shott over their heads and a Musquet now and than from us. In this skirmish only one or two of them was hurt with small Shott, for I avoided killing any one of them as much as possible and for that reason withheld our people from fireing. We had observed that some had hid themselves in a Cave in one of the Rocks, and some time after the whole was over we went towards them, the Chief who I have mintiond to have been on board the Ship happen'd to be one of these he his wife and another man came out to meet us but the rest made off; these three people came and set down by us and we gave them of such things as we had about us. After this we went to another part of the Island where some of the inhabitants came to us and were as meek as lambs. Having taken a Veiw of the Bay from the Island and loaded both boats wth sellery which we found here in great plenty, we returnd on board and at 4 AM hove up the Anchor in order to put to sea with a light breeze at East but it soon falling Calm obliged us to Come too again, and about Eight or 9 oClock seeing no probabillity of our geting to sea I sent the Master with two Boats to sound the harbour, but before this I order'd Math^w Cox, Hen^{ry} Stevens and Man^l Paroyra to be punished with a dozⁿ lashes each for leaving thier duty when a shore last night and diging up Potatoies out of one of the Plantations, the first of the three I remited back to confinement because he insisted that their was no harm in what he had done. All this fore noon had abundance of the Natives about the Ship and some few on board, we trafficked with them for a few trifles in which they dealt very fair and friendly.

[DECEMBER 1769]

FRIDAY 1*st* December. Winds at NNW a Gentle breeze. At 3 PM the Boats having returnd from sounding, I went with them over to the south side of the Harbour and landed upon the Main, accompaned by Mr Banks and Dr Solander; we met with nothing new or remarkable, the place where we landed was in a small sandy Cove where there are two small streams of fresh water and plenty of Wood for fuel, here were likewise sever^l little plantations planted with Potatoes and Yams: the soil and natural produce of the Cuntry was much the same as what we have hitherto met with. The people we saw behaved to us with great marks of friendship. In the evening we had some very heavy showers of rain and this brought us on board sooner then we intended. AM the wind being still contrary I sent some people a shore upon the Island to cut Grass for our Sheep in the doing of which the inhabitants gave them no sort of disturbance and in the same friendly manner did those behave that were along side the Ship. Punished Math^w Cox with half a Doz^n lashes and then dismissed him.

* * *

[*The* Endeavour *spent several days in the Bay of Islands. Cook, Banks and Solander explored on foot, noting the cultivation of yams, and being shown round a* pa, *or as Cook called it 'a* Heppa *or fortified Village'. On 5 December, they began to make their way out of the bay.*]

WEDNESDAY 6*th*. PM had a gentle breeze at NNW, with which we kept turning out of the Bay but gaind little or nothing, in the evening it fell little wind and at 10 oClock it was Calm; At this time the tide or Current seting the Ship near one of the Islands, where we was very near being a shore but by the help of our boat and a light air from the southward we got clear; about an hour after when we thought our selves out of all danger the Ship struck upon a Sunken rock and went immidiatly clear without receiving any perceptible damage; just before the man in the chains had 17 fathom water and immidiatly after she struck 5 fathom, but very soon deepen'd to 20. This rock lies half a Mile WNW from the northermost or outermost Island that lies on the SE side of the Bay. Had light airs from the land and some times Calm untill 9 oClock AM, by this time we had got out of the Bay and a breeze springing up at NNW we stood out to sea. At Noon Cape Brett bore SSE$^{1/2}$E distant 10 Miles. Lat^d Observed 34°59's.

* * *

[*On 10 December Cook sighted what he later called North Cape, but because of very bad weather it took him three weeks to round the cape and the cape to the west 'which we judge to be the same as Tasman calls* Cape Maria Van Diemen'.]

[JANUARY 1770]

MONDAY 1*st* Jan^ry 1770. PM fresh breeze at SWBS and squally, the remainder moderate breezes at SWBS and SW clear weather. At 7 PM Tack'd and Stood to the westward. At this time Mount Camel bore N 83° East and the northermost land or Cape Maria Van Diemen NBW, being distant from the nearest shore 3 Leagues; in this situation had 40 fathom water. Note, Mount Camel doth not appear to lay little more than a Mile from the sea on this side and about the same distance on the other, so that the land here cannot be above 2 or 3 Miles broad from sea to sea, which is what I conjecter'd when we were in Sandy bay on the other side of the coast. – At 6 AM tackd and Stood to the Eastward the Island of the Three Kings NWBN. At Noon tack'd again and stood to the westward being in the latitude of 34°37's. The Island of the 3 Kings bore NWBN distant 10 or 11 Leagues and Cape Maria Vandiemen N 31° E distant 4½ Leagues, in this situation had 54 fathom water. I cannot help thinking but what will appear a little strange that at this season of the year we should be three weeks in geting 10 Leagues to the westward and five weeks in geting 50 Leagues for so long it is sence we pass'd C. Brett but it will hardly be credited that in the midest of summer and in the Latitude of 35° such a gale of wind as we have had could have happen'd, which for its strength and continuence was such as I hardly was ever in before. Fortunately at this time we were at a good distance from land otherwise it might have proved fatal to us.

TUESDAY 2*d*. Fresh breezes at SSW and West accompan'd with a rowling sea from the SW. At 5 PM the wind veering to the westward we tack'd and stood to the Southward. At this time the North Cape bore E¾N and was just open of a point that lies 3 Leagues west and by south from it – being now well assured that it is the Northermost extremity of this Country and is the East point of a Peninsula which stretches out NW and NWBN, 17 or 18 Leag^s and as I have before observe'd is for the most part low and narrow except at its extremity where the land is tollerable high and extends 4 or 5 Leagues every way, Cape Maria Vandeimen is the west point of this peninsula and lies in the Latitude of 34° 30′ Long^{de} 187°18′ West from Greenwich. From this Cape the land trends away SEBS and SE to and behond Mount Camel and is every where a barren shore affording no better a prospect than what ariseth from white sand banks. At ½ past 7 PM the Islands of the Three Kings bore NWBN and Cape Maria Van diemen NEBE dist^t 4 Leagues. At 5 AM C. Maria Van deemen bore NNE½E and Mount Camel East. At Noon was in the Lat^d of 35°17′ and the Cape Maria Van diemen by judgement bore North distant 16 Leagues having no land in sight not daring to go near it as the wind blow'd fresh right on Shore and a high rowling Sea from the same quarter and knowing that there was no harbour that we could put into in case we were caught upon a lee Shore.

* * *

THURSDAY 4*th.* Winds at SW and SWBS mostly a fresh gale accompanied with a rowling sea from the same quarter. Being desirous of taking as near a view of the Coast as we could with safty, we kept edgeing in for it untill 7 oClock pm, being at this time about 6 Leagues from the Land, we then haul'd our wind to the SE and kept on that Course close upon the wind all night sounding several times but had no ground with 100 and 110 fathoms. At 8 oClock AM was about 5 Leagues from the land and a place which lies in the Lat^d of 36°25′ that had the appearence of a Bay or inlet bore East. In order to see more of this place we kept on our Course untill a 11 oClock when we were not above 3 Leagues from it and then found that it was neither a Bay nor inlet but low land bounded on each side by higher lands which caused the deception. At this time we tack'd and stood to the NW. At Noon we were between 3 and 4 Leagues from the land and in the Latitude of 36°31′ and Long^d 185°50′ West. Cape Maria Vandiemen bore N 25° West Distant 44½ Leag^s, from this I form my judgement of the deriction of this Coast which is nearly SSE¾E and NNW¾W and must be nearly a strait Shore. In about the Latitude of 35°45′ is some high land adjoining to the sea, to the Southward of that the land is of a Moderate height and wears a most desolate and inhospitable aspect, nothing is to be seen but large Sand hills with hardly any green thing up[on] them and the great sea which the prevailing westerly winds impell upon the Shore must render this a very dangerous Coast, this I am so fully sencible of that was we once clear of it I am determind not to come so near again if I can possible avoide it unless we have a very favourable wind indeed.

*   *   *

[*Cook stood to the north-west for two days 'in order to get an offing', then turned south again to follow the coast past what is now Auckland and the 'high craggy point' he named Albatross Point. On 11 January he sighted 'a very high Mountain'.*]

SATURDAY 13*th*. Winds Variable, PM Clowdy weather. At 7 oClock sounded and had 42 fathom water, being distant from the shore between 2 and 3 Leagues, and the peaked mountain as near as I could judge bore East. After it was dark saw a fire upon the shore a sure sign that the Country is inhabited. In the night had some Thunder Lightning and rain. At 5 AM saw for a few Minutes the Top of the peaked Mountain above the Clowds, bearing NE; it is of a prodigious height and its top is cover'd with everlasting snow. It lies in the Latitude of 39°16′s and in the Longitude of 185°15′w. I have named it *Mount Egmont* in honour of the Earl of Egmont. This mountain seems to have a pretty large base and to rise with a gradual assent to the peak and what makes it more conspicuous is, its being situated near the Sea, and a flat Country in its neighbourhood which afforded a very good asspect, being cloathed with Wood and Verdure. The shore under the foot of this mountain forms a large Cape which I have named *Cape Egmont*, it lies ssw¹⁄₂w, 27 Leagˢ from Albetross point. On the NE side of the Cape lay two small Islands near to a very remarkable point on the Main that riseth to a good height in the very form of a Sugʳ Loafe: To the Southward of the Cape the land tends away SEBE and ESE and seems to be every where a bold shore. At Noon had variable light airs and clear weather. Latitude Observe'd 39°32′s. Cape Egmont bore about NE and we were about 4 Leagues from the Shore in that direction, in this situation had 40 fathoms water.

SUNDAY 14*th*. PM had a gentle breeze at West which in the Even^g Came to NWBW and continued so all night and blowed a fresh breeze. We steer'd a long shore ESE and SEBE, keeping between two and three Leagues off. At ½ past 7 pm saw for a few minutes Mount Egmont which bore from us N 17° w distant 10 Leagues. At 5 AM steer'd SEBS the land inclineing more southerly, but half an hour after we saw land bearing SWBS which we haule'd up for, at this time the weather was squally attended with showers of rain. At Noon had a steady fresh breeze at WBN and Clowdy weather; the SW extremity of the land in sight bore S 63° West, and some high land which makes like an Island lying under the Main bore SSE distant 5 Leagues: The bottom of the Bay we are now in, and which bears from us south, we cannot see, altho it is very clear in that quarter. Our Latitude by observation is 40°27's, Longitude 184°39' West.

MONDAY 15*th*. Fore and middle parts fresh breezes between the West and NW and fair weather. At 8 PM we were within 2 Leagues of the land we discover'd in the morning, having run 10 Leagues sence Noon. The land seen than bearing S 63° West bore now N 59° West distant 7 or 8 Leag^s and makes like an Island, between this land or Island and Cape Egmont is a very broad and deep Bay or Inlet the SW side of which we are now upon, and here the land is of a considerable height distinguished by hills and Vallies and the shore seems to form several Bays into one of which I intend to go with the Ship in order to Careen her (she being very foul) and to repair some few defects, recrute our stock of Wood, water &c^a with this View we kept plying on and off al[l] night having from 80 to 63 fathoms water. At day light Stood in for an Inlet which runs in SW. At 8 AM we were got within the entrance which may be known by a reef of rocks stretching off from the NW point and some rocky Island[s] lying off the SE point. At 9 oClock being little wind and variable we were carried by the Tide or current within 2 Cable lengths of the NW shore where we had 54 fathoms water, but with the help of our Boats we got clear. At this time we saw rise up twice near the Ship a Sea lyon the head of which was exactly like the head of the male one described [by] Lord Anson. We likewise saw a Canoe with some of the Natives Cross the Bay and a

Village situated upon a point of an Island which lies 7 or 8 Miles with[in] the Entrence.[31] At Noon we were the length of this Island and being little wind had the boats ahead towing.

TUESDAY 16*th*. Variable light airs and clear settled weather. At 1 pm hauled close round the SW end of the Island on which stands the Village before mentioned the Inhabitants of which were all in arms; At 2 oClock we Anchor'd in a very snug Cove[32] which is on the NW side of the Bay faceing the S West end of the Island, in 11 fath. water soft ground and moor'd with the Stream anchor. By this time several of the Natives had come off to the Ship in their Canoes and after heaving a few stones at us and having some conversation with Tupia some of them ventured on board where they made but a very short stay before they went into their boats again and soon after left us all together. I than went a Shore in the bottom of the Cove accompanied by most of the Gentlemen, we found a fine stream of excellent water, and as to Wood the land here is one intire forest. Having the Saine with us we made a few hauls and caught 300 pounds weight of different sorts of fish which were equally distributd to the Ships Compney. AM Careend the Ship scrub'd and pay'd the Larboard side. Several of the Natives Visited us this morning and brought with them some stinking fish which how ever I order'd to be bought up in order to incourage them in this kind of trafick, but trade at this time seem'd [not] to be their object, but were more inclineable to quarrel and as the Ship was upon the careen I thought they might give us some trouble and perhaps hurt some of our people that were in the boats along side; for this reason I fire'd some small Shott at one of the first offenders, this made them keep at a proper distance while they stayd which was not long before they all went away. These people declared to us this morning that they never either saw or heard of a Ship like ours being upon this coast before: from this it appears that they have no Tradition among them of Tasman being here for I beleive Murderers Bay the place where he Anchor'd not to be far from this place but this cannot be it from the Latitude for I find by an observation made this day at Noon

31. Motuara, in Queen Charlotte Sound.
32. Ship Cove.

that we are at an anchor in 41°5′32″s which is 15′ to the southward of Murderers Bay.

WEDNESDAY 17*th*. Light airs Calms and pleasent weath[r] PM righted the Ship and got ready for heeling out the other side, and in the evening hauled the Saine and caught a few fish, while this was doing some of us went in the Pinnace into a nother Cove not far from where the Ship lays; in going thether we met with a Woman floating upon the water who to all appeerence had not been dead many days. Soon after we landed we met with two or three of the Natives who not long before must have been regailing themselves upon human flesh, for I got from one of them the bone of the fore arm of a Man or a Woman which was quite fresh and the flesh had been but lately pick'd off which they told us they had eat, they gave us to understand that but a few days ago they had taken Kill'd and eat a Boats crew of their enemies or strangers, for I beleive that they look upon all strangers as enemies; from what we could learn the Woman we had seen floating upon the water was in this boat and had been drownded in the fray. There was not one of us that had the least doubt but what this people were Canabals but the finding this Bone with part of the sinews fresh upon it was a stronger proof than any we had yet met with, and in order to be fully satisfied of the truth of what they had told us, we told one of them that it was not the bone of a man but that of a Dog, but he with great fervency took hold of his fore-arm and told us again that it was that bone and to convence us that they had eat the flesh he took hold of the flesh of his own arm with his teeth and made shew of eating. – AM Careen'd scrubed and pay'd the Starboard side of the Ship: While this was doing some of the natives came along side seemingly only to look at us, there was a Woman among them who had her Arms, thighs and legs cut in several places, this was done by way of Mourning for her husband who had very lately been kill'd and eat by some of their enimies as they told us and pointed towards the place where it was done which lay some where to the Eastward. M[r] Banks got from one of them a bone of the fore arm much in the same state as the one before mention'd and to shew us that they had eat the flesh they bit a[nd] naw'd the bone and draw'd it thro' their mouth and this in such a manner as plainly shew'd that the flesh to them was a dainty bit.

THURSDAY 18*th*. Winds mostly from the sw a gentle breeze and clear settled weather. PM righted the Ship and sent on Shore all or most of our empty Casks, and in the morning the Coopers went about triming them and the Carpenters went to work to black the bends, Caulk the sides and to repair other defects in the Ship, while the Seamen were employ'd in the hold, cutting Wood &c^a &c^a. I made a little excursion in the Pinnace in order to take a View of the Bay accompanied by Mr Banks and Dr Solander, We met with nothing remarkable and as we were on the west side of the Bay where the land is so closely cover'd with Wood that we could not penetrate into the Country.

FRIDAY 19*th*. Winds and weather as yesterday and the employment of the people the same. In the PM some of our people found in the skirts of the wood three hip bones of Men, they lay near to a hole or hoven, that is a place where the natives dress their Victuals, this circumstance trifleing as it is, is still a farther proff that this people eat human flesh.

In the AM set up the Forge to repair the braces of the Tiller and such other Iron work as was wanting. The natives came along side and sold us a quantity of large Mackerel for nails peices of Cloth and paper, and in this traffeck they never once attemptd to defraud us of any one thing, but dealt as fair as people could do.

SATURDAY 20*th*. Winds Southerly, fair and pleasant weather. Employ'd Wooding Watering &c^a and in the AM sent part of the powder a Shore to be air'd. Some of the Natives brought along side in one of their Canoes four of the heads of the men they had lately kill'd, both the Hairy scalps and skin of the faces were on: Mr Banks bought one of the four, but they would not part with any of the other on any account whatever, the one Mr Banks got had received a blow on the Temple that had broke the skull.

* * *

MONDAY 22*nd*. PM and in the night had Variable light airs and Calms, AM had a fresh breeze South^ly and Clowdy weather. In the morning the people were set about the necessary business of the Ship and I set out in the Pinnace (accompanied by Mr Banks and Dr Solander) with a view of examining the head of the Inlet, but after rowing between 4 and 5 Leagues up it and finding no probabillity of reaching or even seeing the end the wind being againest us and the day already half spent we landed at noon on the SE side in order to try to get upon one of the hills to View the Inlet from thence.

TUESDAY 23*rd*. PM Winds Southerly a fresh breeze. Agreeable to what is mentioned above I took one man with me and climed up to the top of one of the hills but when I came there I was hindred from seeing up the inlet by higher hills which I could not come at for impenetrable woods, but I was abundantly recompenced for the trouble I had in assending the hill, for from it I saw what I took to be the Eastern Sea and a strait or passage from it into the Western Sea a little to the Eastward of the entrance of the Inlet in which we now lay with the Ship, the main land which lies on the SE side of this inlet appeared to me to be a narrow ridge of very high hills and to form a part of the SW side of the Strait. The land on the opposite side seem'd to trend away East as far as the Eye could see, to the SE appear'd as oppen sea and this I took to be the Eastern. I likewise saw some Islands lying on the East side of the Inlet which before I had taken to be a part of the Main land. As soon as I had decended the hill and we had refreshed our selves we set out in order to return to the Ship and in our way pass'd through and examined the Harbours, Coves &c^a that lay behind the Islands above mentioned. In this rout we met with an old Village in which were a good many houses but no body had lived in any of them lately, we likewise saw a nother that was inhabited, but the day being far spent so that we had not time to go to it but made the best [of] our way to the Ship which we reached between 8 and 9 oClock. In the night had much rain with Clowdy hazey weather which continued by intervils untill noon.

WEDNESDAY 24*th*. PM had a fresh breeze Southerly and Clowdy weather. After dinner I employ'd my self in carrying on the Survey of the place and upon one of the Islands where I landed were a number of houses but no inhabitants neither had any been there lately. In the

morning the Gunner was sent a shore with the remainder of the
powder to dry, and the Long-boat was sent with a gang of hands to
one of the Islands to cut grass for our sheep and the rest of the people
were employ'd about the usual work of the Ship. This fore-noon some
of us viseted the Hippa, which is situated on the point of the Island
mentioned on our first arrival. The Inhabitants of this place shew'd
not the least dislike at our coming but on the contrary with a great
deal of seeming good nature shew'd us all over the place, we found
among them some human bones the flesh of which they told us they
had eat, they likewise inform'd us that there was no passage into the
Sea thro' this inlet as I had immagined their might because above
where I was in the Boat it turn'd away to the west ward. Leaving these
people we travel'd to the other end of the Island and there took water
and cross'd over upon the Main where we met with several houses
that were at present or had very lately been inhabited but we saw but
very few of the Inhabitents and these were in there boats fishing. After
viewing this place we returnd on board to dinner.

THURSDAY 25*th*. Winds at NW a gentle breeze and fair weather. PM
The Long-boat having returnd with a load of grass she was employ'd
bringing on board Wood and water and the Caulkers having finish'd
caulking the Ship sides (a thing they have been employ'd upon ever
sence we came here) they were pay'd with tar. Early in the AM the
Long boat was set again for grass, and returnd at Noonwith a Load.

FRIDAY 26*th*. Gentle breezes and pleasent weather. In the PM I made
a little excursion in the Pinnace along shore towards the mouth of the
inlet accompanied by Mr Banks and Dr Solander; we found in a small
cove several of the Natives of whome we purchas'd a quantity of fresh
fish, and upon our return to the Ship we found that the Saine had
been equally as successfull, which we generally haul mornings &
evenings, and seldom fail of geting fish sufficient to serve all hands.
In the AM I made an excursion into one of the Bays which lie on the
East side of the Inlet accompanied by Mr Banks and Dr Solander,
upon our landing we ascended a very high hill from which we had a
full View of the passage I had before descover'd and the land on the
opposite shore which appear'd to be about 4 Leagues from us, but as

it was hazey near the horizon we could not see far to the SE. However, I had now seen enough of this passage to convence me that there was the greatest probabillty in the world of its runing into the Eastern Sea as the distance of that Sea from this place cannot exceed 20 Leagues even to where we were, upon this I resolve'd after puting to sea to search this passage with the Ship. We found on the top of the hill a parcel of loose Stones of which we built a Pyrmid and left in it some Musquet balls, small Shott Beeds and what ever we had about us that was likely to stand the test of time: after this we descended the hill and found along with Tupia and the boats crew several of the natives, seting in the most free and friendly manner immagineable. Tupia always accompanies us in every excursion we make and proves of infinate service. In our return to the ship we Visited the Hippa we had seen on Tuesday last which is situated on a small Island or rather a Rock, the Inhabitants of this place invited us a shore with thier usual marks of friendship and shew'd us all over the place which indeed was soon done, for it was very small yet it contain'd a good number of people and they had in it split & hanging up to dry a prodigious quantity of various sorts of small fish a part of which they sold to us for such trifles as we had about us.

*   *   *

[*Extensive work on the tiller had now been completed by the armourers and some of the carpenters; the coopers were still at work repairing casks; stones were put in the bottom of the bread room to improve the ship's handling.*]

MONDAY 29*th*. Winds as yesterday. PM rainy weather the remainder fair and Clowdy. Pretty early in the AM an old man who made us several Visits upon our first arival here, came on board and told us that one of our boats had fire'd upon and wounded two of their people one of which was dead of his wounds, this affair happen'd on Sunday was a week and never before now came to my knowlidge. On that day the Master and five Petty officers desired to have a small boat to go a fishing, but instead of keeping within the Usual boands and under the protection of the Ship they went over to the Hippa on the Island from which some of the inhabitents put off in two Canoes, as they thought to attack them, this caused the Master to fire and according to the report of the old man wounded two one of which is sence dead: but this last circumstance was soon after contradicted by another of the natives who Mr Green and Tupia saw a Shore and I wish this last report may be true because I find the reasons for fireing upon them are not very justifiable.

This morning I went out to the mouth of the Inlet and landed upon the West point and from the top of a pretty high hill which is there I had a view of the Coast to the NW, the farthest land I could see in that quarter was an Island about 10 Leagues off and lying pretty near the main and is the same as hath been before mentiond; between this Island and the place where I was lay some other Islands close under the Shore which forms several Bays, wherein there appears to be safe anchorage for Shipping. After I had set the different points &c^a we errected upon the Top of the Hill a tower or pile of stones in which we left a peice of Silver Coin, some Musquet Balls Beeds &c^a and left flying upon it a peice of an old pendant: after this we return'd to the boat and in our way to the Ship visited some of the natives we met with a long shore and purchas'd of them a small quantity of fish.

TUESDAY 30*th*. Winds at NW gentle breezes and fair weather. Early in the AM a boat was sent to one of the Islands to get sellery to boil for the peoples breakfasts, whilest our people were gathering of it near some empty hutts about 20 of the Natives landed there, men women and children, they had no sooner got out of their Canoes then 5 or 6 women set down together and cut and scarified their legs, thighs, Arms and faces some with shells and others with peices of jasper. So far as our people could understand them this was done on account of their husbands having been lately kill'd and devoured by their enimies; while the women were performing this ceremony the men went about repairing the hutts without shewing the least concern.

The Carpenter went into the woods with part of his crew to cut and square some timber to saw into boards for the use of the Ship and to prepare two posts to be set up with Inscriptions upon them.

WEDNESDAY 31*st*. Little wind and variable. In the PM the Carpenter having prepared the two Posts with inscriptions upon them seting forth the Ships name month and year, one of them was set up at the

watering place on which was hoisted the Union flag and in the morning
I took the other over to the Island which is known by the Name of
Motu-ouru and is the one that lies nearest to the Sea but before I
attempted to set up the post I went first to the Hippa having along
with me Dr Munkhouse and Tupia, we here met with the old man I
have before spoke of. The first thing I did was to inquire after the
man said to be killd by our people and the one that was wounded at
the same time, when it did not appear to me that any such accidents
had happend. I next, by means of Tupia, explained to the old man
and several others that we were come to set up a mark upon the Island
in order to shew to any ship that might put into this place that we
had been here before, they not only gave their free consent to set it
up, but promise'd never to pull it down. I then gave to every one
present one thing or a nother, to the old men I gave silver threepenny
peices dated 1763 and spike nails with the Kings broad Arrow cut
deep in them things that I thought were most likely to remain long
among them.

After I had thus prepare'd the way for seting up the post we took
it up to the highest part of the Island and after fixing it fast in the
ground hoisted thereon the Union flag and I dignified this Inlet with
the name of *Queen Charlottes Sound* and took formal posession of it and
the adjacent lands in the name and for the use of his Majesty, we then
drank Her Majestys hilth in a Bottle of wine and gave the empty bottle
to the old man (who had attended us up the hill) with which he was
highly pleased. Whilest the post was seting up we asked the old man
about the *Strait* or passage into the Eastern Sea and he very plainly
told us that there was a passage and as I had some conjectors that the
lands to the sw of this strait (which we are now at) was an Island and
not part of a continent we questioned the old man about it who said
that it consisted of two *Wannuaes*, that is two lands or Islands that
might be circumnavigated in a few days, even in four. This man spoke
of three lands, the two above mentioned which he call'd *Tovy-poenammu*
which signifies green Talk or stone such as the[y] Make their tools
on, oramints &c^a and for the third he pointed to the land on the East
side of the Strait, this he said was a large land and that it would take
up a great many moons to sail round it, or some thing to the same

purpose – this he calld *Aeheino mouwe* a name m[an]y others before had call'd it by, that part which borders on the strait he calld *Teirawhitte*. After we had done our business upon the Island we return'd on board bringing the old man along with us who after dinner went ashore in a canoe that came to attend upon him.

*   *   *

[*The* Endeavour *got ready for sea, moved slowly out of Queen Charlotte Sound and headed south. The northerly entrance to the newly discovered strait Cook named Cape Palliser.*]

[FEBRUARY 1770]

THURSDAY 8*th*. In the PM had a fresh breeze at NNE and Clowdy weather. At 3 oClock we were abreast of the Southermost point of land seen at noon which I named *Cape Campbel*, Lat^{de} 41°42′ s. Long^{de} 184°47′ w; it lies SBW dist^t 12 or 13 Leagues from Cape Koamaroo and together with Cape Pallisser forms the Southern entrance of the Straits, the dist^{ce} from the one to the other is 13 or 14 Leagues WBS & EBN.

From this Cape we steer'd along shore SWBS untill 8 oClock when the wind died away, but an hour after a fresh breeze sprung up at SW and we put the Ship right before it. The reasons for my doing this was owing to a notion which some of the officers had just started that *Aeheinomouwe* was not an Island, founding their opinion on a suppotision that the land might extend away to the SE from between Cape Turn-again and Cape Pallisser, there being a space of about 12 or 15 Leagues which we had not seen. For my own part I had seen so far into this Sea the first time I discover'd the Strait, together with many other concurrent testimonies of its being an Island that no such supposition ever enter'd my thoughts, but being resolved to clear up every doubt that might arise on so important an object I took the oppertunity of the shifting of the wind to stand to the Eastward and accordingly steer'd NEBE all night. At 9 oClock AM we were abreast of Cape Pallisser where we found the land trend away NE towards Cape Turn-again which I reckoned to be distant from us about 26 Leagues: but as the weather was hazey so that we could not see above 4 or 5

Leagues ahead we still kept standing to the NE with a light breeze at South. A[t] Noon Cape Pallisser bore N 72° West distant 3 Leagues, our Lat^d by account is 31°30′ South.

FRIDAY 9*th*. Gentle breezes at South and SSE, Hazey Clowdy weather. In the PM three Canoes came off to the Ship wherein were between 30 & 40 of the Natives who had been pulling after us some time; it appear'd from the behaver of these people that they had heard of our being upon the coast, for they came along side and some of them on board the Ship shewing the least signs of fear: they were no sooner on board than they asked for nails: but when nails were given them they asked Tupia what they were which was plain that they had never seen any before, yet they not only knowed how to ask for them but knowed what use to apply them to and therefore must have heard of Nails which they call *Whow*, the name of a tool among them made generally of bone which they use as a chissel in makeing holes &c^a. These people asking so readily for nails proves that their connections must extend as far North as Cape Kidnappers which is 45 Leagues, for that was the southermst place on this side of the coast we had any traffick with the natives, and it is most probable that the Inhabitants of Queen Charlottes Sound got the little knowlidge they seem'd to have of Iron by the connections they may have with the *Terawhetteans* bordering upon them, for we have no reason to think that the inhabitants of any part of this land had the least knowlidge of Iron before we came among them.

After a short stay these people were dismiss'd with proper presents and we continued our Course along shore to the NE until 11 oClock AM when the weather clearing up we saw Cape Turn-again bearing NBE ¼E distant 7 Leagues. I then called the officers upon deck and asked them if they were now satisfied that this land was an Island to which they answer'd in the affirmative and we hauled our wind to the Eastward.

*   *   *

[*Cook sailed south-west for two weeks until he was abreast of the Otago peninsula.*]

SUNDAY 25*th*. In the PM steerd SWBS and SW edgeing in for the land having the advantage of a fresh gale at north which I was over desirious of makeing the most of and by that means carried away the Main Top g^t mast and Fore topmast studding sail boom, but these were soon replaced by others. Altho we kept at no great distance from the shore yet the weather was so hazey that we could see nothing destinct upon the land only that there were a ridge of pretty high hills lying parallel with and but a little way from the sea-coast, which lies SBW and NBE and seem'd to end in a high bluff point to the Southward, which we run the length of by 8 oClock, when being dark and not knowing which way the land trended we brought too for the night having run 15 Leagues upon a SW½S Course sence noon. The point bore at this time West distant about 5 Miles, depth of water 37 fathom the bottom small pebble stones. At 4 AM we made sail, but by this time the northerly wind was gone and was succeeded by one from the southward which proved very variable and unsteady. At day light the point above mentioned bore north distant 3 Leagues and we found that the land trended away from it SWBW as far as we could see. This point of land I have named *Cape Saunders* in honour of Sr Charles (Latitude 45°55′ S, Longitude 189°4′ West), it requ[i]res no description to know it by, the Latitude and the Angle made here by the Coast will be found quite sufficient; however there is a remarkable Saddle hill laying near the shore 3 or 4 Leagues SW of the Cape, by which it may always be known when on that side of it. From one to four Leagues north of the Cape the shore seem'd to form two or three Bays wherein there appeared to be anchorage and Shelter from SW, westerly and NW winds. I had some thoughts of bearing up for one of these places in the morning when the wind came to SW, but the fear of looseing time and the desire I had of pushing to the southward in order to see as much of the coast as possible, or if this land s[h]ould prove to be an Island to get round it, prevented me. Being not far from the shore all this morning we had an opportunity of viewing the land pretty distinctly: it is of a moderate height, full of hills which appear'd green and woody, but we saw not the least sign of Inhabitants. At Noon Cape Saunders bore N 30° W distant 4 Leagues; Lat^{de} per Log, for we had no Observation, 46°0′ S.

*   *   *

[*Cook now took a south-easterly course in very bad weather, then north and then
west until he sighted Cape Saunders again. He then felt his way round the south
coast of South Island, heading for the south of Stewart Island, which he did not
recognize as an island, and having 'a very fortunate escape' from the ledges of rock
which he named The Traps.*]

[MARCH 1770]

SATURDAY 10*th*. PM Moderate breeze at NWBN and north with which
we stood close upon a wind to the westward. At sunset the Southermost
point of land which I afterwards named *South Cape* and which lies on
the Lat^de 47°19′ s, Long^d 192°12′ West from Greenwich bore N 38° E
distant 4 Leagues and the westermost land in sight bore N 2° East,
this last was a small Isl^d lying off the point of the Main. I began now
to think that this was the southermost land and that we should be able
to get round it by the west, for we have had a large hollow swell from
the SW ever sence we had the last gale of wind from that quarter which
makes me think that there is no land in that direction. In the night it
began to blow in so much that at or before day light we were brought
under our two Courses but at 8 AM it fell moderate and we set the
topsails close reef'd, and the Miz^n and Miz^n staysail being split we
unbent them and bent others. At Noon the wind coming to west we
tack'd and stood to the northward, having no land in sight. Our
Latitude by Observation was 47°33′ s, Long^de west from the South
Cape 0°59′.

*   *   *

WEDNESDAY 14*th*. In the PM had a fresh gale from the Southward
attended with squals. At 2 oClock it clear'd up over the land which
appear'd high and Mountainous. At half past 3 double reef'd the
Topsails and haul'd in for a Bay wherein there appear'd to be good
anchorage and into which I had thoughts of going with the Ship, but
after standing in an hour we found the distance too great to run before
dark and it blowed too hard to attempt it in the night or even to keep
to windward, for these reasons we gave it up and bore away aLong
shore. This Bay I have named *duskey Bay* it lies in the Latitude of 45°47′
s, it is about 3 or 4 Miles broad at the entrance and seems to be full

as deep, in it are several Islands behind which there must be shelter from all winds provided there is a sufficient depth of water. The north point of this bay when it bears SEBS is very remarkable there being off it five high peaked rocks standing up like the four fingers and thum of a mans hand on which account I have named it *Point five fingers*. The land of this point is further remarkable by being the only level land near it and extend near two leagues to the northward; it is pretty high, wholy cover'd with wood and hath very much the appearence of an Island by its aspect being so very different from the land behind it which is nothing but barren rocky mountains.

At sun set the Southermost land in sight bore due south distant 5 or 6 Leagues and as this is the westermost point of land upon the whole Coast I have call'd it *West Cape*. It lies about three leagues to the southward of the Bay above mentioned in the Latitude of 45°54′ s and in the Longitude of 193°17′ West. The land of this Cape seems to be of a moderate height next the sea and hath nothing remarkable about it that we could see except a very white Clift two or three leagues to the southward of it; the land to the southward of Cape West trends away towards the SE, to the northward it trends NNE and NE. At 7 oClock brought the Ship too under the fore sail with her head offshore having a fresh gale at SBE. At Midnight it moderated and we wore and lay her head in shore untill 4 AM than made sail and steerd along shore NE$^{1/2}$N having a moderate breeze at SSE. At Noon we were by obser^n in the Lat^{de} of 45°13′ s. Course and distance saild sence yesterday N 41° E. 62 Miles, Long^{de} made from Cape West 0°29′ East, being at this time about 1$^{1/2}$ league from shore; sounded but had no ground with 70 f^{ms} of line. A little before noon we pass'd a small narrow opening in the land where there appear'd to be a very snug harbour form'd by an Island lying in the middle of the opening at least such was the appearences. It lies in the Lat^{de} of 45°16′ s. In land behind this opening were mountains the summits of which were cover'd with snow that seem'd to have fallen lately and this is not to be wonder'd at for we have found it very cold for these 2 days past. The Land on each side of the entrance of this harbour riseth almost perpendicular from the Sea to a very considerable height and this was the reason why I did not attempt to go in with the Ship because I saw clearly that no winds could b[l]ow there but what was either right in or right out. This is Westerly or Easterly, and it certainly would have been highly imprudent in me to have put into a place where we could not have got out but with a wind that we have lately found does not blow one day in a month: I mention this because there were some on board who wanted me to harbour at any rate without in the least considering either the present or future concequences.[33]

* * *

FRIDAY 23rd. Light airs from the southward, at intervals Calm, the fore part hazey, the remainder clear pleasent weather. At Noon our Latitude by observation was 40°36′30″ s, Longitude from Cape West 6°52′ East. The Eastermost point of land in sight bore E 10° North distant 7 Leagues and a bluff head or point, we were abreast off yesterday at noon, off which lay some rocks above water, bore s 18° West distant 6 Leagues: this point I have named *Rocks point*, Latitude 40°50′ South.

Having now nearly run down the whole of this NW Coast [of] *Tovy-poenammu* it is time I should discribe the face of the Country as it hath at different times appeard to us. I have mentioned on the 11th Instant at which time we were off the Southern part of the Island, that the land seen than was Ruged and Mountainous and there is great reason to beleive that the same ridge of Mountains extends nearly the whole length of the Island. From between the Westermost land seen that day and the Eastermost seen on the 13th there is a space of about 6 or 8 Leagues of the Sea Coast unexplored but the mountains inland were Visible enough. The land near the Shore about *Cape West* is rather low and riseth with a gradual assent up to the foot of the mountains and appear'd to be mostly cover'd with Wood; from *Point five fingers* down to the Latitude of 44°20′ there is a narrow ridge of hills rising dire[c]tly from the sea which are cloathed with wood. Close behind these hills lies the ridge of Mountains which are of a prodigious height and appear to consist of nothing but barren rocks, cover'd in many places with large patches of snow which perhaps have laid their

33. Banks's journal shows his irritation at passing by seemingly good harbours which would have allowed him 'to examine the mineral appearances'.

sence the creation. No country upon earth can appear with a more ruged and barren aspect than this doth from the sea for as far inland as the eye can reach nothing is to be seen but the sumits of these Rocky mountains which seem to lay so near one another as not to admit any Vallies between them. From the Latitude of 44°20′ to the Latitude 42°8′ these mountains lay farther inland. The Country between them and the Sea consists of woody hills and Vallies of various extent both for height and depth and hath much the appearence of fertility, many of the Vallies are large low and flat and appeard to be wholy cover'd with Wood but it is very probable that great part of the land is taken up in Lak[e]s Ponds &c^a as is very common in such like places. From the last mentioned Latitude to *Cape Farewell*, (afterwards so call'd)[34] the Land is not distinguished by anything remarkable, it riseth into hills directly from the sea and is cover'd with wood. While we were upon this part of the coast the weather was foggy in so much that we could see but a very little way in land, however we sometimes saw the summits of the Mountains above the fogg and clowds which plainly shew'd that the inland parts were high and Mountainous and gave me great reason to think that thier is a continued chain of Mountains from the one end of the Island to the other.

*   *   *

MONDAY 26*th*. At 3 PM the wind came to north and we steer'd ESE with all the sail we could set untill dark when we shortend sail untill the morning having thick misty weather all night. We kept the lead going continualy and had from 37 to 42 fathoms. At day light we saw the land bearing SEBE and an Island laying near it bearing ESE distant 5 Leagues, this I knew to be the Island seen from the Entrance of Queen Charlottes Sound[35] from which it bears NWBN distant 9 Leagues. At Noon it bore SE distant 4 or 5 Miles and the NW head of Queen Charlottes Sound bore SEBS distant 10½ Leagues. Latitude Observed 40°33′ S.

TUESDAY 27*th*. Fresh breeze of wind westerly and hazey misty weather

34. The name '*Cape Farewell*' was inserted later, as were the words '(afterwards so call'd)' – an interlinear insertion.
35. Stephens Island.

with drizling rain. As we have now circumnavigated the whole of this Country it is time for me to think of quiting of it, but before I do this it will be necessary first to compleat our water especialy as we have on board above 30 Tuns of Casks empty and knowing that there is a bay between the above mentioned Island and Queen Charlottes Sound, wherein no doubt there is anchorage and convenient watering places, accordingly in the PM we hauled round the Island and into the bay, leaving three more Islands on our starboard hand which lay close under the west shore 3 or 4 miles within the entrance. As we run in we kept the lead going and had from 40 to 12 fathom. At 6 oClock we anchord in a 11 fathom water a Muddy bottom under the west shore in the second Cove within the fore mentioned Islands.[36]

At day light AM I took a boat and went to look for a watering place and a proper birth to moor the Ship in both of which I found convenient enough. After the Ship was Moord I sent an officer ashore to superintend the watering and the Carpenter with his crew to cut wood while the long-boat was employ'd carrying a shore empty casks.

WEDNESDAY 28*th*. Winds Westerly which in the AM blowed a fresh gale attend[ed] with rain. Employ'd geting on board Wood and water and fishing in the latter of which we are pretty successfull.

THURSDAY 29*th*. In the PM had a strong gale from the westward, in the AM had variable light airs from the eastward and hazey rainy weather the whole day which however did not prevent us from geting on board wood and water.

FRIDAY 30*th*. Winds at SE a moderate breeze, the first and middle parts dark hazy weather with rain the latter fair. In the AM as the wind seem'd to be settled at SE and having nearly compleated our water we warp'd the Ship out of the Cove in order to have room to get under sail, before this was done it was Noon at which time I went away in the Pinnace in order to examine the Bay and to explore as much of it as the little time I had would admit.

36. This was off D'Urville Island, just south of Old Man's Point.

SATURDAY 31*st*. In the PM after rowing a League and a half or two Leagues up the Bay I landed upon a point of land on the west side where from an eminency I could see this western arm of the bay run in SWBW about 5 Leagues farther yet did not see the head of it. There appear'd to be several other inlets or at least small bays, between this and the NW head of Queen Charlottes sound in every one of which I make no doubt but what there is anchorage and shelter for ship[s] as they are partly cover'd from the sea wind by the Islands which lay without them. The land about this bay at least what I could see of it is of a very hilly uneven surface and appears to be mostly cover'd with wood, shrubs, Firns &c^a which renders traveling both difficult and fatigueing. I saw no inhabitants neither have we seen any sence we have been in the bay, but met with several of there hutts all of which appear'd to have been at least twelve months deserted. Upon my return to the Ship in the evening I found the water &c^a all on board and the Ship ready for sea and being now resolved to quit this country altogether and to bend my thoughts towards returning home by such a rout as might conduce most to the advantage of the service I am upon, I consulted with the officers upon the most eligible way of puting this in execution. To return by the way of *Cape Horn* was what I most wish'd because by this rout we should have been able to prove the existence or non existence of a Southern Continent which yet remains doubtfull; but in order to ascertain this we must have kept in a high latitude in the very depth of winter but the condition of the ship in every respect was not thought sufficient for such an undertaking. For the same reason the thoughts of proceeding directly to the Cape of Good Hope was laid a side especialy as no discovery of any moment could be hoped for in that rout. It was therefore resolved to return by way of the East Indies by the following rout: upon leaving this coast to steer to the westward untill we fall in with the East Coast of New Holland and than to follow the deriction of that Coast to the northward or what other direction it may take untill we arrive at its northern extremity, and if this should be found impractical than to endeavour to fall in with the lands or Islands discover'd by Quiros. With this View at day light in the morning we got under sail and put to sea having the advantage of a fresh gale at SE and clear weather. At Noon the Island which lies off the NW Point of the Bay bore E 9° distant 10 Miles. Our Latitude by observation was 40°35′ S. This Bay I have named *Admiralty Bay* the NW Point *Cape Stephens* and the SE point *Point Jackson* after the two Secretaries. It may always be know[n] by the Island above Mentioned which is pretty high and lies NE 2 Miles from Cape Stephens Lat^{de} 40°37′ S, Longitude 185°6′ West. Between this Island and Cape Farewell which is WBN and EBS distant 14 or 15 Leagues from each other the Shore forms a large deep bay the bottom of which we could hardly see in sailing in a straight line from the one Cape to the other: but it is not attall improbable but what it is all low land next the sea as we have met with less water here than on any other part of the Coast at the same distance from land. However a Bay there is and is known [on] the Chart by the name of *Blind Bay*. But I have reason to believe this to be Tasmans Murderers Bay.[37]

*   *   *

[*Cook now gives a long description of New Zealand and its inhabitants as far as he has been able to observe them. This country 'which before now was thought to be a part of the imaginary southern continent' is seen to be two islands. The south island seemed for the most part mountainous and barren, but the north island, despite being a 'hilly mountainous Country', appeared rich and fertile. 'Was this country settled by an Industrus people they would very soon be supply'd not only with the necessarys but many of the luxuries of life.' The best areas for settlement would be in the River Thames or the Bay of Islands. 'The Natives . . . are a strong raw boned well made Active people.' Cook describes their dress, their tattooing, their food, houses, canoes, tools and the evidence concerning cannibalism. 'With respect to Religion, I believe these People trouble themselves very little about it.' He appends a brief vocabulary, pointing out that the similarity of the language to that of the South Sea islanders argues that the people 'had one Origin or Source'. He concludes his essay with thoughts about future exploration. So far as the southern continent is concerned, although 'there is left but a small space to the northward of 40° where the grand Object can lay', this area should be explored, and if nothing is discovered the navigator could turn his attention to 'those multi-*

37. Blind Bay is now Tasman Bay. Murderers Bay, later Massacre Bay and then Golden Bay, is in fact the north-westerly continuation of the main bay, beyond Separation Point.

tude of Islands' thought to exist 'within the Tropical Regions to the South of the line'.]

[APRIL 1770]

SUNDAY 1*st*. In the PM had a Moderate breeze at East which in the night Veer'd to the NE and was attended with hazey rainy weather. I have before made mention of our quiting *New-Zeland* with an intention to steer to the westward which we accordingly did takeing our departure from *Cape Fare-well* in the Latitude of 40°30′ s and Longitude 185°58′ w from Greenwich, which bore from us at 5 PM West 18° north distance 12 Miles. After this we steer'd NW and WNW in order to give it a good birth untill 8 oClock am at which time we steer'd West having the advantage of a fresh gale at NBE. At Noon our Latitude by account was 40°12′ s. Longitude made from Cape Fare-well 1°11′ West.

*   *   *

[*The* Endeavour *took its westerly course covering approximately 1200 miles in the next sixteen days. The weather was good at first but they ran into strong winds on 15 April, turning into a strong gale on the 17th.*]

WEDNESDAY 18*th*. Winds southerly a hard gale with heavy squals attended with showers of rain and a great sea from the same quarter. At 3 PM Close reef'd the Topsails, handed the Main & Miz^n topsail & got down top gallant yards. At 6 oClock the gale increased to such a height as to Oblige us to take in the Fore topsail and Main sail and to run under the Fore sail and Mizen all night sounding every 2 hours but found no ground with 120 fathoms. At 6 am set the Main-sail and soon after the fore topsail and before noon the Main-topsail both close reef'd. At Noon our Latitude by Obser^n was 38°45′ s. Longitude from Cape Fare-well 23°43′ w and Course and distance run sence yesterday noon N 51° West 82 Miles. Last night we saw a Port Egmont Hen and this morning two more, a Pintado bird several Albetrosses and black sheer-waters. The first of these birds are certain signs of the nearness of land, indeed we cannot be far from it for by our Longitude we are a degree to the westward of the East side of Vandieman Land according to *Tasmans* the first discoverers Longitude of it, who could not err much in so short a run as from this land to Newzeland and by our Latitude we could not be above 50 or 55 Leagues to the northward of the place where he took his departure from.

THURSDAY 19*th*. In the PM had fresh gales at ssw and Clowdy Squaly weather with a large Southerly Sea. At 6 took in the Topsails and at 1 am brought too and sounded but had no ground with 130 fathoms of line. At 5 Set the Topsails Close reef'd and at 6 saw land extending from NE to West at the distance of 5 or 6 Leagues having 80 fathom water a fine sandy bottom. We continued Standing to the westward with the wind at ssw untill 8 oClock at which time we got topg^t yards aCross, made all sail and bore away along shore NE for the Eastermost land we had in sight, being at this time in the Latitude of 37°58′ s and Long^d of 210°39′ West. The Southermost Point of land we had in sight which bore from us w¼s I judged to lay in the Latitude of 38°0′ s and in the Longitude of 211°07′ w from the Meridion of Greenwich. I have Named it *Point Hicks*, because Leuit^t Hicks was the first who discover'd this land.

To the Southward of this point we could see no land and yet it was very clear in that quarter and by our Longitude compared with that of Tasmans the body of Vandiemens land ought to have bore due south from us and from the soon falling of the Sea after the wind abated I had reason to think it did, but as we did not see it and finding this coast to trend NE and sw or rather more to the westward makes me doubtfull whether they are one land or no: however every one who compares this Journal with that of Tasmans will be as good a judge [as] I am, but it is necessary to observe that I do not take the situation of Vandiemens from the prented Charts but from the extract of Tasmens *Journal* published by *Dirk Rembrantse*.

At Noon we were in the Lat^{de} of 37°50′ and Long^d of 210°29′ w, the extremes of the land extending from NW to ENE, a remarkable Point bore N 20° East distant 4 Leagues. This point rises to a round hillick, very much like the *Ram head* going into Plymouth Sound on which account I called it by the same name. Lat^d 37°39′, Longitude 210°22 w. The Variation by an Azimuth taken this morning was 8°7′

East. What we have as yet seen of this land appears rather low and not very hilly, the face of the Country green and woody but the sea shore is all a white sand.

FRIDAY 20*th*. In the PM and most part of the night had a fresh gale westerly with squals attended with showers of rain. In the AM had the wind at SW with serene weather. At 1 pm saw three water spouts at once, two were between us and the shore and one at some distance upon our Larboard quarter. At 6 oClock shortend sail and brought too for the night having 56 fathom water a fine sandy bottom, the Northermost land in sight bore NBE½E and a small Island lying close to a point on the Main bore west distant 2 Leagues. This point I have named *Cape Howe*, it may be known by the Trending of the Coast which is north on the one side and sw on the other (Latitude 37°28′ s, Long^de 210°3′ West) it may likewise be known by some round hills upon the Main just within it. Having brought too with her head off shore we at 10 oClock wore and lay her head in untill 4 am at which time we made sail along Shore to the northward. At 6 oClock the northermost land in sight bore North being at this time about 4 Leagues from the land. At Noon we were in the Latitude of 36°51′ s and Longitude of 209°53′ West and 3 Leagues from ye land. Courses saild along shore sence yesterday at noon was first N 52° East 30 Miles than NBE and NBW 41 Miles. The weather being clear gave us an oppertunity to View the Country which had a very agreeable and promising Aspect, the land is of a moderate height diversified with hills, ridges, planes and Vallies with some few small lawns, but for the most part the whole was cover'd with wood, the hills and ridges rise with a gentle slope, they are not high neither are there many off them.

* * *

[*Cook sailed north up the coast of New Holland (Australia), observing a good deal of smoke indicating habitation, and being at times near enough to make out figures 'of a very dark or black Colour'. He named Cape Dromedary and Cape St George ('we having discover'd it on that Saints day').*]

THURSDAY 26*th*. Clear Serene weather. In the PM had a light breeze at NNW untill 5 oClock at which time it fell calm we being then about

3 or 4 Leag[s] from the land and in 48 fathom water. Variation p[r] Azimuth 8.48 East, the extremes of the land from NEBN to SWBS. Saw several smooks along shore before dark and two or 3 times a fire in the night. We lay becalm'd driving in before the Sea untill 1 oClock AM at which time we got a breeze from the land with which we steerd NE being then in 38 fathom water. At Noon it fell little wind and Veerd to NEBN, we being than in the Latitude of 34°10′ and Longitude 208°27′ w and about 5 Leag[s] from the land which extended from s 37° w to N½E. In this Latitude are some white clifts which rise perpendicularly from the sea to a moderate height.

FRIDAY 27th. Variable light airs between the NE and NW and clear pleasent weather. In the PM stood off shore untill 2 oClock than tack'd and stood in untill 6 at which time we tack'd and stood off being than in 54 fathoms water and about 4 or 5 Miles from the land, the extremes of which bore from s 28° West to N 25°30′ East. At 12 oClock we tackd and stood in untill 4 AM than made a trip off untill day light, after which we stood in for the land; in all this time we lost ground owing a good deal to the Variableness of the winds, for at Noon we were by observation in the Latitude of 34°21′, Red Point bearing s 27 w distant 3 Leagues. In this situation we were about 4 or 5 Miles from the land which extended from s 19°30′ West to North 29° East.

SATURDAY 28th. In the PM hoisted out the Pinnace and yawl in order to attempt a landing but the Pinnace took in the water so fast that she was obliged to be hoisted in again to stop her leakes. At this time we saw several people a Shore four of whome were carrying a small boat or Canoe which we imagined they were going to put into the water in order to come off to us but in this we were mistaken. Being now not above two Miles from the Shore M[r] Banks D[r] Solander Tupia and my self put off in the yawl and pull'd in for the land to a place where we saw four or five of the natives who took to the woods as we approachd the Shore, which disapointed us in the expectation we had of geting a near view of them if not to speak to them; but our disapointment was heighten'd when we found that we no where could effect a landing by reason of the great surff which beat every where upon the shore. We saw hauld up upon the beach 3 or 4 small Canoes which to us appear'd not much unlike the small ones of New Zeland, in the woods were several trees of the Palm kind and no under wood and this was all we were able to observe from the boat after which we returnd to the Ship about 5 in the evening. At this time it fell calm and we were not above a mile and a half from shore in a 11 fathom water and within some breakers that lay to the southward of us, but luckily a light breeze came off from the land which carried us out of danger and with which we stood to the northward. At day light in the morning we discoverd a Bay which appeard to be tollerably well shelterd from all winds into which I resoloved to go with the Ship and with this view sent the Master in the Pinnace to sound the entrance while we kept turning up with the Ship haveing the wind right out. At Noon the entran[c]e bore NNW distance 1 Mile.

SUNDAY 29*th*. In the PM winds southerly clear weather with which we stood into the bay and Anchor'd under the South shore about 2 Mile within the entrence in 6 fathoms water, the south point bearing SE and the north point East. Saw as we came in on both points of the bay Several of the natives and a few hutts, Men, women and children on the south shore abreast of the Ship, to which place I went in the boats in hopes of speaking with them accompaned by Mr Banks Dr Solander and Tupia; as we approached the shore they all made off except two Men who seemd resolved to oppose our landing. As soon as I saw this I orderd the boats to lay upon their oars in order to speake to them but this was to little purpose for neither us nor Tupia could understand one word they said. We then threw them some nails beeds &c^a a shore which they took up and seem'd not ill pleased in so much that I thout that they beckon'd to us to come a shore; but in this we were mistaken, for as soon as we put the boat in they again came to oppose us upon which I fired a musket between the two which had no other effect than to make them retire back where bundles of thier darts lay, and one of them took up a stone and threw at us which caused my fireing a second Musquet load with small shott, and altho some of the shott struck the man yet it had no other effect than to make him lay hold of a Shield or target to defend himself. Emmidiatly after this we landed which we had no sooner done than they throw'd two darts at us, this obliged me to fire a third shott soon after which they both made off, but not in such haste but what we might have taken one, but Mr Banks being of opinion that the darts were poisoned, made me cautious how I advanced into the woods. We found here a few Small hutts made of the bark of trees in one of which were four or five small children with whome we left some strings of beeds &c^a. A quantity of darts lay about the hutts these we took away with us. Three Canoes lay upon the bea[c]h the worst I think I ever saw, they were about 12 or 14 feet long made of one peice of the bark of a tree drawn or tied up at each end and the middle kept open by means of peices of sticks by way of Thwarts.

After searching for fresh water without success except a little in a small hole dug in the sand, we embarqued and went over to the north point of the bay w[h]ere in coming in we saw several people, but when we now landed there were no body to be seen. We found here some fresh water which came trinkling down and stood in pools among the rocks; but as this was troblesome to come at I sent a party of men a shore in the morning to the place where we first landed to dig holes in the sand by which means and a small stream they found fresh water sufficient to water the ship. The strings of beeds &c^a we had left with the children last night were found laying in the hut this morning, probably the natives were afraid to take them away. After breakfast we sent some empty casks a shore and a party of men to cut wood and I went my self in the Pinnace to sound and explore the Bay, in the doing of which I saw sever^l of the natives but they all fled at my approach. I landed in two places one of which the people had but just left, as there were small fires and fresh muscles broiling upon them – here likewise lay vast heaps of the largest oyster shells I ever saw.

MONDAY 30*th*. As soon as the wooders and watere[r]s were come on board to dinner 10 or 12 of the natives came to the watering place and took away there canoes that lay there but did not offer to touch any one of our Casks that had been left ashore, and in the after noon 16 or 18 of them came boldly up to within 100 yards of our people at the watering place and there made a stand. Mr Hicks who was the officer ashore did all in his power to entice them to him by offering them presents &c^a but it was to no purpose, all they seem'd to want was for us to be gone. After staying a short time they went away. They were all arm'd with darts and wooden swords, the darts have each four prongs and pointed with fish bones, those we have seen seem to be intend[ed] more for strikeing fish than offensive weapons neither are they poisoned as we at first thought. After I had returnd from sounding the bay I went over to a Cove on the north side where in 3 or 4 hauls with the saine we caught above 300 pounds weight of fish which I caused to be equally divided among the Ships Company. In the AM I went in the Pinnace to sound and explore the North side of the bay where I neither met with inhabitants or any thing remarkable. Mr Green took the Suns Meridion Altitude a little with[in] the south entrence of the bay which gave the Latitude 34°0's.

[MAY 1770]

TUESDAY 1*st*. Gentle breezes northerly. In the PM ten of the natives again Viseted the watering place. I being on board at this time went emmidiatly ashore but before I got there they were going away, I follow'd them alone and unarm'd some distance along the shore but they would not stop untill they got farther off than I choose to trust my self; these were arm'd in the same manner as those that came yesterday. In the evening I sent some hands to haul the Saine but they caught but a very few fish. A little after sun rise I found the Variation to be 11°3' East. Last night Torby Sutherland seaman departed this life and in the AM his body was buried a shore at the watering place which occasioned my calling the south point of this Bay after his name. This morning a party of us went ashore to some hutts not far from the watering place where some of the natives are daly seen, here we left several articles such as Cloth, Looking glasses, Combs, Beeds Nails &c^a. After this we made an excursion into the country which we found deversified with woods, Lawns and Marshes; the woods are free from under wood of every kind and the trees are at such a distance from one a nother that the whole Country or at least great part of it might be cultivated without being oblig'd to cut down a single tree; we found the soil every where except in the Marshes to be a light white sand

and produceth a quant[it]y of good grass which grows in little tufts about as big as one can hold in ones hand and pretty close to one another, in this manner the surface of the ground is coated in the woods between the trees. Dr Solander had a bad sight of a small Animal some thing like a rabbit and we found the dung of an Animal which must feed upon grass and which we judged could not be less than a deer, we also saw the track of a dog or some such like Animal. We met with some hutts and places where the natives had been and at our first seting out one of them was seen the others I suppose had fled upon our approach. I saw some trees that had been cut down by the natives with some sort of a blunt instrument and several trees that were barked the bark of which had been cut by the same Instrument, in many of the trees, especialy the palms, were cut steps about 3 or 4 feet asunder for the conveniency of climeing them. We found 2 sorts of Gum one sort of which is like Gum Dragon and is the same as I suppose Tasman took for gum lac, it is extracted from the largest tree in the woods.

WEDNESDAY 2d. Between 3 and 4 o'Clock in the PM we returnd out of the Country and after dinner went a shore to the watering place where we had not been long before 17 or 18 of the natives appear'd in sight. In the morning I had sent Mr Gore with a boat up to the head of the bay to dridge for oysters; in his return to the ship he and another person came by land and met with these people who follow'd him at the distance of 19 or 20 yards; when ever Mr Gore made a Stand and face'd them they s[t]ood also and not withstanding they were all arm'd they never offerd to attack him, but after he had parted from them and they were met by Dr Munkhouse and one or two more who upon makeing a sham retreat they throw'd 3 darts after them, after which the[y] began to retire. Dr Solander, I, and Tupia made all the haste we could after them but could by neither words nor actions prevail upon them to come near us. Mr Gore saw some up the bay who by signs invited him ashore which he prudantly declined. In the AM had the wind at SE with rain which prevented me from makeing an excursion up to the head of the Bay as I intended.

THURSDAY 3rd. Winds at SE a gentle breeze and fair weather. In the PM I made a little excursion along the Sea Coast to the southward accompaned by Mr Banks and Dr Solander. At our first entering the woods we saw 3 of the natives who made off as soon as they saw us; more of them were seen by others of our people who likewise made off as soon as they found they were discover'd. In the AM I went in the Pinnace to the head of the Bay accompan'd by Drs Soland[er] and Munkhouse in order to examine the Country and to try to form some Connections with the natives: in our way theither we met with 10 or 12 of them fishing each in a small Canoe who retired in to shoald water upon our approach, others again we saw at the first place we landed at who took to their Canoes and fled before we came near them: after this we took water and went almost to the head of the inlet where we landed and travel'd some distance inland. We found the face of the Country much the same as I have before described but the land much richer, for in stead of sand I found in many places a deep black Soil which we thought was capable of produceing any kind of grain, at present it produceth besides timber as fine meadow as ever was seen. However we found it not all like this, some few places were very rocky but this I beleive to be uncommon; the stone is sandy and very proper for building &c^a. After we had sufficiently examined this part we return'd to the boat and seeing some smook and Canoes at a nother part we went theither in hopes of meeting with the people but they made off as we approached. There were Six Canoes and Six small fires near the shore and Muscles roasting upon thim and a few Oysters laying near, from this we conjecterd that there had been just Six people who had been out each in his Canoe picking up the Shell fish and come a shore to eat them where each had made his fire to dress them by; we taisted of their cheer and left them in return strings of beeds &c^a. Near to this place at the foot of a tree was a small well or Spring of w[ate]r. The day being now far spent we set out on our return to the Ship.

FRIDAY 4*th*. Winds Northerly serene weather. Upon my return to the Ship in the evening I found that none of the natives had appear'd near the watering place but about 20 of them had been fishing in their Canoes at no great distance from us. In the AM as the wind would not permit us to sail I sent out some parties into the Country to try to form some Connections with the natives. One of the Midshipmen met with a very old man and woman and two small Children; they were close to the water side where several more were in their canoes gathering shell fish and he being alone was afraid to make any stay with the two old people least he should be discoverd by those in the Canoes. He gave them a bird he had shott which they would not touch neither did they speak one word but seem'd to be much frighten'd, they were quite naked even the woman had nothing to cover her nuditie. Dr Munkhouse and a nother man being in the woods not far from the watering place discoverd Six more of the natives who at first seemd to wait his coming but as he was going up to them had a dart thrown at him out of a tree which narrowly escaped him, as soon as the fellow had thrown the dart he desended the tree and made off and with him all the rest and these were all that were met with in the Course of this day.

SATURDAY 5*th*. In the PM I went with a party of Men over to the North shore and while some hands were hauling the Saine a party of us made an excursion of 3 or 4 Miles into the Country or rather along the Sea Coast. We met with nothing remarkable, great part of the Country for some distance in land from the sea Coast is mostly a barren heath diversified with marshes and Morasses. Upon our return to the Boat we found they had caught a great number of small fish which the sailors call leather Jackets on account of their having a very thick skin, they are known in the West Indias. I had sent the yawl in the morning to fish for *sting rays* who return'd in the evening with upwards of 4 hundred weight; one single one wieghd 240 lb exclusive of the entrails. In the AM as the wind still continued northerly I sent the yawl again afishing and I went with a party of Men into the Country but met with nothing extraordinary.

SUNDAY 6*th*. In the evening the yawl return'd from fishing having caught two Sting rays weighing near 600 pounds. The great quantity of New Plants &c^a Mr Banks & Dr Solander collected in this place occasioned my giveing it the name of *Botany Bay*.[38] It is situated in the

38. It had earlier been given the name Stingray Harbour, and then Botanist Harbour, and Botanist Bay.

Latitude of 34°0′ s, Longitude 208°37′ West; it is Capacious safe and commodious, it may be known by the land on the Sea-coast which is of a pretty even and moderate height, rather higher than it is farther inland with steep rocky clifts next the Sea and looks like a long Island lying close under the Shore: the entrance of the harbour lies about the Middle of this land, in coming from the Southward it is discoverd before you are abreast of it which you cannot do in coming from the northward; the entrance is little more than a Mile broad and lies in wnw. To sail into it keep the south shore on board untill within a small bare Island which lies close under the north shore, being within that Island the deepest water is on that side 7, 6 and five fathom a good way up. There is shoal'd water a good way off from the South Shore from the inner South point qu[i]te to the head of the harbour, but over towards the north and nw shore is a channell of 12 or 14 feet water at low water 3 or 4 leagues up to a place where there is 3 & 4 f^m but here I found very little fresh water. We anchord near the south shore about a Mile within the entrance for the conveniency of sailing with a Southerly wind and the geting of fresh water but I afterwards found a very fine stream of fresh water on the north shore in the first sandy cove within the Island before which a Ship might lay almost land lock'd and wood for fual may be got every where: altho wood is here in great plenty yet there is very little variety, the largest trees are as large or larger than our oaks in England and grows a good deal like them and yeilds a redish gum, the wood itself is heavy hard and black like Lignum Vitae; another sort that grows tall and strait some thing like Pines, the wood of this is hard and Ponderous and something of the nature of American live oaks, these two are all the timber trees I met with. There are a few sorts of Shrubs and several Palm trees, and Mangroves about the head of the harbour. The Country is woody low and flat as far inland as we could see and I believe that the soil is in general sandy, in the wood are a variety of very boutifull birds such as Cocatoo's, Lorryquets, Parrots &c^a and Crows exactly like those we have in England. Water fowl are no less plenty about the head of the harbour where there are large flats of sand and Mud on which they seek their food, the most of these were unknown to us, one sort especialy which was black and white and as large as a goose but most like a pelican. On the Sand and Mud banks are Oysters, Muscles, Cockles &c^a which I beleive are the cheif support of the inhabitants, who go into shoald water with their little Canoes and pick them out of the sand and Mud with their hands and sometimes roast and eat them in the Canoe, having often a fire for that purpose as I suppose, for I know no other it can be for. The Natives do not appear to be numberous neither do they seem to live in large bodies but dispers'd in small parties along by the water side; those I saw were about as tall as Europeans, of a very dark brown colour but not black nor had they wooly frizled hair, but black and lank much like ours. No sort of cloathing or ornaments were ever seen by any of us upon any one of them or in or about any of their hutts, from which I conclude that they never wear any. Some we saw that had their faces and bodies painted with a sort of white paint or Pigment. Altho I have said that shell fish is their chief support yet they catch other sorts of fish some of which we found roasting on the fire the first time we landed, some of these they strike with gigs and others they catch with hook and line; we have seen them strike fish with gigs & hooks and lines were found in their hutts. Sting rays I believe they do not eat because I never saw the least remains of one near any of their hutts or fire places. However we could know but very little of their customs as we never were able to form any connections with them, they had not so much as touch'd the things we had left in their hutts on purpose for them to take away. During our stay in this Harbour I caused the English Colours to be display'd ashore every day and an inscription to be cut out upon one of the trees near the watering place seting forth the Ships name, date &c^a. Having seen every thing this place afforded we at day light in the Morning weigh'd with a light breeze at NW and put to sea and the wind soon after coming to the Southward we steer'd along shore NNE and at Noon we were by observation in the Latitude of 33°50′ s about 2 or 3 Miles from the land and abreast of a Bay or Harbour wherein there apper^d to be safe anchorage which I call'd *Port Jackson*. It lies 3 Leag^s to the northward of Botany Bay. I had almost forgot to mention that it is high water in this Bay at the full and change of the Moon about 8 o'Clock and rises and falls upon a perpendicular about 4 or 5 feet.

MONDAY 7*th*. Little wind southerly and serene pleasent weather. In the PM found the Variation by Several Azimuths to be 8° East. At sunset the Northermost land in sight bore N 26° East, and some broken land that appear'd to form a Bay boare N 40° West distant 4 Leagues, this bay I named *Broken Bay*, Latitude 33°36′ s. We steerd along shore NNE all night at the distance of about 3 Leagues from the land having from 32 to 36 fathom a hard sandy bottom. A little after Sun rise I tooke several Azimuths with four Needles belonging to the Azimuth Compass the mean result of which gave the Variation 7°56′ East. At Noon we were by observation in the Latitude of 33°22′ s and about 3 Leagues from the land, the northermost part of which in sight bore N 19° East. Some pritty high land which projected out in three bluff points and occasioned my calling it *Cape Three points* (Lat^de 33°33′) bore sw distant 5 Leagues. Longitude made from Botany Bay 0°19′ East.

*   *   *

[*Cook continued cautiously up the coast, without incident, beyond modern Brisbane and round Sandy Cape.*]

WEDNESDAY 23*rd*. Continued our Course along shore at the distance of about 2 Miles off having from 12 to 9, 8 and 7 fathom water untill 5 oClock at which time we were abreast of the South point of a large open bay where in I intended to anchor, accordingly we hauld in close upon a wind and sent a boat ahead to sound. After making some trips we anchor'd at 8 oClock in 5 fathom water a Sandy bottom. The South point of the Bay bore E¾South distance 2 Miles, the north point NW¼N about 2 Miles from the Shore in the bottom of the bay. Last Night some time in the Middle watch a very extraordinary affair happend to Mr Orton my Clerk, he having been drinking in the Evening, some Malicious person or persons in the Ship took the advantage of his being drunk and cut off all the cloaths from off his back, not being satisfied with this they some time after went into his Cabbin and cut off a part of both his Ears as he lay asleep in his bed. The person whome he suspected to have done this was Mr Magra one of the Midshipmen, but this did not appear to me upon inquirey. However as I know'd Magra had once or twice before this in their drunken frolicks cut of his Cloaths and had been heard to say (as I was told) that if it was not for the Law he would Murder him, these things consider'd induce'd me to think that Magra was not altogether innocent. I therefore, for the present dismiss'd him the quarter deck and susspended him from doing any duty in the Ship, he being one of those gentlemen, frequently found on board Kings Ships, that can very well be spared, or to speake more planer good for nothing. Besides it was necessary in me to show my immediate resentment against the person on whome the suspicion fell least they should not have stoped here. With respect to Mr Orton he is a man not without faults, yet from all the enquiry I could make, it evidently appear'd to me that so far from deserving such treatment he had not designedly injured any person in the Ship, so that I do and shall all ways look upon him as an enjure'd man. Some reasons might however be given why this misfortune came upon him in which he himself was in some measure to blame, but as this is only conjector and would tend to fix it up [on] some people in the Ship whome I would fain believe would hardly be guilty of such an act[i]on, I shall say nothing about it unless I shall hereafter discover the Offenders which I shall take every method in my power to do, for I look upon such proceedings as highly dangerous in such Voyages as this and the greatest insult that could be offer'd to my authority in this Ship, as I have always been ready to hear and redress every complaint that have been made against any Person in the Ship.[39]

In the AM I went a shore with a party of men in order to examine the Country accompaned by Mr Banks and the other gentlemen. We landed a little within the South point of the Bay where there is a channel leading into a large Lagoon. The first thing I did was to sound and examine this channel in which I found 3 fathom water untill I got about a Mile up it, where I met with a Shoal whereon was little more than one fathom, being over this I had 3 fathom again. The entrance into this channel lies close to the South point of the Bay

39. Three weeks later Cook decided that Magra was innocent and restored him to duty. The midshipman Patrick Saunders was disrated to AB on this day, presumably because of his part in the affair. At Batavia, a reward was offered for information about the person responsible. Saunders deserted (never to be heard of again) and it was assumed that it was he who mutilated Orton.

being form'd on the East by the shore and on the West by a large spit
of sand, it is about a quarter of a Mile broad and lies in SBW; here is
room for a few ships to lay very secure and a small Stream of fresh
water. After this I made a little excursion into the woods while some
hands made 3 or 4 hauls with the Sain but caught not above a dozen
very small fish; by this time the flood was made and I embarqued in
the boat in order to row up the Lagoon but in this I was hindred by
meeting every where with shoal water. As yet we had seen no people
but saw a great deal of smook up and on the west side of the Lagoon
which was all too far off for us to go by land excepting one; this we
went to and found 10 small fires in a very small compass and some
cockle shells laying by them but the people were gone. On the windward
or South side of one fire was stuck up a little bark about a foot and a
half high and some few pieces lay about in other places; these we
concluded were all the covering they had in the night and many of
them I firmly believe have not this but naked as they are Sleep in the
open air, Tupia who was with us observed that they were *Taata Eno's*
that is bad or poor people. The Country is vissibly worse than at the
last place we were at, the Soil is dry and Sandy and the woods are
free from under-wood of every kind. Here are of the same sort of trees
as we found in Botany Bay with a few other sorts; one sort which is
by far the most numerous of any in the woods grows something like
birch, the bark at first sight looks like birch bark but upon examanation
I found it to be very different and so I believe is the wood, but this I
could not examine as having no ax or any thing with me to cut down
a tree. About the skirts of the Lagoon grows the true Mangrove such
as are found in the West Indias and which we have not seen during
the Voyage before, here is likewise a sort of a Palm tree which grows
on low barren and sandy places in the South Sea Islands. All or most
of the same sorts of land and water fowl as we saw at Botany Bay we
saw here, besides these Black & white Ducks, and Bustards such as
we have in England one of which we killd that weigh'd 17½ pounds
which occasioned my giving this place the name of *Bustard Bay* (Lat^d
24°4' Long^d 208°22'). Here are plenty of small oysters sticking to the
Rocks, stones and Mangrove trees and some few other shell fish
such as large Musels, Pearl oysters, Cockels &c^a. I measured the

perpendicular height of the last tide and found it to be 8 feet above low-water mark and from the time of low-water to day I found that it must be high water at the full and change of the Moon at 8 oClock.

*   *   *

[*Now began the most difficult navigation of the entire voyage as the* Endeavour *groped its way along the coast through shoals and islands, usually with two boats ahead, in the charge of the Master (Robert Molyneux), taking soundings.*]

TUESDAY 29*th.* Fresh gales between the SSE and ESE Hazy we[r] with some showers of rain in the PM. Having sounded about the Ship and found that there was sufficient water for her over the Shoal we at 3 oClock weigh'd and came to sail and stood to the westward as the land lay having first sent a boat ahead to sound. At 6 o'Clock we Anchord in 10 fathom water a sandy bottom about 2 Miles from the Main land, the westermost part of which bore WNW having still a number of Islands in sight a long way without us. At 5 oClock in the AM I sent away the Master with two boats to sound the entrance of an inlet which bore from us west distant about one League, into which I intended to go with the Ship to wait a few days untill the Moon increased and in the Mean time to examine the Country. By such time as we had got the Ship under Sail the boats made the signal for anchor[a]ge upon which we stood in with the Ship and Anchord in 5 fathom water about a League within the entrance of the inlet, which we judged to be a River runing a good way inland. As I observed the tides to flow and Ebb something considerable I had some thoughts of laying the Ship a shore to clean her bottom. With this View both the Master and I went to look for a convinient place for that purpose and at the same time to look for fresh water, not one drop of which we could find, but met with several places where a Ship might be laid a shore with safety.

WEDNESDAY 30*th.* In the PM I went again in search of fresh water but had no better success than before, wherefore I gave over all thoughts of laying the Ship a shore being resolved on spending as little time as possible in a place that was likely to afford us no sort of refreshment, but as I had observed from the hills the Inlet to run a good way in land I thought this a good time to penetrate into the Country to see a little of the inland parts. Accordingly I prepar'd for makeing that excursion in the morning, but the first thing I did was to get upon a pritty high hill which is at the NW entrance of the inlet before sunrise in order to take a view of the Sea coast and Islands &c^a that lay off it, and to take their bearings. . . . As soon as I had done here I proceeded up the Inlet. I set out with the first of the flood and long before high-water got above 8 Leagues up it, its breadth thus far was from 2 to 4 or 5 Miles upon a SWBS dire[c]tion, but here it spread every way and formd a large lake which commun[i]cates with the Sea to the NW; I not only saw the Sea in this direction but found the tide of flood coming Strong in from the NW. I likewise observed an arm of this lake extending to the eastward and it is not att all improbable but what it communicates with the sea in the bottom of the bay which lies to the westward of *C. Townshend*. On the south side of the lake is a ridge of pretty high hills which I was desireous of going upon, but as the day was far spent and high-water I was afraid of being bewilderd among the Shoals in the night, which promised to be none of the best being already rainy dirty weather, and therefore I made the best of my way to the Ship. In this little excursion I saw only two people and those at a distance and are all that we have seen in this place, but we have met with several fire places and seen smooks at a distance. This Inlet which I have named *Thirsty Sound* by reason we could find no fresh water lies in the Latitude of 22°05′ s and Longitude 210°24′ West. It may be known by a Group of small Islands laying under the shore from 2 to 5 Leagues NW from it, there is likewise another Group of Islands laying right before it between 3 and 4 Leagues out at Sea. Over each of the points that form the entrance is a pretty high round hill, that on the NW is a peninsula surrounded by the Sea at high-water, the distance from the one to the other is about two Miles bold to both shores. Here is good anchorage in 7, 6, 5 & 4 fathom water and very convenient places for laying a Ship aShore where at Spring tides the tides doth not rise less then 16 or 18 feet and flowes at full and change of the Moon about a 11 oClock. We met with no fresh water or any other kind of refreshments whatever, we saw two turtle but caught none nor no sort of fish or wild fowl except a few small land birds.

Here are the same sort of water fowl as we saw in *Botany Bay* and like
them so Shy that it is hardly possible to get within shott of them. No
signs of fertillity is to be seen upon the land, the Soil of the uplands is
mostly a hard redish Clay and produceth several sorts of trees such
as we have seen before and some others and clear of all under wood.
All the low lands are mostly over run with Mangroves and at spring
tides over flowed by the Sea, and I beleive in the rainy seasons here
are large land floods as we saw in many places gullies which seem'd
to have been made by torrents of water coming from the adjacent
hills, besides other vissible signs of the water having been a considerable
height above the common spring tides. Dr Solander and I was upon
a rising ground up the Inlet which we thought had at one time or a
nother been over flowed by the Sea, and if so great part of the Country
must at that time been laid under water. Up in the lakes or Lagoons
I suppose are shell fish on which the few natives subsist. We found
oysters sticking to most of the rocks upon the Shore which were so
small as not to be worth the picking off.

*   *   *

[*The tortuous progress continued. There were regular indications of the inhabitants,
who kept their distance. On 4 June they negotiated the passage between Whitsunday
Island and the main. An additional problem for Cook was finding names for all
the bays and points they encountered, and the journal shows considerable uncertainty
about which notable was to be offered which bay. On 8 June Hicks, Banks and
Solander went ashore to get coconuts, but the trees proved to be 'a small kind of
Cabbage Palms'. They were now (unbeknownst) entering the funnel where the
Great Barrier Reef converges with the coast.*]

[JUNE 1770]

SATURDAY 9*th*. Winds between the South and SE a gentle breeze and
clear weather: with which we steer'd NBW as the land lay, the northern
extreme of which at sun set bore N 25° West. We kept on our Course
under an easy sail all night having from 12 to 15 fathom water at the
distance of about 3 or 4 Leagues from the land. At 6 oClock in the
AM we were abreast of some small Islands which we call'd *Frankland
Isles* that lay about two Leagues from the main land the northern point

of which in sight bore NBW½W but this we afterwards found to be an Island tolerable high and about 4 Miles in circuit. It lies about 2 Miles from the point on the Main between which we went with the Ship and were in the Middle of the Channel at Noon and by observation in the Latitude of 16°55′, where we had 20 fathom water. The point of land we were now abreast off I call'd *Cape Grafton* (Lat^de 16°55′ s, Long^de 214°11′ west) it is tolerable high land and so is the whole coast for 20 Leagues to the southward and hath a very rocky surface which is thinly cover'd with wood. In the night we saw several fires along shore and a little before noon some people.

SUNDAY 10*th*. After hauling round *Cape Grafton* we found the land trend away NWBW. Three miles to the Westward of the Cape is a Bay wherein we anchord about 2 Miles from the shore in 4 fathom water an owsey bottom. The East point of the bay bore s 74° East, the west point s 83° West and a low green woody Island laying in the offing bore N 35° East. This Island lies NBE½E distant 3 or 4 Leg^s from *Cape Grafton*, and is known in the Chart by the name of *Green Island*. As soon as the Ship was brought to an Anchor I went ashore accompanied by Mr Banks and Dr Solander, the first thing I did was to look for fresh water and with that View rowed out towards the Cape because in the bottom of the Bay was low mangrove land and little probability of meeting with any there, but the way I went I found two small streames which were difficult to get at on account of the surff and rocks upon the shore. As we came round the Cape we saw in a Sandy Cove a small stream of water run over the beach, but here I did not go in the boat because I found that it would not be easy to land. We hardly advance[d] any thing into the Country, it being here hilly which were steep and rocky and we had not time to viset the low lands and therefore met with nothing remarkable. My intention was to have stay'd here at least one day to have looked into the Country had we met with fresh water convenient or any other refreshment, but as we did not I thought it would be only spending time and looseing so much of a light moon to little purpose, and therefore at 12 oClock at night we weigh'd and stood away to the NW, having at this time but little wind attended with showers of rain. At 4 oClock the breeze freshend at SBE with fair weather. We continued steering NNW½W as the land lay haveing 10, 12 and 14 fathom at the distance of 3 Leagues from the land. At 10 oClock we hauld off north in order to get without a small low Island which lay about 2 Leagues from the Main; it being about high water at the time we passd it great part of it lay under water. About 3 Leagues to the northwestward of this Island close under the Main land is a nother Island tolerable high which bore from us at Noon N 55° west distant 7 or 8 Miles, we being at this time in the latitude of 16°20′ S. *Cape Grafton* bore S 29° East distant 40 Miles and the northermost point of land in sight N 20° W and in this situation had 15 fathom water. The shore between *Cape Grafton* and the above northern point forms a large but not very deep Bay which I named *Trinity Bay* after the day on which it was discoverd, the north point *Cape Tribulation* because here begun all our troubles. Latitude 16°6′S, Long^de 214°39′ W.

MONDAY 11*th*. Wind at ESE with which we steer'd along shore NBW at the distance of 3 or 4 Leagues off having from 14 to 10 & 12 fm [with] two small Islands in the offing which lay in the latitude of 16°0′ S and about 6 or 7 Leagues from the Main. At 6 oClock the northermost land in sight bore NWB½W and two low woody Islands which some took to be rocks above water bore N½W. At this time we shortend sail and hauld off shore ENE and NEBE close upon a wind. My intention was to stretch off all night as well to avoid the dangers we saw ahead as to see if any Islands lay in the offing, especialy as we now begin to draw near the Latitude of those discover'd by Quiros which some Geographers, for what reason I know not have thought proper to tack to this land, having the advantage of a fine breeze of wind and a clear moonlight night. In standing off from 6 untill near 9 oClock we deepen'd our water from 14 to 21 fathom when all at once we fell into 12, 10 and 8 fathom. At this time I had every body at their stations to put about and come too an anchor but in this I was not so fortunate for meeting again with deep water I thought there could be no danger in stand^g on. Before 10 oClock we had 20 and 21 fathom and continued in that depth untill a few Minutes before a 11 when we had 17 and before the Man at the lead could heave another cast the Ship Struck and stuck fast. Emmidiatly upon this we took in all our sails hoisted out the boats and sounded round the Ship, and found that we had got upon the SE edge of a reef of Coral rocks having in some places round the Ship 3 and 4 fathom water and in other places not quite as many feet, and about a Ships length from us on our starboard side (the ship laying with her head to the NE) were 8, 10 and 12 fathom. As soon as the long boat was out we struck yards and Topm^ts and carried out the stream Anchor upon the starboard bow, got the Costing anchor and cable into the boat and were going to carry it out the same way; but upon my sounding the second time round the Ship I found the most water a stern, and therefore had this anchor carried out upon the Starboard quarter and hove upon it a very great strean which was to no purpose the Ship being quite fast, upon which we went to work to lighten her as fast as possible which seem'd to be the only means we had left to get her off as we went a Shore about the top of high-water. We not only started water but throw'd over board our guns Iron and stone ballast Casks, Hoops staves oyle Jars, decay'd stores &c^a, many of these last articles lay in the way at coming at heavyer. All this time the Ship made little or no water. At a 11 oClock in the AM being high-water as we thought we try'd to heave her off without success, she not being a float by a foot or more notwithstanding by this time we had thrown over board 40 or 50 Tun weight; as this was not found sufficient we continued to Lighten her by every method we could think off. As the Tide fell the Ship began to make water as much as two Pumps could free. At Noon she lay with 3 or 4 Strakes heel to Starboard. Latitude Observed 15°45′ South.

TUESDAY 12*th*. Fortunatly we had little wind fine weather and a smooth Sea all these 24 hours which in the PM gave us an oppertunity to carry out the two bower Anchors, the one on the Starboard quarter and the other right a stern. Got blocks and tackles upon the Cables brought the falls in abaft and hove taught. By this time it was 5 oClock in the pm, the tide we observed now begun to rise and the leak increased upon us which obliged us to set the 3rd Pump to work as we should have done the 4th also, but could not make it work. At 9 oClock the Ship righted and the leak gaind upon the Pumps considerably. This was an alarming and I may say terrible Circumstance and threatend immidiate destruction to us as soon as the Ship was afloat. However I resolved to resk all and heave her off in case it was practical and accordingly turnd as many hands to the Capstan & windlass as could be spared from the Pumps and about 20′ past 10 oClock the Ship floated and we hove her off into deep water having at this time 3 feet 9 Inches water in the hold. This done I sent the Long boat to take up the stream anchor – got the anchor but lost the Cable among the rocks, after this turn'd all hands to the Pumps the leak increasing upon us. A Mistake soon after happened which for the first time caused fear to operate upon every man in the Ship. The man which attend[ed] the well took ye depth of water above the ceiling, he being relieved by another who did not know in what manner the former had sounded, took the depth of water from the out side plank, the difference being 16 or 18 Inches and made it appear that the leak had gain'd this upon the pumps in a short time, this mistake was no sooner clear'd up than [it] acted upon every man like a charm; they redoubled their Vigour in so much that before 8 oClock in the Morning they gain'd considerably upon the leak. We now hove up the best bower but found it impossible to save the small bower so cut it away at a whole Cable. Got up the fore topmast and fore yard, warped the Ship to the SE and at a 11 got under Sail and Stood in for the land with a light breeze at ESE, some hands employ'd sowing ockam wool &c^a into a lower Studding sail to fother the Ship, others emplo'd at the Pumps which still gain'd upon the leak.

WEDNESDAY 13*th*. In the PM had light airs at ESE with which we kept edgeing in for the land, got up the Main topmast and Main yard and having got the sail ready for fothering the Ship we put it over under the Starboard fore chains where we suspected the Ship had sufferd most and soon after the leak decreased so as to be kept clear with one Pump with ease, this fortunate circumstance gave new life to every one on board. It is much easier to conceive then to discribe the satisfaction felt by every body on this occation, but a few minutes before our utmost wishes were to get hold of some place upon the Main or an Island to run the Ship ashore where out of her Materials we might build a vessel to carry us to the East Indias; no sooner were we made sensible that the outward application to the Ships bottom had taken effect than the feild of every mans hopes inlarged so that we now thought of nothing but rainging along shore in search of a harbour where we could repair the damages we had susstaind. In justice to the Ships Company I must say that no men ever behaved better than they have done on this occasion, animated by the beheavour of every gentleman on board, every man seem'd to have a just sence of the danger we were in and exerted himself to the very utmost.

The Ledge of rocks or Shoal we have been upon lies in the Lat^de of 15°45′ and about 6 or 7 Leagues from the Main land, but this is not the only shoal that lay upon this part of the Coast especialy to the northward, and one which we now saw to the Southward the tail of which we past over when we had the uneven soundings two hours before we Struck; a part of this shoal is always above water and looks to be white sand. Part of the one [we] were upon drys at low-water and in that place consists of Sand and stones but every where else coral rocks. At 6 oClock we Anchor'd in 17 fathom water about 5 or 6 Leagues from the land and one from the Shoal. At this time the Ship made about 15 Inches water p^r hour. At 6 oClock in the AM we weigh'd and stood to the NW edging in for the land having a gentle breeze at SSE. At 9 oClock we past close without two small low Islands laying in the latitude of 15°41′ and about 4 Leagues from the Main. I have named them *Hope Islands* because we were always in hopes of being able to reach these Islands.

At Noon we were about 3 Leagues from the land and in the latitude of 15°37′ South, the northermost part of the Main in sight bore N 3° west and the above Islands extending from S 30° E to South 40° E, in this situation had 12 fathoms water and sever^l Sand Banks without us. The leak now decreaseth but for fear it should break out again we got the Sail ready fill'd for fothering. The manner this is done is thus, we Mix ockam & wool together (but ockam alone would do) and chop it up small and than stick it loosly by handfulls all over the sail and throw over it sheeps dung or other filth. Horse dung for this purpose is the best. The sail thus prepared is hauld under the Ships bottom by ropes and if the place of the leak is uncertain it must be hauld from one part of her bottom to a nother untill the place is found where it takes effect; while the sail is under the Ship the ockam &c^a is washed off and part of it carried along with the water into the leak and in part stops up the hole. Mr Munkhouse one of my Midshipmen was once in a Merchant ship which sprung a leak and made 48 inches water per hour but by this means was brought home from Virginia to London with only her proper crew, to him I gave the deriction of this who exicuted it very much to my satisfaction.

THURSDAY 14*th*. In the PM had a gentle breeze at SEBE. Sent the Master with two boats as well to sound ahead of the Ship as to look out for a harbour where we could repair our defects and put the Ship into a proper trim both of which she now very much wanted. – At 3 oClock saw an opening that had the appearence of a harbour. Stood off and on while the boats were examining it who found that there was not a sufficient depth of water for the Ship. By this time it was almost sun set and seeing many shoals about us we anchord in 4 fathom water about 2 Miles from the shore the Mainland extending from N½E to SBE½E. At 8 oClock the Pinnace in which was one of the Mates return'd on board and reported that they had found a good harbour about 2 Leagues to leeward. In concequence of this information we at 6 in the AM weighd and run down to it, first sending two boats ahead to lay upon the Shoals that lay in our way and notwithstanding this precaution we were once in 3 fathom water with the Ship; having pass'd these shoals the boats were sent to lay in the C[h]annel leading into the harbour. By this time it begun to blow in so much that the Ship would not work having miss'd stays twice, and being intangled among shoals I was afraid of being drove to leeward before the boats could place themselves, and therefore Anchor'd in 4 fathom about a Mile from the shore and than made the signal for the boats to come on board, after which I went my self and buoy'd the Channel which I found very narrow and the harbour much smaller than I had been told but very convenient for our purpose. At Noon Latitude observed 15°26′ South.

FRIDAY 15*th*. A fresh gale at SE and Clowdy weather attended with showers of rain in the night. As it blowed too fresh to break the Ship loose to run into the harbour we got down topgallant yards, unbent the Main sail and some of the small Sails, got down the Fore topg^t Mast and the Jibb boom and spritsail yard in, intending to lighten the Ship forward as much as possible in order to lay her ashore to come at the leak.

SATURDAY 16*th*. Strong gales at SE and Clowdy hazey weather with showers of rain. At 6 oClock in the AM it moderated a little and we hove short intending to get under sail, but was obliged to desist and bear away again. Some People were seen ashore to day.

SUNDAY 17*th*. Most part strong gales at SE with some heavy showers of rain in the PM. At 6 in the AM being pretty moderate we weigh'd and run in to the Harbour in doing of which we run the Ship a shore twice, the first time she went off without any trouble but the second time She stuck fast, but this was of no concequence any farther then giving us a little trouble and was no more than what I expected as we had the wind. While the Ship lay fast we got down the fore yard Fore topmast booms &c^a over board and made a raft of them along side.

MONDAY 18*th*. Fresh gales and clowdy with showers of rain. At 1 PM the Ship floated and we warped her into the harbour and moor'd her along side of a Steep beach on the south side. Got the anchors Cables and All the Hawsers a shore. In the AM made a stage from the Ship to the shore; errected two tents one for the Sick and the other for the Stores and Provisions; landed all the empty casks and part of the Provisions; and sent a boat to haul the sene who return'd without success.

TUESDAY 19*th*. Fresh gales at SE and clowdy weather with frequent showers of rain. In the PM landed all the provisions and part of the stores; got the sick a Shore which amounted at this time to 8 or 9 afflicted with different disorders but none very dangerously ill. This afternoon I went upon one of the highest hill[s] over the harbour from which I had a perfect View of the inlet or River and adjacent country which afforded but a very indifferent prospect, the low lands near the River is all over run with mangroves among which the salt water flowes every tide and the high land appear'd to be barren and stoney. In the AM got the 4 remaining guns out of the hold and Mounted them on the quarter deck. Got a spare anchor and anchor stock a shore and the remaining part of the stores and ballast that were in the hold. Set up the smiths forge and set the Armourer and his mate to work to make nails &c^a to repair the Ship.

WEDNESDAY 20*th*. Winds at SE a fresh breeze, fore & Middle parts rainy the latter fair. This day got out all the officers stores and the ground tier of water having now nothing in the Fore and Main hold but the Coals and a little stone ballast.

THURSDAY 21*st*. In the PM landed the Powder, got out the stone ballast wood &c^a which brought the Ships draught of water to 8^F 10^I forward and 13 feet abaft; this I thought by triming the Coals aft wou'd be sufficient as I find the tides will rise and fall upon a perpendicular 8 feet at spring tides, but after the coals was trim'd away from over the leak we could hear the water come gushing in a little abaft the fore mast & about 3 feet from her keel; this determined me to clear the hold intirely. Accordingly very early in the morning we went to work to get out the Coals which was employment for all hands.

FRIDAY 22*d*. Winds at SE fair weather. At 4 In the PM having got out most of the Coals, cast loose the moorings and warped the Ship a little higher up the harbour to a place I had pitched upon to lay a Shore for stoping the leak, her draught of Water forward 7 feet 9 Inches and abaft 13 feet 6 Inches. At 8 being high water hauld her bow close a shore but kept her stern a float because I was afraid of neeping her, and yet it was necessary to lay the whole of her as near the ground as possible. At 2 oClock in the AM the tide left her which gave us an oppertunity to examine the leak which we found to be at her floor heads a little before the Starboard fore chains. Here the rocks had made their way thro' four Planks quite to and even into the timbers and wound'd three more. The manner these planks were damaged or cut out as I may say is hardly credable, scarce a splinter was to be seen but the whole was cut away as if it had been done by the hands of Man with a blunt edge tool. Fortunatly for us the timbers in this place were very close, other ways it would have been impossible to have saved the ship and even as it was it appear'd very extraordinary that she made no more water than what she did. A large piece of Coral rock was sticking in one hole and several pieces of the fothering, small stones, sand &c^a had made its way in and lodged between the timbers which had stoped the water from forceing its way in in great quantities. Part of the sheathing was gone from under the larboard bow, part of the false keel was gone and the remainder in such a shatter'd condition that we should be much better of, was it gone also; her fore foot and some part of her Main keel was also damaged but not materialy, what damage she may have received abaft we could not see but beleive not much as the Ship makes but little water while the tide keeps below the leak forward. At 9 oClock the Carpenters went to work upon the Ship while the Smiths were busy makeing bolts nails &c^a.

SATURDAY 23*d*. Winds south easterly a fresh gale and fair weather. Carpenters emp^d shifting the damaged Planks as long as the tide would permit them to work. At low water in the PM we examined the Ships bottom under the starboard side she being dry as far aft as the after part of the fore chains, we could not find that she had received any other damage on this side but what has been mentioned. In the Morning I sent 3 Men into the Country to shoot Pigeons as some few of these birds had been seen flying about, in the evening they returnd with about half a dozen; one of the men saw an animal something less than a grey hound, it was of a Mouse Colour very slender made and swift of foot. In the AM I sent a boat to haul the saine who return'd at Noon having made three hauls and caught only three fish, and yet we see plenty jumping about the harbour but can find no method of catching them.

SUNDAY 24*th*. Winds and weather as yesterday. In the PM the Carpenters finish'd the Starboard side and at 9 oClock heel'd the Ship the other way and hauld her off about 2 feet for fear of neeping. In the AM they went to work upon repairing the sheathing under the larboard bow where we found two planks cut about half thro'. Early in the morning I sent a party of men into the Country under the direction of Mr Gore to seek for refreshments, they returnd about noon with a few Palm Cabbages and a bunch or two of wild Plantains, these last were much smaller then any I had ever seen and the Pulp full of small stones otherwise they were well taisted. I saw my self this morning a little way from the ship one of the Animals before spoke off, it was of a light Mouse colour and the full size of a grey hound and shaped in every respect like one, with a long tail which it carried like a grey hound, in short I should have taken it for a wild dog, but for its walking or runing in which it jumped like a Hare or a dear; Another of them was seen to day by some of our people who saw the first, they describe them as having very small legs and the print of the foot like that of a goat, but this I could not see my self because the ground the one I saw was upon was too hard and the length of the grass hinderd my seeing its legs.

MONDAY 25*th*. At low-water in the PM while the Carpenters were busey in repairing the sheathing and plank under the larboard bow I got people to go under the ships bottom to examine all her larboard side, she only being dry forward but abaft were 9 feet water. They found part of the sheathing off abreast of the Main mast about her floor heads and a part of one plank a little damaged. There were three people who went down who all agree'd in the same story, the master was one who was positive that she had received no material damage besides the loss of the sheathing. This alone will be sufficient to let the worm into her bottom which may prove of bad concequence; however we must run all resk for I know of no method to remedy this but by heaving her down which would be a work of emince labour & time, if not impractical in our present situation.

The Carpenters continued hard at work under her bottom untill put off by the tide in the eveng, and the morning tide did not ebb out far enough to permit them to work, for here we have only one tolerable low and high tide in 24 hours. In the AM a party of men were emp^d ashore filling water while others were employ'd in overhauling the rigging.

TUESDAY 26*th*. Fair weather winds a[t] s, a fresh gale. At low-water in the pm the Carpenters finished under the larboard bow and every other place the tide would permit them to come at. Lashed some Casks under the Ships bows in order to help to float her and at High-water in the night Attempted to heave her off but could not, she not being a float partly owing to some of the Casks not holding that were lash'd under her. In the AM employ'd geting more Casks ready for the same purpose; but I am much afraid that we shall not be able to float her now the tides are takeing off.

WEDNESDAY 27*th*. Winds at SE a fresh breeze and Clowdy weather. In the PM lashed 38 empty Butts under the ships bottom in order to float her off which proved ineffectual and therefore gave over all hopes of geting her off untill the next spring tides. At day light got a consider[able] weight of sundry articles from aft forward to ease the ship. The Armourers at work at the Forge repairing Iron work &c^a, Carpenters caulking the Ship and stocking one of the spare anchors, Seamen employd filling water and overhauling the riging; and I went in the Pinnace up the harbour and made several hauls with the Sain but caught only between 20 and 30 lb of fish which were given to the sick and such as were weak and ailing.

THURSDAY 28*th*. Fresh breezes and Cloudy; all hands employ'd as yesterday.

FRIDAY 29*th*. Winds and weather as yesterday and the Employment of the people the same. Lieutenant Gore having been 4 or 5 Miles in the Country where he met with nothing remarkable, he saw the foot steps of Men and likewise those of 3 or 4 sorts of wild beasts but saw neither man nor beast; some others of our people who were out yesterday on the north side of the River met with a place where the natives had just been, as there fires we[re] still burning but they saw no body nor have we seen one sence we have been in Port. In these excursions we found some wild Yamms or Coccos growing in the swampy grounds and this afternoon I sent a party of men to gather some, the tops we found made good greens and eat exceeding well when boild but the roots were so Acrid that few besides my self could eat them. This night Mr Green and I observed an Emersion of Jupiter first Satellite which happen'd at $2^h58'53''$ in the AM, the same Emersion happend at Greenwich according to calculation on the 30th at 5^{h}17′43″ in the PM; the difference is 14^{h}18′50″ equal to 214°42′30″ of Longitude which this place is west of Greenwich, and its Latitude is 15°26′ South. In the AM I sent some hands with a boat up the River to haul the sain while the rest were employ'd about the rigging and sundry other duties.

SATURDAY 30*th*. Moderate breezes at SE and clear serene weather. In the PM the Boat returnd from hauling the sain having caught as many fish as came to a pound and a half a man. In the AM I sent her again to haul the Sain and some hands to gather greens while others were employ'd about the rigging &c^a &c^a. I likewise sent some of the young gentlemen to take a Plan of the harbour and went my self upon the hill which is over the south point to take a view of the Sea, at this time it was low-water and I saw what gave me no small uneasiness which were a number of Sand banks or shoals laying all along the coast; the innermost lay about 3 or 4 Miles from the shore and the outermost extend[ed] off to sea as far as I could see with my glass, some just appeard above water. The only hopes I have of geting clear of them is to the northward where there seems to be a passage for as the winds blowe constantly from the SE we shall find it difficult if not impractical to return back to the southward.

[JULY 1770]

SUNDAY 1*st*. Gentle breezes at SE and clowdy weather with some gentle showers in the morning. In the PM the People returnd from hauling the Sain having caught as much fish as came to 2½ pound a Man, no one on board having more than another, the few greens we got I cause[d] to be boild a mong the Pease and makes a very good mess, which together with the fish is a great refreshment to the people. In the AM a party of men (one from each mess) went again afishing and all the rest I gave leave to go into the Country knowing that there was no danger from the natives. To day at noon the Thermometer in the shade ris to 87° which is two or three degrees higher then it has been on any day before.

MONDAY 2*d*. D° Weather. In the PM the fishing party caught as much fish as came to 2 pound a man, those that were in the Country met with nothing new. Early in the AM I sent the Master in the Pinnace out of the Harbour to Sound about the Shoals in the offening and to look for a Channel to the northward. At this time we had a breeze of wind from the land which continued till about 9 oClock, what makes me mention this is because it is the first land breeze we have had sence we have been in this River. At low-water lashed some empty Casks under the Ships bows being in some hopes of floating her the next high-water and sent some hands afishing while others were employ'd in refiting the Ship.

TUESDAY 3*rd*. Winds at SE, fore and middle parts a gentle breeze the remainder a fresh gale. In the evening the fishing party returnd having got as much fish as came to 2 lb a man; at High-water Attempted to heave the Ship off but did not succeed. At Noon the Master returnd and reported that he had found a passage out to sea between the shoals which passage lies out ENE or EBN from the Rivers mouth, he found these shoals to consist of Coral rocks; he landed upon one which drys at low-water where he found very large cockles and a variety of other shell fish a quantity of which he brought away with him. He told me that he was 5 Leagues out at sea having at that distance of 21 fathom water and judged him self to be without all the shoals, which I very much doubted; after this he came in shore and stood to the northward where he met with a number of shoals laying a little distance from the shore, about 9 oClock in the evening he landed in a bay about 3 Leagues to the northward of this place where he disturbed some of the natives whome he supposed to be at supper; they all fled upon his approach and left him some fresh Sea Eggs and a fire ready lighted behind them, but there was neither house or hut near.

Altho these Shoals lay within sight of the coast and abound very much with shell fish and other small fish which are to be caught at low-water in holes in the rocks, yet the natives never visit them for if they did we must have seen of these large shells on shore about their fire places, the reason I do suppose is that they have no boats that they dare venture so far out at Sea in.

WEDNESDAY 4*th*. St[r]ong gales at SE and fair weather. In the PM the fishing party returnd with the usual success. At High-water hove the Ship a float. In the AM Employ'd triming her upon an even keel intending to lay her a shore once more to try to come at her bottom under the larboard Main chains.

THURSDAY 5*th*. Strong breezes at SE and fair weather. In the PM warped the ship over and at high-water laid her a shore on the sand bank on the south side of the River for I was afraid to lay her broad side to the shore where she lay before because the ground lies with too great a decent and she hath already received some damage by laying there these last neep tides, at least she still makes water.

FRIDAY 6*th*. D° Weather. At low water in the PM had hardly 4 feet water under the ship yet could not repair the sheathing that was beat off the place being all under water. One of the Carpenters crew, a Man I could trust, went down and examined it and found three streaks of the sheathing gone about 7 or 8 feet long and the Main plank a little rub'd: this accou[n]t agrees with the report of the Master and others that were under her bottom before. The Carpenter who I look upon to be well skilld in his profission and a good judge of these matters was of opinion that this was of little concequence, and as I found that it would be difficult if not impractical for us to get under her bottom to repair it I resolved to spend no more time about it. Accordingly at High-water hove her off and Moor'd her along side the beach where the stores &c^a lay and in the AM got everything in readiness for takeing them on board, and at the same time got on board 8 tuns of water and stowed in the ground tier in the after hold. In the Morning Mr Banks and Lieut^t Gore with three men went in a small boat up the River with a view to stay two or 3 days to try to kill some of the animals we have so often seen about this place.

*   *   *

SUNDAY 8*th*. Gentle breezes at SE and clear weather. Early I sent the Master in a boat out to sea to sound again about the shoals because the account he had given of the Channell before mentioned was to me by no means satisfactory, like wise sent some hands to haul the sain who caught near 80 pound of fish, the rest of the people I gave leave to go into the country.

MONDAY 9*th*. Gentle breezes in the day at SE and in the night calm. In the PM Mr Gore and Mr Banks returnd having met with nothing remarkable, they were about 3 or 4 Leag^s up in the country without finding hardly any Variation either in the soil or produce. In the evening the Master returnd having been seven Leagues out at sea and at that distance off saw shoals without him and was of opinion that there was no geting out to sea that way. In his return he touched upon one of the shoals the same as he was upon the first time he was out, here he saw a great number of turtle three of which he caught weighing 791 pounds. This occasioned my sending him out again this morning provided with proper geer for strikeing them he having before nothing but a boat hook. Carpenters smiths and Coopers at their respective employments and the seam^n employ'd geting on board stone ballast. This day all hands feasted upon turtle for the first time.

TUESDAY 10*th*. Winds and weather as yesterday. Employ'd hoisting on board and stowing away the ground tier of water. In the PM saw Seven or eight of the Natives on the South side of the River and two of them came down upon the sandy point opposite the ship but as soon as I put off in a boat in order to speak with them they run away as fast as they could. At 11 oClock Mr Banks, who had gone out to sea with Mr Molineux the Master, returnd in his own small boat and gave but a very bad account of our turtle catchers. At the time he left them which was about 6 oClock they had not got one nor were they likely to get any, and yet the Master was so obstinate that he would not return; which obliged me to send Mr Gore out in the yawl this mor[n]ing to order the boat and people in, in case they could not be imploy'd there to some advantage.

In the AM 4 of the natives came down to the sandy point on the north side of the harbour having along with them a small wooden Canoe with outriggers in which they seemd to be employ'd striking fish &c^a. Some were for going over in a boat to them but this I would not suffer but let them alone without seeming to take any notice of them, at length two came in the Canoe so near the Ship as to take some things we throw'd them, after this they went away and brought over the other two and came again along side nearer then they had done before and took such trifles as we gave them. After this they landed close to the Ship and all 4 went a shore carrying their arms with them, but Tupia soon prevaild upon them to lay down their arms and come and set down by him, after which more of us went to them, made them again some presents and stay'd by them untill dinner time, when we made them understand that we were going to eat and ask'd them by signs to go with us, but this they declined and as soon as we left them they went away in their canoe. One of these men was some thing above the Middle age, the other three were young, none of them were above 5½ feet high and all their limbs proportionaly small; they where wholy naked their skins the Colour of wood soot or a dark chocolate and this seem'd to be their natural Colour, their hair was black, lank and crope'd short and neither wooly nor frizled nor did they want any of their fore teeth, as Dampier has mentioned those did he saw on the western side of this Country. Some part of their bodies had been painted with red and one of them had his uper lip and breast paint[ed] with streakes of white which he call'd *Carbanda*: their features were far from being disagreeable, the Voices were soft and tunable and they could easily repeat many words after us, but neither us nor Tupia could understand one word they said.

WEDNESDAY 11*th*. Gentle land and sea breezes. Employ'd airing the bread, stowing away water stores &c^a. In the night Mr Gore and the Master returnd with the long-boat and brought with them one turtle and a few shell fish, the Yawl Mr Gore left upon the shoal with Six men to endeavour to Strike more turtle. In the morning four of the natives made us another short visit, 3 of them had been with us the preceeding day and the other was a stranger. One of these men had a hole through the Bridge of his nose in which he stuck a piece of bone as thick as my finger, seeing this we examined all their noses and found that they had all holes for the same purpose, they had likewise holes in their ears but no ornaments hanging to them, they had bracelets upon their arms made of hair and like hoops of small cord; they some times must wear a kind of fillet about their heads for one of them had applied some part of an Old shirt I had given them to this use.

THURSDAY 12*th*. Winds and weather as yesterday and the employment of the people the same. At 2 oClock in the AM the Yawl came on board and brought three turtle and a large skeat and as their was a probabillity of succeeding in this kind of fishery I sent her out again after breakfast. About this time 5 of the natives came over and stay'd with us all the forenoon, there were 7 in the whole 5 Men a woman and a boy, these two last stay'd on the point of sand on the other side of the River about 200 Yards from us, we could very clearly see with our glasses that the woman was as naked as ever she was born, even those parts which I allways before now thought nature would have taught a woman to conceal were uncover'd.

FRIDAY 13*th*. Gentle breezes from the SE in the day and Calm or light airs from the land in the night. Employ'd takeing on board water stores &cᵃ. At noon the Yawl returnd with one turtle and a large sting-ray.

SATURDAY 14*th*. Gentle breezes at SE and Hazey weather. In the PM compleated our water got on board all the Bread and part of the Boatswains stores; in the evening sent the turtlers out again. In the AM employd geting on board stone ballast and airing the Spare sails. Mʳ Gore being out in the Country shott one of the Animals before spoke of, it was a small one of the sort weighing only 28 pound clear of the entrails. The head neck and shoulders of this Animal was very small in proportion to the other parts; the tail was nearly as long as the body, thick next the rump and tapering towards the end; the fore legs were 8 Inch long and the hind 22, its progression is by hoping or jumping 7 or 8 feet at each hop upon its hind legs only, for in this it makes no use of the fore, which seem to be only design'd for scratching in the ground &cᵃ. The Skin is cover'd with a short hairy fur of a dark Mouse or Grey Colour. Excepting the head and ears which I thought was something like a Hare's, it bears no sort of resemblance to any European Animal I ever saw; it is said to bear much resemblance to the Gerbua excepting in size, the Gerbua being no larger than a common rat.

SUNDAY 15th. Gentle breezes at SE and East. In the PM got on board the spare sails and sundry other Articles. In the AM as the People did not work upon the Ship one of the Petty officers was disireous of going out to catch turtle; I let him have the Pinnace for that purpose and sent the long boat to haul the Sain who caught about 60 pounds of fish. Today we din'd of the animal shott yesterday & thought it excellent food.

*   *   *

WEDNESDAY 18th. Winds at ESE a gentle breeze. In the PM I sent the Master and one of the mates in the Pinnace to the northward to look for a Channell that way clear of the shoals. Mr Banks, Dr Solander and my self took a turn into the woods on the other side of the water where we met with five of the natives and altho we had not seen any of them before they came to us without shewing the least signs of fear, two of these wore necklaces made of shells which they seem'd to Value as they would not part with them. In the evening the yawl came in with three turtle and early in the AM she went out again. About 8 oClock we were viseted by several of the natives who now became more familiar then ever. Soon after this Mr Banks and I went over to the south side of the River and travel'd six or 8 Miles along shore to the northward, where we assended a high hill from whence we had an extensive view of the Sea Coast to leward; [which] afforded us a Meloncholy prospect of the difficultys we are [to] incounter, for in what ever direction we turn'd our eys Shoals inum[erable] were to be seen.[40] After this we return'd to the Ship without meeting with any thing remarkable and found several of the natives on board; at this time we had 12 Turtle upon our decks which they took more notice of then any thing else in the ship, as I was told by the officers for their curiosity was satisfied before I got on board and they went away soon after.

THURSDAY 19th. Gentle breezes at SE and fair weather. Employ'd geting every thing in readiness for sea. In the AM we were viseted by 10 or 11 of the natives, the most of them came from the other side of

40. Cook has borrowed this last sentence from Banks's journal.

the River where we saw six or seven more the most of them women
and like the men quite naked; those that came on board were very
desirous of having some of our turtle and took the liberty to haul two
to the gang way to put over the side, being disapointed in this they
grew a little troublesome and were for throwing every thing over board
they could lay their hands upon; as we had no victuals dress'd at this
time I offer'd them some bread to eat, which they rejected with scorn
as I believe they would have done any thing else excepting turtle.
Soon after this they all went a shore, Mr Banks my self and five or six
of our people being a shore at the same time; emmidiatly upon their
landing one of them took a handfull of dry grass and lighted it at a
fire we had a shore, and before we well know'd what he was going
about he made a large circuit round about us and set fire to the grass
in his way and in an Instant the whole place was in flames, luckily at
this time we had hardly any thing ashore besides the forge and a sow
with a Litter of young pigs one of which was scorched to death in the
fire. As soon as they had done this they all went to a place where some
of our people were washing and where all our nets and a good deal
of linnen were laid out to dry, here with the greatest obstinacy they
again set fire to the grass which I and some others who were present
could not prevent, untill I was obliged to fire a musquet load[ed] with
small shott at one of the ri[n]g leaders which sent them off. As we
were apprised of this last attempt of theirs we got the fire out before
it got head, but the first spread like wild fire in the woods and grass.
Notwithstanding my fireing, in which one must have been a little hurt
because we saw a few drops of blood on some of the linnen he had
gone over, they did not go far from us for we soon after heard their
Voices in the woods; upon which Mr Banks and I and 3 or 4 More
went to look for them and very soon met them comeing towards us.
As they had each 4 or 5 darts a piece and not knowing their intention
we seized upon six or seven of the first darts we met with, this alarmed
them so much that they all made off and we followd them for near
half a Mile and than set down and call'd to them and they stoped
also; after some little unintelligible conversation had pass'd they lay
down their darts and came to us in a very friendly manner; we now
returnd the darts we had taken from them which reconciled every

thing. There were 4 strangers among them that we had not seen before and these were interduced to us by name by the others: the man which we suppos'd to have been struck with small shott was gone off but he could not be much hurt as he was at a great distance when I fired. They all came along with us abreast of the ship where they stay'd a short time and then went away, and soon after set the woods on fire about a Mile and a half and two miles from us.

FRIDAY 20*th*. Fresh breezes at SE and fair weather. In the PM got every thing on board the Ship, new birth'd her and let her swing with the tide. In the night the Master return'd with the Pinnace and reported that there was no safe passage for the Ship to the northward. At low-water in the AM I went and sounded and buoy'd the bar, being now ready to put to sea the first oppertunity.

* * *

[*Conditions remained unfavourable for several days.*]

[AUGUST 1770]

SATURDAY 4*th*. In the PM having pritty Moderate weather I order'd the Coasting anchor and Cable to be laid without the barr to be ready to warp out by, that we might not loose the least oppertunity that might offer, for laying in Port spends time to no purpose, consumes our provisions of which we are very short in many articles, and we have yet a long Passage to make to the East Indias through an unknown and perhaps dangerous Sea; these circumstances considerd makes me very anxious of geting to sea. The wind continued moderate all night and at 5 oClock in the morning when it fell calm, this gave us an oppertunity to warp out. About 7 we got under sail having a light air from the land which soon died away and was succeeded by the Sea breeze from SEBS with which we stood off to Sea EBN, having the Pinnace a head sounding. The Yawl I sent to the Turtle bank to take up the net that was left there but as the wind freshend we got out before her, and a little after noon anchor'd in 15 fathom water Sandy bottom; for I did not think it safe to run in among the Shoals untill I had well View'd them at low-water from the Mast head, that I might

be better able to judge which way to steer for as yet I had not resolved
whether I should beat back to the Southward round all the shoals or
seek a passage out to the Eastward or to the north[rd], all of which
appear'd to be equally difficult and dangerous. When at Anchor the
harbour sail'd from bore s 70° West distant 4½ or 5 Leagues; the
northermost point of the Main land we had in sight which I name'd
Cape Bedford (Lat[de] 15°15′ s, Longitude 214°45′ w) bore N 20° West
distant 3½ Leagues, but we could see land to the NE of this Cape
which made like two high Islands, the Turtle banks bore East distant
1 Mile, Latitude by observation 15°23′ s, our depth of water in standing
off from the land was from 3½ to 15 fathom.

* * *

[*Cook gives a description of the 'harbour or River we have been in' which he names
'Endeavour River'. He is now able to say that the animal which has so perplexed
them is called by the natives 'Kangooroo' or 'Kanguru'.*]

SUNDAY 5*th*. In the PM had a gentle breeze at SE and clear weather.
As I did not intend to weigh untill the Morning I sent all the boats to
the reef to get what Turtle and shell fish they could. At low-water
from the Mast head I took a View of the shoals and could see several
laying a long way without this one, a part of several of them appearing
above water, but as it appear'd pretty clear of Shoals to the NE of the
turtle reef, I came to a resolution to stretch out that way close upon
a wind, because if we found no passage we could always return back
the way we went. In the evening the boats returnd with one turtle a
sting-ray and as many large Clams as came to one and a half pound
a man, in each of these Clams were about two pounds of meat, ad[d]ed
to this we caught in the night several Sharks. Early in the morning I
sent the Pinnace and Yawl again to the reef as I did not intend to
wiegh untill half Ebb at which time the shoals began to appear, before
8 oClock it came on to blow and I made the signal for the boats to
come on board which they did and brought with them one turtle. We
afterwards began to heave, but the wind freshing obliged us to bear
away again and lay fast.

MONDAY 6*th*. Winds at SE. At 2 oClock in the PM it fell pretty moderate

and we got under sail and stood out upon a wind NEBE having the
Turtle Reef to windward, having the Pinnace ahead sounding. We
had not stood out long before we discover'd shoals ahead and on both
bows. At half past 4 oClock having run off 8 Miles the Pinnace made
the Signal for shoal water in a place where we little expected it, upon
this we tack'd and stood on and off while the Pinnace stretched farther
to the Eastward, but as night was approaching I thought it safest to
anchor which we accordingly did in 20 fathom water a muddy bottom.
Endeavour River bore s 52° West, *Cape Bedford* WBN½N distant 5 Leagues,
the northermost land in sight which made like an Island North, and
a shoal a small sandy part of which appear'd above water bore NE
distant 2 or 3 Miles. In standing off from the Turtle Reef to this place
our soundings were from 14 to 20 fathoms, but where the Pinnace was
about a Mile farther to the ENE were no more then 4 or 5 feet water
rocky ground, and yet this did not appear to us in the Ship. In the
morning we had a strong gale from the SE, that instead of weighing
as we intended we were obliged to bear away more Cable and to
strike topgallant yards.

TUESDAY 7*th*. Strong gales at SE, SEBS & SSE with clowdy weather. At
Low-water in the PM I and several of the officers kept a lookout at the
Mast head to see for a passage between the Shoals, but we could see
nothing but breakers all the way from the South round by the East as
far as NW, extending out to sea as far as we could see, it did not appear
to be one continued shoal but several laying detach'd from each other,
on the Eastermost that we could see the Sea broke very high which
made me judge it to be the outermost, for on many of those within,
the sea did not break high attall; and from about half flood to half
Ebb they are not to be seen, which makes the Sailing among them
the more dangerous and requires great care & circumspection, for
like all other shoals or reefs of Coral Rocks they are quite steep too;
altho the most of these shoals consists of Coral rocks yet a part of
some of them is sand, the Turtle Reef and some others have a small
patch of sand generaly at the north end that is only cover'd at
High-water. These generaly discover themselves before we come near
them. Altho I speak of this as the Turtle Reef yet It is not to be doubted

but what there are Turtle upon the most of them as well as this one. After having well View'd our situation from the mast head I saw that we were surrounded on every side with Shoals and no such thing as a passage to Sea but through the winding channels between them, dangerous to the highest degree in so much that I was quite at a loss which way to steer when the weather would permit us to get under sail; for to beat back to the SE the way we came as the Master would have had me done would be an endless peice of work, as the winds blow now constantly strong from that quarter without hardly any intermission – on the other hand if we do not find a passage to the north[d] we shall have to come [back] at last. At 11 oClock the Ship drove and obliged us to bear away to a Cable and one third which brought her up again, but in the Morning the Gale increaseing she drove again. This made us let go the Small Bower anchor and to bear away a whole cable on it and two on the other, and even after this she still kept driving slowly untill we had got down Topgallant Mast, struck Yards and Topmasts close down and made all Snug, than she rid fast, *C. Bedford* bearing WSW distant 3½ Leagues. In this situation we had shoals to the eastward of us extending from the SEBS to the NNW, distant from the nearest part of them about two miles.

WEDNESDAY 8*th*. Strong gales at SSE all this day in so much that I dirst not get up yards and Topmasts.

THURSDAY 9*th*. In the PM the weather being something moderater we got up the Topmast but kept the lower Yards down. A[t] 6 oClock in the Morning we began to heave in the Cable thinking to get under sail, but it blowed so fresh together with a head sea that we could hardly heave the Ship ahead and at last was oblig'd to desist.

FRIDAY 10*th*. Fresh gales at SSE and SEBS. In the PM the wind fell so as we got up the small bower Anchor and hove in to a whole Cable on the best bower. At 3 oClock in the morning we got up the lower yards and at 7 weigh'd and stood in for the land (intending to seek a passage along shore to the northward) having a boat ahead sounding, depth of water as we run in from 19 to 12 fathom: after standing in an hour we edge'd away for 3 small Island[s] that lay NNE½E 3 Leagues from *Cape Bedford*, to these Islands the Master had been in the Pinnace when the Ship was in Port. At 9 oClock we were abreast of them and between them and the Main having another low Island between us and the latter which lies WNW, 4 Miles from the Three Island[s], in this Channell had 14 fathom water: the northermost Point of the Main we had in sight bore from us NNW½W distant 2 Leagues. Four or 5 Leagues to the NE of this head land appear'd three high Islands with some smaller ones near them, and the Shoals and reefs without us we could see extending to the northward as far as these Islands: we directed our Course between them and the above headland leaving a small I^d to the Eastw^d of us which lies NBE 4 M. from ye 3 I^s having all the while a boat ahead sounding. At Noon we were got betwixt the headland and the 3 High Islands distant from the former 2 and from the latter 4 Leagues, our Latitude by observation was 14°51' s. We now judged our selves to be clear of all danger having as we thought a clear open sea before us, but this we soon found otherwise and occasiond my calling the headland above mentioned *Cape Flattery* (Lat^{de} 14°56' s, Long^d 214°43' West) it is a lofty Promontary makeing in two hills next the Sea and a third behind them with low sandy land on each side, but it is better known by the Three high Islands out at sea, the northermost which is the largest lies from the Cape NNE distant 5 Leagues. From this Cape the Mainland trends away NW & NWBW.

SATURDAY 11*th*. Fresh breezes at SSE and SEBS with which we steerd along shore NWBW untill one oClock when the Petty officer at the mast head call'd out that he saw land ahead extending quite round to the Islands without us and a large Reef between us and them. Upon this I went to the mast head my self, the Reef I saw very plain which was now so far to windward that we could not weather it, but what he took for main land ahead were only small Islands, for such they appear'd to me but before I had well got from the mast head the Master and some others went up, who all asserted that it was a continuation of the main land, and to make it still more alarming they said that they saw breakers in a manner all round us. We emmidiatly hauld upon a wind in for the land and made the Signal for the boat which was ahead sounding to come on board, but as she was well to leeward we were obliged to edge away to take her up, and soon after came too an Anchor under a point of the Main in ¼ less 5 fathom about a Mile from the Shore, *Cape Flattery* bearing SE distant 3½ Leagues. After this I landed and went upon the point which is pretty high, from which I had a view of the sea-Coast which trended away NWBW 8 or 10 Leagues which was as far as I could see, the weather not being very clear. I likewise saw 9 or 10 small low Islands and some shoals laying of[f] the Coast and some large shoals between the Main and the three high Islands without, which I was now well assured were Islands and not a part of the Main land as some had taken them to be. Excepting *Cape Flattery* and the Point I am now upon, which I have named *Point Lookout*, the Mainland next the Sea to the Northward of *Cape Bedford* is low and Chequer'd with White Sand and Green Bushes &c^a for 10 or 12 Miles in land, behind which is high lands. To the northward of *Point Lookout* the shore appeard to be shoald and flat some distance off, which was no good sign of meeting with a channel in with the land as we have hitherto done. We saw the foot steps of People upon the Sand and smook and fire up in the Country, and in the evening returnd on board where I came to a resolution to Visit one of the high Islands in the offing in my Boat, as they lay at least 5 Leagues out to sea and seem'd to be of such a hieght that from the top of one of them I hoped to see and find a Passage out to sea clear of the shoals: accordingly in the morning I set out in the Pinnace for the northermost and largest of the three accompanied by Mr Banks, at the same time I sent the Master in the Yawl to lee-ward to sound between the low Islands and the Main. In my way to the Island I pass'd over a large Reef of Coral Rocks and sand which lies about two leagues from the Island. I left a nother to leeward which lays about 3 Miles from the Island; on the North part of this is a low sandy Isle with trees upon it. On the Reef we pas'd over in the boat we saw several turtle and chased one or two, but caught none it blowing too hard and I had no time to spare being otherways employ'd. I did not reach the Island untill half an hour after one oClock in the PM of

SUNDAY 12*th*. when I immediatly went upon the highest hill on the Island where to my mortification I discoverd a Reef of Rocks laying about 2 or 3 Leagues without the Island, extending in a line NW and SE farther than I could see on which the Sea broke very high. This however gave me great hopes that they were the outermost shoals, as I did not doubt but what I should be able to get without them for there appear'd to be several breaks or Partitions in the reef and deep water between it and the Islands. I stay'd upon this hill untill near sun set but the weather continued so hazy all the time that I could not see above 4 or 5 Leagues round me, so that I came down much disapointed in the prospect I expected to have had, but being in hopes that the morning might prove Clearer and give me a better View of the Shoals. With this view I stay'd all night upon the Island, and at 3 in the Morning sent the Pinnace with one of the Mates I had with me to sound between the Island and the Reefs and to examine one of the breaks or Channells, and in the mean time I went again upon the hill where I arrived by sun rise but found it much hazier than in the evening. About noon the Pinnace return'd haveing been out as far as the Reef and found from 15 to 28 fathom water. It blowed so hard that they durst not venture into one of the Channells which the mate said seem'd to him to be very narrow but this did not discourage me for I thought from the place he was at he must have seen it at a disadvantage. Before I quit this Island I shall describe it. It lies as I have before observed about 5 Leagues from the Main, it is about 8 Miles in circuit and of a height sufficient to be seen 10 or 12 Leagues; it is mostly high land very rocky and barren except on the NW side where there are some Sandy bays and low land, which last is cover'd with thin long grass Trees &c^a the same as upon the Main. Here is also fresh water in two places the one is a runing stream the water a little brackish where I tasted it which was close to the sea, the other is a standing Pool close behind the sandy beach of good sweet water, as I dare say the other is a little way from the Sea beach. The only Land-animals we saw here were Lizards and these seem'd to be pretty plenty which occasioned my nameing the Island *Lizard Island*. The Inhabitants of the Main Visit this Island at some seasons of the year for we saw the ruens of several of their hutts and heaps of Shells &c^a. SE 4 or 5 Miles from this Island lay the other two high Islands which are very small compared to this, and near them lay three other yet smaller and lower Islands and several Shoals or Reefs especially to the SE. There is however a clear passage from *Cape Flattery* to these Islands and even quite out to the outer Reefs leaving the above Islands to the SE and Lizard Islands to the NW.

MONDAY 13*th*. At 2 oClock in the PM we left Lizard Isl^d in order to return to the Ship and in our way landed upon the low sandy Isle mentioned in coming out. We found on this Island a great number of birds the Most of them Sea fowl, except Eagles, we likewise saw some Turtle but caught none for the reasons before assigned. We found that the Natives resort to this Island as we saw several turtle Shells piled one upon another. After leaving *Eagle Island* we stood SW directly for the Ship, sounding all the way, had not less than 8 f^m nor more than 14 f^m. I found the same depth of water between Lizard and Eagle Island. After we got on board the Master informed me that he had been down to the Islands I had directed him to go to which he judged to lay about 3 Leagues from the Main, he found 10, 12 & 14 fathom water without them and 7 between them & Main, this last channell was narrow because from the[m?] run off a flat above 2 Leagues. He found upon the Islands piles of Turtle shells and some fins that were so fresh that both he [and] the boats crew eat of them, this shew'd that the Natives must have been there lately.

After well considering both what I had seen my self and the report of the Master, who was of opinion that the Passage to Leeward would prove danger[ou]s; this I was pretty well convince'd of my self that by keeping in with the main land we should be in continual danger besides the risk we should run of being locke'd in within the Main reef at last and have to return back to seek a passage out, an accident of this kind or any other that might happen to the Ship would infallibly loose our passage to the East Indias this season and might prove the ruin of the Voyage, as we have now little more than 3 Months provisions on board and that short allowance in many Arti[c]les. These reasons had the [same] weight with all the officers, I therefore resolved to weigh in the morning and endeavour to quet the coast altogether untill we could approach it with less danger: With this View we got under sail at day light and stood out NE for the NW end of Lizard

Island, leaving Eagle Island to windward of us and some other Islands & Shoals to leward having the Pinnace a head sounding, in this channell we had from 9 to 14 fathom. At Noon the NW end of Lizard Island bore ESE distant one mile, Lat^{de} observed 14°38′ s, depth of water 14 fathom. – We now took the Pinnace in tow knowing that there was no danger till we got out to the Reefs without the Island.

TUESDAY 14*th*. Winds at SE a steady fresh gale. By 2 oClock we just fetched to windward of one of the Channels in the outer Reef I had seen from the Island, we now tacked and made a short trip to the SW while the Master in the Pinnace examind the channell, he soon made the Signal for the Ship to follow which we accordingly did and in a short time got safe out, we had no sooner got without the breakers than we had no ground with 150 fathom of line and found a well growen Sea rowling in from the SE, certain signs that nither land nor shoals were in our neighbourhood in that direction, which made us quite easy at being free'd from fears of Shoals &c^a – after having been intangled among them more or less ever sence the 26th of May, in which time we have saild 360 Leagues without ever having a Man out of the cheans heaving the Lead when the Ship was under way, a circumstance that I dare say never happen'd to any ship before and yet here it was absolutely necessary. It was with great regret I was obliged to quit this coast unexplored to its No[r]thern extremity which I think we were not far off, for I firmly believe that it doth not join to *New Guinea*, however this I hope yet to clear up being resolved to get in with the land again as soon as I can do it with safety and the reasons I have before assigned will I presume be thought sufficient for my haveing left it at this time.

The Passage or Channell we now came out by lies in the Latitude of 14°32′, it may always be found and known by the three high Islands within it which I have call'd the *Islands of direction* because by them a safe passage may be found, even by Strangers, in within the reef and quite in to the Main; the Channell lies from Lizard Island NE½N distant 3 Leagues and is about one third of a Mile broad and not more in length. . . .

As soon as we were without the reef we brought too and hoisted in the boats, than stood off an[d] on upon a wind all night as I did not care to run to leeward untill we had a whole day before us. We now began to find that the Ship had received more damage than we immagined and soon felt the effect the high rowling sea had upon her by increasing her leaks considerably so that it was as much as one Pump could keep her free kept continualy at work; however this was looked upon as trifeling to the danger we had lately made our escape from. At Day light in the Morning Lizard Island bore s 15° E Distant 10 Leagues, we now made sail and stood away NNW½W and at 9 oClock NW½N, having the advantage of a fresh gale at SE. At Noon we were by observation in the Latitude of 13°46′ s having at this time no land in sight.

WEDNESDAY 15*th*. Fresh Trade at SE and clear weather. At 6 oClock in the evening shortend sail and brought too with her head to the NE. At 6 oClock in the AM made sail and steer'd West in order to make the land being fearfull of over shooting the Passage supposeing there to be one between this land and New Guinea. At Noon we had no land in sight, our latitude by observation was 13°2′ South, Longitude 216°0′ West which was 1°23′ West of Lizard Island.

THURSDAY 16*th*. By one oClock in the PM or before we saw high land from yᵉ Masthead bearing WSW and at 2 oClock saw more land to the NW of the former makeing in hills like Islands but we judged it to be the continuation of the Main land. An hour after this we saw breakers between us and the land extending to the Southward farther than we could see, but we thought we saw them terminate to the northward abreast of us, this however proved only an opening for soon after we saw the Reef or breakers extend away to the northward as far as we could see, upon this we hauld close upon a wind which was now at ESE. We had hardly trimed our sails before the wind came to EBN which was right upon the Reef and of Course made our clearing of it doubtfull, the northermost of it that we could see at sun set bore from us NBE distant about 2 or 3 Leagues. However this being the best tack to clear it we kept standing to the northward with all the Sail we could set untill 12 oClock at night when fearing to Stand too far up this tack we tacked and stood to the Southward having run 6 Leagues North and NBE sence Sun set. We had not stood above 2 Miles SSE before it fell quite Calm, we both sounded now and several times in the night but had no ground with 140 fathoms of line. A little after 4 oClock the roaring of the Surf was plainly heard and at day break the vast foaming breakers were too plainly to be seen not a Mile from us towards which we found the Ship was carried by the waves surprisingly fast. We had at this time not an air of wind and the depth of water was unfathomable so that there was not a possibillity of Anchoring, in this distressed situation we had nothing but Providence and the small Assistance our boats could give us to trust to; the Pinnace was under a repair and could not immidiately be hoisted out, the Yawl was put into the water and the Long-boat hoisted out and both sent ahead to tow which together with the help of our sweeps abaft got the Ships head round to the northward which seem'd to be the only way to keep her off the reef or at least to delay time, before this was effected it was 6 oClock and we were not above 80 or 100 Yards from the breakers, the same Sea that washed the sides of the Ship rose in a breaker prodigiously high the very next time it did rise so that between us and distruction was only a dismal Vally the breadth of one wave and even now no ground could be felt with 120 fathoms. The Pinnace by this time was patched up and hoisted out and sent ahead to tow; still we had hardly any hopes of saving the Ship and full as little our lives as we were full 10 Leagues from the nearest land and the boats not sufficient to carry the whole of us, yet in this truly terrible situation not one man ceased to do his utmost and that with as much calmness as if no danger had been near. All the dangers we had escaped were little in comparison of being thrown upon this Reef where the Ship must be dashed to peices in a Moment. A Reef such as is here spoke of is scarcely known in Europe, it is a wall of Coral Rock rising all most perpendicular out of the unfathomable Ocean, always overflown at high-water generally 7 or 8 feet and dry in places at low-water; the large waves of the vast Ocean meeting with so sudden a resistance make a most terrible surf breaking mountains high especially as in our case when the general trade wind blowes directly upon it. At this critical juncture when all our endeavours seem'd too little a small air of wind sprung up, but so small that at any other time in a Calm we should not have observed it, with this and the assistance of our boats we could observe the Ship to move off from the Reef in a slanting direction, but in less than 10 Minutes we had as flat a Calm as ever when our fears were again renewed for as yet we were not above 200 Yards from the breakers. Soon after our friendly breeze Viseted us again and lasted about as long as before. A small opening was now seen in the Reef about a quarter of a Mile from us which I sent one of the Mates to examine, its breadth was not more than the length of the Ship but within was smooth water, into this place it was resolve'd to push her if possible haveing no other probable Views to save her,[41] for we were still in the very jaws of distruction and it was a doubt whether or no we could reach this opening, however we soon got off it when to our surprise we found the Tide of Ebb gushing out like a Mill stream so that it was impossible to get in; we however took all the advantage possible of it and it carried us out about a ¼ of a Mile from the breakers, but it was too narrow for us to keep in long; how ever what with the help of Ebb and our boats we by noon had got an offing of one and a half or two Miles, yet we could hardly flater our selves with hopes of geting clear even if a breeze should spring up as we were by this time imbayed by the Reef, and the Ship in spite of our endeavours driving before the Sea into the bight, the Ebb had been in our favour and we had reason to suppose that the flood which was now making would be againest us, the only hopes we had was another opening we saw about a Mile to the Westward of us which I sent Lieut[en]ant Hick[s] in the Small boat to examine. Latitude Observed 12°37′ s, the Main land in sight distant about 10 Leagues.

FRIDAY 17*th*. While Mr Hicks was examining the opening we strugled hard with the flood some times gaining a little and at other times looseing. At 2 oClock Mr Hicks returnd with a favourable account of the opening, it was immidiately resolved to try to secure the Ship in it, narrow and dangerous as it was it seem'd to be the only means we

41. Two boats were ahead sounding; the ship was being towed by the other two, and had the assistance of the sweeps (large oars) out of the gunroom ports.

had of saving her as well as our selves. A light breeze soon after sprung up at ENE which with the help of our boats and a flood tide we soon enter'd the opening and was hurried through in a short time by a rappid tide like a Mill race which kept us from driving against either side, tho the c[h]annell was not more than a quarter of a Mile broad, we had however two boats a head to direct us through, our depth of water in the Channell was from 30 to 7 fathom very erregular soundings and foul ground untill we had got quite within the Reef where we anchor'd in 19 fathom a Corally & Shelly bottom happy once more to incounter those shoals which but two days ago our utmost wishes were crowned by geting clear of, such are the Vicissitudes attending this kind of service and must always attend an unknown Navigation: Was it not for the pleasure which naturly results to a Man from being the first discoverer, even was it nothing more than sands and Shoals, this service would be insuportable especialy in far distant parts, like this, short of Provisions and almost every other necessary. The world will hardly admit of an excuse for a man leaving a Coast unexplored he has once discover'd, if dangers are his excuse he is than charged with *Timorousness* and want of Perseverance and at once pronounced the unfitest man in the world to be employ'd as a discoverer; if on the other hand he boldly incounters all the dangers and obstacles he meets and is unfortunate enough not to succeed he is than charged with *Temerity* and want of conduct. The former of these aspersins cannot with Justice be laid to my charge and if I am fortunate enough to surmount all the dangers we may meet the latter will never be brought in question. I must own I have ingaged more among the Islands and shoals upon this coast than may be thought with prudence I ought to have done with a single Ship and every other thing considered, but if I had not we should not have been able to give any better account of the one half of it than if we had never seen it, that is we should not have been able to say whether it consisted of main land or Islands and as to its produce, we must have been totally ignorant of as being inseparable with the other.

I now came to a fix'd resolution to keep the Main land on board in our rout to the norward let the concequence be what it will, indeed now it was not adviseable to go without the reef, for by it we might be carried so far from the Coast as not to be able to determine whether or no New Guinea joins to or makes a part of this land. This doubtfull point I had from my first coming upon the Coast determined if possible to clear up, but as I had lately experienced the ilconveniency of a boat under repair I intend to lay fast with the Ship tomorrow to have the Pinnace repaired and as I had no employ't for the other boats I sent them all out in the morning to the reef to get such refreshments as they could find. Found the Variation by the Amp^d and Azth to be 4°9′ East. At noon Latitude observed 12°38′ s, Longitude in 216°45′ w, the Main land extending from n 66° West to swbs, distant off the nearest part 8 or 9 Leagues. The opening we came in by, which I have named *Prov[i]dential Channell*, bore ENE distant 10 or 12 Miles. On the Main land within us was a pretty high Promontory which I call'd *Cape Weymouth*, on the north side of the Cape is a Bay known by the same name (Lat^{de} 12°42′, Longitude 217°15′ w).

* * *

[*For several days, with two boats ahead taking soundings, and a lookout at the masthead, Cook nudged his way through islets, shoals and 'keys' along the final stretch of the eastern coast until he was convinced he had reached the northernmost point, which he named York Cape, 'in honour of His late Royal Highness the Duke of York'. He then steered west-south-west through the Endeavour Strait between the mainland and Prince of Wales Island.*]

WEDNESDAY 22d. Gentle breezes at EBS and clear weather. We had not stood above 3 or 4 Miles along shore to the westward before we discoverd the Land ahead to be Islands detach'd by several channells from the Main land; upon this we brought too to wait for the yawl and called the other boats on board, and after giving them proper Instructions sent them away again to lead us through the Channell next the Main, and as soon as the yawl was on board made sail with the Ship after them; soon after we discoverd Rocks & shoals in this Channell, upon which I made the Signal for the boats to lead through the next Channel to the Northward laying between the Islands, which they accordingly did we following with the Ship, and had not less than 5 fathom water and this in the narrowest part of the Channell which was about a Mile and a half broad from Island to Island, At 4 oClock we anchor'd about a Mile and a half or 2 Miles within the entrance in 6½ fathom clear ground, distant from the Islands on each side of us one mile, the Main land extending away to the sw, the farthest point of which that we could see bore from us s 48° West and the South-wester-most point of the Islands on the nw side of the Passage bore s 76° West. Between these two points we could see no land so that we were in great hopes that we had at last found a Passage into the Indian Seas, but in order to be better informd I landed with a party of Men accompan'd by Mr Banks and Dr Solander upon the Island which lies at the se point of the Passage.[42] Before and after we Anchor'd we saw a number of People upon this Island arm'd in the same manner as all the others we have seen, except one man who had a bow and a bundle of Arrows, the first we have seen on this coast. From the appeerence of these People we expected that they would have opposed our landing but as we approachd the Shore they all made off and left us in peaceable posession of as much of the Island as served our purpose. After landing I went upon the highest hill which however was of no great height, yet not less than twice or thrice the height of the Ships Mast heads, but I could see from it no land between sw and wsw so that I did not doubt but what there was a passage. I could see plainly that the Lands laying to the nw of this passage were composed of a number of Island[s] of various extent both for height and circuit, rainged one behind another as far to the Northward and Westward as I could see, which could not be less than 12 or 14 Leagues. Having satisfied my self of the great Probabillity of a Passage, thro' which I intend going with the Ship, and therefore may land no more upon this Eastern coast of *New Holland*, and on the Western side I can make no new discovery the honour of which belongs to the Dutch Navigators; but the Eastern Coast from the Latitude of 38° South down to this place I am confident was never seen or viseted by any European before us, and Notwithstand I had in the Name of His Majesty taken posession of several places upon this coast, I now once more hoisted English Coulers and in the Name of His Majesty King George the Third took posession of the whole Eastern Coast from the

42. Possession Island.

above Latitude down to this place by the name of *New South Wales*,[43] together with all the Bays, Harbours Rivers and Islands situate upon the said coast, after which we fired three Volleys of small Arms which were Answerd by the like number from the Ship. This done we set out for the Ship but some time in geting on board on accou[n]t of a very rappid Ebb Tide which set NE out of the Passage. Ever sence we came in among the Shoals this last time we have found a Moderate Tide the Flood seting to the NW and Ebb to the SE. At this place it is High-water at the Full and Change of the Moon about 1 or 2 o'Clock and riseth and falls upon a perpendicular about 10 or 12 feet. We saw on all the Adjacent Lands and Islands a great number of smooks, a certain sign that they are Inhabited, and we have dayly seen smooks on every part of the coast we have lately been upon. . . .

[*Next day, with the* Endeavour *now on a north-westerly course, Cook took advantage of the wind dropping to make a brief visit with Banks to 'Booby Island'.*]

THURSDAY 23d. . . . I made but a very short stay at this Island before I returnd to the Ship. In the mean time the wind had got to SW and altho it blowed but very faint yet it was accompaned with a swell from the same quarter; this together with other concuring circumstances left me no room to doubt but we were got to the Westward of *Carpentaria* or the Northern extremety of *New-Holland* and had now an open Sea to the westward, which gave me no small satisfaction not only because the dangers and fatigues of the Voyage was drawing near to an end, but by being able to prove that New-Holland and New-Guinea are two Seperate Lands or Islands, which untill this day hath been a doubtfull point with Geographers. The NE entrance of this Passage or Strait lies in the Latitude of 10°27′ s and in the Longitude of 218°36′ West from the Meridian of Greenwich. It is form'd by the Main or the Northern extremety of New-Holland on the SE and by a Congeries of Islands to the NW which I Named *Prince of Wales's Islands*. It is very probable that these Islands extend quite to New-Guinea, they are of

43. This name is written in over another deleted and indecipherable name, and it is clear that the name New South Wales was bestowed at some time after possession was taken.

Various extent both for height and circuit and many of them seem'd to be indifferently well cloathed with wood &c^a and from the smooks we saw some if not all of them must be inhabited. It is also very probable that among these Islands are as good if not better passages than the one we have come thro', altho one need hardly wish for a better was the Access to it from the Eastward less dangerous, but this difficulty will remain untill some better way is found out than the one we came, which no doubt may be done was it ever to become an object to be look'd for; the Northern extent of the Main or outer Reef which limets or bounds the Shoals to the Eastward seems to be the only thing wanting to clear up this point, and this was a thing I had neither time nor inclination to go about, having been already sufficiently harrass'd with dangers without going to look for more.

This Passage, which I have named *Endeavours Straight* after the name of the Ship, is in length NE and SW 10 Leagues and about 5 Leagues broad, except at the NE entrance where it is only 2 Miles broad by reason of several small Islands which lay there, one of which call'd *Posession Island* is of a moderate height and circuit; this we left between us and the Main, passing between it and two small round Islands which lay NW 2 Miles from it. There are also two small low Islands call'd Wallice's Isles laying in the Middle of the SW entrance which we left to the Southward. The depth of water we found in the Straight was from 4 to 9 fathom every where good anchorage; only about 2 Leagues to the northward of Wallice's Islands is a Bank whereon is not more than three fathom at low-water but probably there might be found more was it sought for. I have not been particular in discribing this Strait no more than I have been in pointing out the respective situations of the Islands Shoals &c^a on the eastern coast of *New Wales*. For these I refer to the Chart, where they are delineated with all the Accuracy that circumstances would admit of; with respect to the Shoals that lay upon this Coast I must observe for the benifit of those who may come after me, that I do not beleive the one half of them are laid down in my chart, for it would be obsurd to suppose that we could see or find them all, and the same thing may in some measure be said of the Islands especially between the Latitude of 20° & 22°, where we saw Islands out at Sea as far as we could distinguish any thing. However take the Chart in general and I beleive it will be found to contain as few errors as most Sea Charts which have not under gone a thorough correction, the Latitude and Longitude of all or most of the principal head lands, Bays &c[a] may be relied on, for we seldom faild of geting an Observation every day to correct our Latitude by, and the observation for Settleing the Longitude were no less numberous and made as often as the Sun and Moon came in play, so that it was impossible for any material error to creep into our reckoning in the intermidiate times. In justice to M[r] Green I must say that he was Indefatigable in making and calculating these observations which otherwise must have taken up a great deal of my time, which I could not at all times very well spare. Not only this, but by his Instructions several of the Petty officers can make and Calculate these observations almost as well as himself: it is only by such means that this method of finding the Longitude at Sea can be put into universal practice – a method that we have generally found may be depended upon to within half a degree; which is a degree of accuracy more than Sufficient for all Nautical purposes. Would Sea officers once apply themselves to the makeing and calculating these observations they would not find them so very difficult as they at first imagine, especially with the assistance of the Nautical Almanac and Astronomical Ephemeris, by the help of which the calculations for finding the Long[de] takes up but little more time than that of an Azimuth for find[ing] the Vari[n] of the compass; but unless this Ephemeris is publish[d] for some time to come more than either one or two Years it never can be of general use in long Voyages, and in short Voyages its not so much wanting; without it the Calculations are laborious and discouraging to beginers and such as are not well Verse'd in these kind of calculations.

* * *

[*Cook now enters on a description of New Holland and its people, observing that as far as they could tell the country produced nothing that 'can become an Article in trade to invite Europeans to fix a settlement upon it', but that its natural fertility suggested that almost anything would grow if 'planted and cultivated by the hand of Industry'. Concerning the 'timorous and inoffensive race' inhabiting the country, he had this to say, taking a hint from some reflections in Banks's journal.*]

From what I have said of the Natives of New-Holland they may appear to some to be the most wretched people upon Earth, but in reality they are far more happier than we Europeans; being wholy unacquainted not only with the superfluous but the necessary Conveniencies so much sought after in Europe, they are happy in not knowing the use of them. They live in a Tranquillity which is not disturb'd by the Inequality of Condition: The Earth and sea of their own accord furnishes them with all things necessary for life, they covet not Magnificent Houses, Houshold-stuff &c^a, they live in a warm and fine Climate and enjoy a very wholsome Air, so that they have very little need of Clothing and this they seem to be fully sencible of, for many to whome we gave Cloth &c^a to, left it carlessly upon the Sea beach and in the woods as a thing they had no manner of use for. In short they seem'd to set no Value upon any thing we gave them, nor would they ever part with any thing of their own for any one article we could offer them; this in my opinion argues that they think themselves provided with all the necessarys of Life and that they have no superfluities.

*　　*　　*

[SEPTEMBER 1770]

[*Cook now sailed north, and on 3 September touched on the New Guinea coast. He went ashore with Banks and Solander, but they 'were attacked by 3 or 4 Men who came out of the woods', on whom they fired. He had no wish to explore further, and left the coast, 'to the no small satisfaction of I beleive the Major part of ye Ships company'. He sailed to the west, voicing his exasperation at the inadequacy of the charts available to him from his predecessors in the region, blaming publishers for their boasts of accuracy as much as the seamen for their lack of skill. On 11 September they saw land which Cook rightly judged to be Timor. He resisted the urging of some of his officers to call in at the Dutch settlement at Concordia, being uncertain of his reception. He weakened, however, when they reached the island of Savu, and saw 'Houses, Cocoa-nutt Trees and Flocks of cattle grazing'. He sent Gore in the pinnace to investigate.*]

TUESDAY 18*th*. As soon as Mr Gore Landed he was met on the beach by several people both Horse and Foot who gave him to understand that there was a Bay to Leeward where we could Anchor and likewise get refreshments, upon Mr Gores return with this intelligence we bore away for the Bay, in which we anchord at 7 oClock in 38 fathom water a Clean Sandy bottom about a Mile from shore. The North point of the Bay bore N 30° East 2½ Miles and the South point or West end of the Island bore s 63° West. Two hours before we Anchor'd we saw Dutch Colours hoisted in a Village which stands about a Mile inland and at Day-light in the Morning the same Colours were hoisted on the beach abreast of the Ship: by this I was no longer in doubt but what here was a Dutch Settlement and accordingly sent Lieut^t Gore a shore to wait upon the Governor or Chief person residing here, to acquaint him with the reasons that induce'd us to touch at this Island. Upon Mr Gores landing we could see that he was received by a guard of the Natives and not Dutch Troops and conducted up to the Village where the Colours were hoisted last night. Sometime after this I received a Message from him acquainting me that he was then with the King of the Island, who had told him that he could not supply us with any thing without leave from the Dutch Governor who resided at a nother part of the Island, but that he had sent to acquaint him of our arrival and request.

WEDNESDAY 19*th*. At 2 oClock in the PM the Dutch Governor and King of this part of the Island with his attendance came on board with Mr Gore (he having left two gentlemen a shore as hostages). We entertaind them at dinner in the best Manner we could, gave them plenty of good Liquor, made them some considerable presents and at their going away saluted them with 9 Guns. In return for these favour[s] they made many fair promises that we should be immideatly furnished with every thing we wanted at the same price the Dutch East India Company had it, and that in the Morning Buffaloes, Hogs Sheep &c^a should be down on the beach for us to look at and agree upon a price. I was not attall at a loss for Interpreters for both Dr Solander and Mr Sporing understood Dutch enough to keep up a conversation with the Dutchman, and several of the Natives could speak Portuguese which Language two or 3 of my people understood. In the Morning I went aShore accompined by Mr Banks and sever[al] of the Officers and Gentlemen to return the Kings Viset, but my chief business was to see how well they would perform their promises in regard to the things I wanted. We had not been long a shore before we found that they had promised more than they ever intended to perform.

* * *

[*Excuses were made for the non-appearance of the cattle except for 'one small Buffaloe which they ask'd five Guines for'. After further difficulties were put in their way, Cook ended up with nine buffaloes, 'a number of Fowles and a Large quantity of Syrrup'. He then 'resolved to make no longer stay' and prepared to sail to Java.*]

FRIDAY 21st. We got under sail and stood away to the westward along the north side of the Island and a nother smaller Island which lies farther to the westward which last bore from us at Noon SSE distant 2 Leagues.

* * *

SATURDAY 29th. Moderate breezes at SE and clear pleasent weather. Steer'd NW all this Day in order to make the Land of Java. At Noon we were by observation in the Latitude of 9°31′ S and Longitude 254°10′ West.

SUNDAY 30th. Fresh gales and fair weather. In the AM I took into my posission the Officers, Petty officers and Seamens Log Books & Journals, at least all that I could find and enjoyn'd every one not to divulge where they had been. At Noon our Course and distance saild sence yesterday Noon is N 20° West 126 Miles, which brought us into the Latitude of 7°34′ and Longitude 255°13′ W.

[OCTOBER 1770]

MONDAY 1st Octr. First and latter parts fresh breezes at SE and fair weather, the Middle Squaly with Lightning and Rain. At 7 o'Clock in the PM, being then in the Latitude of *Java Head* and not seeing any land assured us that we had got too far to the westward, upon which

we hauld up ENE having before steerd NBE. At 12 oClock saw the Land
bearing East. Tackd and stood to the sw untill 4 o'Clock than stood
again to the Eastward having very unsettled Squally weather, which
split the Main Topsail Very much and obliged us to bend the other,
many of our sails are now so bad that they will hardly stand the least
puff of wind. At 6 oClock Java head or the west end of Java bore
SEBE distant 5 Leagues, soon after this saw Princes Island bearing
E½s and at 10 oClock Saw the Island of Cracatoa bearing NE, this
is a remarkable high Peaked Island which at Noon bore N 40 E distant
7 Leagues. Princes Island Extending from s 53° E to SBW Distant 3
Leagues. Course and Distance saild sence yesterday at Noon is N
24°30′ E 70 Miles. Latitude in pʳ observation 6°29′ s, Longitude 254°44′
West. Note, in our run from Savou I have allow'd 20′ per day for
the westerly current which no doubt must run strong at this time
of yᵉ Year especially of the Coast of Java, this allowance I find
Answers.

TUESDAY 2*nd* Octʳ. In the PM had the wind at SSE and SEBS and SSE
with which we stood to the Eastward close upon a wind. At 6 oClock
the Hill on Princes Island bore SWBS and Cracatoa Island North 10
Miles, in this situation had 58 fathom water; standing still to the
Eastward at 8 oClock had 52 fathom a Muddy bottom; at 10, 23 fᵐ.
By 4 oClock in the Morning we fetched close in with the Java Shore
in 15 fathom, than steer'd along shore. At 5 oClock it fell Calm which
continued with some Variable light airs untill Noon, at which time
Anger Point bore NE distant 1 League and Thwart the way Island
North. In the Morning I sent a boat ashore to try to get some fruits
for Tupia who is very ill, and likewise to get some grass &cᵃ for the
Buffaloes we have still left: the boat returnd with only 4 Cocoa-Nutts,
a small bunch of Plantains which they purchased of the Natives for a
Shilling and a few Shrubs for the Cattle.

WEDNESDAY 3*rd*. Soon after 12 oClock it fell quite Calm which obliged
us to anchor in 18 fᵐ a muddy bottom about 2 Miles from shore where
we found a Strong Current seting to the sw. Not long before we
anchord we saw a Dutch Ship laying off Anger Point, on board which
I sent Mʳ Hicks to inquire after news. Upon his return he inform'd

me that there were Two Dutch Ships from Batavia the one bound to Ceylon and the other to the Coast of Mallabar, besides a small Fly Boat or Packet which is stationed here to carry Packets, Letters &c^a from all Dutch Ships to Batavia, but it seems more Probable that she is stationed here to examine all Ships that pass and repass these Streights. We now first heard the Agreeable News of His Majestys Sloop the Swallow being at Batavia about two years ago.[44] At 7 oClock a breeze sprung up at ssw with which we weigh'd and stood to the NE between Thward the way Island and the Cap. Soundings from 18 to 26 fathom. We had but little wind all night and having a strong Current against us we got no farther by 8 oClock in the Morning than under *Bantam Point*, at this time the Wind came to NE and obliged us to Anchor in 22 fathom about 2 Miles from the Shore, the above Point bore NEBE distant 1 League. here we found a Strong Current seting to the NW.

In the Morning we saw the Dutch Packet Standing after us, but after the wind shifted to NE she bare away. One of the Dutch Captains told Mr Hicks Yesterday that the Current sets Constantly to the sw ward and that it would continue to set so for a Mo[n]th or Six Weeks longer.

THURSDAY 4*th*. In the PM had the Wind at NEBN which obliged us to lay fast. About Six oClock in the Evening one of the Country boats Came a long side in which was the Commander of the Packet before Mentioned. He seem'd to have two Montives for Coming, the one to take an account of the Ship and the other to sell us refreshments, for in the boat were Turtles, Fowls, Birds &c^a, all of which they held at a pretty high price and had brought to a bad Market as our *Savu* Stock was not yet expended. I gave a Spanish Dollor for a small Turtle which wieghd only 36 pounds. With respect to the Ship he wanted to know her Name, the Captains, the place we came last from and where bound; as I would not see him my self I orderd that no account should be given him from whence we came, but Mr Hicks who wrote the

---

44. Philip Carteret had become separated from Wallis in the *Dolphin* and was feared lost. He reached England in the *Swallow* in March 1769, six months after Cook had sailed.

Ships Name down in his Book put down from Europe, seeing this he express'd some surprise and said that we might write down what we please'd for it was of no other use than for the information of such of our Countrymen as might pass these Streights.

At 7 oClock a light breeze sprung up at sse with which we got under sail, at 1 o'Clock in the Morning Anchord again having not wind to stem the Current which we found to run 3 Knotts. At 2 oClock we wieghd again but finding that we lost ground we were obliged to Anchor in 18 fathom; the Island *Pulo Morock* which lies Close under the Shore 3 Miles to the westward of *Bantam Point*, bore sebs distant 1½ Mile. Latitude Observed 5°55′ s.

FRIDAY 5*th*. At 5 oClock in the PM we wiegh'd with a light breeze at swbs which continued not long before it fell Calm and obliged us to Anchor again. At 1 oClock we weigh'd with the Land wind at sse which died away in the Morning and the Current runing strong againest us we Anchor[d] in 17 fathom. A little before this a Proe came along side wherein was a Dutch Officer who came upon the same business as the other he sent me down a printed paper in English Containing 9 Articles or Questons of which the following is a Copy:

The Commanders and officers of the Ships, where this Paper may be presented, Will be please'd to Answer on the following Questions Vidz⁺ –

1 To What Nation the Ship belongs and its Name.
2 If it comes from Europe or any other place.
3 From what place it lastly departed from.
4 Where unto design'd to go.
5 What and how many Ships of the Dutch Comp. by departure from the last Shore there layed and their Names.
6 If one or more of these Ships in Company with this is departed for this or any other place.
7 If during the Voyage any particularitys is happend or Seen.
8 If not any Ships in Sea, or the Streights of Sunda have seen or hail'd in, and which.

9 If any other News worth of Attention at the place from whence the Ship
    lastly Departed or during the Voyage is happen'd.
Batavia in the Castle
the
    By order of the Governour
    General & the Counselors of India
        J BRANDER BUNGL
            Sec[t]

The first and fourth of these questions I only Answer'd which when
the Officer saw, he made use of the very same words the other had
done before, viz, that we might write what we please'd for it was of
no concequence &c[a] and yet he immidiatly said that he must send
that very paper away to Batavia by water and that it would be there
by to Morrow Noon, which shews that the Governor and Counselors
of India look upon such papers to be of some Concequence. Be this
as it may, My reasons for takeing notice of it in this Journal is because
I am well inform'd that it is but of very late Years that the Dutch have
taken upon them to examine all ships that pass these Streights.

    At 10 oClock we wieghd with a light breeze at sw, but did little
more than Stem the Current. At Noon Bantam Point and Pula baby
in one bearing EBN, distant from the Point 1½ Mile, Latitude Observed
5°53′ s.

*   *   *

[*Cook had considerable difficulty in making his way through the Sunda Strait,
between Java and Sumatra, in order to reach Batavia (Djakarta) in the north-west
of the island.*]

WEDNESDAY 10*th*. according to our reckoning, but by the Peop[l]e
here

THURSDAY 11*th*. At 4 oClock in the PM Anchor'd in Batavia Road
where we found the Harcourt Indiaman from England, 2 English
Country Ships, 13 Sail of Large Dutch Ships and a number of Small
Vesels. As soon as we anchor'd I sent Lieut[t] Hicks a Shore to acquaint
the Governor of our Arrival and to make an Excuse for not Saluting,

as we could only do it with three Guns, I thought it was better let a lone for it was thought the swivles could not be heard. The Carpenter now deliverd me in the Defects of the Ship, of which the following is a Copy:

The Defects of His Majestys Bark Endeavour
Lieut' James Cook Commander.

The Ship very Leakey (as she makes from twelve to six Inches p' Hour) Occationd by her Main Keel being wounded in many places and the Scarph of her stem being very open. The False Keel gone beyond the Midships (from forward and perhaps farther) as I had no opportunity of seeing for the water when haul'd a shore for repair). Wounded on her Larboard side under the Main Channel where I immagine the greatest Leak is (but could not come at it for the water). One Pump on the Larboard side useless the others decay'd within 1½ Inch of the bore. Otherwise Masts, Yards, Boats & Hull in prety good condition.

Dated in Batavia Road
this 10th of Oct' 1770   J. SEETTERLY

Previous to the above I had consulted with the Carpenter and all the other officers concearning the Leake, and they were all unanimously of opinion that it was not safe to proceed to Europe without first seeing her bottom. Accordingly I resolved to apply for Leave to heave her down at this place, and as I understood that this was to be done in writeing I drew up a Request and in the Morning had it translated into dutch in order to be laid before the Governor.

FRIDAY 12*th*. At 5 oClock in the PM I was interduced to the Governor General who Recieved me very politly and told me that I should have every thing I wanted, and that in the Morning my Requist should be laid before the Councel where I was desired to attend.

About 9 oClock in the Evening we had much Rain with some very heavy Claps of Thunder, one of which carried away a Dutch Indiaman's Main Mast by the Deck and split it, the Mⁿ Topmᵗ & Topgᵗ mast all to shivers, she had had a Iron spindle at the Main

Topgallant Mast head which had first Attracted the Lightning. This Ship lay about two Cables lengths from us and we were struck with the Thunder at the same time and in all probabillity we should have shared the same fate as the Dutchman, had it not been for the Electrical Chain which we had but just before got up, this carr[i]ed the Lightning or Electrical matter over the side Clear of the Ship, the Shock was so great as to shake the whole ship very sencibly. This instance alone is sufficient to recommend these Chains to all ships whatever, and that of the Dutchman ought to caution people from having Iron spindles at their Masts heads.

In the Morning I went a shore to the Councel Chamber and laid my Request before the Governor and Councel, who gave me for answer that I should have every thing I wanted.

SATURDAY 13th. Receiv'ed on board a Cask of Arrack and some Greens for the Ships Company.

SUNDAY 14th. Early in the Morning a ship saild from hence for Holland, by which I had just time to write two or three lines to Mr Stephens Secretary of the Admiralty to acquaint him of our Arrival, after which I went a shore and waited upon the Shabander, who has the derection of the Town, port &c^a to get an order to the Superintendant at Unrust to Receive us at that Island, but this I was told would not be ready before Tuesday next. Received from the Shore fresh beef and greens for the Ships Compney.

MONDAY 15th. Fresh Sea and land breezes and fair weather. I had forgot to mention that upon our arrival here I had not one man upon the Sick list, Lieut^t Hicks Mr Green and Tupia were the only People that had any complaints Occasion'd by a long continuence at sea.

TUESDAY 16th. Finding by a strict inquiry that there were no private person or persons in this place that could at this time advance me a sufficient sum of Mony to defray the Charge I might be at in repairing and refiting the Ship, at least if there were any they would be afraid to do it without leave from the Governor: Wherefore I had nothing left but to apply to the Governor himself and accordingly drew up a request which I laid before the Governor and Counc[e]l this Morning in concequence of which the Shabander had orders to supply me with what mony I wanted out of the Companys Treasure:

Lieutenant James Cook Commander of His Brittannick Majestys Bark the Endeavour begs leave to represent to His Excellency The Rig^t Honble Petrus Albertus Van der Parra Governor General & ca & ca & ca.

That he will be in want of a Sum or Sums of Mony in order to defray the Charge he will be at in repairing and refiting His Brittannick Majestys Ship at this place; which sum or Sums of Mony he is directed by his in[s]tructions and empower'd by his Commission to give Bills of Exchange on the respective offices which Superintend His Brittannick Majestys Navy –

The said Lieut^t Jam^s Cook Requests of His Excellency

That he will be pleased to order him to be supply'd with such Sum or Sums of Money as he may want for the Use above mention'd either out of the Companys Treasure or permit such private persons to do it as may be willing to advance Mony for Bills of Exchange on The Honble the Principal Officers and Commissioners of His Brittannick Majestys Navy, The Comission^rs for Victualing His Majestys Navy and the Commissioners for taking Care of the Sick and Hurt.

> Dated on Board His Brittannick
> Majestys Bark the Endeavour
> in Batavia Road the 16th Octr 1770.
> JAMES COOK

WEDNESDAY 17*th.* In the PM I waited upon the Superintendant of Unrust with an order from the Shabander to receive us at that Island, but this order the Superintendant told me was not sufficient to impower him to give me the conveniences and assistance I wanted; and when I came to call upon the Shabander I found this mistake was owing to the word, heave down, being wrong translated, this circumstance trifling as it is will cause a delay of some days as it cannot be set to rights untill next Councel day which is not till Friday.

THURSDAY 18*th.* In the PM Received on board 2 live Oxen, 150 Gall^ns of Arrack, 3 bar^{ls} of Tarr and one of Pitch. At Day light in the AM took up our Anchor and Run down to Onrust. At 9 Anchord in 8 fathom off Coopers Island which lies close to Onrust, there are Warfes at both of these Islands and ships land there stores some times on the one and some-times on the other, but it is only at Onrust where the proper conveniences are for heaving down. Soon after we Anchord I went ashore to the officers of the Yard to see if they could not allow us some place to land our stores but this could not be granted without orders.

FRIDAY 19*th*. In the PM I sent a petty officer to Mr Hicks, who lodges ashore at Batavia for the recovery of his hilth, with orders to desire him to wait upon the Shabandar in order to get the necessary orders respecting us despatch'd to this place as soon as possible.

SATURDAY 20*th*. Employ'd unrigging the Ship &c^a.

SUNDAY 21*st*. In the PM orders came down to the officers of the Yard to comply with every thing I wanted, but we could not yet get to a warfe to land our stores, they being all taken up by shipping.

MONDAY 22*nd*. In the AM Two ships went from the Warfes at Coopers Island, when we prepar'd to go along side one of them.

TUESDAY 23*rd*. In the PM hauld along side one of the Warfes, in order to take out our stores &c^a, after which the Ship is to be deliverd into the Charge of the proper officers at Onrust, who will (as I am inform'd) heave her down and repair her with their own people only, while ours must stand and look on.

WEDNESDAY 24*th*. Emp^d clearing the Ship having a store House to put our stores &c^a in. In the PM I went up to Town in order to put on board the first Dutch Ship that Sails a Packet for the Admiralty containing a Copy of my Journal, a Chart of the South Sea, a nother of New Zeland and one of the East Coast of New Holland. In the Morning the General accompanied by the Water Fiscall, some of the Councel and the Commodore each in their Respective boats went out into the Road on board the Oldest Captain in order to appoint him Commodore of the Fleet ready to Sail for Holland. The Ships were drawn up in two lines between which the General past to the New Commodores Ship which lay the farthest out. . . .

THURSDAY 25*th*. In the Evening I sent the Admiralty Packet on board the Kronenburg Cap[t] Fredrick Kelger, Commodore who together with a nother Ship sails emmidiatly for the Cape where he waits for the remainder of the fleet.

FRIDAY 26*th*. Set up the Ships Tents for the reseption of the Ships Company, several of them begin to be taken ill owing as I suppose to the extreem hot weather.

SATURDAY 27*th*. Employ'd geting out Store[s], Ballast &c[a].

SUNDAY 28*th*. Employ'd as above.

MONDAY 29*th*.
TUESDAY 30*th*. } Employ'd clear[ing] the Ship.
WEDNESDAY 31*st*.

[NOVEMBER 1770]

THURSDAY 1*st*. Got every thing out of the Ship and all Clear for going along side the Carreening Warfe, but about Noon I Received a Message from the Officers at Onrust acquainting me that they could not Recieve us there untill they had first despatched the Ships bound to Europe which were down here taking in Peper.

FRIDAY 2*d*.
SATURDAY 3*d*. } Emp[d] overhauling the Riggings &c[a] makeing Rope,
SUNDAY 4*th*. makeing and repair'g Sails.

MONDAY 5*th*. Clear hot sultry weather. In the AM Transported the Ship over to Onrust along side one of the Carreening warf's.

TUESDAY 6*th*. In the AM the Officers of the Yard took the Ship in hand and sent on board a number of Carpenters, Caulkers, Riggers Slaves &c[a] to make ready to heave down.

WEDNESDAY 7*th*. Employ'd geting ready to heave down. In the PM we had the Missfortune to loose M[r] Monkhouse the Surgeon who died at Batavia of a Fever after a Short illness of which desease and others, several of our people are daly taken ill which will make his loss be the more severly felt. He was succeeded by Mr Perry his mate, who is equally well if not better skilld in his profession.

THURSDAY 8*th*. In the night had much Thunder, Lightning and rain, during the day fair weather which gave us time to get every thing in readiness for heaving down.

FRIDAY 9*th*. In the PM Hove the Larboard side of the Ship Keel out and found her bottom to be in a far worse condition than we expected, the False Keel was gone to within 20 feet of the stern post, the Main Keel wounded in ma[n]y places very considerably, a great quantity of Sheathing [off], several planks much damaged especially under the Main channell near the Keel, where two planks and a half near 6 feet in length were within ⅛ of a Inch of being cut through, and here the worms had made their way quite into the Timbers, so that it was a Matter of Surprise to every one who saw her bottom how we had kept her above water; and yet in this condition we had saild some hundreds of Leagues in as dangerous a Navigation as is in any part of the world, happy in being ignorant of the continual danger we were in. In the Evening righted the Ship, Having only time to patch up some of the worst places to prevent the water geting in in large quantitys for the present. In the Morning hove her down again and most of the Carpenters and Caulkers in the yard (which are not a few) were set to work upon her bottom, and at the same time a number of slaves were employ'd bailing the water out of the hold. Our people altho they attend were seldom called upon, indeed by this time we were so weake[n]d by sickness that we could not muster above 20 Men and officers that were able to do duty, so little should we have been able to have hove her down and repair'd her our selves as I at one time thought us capable of.

SATURDAY 10*th*. In the PM we were obliged to right the Ship before night by reason of her makeing water in her uper works faster than we could free, this made it necessary to have her weather works inside and out caulk'd which before was thought unnecessary.

SUNDAY 11*th*. In the AM having caulkd the uper works hove out the Larboard side again which a number of workmen were employ'd repairing.

MONDAY 12*th*. In the PM finishd the Larboard side and in the AM began to get ready to heave out the other.

TUESDAY 13*th*. This day they hove the starb^d side keel out which we found very little damage'd and was therefore soon done with.

WEDNESDAY 14*th*. Employ'd clearing the Ship of the Carreening geer her bottom being now throughaly repaird and very much to my satisfaction. In justice to the Officers and workmen of this Yard I must say that I do not believe that there is a Marine Yard in the world where Work is done with more alertness than here or where there are better conveniences for heaving Ships down both in point of safety and dispatch. Here they heave down by two Masts which is not now practised by the English but I hold it to be much safer and more expaditious than by heaving down by one mast; a man must not only be strongly bigoted to his own customs but in some measure divested of reason that will not allow this after seeing with how much ease and safety the Dutch at Onrust heave down their largest Ships.

THURSDAY 15*th*. In the AM Transport the Ship from Onrust to Coopers Island and moor'd her a long side the warfe.

FRIDAY 16*th*. Emp^d takeing in Coals and Ballast. Sent one of the decay'd Pumps up to Batavia to have a New one made by it.

SATURDAY 17*th*.
SUNDAY 18*th*.
MONDAY 19*th*.   Employd Rigging the Ship, geting on board
TUESDAY 20*th*.   Stores and water which last we have sent from
WEDNESDAY 21*st*.   Batavia at the rate of Six Shillings and 8 pence
THURSDAY 22*nd*.   a Leager or 150 Gall^{ns}. We are now become
FRIDAY 23*rd*.   so sickly that we seldom can muster above 12
SATURDAY 24*th*.   or 14 hands to do duty.
SUNDAY 25*th*.

MONDAY 26*th*. In the night had much rain after Which the Westerly Monsoon set in, which blows here generally in the night from the SW or from the land in the day from the NW or North.

TUESDAY 27*th*.	
WEDNESDAY 28*th*.	Employ'd geting on board Stores, Provisions,
THURSDAY 29*th*.	Water, Rigging the Ship, repairing and
FRIDAY 30*th*.	bending the sails.
DECEMBER	
SATURDAY 1*st*.	On the last of these Days having got all the
SUNDAY 2*d*.	Sick on board and every other thing from
MONDAY 3*rd*.	the Island, we hauld off from the Warfe
TUESDAY 4*th*.	with a design to run up to Batavia Road
WEDNESDAY 5*th*.	but the wind proving scant obliged us to
THURSDAY 6*th*.	lay at Anchor.
FRIDAY 7TH	

SATURDAY 8*th*. Fresh breezes Westerly and fair weather. At 10 AM weigh'd and run up to Batavia Road where we Anchor'd in 4½ fathom water.

SUNDAY 9*th*. First and latter parts D° weather, Middle Squally with rain. In the PM sent a shore a Boat Load of Empty Casks and at the same [time] went my self in order to forward the things we wanted, and this same evening sent on board the New Pump with some other stores that were immidiatly wanting.

MONDAY 10*th*. For the Most part Squally weather with rain: The People Employ'd scraping the paint Work.

TUESDAY 11*th*.	For the most part of these Days fair weather.
WEDNESDAY 12*th*.	Emp^d takeing on board Provisions and Water,
THURSDAY 13*th*.	this last is put on board at 5/- a Leager
FRIDAY 14*th*.	or 150 Gall^{ns}.

SATURDAY 15*th*. In the PM Anchor'd here the Earl of Elgin Capt Cook an English East India Company ship from Madrass, bound to China, but having lost her passage put in here to wait for the next season.

SUNDAY 16*th*. ⎱ Emp^d takeing on board provisions, Scraping and
MONDAY 17*th*. ⎰ painting the Ship.

TUESDAY 18*th*. Gentle breezes and fair weather. Anchor'd here the
Phenix Capt Black an English Country Ship from Bencoolen.

WEDNESDAY 19*th*. ⎫
THURSDAY 20*th*. ⎪ Fresh breezes and for the most part fair
FRIDAY 21*st*. ⎪ weather. Employ'd takeing on board Pro-
SATURDAY 22*nd*. ⎬ visions water &c^a and geting the Ship ready
SUNDAY 23*rd*. ⎪ for Sea.
MONDAY 24*th*. ⎭

TUESDAY 25*th*. Having now compleatly refited the Ship & taken in a
sufficient quantity of Provisions of all kinds, I this afternoon tooke
leave of the General and such others of the principal Gentlemen as I
had any connections with, all of whome upon every occasion gave me
all the assistance I required. . . .

WEDNESDAY 26*th*. In the PM My self Mr Banks and all the Gentlemen
came on board and at 6 in the AM we wiegh'd and came to sail with
a light breeze at SW. The Elgin Indiaman saluted with three Cheers
and 13 Guns and soon after the Garrison with 14 both of which we
returnd. Soon after this the Sea breeze set in at NBW which obliged
us to anchor just without the Ships in the Road. The Number sick on
board at this time amounts to 40 or upwards and the rest of the Ships
company are in a Weakly condition, having been ev[er]y one sick
except the Sail maker an old Man about 70 or 80 Years of age, and
what was still more extraordinary in this man his being generally more
or less drunk every day. But notwithstanding this general sickness we
lost but Seven Men in the whole: the Surgeon three Seamen, M^r
Greens Servant and Tupia and his servant, both of which fell a sacrifice
to this unwholsom climate before they had reached the Object of their
wishes. Tupia['s] death indeed cannot be said to be owing wholy to
the unwholsom air of Batavia, the long want of a Vegetable diat which
he had all his life before been use'd to had brought upon him all the
disorders attending a sea life. He was a Shrewd Sensible, Ingenious

Man, but proud and obstinate which often made his situation on board both disagreable to himself and those about him, and tended much to promote the deceases which put a period to his life. . . .

Batavia is certainly a place that Europeans need not covet to go to, but if necessity obliges them they will do well to make their stay as short a[s] possible otherwise they will soon feel the effects of the unwholsome air of Batavia which I firmly beleive is the death of more Europeans than any other place upon the Globe of the same extent, such at least is my opinion of it which is founded on facts. We came in here with as healthy a ships company as need [go] to Sea and after a stay of not quite 3 Months lift it in the condition of an Hospital Ship besides the loss of 7 Men and yet all the Dutch Captains I had an oppertunity to convers with said that we had been very lucky and wondered that we had not lost half our people in that time.

THURSDAY 27th. Moderate breezes at West and NW with fair weather. At 6 AM weighd and stood out to Sea. At Noon the Island of Edam bore NBE distant 3 Miles.

*   *   *

[*The* Endeavour *took a week to negotiate the Sunda Strait.*]

[JANUARY 1771]

SUNDAY 6th. At 3 oClock in the PM Anchor'd under the SE side of Princes Island in 18 fathom water, in order to recrute our wood and water and to procure refreshments for the People which are now in a much worse state of hilth then when we left Batavia. After the Ship coming to an Anch[or] I went a shore to look at the watering place and to speak with the Natives some of whome were upon the beach. I found the watering place convenient and the water to all appearence good provide[d] proper care was taken in the filling of it; The Natives seem'd inclined to supply us with Turtle Fowles &c[a], Articles that I intended laying in as great a stock as possible for the benefit of the sick and to suffer every one to purchas what they pleased for themsilves, as I found these people as easy to Traffic with as Europeans. In the Morning sent the Gunner ashore with some hand[s] to fill water, while others were employ'd puting the hold to rights Sending on shore empty casks &c^a. Served Turtle to the Ships company, Yesterday was the only salt Meat Day they have had sence our arrival at Savu which is now near 4 Months.

MONDAY 7*th*. From this Day till MONDAY 14*th* We were employ'd Wooding and watering being frequently interrup[t]ed by heavy rains; having now compleated both we hoisted in the Long boat and made ready to put to Sea, having on board a pretty good stock of refreshments which we purchasd from the Natives, such as Turtle, Fowles, Fish, Two species of Dear, one about as big as a small Sheep, the other no bigger then a Rabbit; both sorts eat very well, but are only for present use as they seldom lived above 24 hours in our possesion. We likewise got fruit of several sorts, such as Coca nutts, Plantains, Limes &c^a. The Trade on our part was carried on chiefly with mony (Spanish Dollars) the natives set but little Value upon any thing else, such of our people as had not this article traded with old Shirts &c^a at a great disadvantage.

TUESDAY 15*th*. Had Variable light Airs of wind, with which we could not get under sail untill the Morning when we weighd with a light breeze at NE which was soon succeeded by a Calm.

WEDNESDAY 16*th*. Had it calm all PM which at 5 oClock obliged us to anchor under the South point of Princes Island, the said point bearing SWBW distant two Miles. At 8 oClock in the AM a light breeze sprung [up] at North [with] which we we[i]gh'd and stood out to Sea. At Noon Java Head bore SE¼S distant 2 Leagues and the West point of Princes Island NNW distant 5 Leagues. Lat^d Ob. 6°45′ s. Java Head from which I take my Departure Lies in the Latitude of 6°49′ s and Longitude 255°12′ West from the Meridion of Greenwich, deduced from Several Astronomical Observations made at *Batavia* by the *Rever^d Mr Mohr*.

* * *

[*Cook now began the eight-week voyage to the Cape of Good Hope.*]

THURSDAY 24*th*. *Winds SWBS to SSE. Course Correct South. Distce sail'd*

4 M. Lat in 9°34′. Long West from Greenw^h 256°50′. First part light airs the remainder Calm. In the AM died Jn° Truslove Corp^l of Marines, a Man much esteem'd by every one on board. Many of our people at this time lay dangerously ill of Fevers and fluxes. We are inclinable to atribute this to the water we took in at Princes Island and have put lime into the Casks in order to purifie it.

FRIDAY 25*th*. Winds Var^l & Calm. Courses S 30° E. Distce sail'd 12 M. Lat. in South 9°44′. Long in West from Greenw^h 256°44′. Light Airs and Calms, hot and Sultry weather. Departed this Life Mr Sporing a Gentleman belonging to Mr Banks's retinue.

SATURDAY 26*th*. Winds SWerly. Courses SE. Distce sail'd 17 M. Lat in South 9°56′. Long in West from Greenw^h 256°32′. First part little wind, the remainder Calm and very hot. Set up the Topmasts rigging and clean'd Ship between decks and wash'd with Vinegar.

SUNDAY 27*th*. Winds Var^l. Courses S 30° W. Distce sail'd 19 M. Lat in South 10°12′. Long in West from Greenw^h 256°41′. Little wind and some times calm. In the Evening found the Variation to be 2°51′ w. Departed this Life Mr Sidney Parkinson, Natural History Painter to Mr Banks, and soon after Jn° Ravenhill, Sailmaker, a Man much advanced in years.

MONDAY 28*th*. Winds WNW, NE. Courses S 43° W. Distce sail'd 66 M. Lat in South 11°0′. Long in West from Greenw^h 257°27′. Moderate breezes with some squalls attended with Showers of rain.

TUESDAY 29*th*. Winds NWerly. Courses S 40° W. Distce sail'd 74 M. Lat in South 11°57′. Long in West from Greenw^h 258°15′. Very variable weather, some times squally with rain, other times Little wind and Calms. In the night Died Mr Charls Green who was sent out by the Royal Society to Observe the Transit of Venus; he had long been in a bad state of hilth, which he took no care to repair but on the contrary lived in such a manner as greatly promoted the disorders he had had long upon him, this brought on the Flux which put a period to his life.

WEDNESDAY 30*th*. Winds East^{ly}. Courses S 40° W. Distce sail'd Miles 67. Lat in South 12°48′. Long in West from Greenw^h 258°59′. First and Latter parts Moderate breezes and clowdy weather, the middle Squally with rain Thunder and Lightning. Died of the Flux Saml Moody and Francis Hate, two of the Carpenters Crew.

THURSDAY 31st. *Winds ESE. Courses SW. Distce sail'd miles* 80. *Lat in South* 13°42'. *Long in West from Greenw^h* 259°55'. First part Moderate and fair, the remainder frequent squalls attended with showers of rain. In the Course of this 24 hours we have had four Men died of the Flux, viz. Jno Thompson Ships Cook, Benj. Jordan Carpenters Mate, James Nicholson and Arch^d Wolfe Seamen. A Melancholy proff of the Calamitous Situation we are at present in, having hardly well men enough to tend the Sails and look after the Sick, many of the latter are so ill that we have not the least hopes of their recovery.

[FEBRUARY 1771]

FRIDAY 1st. *Winds SEBS. Courses S* 58½ *W. Distce sail'd miles* 119. *Lat in South* 14°44'. *Long in West from Greenw^h* 261°40'. Fresh gales with flying showers of Rain. Clean'd between Decks and Wash'd with Vineg^r.

SATURDAY 2nd. *Winds SSE. Courses S* 61° *W. Distce sail'd miles* 131. *Latd in South* 15°48'. *Longd in West from Greenw^h* 263°40'. A Fresh Trade and mostly fair weather. Departed this Life Danl Roberts Gunners Servant who died of the flux. Sence we have had a fresh Trade wind this fatall disorder hath seem'd to be at a stand, yet there are several people which are so far gone and brought so very low by it that we have not the least hopes of their recovery.

SUNDAY 3rd. *Winds Do. Courses S* 65° *W. Distce sail'd miles* 128. *Latd in South* 16°40'. *Longd in West from Greenw^h* 265°40'. D° Weather. In the Evening found the Variation to be 2°56' West. Departed this Life John Thurman Sailmakers assistant.

MONDAY 4th. *Winds SE. Courses S* 69° *W. Distce sail'd miles* 141. *Latd in South* 17°30'. *Longd in West from Greenw^h* 267°56'. A Fresh Trade and hazey weather, with some Squalls attend[ed] with small rain. Unbent the Main Topsail to Repair and bent a nother. In the night died of the Flux Mr John Bootie Midshipman and Mr Jno Gathrey Boatswain.

TUESDAY 5*th*. *Winds EBS. Courses W* 15° *S. Distce sail'd miles* 141. *Latd in South* 18°6′. *Longd in West from Greenw*[h] 270°18′. A Fresh Trade wind and hazey Clowdy weather. Emp[d] repairing sails. Appointed Sam[l] Evans one of the Boatswains mates and Coxswain of the Pinnace to be Boatswain in the room of M[r] Gathrey deceased and order'd a Survey to be taken of the Stores.

WEDNESDAY 6*th*. *Winds SE. Course W* 12° *S. Distce sail'd miles* 126. *Latd in South* 18°30′. *Longd in West from Greenw*[h] 272°28′. A Fresh Trade wind and fair weather. In the night died M[r] Jon[n] Monkhouse Midshipman and Brother to the late Surgeon.

*   *   *

SATURDAY 9*th*. *Winds SE. Course S* 74°30′ *W. Distce sail'd miles* 127. *Latd in South* 19°58′. *Longd in West from Greenw*[h] 278°50′ *pr Log* 281°0′ *pr Obn*. Gentle gales and fair weather. In the Morning saw a Ship on our Starboard Quarter which hoisted Dutch Colours.

SUNDAY 10*th*. *Winds SE qrter. Course S* 77°15′ *W. Distce sail'd miles* 136. *Latd in South* 20°28′. *Longd in West Greenwh* 281°12′ *pr. Log* 283°22′ *pr Obn*. Fresh breezes and Hazey weather. Lost sight in the night of the Dutch Ship she having out Saild us.

MONDAY 11*th*. *Winds Do. Course S* 75° *W. Distce sail'd miles* 126. *Latd in South* 20°58′. *Longd in West of Greenw*[h] 283°22′ *pr. Log* 285°32′ *pr Obsn*. Winds and weather as yesterday. Some hands constantly Employ'd repairing Sails.

TUESDAY 12*th*. *Winds SSE. Course S* 71° *W. Distce sail'd miles* 83. *Latd in South* 21°25′. *Longd in West Greenw*[h] 284°46′ *pr. Log* 286°56′ *pr Obn*. Gentle breezes and fair weather. At 7 in the AM died of the flux after a long and painfull illness M[r] John Satterly, Carpenter, a Man much Esteem'd by me and every Gentleman on board, in his room I apoint George Knowel one of the Carpenters Crew, having only him and one More left.

WEDNESDAY 13*th*. *Winds Do. Course S* 72°30′ *W. Distce sail'd miles* 87. *Latd in South* 21°51′. *Longd in West Greenw*[h] 286°15′ *pr. Log* 288°25′ *pr Obn*.

Weather as yesterday. Employ'd surveying the Carpenters Stores and repairing sails.

THURSDAY 14*th*. *Winds Do. Course S* 73°15' *W. Distce sail'd miles* 105. *Latd in South* 22°21'. *Longd in West Greenw*^{h} 288°3' *pr. Log* 290°13' *pr. Obn.* Moderate breezes and Clowdy with some Showers of rain. Variation p^r Azth 4°10' w. Departed this Life Alex^r Lindsey Seaman; this man was one of those we got at Batavia and had been some time in India.

FRIDAY 15*th*. *Winds SEBE. Course S* 81°15' *W. Distce sail'd miles* 123. *Latd in South* 22°40'. *Longd in West Greenw*^{h} 290°15' *pr. Log* 292°25' *pr. Obn.* Weather as yesterday. Died of the flux Danl Preston Marine.

* * *

WEDNESDAY 20*th*. *Winds South. Course S* 75°45' *W. Distce sail'd miles* 127. *Latd in South* 24°57'. *Long in West from Greenw*^{h} 302°21' *pr. Log* 304°31' *pr. Obn.* Fresh gales and clear weather. Variation p^r Azth 12°15' West. This Morning the Carpenter and his Mate set about repairing the Long-boat, being the first day they have been able to work sence we left Princes Island.

THURSDAY 21*st*. *Winds South to ESE. Course WBS. Distce sail'd miles* 126. *Latd in South* 25°21'. *Long in West from Greenw*^{h} 304°39' *Pr. Accot.* 306°34' *pr. Obsn.* First and Middle parts fair weather, Latter Squally attended with Shower of rain. Between 2 and 3 o Clock in the PM took Several observation[s] of the Sun and Moon, the Mean Result of them gave 304°33' w Longitude from Greenwich, which is 1°55' west of Account and corisponds very well with the last observations, for at that time the Ship was 2°10' West of account. In the night died of the flux Alex^r Simpson a very good Seaman. In the Morning Punished Thos Rossiter with Twelve Lashes for geting Drunk, grossly Asaulting the Officer of the Watch and beating some of the Sick.

* * *

WEDNESDAY 27*th*. *Winds EBS, EBN, NE. Courses S* 77°15' *W. Dist sail'd miles* 108. *Lat In South* 29°30'. *Longd in West* 317°25' *pr. Log* 320°25' *pr. Obn.* D° Gales and clowdy. In the AM Died of the Flux Henry Jeffs, Emanuel Pharah and Peter Morgan Seamen, the last came Sick on board at Batavia of which he never recoverd and the other two had long been past all hopes of recovery, so that the death of these three men in one day did not in the least alarm us; on the contrary we are in hopes that they will be the last that will fall a Sacrefice to this fatal desorder, for such as are now ill of it are in a fair way of recovering.

THURSDAY 28*th. Winds NEBE, North, & SW. Courses S* 85½° *W. Distce saild miles* 88. *Lat in South* 29°37'. *Longd in West* 319°5' *pr. Log* 322°5' *pr. Obn.* Moderate breezes and fair weather untill near 5 oClock in the AM, when a heavy squall from the SW attended with rain took us all a back and obliged us to put before the wind the beter to take in our sails, but before this could be done the Fore Tops^l was split in many places; by 6 oClock the Topsails & M^n Sail were handed and we brought too under the Fore sail and Miz^n. At 8 oClock it fell more Moderate and we set the Main sail and brought another Fore Topsail to the Yard. At Noon had strong gales and Clowdy weather.

*   *   *

[MARCH 1771]

TUESDAY 5*th. Winds SSW to SE. Courses pr. Log N* 31° *W. Dist saild miles* 32. *Lat in South* 31°52' *p^r Ob^n* 31°7' *p^r Reckoning. Longd in West* 331°19' *pr. Obn* 324°56' *pr. Reckoning.* Fresh gales from the SSW with Squally rainy w^r with which we stood to the Westward. In the evening some people thought they saw the appearence of land to the Northward, but this appear'd so improbable that I who was not on deck at this time was not acquainted with it untill dark, when I order'd them to sound but found no ground with 80 f^m upon which we concluded that no land was near, but day light in the Morning proved this to be a Mistake by shewing us the land at the Distance of a bout 2 Leagues off. We had now the wind at SE blowing fresh right upon the land. When we made the land we were standing to the westward, but thinking the other the best tack to get off on we wore and hauld off to Eastward and by now had got an offing of a bout 4 Leagues, the land at this time extending from NEBN to WSW. This part of the Coast of Africa that we fell in with lies in about the Latitude of 32° 0' and Longitude of 331°29' W/28°31' E, and near to what is call'd in the Charts Point

Natall, it was a steep cragy point, very much broke and look'd as if the high Cragy rocks were Islands; to the NE of this point the land in gener¹ appeared to rise sloaping from the Sea to a moderate height, the shore Alternately Rocks and Sand. About 2 Leagues to the NE of the point appeared to be the Mouth of a River which probably may be that of Sᵗ Johns. At this time the weather was very Hazey so that we had but a very imperfect View of the land which did not appear to great advantage.

* * *

MONDAY 11*th*. *Winds Do, SE. Courses N* 85° *W. Distce saild miles* 79. *Lat in South* 34°45′. *Longd in West* 338°48′ *pr. Obn* 328°35′ *pr. R.* First part light Airs at West. The remainder had a fresh gale at SE with which we steerd west and WNW in order to make the Land which was seen from the Deck at 10 AM. At Noon it Extended from NE to NW distant 5 Leagues. The Middle appear'd high & Mountainous and the two extremes low. Took sever¹ obⁿˢ of yᵉ ☉ & ☽ which gave the Longᵈ reduced to noon as pʳ Column.

TUESDAY 12*th*. *Winds East, SE, and Southerly. Courses S* 69°30′ *W. Distce saild miles* 37. *Lat in South* 34°58′. *Longd In West* 339°30′ *pr. Obn* 329°17′ *pr. R.* In the PM had the wind a[t] SE & East with which we steer'd a long shore West & WSW. At 6 Cape Laguillas⁴⁵ bore West distant 3 Leagues. At 8 the wind being than at South we Tackd and stood off being about 2 Leagues from the Cape which bore about WNW, in this Situation had 33 fᵐ water. The wind continued between SW and South all night in times very squally with rain. At 2 AM Tack'd to the westward untill near 8 when we again stood off, Cape Laguillas NW distant 2 or 3 Leagues. At 9 the weather clear'd up and the wind fix'd at SBW, we Tackd and stood to the westward. At Noon Cape Laguillas bore NEBN distᵗ 4 Leagues; the Land of this Cape is very low & sandy next the Sea, inland it is of a Moderate height. Latitude 34°50′, Longᵈ 339°23′ W or 20°37′ E, deduce'd from yterdys Observations.

WEDNESDAY 13*th*. In the PM having the Wind at South we steerd a long shore WBS½S until 3 oClock, when finding this Course carried

45. L'Agulhas. Cape Agulhas is the most southerly point of Africa.

us off from the land we Steerd WBN. At 6 oClock Cape Laguillas or the high land over it bore EBN Distant 12 Leagues and the Westermost land in sight NW½W. We continued a WBN Course with the wind at SE untill day light in the Morning, when we hauld in NW and NWBN, At 8 the Cape of Good hope NWBN and at 10 we were abreast of it, and distant off about 1 League or little more. We pass'd close without a rock on which the Sea brok[e] very high, it lies about a League right out to sea from the Cape. After passing the Cape we keept along shore at the distance of about one League off having a fresh gale at SE. At Noon the Cape bore SE distant 4 L[eagues]. Latitude observed 34°15′ s, Longitude in by our reckoning, corrected by the last Observation, 341°7′ West or 18°53′ E from Greenwich, by which the Cape lies in 34°25′ South Latitude and 19°1′ East Longitude from Greenwich, which nearly agrees with the observations made at the Cape Town by Mes^{rs} Mason and Dixon in 1761 – a prooff that our observations have been well made and that as such they may always be depended on to a Surprising degree of Accuracy. If we had had no such guide we should have found an error of 10°13′ of Longitude or perhaps more to the East, such an effect the Currents must have had upon the Ship.

THURSDAY 14*th*. Winds at SE a fresh gale but as we approached the Lyons Tail on West point Table Bay we had flurries of wind from all points of the Compass; this was occasion'd by the high land for clear of it the wind was still at SE and blow'd so Strong out of the Bay that we could not work the Ship in, we were therefore obliged to Anchor a good way without all the Ships at Anchor in the road, in the whole 16 Sail (viz) 8 Dutch, 3 Dains, 4 French a Frigate and 3 Store Ships, and one English East Indiman who Saluted us with a 11 Guns which compliment we returnd with 9. The gale continued which obliged us to lay fast all the Morning.

FRIDAY *the* 15*th*. Strong gales at SE all the after noon and most part of the night tho in the Evening it fell a little moderate, which gave the Indimans boat an oppertunity to come on board us with a compliment of a Basket of fruit &c^a. She was the Admiral Pocock Captain Riddell homeward bound from [Bombay]. In the Morning we got under sail

& stood into the Road having variable light airs mostly from the sea. A Dutch Boat from the shore came on board in which was the Master Attendant and some other Gentlemen; the former directed us to a proper birth where about 10 oClock we anchord in 7 fathom water a Owsey bottom, the Lyons Tail or West point of the Bay bore WNW, and the Castle SW distant 1½ Miles. I now sent a petty officer ashore to know if they would Answer our salute but before he returnd we saluted, which was immidiatly returnd by the same number of Guns. After this I waited my self upon the Governor who was pleased to tell me that I should have every thing I wanted that the place afforded. My first care was to provide a proper place a Shore for the r[e]seption of the Sick, for which purpose I order'd the Surgeon to look out for a house where they could be Lodged and diated; this he soon found and agree'd with the people of the house for two Shillings a Day per Man, which I found was the Customary price and method of proceeding and I afterwards gave the Surgeon an order to superintend the whole.

Few Remarks have happend sence we left Java head that can be of much use to the Navigator or any other person into whose hand this Journal may fall, Such however as have occurd I shall now insert. After our leaving Java head we were a 11 Days before we got the general SE Trade wind in which time we did not advance above 5° to the South and 3° to the West, having all the time Variable light Airs of Wind interrupted by frequent Calms; the weather all the time hot and sultry and the Airs unwholsome, occasioned most probably by the vast Vapours brought into these Latitudes by the Easterly Trade wind and Westerly Monsoon, both of which blow at this time of the Year in this sea; the Easterly wind prevail[s] as far as 12° or 10° South and the westerly winds as far as 6° or 8°. Between them the winds are variable and I beleive always more or less unwholsome, but to us it was remarkable from the fatal concequences that attended it; for what ever might be the cause of first bringing on the flux among our people, this unwholsome air had a great share in it & increased it to that degree that a man was no sooner taken with it than he look'd upon himself as dead, such was the despondency that reign'd among the sick at this time, nor could it be by any means prevented when every man saw that Medicine however skilfully administred had not the least Effect. I shall mention what effect only the imagery approach of this disorder had upon one man. He had long tended upon the Sick and injoy'd a tolerable good state of hilth: one morning coming upon deck he found himself a little griped and immidiatly began to stamp with his feet and exclaim I have got the Gripes, I have got the Gripes, I shall die, I shall die! – in this manner he continued untill he threw himself into a fit and was carried off the deck in a manner dead, however he soon recover'd and did very well.

We had no sooner got into the se Trade wind then we felt its happy effects, tho we lost several men after, but they were such as were brought so low and week that there was hardly a possibillity of their recovering, and yet some of them linger'd out in a state of suspence a month after who in all probabillity would not have lived 24 hours before this change happen'd. Those that were not so far gone remaind in the same state for some time and at last began to recover; some few however were seiz'd with the disorder after we got into the Trade wind but they had it but slitely and soon got over it. It is worth remarking that of all those who had it in its last stage only one man live'd who is now in a fair way of recovering, and I think Mr Banks was the only one that was cure'd at the first Attack'd that had it to a great degree, or indeed attall before we got into the se Trade, for it was before that time that his cure was happily effected.

It is to be wish'd for the Good of all Seamen and Mankind in General that some preventative was found out against this disease and put in practice in climates where it is common; for it is impossible to Victual and water a ship in those climates but what some one Article or a nother, according to different peoples opinions, must have been the means of bringing on the flux. We were inclinable to lay it to the Water we took in at Princes Island and the Turtle we got their, on which we lived for several days, but there seems to be no reason for this when we consider that all the Ships from Batavia this year suffered by the same disorder as much as we have done, and many of them arrived at this place in a far worse state, and yet not one of these Ships took in any water at Princes Island; the same may be said of the Harcourt Indiman Capt Paul who saild from Batavia soon after our arrival, directly for the Coast of Sumatra – we afterwards heard that she in a very short time lost by sickness above twenty Men. Indeed this seems to have been a year of General sickness over most parts of India, the Ships from Bengall and Madrass bring melancholy accounts of the havock mad[e] there by the United force of sickness and famine. . . .

SATURDAY 16*th*. Variable Light airs all this Day. Moor'd the Ship and struck Yards and Topmasts and in the Morning got all the Sick (28) ashore to quarters provided for them and got off fresh meat and greens for the people on board.

SUNDAY 17*th*. In the AM saild for England the Admiral Pocock Capt Riddel by whome I sent letters to the Admiralty & Royal Society. About Noon came on a hard dry gale from the SE.

MONDAY 18*th*. In the PM Anchored in the offing An English Ship which prov'd to be the Holton Indiaman from Bengal. In the AM it fell Moderate and we began to water the Ship.

TUESDAY 19*th*. Variable gentle breezes all this Day. Employ'd repairing sails, Riging, Watering &c^a.

WEDNESDAY 20*th*. In the PM saild the Holton Indiaman who saluted us with a 11 Guns, which Compliment we returnd. This Ship during her stay in India lost by sickness between 30 and 40 Men and had at this time a good ma[n]y down with the scurvy, other Ships suffer'd in the same proportion, thus we find that Ships which have been little more than Twelve Months from England have suffer'd as much or more by Sickness than we have done who have been out near three times as long. Yet their sufferings will hardly if atall be mentioned or known in England when on the other hand those of the Endeavour, because the Voyage is uncommon, will very probable be mentioned in every News paper, and what is not unlikely with many additional hardships we never experienced; for such are the disposission of men in general in these Voyages that they are seldom content with the hardships and dangers which will naturaly occur, but they must add others which hardly ever had existence but in their imaginations, by magnifying the most trifling accidents and Circumstances to the greatest hardships, and unsurmou[n]table dangers without the imidiate interposion of Providence, as if the whole Merit of the Voyage consisted in the dangers and hardships they underwent, or that real ones did not happen often enough to give the mind sufficient anxiety; thus posteriety are taught to look upon these Voyages as hazardous to the highest degree.

THURSDAY 21*st*. Fine pleasent weather. Employ'd geting on board water, overhauling the Riging and repairing Sails. Saild for Batavia a Dutch Ship.

FRIDAY 22*nd*. ⎫ Mostly fine pleasent weather, on the 23rd we
SATURDAY 23*rd*. ⎪ compleated our water after which I gave as
SUNDAY 24*th*. ⎬ many of the people leave to go aShore to
MONDAY 25*th*. ⎪ refresh themselves, as could be Spar'd at one
TUESDAY 26*th*. ⎭ time.

WEDNESDAY 27*th*. Winds Variable and clear pleasent weather. Saild for Holland four sail of Dutch Ships.

THURSDAY 28*th*. ⎫ Winds and weather as above. Emp^d fixing New
FRIDAY 29*th*. ⎬ Topmast Backstays, repairing Sails &c^a.

SATURDAY 30*th*. In the PM Anchor'd here the Duke of Gloucester English East India Ship from China. In the Evening a prodigious hard gale of wind came on at SE which continued till about 3 oClock in the morning. During the gale the Table Mountain and adjacent hills were Cap'd with extraordinary white clowds, the remainder of the Day light airs and pleasent weather.

SUNDAY 31*st*. Clear pleasent weather all this day. In the morning we got on board a whole Ox which we cut up and salted. I had eat ashore some of as good and fat beef as ever I eat in my life and was told that I might have as good to salt, but in this I was very much disapointed; the one I got was thin and lean, yet well taisted, it weighed 408 lb^s.

[APRIL 1771]

MONDAY 1*st.* Ap^l. In the PM I observ'd a dark dence haze like a fog bank in the SE Horizon and white clowds began to gather over the Table Mountain, certain signs of an aproaching gale from the same quarter, which about 4 oClock began to blow with great Voylance and continued more or less so the remainder of these 24 hours, the Table mountain Cap'd with white Clowds all the time, the weather dry and clear.

*   *   *

TUESDAY 9*th.* Little wind at SW, with Fogy hazey weather. Employ'd makeing ready for sea.

WEDNESDAY 10*th.* Gentle breezes at SSE and fair weather. Took on board 11 of our People from Sick quarters.

THURSDAY 11*th.* Winds and weather as yesterday. Employ'd geting on board various Articles of Provisions from the Shore.

FRIDAY 12*th.* Winds at SW fair weather. Set up the Topmast rigging and bent the sails.

SATURDAY 13*th.* Fresh breezes at SW and Clowdy hazey weather. In the night Anchord here a Dutch Ship from Holland; she saild about 3 Months ago in company with two more, the news brought by this Ship is that a War was Dayly expected between England and Spain. Signals out for 4 or 5 sail more being in the offing one of which is said to be a Ship from England. Took leave of the Governor intending to Sail to morrow.

SUNDAY 14*th.* Winds Westerly gentle breezes. In the PM got all the sick on board many of whome was yet in a very bad state of hilth: three died here[46] but this loss was made up by the oppertunity we had of compleating our full Compliment. In the Morning unmoor'd and got ready for sailing.

46. The muster-books record the deaths of John Dozey and John Lorrain, both seamen, at the Cape. Banks records the death of 'Theodosio', a seaman, on 3 April. [E]

MONDAY 15*th*. None of the Ships in the Offing are yet arrived. Diserous as we must be of hearing news from England I determine'd not to wait the arrival of these Ships, but took the advantage of a breeze of wind from the wsw, wiegh'd and stood out of the Bay. Saluted with 13 Guns which compliment was returnd both by the Castle and Dutch Commodore, the Europa saluted us as we pass'd her, which we returnd; this Ship was to have saild with or before us, but not likeing the oppertunity she lay fast. At 5 in the Evening Anchor'd under Penguin or Robin Island in 10 fathom water, this Island Extending from wnw to ssw, distant 1½ or 2 Miles. . . .

The *Cape of Good Hope* hath been so often discrib'd by Authors and is so well known to Europeans that any discriptions I can give of it may appear unnecessary. However I cannot help observing that most Authors, particularly the Author of Mr Byrons Voyage, have heighten'd the picture to a very great degree above what it will bear, so that a stranger is at once struck with surprise and disapointment, for no Country we have seen this Voyage affords so barren a prospect as this, and not only so in appearence but in reallity. The land over the Cape which constitutes the Peninsula form'd by Table Bay on the north and False Bay on the South consists of high barren Mountains, behind these to the East or what may be call'd the Isthmus is a vast extensive Plain, not one thousand part of which either is or can be cultivated. The soil consists mostly of a light kind of Sea Sand produceing hardly any thing but heath, every Inch of ground that will bear cultivation is taken up in small Plantation[s] consisting of Vineyards, Orchards, Kitchen Gardens &c^a, hardly any two lay together, but are despers'd at some distance one from another. If we may Judge from circumstances the Interior parts of this Country is not more fertile, that is the fertile land bears a very small proportion to the whole; we were told that they have settlements 28 days Journey inland which is computed at 900 English Miles, and thus far they bring provisions to the Cape by land Carriage. It is also said that the Dutch farmers are so despers'd about the Country that some have no neighbours within four or five days Journey of them; admitting these to be facts and it will at once appear that the Country in general cannot be very fertile, for it would be absurd to suppose that they would raise provisions at such an emence distance, where the trouble and expence of bringing them to market must increase in proportion, could it be done nearer. The Dutch assign another reason for being oblige'd to extend their scater'd settlements so far inland, which is that they never disturb the original Natives but always leave them in peaceable posession of whatever lands they may have approbated to their own use, which in some places is pretty extensive and that probably none of the worst, by which good policy the new settlers very seldom if ever meet with any disturbance from the natives; on the Contraory many of them become their servants and mix among them and are usefull members to Society. Notwithstanding the many disadvantages this Country labours under such is the Industry, Oconomy and good management of the Dutch that not only the necessarys but all the luxuries of life are rais'd here in as great abundance, and are sold as cheape if not cheaper then in any part of Europe some few articles excepted. Naval Stores however do not want for Price any more here than they do at Batavia, these are only sold by the Company who have a certain fix'd exorbitant price from which the[y] never deviate.

The Inhabitants of the Cape Town are in general well bred and extremely civile and polite to all strangers, indeed it is their Intrest so to do for the whole Town may be consider'd as one great Inn fited up for the reception of all comers and goers. Upon the whole there is perhaps not a place in the known World that can equal this in affording refreshments of all kinds to Shipping. The Bay is Capacious, pretty safe and commodious, it lies open to the NW winds, which winds we are told very Seldom blow strong, but some times sends in a great sea for which reason Ships moor NE and SW and in such a manner as to have an open hawse with NW winds; the SE winds blows frequently with great Volience but as this is right out of the Bay it is attended with no danger. . . .

TUESDAY Apl. 16*th*. At 2 oClock in the PM saw a Large Ship behind the Island under French Colours standing into Table Bay. At 3 Wieghd with a light breeze at SE and put to Sea. At 4 Departed this Life Mr Robt Molineux Master, a young man of good parts but had unfortunately given himself up to extravecancy and intemperance which brought on disorders that put a pirod to his life. At 6 we had the Table mountain and the Penguin Island in one bearing sse, distant from the latter about 4 or 5 miles. Had it calm most part of the night, in the morning a light breeze sprung up Southerly with which we steer'd nw. At Noon we were by observation in Lat. 33°30′ South. The Table mountain bore s 54° e distant 14 Leagues. – N.B. The Table Mountain lies dire[c]tly over the Cape Town from which last I take my departure, it lies in the Latitude of 33°56′ South and Longitude 341°37′ West from Greenwich.

* * *

MONDAY 29*th. Winds SE. Courses N 53° Wt. Distce saild miles 136. Latitude in South 17°19′. Longd in West from Greenwich 0°50′. D° Gales. Variation 13°53′ w.* In the am cross'd the line of our first Meredean, viz. that of Greenwich having now circumnavigated the Globe in a west direction.

TUESDAY 30*th. Winds SE. Courses N 58° Wt. Distce saild miles 126 Ms. Lat. in South 16°11′. Long in West 2°42′.* Fresh gales & pleasant weather. Exercised the People at Great Guns & Small Arms.

[MAY 1771]

WEDNESDAY 1*st. Winds SE.* Fresh Trade and pleasant weather. At 6 in the am Saw the Island of St Helena bearing West distant 8 or 9 Leagues. At Noon Anchord in the Road before James Fort in 24 fathom water. Found riding here His Majestys Ship Portland, Swallow Sloop and 12 sail of Indiamen. At our first seeing this fleet in the Road we took it for granted that it was a war, but in this we were soon agreeably deceived. The Europa Indiaman Anchor'd here a little before us, she saild from the Cape two days after us and brings an account the French Ship we saw standing into Table Bay was a French Man of War of 64 Guns bound to India and that more were on their passage.

THURSDAY 2*nd. Winds SE. At Anchor in St Helena Road.* Clear pleasant weather. In the pm Moor'd with the Kedge Anchor, and in the am recieved some few Officers stores from the Portland.

FRIDAY 3*rd. Winds Do. At Anchor in St Helena Road.* D° Wea^r. Employ'd repairing sails, overhauling the Rigging &c^a.

SATURDAY 4*th. Winds Do. At Anchor in St Helena Road.* Little wind and pleasent weather. At 6 In the AM the Portland made the Signal to unmoor and at Noon to wiegh at which time the Ships began to get under sail.

SUNDAY 5*th. Winds EBS. Courses N* 50°30' *Wt. Distce saild miles* 71. *Lat. in South* 15°5'. *Longd in West* 6°46'. Gentle breezes and clear wea^r. At 1 PM weigh'd and Stood out of the Road in Company with the Portland and 12 Sail of Indiamen. At 6 oClock James Fort St Helena bore E^1/$_2$s distant 3 Leagues. In the AM found the Variation to be 13°10' W.

MONDAY 6*th. Winds ESE. Courses N* 47^1/$_2$° *Wt. Distce saild miles* 122. *Lat. in South* 13°42'. *Longd in West* 8°27'. Moderate breezes and Clowdy weather. Sailing in Company with the fleet.

TUESDAY 7*th. Winds SE. Courses N* 46° *Wt. Distce saild miles* 137. *Lat. in South* 12°5'. *Longd in West* 10°9'. Weather as yesterday. In the AM found the Var^n to be 12°5' West. Exercized the people at Great Guns & Small Arms.

WEDNESDAY 8*th. Winds SE. Courses N* 46°45' *Wt. Distce saild miles* 126. *Lat. in South* 10°39'. *Longd in West* 11°42'. A Steady breeze and pleasent weather. All the Fleet in company.

THURSDAY 9*th. Winds SEBS. Courses NW. Distce saild miles* 118. *Lat in South* 9°16'. *Longd in West* 13°7'. No Alteration in the weather. In the evening found the Variation to be 11°42' West.

FRIDAY 10*th. Winds Do. Courses NW. Distce saild miles* 120. *Lat in South* 7°51'. *Longd in West* 14°32'. At 6 in the AM saw the Island of Ascension bearing NNW distant 7 Leagues. Made Signal to speak with the Portland and soon after Capt Elliot himself came on board to whome I dilivered a letter for the Admiralty and a box containing the Ships common Log books and some of the Officers Journals &c^a. I did this because it seem'd probable that the Portland would get home before [us] as we sail much heavier than any of the fleet. At Noon the Island of Ascension bore EBS Distant 4 or 5 Leagues – by our Observations it lies in the Latitude of 7°54′ s and Longitude of 14°18′ West. A NWBN Course by Compass or NW a little westerly by the Globe, from Sᵗ Helena will bring you directly to this Island.

SATURDAY 11*th. Winds SEBS. Courses N 42° Wt. Distce saild miles* 117. *Lat. in South* 6°24′. *Longd in West of Greenw*ʰ 15°51′. A Steady Trade wind and pleasent weather. At ½ past 6 PM the Island of Ascension bore SE³⁄₄E Distᵗ 11 or 12 Leagues. Sailing in company with the fleet.

*   *   *

SUNDAY 19*th. Winds SE to SBE. Courses N 20° Wt. Distce saild miles* 98. *Lat in North* 4°32′. *Longd in West of Greenw*ʰ 21°58′. Clowdy unsettled weather with some rain. In the AM found the Variation by the Ampᵈᵉ and Azᵗʰ 7°40′ West. Hoisted a boat out and sent on board the Houghton for the Surgeon Mʳ Carret in order to look at Mʳ Hicks who is so far gone in a Consumption that his Life is de[s]paired of. Obserⁿ at Noon 16 Miles to the northward of the Log.

*   *   *

WEDNESDAY 22*nd. Winds Do. Courses NNW*³⁄₄*W. Distce saild miles* 58. *Lat in North* 6°58′. *Longd in West* 25°38′. Variable unsettled weather with rain. About 9 oClock in the AM the Portland shortend Sail for the Sternmost Ships to come up as we emagined, this gave us an oppertunity to get a head of the fleet after which we made such Sail as was necessary to keep in company.

THURSDAY 23*rd. Winds East to NE. Courses N 25° Wt. Distce saild miles* 56. *Lat in North* 7°49′. *Longd in West* 26°2′. Little wind from the Eastward with frequent Showers of Rain and hazey weather. The fleet a Stern of us all this Day. At Noon we shorten'd Sail for them to come up the headmost being about 2 Leagues off.

FRIDAY 24*th. Winds NE & NNE. Courses N 54° Wt. Distce saild miles* 92. *Lat in North* 8°42′. *Longd in West* 27°18′. First part Moderate breezes and hazey with rain, the latter a fresh breeze and fair. At 3 oClock in the PM find[ing] the fleet to come fast up with us we made all the Sail we could. Soon after it became hazey and we lost sight of them untill near 6 when it cleared up a Little and we saw three Sail abreast of us, bearing East about 2 or 3 Miles distance, by this we saw that they not only kept a better wind but out saild us upon a wind. It became again hazey and we lost sight of them and notwithstanding we kept close upon a Wind alnight with as much sail out as we could bear there was not one sail in sight in the Morning.

SATURDAY 25*th. Winds NNE. Courses N* 50°15′ *Wt. Distce saild miles* 92. *Lat in North* 9°41′. *Longd in West* 28°30′. Moderate Trade wind and clowdy weather.

SUNDAY 26*th. Winds NEBN. Courses N* 46° *Wt. Distce saild miles* 92. *Lat in North* 10°47′. *Longd in West* 29°35′. A Steady Trade and Clowdy weather. About one oClock in the pm departed this life Lieut[t] Hicks and in the evening his body was commited to the Sea with the usual ceremonies; he died of a Consumption which he was not free from when we saild from England so that it may be truly said that he hath been dieing ever sence, tho he held out tollerable well untill we got to Batavia.

MONDAY 27*th. Winds NE. Courses N* 39° *Wt. Dist saild miles* 103. *Lat in North* 12°7′ *Longd in West Greenw[h]* 30°40′. A Steady fresh Trade and Clowdy weather. This day I gave M[r] Charles Clerk an order to Act as Lieutenant in the Room of M[r] Hicks deceased, he being a young Man extremely well quallified for that station.

*   *   *

[JUNE 1771]

WEDNESDAY 19*th. Winds S to SW. Courses N* 73° *E. Distce saild miles* 127. *Lat in North* 40°9′. *Longde in West of Greenwich* 36°44′. Fresh gales and Clowdy. At 2 oClock in the PM found by observation the Same error in our Longitude as yesterday which I have now Corrected, the Long[de] of this day is that resulting from observation. At 10 oClock in the AM Saw a Sail ahead which we soon came up with and sent a boat on board she was a Schooner from Road Island out upon the Whale fishery – from her we learnt that all was peace in Europe and that the

America disputes were made up, to Confirm this the Master said that the Coat on his back was made in Old England.[47] Soon after leaving this Vessel we spoke anothir from Boston and saw a third all out on the same account.

THURSDAY 20*th. Winds SW, NW, North. Courses N 80½° E. Distce saild miles* 121. *Lat in North* 40°29'. *Longde in West of Greenwich* 33°10'. Fresh gales & Clowdy with some showers of rain. At day light in the morning saw a Sail a head standing to the E. A Swell from the NNW.

FRIDAY 21*st. Winds Northerly. Courses EBN. Distce saild miles* 128. *Lat in North* 40°53'. *Longde in West of Greenwich* 30°20'. Fresh gales & Clowdy. In the PM Saw a Sail a Stern Standing to the SE and at 11 oClock AM Saw from the Mast head 13 Sail of Stout Ships which we took to be the East India fleet.

SATURDAY 22*nd. Winds N to NE. Courses North* 81° E. *Distce saild miles* 114. *Lat in North* 41°11'. *Longd in West* 27°52'. Fresh gales with Squalls attend[ed] with Rain. In the Evening had 14 Sail in sight, 13 upon our lee quarter and a Snow upon our lee bow. In the night Split both Topg^t Sails so much that they were obliged to be unbent to repair. In the Morning the Carpenter reported the Main Top m^t to be sprung in the Cap which we supposed happen'd in the PM when both the weather backstays broke, our Rigging and Sails are now so bad that some thing or another is giving way every day. At Noon had 13 Sail in Sight which are well assured are the India fleet and are all now upon our weather quarter.

SUNDAY 23*rd. Winds NEBN to ENE. Courses S* 69½° E. *Distce saild miles* 80. *Lat in North* 40°43'. *Longd in West* 26°13'. Fresh gales & Squally attend[ed] with showers of Rain. In the Evening all the fleet were to windward of us and in the Morn not one was to be seen.

*   *   *

---

47. A reference to the colonial non-importation agreements of 1768-9, which set American patriots to wearing home-spun. [B]

[JULY 1771]

SUNDAY 7*th*. *Winds NNE & NW. Courses N* 50° *E. Distce saild in miles* 49. *Lat in North* 46°16'. *Longde in West* 9°39' *Accot* 9°29' *Obn.* Gentle Breezes & Clear weather. In the evening found the Variation by the Amp^{de} to be 22°30' w. At 9 AM spoke a Brig from Liverpool bound to Porto and some time after another from London bound to the Grenades, she had been three Days from Scilly and reckoned her self in the Longitude of a bout 10° West, which was about 40' to the westward of what we found our selves to day by Observ^n. We learnt from this Vessell that no accounts had been received in England from us and that Wagers were held that we were lost, it seems highly improbable that the letters sent by the Dutch Ships from Batavia should not be come to hand, as it is now five months sence these Ships Saild from the Cape of Good Hope.

MONDAY 8*th*. *Winds NNW to SW. Courses N* 46°45' *E. Distce saild in miles* 43. *Lat in North* 46°45'. *Longde in West* 8°54'. Little wind and hazey weather. Swell from ye Northward.

TUESDAY 9*th*. *Winds S Westerly. Courses N* 21° *E. Distce saild in miles* 100. *Lat in North* 48°19'. *Longde in West* 8°1' *pr Accot* 8°7' *pr Obn.* Fore & Middle parts a Gentle breeze & thick Foggy weather, remainder a fresh breeze & Clowdy, a Swell from the NNW all day.

WEDNESDAY 10*th*. *Winds Westerly. Courses N* 44° *E. Distce saild in miles* 97. *Lat in North* 49°29'. *Longde in West* 6°18'. Pleasent breezes & Clear weather. At 6 o'Clock in the Morning Sounded and Struck ground in 60 fathom, Shells & Stones by which I judged we were the Length of Scilly Isles. At Noon we saw Land from the Mast head bearing North which we judged to be about the Lands end. Soundings 54 f^m Course grey sand.

THURSDAY 11*th* July. Steady fresh breeze and Clear weather. At 2 In the PM saw the Lizard land and at 6 o'Clock the Light Houses bore NW Distant 5 Leagues, we being at this time by my Reckoning in the Longitude of 5°30 w. Soon after saw two Ships under their Topsails between us and the [land] which we took for Men of War. At 7 oClock in the Morning the Start Point bore NWBN distant 3 Leagues, and at Noon we Reckoned our selves about 5 Leagues short of Portland. This Fore noon a small cutter built Vessel came under our Stern and enquired after the India fleet, which they said they were cruzing for and had not seen.

FRIDAY 12*th*. Winds at sw a fresh gale with which we Run briskly up Channell. At ½ past 3 PM pass'd the Bill of Portland and at 7 Peverell point. At 6 AM pass'd Beachy head at the distance of 4 or 5 Miles, at 10 Dungenness at the distance of 2 Miles and at Noon we were abreast of Dover.

*   *   *

[*On Saturday, 13 July, the* Endeavour *anchored in the Downs, off Kent, and Cook went ashore 'in order to repair to London'. A pilot came aboard and took the ship into Galleon's Reach in the Thames. Cook added a postscript to his journal, which concludes as follows.*]

I hope it will not be taken a Miss if I give it as my opinion that the most feasable Method of making fu[r]ther discoveries in the South Sea is to enter it by the way of New Zeland, first touching and refreshing at the Cape of Good Hope, from thence proceed to the Southward of New Holland for Queen Charlottes Sound where again refresh Wood and Water, takeing care to be ready to leave that place by the latter end of September or beginning of October at farthest, when you would have the whole summer before you and after geting through the Straight might, with the prevailing Westerly winds, run to the Eastward in as high a Latitude as you please and, if you met with no lands, would have time enough to get round Cape Horne before the summer was too far spent, but if after meeting with no Continent & you had other Objects in View, than haul to the northward and after visiting some of the Islands already discover'd, after which proceed with the trade wind back to the Westward in search of those before Mintioned, thus the discoveries in the South Sea would be compleat.

Jam.^s Cook

THE SECOND VOYAGE

1772–1775

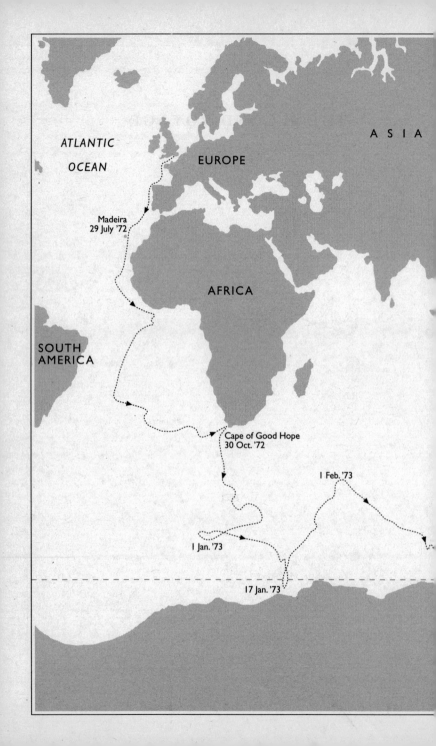

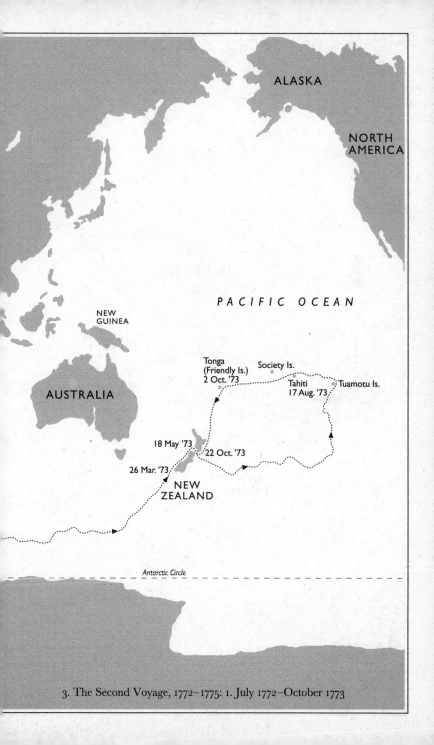

ALASKA

NORTH
AMERICA

PACIFIC OCEAN

NEW
GUINEA

AUSTRALIA

Tonga
(Friendly Is.)
2 Oct. '73

Society Is.

Tahiti
17 Aug. 1773

Tuamotu Is.

18 May '73

22 Oct. '73

26 Mar. '73

NEW
ZEALAND

Antarctic Circle

3. The Second Voyage, 1772–1775: 1. July 1772–October 1773

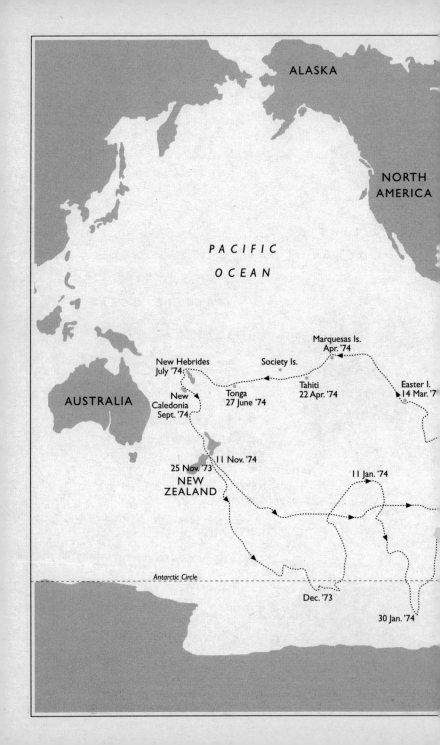

ALASKA

NORTH
AMERICA

PACIFIC

OCEAN

Marquesas Is.
Apr. '74

New Hebrides   Society Is.
July '74

AUSTRALIA   Tahiti   Easter I.
                                          22 Apr. '74   14 Mar. '7
          New   Tonga
          Caledonia 27 June '74
          Sept. '74

              11 Nov. '74

25 Nov. '73   11 Jan. '74
   NEW
ZEALAND

Antarctic Circle

                        Dec. '73

                                    30 Jan. '74

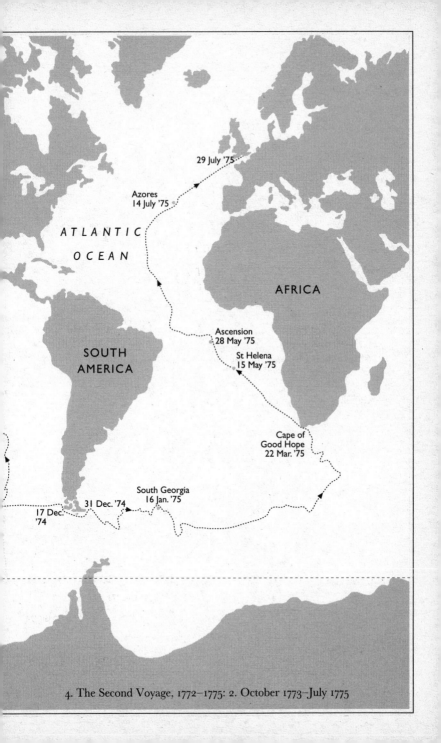

29 July '75

Azores
14 July '75

ATLANTIC

OCEAN

AFRICA

SOUTH
AMERICA

Ascension
28 May '75

St Helena
15 May '75

Cape of
Good Hope
22 Mar. '75

South Georgia
16 Jan. '75

31 Dec. '74

17 Dec.
'74

4. The Second Voyage, 1772–1775: 2. October 1773–July 1775

INTRODUCTION

On 14 August 1771 Lord Sandwich presented Cook to King George III in order to give him an account of the recently completed voyage; the king warmly complimented him on his achievement, and gave him the commission of his promotion from lieutenant to commander. Talk of a second voyage, chiefly to make a definitive search for the southern continent, was soon in the air. The *Endeavour* was being refitted to carry stores to the Falklands, and on 25 September the Admiralty instructed the Navy Board to purchase two proper vessels of about 400 tons 'for service in remote parts'. Cook had written to his old Whitby employer John Walker, saying of the *Endeavour* that 'a better ship for such a Service I could never wish for', and the new ships were both Whitby-built colliers, the *Marquis of Granby* and the *Marquis of Rockingham*. They were renamed *Drake* and *Ralegh*, but on consideration, the Admiralty not wishing to give offence to the Spaniards, they became *Resolution* and *Adventure* ('much properer', said Cook).

The new voyage was seen as an opportunity for a thorough test of the chronometer as a means of establishing longitude. A chronometer which remains accurate during months at sea in a pitching and rolling ship, with great variations in temperature, and which can tell the time at Greenwich when it is noon in one's location, will provide an indication of longitude more quickly and less painfully than the alternative method of celestial observation and lunar tables. The prolonged labours of John Harrison had produced the beautiful and compact watch 'H4', and an exact model of this by Larcum Kendall was to be carried on *Resolution*, while *Adventure* was to carry three chronometers made by John Arnold. The Board of Longitude made grants to enable two observers to join the expedition, one for each ship: William Wales and William Bayley.

Joseph Banks, maintaining his proprietary interest in Cook's endeavours, was making his own ambitious preparations for the scientific capability of the new voyage. He and Solander were to be accompanied by Dr James Lind of Edinburgh, for whom a Parliamentary grant of £4000 was obtained. (He is to be distinguished from the older James Lind, author of the revolutionary *Treatise of the Scurvy*, 1753.) Among the large entourage was the painter Zoffany and two horn-players. The early pages of Cook's journal give an unemotional account of the extraordinary story of the redesigning of the upper deck of the *Resolution* and the building of superstructures in order to provide accommodation for Banks and his team and their equipment, against the wishes not only of Cook but of Admiral Palliser, Comptroller of the Navy and Cook's long-time patron. When she left dock at Deptford and made her way down the Thames, the *Resolution* proved so over-laden and top-heavy that she was unsafe. Cook insisted that she be restored to her original condition, and in spite of fierce opposition from Banks he was supported by the Admiralty and the Navy Board. Midshipman Elliott wrote that when Banks saw the refashioned ship at Sheerness 'he swore and stamped upon the Warfe, like a Mad Man, and instantly ordered his Servants and all his things out of the Ship'.

A hurried replacement had to be made, and the German scientist Johann Reinhold Forster was appointed, with the grant intended for Lind. He took with him his seventeen-year-old son George. Forster was not at all an easy man to get on with, and there was to be a good deal of friction between him and the officers, including Cook. But he was a learned and able scientist, and his son was something of a genius. Beaglehole's intense loyalty to Cook made him constantly characterize Forster as a foolish mischief-maker, an 'incubus' on the voyage. At the Cape of Good Hope Forster brought in the Swedish scientist, Andreas Sparrman, as his assistant.

Cook's first lieutenant was Robert Palliser Cooper, his second Charles Clerke and his third Richard Pickersgill. Joseph Gilbert was master, and James Patten the surgeon. Among the midshipmen were James Burney, son of Dr Charles Burney the musicologist, later transferring to *Adventure* as second lieutenant, and the fourteen-year-old George Vancouver. William Hodges, a pupil of Richard Wilson, was the expedition's energetic and accomplished artist. In command of the *Adventure* was Tobias Furneaux, who had been Wallis's second lieutenant on the *Dolphin*.

Cook's instructions were really a version of his own desired plan, and gave him a great deal of freedom within the main intent of 'further discoveries towards the South Pole'. He was to concentrate on finding Cape Circumcision, which Bouvet had come across in 1739, and to ascertain whether or not it was the tip of the southern continent. (In fact it was the tip of a very small island which Cook never found and which by the end of the voyage he thought must have been an iceberg; see 21 February 1775.) He was to prosecute his discoveries in as high a latitude as possible, circumnavigating the globe until he reached the supposed position of Cape Circumcision again ('nearly in the Latitude of 54°00' South, and in about 11° 20' of Longitude East of Greenwich'; actually Bouvet Island is 54° 26' s, 3° 24' e). When the season made it unsafe to continue in high latitudes, he was to retire to the north until it was time to resume his quest.

The voyage itself was a series of probes into the Antarctic alternating with seasons of exploration in the Tropics, with New Zealand (visited three times) as a kind of hub in the great circling wheels of navigation. Twice the two ships lost contact for long periods. The first occasion was in February 1773 near Kerguelen Island. The ships were reunited in Queen Charlotte Sound, New Zealand, in mid-May; during the separation Furneaux made the first English contact with Van Diemen's Land (Tasmania). The second occasion was a complete separation as the ships were returning to New Zealand in October 1773. Cook took the *Resolution* unaccompanied on its second and most southerly probe of the Antarctic and its second and widest sweep among the islands to the north. The *Adventure*, which had suffered the cruel blow of the massacre of a boat's crew when it eventually reached Queen Charlotte Sound, set off alone on a southern route towards Cape Horn, and then made for home via the Cape of Good Hope.

As regards what Cook called 'the great object of my researches (viz) the Southern Continent' (see 2 August 1773), the results of the second voyage with the great and persistent daring of its challenge to ice and fog were negative: there was no southern continent, at least not in the form people hoped, though Cook agreed there might well be an icy continent near the Pole, useless to every one (see 21 February 1775). However, Cook spent less than half his time south of New Zealand, and much of the interest of his journal of this voyage is in the story of his encounters with places and people both familiar and unfamiliar – and sometimes totally unexpected: Tahiti and the Society Islands, the Tonga group (the Friendly Isles), Easter Island, the Marquesas, New Hebrides, New Caledonia.

Beaglehole had two versions of the journal in Cook's own hand to choose from. Both manuscripts are in the British Library (Add. MSS 27886 and 27888). Beaglehole rightly chose the first of these. The second, which he called 'B', is much fuller, but the narrative (which keeps civil time rather than the ship's time of the first) is muddled and messy. It is a version which is on its way to becoming something else, something much more ambitious than the first version. Beaglehole inserted many of B's amplifications into his text; these are not included here. However, MSS 27886 gives out as the *Resolution* leaves New Zealand for the last time (10 November 1774); what follows is from B, the second manuscript.

JOURNAL OF THE
SECOND VOYAGE
1772–1775

JOURNAL ON BOARD HIS MAJESTY'S BARK
RESOLUTION

NOVEMBER 28*th* 1771.[1] I received a Commission to command His
Majestys sloop Drake at this time in the Dock at Deptford, Burdthen
462 Tons to be man'd with 110 Men including officers & to carry
twelve guns: at the same time Captain Tobias Furneaux was appointed
to the command of the Raleigh at Woolwich Burdthen 336 Tons 80
Men & ten guns. These two sloops were both built at Whitby by M^r
Fis[h]burn the same as built the Endeavour Bark, the former about
fourteen and the latter eightteen months ago, and had just been
purchased into the Navy from Cap. William Hammond of Hull in
order to be sent on discoveries to the South Sea under my directions.
The Admiralty gave orders that they sould be fitted in the best manner
possible, the Earl of Sandwich at this time first Lord intrested himself
very much in the Equipment and he was well seconded by Mr Palliser
and Sr J^no Williams the one Comptroller and the other Surveyor of
the Navy, the Victualling Board was also very attentive in procuring
the very best of every kind of Provisions in short every department
seem'd to vie with each other in equiping these two Sloops: every
standing Rule and order in the Navy was dispenced with, every

1. Although as Cook notes on p. 230 this journal is kept in ship's time (with the day
running from noon to noon), he reverted to normal civil time when the ship was in
harbour for any length of time. The other version of Cook's journal ('B'), which takes
over on 11 November 1774, is in civil time throughout.

alteration, every necessary and usefull article was granted as soon as ask'd for.

Two days after I received my Commission I hoisted the Pendant and took charge of the Sloop accordingly and began to enter Seamen. . . .

Decem^r 25*th.* The Admiralty changed the sloops Names to Resolution and Adventure and the officers were order'd to take out new Comisions & Warrants accordingly.

Mr Banks and Dr Solander who accompanied me in my last Voyage intended to embark with me in this in order to prosecute their discoveries in Natural History and Botany and other usefull knowlidge, for this purpose Mr Banks intend to take with him several Draughtsmen &c^a. The Board of Longitude also came to a Resolution to send out an Astronomer in each sloop to make Astronomical Observations and also to make tryal of Mr Arnolds Watches and Mr Kendals Timepiece which were intended to be sent out with them. The Parliament voted Four thousand pounds towards carrying on Discoveries to the South Pole, this sum was intinded for Dr Lynd of Edinburgh as an incouragement for him to embark with us, but what the discoveries were, the Parliament meant he was to make, and for which they made so liberal a Vote, I know not. Mr Zoffani the famous portrait painter was one of those who had engaged to accompany Mr Banks, all these gentlemen except one Astronomer were to embark in the Resolution and to have large and seperate apartments: three of these gentlemen were not thought of when the sloop was purchased (viz.) the Astronomer, Dr Lynd and Mr Zoffani. The addition of these three persons intirely altered the plan of accommodations and it was found difficult to find room for the whole and at the same time to leave room for her officers and crew and stowage for the necessary stores and provisions, for this end the Navy Board was prevailed upon, tho contrary to the opinion of some of the members particularly the Comptroller, to alter their former plan which was to leave her in her original state and to raise her upper Works about a a foot, to lay a spar deck upon her from the quarter deck to the forecastle (she having at this time a low waist) and to build a round house or couch for my accommodations so that the great Cabbin might be appropriated to the use of Mr Banks alone. Things being thus resolved upon they were carried into execution with all possible dispatch and were about finished by the 6th of Feb[ry] following on which day we hauld out of the dry into the Wet Dock, and began to taken in Ballast, stores and to Rigg the masts &c[a] having by this time compleated our complement of men. On Wednesday 19th the Carpenters having nearly finish[ed] the different appartments of the Sloop, we hauld out of the Dock into the River and began to take in Provisions and the remainder of our stores &c[a] which was not compleated untill the 9th of Ap[r] when we saild from Deptford and the same evening stop'd a long side the sheer hulk at Woolwich where we were detain'd by contrary Winds untill the 22nd on which day with the Advantage of a Westerly wind we reached long reach and two days after were join'd by the Adventure. On the 25th we got on board our guns Powder & other ordnance stores, our draught of Water at this time was 17 feet. Notwithstanding this great depth of water we had reson to think that she would prove Crank and that she was over built; but as all the Gentlemens appartments were full of heavy baggage and the sloop a good deal lumber'd a loft with heavy, and some useless articles, which we might soon get rid of, or get into the hold after we had consumed some of our Provisions I still entertain'd hopes that she would bear all her additional Works and suspended giving any other opinion untill a full tryal had been made of her foreseeing what would be the consequence in case she did not Answer in the manner she was now fitted.

*   *   *

MAY 2*nd.* M[r] Banks gave an entertainment on board to the Earl of Sandwich, the French Embassador Cont de Guines and several other persons of distinction, the[y] were complimented at their coming on board and going a shore with all the honours due to their high ranks: the Earl of Sandwich was so attentive to the equipment of these two sloops that he had honour'd us with his presence on board several times before in order to be an eye witness of their state and condition, a laudable tho rare thing in a first Lord of the Admiralty. . . .

Captain Furneaux having received orders to proceed to Plymouth she sail'd accordingly, at the same time the Resolution had orders to proceed to the Downs under the direction of the first Lieutenant, I having obtain'd leave to be absent untill she arrived at that place, accordingly on the 10th in the morning they got under sail with a light breeze at North where it did not continue long before it came to the Eastward and obliged her to work down the River in which she made so little progress that it was the 14th before she reached the Nore, in this short passage she was found so crank that it was thought unsafe to proceed any further with her. This being represented to me with all its circumstances by Mr Cooper the first Lieutenant I laid the same before the Admiralty and seeing that it was absolutely necessary that something should be done to remove the evil complain'd of I proposed to cut down her poop, shorten her masts and to change her guns from six to four pounders: the Navy Board who was immidiately consulted upon the matter, propos'd not only to cut down her poop, but to take of her spar deck, lower her waist and to reduce her as near to her original state as could conveniently be done. Orders were now sent down for her to put into Sheerness where she anchor'd on the 18th and the officers of that yard recieved orders to cut her down agreeable to a Plan sent them by the Navy Board and which was confirmable to their proposals. While these matters were under consideration of the Admiralty and Navy Board others of a contrary nature were in aggitation by Mr Banks and his friends, as this gentlemen seem'd not to approve of the Ship at the first he now used all his influence to have her condem'd as totally unfit for the service she was going upon and to have a 40 gun Ship or an East Indiaman fitted out in her room, either of which would have been highly improper for makeing discoveries in remot parts. I shall not mention the arguments made use of by Mr Banks and his friends as many of them were highly absurd and advanced by people who were not judges of the subject one or two sea officers excepted who upon this occasion I beleive sacrificed their jud[ge]ment in support of their friendship, or some other montive, be this as it may the clamour was so great that it was thought it would be brought before the house of commons. The Admiralty and Navy Boards however persevered in their resolution of clearing her of all her superfluous works and remain'd firm in their opinion that after this was done she would answer in every respect better then any ship they could get. I was accordingly ordered to join her immidiately, to inspect into and forward these works and to point out such others as might tend to remove the evil complain'd of, a piece of service I went the more readily about as having not the least doubt with my self but that I must succeed, indeed I had it much at heart as she was the Ship of my choice and as I then thought and still think the properest Ship for the Service she is intended for of any I ever saw. On the 20th I set out for Sheerness and arrived thier the same evening and found every thing in great forwardness, the Poop and Spar deck was already taken away and Mr Huntt the Builder only waited to consult me about some little alteration he proposed to make in the waist from the Navy Boards Plan which the Board afterwards approved of. The next day I proposed to the Navy Board by letter to shorten her lower Masts two feet which they approved of and it was done accordingly. On Sunday 24th Mr Banks and Dr Solander came down to take a view of the Sloop as she was now altered and return'd to town again the same even^g and soon after Mr Banks declared his resolution not to go the Voyage, aledging that the Sloop was neither roomy nor convenient enough for his purpose, nor noways proper for the Voyage, these were the principal reasons Mr Banks assign'd for giving up a Voyage the preparing for which had cost him about five Thousand pounds, he probably had others which he did not care to declare, at least whoever saw the Sloop and the appartments that were alloted to him and his people could not help but think so. Be this as it may, not only Mr Banks and his whole suite but Dr Lind gave up the Voyage and their Baggage &c^a were got out of the Sloop and sent to London, after which no more complaints were heard for want of room &c^a.

On the 30th Mr Palliser the Comptroller of the Navy paid us a Visit in order to inspect into the several alterations that had been & were still to make, for this gentleman had taken upon him in spite of all that had been alledged against her to make her compleatly fit not only for the sea but for the service she was intended for, indeed if his advice had not been over ruled at first a great deal of unnecessary trouble and expence would have been saved not only to the Crown but to Mr Banks and every other person concerned. . . .

On the 10th of June the Earl of Sandwich having imbarked on board the Augusta Yacht in order to Visit the several Dock yards and inspect into the state of the Navy, anchor'd at the Nore and soon after landed in the yard and came on board the Resolution. His Lordship inspected into and was pleased to approve of all the alterations that had been made, after a stay of about an hour he return'd on board the yacht and saild directly for the Downs. Every thing being now nearly upon the point of finishing and having some business to settle in London I set out for that place in the Even^g and upon my arrival learnt that Mr John Reinhold Forster and his Son Mr George Forster were to imbark with me, gentlemen skill'd in Natural history and Botany but more especially the former, who from the first was desireous of going the Voyage and therefore no sooner heard that Mr Banks had given it up then he applyed to go. The Earl of Sandwich favoured his proposals which were approved of by His Majesty and a very handsome stipend allow'd him and his son; their Baggage and other necessarys being sent on board and I having finished my Business in Town I on Sunday morn the 21st tooke leave of my Family and set out, in company with Mr Wales the Astronomer for Sheerness where we arrived that evening and the next day saild out of the Harbour. Mr Hunt the Builder of the yard and some of the other officers attended us to the Nore where we try'd the Sloop upon a wind (having a fresh breeze at South) and found her to answer exceeding well: her draught of Water at this time was 15 f^t 10 In. fore and abaft, a foot lighter than when she first went into Sheerness, one great point gain'd by cutting her down. . . .

*   *   *

[*The* Resolution *reached Plymouth on Friday, 3 July 1772, and found the* Adventure *waiting. The Earl of Sandwich and Sir Hugh Palliser came aboard to make a further inspection. The officers and crew were paid six months' wages, and the seamen received an additional two months' pay in advance 'to enable them to purchase necessarys for so long a Voyage'. Cook received his Instructions – which he already knew – and he gave a sealed copy of them to Furneaux.*]

Every thing being at length compleated we on *Monday* the 13th at Six o'Clock in the morning left Plymouth Sound with the Adventure in Company and stood to the sw with the wind at NW where I shall leave them and for the information of the curious give some account in what manner they are equiped. . . .

* * *

[*There were 118 aboard the* Resolution, *including William Hodges, 'Landskip painter', a late appointment who arrived at the last minute, and eighty-three aboard the* Adventure. *Cook lists the provisions aboard each ship in detail, noting their antiscorbutic value (sometimes optimistically).*]

It will be both unnecessary and tedious to enumerate the Naval Stores that are on board, for besides their Furniture of every kind which are all made of the very best materials, we have on board a variety of spare stores of every sort sufficient for so long a Voyage. We are also well provided with fishing Netts, Lines, Hooks, &cᵃ &cᵃ for catching of fish and in order to inable us to procure refreshments at such inhabited parts of the World as we might touch at where Money is of no Value, the Admiralty caused to be put on board each of the Sloops several Articles of Merchantdize, as well to trade with the Natives for Provisions as to make them presents to gain their friendship, their Lordships also caus'd to be struck a number of Medals, on the one side the Kings head and on the other the two Sloops & the time they were at first intended to sail from England, these Medals are to be distributed to the Natives of, and left upon New Discoveried countries as testimonies of being the first discovereries. I have before mentioned that the Resolution carried Twelve carriage guns 4 pounds and the Adventure Ten, they have likewise an equal number of swivels with all other Arms and ammunition in proportion. On Board each of the Sloops is the frame, or all the parts compleat of a small Vesel of about twenty tons burdthen which can be put together in a little time whenever they may be wanting.

From this general View of the equipment the impartial reader who is a judge of Marine affairs will probably conclude with me that whatever may be the event of the expedition, the Ships are both well choosen and well provided.

The Board of Longitude were not wanting on their part in providing the Astronomers with the very best of I[n]struments both for makeing

Celestial and Nautical Observations but as the principal object these
gentlemen are sent out upon is to assertain the going of Mr Kendall's
Watch and three of Mr Arnolds, they employ'd themselves during our
stay at Plymouth in makeing the necessary Observations on Drakes
Island – & at 7 o'Clock in ye even^g on the Friday before we departed
the Watches were put in motion in the presence of my self Captain
Furneaux, the first Lieutenant of each of the Sloops, the two astronomers and Mr Arnold and afterward put on board: Mr Kendals and
one of Mr Arnolds on board the Resolution and the other two of M^r
Arnolds on board the Adventure: the Commander, First Lieutenant
and Astronomer on board each of the Sloops had each of them Keys
of the Boxes which containd the Watches and were allways to be
present at the winding them up and comparing the one with the other.
Mr Kendalls Watch when put in motion was seven tenths of a second
fast of mean time and its rate of going when try'd at Greenwich was
five eights of a second per day slow of mean time. Mr Arnolds Watch
when put in motion was Ten seconds and a half slow of mean time
and its rate of going at Greenwich was fourteen Seconds & Sixty two
hundreds part of a second Pr Day slow of mean time, from these datas
the rate of their going will hereafter be determined.

By the observations made on Drakes Island its Lat. is 50°21′30″ N
and Longitude 4°20′ West from Greenwich, hence by the help of a
Survey of Plymouth Sound made by Mr Gilbert the Master I find
Ram head from which I take my departure to lay in Latitude 50°19′
N and Longitude 4°23′ W. I shall now return to the Sloops which I left
standing to the SW on the Monday ye 13th on the Noon of which day
Ram head at the West entrance of Plymouth Sound bore NNE¾E
distant Seven Leagues. Before I go on regularly with the Transaction
of each day it will be necessary to premise that the day is supposed to
begen and end at Noon, that is Tuesday will now begin on Monday
Noon and end on Tuesday Noon, at which time Wednesday begins
&c^a, that all the bearings and Courses are the true bearings & Courses
and not by Compass and that the proportion between the length of
the Logg line and half minute glass by which the Sloops Way is
measured, is as 50 feet is to 30 seconds of time, the Longitude is
reckoned west from the Meridian of Greenw^h.

* * *

[*The two ships made their way south, calling at Funchal in Madeira, where they took on board 'a large supply of Wine, fruit & other necessarys', and also at Porto da Praia on S. Tiago (Cape Verde Islands) from 13 to 15 August, to replenish their water for the long haul to the Cape of Good Hope. On 20 August, Henry Smock, one of the carpenter's mates, fell while working over the side and was drowned. They crossed the Line on 9 September and 'the ancient custom of Ducking &c.ᵃ was observed and . . . the People were made not a little merry with the liquor given them by the Gentle''. The ships continued south with little incident, except for the death of two of the* Adventure*'s midshipmen from an unidentified illness, until the end of October.*]

[OCTOBER 1772]

SATURDAY 30*th.* *Therm.* 61. *Winds NNW. Latd in South* 33°53′. Fresh gales with rain in the night. At 2 pm Saw the land of the Cape of Good Hope, the Table Mountain which is over the Cape Town bore ESE Distant 12 or 13 Leagues. At 7 AM Anchored in Table Bay (the Adventure in Company) in 5 fathom Water Green Point or the West point of the Bay NWBW and the Church SWBS, Distant from Shore one Mile. Sent an officer to Notify our arrival to the Governor and on his return saluted the Garrison with Eleven Guns which was returned. Moored NE & SW a Cable each way, hoisted out the Long boat and began to prepare to heel and Water the Sloop &cᵃ. At this time we have not one man on the Sick list, the People in general have injoy'd a good state of health ever since we left England. Last night while we were off Penguin Island the Whole sea became all at once illuminated, or what the Seamen calls all on fire, some Water was taken up from along side in which were an immence number of small Globular Insects about the size of a Common Pins head and quite transparrant; this appeerence of the Sea is very common in all parts I have been in, but the cause is not so generally known.

As soon as I landed I waited upon the Governor Baron Plettenberg, who told me that he had received Instructions from Holland relating to these two Sloops and that I might be assured of every assistance the place could afford. My next care was to procure the necessary

Provisions and stores wanting, to get the Sloops caulked and to prepare the Casks for the Brandy, Wine and other Provisions all which was set about without delay. But as the Bread we wanted was yet unbaked and all the Spirits to be brought out of the Country it was the 18 of the following Month before every thing was got on board and the 22nd before we could put to Sea. During this stay the Crews of both Sloops were served every Day with new baked Bread fresh Beef or Mutton and as much greens as they could eat, they had also leave to go on shore 10 or 12 at a time to refresh themselves.

Messrs Wales and Baily the two Astronomers were on Shore all the time makeing the necessary astronomical observations in order to assertain the going of the Watches and other purposes. Mr Kendalls Watch thus far has been found to answer beyond all expection, but this cannot be said of Mr Arnolds. The Longitude of the Cape Town pointed out by these watches is already mentioned in their proper Columns. By observa^{ns} made here Mr Kendals Watch is found to have altered its rate of going something more than one second p^r Day by gain^g ⅞ of a Second p^r Day on mean time whereas at Greenwich it lost ⅝ p^r day, this variation however is very inconsiderable. Mr Arnolds was found to loose on Mean time by the mean rate of its going for twelve days 1′31″, 0125 per day which is 1′17″, 63 more than at Greenwich and also varied in its rate sometimes more than half a minute p^r Day, however one of Mr Arnolds on board the Adventure kept time in such a manner as not to be complained on. Mr Forster met with a Swedish Gentleman here, one Mr Sparman, who understood something of Botany and Natural History and who was willing to embarque with us, Mr Forster thinking that he would be of great assistance to him in the Course of the Voyage strongly importuned me to take him on board which I accordingly did.

Mr Shank first Lieutenant of the Adventure having been in an ill state of health ever sence we left England and not recovering here, requested my leave to quit in order to return home for the reistablishment of his health, his requist appearing to be well founded I gave him leave accordingly and appointed Mr Burney one of my Midshipmen second Lieutenant of the Adventure in the room of Mr Kemp whom I appointed first.

[NOVEMBER 1772]

MONDAY 23*rd. Winds NBW to NWBW. Course S. 44° W. Distce sail'd* 56
miles. Latd in South 34°36'. *Longd in East of Greenwich* 17°34'. *Longd made
from the Cape of Good Hope* 0°49' *W.* First part moderate and Clowdy,
remainder fresh gales and squally with rain. At 3 pm weighed and
came to sail with the Adventure in Company. Saluted the Garrison
with 15 guns which compliment was returned. Made several trips to
get out of the Bay which we accomplished by 7 o'Clock at which time
the Town bore SE Distant 4 Miles. Stood to the Westw^d all night to
get an offing having the Wind at NNW and NW blowing in Squalls with
rain which obliged us to reef our Topsails, after having got clear of
the land I directed my Course for Cape Circumcision.[2]

TUESDAY 24*th. Winds NW, SW to SE. Course S* 12° *E. Distce sail'd* 50
miles. Latd in South 35°25'. *Longd in East of Greenwch* 17°44'. *Longd made
from the Cape of Good Hope* 0°39' *W.* Moderate gales and Clowdy Weather
with a large swell from Southward. In the PM served to each Man a
Fearnought Jacket and a pair of Trowers which were allowed by the
Admiralty. Many Albatroses about the Ship, some of which we caught
with Hook and line and were not thought dispiseable food even at a
time when all hands were served fresh Mutton.

*　　*　　*

SUNDAY 29*th. Winds WNW. Course South. Distce sail'd* 70 *miles. Latd in
South* 42°9'. *Longd in East of Greenwch* 17°14'. *Longd made from the Cape of
Good Hope* 1°9'. Strong gales with hard Squalls, rain & hail. At 7 pm
brought too under the Fore Sail, and at 3 am Made sail under the
Foresail, Mainsail and close reef'd Main Topsail, this last we were
soon after obliged to take in and at 10 to hand the Main sail and lay-to
under the Fore sail and to get down Topg^t Yards. Adventure in
Company.

MONDAY 30*th. Winds WNW. Course S* 66° *E. Distce sail'd* 33 *miles. Latd
in South* 42°24'. *Longd in East of Greenwch* 17°57'. *Longd made from the Cape
of Good Hope* 0°26'. Very hard gales with rain and hail, lying-to under

2. See introduction to this voyage.

a Mizen Stay-sail most part of these 24 hours, the Sea running very high. At 11 pm the Scuttle of the Boatswain Storeroom (not being properly secured) Washed or broke loose and before it was discovered we had two feet and a half Water in the Sloop, however it was soon secured and the Water Pumped out without any other damage than weting some stores &c^a betwixt Decks.

[DECEMBER 1772]

TUESDAY 1st. *Winds WNW. Course S 13° E. Distce sail'd 58 miles. Latd in South 43°21'. Longd in East Greenwch 18°10'. Longd made from the Cape of Good Hope 0°13'.* Hard gales and fair Weather. At 2 pm made sail under the Fore sail and Staysails and at 4 set the Mainsail. At 8 bro^t to under the Fore-sail untill daylight then set the Mainsail & M^n Topsail which we could not carry Long, being so very squally with rain. At 10 it was more moderate and we set the Main again.

WEDNESDAY 2nd. *Therm. 49½. Winds Westerly. Course S 40° E. Distce sail'd 40 miles. Latd in South 43°52'. Longd in East of Greenwh 18°45'. Longd made C. Good Hope 0°22' E.* First and latter parts fresh gales and Clowdy, the Middle little Wind. In the PM under our Courses and Staysails, in the night lay to under the Foresail, at 4 am made sail under the Courses and close reef'd Topsails. Sea running very high.

*   *   *

MONDAY 7th. *Therm. 42½. Winds SW, North, NW. Course S 10° E. Distce sail'd 83 miles. Latd in South 49°32'. Longd in East of Greenwh 18°46'. Longd made C. Good Hope 0°23' E.* PM Fresh gales and fair Weather, the night clear and serene and the rising Sun gave us such flatering hopes of a fine day that we were induced to Loose all the reefs out of the Topsails and get Topg^t Yards a Cross; before 8 o'Clock the Scene was changed, the Weather became hazey with rain and the gale increased so much as to oblige us to hand the Mainsail and close reefe the Topsails and to get down Topg^t yards again. The Barometer at 28½ which is unusally low.

TUESDAY 8th. *Therm. 40. Winds NW. Course S 84° E. Distce sail'd 39 miles. Latd in South 49°36'. Longd in East of Greenwh 19°45'. Longd made*

C. G. Hope 1°22′. *East*. Very hard gales and Hazey with rain. At 1 PM took in the Topsails and Foresail Wore and brought to under the Mizen Staysail, Struck Topg^t mast and got the Spritsail yard in fore and aft. At 8 am Wore and lay too on the other Tack, the gale something moderater, but the Sea runs very high, this together with the Weather which we think very cold, makes great distruction among our Hogs, Sheep and Poultry, not a night passes without some dying, with us, however, they are not wholy lost for we eat them notwithstanding.

WEDNESDAY 9*th*. *Therm*. 36. *Winds NW to West*. *Course S* 68° *E*. *Distce sail'd* 27 *miles*. *Latd in South* 49°49′. *Longd in East of Greenwh* 20°24′. *Longd made C. G. Hope* 2°1′ *East*. *Var of the Compass* 16°34′. Hard gales and hazy weather. At 2 pm made the Signal for the Adventure to come under our Stern and Set the Fore Topmast Staysail, in the Even saw two Penguins and some Weed, Sounded without finding ground with 100 fathoms. At 8 Wore and lay to on the other Tack till 3 am, then wore again, Squaly with Showers of Snow. At 8 made the Signal for the Adventure to make sail and at 10 made sail our selves under the Courses and close reef'd Topsails, Weather more moderate and fair, but a very high Westerly Sea. Many birds in sight.

THURSDAY 10*th*. *Therm*. 36½. *Winds W to NW*. *Course SBE*. *Distce sail'd* 69 *miles*. *Latd in South* 50°57′. *Longd in East of Greenwh* 20°45′. *Longd made C. G. Hope* 2°22′. Fresh gales with a great Sea from the Westward, in the night Frost and in the am Showers of Snow and Sleet. At 6 pm took in the Topsails and at 8 the Mainsail and bro^t to under Foresail and Mizen. In the Morn made sail under Courses and Topsails and made the Signal for the Adventure to go a head. At 6 saw an Island of Ice to the Westward, the Wind abating Loosed all the Reefs out of the Topsails, got Spritsail and Topsail Yards across and made the Signal for the Adventure to come under our Stern.

FRIDAY 11*th*. *Therm*. 34. *Winds N to Wt*. *Course S* 28° *E*. *Distce sail'd* 65 *miles*. *Latd in South* 51°37′. *Longd in East of Greenwh* 25°28′. *Longd in pr. Kendalls Watch* 25°28′. *Longd made C. G. Hope* 3°7′. Fresh gales Fogy and Hazy with Snow & Sleet. At 1 pm saw an Island of Ice right a head distant one Mile, which the Adventure took for land and made the Signal accordingly and hauled her Wind till I made the Signal for her to come in under our Stern. Reef'd the Topsails and sounded but had no ground at 150 f^{m} Spent the night makeing short trips under an easy Sail, the Wind blowing fresh in Squals with Sleet & Snow. In the Morn stood to the Southward with the wind at West. A little before noon pass'd two Islands of Ice one on each side. Saw some Birds which were about the size of Land Pigions, shaped like Fulmers, Plumage White as Snow, with blackish Bills and feet. I believe them to be intirely new as I never saw any such Sea Birds before and Mr Forster has no knowlidge of them.

SATURDAY 12th. *Winds NW, North, & NW. Course S* 20½° *W. Distce sail'd* 71 *miles. Latd in South* 52°56'. *Longd in E. Greenwhich Reck.g* 20°50'. *Longd made C. G. Hope* 2°27' *East.* Fresh gales and Hazy Foggy weather with sleet and snow. In the PM stood to the SW with the Wind at West & WNW which in the night veer'd to North at which time the Therm^{r} was one degree below the Freezing point, kept on a wind all night under an easy sail and in the Morn made all the Sail we could and Steer'd SW with the Wind at NW. Pass'd Six Islands of Ice this 24 hours, some of which were near two Miles in circuit and about 200 feet high, on the Weather side of them the Sea broke very high, some Gentlemen on Deck saw some Penguins.

SUNDAY 13th. *Therm* 31½. *Winds North, NW to SW. Course S* 10° *E. Distce sail'd* 65 *miles. Latd in South* 54° 0'. *Longd in E. Greenwhich Reck.g* 21°9'. *Longd made C. G. Hope* 2°46' *East.* Continued a SW Course With the Wind at NNW untill 8 PM then hauld close under our Topsails, the Wind soon after came to the west and in the Morn to SW and freshen'd, Hazey with Snow and Sleet all the 24 hours, the Thermometer generally below or at the freezing point so that our Sails and Rigging were chequered with Ice. Pass'd 18 Islands of Ice, many loose pieces and saw more Penguins.

MONDAY 14th. *Therm. In the Night* 29. *Winds Westerly. Course S* 34° *E. Distce sail'd* 66 *miles. Latd in South* 54°55'. *Longd in E. Greenwhich Reck.g* 22°13', *Watch* 22°1'. *Longd made C. G. Hope* 3°50'. Fore and Middle parts fresh gales and hazy with showers of Snow. Stood to the SSE with the Wind at SW from Noon till 8 pm in which time twenty Islands of Ice presented themselves to our View. We now sounded but found no ground with 150 fathoms of line. Tacked and stood to the northward under an easy sail untill Midnight then stood to the South and in the Morn set the Courses and staysails. At half past six we were stoped by an immence field of Ice to which we could see no end, over it to the SWBS we thought we saw high land, but can by no means assert it. We now bore away SSE, SE & SEBS as the Ice trended, keeping close by the edge of it, where we saw many Penguins and Whales and many of the Ice Birds, small grey Birds and Pintadoes. At 8 o'Clock bro^t to under a Point of the Ice and sent on board for Captain Furneaux, fixed on Rendizvouze in case of seperation, agreed on some other matters for the better keeping Company and after breakfast he return'd to his Sloop and we made sail along the Ice, but before we hoisted the boat in we took up several pieces which yeilded fresh Water, at Noon had a good observation both for determining the Latitude and Longitude by the Watch.

TUESDAY 15th. *Winds NW, North, NE, NW. Course S 47½ E. Distce sail'd 23 miles. Latd in South 55°10′. Longd in Greenwich pr. Reck.g 22°43′. Longd in C. G. Hope 4°20′.* Gentle breezes and pretty clear weather in the PM, steer'd SE along the edge of the Ice till one o'Clock when we came to a point round which we hauled SSW there appearing a Clear sea in that direction, after running 4 Leagues upon this Course (always along the edge of the Ice) we found our selves in a manner surrounded by it which extended from the NNE round by the West and South to the East farther then the Eye could reach in one compact body, some few places excepted, where Water was to be seen like Ponds, in other places narrow creeks run in about a Mile or less, high hills or rather Mountains of Ice were seen within this Feild ice and many Islands of Ice without in the open Sea, Whales, Penguins and other Birds. At 5 o'Clock we hauld away East with the Wind at North in order to get clear of the Ice, the extream East point of which at 8 o'Clock bore EBS, over which there appeared clear Water. We spent the night standing off and on under our Topsails as also the remainder of the

Day being so Foggy at times that we could not see a Ships length. Betwixt 12 at night and 7 in the Morn 4 Inches thick of Snow fell on the Decks the Thermometer most of the time five degrees below the Freezing point so that our Rigging and sails were all decorated with Icikles. We found a Current setting SE about ¾ of a Mile pʳ hour, at the same time a Thermometer which in the open air was at 32°, in the Surface of the Sea 30° and after being Imerged 100 fathoms deep for 20 Minutes came up at 34° which is only 2° above freezing.

* * *

THURSDAY 17th. *Therm. 33½. Winds NW. Course S 76° E. Distce sail'd 34 miles. Latd in South 55°16'. Longd in Greenwh pr. Reck.g 23°43'. Watch 23°28'. Longd made C. G. Hope 5°20' East. Varn of the Compass 20°50' West.* At 2 pm the Weather clearing up a little we made sail to the Southward and 4 Saw the Main field of Ice extending from SSW to SE and soon after to East, which obliged us to bear up to the East. At 10 o'Clock hauled upon a Wind to the Northward with an easy sail, Wind at WNW a gentle gale, Foggy and Hazy with Snow. At 4 am we stood to the South and after runing two Leagues was obliged to bear up again for the Ice along the edge of which we Steer'd betwix'd SSW and East, hauling into every opening without finding any inlet, snow showers continued but at times it was pretty clear so as to inable us to get observations for the Watch, Variation and Latitude. Many Islands and a great Deal of loose Ice without the Main feild. . . .

FRIDAY 18th. *Therm. 31. Winds NW to NE. Course N 20° E. Distce sail'd 18 miles. Latd in South 54°57'. Longd in Greenwh pr. Reckg. 24°6' Longd made C. G. Hope 5°43' East.* From Noon till 8 pm kept steering along the Ice, SSW, SE, East & NNE as we found it to trend, more broken Ice and small Islands without the Main Feild than usual, in so much that we had continualy some along side. At 8 we sounded but had no ground with 250 fathoms of line, after this we hauled close upon a Wind to the northward the evening being clear and serene (a rare thing here) we could see the firm Ice extending from SSW to NE but this happened not to be the northern point: for at 11 o'Clock we were obliged to Tack to avoide it, at 2 am we stood again to the northward thinking to clear it upon this Tack, but at 4 o'Clock we found this could not be done, it extending to our Weather bow in somuch that we were quite imbayed, we therefore Tack'd and stood to the Westward under all the Sail we could set, having a fresh breeze and clear weather, but the serenity of the sky lasted not long, at 6 o'Clock the Weather became hazey and soon after a Thick Fog. The gale freshened and brought with it snow and sleet which freezed on our Rigging and Sails as it fell, the Wind however veer'd more & more to the NE which inabled us to clear the Field Ice, though at the same time it carred us among the Islands which we had enough to do to keep clear of, of two evils I thought this the least. Dangerous as it is sailing a mongest the floating Rocks in a thick Fog and unknown Sea, yet it is preferable to being intangled with Field Ice under the same circumstances. The danger to be apprehended from this Ice is the geting fast in it where beside the damage a ship might receive might be detaind some time. I have heard of a Greenland Ship lying nine Weeks fast in this kind of Ice and at present we have no more appearence of thaw than they can have in Greenland; on the Contrary Fahranheits Thermometer keeps generally below the freezing point and yet it may be said to be the middle of summer. We have now sail'd 30 Leagues a long the firm Ice, which has extended nearly East and West, the Several Bays formed by it excepted, every one of which we have looked into without finding one open^g to the South. I think it reasonable to suppose that this Ice either joins to or that there is land behind it and the appearence we had of land the day we fell in with it serves to increase the probabillity, we however could see nothing like land either last night or this Morn, altho' the Weather was clearer than it has been for many days past. I now intend, after geting a few miles farther to the North, to run 30 or 40 Leagues to the East before I haul again to the South, for here nothing can be done.

* * *

SUNDAY 20*th. Thermr.* 34. *Winds NW to NE. Course N* 79°30' *E. Dist Sail'd* 92 *Miles. Lat. in South* 54°0'. *Longde in East pr. Reck.g* 28°14'. *Long. made C.G.H.* 9°50'. In the PM had thick hazy Weather untill 6 o'Clock when it cleared up and continued so till 6 am when the gale freshen'd at NNE and brought with it hazey weather Sleet and Snow the

Thermometer from 31° to 34. Ice Islands as usual of various extent both for height and circuit. Set all the Taylors to Work to lengthen the Sleves of the Seamens Jackets and to make Caps to shelter them from the Severity of the Weather, having order'd a quantity of Red Baize to be converted to that purpose. Also began to make Wort from the Malt and give to such People as had symptoms of the Scurvy; one of them indeed is highly Scorbutick altho he has been taking of the Rob for some time past without finding himself benifited therefrom, on the other hand the Adventure has had two men in a manner cured by it who came, even, from the Cape highly Scorbutick. Such another large brown bird or Albatross as we saw near the feild Ice I saw near the Ship last night: the common sort of Albatross seem not to like an Icey sea for we have only seen one now and then sence we came a mong the Islands.

MONDAY 21st. *Thermr.* 31 *to* 33½. *Winds North to West. Course S* 76° *E. Dist. Sail'd* 42 *Miles. Lat. in South* 54°10'. *Longde. in East pr. Reck.g* 29°24'. *Watch* 29°23'. *Long. made C.G.H.* 11°1'. *Var. of the Compass* 21°47'. Fresh gales and hazy with Snow untill 8 AM the gale then abating and the Weather clearing up, we hauld again to the Southward, the Course I now intend to Steer till I meet with Interruption. Ice Islands not so thick as usual nor quite so large. Had a Meridian observation to day which we have not had for some days past.

*   *   *

WEDNESDAY 23rd. *Thermr.* 32 *to* 34. *Winds Westerly. Course S* 55° *E. Dist. Sail'd* 56 *Miles. Lat. in South* 55°26'. *Longd. in East of Greenwich pr. Reck.g* 31°33'. *Longd. from C.G.H.* 13°10'. *Var. of the Compass* 23°56'. Moderate gales and clowdy with some Showers of Snow and hail in the night. In the pm sounded but had no ground with 130 f^m. In the am having but little Wind hoisted out a Boat to try the Current but found none. . . . Having not much Wind and the day being such as would be called a tolerable good Winters day in England Cap Furneaux dined with us and returned on board in the evening.

*   *   *

FRIDAY 25th. *Thermr.* 31 *to* 35½. *Winds East to South. Course S* 64½° *W.*

Dist. Sail'd 88 *Miles. Lat. in South* 57°50'. *Longd. in East of Greenwich pr.*
Reck.g 29°32'. *Longd. from C.G.H.* 11°9'. Gentle gales fair & Clowdy.
Therm^r from 31 to 35. At 2 pm being near an Island of Ice which was
about 100 feet high and four cables in circuit I sent the Master in the
Jolly Boat to see if any Fresh Water run from it, he soon returned
with an account that their was not one Drop or the least appearence
of thaw. From 8 to 12 am Sailed thro' several Floats or fields of loose
Ice extending in length SE and NW as far as we could see and about
¼ of a Mile in breadth, at the same time we had several Islands of
the same composission in sight. At Noon seeing that the People were
inclinable to celebrate Christmas Day in their own way, I brought the
Sloops under a very snug sail least I should be surprised with a gale
[of] wind with a drunken crew, this auction was however unnecessary
for the Wind continued to blow in a gentle gale and the Weather such
that had it not been for the length of the Day one might have supposed
themselves keeping Christmas in the Latitude of 58° North for the air
was exceeding sharp and cold.

SATURDAY 26*th. Thermr.* 35 *to* 31. *Winds Southerly. Course S* 64½° *W.*
Dist. Sailed 69 *Miles. Lat. in South* 58°31'. *Longde. East of Greenwich Reck.g*
27°37'. *Longd. made from C.G.H.* 8°34'. *Var. Compass* 19°25' *West.* Fresh
gales fair & Clowdy till towards Noon when it cleared up and we had
a very good observation; in the Course of this Days sail we passed
thro' Several Feilds of Broken loose Ice all of which lay in the direction
of NW and SE. The Ice was so close in one that it would hardly admitt
of a Passage thro, the pieces of this Ice was from 4 to 6 or 8 Inches
thick, broke into various sized pieces and heaped 3 or 4 one upon the
other, it appeared to have been constituted from clear water which
occasioned some on board to think that it came from some River.
The Ice in some other of the loose feilds appeared like Corral Rocks,
honey combed and as it were rotten and exhibited such a variety of
figuers that there is not a animal on Earth that was not in some degree
represented by it. We supposed these loose feilds to have broken from
the large feild we had lately left and which I now determined to get
behind, if possible, to satisfy my self whether it joined to any land or
no. To Day we saw some of the White Albatross with black tiped

Wings, some of the snow birds or White Peterls, Blue Peterls &c and a nother kind of a Peterls, which are a good deal like the Pintadoes, these as well as the White we have seen no where but a mong the Ice and but few at a time.

*   *   *

TUESDAY 29th. *Thermr.* 31 *to* 36. *Winds East. Course S* 72° *W. Dist. Saild* 90 *Miles. Lat. in South* 59°12′. *Longd. E. of Greenwh pr. Reck.g* 19°1′. *Long. Cape Good Hope* 0°38′ *E.* First part a fresh breeze, the remainder a gentle Breeze and clowdy with Showers of Snow. At 4 pm called in the Adventure by Signal, the Weather being so hazy that we could but just see her, and at 6 took a reef in the Topsails, having at this time Several Islands of Ice in sight. A[t] 4 am Saw Several Penguin. Loosed the Reefs out of the Topsails and Set Topg^t Sails. To Wards Noon I sent on Board for Captain Furneaux in order to communicate to him a resolution I had taken of runing as far West as the Meridian of Cape Circumcision, provided we met with no impediment, as the Distance is now not more than 80 Leagues the Wind favourable and the Sea pretty clear of Ice.

*   *   *

THURSDAY 31st. *Thermr.* 31 *to* 36. *Winds East to SE. Course S* 60° *W. Dist. Sailed* 71 *Miles. Lat. in South* 59°58′. *Longd. in East of Greenwich pr. Reck.g* 16°19′. *Long. made from C.G.H.* 4°04′ *W.* PM Gentle gales and Clowdy, Steering WBS with some Ice Islands in Sight, at 8 o'Clock steer'd NW being nearly the direct course for Cape Circumcision. At Midnight seeing some loose Ice ahead we hauled three point more to the north in order to avoide it but the very reverse happened, for after standing an hour NBW the Ice was so thick about us that we were obliged to tack and Stand back to the Southward till half past 2 am, when we stood for it again thinking to take some up to serve as Water; but we soon found this impracticable, the Wind which had been at EBN now veered to SE and increased to a fresh gale and brought with [it] such a Sea as made it dangerous for the Sloops to lay among the Ice, this danger was much heightened by discovering at 4 o'Clock (being then in Lat 59°20′) an immence field to the North of us, extending NEBE & SWBW in a compact body farther than the eye could reach, we were now near it and already in the lose parts, we immidiately wore, double reefed the Topsails, got our tacks on board and hauled to the Southward close upon a Wind, and it was not long before we got clear of the ice but not before we had receved several hard knocks for the pieces were of the largest sort. Struck Topg^t yards, at Noon had strong gales and Clowdy hazy Weather and only one Ice Island in sight, indeed they are now become so familiar to us that they are generaly pass'd unnoticed. While we were in the ice a Seal was seen.

[JANUARY 1773]

FRIDAY 1st. *Thermr.* 31 to 31^1/$_2$. *Winds SE to SBW. Course S 78° W. Dist. Sailed 66 Miles. Lat. in South* 60°12'. *Longd. in East of Greenwich pr. Reck.g* 12°13'. *Long. made C.G.H.* 6°12'. PM Strong gales and Hazy, which obliged us to Close reefe our Topsails, and at 8 o'Clock to hand them, at which time we wore and stood to the East ward under our two Courses, having a hard gale blowing in Squals and thick hazy weather with Snow and a very large Swell from the Eastward. At Midnight Wore and stood to the Westward, being in the Latitude 60°21' s wind at South a strong gale which toward noon abate'd so that we could set our Topsails Close reefed, but the Weather still continued thick and hazy with Snow which ornamented our Riging with Icikles.

SATURDAY 2nd. *Thermr.* 31 to 32. *Winds S West. Course N 48° W. Dist. Sailed 91 Miles. Lat. in South* 59°12'. *Longd. in East of Greenwich pr. Reck.g* 9°45' *Watch* 10°17'. *Long. made from C.G.H.* 8°38'. Fresh gales and hazy, with Showers of Sleet and Snow, till 9 am when it became fair and we loosed two Reefs out of the Topsails, the Wind had veered from South to West with which we stood to the Northward Pass'd 7 Ice Islands this 24 hours and saw some Penguins.

SUNDAY 3rd. *Thermr.* 31 to 32. *Winds West, NW to NE. Course S 82° E. Dist. Sailed 44 Miles. Lat. in South* 59°18'. *Longde. in East of Greenwich pr. Reck.g* 11°9'. *Longd. made C.G. Hope* 7°14'. In the PM the Weather cleared up and we were favoured with a Sight of the Moon, which we had seen but once before sence we left the Cape, we did not loose this oppertunity to observe the Distance betwixt her and the Sun, the

Longitude deduced th[e]refrom was 9°34½' East from Greenwich, being the mean of no less than 12 observations, M[r] Kendals Watch at the same time gave 10°6'E and our Latitude was 58°53½'s. The Variation of the Compass by the mean of several Azimuths was 12°8' West. We were now about 1½° or 2° of Longitude to the West of the Meridian of Cape Circumcision and at the going down of the sun 4°45' of Latitude to the Southward of it, the Weather was so clear, that Land even of a Moderate height might have been seen 15 Leagues, so that there could be no land betwixt us and the Latitude of 48°. In short, I am of opinion that what M. Bouvet took for Land and named Cape Circumcision was nothing but Mountains of Ice surrounded by field Ice. We our selves were undoubtedly deceived by the Ice Hills the Day we first fell in with the field Ice and many were of opinion that the Ice we run along join'd to land to the Southward, indeed this was a very probable supposission, the probabillity is however now very much lessened if not intirely set a side for the Distance betwixt the Northern edge of that Ice and our Track to the West, South of it, hath no where exceeded 100 Leagues and in some places not Sixty, from this it is plain that if there is land it can have no great extent North and South, but I am so fully of opinion that there is none that I shall not go in search of it, being now determined to make the best of my way to the East in the Latitude of 60° or upwards, and am only sorry that in searching after those imaginary Lands, I have spent so much time, which will become the more valuable as the season advanceth. It is a general recieved opinion that Ice is formed near land, if so than there must be land in the Neighbourhood of this Ice, that is either to the Southward or Westward. I think it most probable that it lies to the West and the Ice is brought from it by the prevailing Westerly Winds and Sea. I however have no inclination to go any farther West in search of it, having a greater desire to proceed to the East in Search of the land said to have been lately discovered by the French in the Latitude of 48½° South and in about the Longitude of 57° or 58° East.[3]

3. Kerguelen Island, 49° 30' s, 69° 30' E. Cook had heard at the Cape of its discovery by Yves de Kerguélen in 1772. Like Cape Circumcision, it was thought it might be the tip of the great southern continent.

The Clear Weather continued no longer then 4 o'Clock in the AM, by that time the Wind had veered to NE and blowed a strong gale attended with a thick Fogg with snow and sleet which froze on the Rigging as it fell, the fine Even^g had tempted us to loose the Reefs out of the Topsails and get Topg^t yards across, but were now fain to get them down again & close reef the Topsails.

MONDAY *4th. Winds NE to NNW. Course N* 82° *E. Dist. Sailed* 112 *Miles. Lat. in South* 58°55'. *Long. in East of Greenwich per Reck.g* 14°43'. *Long. Cape G. Hope* 3°40'. First and middle parts strong gales attended with a thick Fogg Sleet and Snow, all the Rigging covered with Ice and the air excessive cold, the Crew however stand it tolerable well, each being cloathed with a fearnought Jacket, a pair of Trowsers of the same and a large Cap made of Canvas & Baize, these together with an additional glass of Brandy every Morning enables them to bear the Cold without Flinshing. At Noon we judged our selves to be in or near the same Longitude as we were when we fell in with the last Feild Ice and about Six Leagues farther to the North so that had it remained in the same place we ought to have been in the middle of it, or at least so many Leagues advanced within it; as it cannot be supposed that so large a body of Ice as that appeared to be could be wasted in so short a time as 4 Days, it must therefore have drifted to the northward and if so there can be no land to the north in this meridian, that is between the Latitude of 55° and 59° a part where we have not been and which I believe to be mostly covered with Ice, be this as it may, we have not only met with better weather, but much less Ice of every kind to the Southward of the above mentioned Latitudes, than we did to the northward. We had been steering ENE for some time with a view to make the Ice, but not seeing any thing of it we steer'd EBS ½S in order to get to the Southward of our old Track.

TUESDAY *5th. Winds NW. Course EBS*½*S. Dist. Sailed* 159 *Miles. Lat. in South* 59°51'. *Long. in East of Greenwich per Reck.g* 19°40'. *Long. Cape G. Hope* 1°17' *E.* Strong gales and Foggy with sleet and snow all the pm, in the am Moderate and fair with a large Sea from the NW which indicates no land near in that Quarter, in the Course of this days run we fell in with only 2 Islands of Ice.

WEDNESDAY 6*th. Thermr.* 34½. *Winds NW. Course EBS. Distce. Sailed* 143 *Miles. Lat. in South* 60°18'. *Long. in East of Greenwich Reck.g* 24°21'. *Long. made C. G. Hope* 5°57' *East.* Fresh gales am hazy attended with Snow Showers. We kept on to the East under all the sail we could carry having daylight the whole 24 hours round and the Weather realy milder than it was farther north, the gales more Moderate, and we are less incumbered with Ice having seen only four Islands this 24 hours.

*　　*　　*

SATURDAY 9*th. Thermr.* 35. *Winds NW. Lat. in South* 61°36'. *Var. of the Compass* 30°8'. Gentle gales and clowdy. In the PM passed Several Islands of Ice more than we have seen for some days past, and at 9 o'Clock came to one that had a quantity of loose Ice about it, upon which we hauled our Wind with a view to keep to windward in order to take some of it up in the Morn, at Midnight we tacked and stood for the Island, at this time the Wind shifted two or 3 Points to the Northward so that we could not fetch it, we therefore bore away for the next Island to Leeward which we reached by 8 o'Clock and finding loose pieces of Ice about it, we hoisted out three Boats and took up as much as yeilded about 15 Tons of Fresh Water, the Adventure at the same time got about 8 or 9 and all this was done in 5 or 6 hours time; the pieces we took up and which had broke from the Main Island, were very hard and solid, and some of them too large to be handled so that we were obliged to break them with our Ice Axes before they could be taken into the Boats, the Salt Water that adhered to the pieces was so trifleing as not to be tasted and after they had laid on Deck a little while intirely dreaned of, so that the Water which the Ice yeilded was perfectly well tasted, part of the Ice we packed in Casks and the rest we Milted in the Coppers and filled the Casks up with the Water; the Melting of the Ice is a little tideous and takes up some time, otherwise this is the most expeditious way of Watering I ever met with.

SUNDAY 10*th. Winds NWBN to WNW. Course S* 54° *E. Dist. Saild* 37 *Miles. Lat. in South* 61°58'. *Longd. in East pr. Reckg. Corrected* 36°7' *Watch* 35°48'. *Long. made from C.G.H.* 17°44'. Gentle gales, first part fair and

Clowdy, remainder hazy with showers of snow. In the PM hoisted in the Boats after having taken up all the loose Ice with which our Decks were full; having got on board this seasonable supply of fresh Water, I did not hesitate one moment whether or no I should steer farther to the South but directed my course South East by South, and as we had once broke the Ice I did not doubt of geting a supply of Water when ever I stood in need. We had not stood above one hour and a half upon the above Course before I found it necessary to keep away more East and before the Swell to prevent the Sloops from rowling occasioned in some measure by the great weight of Ice they had on their Decks which by 9 o'Clock in the Morning was a good deal reduced and the Swell gone down we resumed our former Course.

*   *   *

TUESDAY 12*th. Winds NE, East, & SE. Course S* 18½° *E. Dist. Saild* 63 *Miles. Lat. in South* 64°12'. *Longd. in East pr. Reckg. Corrected* 38°14' *Watch* 37°47'. *Long. made from C.G.H.* 19°51'. *Variation of the Compass* 23°52½'. Gentle gales and Clowdy, at 4 in the AM it was clear and I took 12 observations of the Suns Azimuth with Mr Gregorys Compass which gave 23°39½' West Variation. I also took a like number with two of Dr Knights Compass's, the one gave 23°15' and the other 24°42' West Variation, the Mean of all these Means is 23°52¼'; our Latitude and Longitude was the same as at Noon. At 6 o'Clock, having but little Wind, we brought to a mong some loose Ice, hoisted out the Boats and took up as much as filled all our empty Casks and compleated our Water to 40 Tons, the Adventure at the same time filled all her Empty Casks; while this was doing Mr Forster shott an Albatross whose plumage was of a Dark grey Colour, its head, uper sides of the Wings rather inclining to black with white Eye brows, we first saw of these Birds about the time of our first falling in with these Ice Islands and they have accompanied us ever sence. Some of the Seamen call them Quaker Birds, from their grave Colour. These and a black one with a yellow Bill are our only Companions of the Albatross kind, all the other sorts have quite left us. Some Penguins were seen this morning.

WEDNESDAY 13*th. Winds Southerly – Calm. Course ESE. Dist. Sailed* 16 *Miles. Latitude in South* 64°18'. *Longd. in East Greenwich Reck.g Corrct.*

38°48′. *Longd. made Cape G. Hope* 20°25′. At 4 o'Clock in the PM hoisted in the Boats and made sail to the SE with a gentle gale at SBW attended with Showers of Snow. At 2 am it fell calm, and at 9 hoisted out a Boat to try the Current which we found to set NW near one third of a Mile an hour which is pretty confirmable to what I have before observed in regard to the Currants; this is a point worth inquiring into, for was the direction of the Currants well assertained, we should be no longer at a loss to know from what quarter the Islands of Ice we daily meet with comes from. At the time of trying the Currant Fahrenheits Thermometer was sent down 100 fathom and when it came up the mercury was at 32 which is the freezing point, some little time after, being exposed to the surface of the Sea, it rose to 33½ and in the open air to 36. Some curious and intresting experiments are wanting to know what effect cold has on Sea Water in some of the following instances: does it freeze or does it not? if it does, what degree of cold is necessary and what becomes of the Salt brine? for all the Ice we meet with yeilds Water perfectly sweet and fresh.

* * *

FRIDAY 15*th. Winds South to S.E. Course N* 26° *E. Distce Sailed* 23 *Miles. Lat in South* 63°57′. *Longde in East of Greenwich Reck.g* 39°38½′ *Watch* 38°35½′. *Longt. East of C.G.H.* 21°15′. Very gentle breezes of Wind with tolerable Clear and Serene Weather. We have now had five tolerable good Days succeeding one another, which have been usefull to us more ways than one; having on board plenty of Fresh Water or Ice which is the same thing, the People have had an oppertunity to Wash and Dry their Linnen &c[a] a thing that was not a little wanting. We also made the necessary Observ[ns] for finding the Ships place and the Variation of the Compass.

* * *

SUNDAY 17*th. Thermr.* 34. *Winds EBS. Course South. Dist. Sailed* 125 *Miles. Lat. in South* 66°36½′. *Longde. in E. Greenwich Reck.g* 39°35′. *Long*[de] *made E. of C.G.H.* 21°12′. In the PM had fresh gales and Clowdy weather. At 6 o'Clock, being then in the Latitude of 64°56′ S I found the Variation by Gregorys Compass to be 26°41′ West, at this time the Motion of the Ship was so great that I could not observe with D[r]

Knights Compass. In the AM had hazy weather with Snow Showers and saw but one Island of Ice in the Course of these 24 hours so that we begin to think that we have got into a clear Sea. At about a ¼ past 11 o'Clock we cross'd the Antarctic Circle for at Noon we were by observation four Miles and a half South of it and are undoubtedly the first and only Ship that ever cross'd that line. We now saw several Flocks of the Brown and White Pintadoes which we have named Antarctic Petrels because they seem to be natives of that Region; the White Petrels also appear in greater numbers than of late and some few Dark Grey Albatrosses, our constant companions the Blue Petrels have not forsaken us but the Common Pintadoes have quite disapeared as well as many other sorts which are Common in lower Latitudes.

MONDAY 18th. *Winds EBS. Course North. Distce Sailed 44 Miles. Lat. in South* 65°52′. *Longde. in East Greenwich Reck.g* 39°35′. *Longde. East Cape G. Hope* 21°12′. In the PM had a Fresh gale and fair Weather. At 4 o'Clock we discoverd from the Mast head thirty eight Islands of Ice extending from the one Bow to the other, that is from the SE to West, and soon after we discovered Feild or Packed Ice in the same Direction and had so many loose pieces about the Ship that we were obliged to loof for one and bear up for another, the number increased so fast upon us that at ¾ past Six, being then in the Latitude of 67°15′ s, the Ice was so thick and close that we could proceed no further but were fain to Tack and stand from it. From the mast head I could see nothing to the Southward but Ice, in the Whole extent from East to wsw without the least appearence of any partition, this immence Feild was composed of different kinds of Ice, such as high Hills or Islands, smaller pieces packed close together and what Greenland men properly call field Ice, a piece of this kind, of such extend that I could see no end to it, lay to the SE of us, it was 16 or 18 feet high at least and appeared of a pretty equal height. I did not think it was consistant with the safty of the Sloops or any ways prudent for me to persevere in going farther to the South as the summer was already half spent and it would have taken up some time to have got round this Ice, even supposing this to have been practicable, which however is doubtfull. The Winds Continued at East and EBS and increased to a strong gale attended with a large Sea, hazy weather Sleet and Snow and obliged us to close reef our Topsails.

* * *

[*At this time Cook was in fact only about 75 miles away from the Antarctic continent. The ships now took a north-easterly course in search of Kerguelen Island.*]

SATURDAY 30*th. Thermr.* 39½. *Winds North W to North. Course N* 57° *E. Dist. Sailed* 101 *Miles. Lat. in South* 51°34′. *Longde. in East of Greenwich Reck.g* 55°55′. *Long. made from C.G. Hope* 37°32′. Very hard gale and thick hazey weather with drizling rain which obliged us to close reef our Topsails and at 8 o'Clock to hand the Main sail and Fore Topsail. We spent the night, which was dark and stormy, in making a trip to the SW, and in the morning made sail again to the NE under Courses and Double reefed Topsails, the Wind being some thing abated but it yet blew a fresh gale at NW and NNW attended with drizling rain and hazey thick weather. This is the first and only day we have seen no Ice sence we first discovered it.

* * *

[FEBRUARY 1773]

MONDAY 1*st. Thermr.* 41½. *Winds WNW. Course N* 18° *E. Diste. Sailed* 126 *Miles. Lat. in South* 48°51′. *Longde. in East Reck.g* 57°47′. *Long. made from C.G.H.* 39°24′. Fresh gales and Clowdy, at 2 pm passed two Is^ds of Ice. In the AM saw a small piece of rock weed.

TUESDAY 2*nd. Winds NW to WNW. Course N* 78° *E. Diste. Sailed* 73 *Miles. Lat. in South* 48°36′. *Longde. in East* 59°35′ *Watch* 59°33′. *Long. made from C.G.H.* 41°12′. Hazey Clowdy weather and a fresh gale at NW with which we stood NEBN till 4 o'Clock in the PM when being in the Latitude of [48°39′] s and nearly in the Meridian of the Isle of Mauritius, where we were to expect to find the Land said lately to have been discovered by the French, but seeing nothing of it we bore away East and made the Signal to the Adventure to keep on our Starboard beam at 4 miles distance.

* * *

[*Westerly winds took Cook further to the east than he intended, but because the longitude of what they were looking for had been vaguely and incorrectly given, he was actually ten degrees to the west of the island, which they never found. On 6 February Cook gave up the search 'and bore away East a little Southerly all sails set'.*]

MONDAY 8*th. North, East to North. Course S* 54° *E. Distce. Saild* 103 *Miles. Lat. in South* 49°51'. *Longde. in East Reck.g* 63°57'. *Longde. East C.G.H.* 45°34'. At 6 o'Clock in the pm, made the Signal for the Adventure to come under our stern and at the same time took several Az[ths] which gave the var[n] 31°28' but the observations were doubtfull on account of the rowling of the sloop occasioned by a very high Westerly swell. Fair weather continued till Midnight when it became Squally with rain and we took a reef in each Topsail. In the Morning saw several Penguins & Divers and some were heard at different times in the night, these signs of land continuing we at 8 o'Clock sounded but found no ground with 210 fathoms. We were now in the Latitude of 49°53' s, Longitude 63°39' East, Steering South by Compass close upon a Wind which was at ESE the Adventure was about a point or two upon our Larb[d] quarter, distant about one Mile and a half or as some thou[gh]t one Mile, about half an hour after a thick Fogg came on so that we could not see her. At 9 o'Clock we fired a gun and repeated it at 10 and at 11 and at Noon made the Signal to Tack and Tacked accordingly, but neither this last Signal or any of the former were answered by the Adventure which gave us too much reason to apprehend that a seperation would take place. I have said that at 8 o'Clock we laid South by Compass with the wind at ESE but by 9 o'Clock or before the Wind veered to NNE so that we laid E½s, this must have brought the Adventure upon our weather beam or directly to Windward of us, provided she kept her Wind which she ought to have done as no signal was made to the contrary. In short we were intirely at a loss, even to guess by what means she got out of the hearing of the first gun we fired.

TUESDAY 9*th. Winds North, North, NBE & NNW. Course S* 66° *W. Distce. Sailed* 5 *Miles. Lat. in South* 49°53'. *Long[d]. in East Reck.g* 63°53'. *Longde. made C.C.H.* 45°30'. The thick Foggy Weather continuing and being apprehensive that the Adventure was still on the other Tack, we at

2 pm, after having run 2 Leagues to the West, made the Signal and Tacked, to which we heard no Answer, we now continued to fire a gun every half hour. At 3 o'Clock just after fireing our gun the officer of the Watch and others on Deck heard or thought they heard the report of a gun on the Weather bow, about the same space of time after fireing the next gun no one on deck doubted but what they heard the report of a nother gun on our beam, the different situations of these two sounds induced us to think that the Adventure was on the other Tack and standing to the Westward, and being to Windward of us I thought she might not hear our guns, but was only fireing half hour guns as well as us and that her fireing so soon after us was only chance. I therefore orderd a nother gun to be fire'd a quarter of an hour after to which we heard no answer, being now satisfied that she did not hear us both from her not answering and not bearing down, I prepared to Tack at 4 o'Clock but first ordered a Gun to be fired after which Mr Forster alone thought he heard the report of a nother to Windward nearly in the same situation as the last, this occasioned my standing half an hour longer to the Westward in which time we fired two guns to which no answer was heard, we then Tack'd and stood to the Westward after having stood some thing more than 8 Miles to the East. We still continued to fire half [h]our guns and the Fogg dissipated at times so to admit us to see two or three Miles or more round us, we however could niether hear nor see any thing of her. Being now well assured that a Separation had taken place I had nothing to do but to repair to the place where we last saw her, Captain Furneaux being directed to do the same and there to cruze three days, accordingly I stood on to the Westward till 8 o'Clock, than made a trip to the East till Midnight and then again to the West till Day light and fired half hour guns and Bur[n]t false fires all night, the Weather continued Foggy and hazey and the Wind remained invariable at North and NBW, which, if the Adventure kept her Wind during the Fogg, was very favourable for her to return back to the apointed station. After day light at which time we could only see about 2 or 3 Miles round us, we tacked and stood to the East till 8 o'Clock, then again to the West and at Noon we were about 6 or 7 Miles East of the place were we last saw the Adventure and would see about 3 or 4

Leagues round us: the Wind which was now at NNW had increased in such a manner as to oblige us to take in our Topsails and the Sea at the same time began to rise from the same point. We still continued to see Penguins and Divers which made us conjector that land was not far off, it was for this reason I tacked yesterday at Noon which probably was the occasion of my loosing the Adventure for seeing such signs of the Vicinity of land, I thought it more prudent to make short boards during the Fogg, over that part of the Sea we had already made our selves accquainted with, than to continue standing to the Eastward at a time we could not see a quarter of a mile before us.

WEDNESDAY 10*th. Thermr.* 40½. *Winds NNW to WBN. Course S* 68°. *Distce. Sailed* 38 *Miles. Lat. in South* 50°7′. *Longde. in East Reck.g* 64°53′ *Watch* 64°49′. *Longd. C.G.H.* 46°30′. We stood to the Westward till half past 2 o'Clock pm having run 10 Miles sence Noon and neither hearing or seeing any thing of the Adventure, we wore and lay-too under the Mizen Staysail with our head to the Eastward, at 8 o'Clock the gale being somewhat abated we set the Foresail and this Sail we kept under all night; during the height of the gale the Weather was hazey with rain, but towards evening it cleared up so as to see 3 or 4 Leagues round us and in this state it continued all night, we however kept burning false fires at the mast head and fireing guns every hour, but neither the one nor the other had the desired effect for altho we laid too all the morning we could see nothing of the Adventure which if she had been with[in] 4 or 5 Leagues of us must have been seen from the mast head. Having now spent two Days out of the three assign'd to look for each other, I thought it would be to little purpose to wait any longer and still less to attempt to beat back to the appointed station will knowing that the Adventure must have been drove to leeward equally with our selves. I therefore made sail to the SE with a very fresh gale at WBN accompanied with a high Sea, many dark grey Albatrosses, Blue Petrels and Sheerwaters about the Ship but only two or three divers were seen and not one Penguin.

* * *

SATURDAY 13*th. Thermr.* 36. *Winds SW to WBS. Course S* 50°30′ *E. Distce. Sailed* 104 *Miles. Lat. in South* 53°54′. *Longde. in East Reck.g* 72°34′

Watch 72°24′. *Longd. C.G.H.* 54°11′. *Varn.* 33°8′. Gentle gales and pleasant Weather. In the Evening the Variation was 32°32′ w and in the morning 33°8′ w. We were now accompanied by a much greater number of Penguins than at any time before and of a different sort, being smaller, with Redish Bills and brown heads, the meeting with so many of these Birds gave us still some hopes of meeting with land and various were the oppinions among the officers of its situation. Some said we should find it to East others to the North, but it was remarkable that not one gave it as his opinion that any was to be found to the South which served to convince me that they had no inclination to proceed any farther that way. I however was resolved to get as far to the South as I conveniently could without looseing too much easting altho I must confess I had little hopes of meeting with land, for the high swell or Sea which we have had for some time from the West came now gradualy round to SSE so that it was not probable any land was near between these two points and it is less probable that land of any extent can lie to the North as we are not above [160] Leagues South of Tasmans track and this space I expect Captain Furneaux will explore, who I expect is to the North of me.

*   *   *

MONDAY 15*th. Thermr.* 36½. *Winds SWBS. Course SEBE. Dist. Sailed* 162 *Miles. Lat. in South* 56°52′. *Longd. in East Reckg.* 78°48′. *Longd. East Cape G.H.* 60°25′. Fresh gales, with now and then Showers of sleet and snow. In the evening the Variation was found to be 34°48′ West. The Wind now veered to SWBS or SSW and the Swell followed the same direction. About 6 in the AM a nother Seal was seen. Some petty thefts having lately been commited in the Ship, I made a thro' search to day for the stolen things and punished those in whose custody they were found.

*   *   *

WEDNESDAY 17*th. Winds NBE to EBS. Course S* 36½° *E. Dist. Sailed* 57 *Miles. Lat. in South* 57°54′. *Longd. in East Reckg.* 82°4′. *Longd. East Cape G.H.* 63°41′. Gentle gales and dark clowdy weather with frequent Showers of Sleet and snow. At 9 o'Clock am Saw an Island of Ice to the westward distant 3 or 4 Leagues, which we bore down to with the same intention as we stood for the one yesterday. The Wind was now at East by South but the swell still continued to come from the West. Last night Lights were seen in the Heavens similar to those seen in the Northern Hemisphere commonly called the Northern lights, I do not remember of any Voyagers makeing mention of them being seen in the Southern before.

THURSDAY 18*th. Thermr.* 30 *to* 33. *Winds SBW. Course S* 87° *E. Distce. Sailed* 48 *Miles. Lat. in South* 57°57'. *Longd. in East Reckg.* 83°44' *Watch* 83°0'. *Longd. from the Cape G.H.* 65°21'. *Var.* 39°33' *West.* A little past Noon we brought-to under the Island of Ice which was full half a mile in circuit and two hundred feet high. At this time there were but a few loose pieces about it but while we were hoisting out the Boats to take this up an immence quantity broke from the Island, a convincing proof that these Islands must decrease pretty fast while floating about in the Sea. I observed the loose pieces to drift fast to the Westward, that is it quited the Island in that direction and this I suppose to be occasioned by a current, for the Wind which was at ESE could have little or no effect upon the Ice.

At 8 o'Clock we hoisted in the Boats and made sail to the Eastward with a gentle gale at South, having got on board as much Ice as yeilded nine or ten Tons of Water. In the morning the Variation was 39°33' West. At Noon we had twelve Islands of Ice in sight besides an immence number of loose pieces which had broke off from the Island. The Southern lights were again seen last night. The Thermometer was 2° or 3° below the freezing point in consequence of which the Water in the Scuttle cask was froze. Swell still continues to come from the West. The morning being clear Mr Wales and some of the officers took several Observations of the Sun and Moon which gave the Longitude reduc'd to Noon 83°44' E one degree less then the Logg gives carried on from the last observations, which indicates that there is a current seting to the West.

* * *

SUNDAY 21*st. Thermr.* 36. *Winds South, SW to NWBW. Course S* 61° *E. Dist. Sailed* 27 *Miles. Lat. in South* 59°0'. *Longd. in East Reckg.* 92°30'. *Longd. E. of Cape G.H.* 76°27'. Gentle breeze and clowdy Weather. At

1 pm, thinking we saw land to the sw, we Tacked and stood towards it, but at 3 o'Clock found it to be only clowds, which soon dissipated and we again resumed our Course to the sE. In the Evening the Horizon was unusally clear so as to see full 12 or 15 Leagues round. The variation by several Az^{ths} taken with Dr Knights Compass was 40°8' and by Gregorys 40°15' West. Had but little wind all night which increased but very little with the Day and as the Sea was smooth and favourable for the Boats to take up Ice we steered for a large Island were we expected to meet with some and were not disapointed when we reached it. In the morning some Penguins were seen.

MONDAY 22nd. *Winds NBE to EBN. Course S 44° E. Dist. Sailed 49 Miles. Lat. in South 59°35'. Longd. in East Reckg. 93°36'. Longd. E. of Cape G.H. 77°33'. Varn. West 40°51'.* After Dinner hoisted out two Boats and set them to take up Ice while we stood to and from under the Island which was about half a mile in circuit and three or four hundred feet high, yet this huge body turned nearly bottom up while we were near it. At 6 o'Clock having got aboard as much Ice as we could dispence with, we hoisted in the Boats and made sail to the sE with a gentle breeze at NBE having at this time Eight Ice Islands in sight and increased in such a manner as we run to the sE that in the morn^g 23 were seen at one time and yet the Weather was generally hazey with snow showers. Variation p^r Az^{ths} 40°51' West.

*   *   *

WEDNESDAY 24th. *Winds ESE. Course S 16° E. Dist. Sailed 22 Miles. Lat. in South 61°21'. Longd. in East Reckg. 95°15'. Longd. in C.G.H. 79°12'.* Fresh gales & hazey with Snow and sleet. Stood to the South till 8 pm at which time we were in the Latitude of 61°52' s, the Ice Islands were now so numerous that we had passed upwards of Sixty or Seventy sence noon many of them a mile or a mile and a half in circuit, increasing both in number and Magnitude as we advanced to the South, sufficient reasons for us to tack and spend the night making short boards, accordingly we stood to the north under Reefed Topsails and Fore sail till midnight when we tacked and stood South having very thick hazey weather with Sleet & snow together with a very strong gale and a high Sea from the East. Under these circumstances and surrounded on every side with huge pieces of Ice equally as dangerous as so many rocks, it was natural for us to wish for day-light which when it came was so far from lessening the danger that it served to increase our apprehensions thereof by exhibiting to our view those mountains of ice which in the night would have been passed unseen. These obstacles together with dark nights and the advanced season of the year, discouraged me from carrying into execution a resolution I had taken of crossing the Antarctick Circle once more, according at 4 o'Clock in the AM we Tacked and Stood to the North under our two Courses and double reefed Topsails, stormy Weather still continuing which together with a great Sea from the East, made great distruction among the Islands of Ice. This was so far from being of any advantage to us that it served only to increase the number of pieces we had to avoide, for the pieces which break from the large Islands are more dangerous then the Islands themselves, the latter are generally seen at a sufficient distance to give time to steer clear of them, whereas the others cannot be seen in the night or thick weather till they are under the Bows: great as these dangers are, they are now become so very familiar to us that the apprehensions they cause are never of long duration and are in some measure compencated by the very curious and romantick Views many of these Islands exhibit and which are greatly heightned by the foaming and dashing of the waves against them and into the several holes and caverns which are formed in the most of them, in short the whole exhibits a View which can only be discribed by the pencle of an able painter and at once fills the mind with admiration and horror, the first is occasioned by the beautifullniss of the Picture and the latter by the danger attending it, for was a ship to fall aboard one of these large pieces of ice she would be dashed to pieces in a moment.

* * *

SUNDAY 28*th*. *Thermr*. 36½. *Winds South to SW*. *Course N* 77°15′ *E*. *Dist. Sailed* 135 *Miles*. *Lat. in South* 59°58′. *Longd. in East Reck.g* 104°44′. *Long^d East C.G.H*. 86°21′. In the pm the gale abated and the Wind veered to ssw and swbs. Hazey weather with sleet continued till 8 o'Clock in the am when it became fair and tolerable clear, at day light in the morn got Topg^t yards across and set all the sail we could, having a fine fresh gale and but few Islands of Ice to impede us, the late gale having probably distroyed great numbers of them. A large hollow sea hath continued to accompany the Wind that is from the East round by the South to sw, so that no land can be hoped for betwixt these two extreme points. We have a breeding sow on board which yesterday morning Farrowed nine Pigs every one of which were killed by the cold before 4 o'Clock in the afternoon notwithstanding all the care we could take of them, from the same cause several People on board have their feet and hands chilblain'd, from the circumstances a judgement may be formed of the summer weather we injoy here.

*   *   *

[MARCH 1773]

WEDNESDAY 17*th. Thermr.* 33 *to* 35¹/₂. *Winds South to SW. Course N* 86°40'. *Dist^e Sailed* 163 *Miles. Lat. in South* 58°40'. *Longd. in East Reck.g* 147°43'. *Longd. East of C.G.H.* 129°20'. *Varn.* 0°31' *East.* Fresh gales, in the pm showers of Snow and hail, the remainder mostly fair but very dark and gloomy. In the evening being in the Latitude of 58°58' s Longitude 144'27° E I found the variation by several Az^{ths} to be 0°31' East. I was not a little pleased with being able to determine with so much precision this point of the line in which the Compass hath no variation. We continued to steer to the East inclining a little to the South till 5 o'Clock in the am at which time we were in the Latitude of 59°7' s Long 146°53' E. We then bore away NE and at Noon steer'd North inclining to the East with a resolution of making the best of my way to *New Holland* or *New Zealand*, my sole montive for wishing to make the former is to inform my self whether or no Van Diemens Land makes a part of that continent. If the reader of this Journal desires to know my reasons for taking the resolution just mentioned I desire he will only consider that after crusing four months in these high Latitudes it must be natural for me to wish to injoy some short repose in a harbour where I can procure some refreshments for my people of which they begin to stand in need of, to this point too great attention could not be paid as the Voyage is but in its infancy.

* * *

FRIDAY 19*th.* *Thermr.* 43. *Winds WSW to NW. Course N* 34° E. *Dist^e Sailed* 134 *Miles. Lat. in South* 55°1′. *Longd. in East Reck.g* 152°1′. *Longd. E of Cape* 133°38′. Thick hazey weather with rain till the evening when the sky clear'd up and we had fair Weather most part of the night and the Heavens beautifully illuminated with the Southern lights. At 5 o'Clock in the pm the variation by several Az^ths was 13°30′ E being then in the Latitude of 56°15′ Longitude 150°0′ E, soon after we hauld up with the Log a piece of Rock weed which was all covered with Barnacles. At 7 o'Clock in the Morning we saw a Seal and towards Noon some Penguins and more rock Weed, all these are what Navigators have hitherto looked upon as signs of the vicinity of land, however at this time we know of none, nor is it probable that there is any nearer than New Holland or Van Diemens and from which we are distant [260] Leagues.

* * *

THURSDAY 25*th.* *Thermr.* 54. *Winds SE to WBS. Course N* 77°45′ E. *Dist^e Sailed* 80 Miles. *Lat. in South* 46°16′. *Long. in East Reck.g* 166°11′. *Longd. E. of Cape* 147°48′. Foggy wet weather continued till the evening when the Wind abated and the Weather cleared up, about 2 o'Clock we passed a peice of Wood & a quantity of Weed. In the morning the Wind shifted to South and SW when we made all sail, saw more Weed, Egg Birds, Port Egmont Hens &c^a. These signs of the vicinity of land we were to expect for at 10 o'Clock the land of New Zealand was seen from the Masthead and at Noon from the Deck extending from NEBE to East distant 10 Leag^s. For two days past we have had a very large swell from the SW.

[FRIDAY 26*th.*] Intending to put into *Dusky Bay* or any other Port I could find on the Southern part of *Newzealand*, we steered in for the land under all the Sail I could set, haveing the advantage of a fresh gale and tolerable clear weather till half past 4 in the pm when the Weather became very thick and hazey, at this time we were within 3 or 4 Miles of the land and before the Mouth of a Bay which I had mistook for Dusky Bay, being deceived by some Islands which lie before it. Fearing to run into a place in thick weather we were utter strangers to, I tacked in 25 f^m water and stood out to sea. This Bay lies on the SE side of West Cape and may be known by a White clift which is on one of the Islands which lies about the middle of the Mouth of the Bay; this part of the Coast I did not see in my last voyage, indeed we have seen so little of it now and under so many disadvantages, that all I have said of it must be very doubtfull. We stood off to the South under Close reefed Topsails & Courses till 11 o'Clock when we wore and stood to the Northward, at 5 o'Clock in the am the gale abated and we bore up for the land under all the sail we could set, at 8 the West Cape bore EBN½N, for which we steered and entred Dusky Bay about Noon in the mouth of which we found 44 fathom water, a Sandy Bottom, the West cape bearing SSE and the North point of the Bay North, here we found a vast swell roll in from the SW, the Water Shoalden'd to 40 f^m, after which we had no ground with 60, we were however too far advanc^d to return and therefore pushed on not doubting but what we should find anchorage, for in this Bay we were all strangers, in my last Voyage I did no more than discover it.

SATURDAY 27*th.* After runing about two Leagues up the Bay without find'g Anchorage and having pass'd some of the Islands which lie in it, I brought to, hoisted out two Boats and sent one of them with an officer round a point on the Larboard hand and upon her makeing the Signal for anchorage we followed with the Ship and came to an Anchor in 50 f^m water so near the shore as to reach it with a hawser after having been 117 Days at Sea in which time we have Sailed [3660] Leagues without once having sight of land. I cannot however help thinking but that there is some near the Meridian of the Mauritius and about the Latitude of 49° or 50° which I have been unfortunate enough not to find, at least the many Penguins and Divers we saw there seemed to indicate as much, but I shall refer makeing my remarks on this subject till I join the Adventure which cannot be far off if not already in *Queen Charlottes Sound* provided she hath met with nothing to retard her. . . .

My first care after the Ship was moored was to send a Boat &

People afishing, in the mean time some of the Gentle^n went in a Boat to a rock a small distance from the ship on which were many Seals, one of which they killed which afforded us a fresh Meal. As I did not like the place we had anchored in I sent Lieut^t Pickersgill over to the SE side of the Bay to look for a more convenient Harbour while I went my self to the other side for the same purpose, I found an exceeding snugg Harbour, but met with nothing else worthy to be noted. Soon after my return to the Ship Mr Pickersgill returned also and reported that he had also succeeded in find[ing] a good harbour with every other conveniency. As I liked the situation of this harbour better than the one I had found I determined to go to it in the morning, the fishing Boat was equally as successful by returning with as much fish as all hands could eat for supper and in a few hours in the morning supplyed us with a Dinner. This gave us certain hopes of being Plentifully supplyed with fish.

We had rain in the night and untill 9 o'Clock in the Morning when we got under sail and with a small breeze at SW worked over to the NW side of the Bay where we anchored in Mr Pickersgills Harbour which I found full as safe and convenient as he had reported.

SUNDAY 28*th*. In the PM hauled the Sloop into a small creek and moored her head and stern to the Trees and so near the Shore as to reach it with a Brow or stage which nature had in a manner prepared for us by a large tree which growed in a horizontal direction over the Water so long that the Top of it reached our gunwale. Wood for fuel was here so convenient that our yards were locked in the branches of the trees, about one hundred yards from our stern was a fine stream of fresh Water and every place abounded with excellent fish and the shores and Woods we found not distitute of wild fowl, so that we expected to injoy with ease what in our situation might be call'd the luxuries of life. The few sheep and goats we had left were not likely to fair quite so well here being neither pasture nor grass to eat but what is course and harsh, nevertheless we were supprised to find that they would not eat it as they had not tasted either grass or hay for these many Weeks past, nor did they seem over fond of the leaves of more tender plants and shrubs, upon examination we found their teeth loose and that many of them had every symptom of an inveterate Sea Scurvy; out of four Ewes and Two Rams I brought from the Cape with an intent to put a shore in this Country or any other I might have found, I have only been able to preserve one of each and even they are in so bad a state that it is doubtfull if they may recover.

In the AM some of the officers went up the Bay in a small Boat on a shooting party, but returned again before noon and reported that they had seen Inhabitants in an Arm of the Bay and as the Day was rainy and wet they did not think proper to land, but return to the Sloop and acquaint me therewith, they had but just got on board when the Natives appeared in two or three Canoes off a point about a Mile from us and soon after retired behind the point out of sight probably owing to a heavy shower of rain which then fell.

MONDAY 29th. After the rain was over one small double Canoe in which were Eight of the natives appeared again and came within musquet shott of the Ship where they [were] looking at us for about half an hour or more and then retired, all the signs of freindship we could make notwithstanding. After dinner I tooke two Boats and went in search of them in the Cove where they were first seen, accompanied by several of the officers and gentlemen, we found the Canoe hauled upon the Shore, near two small mean hutts where there were several fire places, some fishing netts, a few fish lying on the beach and some in the Canoe; we however saw no people, they probably had retired into the Woods. After a short stay and leaving in the Canoe some medals, Looking glasses, Beeds &c[a] I embarked and rowed to the head of the Cove where we found nothing remarkable; in returning down the Cove we put a shore where we landed before but so still no people, they however could not be far off for we could smell the smoke of fire nor had any thing I had put into the Canoe been touched to which I now added a hatchet and then return with the night aboard.

In the AM no person went from the Ship, all hands were Employed clearing the Woods, making the Brow &c[a].

TUESDAY 30th. Showery Weather. In the PM a party of the officers made an excursion up the Bay and M[r] Forster with his party were out Botanizing, both partys returned in the evening without meeting with any thing remarkable. In the AM cleared places in the Woods near the Brook and set up Tents for the Water[er]s, Coopers, Sail-makers &cᵃ.

WEDNESDAY 31*st*. PM fair weather, Some hands assisting Mʳ Wales to clear a place for his observatory. In the AM very stormy rainy Weather in so much that no Work could go forward.

[APRIL 1773]

THURSDAY 1*st*. Little Wind and tolerable fair. Began to cut down Wood for fuel, got our empty casks ashore to fill with Water and to repair such as were in want of repair, set up the Forge to repair our Iron Work and put the Sail-makers to Work upon the Sails all of which were absolutly necessary occupations. Also began to Brew Beer with the leaves & branches of a tree which resembles the Americo black Spruce Inspissated Juce of Wort and Melasses. . . .

In the afternoon I went to the place where the Natives were first seen to see if any of the articles I had left there were taken away, but I found every thing just as I had left nor did it appear that any body had been there sence. We shott several curious Birds among which was a Duck of Blue grey Plumage with the end of its Bill as soft as the lips of any other animal, as it is altogether unknown I shall endeavour to preserve the Whole in spirits. With the night I returned on board.

FRIDAY 2*nd*. A very pleasent Morning, Lieutˢ Clerk and Edgcomb and the two Mʳ Forsters went in a small Boat to the Indian Cove to search for the productions of Nature while myself with Lieutᵗ Pickersgill & Mʳ Hodges went in the Pinnace to view the North West part of the Bay, in our Way we touched at the Seal rock where we killed three Seals one of which afforded us much sport. After passing several Isles we at length came to the most northern & Western Arm of the Bay the same as is formed by the Land of Point five fingers, in the Bottom of this Arm we found many Ducks, Water Hens and other Wild fowl. Some we killed and returned on board at 10 o'Clock in the evening. . . .

*   *   *

TUESDAY 6*th*. Early in the Morn a Shooting party made up wholly of the officers went in a small Boat to the place where I was on Friday last and my self accompanied by the two Mr Forsters and Mr Hodges set out in the Pinnace upon the Survey of the Bay, my attention was directed to the North side where and about half way up the Bay I discovered a very safe and capacious Cove in the bottom of which is a fresh Water River and on the Western shore several beautiful small Cascades, and the Shores are so steep that a ship may lie near enough to convey ye Water into her with a hose. In this Cove we shott fourteen Ducks which occasioned my naming it Duck Cove: on our return in the evening we had a short interview with three of the Natives, one man and two Women, they first discovered themselves on the NE point of Indian Island, named so on this occasion.

WEDNESDAY 7th. The man called to us as we passed by from the point of a Rock on which he stood with his staff of destruction in his hand, the two Women stood behind him at the skirts of the Woods with each a Spear in her hand, the man seemed rather afraid when we approached the Rock with our Boat, he however stood firm. I threw him a shore two handkerchiefs but he did not desend the Rock to take them up. At length I landed went up and imbraced him and presented him with such articles as I had about me which disapated his fears and presently after we were joined by the two Women, the Gentlemen that were with me and some of the Seamen and we spent about half an hour in chitchat which was little understood on either side in which the youngest of the two Women bore by far the greatest share. We presented them with fish and Wild fowl which we had in our boat, which the young Woman afterwards took up one by one and threw them into the Boat again giving us to understand that such things they wanted not. Night approaching obliged us to take leave of them, when the young Woman gave us a Dance but the man view'd us with great attention. At midnight the sportsmen returned having had but indifferent success. In the morning I went again to the Indians and carried with me various articles which I presented them with, most of which they received with a great deal of indifferency, except hatchets and spike nails, these they seemed to value very much. The interview was at the same place as last night and where we saw the whole Family which consisted of the Man, his two wives, the young Woman before mentioned his daughter, a Boy about 14 or 15 years of age and three small Children the youngest of which was at the breast, they were all well looking people except one Woman, Mother to the young Woman, who had a large Wan on her upper lip which made her look disagreeable enough and seemed to be intirely neglected by the man. They conducted us to their habitation which was but a little within the skirts of the Woods and were two low wretched huts made of the bark of trees. Their Canoe was made fast in a creek near to them, a small double one just capable to transport the whole family from place to place. During our stay with them Mr Hodges made drawens of them which occasioned them to give him the name of Toetoe. When we took leave of them the Chief presented me with a piece of Cloth and some other trifles and immediately after expressed a desire for one of our Boat Cloaks, I took the hint and ordered one to be made for him of red Baize as soon as I came on board.

*   *   *

FRIDAY 9*th*. In the PM I viseted the Natives, we made known our approach by hollowing but they did not meet us at the shore as usual, they were perhaps better employed for when we came to their habitation they were all dressed, Man Women and Children, in their best Cloathing with their hair comb'd oyled and tyed upon the crowns of their heads and oramented with white feathers. I presented the chief with the Cloak with which he seemed well pleased and took his Patta-pattou from his girdle and gave it me, after a short Stay we took leave and rowed over to the North side of the Bay in order to continue the Survey and on this service I spent the day.

SATURDAY 10*th*. Very heavy rain all the night which did not cease at Noon.

SUNDAY 11*th*. Rain continued all the PM but the Morning was clear and Serene which afforded an oppertunity for us to dry our linnen a thing very much wanting, not having had fair weather enough for that purpose sence we put into this Bay. Mr Forster and his party profited by the day in Botanizing. About 10 o'Clock the family of the Natives paid us a visit, seeing that they approachd the Ship with great caution I met them in my Boat which I quited and went into their canoe, nevertheless I could not prevail upon them to put along side the Ship and was at last obliged to leave them to follow their own inclinations; at length they put a shore in a little creek hard by us and afterwards came and set down on the shore abreast of the Ship near enough to speak to us. I caused the Bagpipes and fife to be played and the Drum to be beat, this last they admired most, nothing however would induce them to come a board but they entered with great familiarity into conversation with such of the officers & Seamen as went to them and paid a much greater regard to some more than others and these we had reason to believe they took to be Women, to one man in particular the Girl shewed an extraordinary fondness untill she discovered his sex and then she would not suffer him to come near her, whether it was because that she before realy took him for a Women or that the Man had taken some liberties with her which she thus resented I know not.

MONDAY 12*th*. Being a fine afternoon I took Mr Hodges to a large Cascade which falls down a high mountain on the South side of the Bay about a League higher up than the Cove where we are anchr^d. He took a drawing of it on Paper and afterwards painted it in oyle Colours which exhibits at one view a better discription of it than I can give, huge heaps of stones lies at the foot of this Cascade which have been brought by the force of the Stream from adjacent mountains, the stones were of different sorts, none however appeared to contain either Minerals or Mitals, nevertheless I brought away specimens of every sort as the whole country, that is the rocky part of it, seems to be made up of these sort of stones and no other. . . . When I returnd aboard in the evening, I found that the natives had taken up their quarters not more than one hundred yards from our watering place which was a great mark of the intire confidence they placed in us. After dinner a shooting party made up of the officers went over to the North side of the Bay having the small Cutter to convey them from place to place. In the Morning I went in the Pinnace, accompanied by Mr Forster, to Survey the Isles and Rocks which lie in the mouth of the Bay, I found some of them to shelter a very Snug Cove, on the

SE side of Anchor Isle, from all Winds, which we call'd Lunchen Cove because here we dined on Craw fish on the side of a pleasent brook under the shade of the trees.

TUESDAY 13*th*. After dinner we proceed by rowing out to the outermost Isles where we saw many Seals, fourteen we killed and brought away with us, we might have got many more could we have landed with safty on the other Isles. I returned aboard about 8 o'Clock in the evening and the next morning set out again to continue the Survey. I intend to have landed again on the Seal Isles but there run such a surf that I could not come near them, with some difficulty I rowed out to Sea and round the SW end of Anchor Isle, it happened very lucky that I took this round in which we found the Sportsmen Boat adrift with no one in her, we lay hold of her the very moment she was going to be dashed against the Rocks. I was not at a loss to guess how she came adrift nor was I under any apprehensions for the safty of the People who had been in her; after securing the Boat in a little creek I proceeded to the place where we supposed the Gentlemen to be & which we reached between 7 & 8 o'Clock in the evening and found them upon a small Isle in Goose Cove, where as the tide was out we could not come with the Boat but was obliged to wait till the return of the flood and as this would not happen till 3 o'Clock in the morning we land upon a naked beach, not knowing where to find a better place, and after some time got a fire and broiled some fish on which we made a hearty supper without any other sauce than a good appetite. After this we laid down to sleep having a stoney beach of a bed and the canopy of Heaven four a covering. At length the Tide permited us to take of the sportsmen and with them we imbarqued & proceed for the place where we had left their boat which we soon reached having a breeze of wind in our favour attended with rain. When we came to the Creek which was on the NW side of Anchor Isle we found their an immence number of Blue Peterls, some on the Wing, others in the Woods, in holes in the ground, under the roots of trees and in the creveses of rocks where they had desposited their young; as not one was to be seen in the day time they must be then out at sea seaking for food which they bring to their young in the evening, the noise they made was like the croaking of Frogs. After restoring the sportsmen to their boat we all proceeded for the Ship which we reached at 7 o'Clock not a little fatigued with our nights expedition.

Last night the natives returned to their habitations probably foreseeing that rainy weather was at hand.

* * *

[*It was a month before the* Resolution *left Dusky Sound (via Acheron Passage and Breaksea Sound, to the north of Resolution Island). The officers and gentlemen spent their time shooting wildfowl and seals, botanizing, sketching, exploring and making further contacts with the Maori. The ship was overhauled and ready for sea by 25 April.*]

[MAY 1773]

WEDNESDAY 12*th*. Having quited Dusky Bay as has been already mentioned I directed my Course along shore for Queen Charlottes Sound having a gentle breeze at SE and South with fair weather.

At 4 in the PM Doubtfull Harbour bore ESE dist^t three or 4 Leagues & the North entrance of Dusky Bay SSE distant 5 Leagues. In the night had little Wind with showers of rain, in the morning it was fair but the Weather was dark & gloomy and the Wind veered to NW. At Noon we were distant from the Shore 5 Leagues.

THURSDAY 13*th*. Wind at NW to West a fresh gale, first part rain latter fair. Course made good this 24 hours NEBN dist^c 120 miles.

FRIDAY 14*th*. Winds from West to South, first part fresh gales & Cloudy, Middle a gentle gale with Showers of rain, latter little wind and variable. At Noon we were by Observation in the Lat of 41°53′ and about 7 or 8 Leagues from the land.

SATURDAY 15*th*. Little [wind] and Variable between the South and East and East & North with fair Weather. At Noon observed in Lat 41°12′ Rocks Point ENE.

SUNDAY 16*th*. Wind at NNE and NEBN a fresh gale and Clowdy hazey weather. Plying to Windward, at Noon Rocks point bore NNE distant about 4 Leagues and being about 3 miles from the nearest shore which was a low sandy beach, in this situation had 25 fathom water.

MONDAY 17*th*. At 5 pm the Wind veer'd to West and afterwards to ssw and blew a Strong gale, at Middnight judgeing our selves the length of Cape Farewell, we brought to till 4 am when we made sail, at 8 the above Cape bore west half South distant six Legˢ. At Noon Stephens's Isle bore E ½S dist 5 Legues.

TUESDAY 18*th*. At 4 o'Clock in the PM the sky became suddenly obscured and seemed to indicate much Wind which occasioned us to clew up all our sails, presently after Six Water Spouts were seen, four rose and spent themselves between us and the land, the fifth was at some distance without us and the Sixth pass'd under our Stern at about fifty yards from us, the diameter of the base of this spout I judged to be about fifty or sixty feet, during the time these Spouts lasted which was near a hour we had light puffs of wind from all points of the Compass. Water Spouts are caused by whirl winds which carries the Water in a stream upwards, the Sea below them is much agitated and all in a foam from which a tube or round boddy is formed by which the water is conveyed up to the Clowds, some of our people said they saw a bird in the one near us which was whirled round in the same manner as the fly of a Jack while it was carried upwards; we had thick hazey weather for some hours after with varible Winds, but by middnight the Weather was clear at which time we pass'd Stephens's Isle at the distance of one mile. About Six leagues to the Eastward of Cape Farewell there seems to be a spacious Bay covered from the Sea by a low point of land and is I beleive the same as Tasman first anchored in. Blind Bay, which is to the SE of this seems to extend a long way in to the South, the sight in this direction was not bounded by any land, I think it not improbable but that it may communicate with Queen Charlottes Sound. At Daylight in the Morn we were the length of Point Jackson at the entrance of Queen Charlottes Sound and soon after we discovered the Adventure in Ship Cove by the Signals she made, what little wind we had was out of the Sound so that we had to work in, in the doing of which we discovered a rock which we did not see in my last voyage, it lies SBE¼E from the

outermost of the two Brothers and in a line with the white Rocks on
with the middle of Long Island, the top of it is even or rather above
the Surface of the Sea and there is deep water all round it. At Noon
the Adventure's Boat came on board with Lieut' Kemp and brought
us a dish of fish and some Salleting.

Little Wind and clear pleasent Weather. With the assistance of our
boats and the tide which was in our favour we got to an Anchor in
Ship Cove at Six o'Clock in the evening and the next morning we
moved farther in and moor'd with a hawser to the Shore. A little while
before we anchored Captain Furneaux came on board and informed
me that he arrived here on the 7th of Apr^l having first touched at Van
Diemens Land.

*　　*　　*

[*Cook now gives a transcription of Furneaux's journal. After losing touch with the*
Resolution, *he made for Van Diemen's Land (Tasmania), coming to anchor in*
Adventure Bay. *In exploring the east coast they were unable to ascertain that
Tasmania was an island. Cook thought the evidence made it 'highly probable that
the whole is one continued land and that van Diemen's land is a part of New
Holland'.*]

WEDNESDAY 19*th.* I have some were in this Journal mentioned a desire
I had of Viseting Vandeimens land in order to inform my self whether
or no it made a part of New Holland, but sence Captain Furneaux
hath in a great degree cleared up this point I have given up all thoughts
of going thither, but that I might not Idle away the whole Winter in
Port I proposed to Captain Furneaux to spend that time in exploring
the unknown parts of the Sea to the East and North, acquainting him
at the same time with the rout I intended to take and the time I meant
to spend in this cruze. To this propossition he readily agreed; and in
concequence thereof I disired him to get his Sloop ready for sea as
soon as possible for at this time she was striped. Knowing that sellery
and Scurvey grass and other vegetables were to be found in this Sound
and that when boiled with Wheat or Pease and Portable Soupe makes
a very nourishing and wholesom Diet which is extreemly beneficial
both in cureing and preventing the Scurvey, I went my self at day
light in the Morn in search of some and returned by breakfast with a

boat load and having satisfied my self that enough was to be [got] I gave orders that it should be boild with Wheat or Oatmeal and Portable Soup for the Crew of both Sloops every morning for breakfast and also with Pease every day for dinner and I took care that this order was punctualy complied with at least in my sloop.

THURSDAY 20*th*. This morning I put ashore at the Watering place near the Adventure's Tent, a Ewe and a Ram (the only two remaining of those I brought from the Cape of Good Hope) untill I found a proper place to put them a shore for good for my intention was to leave them in this Country, at the same time I visited the different Gardens Captain Furnea[u]x and his officers had planted with garden seeds roots &c.ᵃ all of which were in flourishing condition and if improved or taken care of by the natives might prove of great use to them.

* * *

SUNDAY 23*rd*. Last Night the Ewe and Ram I had with so much care and trouble brought to this place, died, we did suppose that they were poisoned by eating of some poisonous plant, thus all my fine hopes of stocking this Country with a breed of Sheep were blasted in a moment. Towards noon we were visited for the first time by some of the Natives, they stayed and dined with us and it was not a little they devoured, they were dismiss'd in the evening Loaded with presents.

MONDAY 24*th*. Being a pleasent morning I sent Mʳ Gilbert the Master out to Sea in the Cutter to sound about the Rock we discover'd in coming in, my self accompanied by Captain Furneaux & Mʳ Forster went in the Pinnace to the West Bay on a Shooting party, in our way we met a large Canoe in which were fourteen or fifteen people, one of the first questions they asked was for Tupia the Otaheitean and they seem'd to express some concern when we told them he was dead. They all of them enquired after this man of Captain Furneaux when he first arrived: the people in this canoe seem'd as if they were going to the Ships but when we parted with them they went another way. In the West Bay we had pretty good sport among the Sea Pies and

Shaggs and in the evening return'd a board when I lear[n]t that a Canoe from the northward or some place out of the Sound had been alongside, the people in her, who appear'd to be strangers, also enquired after Tupia, Lieutenant Pickersgill away in the Launch collecting selery and Scurvy grass.

*   *   *

SATURDAY 29*th*. This Morning several of the Natives came along side and brought with them some fish which they exchanged for Nails &c^a. After Breakfast I took one of them over to Motuara and shew'd him the Potatoes planted there by Mr Fannen the Master of the Adventure which he had brought from the Cape of Good Hope, there seems to be no doubt of their succeeding as they were in a very thriving state, the man was so pleased with them that he immidiately began to hough the earth about the plants, I call'd them Coumalla a root common in many parts of *Eahei nomauwe* and is as I could find from this man not unknown to the Inhabitents of *Tavai-poenammoo*.[4] I next carried him to the other of Captain Furneaux's gardens (this gentleman being with me) I explaned to him as well as I could the nature of the Turnips, Carrots & Parsnips roots together with Potatoes that will be of more use to them than all the other vegetables. I gave him a tolerable Idea of the Carrots and Parsnips by calling them Tara a root to which they bear some likeness and is known to the Natives.

SUNDAY 30*th*. We were Viseted again by the Natives this morning who brought with them some fish to market, Two or three families having taken up their aboad near us.

MONDAY 31*st*. This Day I employ'd in clearing and diging up ground on Motuara and planting it with Wheat, Pease and other Pulse Carrots Parsnips and Straw berries.

---

4. The Maori names for North Island and South Island as Cook understood them on his first visit (see 31 January 1770).

[JUNE 1773]

WEDNESDAY 2*nd*. This Morning I went over to the East side of the Sound accompanied by Captain Furneaux and Mr Forster, there I put a Shore two Goats male and female, the latter was old but had two fine Kids, some time before we arrived in *Dusky Bay*, which were both kill'd by the cold as I have already mentioned, the male was something more than twelve months old: Captain Furneaux hath put a Shore in Canibals Cove a Boar and a Breeding Sow so that we have reason to hope that in process of time this Country will be stocked with Goats and Hoggs; there is no great danger that the Natives will destroy them as they are exceedingly afraid of both, besides as they have not the least knowlidge of them being left, they will grow so Wild before they are discovered as not to suffer any one to come near them. The Goats will undoubtedly take to the Mountains and the Hoggs to the Woods where there is plenty of food for both. In this excursion I saw the largest Seal I ever met with, it was Swiming on the Surface of the Water and suffer'd us to come near enough to fire at it but without effect for after a chase of near an hour we were obliged to give it up. By the size of this animal it is probable that it was a Sea-Lioness, it certainly very much resembled the one drawn by Lord Anson, our seeing a Sea Lion when we entred this Sound in my former Voyage increaseth the probabillity. After Loading two Boats with Vegetables and Shooting some Pigeons & other Birds we return'd on board in the evening.

THURSDAY 3*rd*. Sent the Carpenter over to the East side of the Sound to Cut spars, the Boat was chased by some of the natives in a large Canoe but with what intent is not known. Early in the morning our friends the Natives brought us off some fish and we had there company at breakfast. . . . While these people were on board a large double Canoe in which were twenty or thirty people appear'd in sight, our friends on board seem'd much alarmed telling us that the others were enimies, two of them, the one with a Spear and the other with a Stone hatchet in his hand, got upon the Arm Chists which were on the Poop and there in a kind of bravado set those enimies at difiance while the others took to their Canoes and padled ashore probably to secure the Women & Children and effects. All I could do I could not prevail on these men to call the Canoe alongside on the Contrary they seem'd displeased at my doing it, at length after some ceremony perform'd by the people in her they put along side after which the chief was easily prevail'd upon to come aboard followed by many others and Peace was immidiately istablished on all sides indeed it did not appear to me that the people in this Canoe had any intention of making war upon their Brethren at least if they did they were sensible enough to know that this was neither time nor place for them to commit hostillities. One of the first questions these Strangers ask'd was for *Tupia*, and when I told them he was dead, one or two of them express'd their sorrow by a kind of lamentation which appear'd to me to be merely formal. A trade soon Commenced between our people and these, it was not possible to hinder the former from giving the clothes from of their backs for the merest trifles, things that were neither usefull nor curious, such was the prevailing passion for curiosities and caused me to dismiss these strangers sooner than I would have done. When they departed they went over to Moutara where, by the help of our Glasses we discover'd four or five more Canoes and a number of people on the Shore, this induced me to go over in my boat accompanied by Mr Forster and one of the Officers, we were well received by the Chief and the whole tribe which consisted of between 90 & 100 people Men Women and Children, having with them Six Canoes and all their utensils which made it probable that they were come to reside in this Sound, but this is only conjector for it is very common for them when they even go but a little way to carry their whole property with them, every place being equally alike to them if it affords the necessary subsistance so that it can hardly be said that they are ever from home, thus we may easily account for the migration of those few small families we found in *Dusky Bay*. Living thus dispers'd in small parties knowing no head but the chief of the family or tribe whose authority may be very little, subjects them to many inconveniences a well regulated society united under one head or any other form of government are not subject to, these form Laws and regulations for their general security, are not alarm'd at the appeerence of every stranger and if attack'd or invaded by a publick enimy have strong holds to retire to where they can with advantage defend themselves, their property & their Country, this seems to be the state of most of the Inhabitents of *Eahei-nomauwe*, whereas those of *Tavai-poenammoo*, by living a wandering life in small parties are distitute of most of these advantages which subjects them to perpetual alarms, and we generally find them upon their guard traveling and working as it were with their Arms in their hands even the Women are not exempted from carrying Arms as appear'd at the first interview I had with the family in *Dusky Bay* when each of the two Women were Arm'd with a Spear not less than 18 feet in length. I was lead into these reflections, by not being able to recollect the face of any one person I had seen here three years ago, nor hath it appear'd that any one of them had the least knowlidge of me or any other person with me that was here at that time, it is therefore not very improbable but that the greatest part of the Inhabitants that were here in the beginning of the year 1770 are drove out of it or have on their own accord removed some were else; certain it is that not one third the people are here now that were then. Their Strong hold on the point of Moutara hath been some time deserted and we find many forsaken habetation in all parts of the Sound, however we are not wholy to infer from this that this place has been once very populous for each family may, for their own conveniency when they move from place to place, have more hutts than one or two. It may be ask'd, that if these people had never seen the Endeavour or any of her crew, how they became acquainted with the Name of Tupia or to have in their possession such articles as they could only have got from that Ship, to this it may be answered that the Name of Tupia was at that time so popular among them that it would be no wonder if at this time it is known over great part of *New Zealand*, the name of Tupia may be as familiar to those who never saw him as to those who did, had a Ship of any other Nation whatever arrived here they would equally have enquired for him, by the same way of reasoning the Articles left here by the Endeavour may be now in possession of those who never saw her. I got from one of the people I am now with an Ear ornament made of glass very well form'd and polished.

After spending about an hour on Motuara with these people and having distributed among them some presents and shew'd the Chief the gardens we had made, I return'd aboard and spent the remainder of our Royal Masters Birth Day in Festivity, having the company of Captain Furneaux and all his officers and double allowance enabled the Seamen to share in the general joy.

Both Sloops being now ready to put to Sea I gave Captain Furneaux an account in writing of the rout I intended to take which was to proceed immidiately to the East between the Latitudes of 41° and 46° untill I arrived in the Longitude of 140° or 135° West and then, providing no land was discovered, to proceed to *Otaheite*, from thence to return back to this place by the Shortest rout, and after takeing in wood and Water to proceed to the South and explore all the unknown parts of the Sea betw^n the Meridian of New Zealand and Cape Horn and therefore in case of seperation before we reach'd Otaheite I appointed that Island for the place of Rendezvouz where he was to wait untill the 20th of Augt. Not being join'd by me before that time he was then to make the best of his way back to Queen Charlottes Sound and there remain untill the 20th of Novr after which he was to put to Sea & carry into execution their Lordships Instructions. It may be thought by some an extraordinary step in me to proceed on discoveries as far South as 46° in the very depth of Winter for it must be own'd that this is a Season by no means favourable for discoveries. It nevertheless appear'd to me necessary that something must be done in it, in order to lessen the work I am upon least I should not be able to finish the discovery of the Southern part of the South Pacifick Ocean the insuing Summer, besides if I should discover any land in my rout to the East I shall be ready to begin with the Summer to explore it; seting aside all the[se] considerations I have little to fear, having two good Ships well provided and healthy crews. . . .

During our short stay in this Sound I have observed that this Second Visit of ours hath not mended the morals of the Natives of either Sex, the Women of this Country I always looked upon to be more chaste than the generality of Indian Women, whatever favours a few of them might have granted to the crew of the Endeavour it was generally done in a private manner and without the men seeming to intrest themselves in it, but now we find the men are the chief promoters of this Vice, and for a spike nail or any other thing they value will oblige their Wives and Daughters to prostitute themselves whether they will or no and that not with the privicy decency seems to require, such are the concequences of a commerce with Europeans and what is still more to our Shame civilized Christians, we debauch their Morals already too prone to vice and we interduce among them wants and perhaps diseases which they never before knew and which serves only to disturb that happy tranquillity they and their fore Fathers had injoy'd. If any one denies the truth of this assertion let him tell me what the Natives of the whole extent of America have gained by the commerce they have had with Europeans.

SATURDAY 5*th*, SUNDAY 6*th*. Both these days the Wind was at SE and blew a fresh gale so that we neither could sail or have any communication with our friends the natives.

MONDAY 7*th*. At 4 o'Clock in the morning the Wind coming more favourable we unmoor'd and at 7 wieghed and put to Sea with the Adventure in company, as soon as we had got out of the Sound we found the Wind at South so that we had to ply through the Straits. At Noon the two Brothers which lie off Cape Koamaroo bore West distant one mile, the Tide of ebb was now makeing in our favour so that we had some prospect of geting through before night.

TUESDAY 8*th*. At 5 o'Clock in the PM Cape Pallisser on the Island of Eahei-namauwe bore ESE¼s and Cape Koamaroo on Tavai poenam-moo bore NBW¾W, in this situation we had no ground with 75 fathoms of line; the Tide of flood now made against us and being little Wind next to a Calm we were drove fast back to the Northward but at middnight a light breeze afterwards freshen'd which together with the Tide of Ebb carried us by 8 o'Clock in the morning quite clear of the Strait, Cape Pallisser at this time bearing ENE and at Noon NBW distant 7 Leagues. From this Cape I take my departure allowing it to lie in the same Latitude and Longitude as laid down in my Chart of the Islands. To day when we attended the Winding up of the Watches the fusee of Mr Arnolds would not turn round and after several unsuccessfull tryals we were obliged to let it go down, this is the second of this gentlemans Watches that hath fail'd, one of those on board the Adventure stop'd at the Cape of Good Hope and hath not gone since.

WEDNESDAY 9*th*. *Winds West to NNW. Course S* 54°30' *E. Distce Sail'd* 95 *Miles. Lat. in South* 42°52'. Gentle gales and pleasent Weather. At 5 pm Shorten'd Sail, at 4 am made all Sail and betwen 8 and 12 exercized the people at great guns & Sm^l Arms. Swell from SE, several Port Egmont Hens seen.

*   *   *

[*The two ships had an uneventful voyage east for a month, then turned north. Towards the end of July, Cook heard that the crew of the* Adventure *were badly hit with scurvy and that the cook had died.*]

[AUGUST 1773]

MONDAY 2*nd. Therm.r* 68. *Winds NW to SW. Course North. Dist^e. Sailed* 107 *Miles. Lat. in South* 23°14'. *Longde. in West Reck.g* 134°6'. *Long. C. Pallisser* 49°51'. First part fresh gales and Clowdy remainder gentle breeze and clear weather. Being in the Latitude of *Pitcair[n]s* Island discovered by Captain Carteret in 1767 we looked out for it but could see no thing excepting two Tropick birds, we undoubtedly left this Island to the East of us. Having now crossed or got to the north of Captain Carteret's Track, no discovery of importance can be made, some few Islands is all that can be expected while I remain within the Tropical Seas. As I have now in this and my former Voyage crossed this Ocean from 40° South and upwards it will hardly be denied but what I must have formed some judgement concerning the great object of my researches (viz) the Southern Continent. Circumstances seem to point out to us that there is none but this is too important a point to be left to conjector, facts must determine it and these can only be had by viseting the remaining unexplored parts of this Sea which will be the work of the remaining part of this Voyage.

*   *   *

WEDNESDAY 11*th. Winds East. Course N* 87½ *W. Distce Saild* 122 *Miles. Lat. in South* 17°18'. *Long. in West Reck.g* 142°3' *Watch* 142°29'. *Long. made C. Pallisser* 41°54'. Gentle gales and fair weather. At 6 o'Clock in the morning land was seen to the Southward, we soon discovered it to be an Island about 2 Leagues in extent NW & SE, low and cloathed with wood above which the Cocoa-nutts shew'd their lofty heads. I beleive it to be one of the Isles discovered by M de Bougainville (Latitude 17°24′ Longitude 141°39′ West).[5] The Scorbutic state of the Adventures Crew made it necessary for me to make the best of my way to Otaheite where I was sure of finding refreshments for them, concequently I did not wait to examine this Island which appear'd too small to supply our wants.

THURSDAY 12*th. Therm.r* 78. *Winds East. Course N* 85°30′ *W. Distce Sailed* 90 *Miles. Lat. in South* 17°11′. *Long. in West Reck.g* 143°38′ *Watch* 144° 4′. *Long. made C. Pallisser* 40°19′. Gentle breezes and clear weather. At 6 o'Clock in evening land was seen from the Mast head bearing west and by South, probably this was a nother of M. de Bougainville's isles.[6] We steer'd more to the north in order to avoid it and stood on under an easy sail all night, at day break in the morn, land was seen right a head not farther from us than two miles, this proved to be another low Island or rather a large shoal of about 20 Leagues in circuit, the firm land occupied but a small part of this space and laid in little Islets along the north side and connected to each other by the reef as is usual with these low Islands, this reef extended out from each extreme of the Islets in a circular form encircling a large Bason of Water in which was a Canoe under sail. As this Island which is situated in the Latitude 17°5′ s, Longitude 143°16′ w has no place in the Maps I named it   .[7]

FRIDAY 13*th. Winds East. Course S* 86° *W. Lat. in South* 17°16′. *Long. in West Reck.g.* 144°54′ *Watch* 145°20′. *Long. made C. Pallisser* 39°3′. *Varn.* 6°48′. We continued to advance to the West all sails set till 6 o'Clock in the pm when we shortne'd sail to the three Top-sails, at 9 we brought too with our heads to the South till 4 AM when we bore away

5. Tauere Island, in the Tuamotu Archipelago. Cook called it Resolution Island. Its first discoverer was not Bougainville but Domingo de Boenechea in the *Aguila* on the Spanish voyage to Tahiti, 28 October 1772.

6. Tekokota, called by Cook (who was the first discoverer) Doubtful Island.

7. Marutea, called Furneaux Island in the printed voyage.

under our Top-sails and at day-light discovered a nother low Island bearing N½W distant 3 or 4 Leagues.[8] It was lucky we brought too in the night for if we had not we must have been embarrass'd with this Island which is situated in the Latitude of 17°4′ south Longitude 144°36′ West and appear'd to be of too little concequence to devert me from my intended course. We have had a smooth sea sence we came among the Islands.

SATURDAY 14*th. Winds East. Course W* 0°30′ *N. Distce Sailed* 102 *Miles. Lat. in South* 17°15′. *Long. in West Reck.g.* 146°41′ *Watch* 147°8′. *Long. made C. Pallisser* 37°16′. At 5 o'Clock in the pm saw land extending from WSW to SW dist^t 3 or 4 Leagues. I judged it to be Chain Island discovered in my last Voyage.[9] Fearing to fall in with some of these low Islands in night and being desirous of avoiding the delay which lying too occasions I hoisted out the Cutter, equiped her properly and sent her a head to carry a light with proper signals to direct the Sloops in case she met with danger, in this manner we proceeded all night without meeting with any thing, at 6 in the morning I called her on board and hoisted her in as it did not appear that she would be wanted again for this purpose, as we had now a large swell from the South a sure indication that we were clear of the low Islands.

SUNDAY 15*th. Winds EBN. Course S* 71°45′ *W. Distce Sailed* 95 *Miles. Lat. in South* 17°45′. *Long. in West Reck.g.* 148°16′ *Watch* 148°34′. *Long. made C. Pallisser* 35°41′. *Varn.* 5°10′. Gentle breezes and pleasent weather. At 5 am saw Osnaburg Island bearing SBW½W.[10] At 9 o'Clock I sent for Captain Furneaux on board to acquaint him that I intended to put into Oaiti-peha Bay in the SE end of Otaheite in order to get what refreshment we could from that part of the Island before we went down to Matavai Bay. At Noon Osnaburg Island bore ESE distent 5 or 6 Leagues. Swell from the Southward still continues.

At 6 PM saw the Island of Otaheite extending from WBS to WNW distant about 8 Leagues. We stood on till midnight then brought too till 4 o'Clock when we made sail in for the land. I had given directions

8. Motutunga.
9. 9 April 1769. Anaa.
10. Mehetia, discovered by Wallis, 17 June 1767.

in what possision the land was to be kept but by some mistake it was
not properly attended to for when I got up at break of day I found
we were steering a wrong course and were not more than half a league
from the reef which guards the South end of the Island. I immidiately
gave orders to haul off to the Northward and had the breeze of wind
which we now had continued we should have gone clear of every
thing, but the wind soon died away and at last flatened to a Calm.
We then hoisted out our Boats but even with their assistance the
Sloops could not be kept from nearing the reef, but the current seem'd
to be in our favour, we were in hopes of geting round the point of the
reef into the Bay. At this time many of the natives were on board the
Sloops and about them in their canoes, bring[ing] off with them some
fruit and fish which they exchanged for Nails, Beeds, &cᵃ.

TUESDAY 17*th*. About 2 o'Clock in the PM we came before an opening
in the reef by which I hoped to enter with the Sloops as our situation
became more and more dangerous, but when I examined the natives
about it they told me that the Water was not deep and this I found
upon examination, it however caused such an indraught of the Tide
as was very near proving fatal to both the Sloops, the Resolution
especially, for as soon as the Sloops came into this indraught they
were carried by it toward the reef at a great rate; the moment I
preceived this I order'd one of the Warping Machines which we had
in readiness to be carrid out with about 3 or 4 hundred fathoms of
rope to it, this proved of no service to us, it even would not bring her
head to Sea. We then let go an anchor as soon as we could find bottom
but by such time as the Ship was brought up she was in less then 3
fathom water and Struck at every fall of the Sea which broke with
great violence against the reef close under our stern and threatened
us every moment with ship-wreck, the Adventure anchored close to
us on our starboard bow and happily did not touch. We presently
carried out a Kedge Anchor and a hawser and the Coasting Anchor
with an 8 inch Hawser bent to it, by heaving upon these and cuting
away the Bower Anchor we saved the Ship; by the time this was done
the currant or Tide had ceased to act in the same direction and then
I order'd all the Boats to try to tow off the Resolution, as soon as I

saw it was practical we hove up the two small anchors. At that moment a very light air came of from the land which with the assistance of the Boats by 7 o'Clock gave us an offing of about 2 Miles and I sent all the Boats to the assistance of the Adventure, but before they reached her she had got under sail with the land wind, leaving behind her three anchors, her coasting Cable and two Hawsers which were never recovered: thus the Sloops were got once more into safety after a narrow escape of being Wrecked on the very Island we but a few days ago so ardently wished to be at. We spent the night making short boards and in the morning stood in for Oaiti-peha Bay where we anchor'd about Noon in 12 fathom water about 2 Cables length from the shore and moor'd with our stream anchors, both Sloops being by this time surrounded by a great number of the natives in their Canoes, they brought with them Cocoa-nutts, Plantans, Bananoes, Apples, yams and other roots which they exchanged for Nails and Beeds. To Several who call'd themselves *arree's* (Chiefs) I made presents of Shirts, Axes and various other articles and in return they promised to bring me Hogs and Fowls, a promise they neither did nor never intended to perform.

WEDNESDAY 18*th*. In the PM I landed in company with Captain Furneaux in order to examine the Watering place and sound the disposision of the Natives. The latter I found to behave with great Civility and the latter as convenient as could be expected, we also got of some Water for present use, having scarce any left on board. Early in the morning I detached the two Launches and the Resolutions Cutter under the command of M\u02b3 Gilbert to endeavour to recover the Anchors we had lost, they return'd about noon with the Resolutions Bower Anchor but could not recover the Adventures. The Natives crowded about us as yesterday with fruits &c\u1d43 but in no great quantity. I had also a party tradeing on shore under the Protection of a Guard, nothing however but fruit and roots were offered to us tho many Hogs were seen (as I was told) about the Habitations of the natives, the cry was they all belonged to *Oheatooa* the Arree dehi or King and him we could not see or any other Chief of note, many however came on board who call'd themselves Arrees partly with a view of obtaining presents and partly to have an oppertunity to pilfer whatever came in their way, one of these sort of Arrees I had most of the day in the Cabbin, made him and all his friends, which were not a few, presents, at last he was caught takeing things which did not belong to him and handing them out of the quarter Gallery, many complaints of the like kind were made to me against those on deck which induced me to turn them all out of the Ship; my Cabbin guest made good haste to be gone, I was so exasperated at his behaver that after he had got a good distance from the Ship I fired two Musquet balls over his head which made him quet his Canoe and take to the Water. I then sent a boat to take up the Canoe, as soon as she came near the shore the people from thence began to pelt her with stones, the Boat still persuing the Canoe and being unarm'd I began to be in pain for her safety and went my self in another boat to protect her and order'd a 4 pounder to be fire'd a long the Coast, this made them all retire back from the shore and suffered me to bring away two Canoes without the least shew of opposision and in a few hours after the People were as well reconciled as if nothing had happen'd. The Canoes I return'd to the first person who ask'd for them. It was not untill the Evening of this day that any one enquired after Tupia and as soon as they learnt the cause of his death they were quite satisfied, indeed it did not appear to me that it would have caused a moments uneasiness in the breast of any one had his death been occasioned by any other means than by sickness; as little enquiry was made after *Aotourou* the man M. de Bougainville to[ok] away with him, but they were constantly asking after Mr Banks and many others of the Gentlemen and people that were with me last voyage. These people informed us that *Toutaha*, King of the greater Kingdom of Otahiete was kill'd in a Battle which happen'd between the two Kingdoms about five months ago and that Otou was now the Reigning Prince. Tiboura and several more of our principal friends about Matavai fell in the same Battle and likewise a great number of Common people, at present a peace subsisted between the two Kingdoms.[11]

11. There were not in fact two kingdoms in Tahiti. The battle in question was against the region of Taiarapu in March 1773. The death of Toutaha (Tuteha) and Tiboura (Toobouratomita) gave opportunity for the high-ranking Otou (Tu) to assert himself and foster his ambitions for wider power.

THURSDAY 19*th*. Gentle breezes with some smart showers of rain. Early in the morning I sent the Boats again to take up the Adventures anchors, but they return'd after as little success as the day before and we ceased looking for them any longer. In an excursion I made along shore to the sw accompanied by Cap[n] Furneaux we met with a Chief who entertained us with excellent fish and fruit, in return for his hospitality we made him sever[l] presents and he afterwards accompanied us to the Ship where he made but a short stay. Fruit and roots sufficient for both Sloops but no Hogs, those that were lately in the adjacent house are carried off.

*   *   *

[*Cook had a meeting with Vehiatua (whom he calls Oheatooa). This is the titular name of the* arii nui *of Outer Teva. Cook had met the present Chief (Ta'ata-uraura) as a boy in 1769. On 24 August Cook set sail for Matavai. The victims of scurvy in the* Adventure *were improving greatly with the fresh fruit now available.*]

THURSDAY 26*th*. At 4 o'Clock in the PM we anchored in Matavai Bay after which I sent our Boats to assist the Adventure who got in about two hours after. At the time we anchored many of the natives came of to us, several of whom I knew and almost all of them me, a great crowd were got together on the shore among whom was King [Otoo]. I was just going to pay him a visit when I was told he was mataou'd[12] and gone to Oparre.[13] I could not conceive the reason of this Chief being frightned as every one seem'd pleased to see me, a chief whose name was Marritata was at this time aboard and advised me to put of my Viset till the next morning when he would accompany me. Accordingly in the morning, after having given directions about erecting Tents for the reception of the Sick, Coopers and guard, I set out for Oparre accompanied by Captain Furneaux, some of the gentlemen, Maritata and his Wife, as soon as we landed we were conducted to Otoo who we found seated on the ground under the shade of a tree with a crowd of People round him. After the first salutation was over I made him a present of such things as were in most esteem with them

12. i.e., afraid.
13. Pare, to the west of Matavai.

with which he seem'd well pleased, I likewise made presents to several of his attendance and was offer'd in return a large quantity of Cloth which I refused giving them to understand that what I had given was for Tiyo (friendship), the King inquired after Tupia and all the gentlemen that were with me last Voyage by name, altho I do not know that he was personally acquainted with any one or that he had ever been seen by any of us. He promised that we should have Hogs the next day, but I had a good deal to do to perswaid him to come to the Ship, he said he was Mataou Poupoue, that is afraid of the Guns, indeed all his actions shew'd him to be a timerous Prince, he is about 30 or 35 years of age, six feet three inches high and is as fine a person as one can see. All his subjects appeared uncovered before him, even his Wife and Father were not excepted. When I return'd from Oparre I found the Tents set up on the same ground we had occupied when I was here before. Mr Wales and Baily also set up their Instruments at the same place, I had the Sick land, Twenty from the Adventure and one from the Resolution, landed a sufficient number of men to guard the Whole and left the command to Lieut^t Edgcombe of the Marines.

FRIDAY 27*th*. Early in the Morning Otoo with a numerous trane paid me a Viset, he first sent into the Ship a quantity of cloth, a Hog, two large fish and a quantity of fruit and after some perswasions came in himself with his wife a younger Brother and many others, to all of them I made presents and after breakfast took the King and as many of his attendance as I had room for in the Pinnace and carried them to Oparre the place of their residence. I had no sooner landed than I was met by a venerable old Lady mother of the late Toutaha, she seized me by both hands and brust into a flood of tears saying Toutaha Tiyo no Toute matte (Toutaha the friend of Cook is dead). I was so much affected at her behavour that it would not have been possible for me to refrain mingling my tears with hers had not Otoo come and snatched me as it were from her, I afterwards disired to see her again in order to make her a present but he told me she was Mataou and would not come, I was not satisfied with this answer and desired she might be sent for, soon after she appeared I went up to her, she again wept and lamented the death of her son. I made her a present of an Ax and other things and then parted from her and soon after took leave of Otoo and return'd aboard. Captain Furneaux who was with me gave to the King two fine goats male and female which if properly taken care of will no doubt multiply.

SATURDAY 28*th*. At 4 o'Clock in the morning I sent Lieut' Pickersgill with the Cutter as far as Attahourou to endeavour to procure Hogs and a little after Sunrise I had a nother Viset from Otoo he brought me more cloth, a Pig, a large fish and some fruit. The Queen who was with him and some of his attendance came aboard, but he and others went to the Adventure with the like present to Captain Furneaux, it was not long before he left the Adventure and came with Captain Furneaux on board the Resolution when I made him a hansome return for the present he brought me and dress'd the Queen out as well as I could, she, the King's brother and one or two more appear'd covered before him to day. When Otoo came aboard [Ereti] and one or two of his friends were siting in the Cabbin covered, the moment they saw the King enter they undress'd themselves in great haste, that is they put off their ahows or clothes from of their Shoulders, seeing I took notice of it they said it was because the Arree was present, and this was all the respect they paid him for they never rose from their seats or paid him any other obeisence. When the King thought proper to depart I carried him again to Oparre in my Boat and entertained him with the Bag-pipes of which musick he was very fond, and dancing by the Seamen; he in return ordered some of his people to dance also which dancing consisted chiefly in strange contortions of the Body, there were some of them that could however immitate the Seamen tollerable well both in Country dances and Horn pipes. While I was here I had a present of cloth from Toutaha's Mother, this good old Lady could not look upon me without sheding tears, tho she was more composed to day than before. When I took leave the chief told me he shou'd viset me tomorrow but that I must come to him. In the evening M'r Pickersgill return'd empty but with a promise of some in a few days.

SUNDAY 29*th*. After breakfast I took a trip to Oparre in my Boat accomp'd by Cap'n Furneaux and some of the Officers to viset Otoo as he had requested, we made him up a present of such things as he had not seen before, one article was a large Broad sword at the very sight of which he was so intimidated that I had enough to do to perswaid him to have it buckled upon [him] where it remaind but a short time before he asked permission to take it off and send it away, after which we were conducted to the Theatre where we were entertain'd with a Dramatick Heava or Play in which were both Dancing and Comedy, the performers were five Men and one Women, which was the Queen, the Musick consisted of three Drums only, it lasted about an hour and a half or two hours and upon the whole was well conducted; it was not possible for us to find out the meaning of the Play, some parts of it seem'd to [be] adapted to the present time as my name was mentioned several times, other parts were certainly wholy unconnected with us. It apparently differed in nothing, at least the manner of acting, from those we saw at Ulietea in my last Voyage, the dancing dress of the Queen was more elegant than any I saw there by being set off or decorated with long [tasles] made of feathers hanging down from the waste. As soon as the whole was over the King himself desired me to depart and ordered into the Boat different sorts of fruit and some dress'd fish with which we took leave and return'd aboard.

MONDAY 30*th*. The next Morning he sent me more fruit and several small parcells of fish. About 10 o'Clock in the evening we were alarmed by a great noise a Shore near the Bottom of the Bay at some distance from our incampment. I suspected that it was occasioned by some of our people and sent an Officer with an Arm'd Boat a shore to know what was the matter and to bring off such of our people as he should find their. I also sent to the Adventure and to the Post on shore to know what people were missing, the Boat soon return'd with three Marines and a Seaman who belonged to the party on shore, some others belonging to the Adventure were also taken, all of them put in Irons and the next morning I ordered them to be punished according to their [deserts].[14]

14. The charge was for being absent from duty and quarrelling with the natives. It was thought the quarrel arose from the seamen being too free with the women.

TUESDAY 31st. I did not find that any Mischief was done, our people would confess nothing altho some of them were heard to call out Murder several times, the Natives were however so much allarmed that they fled from their habitations in the dead of the night and when I went to viset Otoo in the morning by appointment I found him many Miles removed from the place of his aboad and it was some time before I could see him attall and when I did he complain'd of the last nights riot. As this was intended to be my last Viset I had taken with me a present suteable to the occasion in which were three Cape Sheep, Axes Cloath and several other articles, the Sheep he had seen before and asked for them (for these people never loose any thing for want of asking) he was pleased at geting them tho they were of little Value to either him or us, to us because they were very poor, to him because they were of a sort that could not breed. The presents he got at this interview intirely removed his fears and opened his heart for he sent for three Hogs for us one for me, one for Captain Furneaux and one for Mr Forster, this last was small of which we took notice calling it ete ete, presently after a man came into the circle and spoke to the King with some warmth and in a very peremptory manner something or other about Hogs, we at first thought that he was angery with the King for giving us so many especially as he took the little Pig away with him; the contrary however seem'd to be the true cause of his displeasure for presently after he was gone a Hog larger than either of the other two was brought us. I acquainted the King when I took leave that I should leave the Island the next day at which he seem'd moved and embraced me several times. We embarqued in our Boat to return aboard and he directed his March back to Oparre. Yesterday I sent Mr Pickersgill again to Attahourou for the Hogs he had promised him.

[SEPTEMBER 1773]

WEDNESDAY 1st. The Sick being all pretty well recovered, our Water Casks repaired and fill'd and the necessary repairs of the Sloops compleated I determined to put to sea without Loss of time, accordingly I ordered every thing to be got off from the Shore and the Sloops to be unmoor'd. At 3 o'Clock in the afternoon the Boat return'd from Attahourou with my old friend Potattou the chief of that district his Wife and some more of his friends, they brought me a present of two Hogs and Mr Pickersgill had got two more by exchanges from *Oamo* for he went in the Boat as far as Paparra where he saw old *Obarea*, she seem'd to be much altered for the worse, poor and of little concequence: the first words she said to Mr Pickersgill Arree Mataou ina Boa (the aree is frightned, you can have no Hogs) from this it should seem that she had little or no property and was her self subject to the Aree which I believe was not the case when I was here before. The wind which had blowen Westerly all day shifted at once to the East with which we put to sea, on this account I was obliged to dismiss my friends sooner then they wished to go loaded with presents and well satisfied. Some hours before we got under sail a young man whose name was Poreo came to me and desired I would take him with me. I consented thinking he might be of service to us on some occasion, many more would have gone if I would have taken them. He beg'd a hatchet and a Nail for his father who was on board as we got under sail, he had them and gave them to his father after which they parted more like two strangers than father and son which gave me reason to think that this man was not his father, but that he had only call'd him so with a view of geting the Ax and Nail; as we were standing out of the Bay a Canoe conducted by two men came a long side and demanded him in the name of Otoo. I now saw that the whole was a trick to get some thing from me and ask'd if they had brought the Hatchet and Nail with them, they said that was ashore, I told them to go and bring them and then he should go, this they said they could not do and so went away, the young man seem'd satisfied. He however could not refrain from Weeping when he view'd the land a stern. . . .

THURSDAY 2*nd*. After leaving the Bay of Matavai as before mentioned I directed my course for the Island of *Huaheine* and at 6 o'Clock the following evening we were with[in] two or three Leagues of its northern point where we spent the night laying too and makeing short boards, and on Friday morning at day light made sail round the point for the Harbour Owharre where we anchored at 9 o'Clock in 24 fathom water, as the wind blew out of the Harbour I choose to turn in by the southern channell, the Resolution turn'd in very well, but the Adventure missing stays got a shore on the reef on the north side of the channell.

FRIDAY 3*rd*. I had the Resolutions Launch in the Water ready in case of an axcedent of this kind, and sent her immidiately to the Adventure by this timely assistance she was got off without receiving any damage. As soon as the Sloops were in safety I landed and was received by the natives with the utmost cordiality. I distributed some presents among them and presently they brought down Hogs, Fowls and fruit which they exchanged for Hatchets, Nails, Beeds, &cᵃ, a like trade was soon opened aboard the Sloops, the natives bring[ing] them off in their Canoes so that every thing promised us a plentifull supply of fresh pork and Fowls which to people who had been living Ten months on salt meat was no unwelcome thing. I learnt that my old friend Oree was still living and chief of the Island and that he was hastning to this part to see me.

SATURDAY 4*th*. Early in the morning I sent Lieutenant Pickersgill with the Cutter on a tradeing party towards the South end of the Island and also a nother on shore near the Sloops, with this I went my self in order to see it was properly conducted at the first seting out, a very necessary point to be attended to, this being settled to my mind I went to pay my first Viset to Oree the Chief who I was told was waiting for me, accompanid by Captain Furneaux and Mʳ Forster. We were conducted to the place by one of the natives, but we were not permitted to go out of the Boat without going through the following ceremony usual at this Isle on such occasions. The Boat being landed before the chiefs House which was close by the Water side Five young Plantan trees, which are their Emblems of Peace, were brought seperately and with some ceremony into the Boat. Three small Pigs accompanied the first three and a Dog the fourth, each had its particular name and purpose rather too mysterious for us well to understand, lastly the Chief sent me the Inscription engraved on a small peice of Pewter which I left with him when [I saw] him in 1769, it was in the same bag I had made for it together with a peice of counterfeit English coin and a few Beads given him at the same time, this shews how well he had taken care of the whole. After they had done sending the things above mentioned to the Boat, our guide who still remained in the Boat with us desired us to decorate three young Plantan plants with Nails, looking glasses Medals, &c^a &c^a, which was accordingly done, we landed with these in our hands and walked up towards the Chief a lane being made by the people between us and him for here were a vast crowd. We were made to sit down before we came to the chief, our Plantains were then taken from us one by one and laid down by him, one was for Eatoua or God, the Second for the Arree or King and the third for Tyo or friendship. This being done Oree rose up came and fell upon my neck and embraced me, this was by no means ceremonious, the tears which trinckled plentifully down his Cheeks sufficiently spoke the feelings of his heart. All his friends were next interduced to us among whome was a beautifull Boy his grandson. The whole ceremony being now over I made him the present I had prepared consisting of the most Valuable articles I had for this purpose and in return he gave me a Hog and a quantity of Cloth and promised that all our wants should be supplied and it will soon appear how well he kept his word, at length we took leave and return'd aboard to dinner and some time after the Cutter arrived with 14 Hogs, many more were purchased on shore and a long side the Sloops.

*   *   *

MONDAY 6*th*. In the morning I sent the tradeing party a shore as usual and after breakfast went my self when I found that one of the natives had been a little troublesome, this fellow being pointed out to me compleatly equiped in the War habit with a club in each hand, as he seem'd to be intent on Mischief I took from him the two clubs and broke them and with some difficulty forced him to retire from the place, they told me that he was an Aree which made me the more suspicious of him and occasioned me to send for a guard which before I had thought unnecessary. About this time Mr Sparman being out alone botanizing was set upon by two men who striped him of every thing he had but his Trowsers, they struck him several times with his own hanger but happily did him no harm, as soon as they had accomplished their end they made off after which a man came to him, gave him a piece of cloth to cover himself and conducted him to me. I went immidiately to Oree to complain of this outrage takeing with me the man who came back with Mr Sparman to confirm the complaint, as soon as the chief heard it he wept a lowd as did several others and after the first transports of his grief was over expostulated with the people shewing them how well I had treated them both in this and my former voyage or some thing to this purpose, he then promised to do all in his power to recover what was taken from Mr Sparman and took a very minute account of every article after which he rose up and went to the Boat desiring me to follow, his people seeing this and being apprehensive of his safety they opposed his going into the Boat, he step'd in notwithstanding their opposision and intreaties. When the people saw their beloved chief wholy in my power they set up a great outcry and with Tears flowing down their cheeks intreated him once more to come out of the Boat. I even joined my intreaties to theirs, it was to no purpose, he insisted of my coming into the Boat and as soon as I was in ordered her off him self, his Sister with Spirit equal to her Royal Brother was the only person that did not oppose his going: as his intention for coming into the Boat was to go with us in search of the Robbers we put off and proceeded accordingly as far as we could by Water, then land and entered the Country and traveled some miles, the chief leading the way inquiring of every one he saw, at length he step'd into a house which was by the road side and order some Cocoa-nutts to be brought for us to drink. After we had refreshed ourselves he wanted to proceed farther, this I opposed and insisted upon his returning back which he was obliged to comply with when he saw I would not follow him. I disired him to send some people for the stolen things for I saw it was to little purpose going farther, for the thieves had already got so much start of us that we might have pursued them to the very remote part of the Island, besides as I intended to sail the next day, this occasioned a loss to us by puting a stop to all manner of trade for the natives were so Allarmed that none came near us but those that were about the chief, the accedent which befell Mr Sparman was first made known to us at the tradeing place by the precipitate retiring of all the people without my being able to conceive the meaning till Mr Sparman appeard, it became therefore the more necessary for me to return to endeavour to restore things to their former state, accordingly we return'd to our boat where we found the chief's sister and several more people who had traveled by land to the place. We immidiately embarqued in the Boat in order to go aboard without so much as asking the Chief to accompany us, he however insisted on going with us in spite of the opposition he met with from those about him, his Sister followed his example contrary to the tears and intreaties of her Daughter a young woman about 16 or 18 years of age. The Chief sit at Table with us and made a hearty meal, his sister sit behind us as it is not the custom for the Women to eat with the men. After dinner I made them both presents and in the Evening carried them a shore to the place were I first took him in where some hundreds waited to receive him many of whome imbracced him with tears of joy in their eyes, all was now harmony and Peace, the people crowded in from every part with Hogs, Fowls and Fruit so that we presently loaded two Boats, the Chief himself made me a present of a large Hog and some fruit, the hanger, the only thing of value Mr Sparman had lost, and part of his waist coat was brought us and we were told we should have the others the next day. Some of the officers who were out on a Shooting party had some things stolen from them which were returned in like manner, thus ended the transactions of this day which I have been rather particular in enumerating because it shews what great confidence this Brave old Chief put in us, it also in a great degree shews that Friendship is Sacred with these people. Oree and I were profess'd friends in all the forms customary among them and he had no idea that this could be broke by the act of any other person, indeed this seem'd to be the great Argument he made use on to his people when they opposed his going into my boat, his words were to this effect: Oree (for so I was always calld) and I am friends, I have done nothing to forfeit his friendship, why should I not go with him. We however may never meet with a nother chief who will act in the same manner on any semiliar occasion.

TUESDAY 7*th*. Early in the morn we began to unmoor, while this was doing I went to take my leave of the chief accompanied by Captain Furneaux and Mr Forster. I tooke with me such things for a present as I knew were most useful and valuable to him. I also left with him the Inscription plate he had before in keeping and another small copper plate on which was engraved these words: Anchor'd here His Britannic Majestys Ships Resolution and Adventure September 1773, together with some Midals all put up in a Small Bag, the chief promised to take great care of the whole and to produce them to the first Ship that should come to the Isle. He next gave me a Hog and after trading for six or eight more and loading the boat with fruit we took leave at which the good old Chief imbraced me with Tears in his eyes. At this interview nothing was said about the remainder of Mr Sparmans Clothes. I judged they were not brought in and for that reason did not mention them least I should give the chief pain about a thing I did not give him time to recover. When I came aboard I found the Sloops crowded round with Canoes full of Hogs, Fowls and Fruit as at our first arrival. Soon after Oree himself came aboard to inform me (as we at first understood him) that the robbers were taken and wanted me to go on Shore either to punish or see them punished, but this could not be done as the Resolution was just under sail and the Adventure already out of the Harbour. I likewise understood from him that four or five of his people were gone away in the Adventure and that he wanted to have them return'd, but in this the chief had either been misinformed or we misunderstood him for I immidiately sent on board Captain Furneaux for them, when the Boat returned she brought only one[15] no more being on board and as this man had been on board the Adventure from the first hour of her arrival at the Isle and it being known to all the natives that he intended to go away with us, without being once demanded and as Captain Furneaux being desireous of keeping [him] I did not think it was necessary to send him on Shore for the Chief was now gone, he[16] stayed aboard till we were a full half League out at Sea then went away in a small Canoe conducted by one man and himself. While we lay in this Port several of the common people frequently desired me to Kill the Bolabola men (the people of a neighbouring isle).[17] Oree probably heard of this and took an oppertunity when he was left aboard to disire that I would

15. Omai.   16. i.e., the Chief.   17. Bora-Bora.

not, teling me that Opoone their King was his Friend, the Common people in general seem to bear an implacable hatred against the Bolabola men nor is this to be much wondred at sence they have made a conquest of most of the neighbouring iles, the little Island of Huaheine under the brave and wise conduct of Oree still preserves its independancy, not a Bolabola man have yet been able to get a footing there tho' we have been told some attempts have been made but of this we have no absolute certainty, from the great plenty of everything on the Isle one might conclude that it had injoyed the b[l]esings of Peace for many years, during our short stay we procured not less than 300 Hogs to both Sloops, besides Fowls and Fruit and had we made a longer stay might have got many more for neither Hogs nor Fowls were apparently diminished but every where appeared as numberous as ever, such is the state of the little but fertile Isle of Huaheine. My friend Oree was no sooner gone than we made sail for Ohamaneno Harbour[16] on the West side of Ulietea where I intended to stop a few days to procure an addition of Fruit to our present stock.

* * *

THURSDAY 9*th*. In the Morning we paid a formal Viset to the Chief of this part of the Isle whose name is Oreo, the same as when I was here before. We went through no sort of ceremony at landing but were conducted to the Chief at once who was seated in his House which stands close to the Water side. The Chief and his friends received us with great Cordiallity, express'd much satisfaction at seeing me again, desired that he might be call'd Cook (or Toote) and I Oreo which was accordingly done, he then ask'd after Tupia and several other gentlemen by name who were with me last voyage. Now I have mentioned Tupia it is necessary to observe that scarce a person here or at Huaheine that did not enquire after him and the occasion of his death and like true Philosophers were perfectly satisfied with the answers we gave them, indeed as we had nothing but the truth to tell the story was always the same by whom soever told. After I made the Chief and his friends the necessary presents we return'd aboard with a Hog and some fruit which the Chief gave me in return; in the

16. Haamanino.

after-noon he gave me a nother Hog'still larger without asking for the least return. Fruit in abundance were brought off to the Sloops and exchanged for Nails &c[a].

FRIDAY 10*th*. In the Fore-noon Captain Furneaux and I paid Oreo a Viset and made him some returns for what he gave me yesterday. The Chief entertain'd us with a Comedy or Dramatick Heava such as is usually acted in the Isles, the Musick consisted of three Drums, the actors were Seven Men and one Woman, the chief's Niece, the Play seemed to be nearly if not quite the same as was acted at Otaheite. The only entertaining part in it was a Thift committed by a man and his accomplice, this was done in such a manner as sufficiently desplayed the Genius of the people in this art. The Thift was discovered before the thief had time to carry of his prize and a scuffle essued between him his accomplice and those set to guard it and altho' they were four to two they were beat off the Stage and the others carried off their prise in triumph. I was very attentive to the whole of this part in expectation that it would have had a quite different end, for I had before been told that Teto, that is the thief, was to be acted and had understood that the Theift was to be punished with death or with a good Tiparrahying (beating) but I found my self misstaken in both. We are however told that this is the punishment they inflict on those who are guilty of this crime, be this as it may strangers certainly have not the Protection of this Law, them they rob with impunity at every oppertunity. As soon as the Play was over we return'd aboard to dinner after which went ashore again where we spent the remainder of the day. Learnt from one of the Natives that Nine Islands laid to the Westward at no great distance from hence, they are all small and two of them uninhabited. Brisk trade for fruit &c[a].

* * *

SUNDAY 12*th*. Viseted Oreo according to promise, who entertain'd us with a Heva some what different from the one we saw before, he after wards came aboard and dined with us together with two of his friends. Many of the Gentlemen and Seamen were on Shore to day rambling about the Country and met every were with sevel treatment from the Natives.

MONDAY 13*th*. Nothing happen'd worthy of note.[17]

TUESDAY 14*th*. Early in the Morning I sent Lieutenant Pickersgill with the Resolutions Launch and the Adventures Cutter to Otaha to procure fruit, especially Plantains, for a Sea Store. Had a Veset from Oreo and some of his Friends, acquainted the Chief that I should dine with [him] a Shore and desired he would order two Pigs to be dress'd for us in their own way, giving him the Value of the Pigs before hand, but this was not absolutely necessary, he accordingly went a shore to prepare the dinner and about one o'Clock I and the officers of both Sloops went to pertake of it, when we came to the Chiefs house we found the Cloth already laid, that is green leaves were laid thick on the floor round which we seated our selves, the chief then asked me if the Victuals should be brought. I told him yes and presently after one of the Pigs came over my head souce upon the leaves and immidiatly after the other, both so hott that it was scarce possible to touch them, the dish was garnished with hot bread fruit and Plantains and a quantity of Cocoa-nutts were brought for drinks. There were several Women at table and no doubt some of them might be in a longing condition but as it is not the Custom here for the Women to eat with the men, we were not delayed or the victuals suffered to cool by carving out their longing bits. Each man being ready with his knife in his hand we turn'd to without ceremony. Never was Victuals cleaner or better dress'd, the Pigs were dress'd whole, one wieghed between 50 and 60 pound the other about half as much and yet all the parts were equally well done and with all its juces in it and eat by far sweeter than it would have done had it been dress'd by any of our methods. The Chief his Son and some other of his Male friends eat with us and pieces were handed to siveral others who sat behind for we had a vast crowd about us. The Chief never faild to drink his glass of Madeira when ever it came to his turn not only now but at all other times when

17. Cook is silent about a major row with his scientist, J. R. Forster. Forster's son George had had his gun wrested from him by an islander, and Forster had shot at the culprit. Cook first laughed at the incident, and then rebuked Forster for firing. Forster refused to accept this; there was a quarrel, and Cook forcibly expelled Forster from the great cabin. Reconciliation came three days later, when the two men shook hands. [E]

he dined with us without ever once being the least affected by it. As soon as we had dined the Boats crew took the remains to the Boat where by them and the people about them the whole was consum'd. When we rose up many of the Common people rushed in to pick up the Crums which fell from our Table, this led me to think that as plenty as Pork is at these Isles but little falls to the share of the Common people. Some of our gentlemen being present when these two Pigs were dress'd and kill'd saw the chief divide the intrails, lard &c^a into ten or twelve equal parts and serve it out to certain people. Several dayly attended the Sloops and assisted the butchers for the sake of the intrails of the hogs we kill'd: probably little else falls to the share of the Common people, it must however be owned that they are exceeding carefull of all their Provisions and waste nothing that can be eat by man, flesh and fish especially. In the afternoon we were entertained with a Play with which ended the principal transactions of the day, Plays have indeed generally been acted every day sence we have been here either to entertain us or for their own amusement. Many fine large Hogs were offered us to Day for Axes and Hatchets which we were obliged to refuse having already got more than we know what to do with.

*   *   *

THURSDAY 16*th*. . . . Having got a board a large supply of refreshments I determined to put to Sea in the morning and made the same known to the chief who promised to come and take leave of me on board the Ship.

FRIDAY 17*th*. At 4 o'Clock in Morning we began to unmoor and as soon as it was light Oreo and some of his friends came to take leave, many Canoes also came off with Hogs and fruit, the former they even beged of us to take from them, calling out, Tyo Boa Atoi which was as much as to say, I am your friend take my Hog and give me an ax, but our decks were already so full of them that we could hardly move, having on board the Resolution about 230 and on board the Adventure about 150. The increase of our Stock together with what we have consumed sence we came to this Isle I judge we have got here about 500 Hogs, big and little, some were only roasters, others wieghed 100 lb and upwards, it is not easy to guess how many we might have got could we have dispenced with all that were offered us.

The Chief and his friends did not leave us till the Anchor was a weigh. At parting I made him a present of a Broad Ax and several other things with which he went away well satisfied. He was extremely desirous to know if, and when I would return, these were the last questions he asked me. After we were out of the Harbour and had made sail we discovered a Canoe conducted by two men following us, upon which I brought to and they presently came a long side with a present of fruit from Oreo, I made them some return for their trouble, dismissed them and made sail to the Westward with the Adventure in company. The young man I got at Otahiete left me at Ulietea two days before we sailed being inticed away by a young Woman for whom he had contracted a friendship. I took no methods to recover him as their were Volanteers enough out of whome I took one, a youth about [17 or 18] years of age who says he is a relation of the great Opoony and is a great advocate for Bolabola of which Island he is a native, his name is Oediddee,[18] he may be of use to us if we should fall in with and touch at any isles in our rout to the west which was my only montive for takeing him on board.

SATURDAY 18th. *Winds EBS. Courses S 69° W. Dist. Sailed 75 Miles. Lat. in S. 17°17'. W. Longd. Greenwich pr. Reck.g. 153°10'. Longd. West of Ulietea 1°31'.* Having left Ulietea as before related, I directed my Course to the West inclining to the South as well to avoid the tracks of former Navigators as to get into the Latitude of Amsterdam Island[19] discovered by Tasman in 1643, my intention being to run as far west as that Island and even to touch there if I found it convenient before I proceeded to the South.[20] In the PM we saw the Island of Maurua, one of the Society Isles bearing NBW distant 10 Leagues. A little after Sun

18. Properly Hitihiti. His former name, always used by the Forsters, was Mahine. The young man who left was Poreo (see 1 September).

19. Tongatapu.

20. This decision to investigate the discoveries of Tasman among the islands of Tonga is a change of plan with important consequences. Cook came back to the islands (which he named the Friendly Islands) the following year, and again on his final voyage.

set shorten'd Sail to single reefed Top-sails and brought to during the night, but in the day made all the sail we could. This we continued to do for several suceeding nights.

*   *   *

[*The ships proceeded west by south for the rest of the month, passing islands which Cook first named the Sandwich Islands and then the Hervey Islands after another Lord of the Admiralty. At the beginning of October they were approaching the Tonga group of islands.*]

[OCTOBER 1773]

FRIDAY 1st. *Ther.r 70. Winds SE to East. Course S 82°30' W. Dist. Sailed 85 Miles. Lat. South 21°21'. West Longd. Greenwich Reck.g. 174°4'. West Longd. Ulietea 22°36.* First part fresh gales remainder gentle gales and Clowdy. At Sun set the People at the mast head said they saw land to the westward, this occasioned us bring[ing] to during the night. Day light shew us our misstake when we again made sail to the West.

SATURDAY 2nd. *Winds Easterly.* Fresh gales and fair Weather. At 2 pm Saw the Island of Middleburg[21] bearing wsw. At 6 o'Clock we were about 12 miles from the East side the extreams bearing from swbw to NW and another land bearing NNW, at this time we hauled to the Southward in order to get round the South end of the Island. At 8 o'Clock we discovered a small Island lying wsw from the South end of Middleburg, not knowing but these two Islands might be connected to each other by a reef the extent of which we must be ignorant of and in order to guard against the worst, we haul'd the wind and spent the night makeing short boards under an easy sail.

At the return of Day-light we made Sail and bore up for the sw side of the Island, passing between it and the little Island above mentioned where we found a Channell of 2 miles broad. We rainged the sw side of the Island at the distance of half a mile from shore on which the Sea broke with great [violence] as to leave us no hopes of finding Anchorage this continuing till we came to the most western point of the Island (from which the land trend NNE and NEBN) we bore

21. So called by Tasman. It is Eua, in the Tongatapu group in the south.

up for the Island of Amsterdam which we had in sight but before we had time to trim our sails the Shore of Middleburg assumed another asspect and promised fair to afford Anchorage, upon this I hauled the wind again in order to get under the land. Soon after two Canoes, each conducted by two or 3 men came along side and some of the people into the Ship without the least hesitation, this mark of confidence gave me a good opinion of these Islanders and determined me to anchor if I found a convenient place and this we soon met with and came to in 25 fathom water about 3 Cables length from the shore and before a small creek formed by the Rocks which made landing in Boats easy. . . . By this time we had a great number of Canoes about the sloops and many of the Islanders aboard, some bringing with them Cloth and other Curiosities which they exchanged for Nails &c^a. There was one man aboard who from the authority he seem'd to have over the others I discovered to be a chief and accordingly made him a present of a hatchet, Nails and several other things with which he seemed will pleased, thus a frienship between this chief, whose name is Tioonee, and me commenced. Soon after we had come to an Anchor, I went a shore with Captain Furneaux and some of the officers and gentlemen, having in the Boat with us Tioonee who conducted us to the proper landing place where we were welcomed a shore by acclamations from an immence crowd of Men and Women not one of which had so much as a stick in their hands, they crowded so thick round the boats with Cloth, Matting, &c^a to exchange for Nails that it was some time before we could get room to land, at last the Chief cleared the way and conducted us up to his house which was situated hard by in a most delightfull spot, the floor was laid with Matting on which we were seated, the Islanders who accompanied us seated themselves in a circle round the out sides. I ordered the Bag-pipes to be played and in return the Chief ordered three young women to sing a song which they did with a very good grace. When they had done I gave each of them a necklace, this set most of the Women in the Circle a singing, their songs were musical and harmonious, noways harsh or disagreeable. After we had sat here some time I disired to see the adjoining Plantations which were fenced in on every side, accordingly we were conducted into one of them through a door way, the door was hung in such a manner as to shut of itself. In this Plantation the Chief had a nother house into which we were interduced, Bananas and Cocoa nuts were brought to us to eat and a bowl of liquor, made in our presence of the [22] Plant, to drink of which none of the gentlemen tasted but my self, the bowl was however soon emptied of its Contents of which both men and Women pertook, by this time it was noon when we return'd aboard to dinner with the Chief in our company, he sat at table but did [not] eat any of our victuals. In the after-noon went a shore again and was received by the crowd as before. Mr Forster and his party and some of the officers walked into the country as soon as we landed, Captain Furneaux and I were conducted to the Chiefs house where we had fruit brought us to eat, afterwards he accompanied us into the Country through several Plantations Planted with fruit trees, roots &cᵃ in great tast and ellegancy and inclose by neat fences made of reeds. In the lanes and about their house[s] were runing about Hogs and large fowls which were the only domistick Animals we saw and these they did not seem desireous to part with, nor did they during this day offer to exchange any fruit or roots worth mentioning, this determined me to leave the Island in the morning and go down to that of Amsterdam where Tasman in 1643 found refreshments in plenty. In the evening we all returned aboard every one highly dilighted with his little excursion and the friendly behaver of the Natives who seem'd to [vie] with each other in doing what they thought would give us pleasure.

SUNDAY 3rd. Early in the morning while the Sloops were geting under sail I went a shore in company with Captain Furneaux and Mr Forster to take leave of the Chief and to carry him an assortment of garden seeds and to make him some other presents. I gave him to understand that we were going away at which he neither seem'd pleased nor sorry, he came into our boat with an intent to accompany us aboard and came off about half way, but when he saw that the Resolution was already under sail he call'd to a Canoe to come and take him in together with a nother or two of his friends who were in the boat. As soon as I was aboard we bore away for the Island of Amsterdam all

22. Kava (see Glossary).

sails set, we ran a long the South Side of the Isle half a mile from
shore and had an oppertunity with the assistance of our glasses to
view the face of the Country every acre of which was laid out in
Plantations, we could see the natives in different parts runing a long
the shore, some having little white flags in their hands which we took
for signs of Peace and answered them by hoisting a St Georges Ensign.
The people were as little afraid of us as those of Middleburg, while
we were but middway between the Isles we were met by 3 or 4 Canoes,
each conducted by 2 or 3 men, who strove hard to get aboard, but
this was not to be done as we were runing at the rate of 5 or 6 Knots,
we threw the end of a lead-line into one which they held fast till it
brok, they afterward made the like but unsuccessfull attempt to get
aboard the Adventure who was a stern of us. After we had opened
the West side of the Isle we were met by sever^l more Canoes with two
and 3 men in each, they brought with them and presented to us some
of the [Pepper] root after which they came a board without farther
ceremony. After makeing a board or two we anchored in Van diemens
Road in 18 fathom water about a Cables length from the Rocks or
breakers off the shore and moored with the Coasting Anchor and
Cable out to sea to prevent the Ship from tailing ashore in case of a
shift of wind or a Calm. By this time we had a great number of the
Islanders aboard and about the sloops, some coming off in Canoes
and others swiming off, bringing little else with them but Cloth and
other curiosities, things which I did not come here for and for which
the Seamen only bartered away their clothes. In order to put a stop
to this and to obtain the refreshments we wanted, I gave orders that
no Curiosities should be purchassed by any person whatever either
aboard or along side the Sloops or at the landing place on shore; this
had the desired effect for in the morning the Natives came off with
Bananas and Cocoa-nutts in abundance and some Fowls and Pigs
which they exchanged for Nails, and pieces of Cloth.

MONDAY 4*th*. After breakfast I went a shore with Captain Furneaux,
Mr Forster and several of the officers, a chief, or man of some note,
to whom I had made several presents was in the Boat with us, his
name was Hātago by which name he desired I might be called and

he by mine (Otootee). We were lucky in having anchored before a narrow creek in the rocks which just admitted our Boats within the breakers where they laid secure and at high water we could land dry on the shore; into this place Hatago conducted us, there [were] on the shore an immence crowd of men Women and children who Welcomed us in the same manner as those of Middleburg and were like them all unarm'd. All the officers and gentlemen set out into the Country as soon as we land, excepting Captain Furneaux who stayed with me on the shore, we two Hatago seated on the grass and ordered the People to set down in a circle round us which they did, never once attempting to push themselves upon us as the Otahieteans and the people of the neighbouring Isles generally do. After distributing some trifles among them we signified our desire to see the Country, this was no sooner done than the chief shewed us the way, conducting us along a lane which led us to an open green on the one side of which was a house of Worship built on a mount which had been raised by the hand of Man about 16 or 18 feet above the common level, it had an oblong figure and was supported by a Wall of Stone about three feet high, from the top of this Wall the mount rose with a gentle slope and was covered with a green turf, on the top of the mount stood the house which was of the same figure as the mount about 20 feet long and 14 or 16 broad. As soon as we came before this place every one seated him self on the ground about 50 or 60 yards from the house, presently after came three elderly men and seated them selves between us and the house and began to speak what I understood to be a prayer, their discourse being wholy directed to the house, this lasted about ten minutes and then the three priests, for such we took them to be, came and sit down with us and the rest of the people when both Captain Furneaux and I made them presents of Nails, Medals &c^a giving them to understand that we did it to shew our respect to that house which I now desired leave to examine, the chief contrary to my expectations immidiately went with us without shewing the least backwardness and gave us full liberty to examine every part of it. In the front were two steps leading up to the top of the wall, after which the assent was easy to the house round which was a fine good Walk, the house was built in all respects like to their common dwelling houses (viz) with Posts and rafters and the Covering of Palm thatch, the eves came down to within 3 feet of the ground which space was fill'd up with strong Matting made of Palm leaves which formed a kind of Wall, the floor of the house was laid with gravel, except in the middle where it was raised with fine blew pebbles to the height of about Six Inches and had the same form as the house that is oblong. At one corner of the house stood a rude image and on one side laid a nother, each about two feet in length, I who had no intention to offend either them or their gods, did not so much as touch them, but asked the chief as well as I could if they were Eatua's; whether he understood me or no I cannot say, but he immidiatly turned them over in the doing of which he handled them as roughly as he would have done any other log of wood, which raised a doubt in me that they were representations of the Divinity. I was curious to know if their dead were enterr'd in these Mounts and asked my friend several questions relating thereto but I was not certain that he understood any of them, at least I did not understand the answers he made. Before we queted the house we laid upon the blue Pebbles some Medals, Nails and other things which my friend took up and carried away with him. The Stones on which the wall was made that inclosed the Mount were like flags, some of them 9 or 10 feet by 4, and about Six inches thick, it is difficult to conceive how they could cut such stones out of the coral rocks. This Mount stood in a kind of grove open only on one side which fronted the high road and green on which the people were seated, at this green was a junction of five roads and two or three of them appeared to be very publick ones: the grove was composed of several sorts of trees among which was the [Etoa] tree or   and a kind of low Palm which is very common in the northern parts of New Holland. After we had [d]one examining this place of worship which in their Language is called *Afiā-tou-ca*, we desired to return, but instead of conducting us directly to the Water side they struck into a road leading into the Country, this road which was a very publick one, was about [16] feet broad and as even as a B[owling] green, there was a fence of reeds on each side and here and there doors which opened into the adjoining Plantations; several other Roads from different parts joined this, some equally as broad and others narrower, the most part of them shaded from the Scorching Sun by fruit trees. I thought I was transported into one of the most fertile plains in Europe, here was not an inch of waste ground, the roads occupied no more space than was absolutely necessary and each fence did not take up above 4 Inches and even this was not wholly lost for in many of the fences were planted fruit trees and the Cloth plant, these served as a support to them, it was every were the same, change of place altered not the sene. Nature, assisted by a little art, no were appears in a more florishing state than at this isle. In these delightfull Walks we met numbers of people some were traveling down to the Ships with their burdthens of fruit, others returning back empty, they all gave us the road and either sit down or stood up with their backs against the fences till we had pass'd. At several of the cross Roads or at the meeting of three or more roads, were generally an Afiā-tou-cā, such as above discribed with this difference, that the Mounts were Pallisaded round in stead of a stone wall. At length we came to one larger than common, near to which was a large House belonging to a Chief which was with us, here we were desired to stop which we accordingly did and had some Cocoa-nutts brought us; we were no sooner seated in the house than the oldest of the Priests began a speach or prayer which was first directed to the Afiā-tou-cā and then to me and it altarnetly, when he adress'd me he paused at each sentance, till I gave a nod of approbation. I however did not understand one single word he said. At times the old man seem'd to be at a loss what to say, or perhaps his memory fail'd him, for every now and then he was prompt by a nother who sat by him. Both during this Prayer and the one before mentioned the people were silent but not attentive. At this last place we made but a short stay, our guides conducted us down to our Boat and returned with my friend Ata-go aboard to dinner. We had but just got aboard when an old gentleman came a long side who I understood from Atago was some King or great man, he was according interduced into the Ship when I made him a present of some red Cloth, Nails &c^a and seated him at Table to dinner, we now saw that he was certainly a man of some concequence for Ata-go would not sit down and eat before him, but as the old gentleman was almost blind, he got to the other end of the table and sat and eat with his back towards him, the old gentleman eat a bit of fish and drank a glass of Wine and then returned a shore. After Ata-go had seen him out of the ship he came and took his place at Table finished his dinner and drank about two glasses of wine. As soon as dinner was over we all went a shore again were we found the old Chief who presented me with a Hog and he and some others took a Walk with us into the Isle, our rout was by the first mentioned Afiá--tou-ca before which we again seated our selves, but had no praying on the contrary here the good natured old Chief interduced to me a woman and gave me to understand that I might retire with her, she was next offered to Captain Furneaux but met with a refusal from both, tho she was neither old nor ugly. Our stay here was but short. The Chief, probably thinking that we might want water on board the Sloops conducted us to a Plantation hard by and there shewed us a pool of fresh Water without our makeing the least enquiry after such a thing. I believe it to be the same as Tasman calls the Washing place for the King and his nobles, from hence we were conducted down to the shore of Maria Bay or NE side of the Isle, where in a Boat house the old chief shewed us a large double Canoe not yet launched and did not fail to make us sencible that it belonged to him, here we left him, and returned aboard. Mr Forster and his party spent the day in the Country botanizing and several of the officers were out Shooting, every one met with sevel treatment from the natives and found the Country just as I have described. We had also a brisk trade for Bananas, Cocoa-nutts, yams, Pigs and fowls all of which were purchass'd with nails and pieces of Cloth, a Boat from each Sloop was employed tradeing a shore bring[ing] off their cargo as soon as they were loaded which was generally in a short time, by this method we got a good quantity of fruit as well as other articles from people who had no canoes to bring them aboard, bought them cheaper and with less trouble.

* * *

WEDNESDAY 6*th*. My friend Otago viseted me this morning as usual, brought with him a Hog and assisted me in purchasing several others, after this I wint a shore, viseted the old Chief where I stayed till noon and then returned aboard to dinner with my friend who never quited me. As I intended to sail the next day, I made up a present for the old Chief whom I proposed to take leave of in the Evening, when I landed for this purpose I was told by the officers on shore that there was a far greater Chief no less than the King of the whole Island, come to viset us; he was first seen by Mr Pickersgill and some others of the officers who were in the Country and found him seated in a lane with a few people about him and soon saw that he was a man of some concequence by the extraordinary respect paid him, some when they approached him fell on their faces and put their heads between his feet and what was still more no one durst pass him till he gave them leave. Mr Pickersgill took hold of one arm and a nother of the gentlemen the other and conducted him down to the landing place where I found him seated with so much sullen and stupid gravity that I realy took him for an ideot which the people were ready to worship from some superstitious notions, I salluted him and spoke to him, he answered me not, nor did he take the least notice of me or alter a single feature in his countenance, this confirmed my former opinion and [I was] just going to leave him when one of the natives an intelligent youth under took to undeceive me which he did in such a manner as left me no doubt but that he was the principal man on the Island, accordingly I gave him the present I had intended for the old chief which consisted of a Shirt, An axe, a piece of Red Cloth, a looking glass & some Medals and Beeds, he still preserved his sullen gravity, I got not one word from him nor did he so much as turn his head or eyes either to the right or left but sit like a Post stuck in the ground just as I found him so I left him and soon after he retired. I had not been long aboard before word was brought me that a quantity of Provisions was sent me from this chief, a boat was sent to bring it aboard, it consisted of about 20 baskets containing roasted Bananas, sour bread and yams and a Pig of about twenty pound weight. Mr Edgcumb with his party was just imbarking when these came down to the Water side, the bearers thereof told him that it was a present from the King of the Island to me, that is the same person as I have been speaking of, after this I was no longer to doubt his dignity.

*　　*　　*

FRIDAY 8*th. Winds Easterly. Course S* 17° *W. Dist. sailed* 63 *Miles. Lat. in South* 22°3′. *Longde in West Reckg.* 175°30′. *Longde. made Amsterdm* 0°19′ *West.* It was 5 o'Clock in the PM before we were in a condition to make sail at which time Van Diemens Road, Lat 21°40′, Long^d 275°11′, from whence I take my departure, bore NE dist^t two miles, at this time a Canoe conducted by four Men came along side with one of those Drums already mentioned on which one man kept continually beating, thinking no doubt that we should be charm'd with his musick. I gave them a piece of Cloth and a Nail for their Drum and took this oppertunity to send to my friend Attago some Wheat, Pease & Beans which I had forgot to give him when he had the other seeds. After this Canoe was gone we stretched to the Southward with a gentle gale at SEBE, it being my intention to make the best of my way to New Zealand and there take in Wood and Water and then proceed to the South.

*   *   *

[*It is approximately 1200 miles from Tongatapu to New Zealand. The ships reached it in twelve days.*]

WEDNESDAY 20*th. Winds Northerly, North to Westerly. Course S*½*W. Dist. Sailed* 110 *Miles. Lat. in South* 37°48′. *Longde. in East Reckg.* 179°38′. *Longde. made West* 5°11′. First part frish gales and fair weather, at 7 in the evening it blew in squalls attended with rain, the Adventure being about 3 Miles a stern I shortned sail to the three Top-sails for her to come up. At 8 o'Clock the wind Veered to NBW upon which I altered the Course from South to SWBS and made the same known to the Adventure by Signal. About 11 o'Clock I was informd that land was seen extending from the South to the West and that we were very near it, when I got on deck I soon saw that it was only a black clowd forming in the Horizon which soon broke in a very heavy shower of rain, the Wind too shifted to the same quarter were it remained unsettled for some houres and then fixed at West and blew a fresh gale with which we stretched to the Southward. The night was so obscure that we were frequently obliged to fire guns and burn false fires to prevent being seperated.

THURSDAY 21*st*. *Winds Westerly. Course* S 27° W. *Dist. Sailed* 87 *Miles. Lat. in South* 39°6′. *Longde. in East Reckg.* 179°22′. *Londge. made West* 6°11′. Fresh gales and fair Weather. At 3 o'Clock in the PM our Longitude by observations of the Sun and Moon was 180°11′ West. At 5 o'Clock in the AM we saw the land of New Zealand extending from NWBN to WSW. At Noon Table Cape bore West distant 8 or 10 Leagues.

FRIDAY 22*nd*. *Winds Variable*. We stretched in for the land with a fresh gale at North and NW. I was desirous of having some communication with the Inhabitants of this Country as far north as possible in order to give them some Hogs, Fowls, Seeds, roots &c^a I had provided for the purpose, we fetched in with the land a little to the Northward of the Isle of Portland and stood as near the shore as we could with safety do, we saw several people on the Shore but none attempted to come off to us, seeing this I bore away under Portland were we lay to some time as well to give time for the Natives to come off as to wait for the Adventure which was some distance a stern, the wind blew fresh from off the land which might be the reason why no boddy came off therefore as soon as the Adventure was up with us I made Sail and Steered for Cape Kidnappers, having a moderate breeze at SW and West, hazy dirty weather. At middnight the Sky cleared up and the wind fixed at NW. At 5 o'Clock we passed the above mentioned Cape and at half past 9 o'Clock (being about 3 Leagues short of Black head) we saw some Canoes put off from the Shore upon which I brought to in order to give them time to come on board and made the Signal to the Adventure to continue her Course. It was not long before three Canoes reached us in which were about 18 people, the first that came were fishers and exchanged some fish for Cloth and Nails, I was not over desireous of geting any of the Men in this Canoe aboard because in one of the other two I expected to find a Chief, nor was I misstaken for in the Second Canoe which came was one or two as appear'd by their dress and manner of acting, the principal of these two came aboard without hesitation and was soon after followed by the other. I conducted him into the Cabbin and presented him with several large nails which he coveted so much that he seized hold of all he could cast his eyes upon and with such eagerness as plainly shewed that they were the most Valuable things in his eyes in our posession. I also gave him a peice of Cloth and a looking glass and then brought before him the Piggs, Fowls, Seeds and roots I intend'd for him, the Piggs and Fowls he at first took but little notice of till he was given to understand that [they] were for himself, nor was he then in such raptures as when I gave him a spike nail half the length of his arm, I however took notice that at going away he very well remember'd how many were brought before and took care that he had them all and kept a watchfull eye over them least any should be taken away; he made me a promise not to kill any, if he keeps his word and proper care is taken of them there were enough to stock the whole Island in due time, there being two Boars, two Sows, two Cocks and four Hens; the seeds and roots were such as are most usefull (viz) Wheat, French and Kidney Beans, Pease, Cabages, Turnips, Onions, Carrots, Parsnips, Yams &cᵃ &cᵃ, with these Articles I dismissed my two chiefs and made sail again but by this time the wind had Shifted from NW to WSW with which we stretched off to the Southward. At Noon our Latitude was 4 °   ′ s [Cape Turnagain] bearing   distant   Leagues. It was evidant that these people had not forgot the Endeavour being on their Coast for the first words they said to us was we are affraid of the guns [Mataou no te poupou], probably they were no strangers to the affair which happened of Cape Kidnappers.

SATURDAY 23*rd.* In the PM the wind blew fresh at West and WBN and in squals. I carried a press of sail in order to keep the land aboard which occasioned the loss of our fore-top-gallant mast which went away close to the cap. At half passed 7 we tacked and stretched in shore, Cape Turnagain at this time bore about NW½N, 6 or 7 Leagues distant, the Adventure being too far to leeward to distinguish any Signal was seperated from us, the Squals increasing and obliged us to Double Reef the Main Top-sail and to single-reef the Fore and Mizen Top-sails, the latter was no sooner set than it split in two from the one leach to the other. We spent the night stretching off and on, at 6 o'Clock in the Morning we found our selves about 7 Leagues from the land which we now stood in for under our Courses the gale having increased in such a manner as not to admit of carrying more sail, the wind too had veered to sw and ssw and was attend with rainy weather. At 9 o'Clock the sky began to clear up and the gale abated so as to admit of our carrying close reefed Top-sails. At 11 o'Clock we were close in with Cape Turnagain accordingly Tacked and Stood off. At Noon it bore West a little northerly distant 6 or 7 miles, our Latitude by observation was 40°30' s.

SUNDAY 24*th*. Soon after noon the Wind flat'ned almost to a Calm and we were in hopes that it would be succeeded by one more favourable, according we got up a nother Topgall^t Mast loosed the reefs out of the Top-sails and got topg^t yards a Cross. At 4 o'Clock a breeze sprung up at WBN with which we stretched along shore to the Southward as near the wind as we could lay, which began to increase in Such a manner as to oblige us to close reef our topsails and strike top-gallant yards. We continued to stretch to the Southward all night under two Courses and two close reef'd Top-sails, having a very strong gale attended with heavy Squals, towards day-light the gale abated and we were again tempted to shake out the reefs and get topgall^t yards a Cross, this was again all labour lost for before 9 o'Clock we were reduced to the same sail as before, the wind was at WNW and blew as hard as ever attended with very heavy squalls. Soon after the Adventure joined us and at Noon Cape Palliser the Northern[23] point of *Eaheinomauwe* bore west distant 8 or 9 Leagues.

MONDAY 25*th*. The gale continued without the least variation for the better till middnight when it fell little wind and shifted to SE. Three hours after it fell Calm, during this time we loosed the reefs out of the Top-sails and rigged top-g^t yards with the vain hopes that the next wind which came would be favourable, we were misstaken, the wind only tooke this little repose in order to gain strength to fall the heavier upon us, for at 6 o'Clock a gale sprung up at NW with which we attempted to stretch to the sw. Cape Palliser at this time bore NNW distant about 8 or 9 Leagues, as the gale increased we reduced our sails till about 11 o'Clock when it came on in such fury as to oblige us to take in all our sails with the utmost expedition and to lay-to under

23. He means southern.

our bare poles with our heads to the sw. The brails of the Mizen giving way the wind took hold of the sail and tore it in several places, we presently lowered down the yard and bent a nother sail. The Sea rose in proportion with the Wind so that we not only had a furious gale but a mountainous Sea also to incounter, thus after beating two days against strong gales and arriving in sight of our Port we had the mortification to be drove off from the land by a furious storm; two favourable circumstances attended it which gave us some consolation, the Weather continued fair and we were not apprehinsive of a lee-shore.

TUESDAY 26*th*. The Storm continued all the PM without the least intermission. At 7 o'Clock the Adventure being to leeward and out of sight we bore down to look for her and after runing the distance we supposed her to be off, brought to again without seeing her, it being very hazey in the horizon occasioned in a great measure by the spray of the Sea which was lifted up to a great height by the force of the wind. At middnight the gale abated so that we could bear the Mizen stay sail and soon after it fell little wind and at 4 o'Clock shifted to sw when we wore, set the Courses and close reefed Top-sails and stood in for the land. The Wind soon after freshned and fixed at South but as the Adventure was some distance a stern we lay-by for her to come up till 8 o'Clock when we made all the sail we could and steered NBW½w for the Straits. At Noon our Latitude by observation was 42°27′ s. Cape Palliser by judgement bore North distant 17 Leag⁵.

WEDNESDAY 27*th*. Our favourable wind was not of sufficient duration, it fell by degrees and at last at 7 in the evening flatned to a Calm which at 10 was succeeded by a fresh breeze from the North with which we stretched to the Westward till 3 in the Morning when being near the land of Cape Campbel we tacked and stretched over for Cape Pallisser under our Close reef'd Top-sails and Courses, being as much sail as we could carry. At day-light we could but just see the Adventure from the Mast head to the Southward. At Noon the last mentioned Cape bore West distant 4 or 5 Leagues, we now Tacked and stretched to the sw having a strong gale and fair weather.

THURSDAY 28*th*. Wind and weather continues the same, the former rather increaseing for at 4 pm we were obliged to take in the Top-sails. At 6 Cape Pallisser bore NBW½W distant 6 Leagues. At middnight wore and stood to the Northward. At 6 am set the Top-sails close reefd, the Adventure in sight to the South. At 8 wore and Stretched to the sw, at Noon we were by Observation in the Latitude 42°17′ s the high land over Cape Campell west distant 10 or 12 Leagues. By this time the gale had increased so as to make it necessary to take in the Top-sails and main-sail and to lay too under the fore-sail and Mizen stay-sail, the Adventure 4 or 5 Miles to lee-ward.

FRIDAY 29*th*. We continued to lie to untill 4 o'Clock in the pm when the gale being some thing abated we wore and set the Main Top-sail close reefed, some time after set the main-sail, under these sails we stretched to the Northward all night with the wind at WNW and WBN, a strong gale attended with squalls which at 4 o'Clock in the morning began to abate so that we could bear the Fore top-sail. Soon after the wind shifted to sw and blew a gentle gale. We took immidiate advantage of it and set all our sails and stretched in for Cape Pallisser which at Noon bore WBN½N distant about 6 Leagues. Latitude Observed 41°44′ s.

SATURDAY 30*th*. The breeze continued between the sw and South till 5 o'Clock in the PM when it fell calm, we being about 3 Leagues short of Cape Pallisser. At 7 o'Clock a breeze sprung up at NNE which was as favourable as we could wish, it proved however of short duration for about 9 the wind shifted into its old quarter NW and increased to a fresh gale with which we stretched to the sw under Courses and single-reefed top-sails. At Middnight the Adventure was two or three Miles a stern, soon after she disapeared nor was she to be seen at day-light, we supposed she had tacked and stood to the NE by which means we had lost sight of her; we however continued to stand to the westward with the wind at NNW and which increased in such a manner as at last to bring us under our two Courses, after splitting a new Main top-sail. At Noon Cape Campbell bore NBW distant 7 or 8 Leagues.

SUNDAY 31*st*. At 8 o'Clock in the pm the gale became somewhat more moderate and veered more to the north so that we fetched in with the shore under the Snowey mountains[24] about four or five leagues to windward of the Lookers on,[25] where there was all the appearence of a large bay. Had the Adventure been now with me I should have given up all thoughts of going to Queen Charlottes Sound to Wood and Water and sought for these articles farther South as the wind was now favourable for rainging a long the coast but as we were now seperated I was under a necessity [of] going to the Sound as being the place of rendezvouz. As we drew near the land we sounded and at the distance of 3 Miles found 47 fathom which decreased in such a manner that at the distance of 1 Mile there was 25 fathom, we then wore and stood to the Eastward, under the two Courses and Close reefed Top-sails, but these last we were soon put past and at 7 o'Clock in the Morning we wore and brought to under the Fore-sail and Mizen Stay sail the wind being now at NNW and blew with great fury till 9 when it abated a little and we set the Main Sail and two close reef'd Top-sails but the latter we were obliged to take in again at Noon at which time the snowey mountains bore WNW distant 12 or 14 Leagues. Our Latitude by observation was 42°22′ s.

* * *

[NOVEMBER 1773]

[*The good fortune of the northerly gale abating followed by a southerly breeze enabled Cook to head for Queen Charlotte Sound, but the wind changing again forced him into the inlet east of Cape Terawhiti (where Wellington now stands). He anchored there overnight and next day in spite of very difficult conditions made the rendezvous of Queen Charlotte Sound and Ship Cove. But there was no sign of the* Adventure.]

THURSDAY 4*th*. Gentle breezes and clear pleasent weather. Sent on shore all our empty Casks in order to be repaired cleaned and fill'd with Water, set up tents for the reception of the Sail-makers, Coopers and others whose business made it necessary for them to be on Shore,

24. The Kaikoura ranges.
25. Kaikoura Peninsula. The name was given on the first voyage.

began to caulk the decks and sides, Overhaul the rigging, to cut firewood and set up the forge to repair the Iron work all of which were absolutely necessary occupations. In the Morning I made some hauls with the seine but got no fish, the natives in some measure made up for this difficiency by bring[ing] us a good quantity which they exchang'd for pieces of cloth &c^a.

FRIDAY 5*th*. PM fair weather, AM clowdy with rain which hindered us from finishing boot-toping the Starboard side which we had begun. In opening some of our Bread Casks we found to our irrepairable loss a good deal of the bread very much damaged, owing as we supposed to the Casks being made of green Wood. I ordered the Oven to be set up to bake or dry such as was damp and not so bad but that it might be eat. This mor[n]ing some of the natives stole from out of one of the tents some of our peoples Cloaths, as soon as I was informed of it I went to their habitations in an adjoining Cove and demanded them again and after some time recovered the most of them, here I saw the youngest of the two Sows Capt Furneaux left in *Canibal Cove*, it was lame in one of its hind legs otherwise in good case; if we understood these people right, the Boar and other Sow was also taken away and the one carried towards the East and the other to the west, we have also been informed that the two Goats have likewise been caught killed and eat, thus all our endeavours for stocking this Country with usefull Animals are likely to be frusterated by the very people whom we meant to serve; our gardens had faired some thing better, every thing in them excepting the Potatoes, they had left intirely to nature who had acted her part so well that we found most articles in a florishing state, the Potatoes they had dug up, some few, however remained and were growing.

SATURDAY 6*th*. PM hard rain so that no work could go forward. AM fair weather. In the morning I went to the cove where the natives resided to haul the Seine and took with me a young boar and a sow, two Cocks and two hens I had brought from the Isles and gave them to the Natives who seemed as if they would take proper care of them, at least I had good reason to think so sence they had kept Captain

Furneaux's young sow near five month for I must suppose that it fell into their hands soon after we left the place.

Towards Noon several Indians came from up the Bay in four or five Canoes, these together with what might be in the Cove before made up about one hundred and fifty, these new commers took up their quarters near us but very early the next morning moved off with Six of our small water-casks and with them all the others that we found here upon our arrival, the precipitate retreat of these last we supposed was owing to the theeft the others had committed, they left behind them some of their dogs and the boar I had given them and which I now took back again, our Casks will be the least loss we shall sustain by these people leaving us as they were very usefull in providing us with fish which they were far more expert in catching than we.

MONDAY 8*th*. Hazy weather with drizling rain which proved rather unlucky as it hindered us from working upon our Bread, but the next day proved very favourable for this as well as our other works, the wind too was at NE which gave us some hopes of seeing the Adventure but these hopes vanished in the after-noon when the Wind shifted to the West. Pretty early this morning some of our friends the Natives paid us a viset and brought with them a quantity of fish which they exchanged for two hatchets.

WEDNESDAY 10*th*. Showery most part of the day and the wind variable.

THURSDAY 11*th*. Wind Southerly with Showery weather.

FRIDAY 12*th*. Wind as yesterday but fair weather which gave us an oppertunity to finish over hauling the bread [4292] pounds of which we found Mouldy and rotten and totally unfit for men to eat [3000] pounds more that few would eat but such as were in our circumstances, this damage our bread had susstained was wholy owing to the Casks being made of green wood and not well seasoned before the Biscuit was packed in them for all the biscuits that were in co[n]tact or near the insides of the Casks were damaged while those in the middle were not the least injured. Mr Forster and his party in the Country botanizing.

SATURDAY 13*th*. Clear pleasant weather. Early in the Morning the Natives brought us a quantity of fish which they exchanged as usual for Cloth &cᵃ but their greatest branch of trade is for the green-talk or stone (called by them Poenammoo) a thing of no sort of Value, nevertheless it is so much sought after by our people that there is hardly any thing that they would not give for a piece. Great part of our Coals being expended we took into the Main hold two launch loads of ballast after taking out all the Coals.

SUNDAY 14*th*. Weather as yesterday. In the Morning had a plentifull supply of fish from the Natives, who remained with us the most part of the day.

MONDAY 15*th*. Fair weather winds notherly a gentle breeze. In the Mornᵍ I went in the Pinnace over to the East Bay, accompanied by some of the officers and gentlemen; as soon as we landed we went upon one of the hills in order to take a view of the Straits, to see if we could discover any thing of the Adventure, we had a fatiguing walk to little purpose for when we got to the top of the hill we found the Eastern horizon so foggy that we could not see above two or three miles. Mʳ Forster who was one of the party profited by this excursion in collecting some new plants; as to the Adventure I dispair of seeing her any more but am totally at a loss to conceive what is become of her till now. I thought that she might have put into some port in the Strait when the wind came at NW the day we Anchor'd in Ship Cove and there stayed to compleat her wood and Water; this conjector was reasonable enough at first, but the elapsation of twelve days has now made it scarce probable. The hill we were upon is the same as I was upon in 1770 on which we then built a tower of Stones which was now leveled to the very ground, done no doubt by the Natives with a view of finding some thing hid in it. When we returned from the hill we found a number of the natives collected round our boat, we made some exchanges with them and then returned on board and in our way viseted some others.

*   *   *

MONDAY 22*nd*. Clear pleasent Weather, winds variable. . . . I took four

Hogs, three sows and one boar, two hens and three cocks and carried them a little way into the woods in the very bottom of West Bay where I left them with as much food as would serve them a week or ten days. . . . Having now got the principal parts of the Sloop caulked, the rigging over hauled and in other respects in a condition for Sea, I ordered the tents to be struck and every thing to be got on board. . . .

TUESDAY 23*rd*. Calm or light airs from the Northward so that we could not get to sea as I intended, some of the officers went on shore to amuse themselves among the Natives where they saw the head and bowels of a youth who had lately been killed, the heart was stuck upon a forked stick and fixed to the head of their largest Canoe, the gentlemen brought the head on board with them, I was on shore at this time but soon after returned on board when I was informed of the above circumstances and found the quarter deck crowded with the Natives. I now saw the mangled head or rather the remains of it for the under jaw, lip &c^a were wanting, the scul was broke on the left side just above the temple, the face had all the appearence of a youth about fourteen or fifteen, a peice of the flesh had been broiled and eat by one of the Natives in the presince of most of the officers. The sight of the head and the relation of the circumstances just mentioned struck me with horor and filled my mind with indignation against these Canibals, but when I considered that any resentment I could shew would avail but little and being desireous of being an eye wittness to a fact which many people had their doubts about, I concealed my indignation and ordered a piece of the flesh to be broiled and brought on the quarter deck where one of these Canibals eat it with a seeming good relish before the whole ships Company which had such effect on some of them as to cause them to vomit. [Oediddee] was [so] struck with horor at the sight that [he] wept and scolded by turns, before this happened he was very intimate with these people but now he neither would come near them or suffer them to touch him, told them to their faces that they were vile men and that he was no longer their friend, he used the same language to one of the officers who cut of the flesh and refused to except, or even touch the knife with which it was cut, such was this Islanders aversion to this vile custom. I could not find out the reason of their undertaking this expedition, all I could understand for certain was that they had gone from hence into Admiralty Bay and there fought with their enemies many of whom they killed, they counted to me fifty a number which exceeded all probabillity by reason of the smallness of their own number, I think I understood them for certain that this youth was killed there and not brought away a prisoner, nor could I learn that they had brought away any more which increased the improbabillity of their having killd so many. We had reason to beleive that they did not escape without some loss, a young woman was seen, more than one, to cut and scar herself as is the custom when they loose a friend or relation.

That the New Zealanders are Canibals can now no longer be doubted, the account I gave of it in my former Voyage was partly founded on circumstances and was, as I afterwards found, discredited by many people. I have often been asked, after relateing all the circumstance, if I had actualy seen them eat human flesh my self, such a queston was sufficient to convence me that they either disbelieved all I had said or formed a very different opinion from it, few considers what a savage man is in his original state and even after he is in some degree civilized; the New Zealanders are certainly in a state of civilization, their behavour to us has been Manly and Mild, shewing allways a readiness to oblige us; they have some arts a mong them which they execute with great judgement and unweared patience; they are far less addicted to thieving than the other Islanders and are I believe strictly honist among them-selves. This custom of eating their enimies slain in battle (for I firmly believe they eat the flesh of no others) has undoubtedly been handed down to them from the earliest times and we know that it is not an easy matter to break a nation of its ancient customs let them be ever so inhuman and savage, especially if that nation is void of all religious principles as I believe the new zealanders in general are and like them without any settled form of goverment; as they become more united they will of concequence have fewer Enemies and become more civilized and then and not till then this custom may be forgot, at present they seem to have but little idea of treating other men as they themselves would wish to be treated, but treat them as they think they should be treated under the same circumstances. If I remember right one of the arguments they made use on against Tupia who frequently expostulated with them against this custom, was that there could be no harm in killing and eating the man who would do the same by you if it was in his power, for said they 'can there be any harm in eating our Enimies whom we have killed in battle, would not those very enimies have done the same to us?' I have often seen them listen to Tupia with great attention, but I never found that his arguments had any weight with them or that they ever once owned that this custom was wrong and when [Oediddee] shewed his resentment against them they only laughed at him, indeed it could not be supposed that they would pay much attention to a youth like him. I must here observe that [Oediddee] soon learnt to convirse with these people tolerable well as I am perswaided he would have done with those of Amsterdam had he been the same time with them.

WEDNESDAY 24*th*. At 4 o'Clock in the Morning we unmoored with an intent to put to Sea, but the wind being Northerly or NE without and blew in strong pufs into the Cove so that we were obliged to lay fast. While we were unmooring, some of our old friends the Natives came to take their leave of us and after wards took all their effects into their Canoes and left the Cove, but the party which had been out on the late expedition remained, these some of the gentlemen viseted and found the heart still remaining on the Canoe and the bowels and lungs lying on the beach, but the flesh they believed was all devoured.

THURSDAY 25*th*. At 4 o'Clock in the Morning we weighed with a light breeze out of the Cove which carried us no farther than betwen Motuara and Long-island where we were obliged to anchor, presently after a breeze sprung up at North with which we weighed and turned out of the Sound by 12 o'Clock. . . .

The morning before we sailed I wrote a memorandum seting forth the time we arrived last here, the day we sailed, the rout I intended to take & such other information as I thought necessary for Captain Furneaux to know and buried it in a bottle under the root of a tree in the garden in the bottom of the Cove in such a manner that it must be found by any European who may put into the Cove. I however have not the least reason to think that it will ever fall into the hands of the person I intended it for, for it is hardly possible that Captain Furneaux can be in any part of New Zealand and I not have heard of him in all this time, nevertheless I was determined not to leave the country without looking for him where I thought it was most likely for him to be found; accordingly as soon as we were clear of the Sound I hauld over for Cape Teerawhitte and ran along the shore from point to point to Cape Pallisser fireing guns every half hour without seeing or hearing the least signs of what we were in search after. . . .

The next Morning at day-light we made Sail round Cape Pallisser fireing guns as usual but saw not the least signs of the Adventure and therefore bore away for Cape Campbell on the other side of the Strait having a light breeze at NE. Soon after we discovered a smoak to the NE a little way in-land, it was improbable enough that this should be made by any of the Adventures crew, I however determined to put it out of all manner of doubt and accordingly hauled the wind again, we kept plying till 6 o'Clock in the evening, several hours after this smoke and every other sign of people disapeared. All the officers being unanimous of opinion that the Adventure could neither be stranded on the Coast or be in any of the Ports in this Country determined me to spend no more time in search of her, but to proceed directly to the Southward. I am under [no] apprehensions for the safety of the Adventure nor can I even guess which way she is gone, the manner she was seperated from me and [not] coming to the rendezvouze has left me no grounds to form any conjectors upon, I can only suppose that Captain Furneaux was tired with beating against the NW winds and had taken a resolution to make the best of his way to the Cape of good hope, be this as it may I have no expectation of joining him any more.

*   *   *

[*The* Adventure, *much less able than the* Resolution *to cope with adverse weather conditions, was constantly defeated in her attempts to battle her way to Queen Charlotte Sound, and it was not until 30 November that she succeeded — five days after Cook had left. They found the bottle, but necessary repairs etc. meant that they were not ready to sail until 17 December. Then disaster struck. The cutter did not return from a mission, and Furneaux found that the crew had been killed by the Maoris. It was not until 23 December that they finally left. By the time they reached the vicinity of Cape Horn, neither the ship nor the crew, nor their provisions, were in good shape, and Furneaux made the best of his way to the Cape of Good Hope and to England, which he reached on 14 July 1774.*

Meanwhile Cook set off towards the Antarctic without a consort, claiming that no one was dejected at the prospect of proceeding on their own 'to the South or wherever I thought proper to lead them'. By the middle of December they had reached the ice.]

[DECEMBER 1773]

WEDNESDAY 15*th. Therm.r. Noon* 31. *Winds* WBN, NNW, & West. *Course* S 60°15′ E. *Dist. Sailed* 116 Miles. *Lat. in South* 65°52′. *Longde. in West Reck.g.* 159°20′. *Long. made from C. Pallisser* 25°19′. Fresh gales and thick Foggy weather with snow, except in the pm when we had some intervals of clear Weather in one of which we found the Variation to be 14°12′ E. At 6 o'Clock double reefed the Top-sails and handed the Main sail and Mizen Top-sail. The Ice begins to increase fast, from Noon till 8 o'Clock in the evening we saw but two islands, but from 8 to 4 am we passed fifteen, besides a quantity of loose Ice which we sailed through, this last increased so fast upon us that at 6 o'Clock we were obliged to alter the Course more to the East, having to the South an extensive feild of loose ice; there were several partitions in the feild and clear water behind it, but as the wind blew strong the Weather foggy, the going in among this Ice might have been attended with bad concequences, especially as the wind would not permit us to return. We therefore hauled to the NE on which course we had stretched but a little way before we found our selves quite imbayed by the ice and were obliged to Tack and stretch back to the sw having the loose field ice to the South and many large islands to the North. After standing two hours on this tack the wind very luckily veered to the westward with which we tacked and stretched to the Northward (being at this time in Lat 66°0′ s) and soon got clear of all the loose ice but had yet many huge islands to incounter, which were so numerous that we had to luff for one and bear up for a nother. One of these mases was very near proving fatal to us, we had not weather[ed] it more than once or twice our length, had we not succeeded this circumstance could never have been related. According to the old proverb a miss is as good as a mile, but our situation requires more misses than we can expect, this together with the improbability of meeting with land to the South and the impossibility of exploreing it for the ice if we did find any, determined me to haul to the north. This feild or loose ice is not such as is usually formed in Bays or Rivers, but like such as is broke off from large Islands, round ill-shaped pieces from the size of a small Ship's Hull downwards, whilest we were amongest it we frequently, notwithstanding all our care, ran against some of the large pieces, the shoks which the Ship received thereby was very considerable, such as no Ship could bear long unless properly prepared for the purpose. Saw a great number of Penguins on an ice island and some Antartick Petrels flying about.

THURSDAY 16th. Therm.r. Noon 31 to 33. Winds West, Calm, SE. Course N 19½° E. Dist. Sailed 102 Miles. Lat. in South 64°16'. Longd. in West Reck.g. 158°0'. Longd. made from C. Palliser 26°39'. Continued to stretch to the Northward with a very fresh gale at west which was attended with thick snow showers till 8 pm when the weather began to clear up and the gale to abate. At 6 o'Clock in the am it fell Calm and continued so till 10 when a breeze sprung up at SEbS with which we stretched to the NE. Weather dark and gloomy and very cold our sails and rigging hung with icicles for these two days past. At present but few ice islands in sight but have past a great many this last 24 hours.

* * *

TUESDAY 21st. Therm.r. Noon 33. Winds NE. Course S 41° E. Dist. Sailed 70 Miles. Lat. in South 66°50'. Longde. in West Reck.g. 66°50'. Long. made C. Pallisser 38°11'. In the pm the wind increased to a strong gale attended with a thick fogg sleet and rain which constitutes the very worst of weather, our rigging was so loaded with ice that we had enough to do to get our Top-sails down to double reef. At 7 o'Clock we came the second time under the Polar Circle and stood to the SE till 6 o'Clock in the am when being in Lat 67°5' South, Longitude 145°49' West, the fogg being exceeding thick we came close aboard a

large Island of ice and being at the same time a good deal embarrass'd
with loose ice we with some difficulty wore and stood to the NW untill
Noon when the fogg being some what disipated we resumed our
Course again to the SE. The ice islands we fell in with in the morning,
for there were more than one, were very high and rugged terminating
in many Peaks, whereas all those we have seen before were quite flat
at top and not so high. A great Sea from the North. Grey Albatroses
and a few Antarctick Petrels.

*   *   *

FRIDAY 24*th*. *Therm.r. Noon* 32. *Winds Northerly. Course S* 40° *W. Dist.
Sailed* 9 *Miles. Lat. in South* 67°19'. *Longde. in West Reck.g.* 138°15'. *Long.
made C. Pallisser* 46°24'. At 4 o'Clock in the PM as we were standing to
the SE, fell in with such a vast quantity of field or loose ice as covered
the whole Sea from South to East and was so thick and close as to
obstruct our passage, the wind at this time being pretty moderate,
brought to in the edge of this feild, hoisted out two boats and sent
them to take some up, and in the mean time we slung several large
pi[e]ces along side and hoisted them in with our tackles; by such time
as the Boats had made two trips it was Eight o'Clock when we hoisted
them in and made sail to the westward under double reef'd Top-sails
and Courses, with the wind notherly a strong gale attended with a
thick fog Sleet and Snow which froze to the Rigging as it fell and
decorated the whole with icicles. Our ropes were like wires, Sails like
board or plates of Metal and the Shivers froze fast in the blocks so
that it required our utmost effort to get a Top-sail down and up; the
cold so intense as hardly to be endured, the whole Sea in a manner
covered with ice, a hard gale and a thick fog: under all these unfavourable circumstances it was natural for me to think of returning more
to the North, seeing there was no probability of finding land here nor
a possibility of get[ting] farther to the South and to have proceeded
to the East in this Latitude would not have been prudent as well on
account of the ice as the vast space of Sea we must have left to the
north unexplored, a space of 24° of Latitude in which a large track of
land might lie, this point could only be determined by makeing a
stretch to the North. While we were takeing up the ice two of the

Antarctick Petrels so often mentioned were shott; we were right in our conjectures in supposeing them of the Petrel tribe; they are about the size of a large pigeon, the feathers of the head, back and part of the upper side of the wings are a lightish brown, the belly and under side of the wings white, the tail feathers which are 10 in number are white tiped with brown. At the same time we got another new Petrel smaller than the former, its plumage was dark grey. They were both casting their feathers and yet they were fuller of them than any birds we had seen, so much has nature taken care to cloath them sutable to the climate in which they live. At this time we saw two or three Chocolate coloured Albatrosses with yellowish Bills, these as well as the Petrels above mentioned are no were seen but among the ice. The bad weather continuing without the least variation for the better which made it necessary for us to proceed with great caution and to make short boards over that part of the Sea we had in some measure made our selves accquainted with the preceeding day, we were continually falling in with large ice islands which we had enough to do to keep clear of.

SATURDAY 25*th*. *Therm.r. Noon* 34. *Winds NW. Course N* 48¼° *E. Dist. Sailed* 84 *Miles. Lat. in South* 66°23'. *Longde. in West Reck.g.* 135°7'. *Long. made C. Pallisser* 49°32'. In the PM the wind veer'd more to the West, the gale abated and the sky cleared up and presented to our view the many islands of ice we had escaped during the Fog. At 6 o'Clock being in Latitude 67°0' s, Long^de the same as yesterday at noon, the variation was observed to be 15°26' East. As we advanced to the NE with a gentle gale at NW the ice increased so fast upon us that at Noon no less than 90 or 100 large islands were seen round us besides innumberable smaller pieces.[26]

SUNDAY 26*th*. *Therm.r.* 37. *Winds NNW, Calm, WSW. Course N* 66° *E. Dist. Sailed* 20 *Miles. Lat. in South* 65°15'. *Longde. in West Reck.g.* 134°22'. *Long. made C. Pallisser* 50°17'. *Varn.* 16°2' *East.* At 2 o'Clock in the pm it fell calm, we had before preceived this would happen and got the

26. The usual Christmas celebrations were observed, rather muted because (according to Forster) 'a great many people in the ship', including himself, were 'very ill'.

ship into as clear a birth as we could where she drifted along with the ice islands and by takeing the advantage of every light air of wind was kept from falling foul of any one; we were fortunate in two things, continual day light and clear weather, had it been foggy nothing less than a miracle could have kept us clear of them, for in the morning the whole sea was in a manner wholy covered with ice, 200 islands and upwards, none less than the Ships hull and some more than a mile in circuit were seen in the compass of five miles, the extent of our sight, and smaller peices innumberable. At 4 in the AM a light breeze sprung up at WSW and enabled us to Steer north the most probable way to extricate our selves from these dangers.

*   *   *

[JANUARY 1774]

TUESDAY 4*th. Therm.r. Noon* 46¼. *Winds Westerly. Course NBE. Dist. Sailed* 114 *Miles. Lat. in* 54°55′. *Longd. in West Greenwich Reck.g.* 139°4′, *East C. Pallisser* 45°45′. Fresh gales and Clowdy with some Showers of Sleet. In the PM saw a few more of the small divers, and some small pieces of weed which appeard to be old and decayed and not as if it had lately been broke from rocks. I can not tell what to think of the divers, had there been more of them I should have thought them signs of the vicinity of land, as I never saw any so far from known land before, probably these few may have been brought out thus far to Sea by some Shoal of fish, such were certainly about us by the vast number of Blue Petrels and Albatrosses, all of which left us before the evening. As the wind seems now fixed in the western board, we shall be under a necessity of leaving unexplored to the west a space of Sea containing 40° of Longitude and 20° or 21° of Latitude, had the wind been favourable I intended to have run 15° or 20° of longitude to the west in the Latitude we are now in and back again to the East in the Latitude of 50° or near it, this rout would have so intersected the space above mentioned as to have hardly left room for the bare supposission of any large land lying there. Indeed as it is we have no reason to suppose that there is any for we have had now for these several days past a great swell from west and NW, a great sign we have not been

covered by any land between these two points. In the AM saw some
Pie bald porpuses.

*　　*　　*

THURSDAY 6*th. Therm.r.* 47. *Winds West, NW, & WSW. Course* N 36°45'
E. *Dist. Sailed* 128 *Miles. Lat. in* 52°0'. *Longde. in* W. *Greenwh. Reck.g.*
135°32' *Watch* 135°38', *East Cape Pallisser* 49°7'. Very strong gales and
excessive heavy squalls attended with rain. At 8 pm took in the
Top-sails till 8 am when the gale being some what abated set them
again close reef'd. At Noon loosed all the reefs out and bore away NE
with a fresh gale at WSW, fair weather, the distance between us now
and our rout to Otahiete being little more than two hundred leagues
in which space it is not probable there can be any land, and it is less
probable there can be any to the west from the vast high billows we
now have from that quarter.

*　　*　　*

TUESDAY 11*th. Therm.r. Noon* 50. *Winds Westerly. Course* N 81° E. *Dist.
Sailed* 103 *Miles. Lat. in South* 47°51'. *Longde.* W. *Greenwh. Reck.g.* 122°12'
Watch 122°17'307". *Long. EC. Palliser* 62°27'. Little wind continued most
part of the PM. In the night it began to freshen, blew in Squalls attended
with rain, afterwards the weather became clear and the wind sittled.
At Noon being little more than two hundred Leagues from my track
to Otaheite in 1769 in which space it was not probable any thing was
to be found, we therefore hauled up SE with a fresh gale at SWBW.[27]

WEDNESDAY 12*th. Therm.r. Noon* 56. *Winds SWBW to NWBN. Course* S
42°30'. *Dist. Sailed* 138 *Miles. Lat. in South* 49°32'. *Longd.* W. *Greenwh.
Reck.g.* 119°52' *Watch* 119°57'. *Long. E. C. Pallisser* 64°47'. Fresh gales
and pleasent weather. In the pm found the variation 2°34' East. The
Westerly swell still continues. Very few birds seen and these such as
are found all over the Ocean in these Latitudes. At Noon hauled more
to the Southward.

*　　*　　*

27. This alteration of course to the south brought 'utter astonishment' to John Elliott,
who thought they were now on their way home. The captain, he wrote, was 'close
and secret in his intentions at all times'.

THURSDAY 20*th. Therm.r.* 40. *Winds NE & Easterly. Course S* 21° *E. Dist. Sailed* 45 *Miles. Lat. in South* 62°34'. *Longde. in West Reck.g.* 116°24'. *Long. East C. Pallisser* 68°15'. First part fresh gales and hazey with rain, remainder little wind and Mostly fair. At 7 PM saw a large piece of Weed. In the AM two ice islands one of which was very high terminating in a peak or like the Cupala of St Pauls Church, we judged it to be 200 feet high. A great Westerly swell still continues a probable certainty there is no land between us and the Meridian of 133½° which we were under when last in this Latitude.

* * *

TUESDAY 25*th. Therm.r. Noon* 42. *Winds WNW to North. Course SBW*½*W. Dist. Sailed* 109 *Miles. Lat. in South* 65°24'. *Longd. in W. Greenwh. Reck.g.* 109°31', *East C. Pallisser* 75°8'. *Varn. East* 19°27'. First part fresh breeze and clowdy, Middle hazy with Sleet and rain, latter a gentle breeze and pleasent weather and the air very warm considering the Latitude. Not a bit of ice to be seen, which we who have been so much used to it think a little extraordinary and causes various opinions and conjectures.

WEDNESDAY 26*th. Therm.r. Noon* 40. *Winds Northerly. Course South. Dist. Sailed* 72 *Miles. Lat. in South* 66°36'. *Longd. in W. Greenwh. Reck.g.* 109°31', *East C. Pallisser* 75°8'. *Varn. East* 18°20'. Gentle breezes and Clowdy mild weather. At 6 PM Latitude 65°44' s. Variation p^r Azm^{uths} 19°27' E and at 7 AM being then in Latitude 66°20' the Variation was 18°20' East. At this time saw Nine Ice islands, the most of them small, several Whales and a few blue Petrels. At 8 o'Clock we came the third time within the Antarctick Polar Circle. Soon after saw an appearence of land to the East and SE, haul'd up for it and presently after it disapeared in the haze. Sounded but found no ground with a line of 130 fathom. A few whales & Petrels seen.

THURSDAY 27*th. Therm.r.* 37½. *Winds NE. Course S* 21°15' *E. Dist. Sailed* 83 *Miles. Lat. in South* 67°52'. *Longd. in W. Greenwh. Reck.g.* 108°15', *East C. Pallisser* 76°24'. Little wind and foggy with rain and Sleet, at intervals fair and tolerable clear. Continued to stretch to the SE till 8 o'Clock am by which time we were assured our supposed land was vanished into clowds and therefore resumed our Course to the South. A smooth

Sea, what little swell we have is from the NE. A few Blue Petrels, Black Sheer-waters and Mother Caries Chickens are all the Birds we see.

* * *

SATURDAY 29*th. Therm.r.* 36½. *Winds NE, NW, & NNE. Course S* 33° *E. Dist. Sailed* 30 *Miles. Lat. in South* 70°00′ *Obn. Longd. in W. Greenwh. Reck.g.* 107°27′ *Watch* 107°36′, *East C. Pallisser* 77°12′. *Varn. East* 22°41′. At 1 o'Clock in the PM fell in with some loose ice, brought-to, hoisted out two Boats and took a quantity on board; which done made sail to the NW not daring to stand to the South in so thick a fog which hindered us from seeing the extent or quantity of ice we were among. The wind was Variable between NW and North and but little of it. At Midnight Tacked to the Eastwards. At 4 o'Clock the Sky cleared up, the wind fixed at NNE and we bore away SSE passing several large Ice islands. Betwixt 4 and 8 o'Clock found the variation by several trials to be 22°41′ E. Latitude at this time about 69°45′ S. Clear pleasent Weather, Air not cold.

SUNDAY 30*th. Winds ESE. Course S* 20° *E. Dist. Sailed* 51 *Miles. Lat. in South* 70°48′. *Longd. in W. Reck.g.* 106°34′. Continued to have a gentle gale at NE with Clear pleasent weather till towards the evening, when the Sky became Clowded and the air Cold atten[d]ed with a smart frost. In the Latitude of 70°23′ the Variation was 24°31′ East; some little time after saw a piece of Rock Weed covered with Barnacles which one of the brown Albatroses was picking off. At 10 o'Clock pass'd a very large Ice island which was not less than 3 miles in circuit, presently after came on a thick fog, this made it unsafe to stand on, especially as we had seen more Ice Islands ahead; we therefore tacked and made a trip to the North for about one hour and a half in which time the fog dissipated and we resumed our Cou[r]se to the SSE, in which rout we met with several large ice islands. A little after 4 AM we precieved the Clowds to the South near the horizon to be of an unusual Snow white brightness which denounced our approach to field ice, soon after it was seen from the Mast-head and at 8 o'Clock we were close to the edge of it which extended East and West in a streight line far beyond our sight; as appear'd by the brightness of the horizon; in the Situation we were now in just the Southern half of the horizon was enlightned by the Reflected rays of the Ice to a considerable height. The Clowds near the horizon were of a perfect Snow whiteness and were difficult to be distinguished from the Ice hills whose lofty summits reached the Clowds. The outer or Nothern edge of this immence Ice field was compose[d] of loose or broken ice so close packed together that nothing could enter it; about a Mile in began the firm ice, in one compact solid boddy and seemed to increase in height as you traced it to the South; In this field we counted Ninety Seven Ice Hills or Mountains, many of them vastly large. Such Ice Mountains as these are never seen in Greenland, so that we cannot draw a comparison between the Greenland Ice and this now before us: Was it not for the Greenland Ships fishing yearly among such Ice (the ice hills excepted) I should not have hisitated one moment in declaring it as my opinion that the Ice we now see extended in a solid body quite to the Pole, and that it is here, i.e. to the South of this parallel, where the many Ice Islands we find floating about in the Sea are first form'd, and afterwards broke off by gales of wind and other causes, be this as it may, we must allow that these numberless and large Ice Hills must add such weight to the Ice feilds, to which they are fixed, as must make a wide difference between the Navigating this Icy Sea and that of Greenland: I will not say it was impossible anywhere to get in among this Ice, but I will assert that the bare attempting of it would be a very dangerous enterprise and what I believe no man in my situation would have thought of. I whose ambition leads me not only farther than any other man has been before me, but as far as I think it possible for man to go, was not sorry at meeting with this interruption, as it in some measure relieved us from the dangers and hardships, inseparable with the Navigation of the Southern Polar regions. Sence therefore we could not proceed one Inch farther South, no other reason need be assigned for our Tacking and stretching back to the North, being at that time in the Latitude of 71°10′ South, Longitude 106°54′ w. We had not be[en] long tacked before we were involved in a very thick fog, so that we thought our selves very fortunate in having clear weather when we approach'd the ice. I must observe that we saw here very few Birds of any kind; some Penguins were heard but none seen, nor any other signs of land whatever.

MONDAY 31st. *Therm.r. at Noon* 34. *Winds ESE to ENE. Course NBE. Dist. Sailed* 96 *Miles. Lat. in South* 69°13′. *Longd. in W. Reck.g.* 105°39′. Fresh breezes and thick foggy weather with Showers of Snow, piercing cold air; the Snow and Moistness of the fog gave a Coat of Ice to our riging of near an Inch thick. Towards noon had intervals of tolerable clear weather.

*   *   *

[FEBRUARY 1774]

SUNDAY 6th. At 1 pm took the second reef in the Top-sails and got down Top g^t yards which was no sooner done than it fell Calm and soon after had variable breezes between the NW and East, attended with Snow and Sleet. In the AM we got the wind from the South, loosed all the reefs out, got top-g^t yards and set the Sails and steered North-Easterly, with a resolution to proceed directly to the North as there was no probability of finding Land in these high Latitudes, at least not on this side Cape Horn and I thought it equally as improbable any should be found on the other side, but supposing the Land laid down in Mr Dalrymples Chart to exist or that of Bouvets, before we could reach either the one or the other the Season would be too far spent to explore it this Summer, and obliged us either to have wintered upon it, or retired to Falkland Isles or the Cape of Good Hope, which ever had been done, Six or Seven Months must have been spent without being able in that time to make any discovery what ever, but if we had met with no land or other impediment we must have reached the last of these places by April at farthest when the expedition would have been finished so far as it related to the finding a Southern Continent, mentioned by all authors who have written on this subject whose assertions and conjectures are now intirely refuted as all there enquiries were confined to this Southern Pacific Ocean in which altho' there lies no continent there is however room for very large Islands, and many of those formerly discover'd within the Southern Tropick are very imperfectly explored and there situations as imperfectly known. All these things considered, and more especially as I had a good Ship, a healthy crew and no want of Stores or Provisions I thought I cou'd not do better than to spend the insuing Winter within the Tropicks: I must own I have little expectation of makeing any valuable discovery, nevertheless it must be allowed that the Sciences will receive some improvement therefrom especially Navigation and Geography. I had several times communicated my thoughts on this subject to Captain Furneaux, at first he seem'd not to approve of it, but was inclinable to get to the Cape of Good Hope, afterwards he seem'd to come into my opinion; I however could not well give any Instructions about it, as at that time it depended on so many circumstances and therefore cannot even guess how Captain Furneaux will act; be this as it will, my intintion is now to go in search of the Land said to be discovered by Juan Fernandas in the Latitude of 38° s, not finding any such Land, to look for Easter Island, the situation of which is so variously laid down that I have little hopes of finding [it]. I next intend to get within the Tropicks and proceed to the west on a rout differing from former Navigators, touching at, and settling the Situation of such Isles as we may meet with, and if I have time, to proceed in this manner as far west as Quiros's Land or what M. de Bougainville calls the Great Cyclades.[28] Quiros describes this Land, which he calls Tierra Austral del Espiritu Santo, as being very large, M. de Bougainville neither confirms nor refutes this account. I think it a point well worth clearing up; from these isles my design is to get to the South and proceed back to the East between the Latitudes of 50 and 60°, designing if Possible to be the Length of Cape Horn in November next, when we shall have the best part of the Summer before us to explore the Southern part of the Atlantick Ocean. This I must own is a great undertaking and perhaps more than I shall be able to perform as various impediments may—[29]

* * *

28. The New Hebrides, discovered by Quirós in 1606 and rediscovered by Bougainville in 1768.

29. Cook broke off his sentence here. In a later version of his journal he put his intention less doubtfully (deleting however the words in italics). 'Great as this design appeared to be, I however thought it was possible to be done and when I came to communicate it to the officers *who till now thought we were bound directly to the Cape of Good Hope* I had the satisfaction to find that they all heartily concur'd in it.'

[*Cook continued on a northerly course for the rest of the month and into the beginning of March. He crossed the track of the* Endeavour *(1769) and of the* Dolphin *(Wallis, 1767). There was constant observation of possible indications of land – the swell, currents, birds, driftwood, weeds – but Cook was sceptical about 'the discovery of Juan Fernandez', which was not the real island known by his name but an imaginary discovery of his seemingly invented by Juan Luis Arias and enthusiastically adopted by Dalrymple as evidence of the great southern continent. What Cook does not mention is that he fell ill about 23 February. In a later version of the journal he wrote: 'I was now taken ill of the Billious colick and so Violent as to confine me to my bed, so that the Management of the Ship was left to Mr Cooper my first Officer who conducted her very much to my satisfaction.'*]

[MARCH 1774]

TUESDAY 8th. [*Therm.*] 75½. [*Winds*] Easterly. [*Course*] N 52° W. [*Dist.*] 124 *Miles.* [*Lat.*] 27°4′. [*Long. by reckoning*] 103°58′. [*Long. by watch*] 105°3′. Gentle gales and fine pleasant weather. In the AM saw many Birds, such as Tropick, Men of War and Egg Birds of two sorts, grey and White, many sheer-waters or Petrels of two or three sorts, one sort small and almost all black, another sort much larger with dark grey backs and white bellies. Swell not much and from the East.

WEDNESDAY 9th. [*Winds*] Easterly. [*Course*] W 2° S. [*Dist.*] 106 *Miles.* [*Lat.*] 27°7′. [*Long.*] 106°00′. Weather and winds as yesterday. Judgeing our selves by observation to be nearly in the Latitude of Davis's land or Easter Island we steer'd nearly due west meeting with the same sort of Birds as yesterday.

THURSDAY 10th. [*Therm.*] 76¾. [*Winds*] Easterly. [*Course*] West, Southly. [*Dist.*] 102 *Miles.* [*Lat.*] 27°9′. [*Long.*] 107°55′. In the evening took in the Studding Sails and ran under an easy sail during night, at day-light made all sail again, meeting with the same sort of Birds as yesterday and abundance of Albacores & flying fish not one of which we could catch.

FRIDAY 11th. [*Therm.*] 75. [*Winds*] Easterly. [*Course*] W 2° S. [*Dist.*] 60 *Miles.* [*Lat.*] 27°11′. [*Long.*] 109°2′. Gentle breeze and pleasant weather. At Middnight brought to till day-light then made sail and soon after saw the Land from the Mast head bearing West. At Noon it was seen from the deck extending from w¾n to wbs. Distant about 12 Leagues.

SATURDAY 12*th*. At 7 o'Clock in the pm being about 5 Leagues from the island which extending from n 62° w to n 87° w we sounded but had no ground with a line of 140 fathoms; we now Shortned Sail and Stood off se & sse having but very little wind and at 2 am it fell quite calm, and continued so till 10 AM when a breeze sprung up at sw & wsw with which we stood in for the land the extremes of which at Noon bore from nw to west by North distant 4 or 5 Leagues. Lat ob^d 27°   South.

SUNDAY 13*th*. In stretching in for the land we discovered people and those Moniments or Idols mentioned by the Authors of Roggeweins Voyage which left us no room to doubt but it was Easter Island. At 4 o'Clock we were within about half a League of the ne point, bearing nnw where we found 35 fathom a dark sandy bottom. We plyed to windward in order to get into a Bay which appeared on the se side of the isle, but night put a stop to our endeavours, which we spent makeing short boards, Soundings from 75 to 110 fathoms, bottom dark Sand. During night the wind was variable, but in the morning it fixed at se, blew in squals attended with rain which ceased as the day advanced. The wind now blowing right on the se shore on which the Sea broke very high and there being no bay or Harbour as we had immag[in]ed, I steer'd round the South point of the Island in order to explore the western side, accordingly we ran along the western and nw side at the distance of one mile from the Shore, untill we open'd the nothern point without seeing any safe anchoring place. The Natives were collicted together in several places on the shore in small companies of 10 or 12. The most likely anchoring place we had seen was on the West side of the isle   miles to the northward of the South point before a small sandy beach where we found 40 and 30 fathoms one mile from the Shore, Bottom dark sand, here a Canoe conducted by two Men came off and brought us a Bunch of Plantans and then returned a shore. Seeing no better anchorage than the one just mentioned we Tacked and Plyed back to the South in order to gain it.

MONDAY 14th. At half past 6 o'Clock pm Anchored at the place before mentioned in 36 fathom Water, the bottom a fine dark sand. Having sent the boat in shore to sound one of the natives swam off to her, came on board and remained with us all night and next day, this confidence gave us a favourable Idea of the rest of the Natives. At 3 am a breeze from the land drove us of the bank, which after the Anchor was up we plyed in for again and in the mean time I went a shore to inform my self if any refreshments or Water were to be got. We landed at the sandy beach where about 100 of the Natives were collected who gave us no disturbance at landing, on the contrary hardly one had so much as a stick in their hands. After distributing among them some Medals and other trifles, they brought us sweet Potatoes, Plantains and some Sugar cane which they exchanged for Nails &cª; after having found a small Spring or rather Well made by the Natives, of very brackish Water, I returned on board and anchored the Ship in 32 fᵐ Water, the bottom a fine dark sand, something more than a mile from the Shore.

TUESDAY 15th. PM Got on board a few Casks of Water and Traded with the Natives for some of the produce of the island which appeared in no great plenty and the Water so bad as not to be worth carrying on board, and the Ship not in safety determined me to shorten my stay here. Accordingly I sent Lieutenants Pickersgill and Edgcumb with a party of Men, accompanied by Mʳ Forster and several more of the gentlemen, to examine the Country; I was not sufficiently recovered from a fit of illness to make one of the party. At the Ship employed geting on Board Water and tradeing with the Natives.

WEDNESDAY 16th. About 7 in the evening the exploaring party returned and the next morning Mʳ Pickersgill made me the following report. . . .

[*Pickersgill's 'Remarks' dwelt on the barrenness of the island and the poor quality of the scanty water. They were led round the island by a man with a white flag. The great stone images they understood to be of* ariki *or chiefs; many of the images had collapsed. They had a ceremonial meeting with an imposing person whom they understood to be 'the areeke of the Island . . . called Wy-hu'. When one of the islanders caught up a bag which a member of the party had put on the ground, the trigger-happy marine officer Edgecumbe fired at him with small shot; there was a commotion but no apparent consequences.*]

This report of M[r] Pickersgills so far as it regarded the Produce of the Island was confirmed by the whole party and determined me to quit the island without further delay, a breeze of wind about 10 o'Clock Coming in from Sea, attended with heavy showers of rain made this the more necessary, accordingly we got under sail and stood out to Sea, but as we had but little wind I sent a boat a shore to purchase such refreshments as the Natives might have brought to the Water side.

THURSDAY 17*th*. PM Plying off the Island with variable light winds and had a boat and people on Shore tradeing, in the evening they return'd on board when we hoisted the boat in and made Sail NW with the wind at NNE. At Noon the body of the Island bore ESE½s distant 15 Leagues. Lat Ob[d] 26°48′ s.

This is undoubtedly the same Island as was seen by Roggewein in Ap[l] 1722 altho' the descriptions given of it by the authors of that voyage do's by no means correspond with it now; it may also be the same as was seen by Captain Davis in 1686, but this is not altogether so certain, and if it is not than his discovery cannot lie far from the continent of America, for this Latitude seems to have been very well explored between the Meridian of 80 and 110, Captain Carteret carries it much farther, but his Track seems to be a little too far to the South. . . . No Nation will ever contend for the honour of the discovery of Easter Island as there is hardly an Island in this sea which affords less refreshments and conveniences for Shiping than it does; Nature has hardly provided it with any thing fit for man to eat or drink, and as the Natives are but few and may be supposed to plant no more than sufficient for themselves, they cannot have much to spare to new comers. . . .

The Inhabitants of this isle from what we have been able to see of them do not exceed six or seven hundred souls and a bove two thirds of these are Men, they either have but few Women among them or else many were not suffer'd to make their appearence, the latter seems most Probable. They are certainly of the same race of People as the

New Zealanders and the other islanders, the affinity of the Language, Colour and some of thier customs all tend to prove it, I think they bear more affinity to the Inhabitants of Amsterdam and New Zealand, than those of the more northern isles which makes it probable that there lies a chain of isles in about this Parallel or under, some of which have at different times been seen. . . .

Of their Religion, Goverment &c^a we can say nothing with certainty. The Stupendous stone statues errected in different places along the Coast are certainly no representation of any Deity or places of worship; but most probable Burial Places for certain Tribes or Families. I my self saw a human Skeleton lying in the foundation of one just covered with Stones, what I call the foundation is an oblong square about 20 or 30 feet by 10 or 12 built of and faced with hewn stones of a vast size, executed in so masterly a manner as sufficiently shews the ingenuity of the age in which they were built. They are not all of equal height, some are not raised above two or three feet, others much more, and seems to depend on the nature of the ground on which they are built. The Statue is errected in the middle of its foundation, it is about [15 to 30 feet] high and [from 16 to 24] round for this is its shape, all the appearences it has of a human figure is in the head where all the parts are in proportion to its Size; the head is crow[n]ed with a Stone of the shape and full size of a drum, we could not help wondering how they were set up, indeed if the Island was once Inhabited by a race of Giants of 12 feet high as one of the Authors of Roggewein's Voyage tell us, than this wonder ceaseth and gives place to another equally as extraordinary, viz. to know what is become of this race of giants. Besides these Statues which are very numerous and no were but a long the Sea Coast there are many little heaps of stones here and there on the bank along the Sea Coast, two or three of the uppermost stones of these piles are generally white, perhaps always so when the pile is compleat: it can hardly be doubted but these piles of stones have some meaning tho' we do not know it.

From the report of Mr Pickersgill it should seem that the Island is under the goverment of one Man whom they stile Arreeke, that is King or Chief.

Some pieces of Carving were found a mongest these people which were neither ill designed nor executed. They have no other tools than what are made of Stone, Bone, Shells &cᵃ. They set but little value on Iron and yet they knew the use of it, perhaps they obtained their knowlidge of this Metal from the Spaniards who Viseted this Isle in 1769 some Vistiges of which still remained amongest them, such as pieces of Cloth &cᵃ.

*   *   *

[*For three weeks Cook followed a north-westerly and then a westerly course. On 6 April he calculated his position as latitude 9 °20′ s, 138° 1′ w.*]

[APRIL 1774]

THURSDAY 7*th*. At 4 o'Clock in the PM after runing 4 Leagues West sence Noon, Land was seen bearing WBS distant about 9 Leagues, two hours after saw a nother land bearing SWBS and appeared more extensive than the first: hauld up for this land and kept under an easy Sail all night having Squally unsittled weather with rain. At 6 am the Land first seen bore NW the other SW½W and a third West, I directed my Course for the Channell between these two last lands, under all the Sail we could set, having unsittled Squally Showery weather. Soon after we discovered a fourth land still more to the westward and were now well assured that these were the Marquesas discovered by Mendana in 1595. At Noon we were in the Channell which divides Sᵗ Pedro and La dominica.

FRIDAY 8*th*. Continued to rainge a long the SE Shore of La Dominica without seeing any signs of an Anchoring place, till we came to the Channell which divides it from Sᵗ Christina through which we pass'd and haul'd over to the last mentioned Island and ran along the shore to the South westward in search of Mendana['s] Port. After passing Several Coves in which seem'd to be tollerable Anchorage, but a great Surff on the Shore; from some of these places came of some of the Natives in their Canoes, but as we had a fresh of wind and did not shorten Sail none came up with us. At length we came to the Port we were in search after,[30] into which we hauled and made an attempt to turn in, in the doing of which we were attacked by such Violent Squalls from the high lands that we were within a few yards of being driven against the rocks to Leeward. After escaping this danger we stood out again made a stretch to windward and then stretched in and Anchored in the Entrance of the Bay in 34 fathom water, sandy bottom, without so much as attempting to turn farther in. . . . We had no soon anchored then about 30 or 40 of the Natives came round us in a Doz[n] or fourteen Canoes, but it requir'd some address to get them along side, at last a Hatchet and some large Nails induced the people in one Canoe to put under the quarter gallery, after this all the others put along side and exchanged Bread fruit and some fish for small Nails and then retired a shore. But came off again to us very early the next morning in much greater numbers bringing off Bread fruit, Plantains and one Pig which they exchanged for Nails &c[a] but in this Traffick they would frequently keep our goods and make no return, tell at last I was obliged to fire a Musquet ball Close past one man who had served us in this manner after which they observed a little more honisty and at length several of them came on board. At this time we were prepairing to warp the Ship farther into the Bay and I was going in a Boat to look for the most convenient place to mo[o]r her in; observing so many of the Natives on board, I said to the officers, you must look well after these people or they certainly will carry off some thing or other, these words were no sooner out of my mouth and had hardly got into my Boat, when I was told they had stolen one of the Iron Sta[n]chions from the opposite Gang-way, I told the officers to fire over the Canoe till I could get round in the Boat, unluckily for the theif they took better aim than I ever intend and killed him the third Shott, two others that were in the same Canoe jumped overboard but got in again just as I got to the Canoe, the one was a Man and seem'd to laugh at what had happen'd, the other was a youth about 14 or 15 years of age, he looked at the dead man with a serias and dejected countinance and we had after wards reason to believe that he was son to the disceas'd. This accident made all the Canoes retire from us with precipitation.

30. Madre de Dios (Resolution Bay or Vaitahu Bay).

I followed them into the Bay and prevaild upon the people in one Canoe to come along side the Boat and receive some Nails and other things I gave them. When I returnd on board we carried out a Kedge Anchor with 3 hawsers upon an end to warp in by and hove short on the bower. One would have thought that the Natives by this time were fully sencible of the effect of our fire Arms but the event proved other wise for the boat had no sooner left the Kedge anchor than a Canoe put of from the Shore, took hold of the Buoy and attempted, as we supposed, to drag what was fast to the rope a shore, but fearing they would at last take away the Buoy I ordered a Musquet to be fire[d] at them, but as the ball fell short they took no notice of it, but the 2nd ball that was fired pass'd over them on which they let go the buoy and made for the shore and this was the last shott we had occasion to fire and probably had more effect upon them than killing the Man as it shewed them that they were hardly safe at any distance for they afterwards stood in great dread of the Musquet, nevertheless they would very often exercize their tallant of thieving upon us, which I thought necessary to put up with as our stay was likely to be but short among them. The Natives had retarded us so long that before we were ready to heave up the anchor and warp in the wind began to blow in Squalls out of the Bay, so that we were obliged to lay fast where we were.

It was not long before the Natives ventured off to us again, in the first Canoe which came was a man who seem'd of some consequence, he advanced slowly with a Pig upon his Shoulder which he sold for a Spike nail as soon as he got a long side. I made him a present of a Hatchet and several other Articles which induced him to come into the Ship where he made a short stay and then retired; his example was followed by all the other Canoes and trade was presently reestablished. Things being thus Settled on board I went a shore with a party of Men to try what was to be done there, we were received by the Natives as if nothing had happened, traded with them for some Plantains and a few Sm^l Piggs and after Loading the Launch with water returned on board to dinner.

SATURDAY 9*th*. PM sent the boats and a guard a Shore again for Water;

upon their landing the Natives all fleed but one Man and he seemed much frightned, he was disir'd to go and fetch some fruit which he did accordingly and after him one or two more came and these were all that were seen till 8 o'Clock in the AM at which time some made their appearence just as the Boats put off from the Watering place; after breakfast I went a Shore my self before the guard when the Natives crowded round me in great numbers but as soon as the guard landed I had enough to do to prevent them from runing off, at length their fears were dissipated and a trade opened for fruit and Pigs. I beleive the reason of their flying from our people last evening was their not seeing me at the head of them, for they certainly would have done the same now had I not been present. Towards Noon a chief of some consequence, attended by a great number of People, came down to us, I made him a present of Nails and Several other Articles and in return he gave me some of his ornaments, after these Mutal exchanges a good under Standing Seemed to be settled between us and them so that we got by exchanges as much fruit as Loaded two boats and then return on board.

SUNDAY 10*th*. PM Launch Watering and a party Trading with the Natives, went my self into the Southern cove of the Bay where I procured five Pigs, and came to the House which we were told belonged to the Man we had kill'd; there were Six Piggs in it which we were told belonged to the deceased Son who had fled upon our approach. I wanted much to have seen him to have made him a present and by other kind treatment convinced him and the others that it was not from any bad design we had against the Nation we had kill'd his father; it would have been to no purpose my leaving any thing in the house as it certainly would have been taken away by others. Strict honisty was seldom observed amongst them selves when the property of our things came to be disputed, I saw a Striking instance of this. I offered a man a Six Inch Spike for a Pig which he readily excepted of and hand'd the pig to a nother man to give me which was done and the Spike given in return, but in stead of giving it to the Man who sold the Pig he kept it him self and offered him in lieu a Sixpenny Nail, words of course arose and I waited to see how it would end, but as the man who had got posession of the Spike seem'd resolved to keep it I left them before it was desided.

AM Emp^{pd} as usual (viz) in Watering and Trading with the Natives. Some Canoes from more distant parts came and sold us some Pigs so that we had now sufficient to give all hands a fresh meal, the Pigs they bring us are so small that 40 or 50 are hardly sufficient for this purpose.

MONDAY 11*th*. In the PM I made an expedition towards Southward in which I collected 18 Pigs and I believe should have got more had I had more time, in the Morning I went to the same places but instead of geting Pigs as I expected I found every thing quite changed, the Nails and other things they were Mad after the Evening before they now dispised and in stead of them they wanted they did not know what, the reason of this was, some of the young gentlemen having been a Shore the preceeding day and had given them in exchange various Articles such as they had not seen before and which took with them more than Nails, or perhaps they thought they had already enough of these and wanted some thing more curious, which I nor indeed any one else had to give them sufficient to supply us with refreshments, thus our market was at once spoil'd and I was obliged to return with 3 or 4 little Pigs which cost me more than a Dozⁿ would have done the evening before; when I got on board I found that the party at the water place had had no better success. When I saw that this place was not likely to supply us with sufficient refreshments, not very convenient for geting off wood and Water nor for giving the Ship the necessary repairs, I resolv'd forth with to leave it and seack for some place that would supply our wants better, for it must be supposed that after having been 19 Weeks at Sea (for I cannot call the two or 3 days spent at Easter Island any thing else) living all the time upon a Salt Diet, but what we must want some refreshments altho I must own and that with pleasure, that on our arrival here, it could hardly be said that we had one Sick Man on board and not above two or three who had the least complaint, this was undoubtedly owing to the many antiscorbutic articles we had on board and the great care and Attention of the Surgeon who took special care to apply them in time.

TUESDAY 12*th*. At 3 o'Clock in the PM weighed and Stood over for St Dominica in order to take a View of the West side of that Island but as we could not reach it before dark the night was spent Plying between the two Islands. In the morning we had a full View of the SW and western sides of the Isle neither of which seem'd to afford any Anchorage. At 8 o'Clock we were off the NW point from which the land trended NE Easterly, so that this side was not likely to have any safe Port as being exposed to the Easterly winds; we had now but little and that very variable with Showers of Rain: at length we got a breeze at ENE with which we steered to the South ward with a view of leaving these Isles altogether. . . .

WEDNESDAY 13*th*. *Winds NE to ESE. Course S* 36° *West. Distce Sailed* 75 *Miles. Latde in* 10°56'. *Longde in West* 139°54'. Gentle breezes with rain. At 5 o'Clock in the PM the Harbour of Madre de Dios bore ENE½E distant 5 Leagues and the body of the Island Magdalena SE about 9 Leagues; this was the only View we had of this last isle. From hence I directed my Course SSW½W for Otaheite and likewise with a view of falling in with Some of those isles discovered by former Navigators whose Situations are not well determined.

* * *

[*Cook made a brief stop at Takaroa in the Tuamotu archipelago, where he had an uncertain reception. As they left, Cook 'ordered two or three Guns to be fired over the little isle the Natives were upon in order to shew them that it was not their own Superior strength and Numbers which obliged us to leave their isle'.*]

THURSDAY 21*st*. *Winds EBN. Course S* 38°45'. *Dist. Sailed* 113 *M. Lat. in* 17°32'. *Longde. in* 148°42'. First part fresh gales with rain, remainder fair and Clowdy. At 10 AM Saw the high land of Otahiete and at Noon Point Venus bore west-northerly distant 13 Leagues.

FRIDAY 22*nd*. *Winds Easterly. Lat. in* 17°29'. *Longde. in* 149°35', *[watch]* 151°44'. PM Moderate breezes and Clowdy. At 7 Shortned Sail and spent the night plying of and on. AM Squally with heavy Showers of rain. At 8 Anchored in Matavai Bay in 7 fathom Water, which was no sooner done than we were viseted by several of our old friends, who express'd not a little joy at seeing us.

As my reasons for puting in here was to give Mr Wales an oppertunity to know the error of the Watch from the known Longitude of this place and to determine a fresh her rate of going; the first thing we did was to land his Instruments &c^a and to set up tents for the reception of a guard and such others as it was necessary to have on Shore. As to Sick we had none.

SATURDAY 23*rd*. Showery rainy Weather. The Natives begin to bring us in refreshments, such as fruit and Fish, sufficient for all hands.

SUNDAY 24*th*. *Otou* the King with a vast train and several Chiefs of distinction paid us a Viset and brought with them as presents Ten or a Doz^n Hogs which made them exceeding welcome. I was advertised of the Kings coming and met him at the Tents a shore, conducted him on board where he stay'd Dinner, after which he and his attendance were dismiss'd with Suteable presents.

MONDAY 25*th*. Much rain, Thunder and Lightning. Nevertheless I had a nother Viset from Otou who brought with him a quantity of refreshments &c^a. When we were at Amsterdam, among other Curosities we Collected some red Parrot Feathers which were highly Valued by these people; When this came to be known in the isle all the Principal people of both Sex endeavour'd by every means in their power to Ingratiate themselves into our favour in order to obtain these Valuable Jewels by bring[ing] us Hogs and every other thing the Island produced, and generally for Tiyo (Friendship) but they always took care to let us know that Oora (red Feathers) were to be a part of the return we were to make. Having these Feathers was a very fortunate circumstance to us for as they were Valuable to the Natives they became so to us allso, for our Stock of trade was by this time greatly exhausted and if it had not been for them I should have found it difficult to have supplyed the Ships with the necessary refreshments.

When I put in here my intention was to stay but a few days, that is no longer than Mr Wales had made the Obser^{ns} for the purpose already mentioned from a supposition founded on the reception we met with the last time we were here that we should get no Hogs; but the Number the Natives have already brought us and the few excursions we have made which have not exceeded the Plains of Matavai and Oparre hath convinced us of our error. We find at these two places built and building a great number of Canoes and houses both large and small, People living in spacious houses who had not a place to shelter themselves in Eight Months ago, several large hogs near every house and every other Sign of a riseing state.

Judging from these favourable circumstances that we should not mend our Situation by removeing to a nother island I therefore resolved to make a longer stay & to begin with the repairs of the Ship; accordingly I ordered the empty Casks and Sails to be got on shore to repair, the Smiths Forge to be set up to repair our Iron work, the Ship to be Caulked and the rigging &c^a to be overhauled, Works which the high Southern Latitudes had made highly necessary.

TUESDAY 26th. In the Morning I set out for Oparre accompaned by the two Mr Forsters and some of the officers to pay Otoo a formal Viset by appointment, as we approached Oparre we observed a number of large Canoes in Motion; but we were surprised when we got there to see upwards of three-hundred of them all rainged in good order for some distance along the Shore all Compleatly equip'd and Man'd, and a vast Crowd of Men on the Shore; So unexpected an Armament collected together in our Neighbourhood in the space of one night gave rise to various conjectures: we landed however and were received by a Vast Multitude some under Arms and some not, the cry of the latter was Tiyo no Otoo and the former Tiyo no Towha,^{31} this Cheif as we soon after learnt was General or Admiral of the fleet. I was met by him presently after we landed, he received me with great Courtsey and then took hold of my right hand. A Cheif whose name was Tee, Uncle to the King and one of his Prime Ministers, had hold of my left, thus I was draged along as it were between two parties, both declaring themselves our friends, the one wanted me to stay by the fleet and the other to go to the King, at last coming to the general place of Audience a Mat was spread on the ground for me to sit down upon and Tee went to bring the King, Towha was unwilling I should sit down but partly insisted on my going to the fleet but as I knew

31. Taio no Tu, friend of Tu! – Taio no Towha, friend of Towha! [B]

nothing of this Chief I did not comply; presently Tee return'd and wanted to conduct me to the King and took me by the hand for that purpose, this Towha opposed so that between the one party and the other I was like to have been torn to pieces and was obliged to disire Tee to desist, and to go with the Admiral and his party to the fleet. As soon as we came before the Admirals Vessel two lines of Arm'd Men were drawen up on the shore before her to keep of the Crowd and clear the way for me to go in, but as I was determined not to go (unless forced) I made the Water which was between me and the Canoe an excuse, this did not answer for a Man immidiately squated himself down at my feet and offered to carry me in and then I declar'd I would not go and that very moment Towha quited me without my seeing which way he went nor would any one inform me; I therefore turn'd back and inquired for the King, Tee who I beleive never lost sight of me, came and told me he was gone into the Country Mataou and advised me to go to my boat which we according did as soon as we got all together for Mr Edgcumb was the only gentleman that could keep with me, the others were jostled about in the crowd in the same Manner as we were. When we had got into our boat we took our time to view this fleet, the Vessels of War consisted of 160 large double Canoes, very well equip'd, Man'd and Arm'd, altho' I am not sure that they had on board either their full compliment of Fighting men or rowers, I rather think not. The Cheifs ie all those on the Fighting Stages were drist in their War habits, that is in a vast quantity of Cloth Turbands, breast Plates and Helmmets, some of the latter are of such a length as to greatly incumber the wearer, indeed their whole dress seem'd ill calculated for the day of Battle and seems to be design'd more for shew than use, be this as it may they certainly added grandure to the Prospect, as they were complesant enough to Shew themselves to the best advantage, their Vessels were decorated with Flags, Streamers &c^a so that the whole made a grand and Noble appearence such as was never seen before in this Sea, their implements of war were Clubs, pikes and Stones. These Canoes were rainged close along side each other with their heads a Shore and Sterns to the Sea, the Admirals Vesel was, as near as I could guess, in the center. Besides these Vesels of War there were 170 Sail of Smaller double Canoes, all with a little house upon them and rigg'd with Masts and sails which the others had not; These Canoes must be design'd for Transporte or Victulars or both and to receive the wounded Men &cᵃ; in the War Canoes were no sort of Provisions whatever. In these 330 Canoes I judged there were no less than 7760 Men a number which appears incredible, especially as we were told that they all belonged to the districts of Attahourou and Ahopatea. . . .

When we had well view'd this fleet I wanted much to see the Admiral to have gone with him on board the Vesels, I enquired for him as we rowed past the Vesels to no purpose, we then put a shore and inquire'd for him, but the noise and Crowd was so great that no one attended to what we said, at last Tee came and whispered us in the ear that the King was gone to Matavai and advised us to go their also and not to land where we were, we took his advice put off and row'd for the Ship accordingly, this account and advice of Tee gave rise to new conjectures, in short we conclude that this Towha was some disaffected Chief upon the point of making War against his King. We had not long left Oparre before the whole fleet was in Motion and proceeded back to the westward from whence they came.

When we got on board the Ship, we were told that this fleet was a part of the armament intended to go against Eimeo whose Chief had revolted from Otou his Lawfull Sovereign. I was also inform'd that Otou was not nor had been at Matavai, and therefore after dinner I went again to Oparre where I found him, I now learn that his fears and the reason of his not seeing us in the Morning was occasioned by some of his people stealing (owing to the neglect of the washerman) a quantity of my Clothes and was fearfull least I should demand resti-tution, when I assured him I should not disturb the peace of the isle on any such occasion he was satisfied; I likewise understood that Towha was alarm'd partly on this account and partly by my not honoring him with my company on board his fleet when he desired it. I was Jealous at seeing such a Force in our neigherhood without being able to know any thing of its design; thus by misunderstanding one a nother I lost the oppertunity of examining more narrowly into a part of the Naval force of this Island and makeing my self better acquainted how it acts and is conducted. Such a nother oppertunity may never happen again as it was commanded by a brave, Sencible and intelligent Chief who no doubt would have satisfied us in all the questions we had thought proper to ask and as the Objects were before our eyes we could not well have mistook one another. Matter[s] being Thus cleared up and mutual presents having pass'd between Otou and me we return'd on board in the evening.

WEDNESDAY 27*th*. Morning, Received a present from Towha consisting of Two Large hogs and some fruit sent me by two of his Servants who had orders to receive nothing in return. Soon after I took a trip in my boat to Oparre were I found both this chief and the King, after a Short Stay I brought them both on board to dinner together with the Kings Brother, they were shew'd all over the Ship, the Admiral who had never seen such a one before view'd every thing with great attention and express'd much surprise at what he saw. After dinner he put a Hog on board the Ship and retired before I had time to make him any return either for this or what I had in the Morning and soon after the King and his Brother took leave. The King seem'd not only to pay the Admiral much respect himself but was desireous I should do the same, he was nevertheless certainly jelous of him, but on what account we knew not for it was but the day before he frankly told us the Admiral was not his friend. Both these Chiefs when on board to day Solicited me to assist them against the people of Tiarabou altho at this time the two Kin[g]doms are at peace and we were told go with their joint force against Eimeo. To this request of theirs I made an evasive answer which I believe they understood was not favourable to their request.

THURSDAY 28*th*. Remaind on board all day. Had a Present of a Hog sent me by Oheatua the King of Tiarabou, for which in return he disired a few red feathers. In the afternoon Mr Forster and his party set out for the Mountains with an intent to Stay out the night.

FRIDAY 29*th*. Early in the Morn Otoo, Towha and Several other Grandees came on board and brought with them not only provisions but some of the Most Valuable curiosities in the island which they gave to me and for which I made them such returns as they were well pleased with, I likewise took the oppertunity to repay the civilties I had received from Towha.

Last night one of the Natives made an Attempt to Steal one of our Water Casks from the Watering Place, he was caught, sent on board and put in Irons in which Situation he was found by the two Chiefs to whom I made known his crime. Otou beg'd he might be set at liberty which I refused tilling him it was but Just the Man should be punished, accordingly I orderd him a shore to the Tent, where I went my self with the two Chiefs and others, here I ordered the Man to be tyed up to a Post, Otou his Sister and some others beg'd hard for the Man, Towha said not one word but was very attentive to every thing going forward; I expostulated with Otou on the conduct of this Man and his people in general tilling him that neither I nor any of my people took any thing from him or his people without first paying for it and innumirated the Articles we gave for such and such things and that he well knew that when any of my people broke through these rules they were punished for it and that it was but right this man should be punished also, besides I told him it would be the means of saving the lives of some of his people by detering them from commiting crimes of this nature in which some would be kill'd at one time or a nother; I said more to the same purpose most of which I believe he pretty well understood as he was satisfied and only desired the Man might not be kill'd. I then ordered the guard out to keep the Crowd which was very great at a proper distance and in Sight of them all ordered the fellow two dozen lashes with a Cat of Nine tails which he bore with great firmness, he was then set at liberty and Towha the Admiral began to Harangue the crowd for not a man left us on this occasion, he spoke for a full quarter of an hour and with seemingly great Perspicuity and he was heard with great Attention, his speach consisted mostly of short Sentences, nevertheless I could understand but few words, he recapitulated most of what I had said to Otou, named several Advantages they had received from us, condemn'd their present conduct and recommended a different one for the future. Otou on this occasion spoke not one word. As soon as the Chief had ended his speach I order'd the Marines to go through their exercise and to Load and fire which gave the Two Chiefs, especially the

Admiral, much entertainment, this done I invited them on board to dinner but they excused themselves took leave and retired with all their attendance. . . .

*   *   *

[MAY 1774]

SATURDAY 7*th*. On going a Shore in the Morning I found Otou at the Tents and took the Oppertunity to ask his leave to cut down some trees for fuel, he not well understanding me I took him to some standing near the Shore and fit for nothing else, these he gave me leave to cut down, but as they were not Sufficient I desired he would let us know where we could get more, declaring at the same time that I should Cut down no trees which bore any fruit, he was so pleased with this declaration that he told it a loud three times to the people about us.

In the afternoon he and the whole Royal Family (Viz) his Father, Brother and three Sisters with their attendants, made me a Viset on board; His Father made me a present of a compleat Mourning dress, curiosities we most valued, in return I gave him what ever he desired and distributed red feathers to all the others and then conducted them a shore in my boat; Otou was so well pleased with the reception he and his friends had met with that he told me at parting, I might cut down as many and what Trees I pleased.

SUNDAY 8*th*. Last Night in the Middle Watch through the negligence of one of the Sentinels on Shore all our Friendly connections received an interruption, he having either slept or quited his Post gave one of the Natives an oppertunity to carry off his Musquet, the first news I heard of it was brought me in the morning by Tee whom Otou sent for this purpose and to desire I would go to him for he was Mata-ou (frightned, alarmd &ᶜ). I did not fully understand the story of the Musquit till I got on shore and was inform'd of it by the Serjᵗ who had the Command. I found the Natives were all alarm'd and the most of them fled, the Kings Brother slept on board all night and came a Shore with me, but having heard the whole story from Tee he gave me the Slip in a Moment before I knew well what was the matter. I cross'd the River and went alone with Tee and some others into the Woods in search of Otou. As we went a long I endeavoured to allay the fears of the People but at the same time insisted on having the Musquet return'd. After traveling some distance in the woods, enquiring of every one we met where Otou was, Tee stop'd all at once and advised me to go back for that Otou was gone towards the Mountains, that he would go to him and tell him that I was still his friend and that he would use his endeavours to have the Musquet return'd. I was satisfied by this time it was to no purpose my going farther, for altho' I was alone and without Arms, Otou's·fears were such that he dar'd not see me and therefor took Tees advice and return'd. As soon as I got on board I sent Odiddy to Otou to let him know I only requird the return of the Musquet which I knew to be in his power to do. . . .

*   *   *

[*The space which Cook gave to his account of the rest of this affair shows the supreme gravity not so much of the theft but of the possibility that the Tahitians would be equipped with firearms. Attempts to capture canoes and take hostages were exasperatingly frustrated. Cook was fed with information which he did not know whether to believe that the thief was from Taiarapu in the south. Suddenly and mysteriously the missing musket was returned. Cook was unable to clear up the affair because Tu, deeply upset that muskets had been fired at canoes, cut off the supplies which Cook needed. Conciliation was inevitable, and the affair ended with Cook ordering a salvo of the ship's 'great guns' to be fired at Tu's request, and a firework display.*]

WEDNESDAY 11*th.* In the Morning had a very large Supply of Fruit brought us from all parts, some of which came from Towha the Admiral, sent as usual by his Servants with orders to receive nothing in return, only desired to see me at Attahourou as he was ill and could not come to me; as I could not well undertake this Journey now I sent Odiddy along with his Servants with a present sutable to those I had in so genteel a manner received from Towha. As the Most Essential repairs of the Ship were now nearly finished I resolved to leave the isle in a few days, accordingly ordered every thing to be got off from the Shore, that the Natives might see we were about to depart.

THURSDAY 12*th*. Showery Rainy weather. To Day we had a Viset from Old Obarea the Dolphins Queen who looked as well and as young as ever. She presented me with two Hogs, some Cloth &c^a. Presently after her came Otou with a great retinue and a great quantity of Provisions, to every one of them I made large presents thinking it might be the last time I should see them and in the evening entertain'd them with fire works.

FRIDAY 13*th*. Winds Easter, fair Weather. Two things prevented our Sailing this Morning, first Odiddy was not yet return'd from Attahourou, Secondly Otou desired I would not sail till he had seen me again; various were the reports about Odiddy, some said he was return'd, others that he was at Oparre and others said he would not return. In the evening a party of us went down to Oparre to learn more of the truth, here we found not only Odiddy, but Towha also who notwithstanding his ill state of health had resolved to see me before I went away and had got thus far on his Journey, he had got a swelling in his feet and legs which had intirely taken away the use of them; our Viset was short for after seeing Otou we return'd with Odiddy on board, this youth I found was desirous of remaining at this isle and therefore told him he was at liberty to remain here or at Ulietea and Frankly told him that if he went to England it was highly probable he would never return, but if after all he choosed to go I would take care of him and he must look upon me as his Father, he threw his arms about me and wept saying many people persuaded him to stay at the isle. I told him to go a Shore and speak with his friends and then come to me in the morning. He was very well beloved in the Ship for which reason every one was persuading him to go with us, telling what great things he wou'd see and return with immence riches, according to his Idea of riches, but I thought proper to undeceive him, thinking it an Act of the highest injustice to take away a person from these isles against his own free inclination under any promise whatever much more that of bringing them back again, what Man on board can make such a promise as this. At this time it was quite unnecessary to persuade any one to go with us, there were many youths who Voluntary offered themselves to go with us and even to remain and die in Brit-tania.

The King importuned me very much to take one or two to collect red
feathers for him at Amsterdam, willing to risk the chance of their
returning or no; some of the gentle[men] on board were desirous of
takeing some as Servants, but I refused all manner of Solicitations of
this kind, knowing from experience that they would be of no use to
us in the course of the Voyage, but what had the greatest weight with
me was the thinking my self bound to see they were after wards
properly taken care of as they could not be taken from their Native
spot without my consent.

SATURDAY 14th. Early in the Morning Odiddy came on board with a
resolution to stay at the Isle, but Mr Forster prevailed upon him to go
with us to Ulietea. Soon after Towha came a long side and also several
more of our friends with fruit &c^a. Towha was hoisted in and place'd
in a Chair on the Quarter deck, amongst the various articles I gave
this Chief was an English Pendant, told him the use of it and instructed
him in what manner and where it was to be hoisted in his Canoe,
after which he seem'd highly pleased. We had no sooner dispatched
our friends than we saw a Number of War Canoes coming round the
point of Oparre, being desirous to have a nearer view of them I
hastned down to Oparre (accompanied by some of the officers &c^a)
which we reached before the Canoes were all landed and had an
oportunity to see in what manner they approached the shore. . . . This
fleet consisted of Forty sail, were equiped in the same manner as those
we had seen before and belonged to the little district of Tettaha and
were come to Oparre to be reviewed before Otou as those we had
seen before had done. . . . Otou who was present caused some of the
Troops to go through their exercize on Shore, Two parties first began
with Clubs, but this was so soon over that I had no time to make
observations upon it, they then went to Single Combat and went thro'
the Various Mithods of fighting with great allertness and parried off
the blows, pushes &c^a each combatant intended the other with great
dexterity. . . .

   This being over the fleet depart as fast as they were got afloat and
I went with Otou to one of his large double Canoes which was building
and nearly ready to launch. She was by far the largest I had seen at

any of the isles, he beged of me a grapling and grapling rope for her to which I aded an English Jack and Pendant, the use of which he had been before fully instructed in. I desired that these two Joint Canoes, ie what is understood as a double Canoe, might be call'd Britanne (Brit-tania) the name they have addopted for our Country, to which he very readily consented and she was Christened accordingly. . . . The King came on board with us and after dinner took a Most Affectionate leave, he hardly ever ceased to day Soliciting me to return and just before he went out of the Ship took a youth by the hand, presented him to me and disired I would take him on board to Collect red feathers, I told him I could not take him knowing he would never return, but that if any Ship should happen to come here again from Brit-tania I would take care to either bring or send him plenty of red feathers; this seem'd to satisfy him, but the youth was exceedinly disireous of going and had I not made a resolution to carry no one from the isles I believe I should have taken him.

Otou remained along side of the Ship till we were under sail when he put off and we Saluted him with three guns. Our treatment at this isle was such as had induced one of our gunners mates[32] to form a Plan to remain at it, he knew he could not execute it with success while we lay in the Bay, therefore took the oppertunity as soon as we were out and all our Sails set to slip over board (he being a good swimer) but he was discov[er]ed before he had got clear of the Ship, we presently Broug^t to, hoisted out a boat and sent and took him up: a Canoe was observed about half way between us and the Shore seemingly coming after us, she was intended to take him in, but seeing our boat, kept at a distance, this was a preconcerted plan between the Man and the Natives with which Otou was acquainted and had incouraged. I kept the Man in confinement till we were clear of the isles then dismiss'd [him] without any other punishment, for when I considered the situation of the Man in life I did not think him so culpable as it may at first appear, he was an Irishman by birth, a good Seaman and had Saild both in the English and Dutch Service. I pick'd him up at Batavi in my return home from my last Voyage and he had remained with

32. John Marra.

me ever sence. I never learnt that he had either friends or connection to confine him to any particular part of the world, all Nations were alike to him, where than can Such a Man spend his days better than at one of these isles where he can injoy all the necessaries and some of the luxuries of life in ease and Plenty. As soon as the Boat was hoisted in again we directed our Course for Huaheine in order to pay a Viset to our friends there. . . .

SUNDAY 15*th.* I have already mentioned that after leaving Otaheite we directed our Course for Huahine and at one o'Clock in the after noon of this day Anchor'd in the North entrance of Owharre Harbour, hoisted out the boats and Warp'd into a proper birth and there Moor'd the Ship. While this was doing several of the Natives came on board amongest whom was Oree the Chief, he brought with him a Hog and some other Articles which he presented to me with the usual cerimony.

MONDAY 16*th.* In the Morning I return'd Oree's Visset and made my present in return, after which he put two Hogs into my boat and he and several of his friends came on board and dined, after dinner I gave to Oree Axes, Nails &c^a and desired he would distribute them to his friends which he accordingly did seemingly to the satisfaction of every one.

Mr F. and his party being out botanizing his Servt a feeble Man was set upon by five or Six fellows who would have strip'd him if they had not been prevented by a nother of the party.

TUESDAY 17*th.* Being on shore in the after-noon Oree sent for me to a large house where were collected a good number of people, here a kind of Councel was hild. I well understood it regarded us and that the Chiefs all declared they had no hand in asulting M^r F Servant and desired I would Matte[33] the fellows who did. I assured Oree that I was satisfied neither he or any of the people present had any hand in it and that I should certainly do with the fellows as they desird but the Quiry was where and how I was to find them. After this the Councel broke up.

33. *matte*: punish, beat (Tahitian, also used in Tonga).

WEDNESDAY 18*th*. Some Showers of rain. Morning Oree came with a present of fruit, stay'd dinner and in the after noon desired to see some great guns fired, Shotted, which I comply'd with and then he return'd a shore well satisfied. Some of the Petty officers going out into the Country took two men as guides and to carry their money bags, containing hatchets, Nails &c^a the Currant coin of these countries, but the fellows found means to move off with their burdthens and the Method they took was artfull enough, they pointed out to them some birds to shoot, one of the two Musquets they had went of and the other miss'd fire several times, so that they saw they were secure from both and ran off immidiately and left the gentlemen gazeing at them like fools.

* * *

FRIDAY 20*th*. Early in the Morning three of the officers set out on a Shooting party, about 3 o'Clock in the after-noon I received intelligence that they were Seized and stripd of every thing about them, immidiately upon this I went a Shore with Mr F. and a boats crew and took possession of a large house with all the effects in it and two Chiefs, but in such a manner that they hardly knew what we were about being unwilling to alarm the neighbourhood. In this situation we were till the officers returnd safe and had had all their things restored; some insult on their side induced the Natives (who perhaps waited for such an oppertunity) to seize their guns, upon which a scuffle insued, some chiefs interfeer'd and took the officers out of the Crowd and caused what had been taken from them to be restored. I wint to look for Oree to complain of those repeated outrages, but not being in the neghberhood did not see him, after I had got on board I was told he was come to his house and was much grieved at what had happen'd.

SATURDAY 21*st*. Early in the Morn sail'd from hence for Ulietea, upward of Sixty Canoes, we were told the people in them were Arioe's and were going to the neghbouring isles to viset thier Brethren of the same ferternity, one may almost compair these Men to free masons, they tell us they assist each other when need requires and they seem to have Customs amongst them which they either will not or cannot explain, Odiddy says he is one and yet he cannot give us hardly any Idea of them.

Odiddy who generly sleeps on Shore came off with a Message from Oree desiring I would come on shore with 22 Men to go with him to Chastise the robers, the Messenger brought with him 22 pices of leaves least as I suppose he should forget his number, but this is one of their customs. Upon my receiving this extraordinary message I went ashore for better information; all I could learn from the Chief was these fellows were a sort of Banditi that had form'd themselves into a boddy with a resolution to seize and rob our people where ever they found them and therefore he wanted them chastized. I told him they would fly to the Mountains, he said no they had arm'd themselves to fight us.

When I got on board I acquainted the officers with what I had heard and desired to have their opinion of the Matter, in short it was concluded to go upon this consideration, that if we declined it as it was at the request of the cheif, these fellows would thereby be incouraged to commit greater acts of Violence and as these proceeding[s] would soon reach Ulietea, at which isle we intended to touch, the people there might treat us in the same manner or worse as being more numerous. Accordingly we landed 48 Men including my self, Mr F. and officers, the Cheif join'd us with a few people and we set out on our march in good order, the Chiefs party gather'd like a snow ball as we marched thro' the Country, some arm'd and some not; Odiddy who was with us began to be alarm'd and told us that many of the people in our company were of the party we were going against and at last told us that they were only leading us to some place where they could attack us to advantage, whether there was any truth in this or only occasioned by Odiddies fears I will not pretend to say, he however was the only person we could confide in and we regulated our march accordingly; after we had march'd several miles we got intelligence that the people we were going against were fled to the Mountains, but I think we were not told this till I had diclar'd to the Chief that I would March no farther for we were then about crossing a deep Vally bounded on each side with Steep Rocks where a few men with stones only might have cut off our retreat supposeing their intention to be what Odiddy had said and what he still abided by; having therefore no business to proceed farther we return'd back in the same order as we went, and saw in several places people come down from the sides of the hills with their arms in their hands, which they laid down when ever they found they were seen by us, this shews that there must have been some truth in what Odiddy had said, but I must acquit Oree the Chief from having any hand in it. In our return Stoping at a house to refresh our selves with Cocoa-nutts two Chiefs brought each of them a pig and a dog and with the Customary ceremony presented them to me together with some young plantain trees by way of making and ratifying the Peace, after this we continued our march to the landing place where we imbarqued and went on board, soon after the chief follow'd, with a quantity of fruit, and set down with us to dinner, we had scarce dined before more fruit and two Hogs were brought off to the Ship, so that we were likely to get more by this excursion than by all the presents we had made them; it certainly gave them some Alarm to see so strong a party march into the Country and probably gave them a better opinion of our fire Arms, for I had caused the people on our return to the beach to fire several vollies to let the Natives see we could keep up a constant fire for I believe they had but an indifferent or rather contemptable Idea of Musquets in general, having never seen any fired but at birds &c^a by such of our people as used to stragling about the Country, the most of them but indifferent sportsmen and Miss'd generally two Shott out of three, this together with their pieces missing fire, being Slow in charging and before the Natives, all this they no doubt took great Notice of and concluded that Musquets were not such terrible things as they had been tought to believe.

* * *

MONDAY 23*rd*. Winds Easterly, as it has been ever since we have been here. The Ship being unmoor'd and every thing in readiness to Sail, at 8 am wieghed and put to Sea, the good old Chief was the last of the Natives who went out of the Ship, when he took leave I told him we should see each other no more at which he wept saying than let your sons come we will treat them well. Oree is a good Man to the utmost sence of the word, but many of the people are far from being of that disposision and seem to take advantage of his old age. The gentle treatment they have ever met with from me and the careless and imprudent manner many of our people have rambled about in their country from a Vain opinion that fire Arms rendred them invincible hath incouraged some of these people to commit acts of Violence no man at Otaheite ever dar'd attempt.

During our stay at this isle we got bread fruit, Cocoa nuts &c[a] more than we could well consume, but Hogs not by far sufficient for our daily expence and yet they did not appear to be scarce in the isle, it must however be Allowed that the number we took away when last here must have thin'd them much and at the same time Stock'd the Natives with our articles, besides we now wanted a proper assortment of Trade our Stock being nearly exhausted and the few Red feathers we had left was here of little Value when compared to what they bore at Otaheite, this obliged me to set the Smiths to work to make different sorts of Iron tools, Nails &c[a], in order to inable me to procure refreshments at the other isles and to support my Credit and influance among them.

MONDAY 23rd.[34] As Soon as we were clear of Hauheine we made Sail and steer'd over for the South end of Ulietea, one of the Natives of the first isle took a Passage with us as some others had done from Otaheite. Having but little wind all the afternoon it was dark by such time as we reached the West side of the isle where we spent the night. The same light and variable winds continued till 10 o'Clock y[e] next morning when the Trade wind at East prevail'd and we ventured to ply up to the Harbour, first sending a boat to ly in Anchorage; after making a few trips, anchor'd in 20 fathom water, between the two points of the reef which form the entrance on which the Sea broke with Such height and Violence as was frightfull to look at; having all our Boats and Warpes in readiness we presently carried them out and Warped the Ship in to safety where we droped an Anchor for the night. While we were warping into the harbour my old friend Oreo

34. Cook begins another Monday at noon as he moves from civil time to ship's time.

the Chief and Several more came off to see us. The Chief came not empty handed.

WEDNESDAY 25*th*. Rainy Weather, AM Warp'd the Ship up into the Cove which froonts the entrance of the Harbour and higher up than we had ever anchor'd before and there moor'd her, in this situation we commanded the Shores all round us. Whilest this was doing I went on Shore accompanied by Mr F. &c^a to make the Chief the Customary present. At our first entering his house we were met by 4 or 5 old Women, Weeping and lamenting, as it were, most bitterly and at the same time cuting their heads with Instruments made of Sharks teeth so that the blood ran p[l]entifully down their faces and on their Shoulders, and what was still worse we were obliged to submit to the Embraces of these old Hags and by that means got all besmear'd with Blood: this ceremony (for it was meerly such) being over, these women went and Washed themselves and immidiately after appear'd as Cheerfull as any of the Company. After I had given my presents to the Chief and his friends he put a Hog and some fruit into my Boat and came on board with us to dinner. In the after-noon we had a vast number of Canoes and people about us from different parts of the isle, they all took up their quarters in our neighbourhood where they remain'd feasting for two or three days. We understood the most of them were Arioe's.

* * *

FRIDAY 27*th*. In the Morning Oreo, his Wife, Son and Daughters and several more of his friends came aboard and brought with them a supply of refreshments. After dinner we went on Shore and were entertained with a Play which ended with the representation of a Woman in Labour, who at last brought forth a thumping Boy near six feet high who ran about the stage draging what was to represent the [35] after him. I had an oppertunity to see this acted afterward, and observed that as soon as they got hold of the fellow who represented the child they f[l]atned his nose or press'd it to his face which may be a Custom a Mong them and be the reason why they have all in general flat, or what we call pug noses.

35. Afterbirth or umbilical cord. [B]

SATURDAY 28*th*. Mr F. and his party out Botanizing. Spent the day with the Chief and his friends much the same as yesterday.

SUNDAY 29*th*. . . . After dinner we all went a Shore where a play was acted for the entertainment of such as would spend their time in looking at it. Besides the Plays which the Chief now and then caused to be acted for our entertainment there were a Set of stroling Players in the Neghbourhood who acted every day, but they were all so much of a piece that we soon grew tired of them, especially, for want of throughly knowing their Language, no intristing circumstance could be collected from them; we well know they can add to or diminish their plays at pleasure; we, our Ship and our Country they have frequently brought on the Stage, but on what account I know not. I make no doubt but it was intended as a Compliment and not interduced but when some of us were present. I generally appear'd at Oreo's Theatre towards the latter end of the Play and twice at the other in order to give my mite to the actors, the only actress was Oreo's Daughter, a pretty brown girl at whose Shrine, on these occasions, many pretty things were offered by her numerous Votarists and I believe was one great inducement why her father gave us these entertainments so often.

MONDAY 30*th*. Early in the Morning, I set out with two boats accompanied by Messrs F., Odiddy, the Chief, his Wife, Son and Daughter for an Estate which Odidde call'd his, situated at the North end of the Island, here I was promised to have Hogs and fruit in a bundance, but when we arrived I found poor Odidde could not command one single thing whatever right he might have to the Whennooa which was now in possession of his Brother, by whom were presented to me with the usual ceremony two small Hogs, in return I made him presents of three times their Value, One of the Hogs I order'd to be immidiately Kill'd and dress'd for dinner. . . .

Soon after we had dined we set out for the Ship with the other Pig and a few races of Plantans which proved the sum total of our great expectations. Poor Odiddy had drank a little too freely either of the juice of peper or our Grog or both and was brought into the boat dead drunk. In our return to the Ship we put a Shore at a place where in a House we Saw four wooden Images standing upon a shelf each about 2 feet in length, they had Turbands about their heads in which were stuck some long feathers. A person in the house told us they were Eatua's no te Tou tou, that is the gods of the Common people, but this is by no means Sufficient to conclude that they worship them as such or that the Servants or Slaves are not allow'd the same Gods as those of a more elevated rank. I never heard that Tupia made any such distinction, besides these were the first wooden gods we had seen in any of the isles and all the authority we had of their being such was the bare word of, perhaps, a Superstitious person. The people of this isle are in general far more superstitious than at Otaheite or any of the other isles. The first Visit I made the chief after our arrival, he desired I would not suffer any of my people to Shoot the Heron's and Wood Pickers, Birds as Sacred to them as Robin Red-breasts, Swallows, &c^a &c^a are to many old women in England. Tupia who was a Priest, and seem'd well accquaint[ed] with their Religion, Traditions, Customs &c^a paid little or no regard to these Birds. I mention thise things because some among us were inclinable to beleive that they look'd upon these two Birds as Eatua's or Gods. We fell into this opinion when I was here in the Endeavour and some others Still more Obsurd which undoubtedly we should have adopted if Tupia had not undeceived us, a Man of his knowlidge we have not sence met with, concequently have added nothing to his account of their Religion but superstitious Notions.

TUESDAY 31*st*. The Natives being informed that we should sail in a few days began to bring us on board fruit more than usual, amonghest those who came on board was a young man who measured Six feet four Inches and Six-tenths, His Sister, younger than himself, measured five feet ten Inches and a half.

* * *

[JUNE 1774]

SATURDAY 4*th*. Early in the Morn got every thing in readiness to Sail. Oreo the Chief and his whole family came to take their last leave, accompanied by Oo oorou the Aree de hi and Boba the Aree de hi of Otaha, none of them came empty handed, but Oo oorou brought a pretty large present as this was his first and only Viset, my present in return was suteable to his title, I say title because I believe he posess'd very little more. I made all the others presents sutable to their rank and the service they had done me after which they took a very affectionate leave, Oreo's last request was for me to return and when he found I would not make him the Promise, he asked the name of my *Marai* (burial place) a strange quiston to ask a Seaman, however I hesitated not one moment to tell him Stepney the Parish in which I lived when in London. I was made to repeated it several times over till they could well pronounce it, then Stepney Marai no Tootee was echoed through a hundred mouths at once. I afterwards found that the same question was put to Mr F. by a Person a Shore but he gave a different and indeed more proper Answer by saying no man who used the Sea could tell were he would be buried. It is the Custom here as well as in most other Nations for all the great families to have burial places of their own were their bones are entarr'd, these go with the estate to the next heir, as for instance at Otaheite when Toutaha held the sceptre the Marai at Oparre was Marai no Toutaha, but now they say Marai no Otoo. What greater proof could we have of these people Esteeming and loving us as friends whom they wishd to remember, they had been repeatedly told we should see them no more, they then wanted to know the name of the place were our bodies were to return to dust.

As I could not promise or even Suppose that any more English Ships would be sent out to the isles our Companion Odiddee chose to remain in his Native Country, but he left us with great regret, he was a youth of good parts, of a Gentle and Humane disposision but quite ignorant of all their Traditions and Policy both in Religion and goverment, consequently no material knowlidge could have been got from him had I brought him away with us. Just as he was going out of the Ship he ask'd me to Tattaow some Parou[36] for him in order to Shew to any other Europeans who might touch here, I readily complied with his request by giving him a Certificate of his good behavour, the

36. Mark some speech or words – write him a testimonial, in fact. [B]

time and were he had been with us and recommended him to the Notice of those who might come to these isles after me.

It was 11 o'Clock before we could get clear of our friends, when we weigh'd and put to Sea, but Odiddee did not leave us till we were almost out of the Harbour, in order that he might have an oppertunity to fire some of the guns, for being his Majestys Birth Day we gave them the Salute at going away. I believe I should have spent the Day with them had not my stock of Trade been wholy expended, they were continually asking for things which I had not to give them, which to me was exceeding disagreeable and made me very desireous of geting away.

When I first came to these isles I had some thoughts of Viseting the famous Island of Bola bola, but having now got all the necessary repairs of the Ship done and got a plentifull Supply of all manner of refreshments I thought it would be answering no end going there and therefore laid it a side and directed my Course to the West and took our final leave of these happy isles and the good People in them.

*   *   *

[*Cook followed a course west by south towards Tonga, passing by a new island which he named Palmerston Island on 17 June.*]

MONDAY 20*th. Winds East. Course S* 75°30' *W. Dist. Sailed* 99 *Miles. Lat. in South* 18°50'. *Longde. in West Reck.g.* 168°52'. *Longde. made Ulietea* 17°13'. D° gales which freshned towards Noon at which time thought we Saw Land to the ssw and accordingly hauled up for it.

TUESDAY 21*st. Winds East to NE. Course S* 81° *W. Dist. Sailed* 47 *Miles. Lat. in South* 19°23'. *Longde. in West Reck.g.* 170°20'. *Longde. made Ulietea* 18°41'. Gentle breezes and fair Weather. At 2 PM found what we took for land was only Clouds, reassumed our WBS Course, and an hour after saw land from the Mast head in the same direction, as we drew near found it to be an Island the body of which at 5 bore due West distant five Leagues, Shortned Sail and spent the night Plying under Top-sails. At Day break bore up for the Nother point of the Isle and ran along the West Shore at the distance of one Mile from it. A little before Noon preceiveing Some People runing along the Shore and

Seeing landing was Practical, Brought-to, hoisted out and Man'd two Boats in one of which I went my self and Mr Pickersgill in the other. Mr F. and his party and Mr H. accompanied us.

WEDNESDAY 22*nd*. As we came near the Shore some People who were on the rocks retired to the woods, as we supposed to meet us and we afterwards found our conjectures right. We landed with ease and took Post on a high rock to prevent a Surprise as the whole Coast was all over run with woods, Shrubery &c^a and began to Collect plants &c^a under the protection of the Party under Arms, but the approach of the Indians soon made it necessary for us to join which was no sooner done than they appeared in the Skirts of the woods not a Stones throw from us, one of two men who were advanced before the rest threw a Stone which Struck Mr Sparman on the Arm, upon this two Musquets were fired without order which made them all retire under cover of the woods and we saw them no more. Seeing nothing was to be done here we imbarqued and proceeded down a long shore, in hopes of meeting with better Success in a nother place. We proceeded several miles down the Coast without seeing any human being or convenient landing place, at length coming before a small Beach on which lay four Canoes, here we landed by means of a small creek in the rocks, just to take a View of the Boats and to leave in them some trifles to induce the Natives to believe we intended them no harm. I left a party on the rocks under Arms to keep a good lookout while some of us went to the Canoes where we were but a few minutes before the Indians rushed out of the woods upon us, it was to no effect our endeavouring to bring them to a parly, one of them with the ferocity of a wild Boar advanced a head of the others and threw a dart at us, two or three Musquets discharged in the air did not hinder him from advanceing still farther and throwing a nother, at this instant the party on the rocks began to fire at others who appeared on the hieghts over us, this abated the Ardour of the party we were engaged with and gave us time to retire and then I caused the fireing to cease, the last discharge sent them into the woods from whence they did nor return, we had reason to beleive none were hurt. Seeing no good was to be got of these people or at the isle we return'd on board hoisted in the

Boats and made sail to wsw. The Conduct and aspect of these Islanders occasioned my giving it the Name of *Savage Island*,[37] it lies in the Latitude of 19°1', Longitud 169°37' West, is about 11 Leagues in circuit, of a tolerable hieght and seemingly covered with wood amongst which were some Cocoa-nutt trees. These Islanders were Naked except their Natural parts, some were painted black. The Canoes were like those of Amsterdam and full as neatly made.

* * *

SATURDAY 25*th. Winds ENE, Calm, Northerly.* Little Clowdy and Hazey at times. In the Evening judgeing our Selves not far from Roterdam[38] shortned Sail and spent the night under our Top-sails. At 6 AM bore away West, at Day light Saw land (Islands) extending from ssw to NNW; the Wind being at NE hauled to the NW with a view of discovering more distinctly the isles in that Quarter but presently after a reef of rocks were seen lying a thwart our Course extending on each Bow farther than we could see, it therefore became necessary to Tack and bear up to the South in search of a Passage that way. At Noon the most Southermost Isle bore sw distant about 4 Miles, near and to the North of this isle were 3 others and Several more to the west: the first four were joined to one a nother by a reef of rocks, we were not certain if this Reef did not join to the one Seen in the Morning as we saw breakers in the intermidiate space.

SUNDAY 26*th. Winds NE, Southerly.* At 3 PM seeing more breakers ahead and having but little wind and a great Easterly Swell, hauled off SE. In the evening the Southern isle bore WNW distant 5 miles and the Breakers last seen ssw½w; here we spent the night for it presently after fell Calm and continued so till 4 AM when we got breeze at South. At Day-light preceiving a likelyhood of a clear Passage between the Isle and the Breakers we stretched to the West and soon after saw more isles a head and on each Bow, but the Passage seem'd open; at length we found soundings in 45 & 40 fathom a clear bottom, this circumstance greatly lessned the danger sence we now had it in our

37. It was Niue.
38. Nomuka, among the northern Tonga (or Friendly) Islands.

power to Anchor. Towards Noon some people came off in Canoes from one of the isles bring[ing] with them some Cocoa nutts and Shaddocks which they exchanged for Nails, they shewed us Anna-mocka or Rotterdam. . . . They like wise gave us the names of some of the other Isles and wanted us much to go to theirs. The breeze freshning we soon left them a Stern.

MONDAY 27*th*. Gentle breezes and pleasent Weather. In the PM meeting with nothing to obstruct us, at 5 o'Clock Anchored on the North side of Annamocka about ¾ of a mile from the Shore in 20 fathom water, the bottom Coral Sand, the extremes of the isle extending from s 88° E to SW and a Cove with a Sandy beach s 50° East. As soon as we approached the South end of the isle Several of the Natives came off in their Canoes one of which asked for me by name, a proof that these people have a communication with Amsterdam; as soon as we had Anchored they came a long side with yams and Shaddocks which they exchanged for Small Nails and old rags.

Early in the Morn the Master and I went a Shore to look for fresh water, we were received with great Courtesy by the Natives and conducted to a Pond of Brackish Water, the same I suppose as Tasman Water at. In the mean time those in the Boat had loaded her with fruit and roots which the Natives brought down and exchanged for Nails and Beads and on our return to the Ship found the same Traffick carrying there. After breakfast I went a Shore with two Boats to Traffick with the People and ordered the Launch to follow to take in Water. The Natives assisted us to roll the Casks to and from the Pond which was about ⅓ of a Mile, the expence of their labour was a bead or a small Nail. Fruit and roots were brought down in such plenty that the other two Boats were Laden in a trice, sent of cleared and load a second time by Noon at which time the Launch was Laden also and the Botanizing and Shooting parties all come in except the Surgeon for whom we could not wait as the Water was Ebing fast out of the Cove.

TUESDAY 28*th*. In the PM the Launch could not go for Water as there was no geting into the Cove where we landed before and where we took it off, but without the Cove is a very good landing place at all times of the Tide, here some of the Officers landed after dinner, where they found the Surgeon[39] strip'd of his Gun, he having come to the landing place some time after the boats were gone, got a Canoe to bring him on board but he had no sooner got into her than a fellow snatched hold of the gun and ran of with it. . . .

*   *   *

[*This was the start of much confusion. Cook hastened ashore to prevent precipitate retaliation, but he feared that his 'Lenity . . . incourag'd them to commit acts of greater Violence'. A watering party under Clerke was set upon and Clerke's musket and many tools were taken off. Cook went ashore again and this time seized two double canoes and fired small-shot at a protester. He got the two muskets back. The next watering party was not molested.*]

Returning from the Watering place we found some of the Natives collected together near the beach from whom we understood that the Man I had fired at was Matte (dead). I treated the Story as improbable and demanded of one of them, a man who seemed of some concequence, the return of a adze which had been taken from us in the morning and told him to send for it, accordingly two men were dispatched, but I soon found that we had quite misunderstood each other for instead of the Adze the wound'd man was brought on a board and laid down at my feet to appearence dead, but we soon found our mistake and that tho he was wounded both in the hand and thigh neither the one nor the other were dangerous. I however sent for the Surgeon a Shore to dress his wounds, in the Mean time I addressed my self to several people to have the Adze return'd, especially to an elderly woman who had always a great deal to say to me from my first landing, but upon this occasion she gave her Tongue free liberty, not one word in fifty I understood, all I could learn from her Arguments was that it was mean in me to insist on the return of so trifling an article, but when she found I was determined She and 3 or 4 more Women went away and soon after the Adze was brought me, but I saw her no more which I was sorry for as I wanted to make her a present on account of the part she seem'd to take in all our

39. James Patten.

transactions, private as well as publick, for I was no sooner return'd
from the Pond the first time I landed than this woman and a man
presented to me a young woman and gave me to understand she was
at my service. Miss, who probably had received her instructions, I
found wanted by way of Handsel, a Shirt or a Nail, neither the one
nor the other I had to give without giving her the Shirt on my back
which I was not in a humour to do. I soon made them sencible of my
Poverty and thought by that means to have come of with flying Colours
but I was misstaken, for I was made to understand I might retire with
her on credit, this not suteing me niether the old Lady began first to
argue with me and when that fail'd she abused me, I understood very
little of what she said, but her actions were expressive enough and
shew'd that her words were to this effect, Sneering in my face and
saying, what sort of a man are you thus to refuse the embraces of so
fine a young Woman, for the girl certainly did not [want] beauty
which I could however withstand, but the abuse of the old Woman I
could not and therefore hastned into the Boat, they then would needs
have me take the girl on board with me, but this could not be done
as I had come to a Resolution not to suffer a Woman to come on
board the Ship on any pretence what ever and had given strict orders
to the officers to that purpose for reasons which I shall mention in a
nother place.

When the Surgeon arrived he dress'd the mans wounds and let
him blood and was of opinion he was in no sort of danger as the shott
had done little more than penetrate the Skin. In the operation some
poultice was wanting, the Surgeon ask'd for ripe Plantains but they
brought Sugar Cane and Chewed it to a poulp and gave him it to
apply to the wounds, this being more of a Balsamick than the other
shews that these people understand Simples. After the mans wounds
were dress'd I gave him a Spike Nail and a Knife which to them was
of great value, his Master or at least the man who seem'd to own the
Canoe took them, most probably to himself. It was rather unlucky
this man did not belong to the Isle, but had lately come in one of the
two Sailing Canoes from a nother isle in the Nighbourhood. Matters
being once more put in order we all return'd on board to dinner.

WEDNESDAY 29*th*. Having got on board a plentifull Supply of roots and some fruits I resolved to sail as soon as we got any Wind for at present it was Calm. In the evining I went a Shore in Company with Mr F. and some of the officers, they made a little excursion into the isle but I did not quit the landing place, the Natives were every were very submissive and obligeing so that had we made a longer stay its probable we should [have] had no more reason to complain of their conduct; while I was now on Shore I got the names of Twenty Islands which lay between the NW and NE, some of them in Sight. Two which laid most to the West were remarkable on account of their great hight, in the most westermost we judged was a Vulcano by the Continual Column of Smoak we saw assend from the center of the isle; to clear up this point it was necessary we should approach them nearer, accordingly at day-light in the Morning got under Sail with a light breeze at West and Stood to the Northward for these isles, but the wind scanting carried us among the low Islots and Shoals which lie north of Annamocka so that we had to ply to windward. At Noon the middle of Annamocka bore S¼E distant 9 Miles and was at the same time close to one of the islots, those we had in Sight extended from N½W to SEBE½E, and were Sixteen or 18 in Number, the two high Islands bore from NW to NNW½W. Lat Ob^d 20°6′ s. A great Number of Canoes kept about us all the forenoon; the people in them brought for Traffick Various sorts of Curiosities, some roots, fruits and fowls but of these not many; they took in exchange small Nails and Pieces of any kind of Cloth. I believe before they went away they striped the most of our people of the few Clothes the Otaheite Ladies had left them for the Passion for Curiosities was as great as ever.

THURSDAY 30*th*. The Wind being contrary and but little of it the after noon and night was spent in plying with the precaution necessary to such navigation. In the Morning Stretched out for the high Islands having the Advantage of a gentle breeze at WSW. Day no sooner dawned than we saw Canoes coming from all parts, their Traffick was much the same as yesterday or rather better, for out of one Canoe I got two Pigs which were Scarce Articles with them.

[JULY 1774]

FRIDAY 1*st*. Gentle breezes and Clowdy Weather. At 4 o'Clock in the PM we reached the two high Islands, the Southermost and the one on which the Vulcano is or is supposed to be is called by the Natives Amattafoa and the other which is round high and Peaked Oghao.[40] We pass'd between the two, the Channell being two Miles wide, safe and without soundings; both are inhabited but neither of them appeared firtile, they lay from Annamocka NNW¼W Distant 11 or 12 Leagues. Amattafoa which is the largest of the two is about 5 Leagues in Circuit. Unfortunately the Summit of this isle during the whole day was covered with heavy clouds, so that we were not able to veryfy whether or no the Smoak we had seen was occasioned by a Vulcano or the burning of the Country, for we could see that great part of the Brow of the Hill had been consumed by fire, this divided our opinions and nothing determined. While we were in the Passage between the two Isles we had little wind, which gave time for a large Sailing Canoe which had been chasing us all day to get up with us as well as several others with Padles which had been thrown a Stern when the breeze was fresh. . . .

We were hardly through the Passage before we got a fresh breeze from the South, that moment the Natives made haste to be gone and we steer'd to the west all sails set. I had some thoughts of touching at Amsterdam as it lay not much out of the way, but as the Wind was now we could not fetch it and was the occasion of my laying a side going there at all.

Before I proceed with the Sloop to the west it will be necessary to turn back to Annamocka. This Island which is situated in the Latitude of 20°15′, Long^de 174°30′ w was first discovered by Captain Tasman and by him Named Rotterdam. It is of a Triangler form each side where of is about three miles and a half or four miles, a Salt-Water Lake which is in it occupies not a sm^l part of its Surface and in a manner cuts off the SE angle. Round the isle, that is from the NW to the South, round by the North and East lies scatered a number of

40. Tofua and Kao.

Islots, Sand banks and breakers, we could see no end to their extent to the North and its very probable they reach as far to the South as Amsterdam which together with Middleburg and Pylstaerts make one group of Isles, containing about three degrees in Latitude and two of Longitude: this groupe I have named the Friendly Archipelago as a lasting friendship seems to subsist among the Inhabitants and their Courtesy to Strangers intitles them to that Name. Tasman seems to have seen the northern extremity in about 19°. The Inhabitants of Boscawen and Keppels Isles, discovered by Captain Wallis in 15°53' and nearly under the same Meridian as this Archipelago, seem, from the little account I have had of them, to be the same Sort of friendly people as these. The Latitude and discriptions of these two isles point them out to be the same as Cocos and Traitors discovered by Lemaire and Schouten, but if they are the same Mr Dalrymple has placed them above 8° too far to the west in his Chart.

The Inhabitants, Productions, &cª of Rotterdam or Annamocka and the Neighbouring isles are much the Same as at Amsterdam. . . . The people of this isle seem to be more affected with the Leprous or some other Scrofulous disease than any I have yet seen, it breaks out in the face more than in any other parts of the Body. I have seen several who had quite lost their Noses by it. In one of my excursions I happen'd to peep into a house where one or more of these people were, one Man only appeared at the Door or Hole by which I was to enter and he began to Shut me out by drawing a Cord a Cross, but the intolerable Stench which came from his Putrified face was alone sufficient to keep me from entering, his Nose was quite gone and his face ruin'd being wholy covered with ulcers, or rather wholy covered with one ulcer so that the very sight of him was shocking. As our People had not quite got clear of the disease communicated to them by the women of Otaheite I took all immaginable care to prevent its being communicated to these people, and I may venture to assert that my endeavours succeeded.

* * *

[*Following a north-westerly course, Cook paused briefly on 3 July at Vatoa, a south-eastern islet of the Fiji group, the only contact which he made with Fiji.*]

SUNDAY 17*th*. Continued to Steer to the West till 3 o'Clock in the PM when we saw land bearing SW upon which we took in the Small Sails, reef'd the Top-sails and hauled up for it having a very Strong gale at SE thick hazey weather. At half past 5 the land bore from SSW to NWBN½W but we were not certain that we saw the whole extent either way. At half past 7 Tack'd judging our selves at this time about two leagues from the land. We stood off till between 1 and 2 in the AM then Stood in again. It was no wonder to find we had lost ground in the night for it blew exceeding hard at times and there went a great Sea from the SE, besides several of our Sails were Split and torn to pieces in the night, particularly a Fore Top-sail which was rendred quite useless as a Sail. Being desireous of geting round the Southern ends of the lands or at least so far to the South as to be able to judge of their extent in that direction, for I made no doubt but this was the Australia Del Espiritu Santo of Quiros or what M. D. Bougainville calls the Great Cyclades, and the coast we were now upon the East side of Aurora Island[41] whose Longitude by the Observations we have lately had is 17 °   ′ E.

*   *   *

[*Cook made no landing until he reached the large island of Malekula, towards the middle of the group.*]

FRIDAY 22*nd*. Wind at SE a gentle breeze and pleasent Weather. In Standing in for the land we preceived a creek which had the appearence of a good harbour, formed by a point of land or Peninsula projecting out to the North, we just fetched this place at 1 o'Clock PM when we tack'd and stood off till half past 2 in order to gain room and time to hoist the Boats out to examine it. Several people appeared on the Point of the Peninsula and seem'd to invite us a Shore, but the most of them had Bows and Arrows in their hands. In stretching in Shore, by the help of a Tide or Current which we had not before preceived, we fetched two Leagues to windward of this place, and by that means discovered a nother opening which I sent Lieut^t Pickersgill and the

---

41. Bougainville's name (1768) for Maewo, the north-easternmost of the archipelago which Cook later named the New Hebrides.

Master in two Arm'd boats to Sound and look for Anchorage; Upon their makeing the Sign for the latter, we saild in and anchored in 11 fathom Water Sandy bottom, some thing more than a Cables length from the South Shore and a Mile within the entrance.

Some of the Natives came off to us in their Canoes, two of them were induced to come on board where they made a very Short stay as the Sun was already set; the kind reception these met with induced others to come off by moon light, but I would permit none to enter the Ship or even to come along-side, by this means we got rid of them for the night. They exchanged for pieces of Cloth some few Arrows, some of which were pointed with bone and diped in Poison or some green gummy substance that could Answer no other end.[42]

In the Morning a good many came round us, some came in Canoes and others swam off. I soon prevaild on one to come on board which he had no sooner done than he was followed by more than we desired: four I took into the Cabbin and made them various presents which they Shew'd to those in the Canoes, thus a friendly intercourse between us and them was in a fair way of being opened when an accident happened which put all in confution but in the end I believe turn'd out to our advantage. A fellow in a Canoe having been refused admittance into one of our boats a long-side was going to Shoot one of the Poisoned Arrows at the Boat-keeper, some interfeering prevented him from doing it that Moment, the instant I was acquainted with this I ran on deck and saw a nother man strugling with him, one of those as I was told who were in the Cabbin and had jump'd out of the window for that purpose, but the fellow got the better of him and directed his Bow again to the boat keeper, but upon my calling to him he directed it to me and was just going to let fly when I gave him a peppering of Small Shott, this Staggered him for a Moment but did not hinder him from holding his bow in the Attitude of Shooting, another discharge of the same Nature made him drop it and the others in the Canoes to Paddle off as fast as they could. Some began to Shoot Arrows from the other side, a Musquet discharged in the air and a

---

42. It was not poison, but an unguent believed to have magical properties. The surgeon tried it out on a dog who 'lived to be brought home to England'.

four pounder over their heads sent them all off in the utmost confusion; those in the Cabbin leaped out of the Windows, other that were in the ship and on different parts of the Rigging all leaped over board and many quited their Canoes and swam a shore. After this we took no further notice of them, but suffered them to come and pick up their Canoes, and some were soon after prevailed upon to come alongside. We now got every thing in readiness to land in order to try to get some refreshments, for nothing of this kind had been seen in any of thier boats, and to Cut some Wood of which we were in want of.

About 9 o'Clock we landed in the face of about 4 or 500 Men who were assembled on the Shore, arm'd with Bows and Arrows, Clubs and Spears, but they made not the least oppossission, on the contrary one Man gave his Arms to a nother and Met us in the water with a green branch in his hand, which [he] exchanged for the one I held in my hand, took me by the other hand and led me up to the crowd to whom I distributed Medals, Pieces of Cloth &c^a. After Mr Edgcomb had drawn his Marines up on the beach in such a manner as to Protect the workmen in cutting down wood I made Signs to the Natives that we wanted some to take on board, to which they willingly consented. A small Pigg was now brought down and presented to me for which I gave the bearer a Piece of Cloth, this gave us hopes that a trade would soon be opened for refreshments but we were misstaken, this Pig came on some other account probable as a peace offering, for all that we could say or do did not prevail upon them to bring us above half a Dozen small Cocoanutts and a small quantity of fresh water. They set no sort of Value upon Nails nor did they seem much to esteem any thing we had, they would now and then give an arrow for a Piece of Cloth but constantly refused to part with their bows, they were unwilling we should go into the Country and very desireous for us to go on board, we understood not a word they said, they are quite different to all we have yet seen and Speak a different language, they are almost black or rather a dark Chocolate Colour, Slenderly made, not tall, have Monkey faces and Woolly hair.[43] About Noon after

43. Cook had passed from the Polynesian to the Melanesian area of the Pacific.

sending what wood we had cut on board we all embarqued and went of after which they all retired some one way and some a nother.

SATURDAY 23rd. Having now got on board a small quantity of Wood for present consumption and intending to put to Sea the next Morning in order to take advantage of the moonlight nights which now happened we employ'd this after-noon in seting up our lower & Top-mast Rigging which they stood in need of. Some time last night the Natives had taken away the Buoy from the Kedge Anchor we lay moor'd by, which I now saw a fellow bringing along the Strand to the landing place. I therefore took a boat and went for it accompanied by some of the Gentlemen; the moment we landed the Buoy was put into our boat by a man who walked of again without Speaking one word; it ought to be observed that this was the only thing they even so much as attempted to take from us by any means whatever and that they seem'd to Observe Strict honisty in all their dealings. Having landed near some of their houses and Plantations which were just within the Skirts of the Woods, I prevaild on one man to let me see them, they Suffered Mr F. to go with me but were unwilling any more should follow. Their houses are low and covered with thick Palm thatch, their form is oblong and some are boarded at the ends where the entrance is by a Square Port hole which at this time was Shut up; they did not chouse we should enter any of them and we attempted nothing against their inclinations; here were about half a Dozen houses, some small Plantations which were fenced round with reeds, about Twenty Piggs and a few Fowles runing about loose, and a good many fine yams lying piled up upon Sticks or kind of Platforms; here were Bread fruit Trees, Cocoa-nutt and Plantain Trees on which were little or no fruit, we afterwards saw an Orange on the beach, proof sufficient that they have of these fruit. . . .

The people of this country are in general the most Ugly and ill-proportioned of any I ever saw, to what hath been allready said of them I have only to add that they have thick lips flat noses and—[44]

Their Beards as well as most of their Woolly heads are of a Colour between brown and black, the former is much brighter than the latter

44. The sentence is unfinished.

and is rather more of hair than wool, short and curly. The Men go naked, it can hardly be said they cover thier Natural parts, the Testicles are quite exposed, but they wrap a piece of cloth or leafe round the yard which they tye up to the belly to a cord or bandage which they wear round the waist just under the Short Ribbs and over the belly and so tight that it was a wonder to us how they could endure it. They have curious bracelets which they wear on the Arm just above the Elbow, these are work'd with threed or Cord and studed with Shells and are four or five inches broad, they never would part with one, they also wear round the wrist Hoggs Tusks and rings made of large Shells; the bridge of the Nose is pierced in which they wear an ornament of this form, it is made of a stone which is not unlike alabaster, they likewise wear small ear Rings made of Tortise shell. We saw but few Women and they were full as disagreeable as the Men, their head face and Shoulders were painted with a Red Colour, they wear a piece of Cloth wraped round their Middle and some thing over their Shoulders in which they carry their Children. . . .

SUNDAY 24*th*. Gentle breezes and fair Weather. . . .

The Night before we came out of Port two Red fish about the Size of large Bream and not unlike them were caught with hook and line of which Most of the officers and Some of the Petty officers dined the next day. In the Evening every one who had eat of these fish were seiz'd with Violant pains in the head and Limbs, so as to be unable to stand, together with a kind of Scorching heat all over the Skin, there remained no doubt but that it was occasioned by the fish being of a Poisoness nature and communicated its bad effects to every one who had the ill luck to eat of it even to the Dogs and Hogs, one of the latter died in about Sixteen hours after and a young dog soon after shared the same fate. These must be the same sort of fish as Quiros mentions under the name of *Pargos*, which Poisoned the Crews of his Ships, so that it was some time before they recovered. We had reason to be thankfull in not having caught more of them for if we had we should have been in the Same Situation.

* * *

[*Cook continued exploring to the south until he reached Eromanga. Here he anchored and took two boats to a sandy beach. He stepped out holding out a green branch in the face of 'a great multitude'. He 'was charmed with their behaviour', but they misinterpreted Cook's attempt to have the boats hauled up on the sand as an intention to leave, and they tried to prevent this. Fighting broke out, muskets (which kept misfiring) against darts and arrows. Back on board, Cook fired a four-pound shot as a parting gesture.*]

[AUGUST 1774]

FRIDAY 5*th*. . . . After leaving this Island we shaped our Course for the East end of the one to the South, being guided by a great fire we saw upon it. At 1 o'Clock we came near the Shore and made it necessary to shorten Sail and spend the remainder of the night making Short boards. At day break we discover'd a high table land bearing EBS and a smal low isle bearing NNE which we had passed in the night, Traitors head[45] was still in sight bearing N 20° west and the Island to the Southward extending from s 7° w to s 87° w distant about one League, we now found that what we had taken for a common fire in the Night was a Volcano which threw up vast quantaties of fire and smoak and made a rumbling noise which was heard at a good distance. Soon after we had made Sail for the East end of the island we discovered an Inlet which had the appearence of a harbour, as soon as we drew near I sent two Arm'd Boats under the command of Lieut.ᵗ Cooper and the Master to examine and Sound it while we stood on and off with the Ship to be ready to follow or give them any assistance they might want. On the East point were a great number of People Hutts and Canoes, some of the latter they put into the Water and followed our boats but came not near them. It was not long before our boats made the Signal for Anchorage and we stood in accordingly: the Wind being at West, we borrowed close to the west point and pass'd over some Sunken Rocks which would been have avoided by keeping a little more to the East. The wind left us as soon as we were within the entrance and obliged us to drop an anchor in 4 fathom water when the boats were sent again to Sound and in the mean time the Launch

45. A promontory on the east coast of Eromanga, so named because of what Cook regarded as the treacherous behaviour of the inhabitants.

was hoisted out and as soon as we were acquainted with the Channel, laid out warps and warped farther in. While this work was going forward Vast numbers of the Natives had collected together on the Shores and a great many came off in Canoes and some even Swam off, but came not nearer than a stones throw and those in the Canoes had their Arms in constant readiness; insensibly they became bolder and bolder and at last came under our Stern and exchanged some Cocoa nutts for pieces of Cloth &c^a; some more daring than the others were for carrying off every thing they could lay their hands upon and made several attempts to knock the rings of[f] the rudder, the greatest trouble they gave us was to look after the Buoys of our anchors which were no soon let go from the Ship or thrown out of the boats than they lay hold of them, a few Musquets fired without any design to hit had no effect, but a four pounder threw them into great confusion, made them quit their Canoes and take to the water but seeing none were hurt they presently recoverd their fright and returned to their Canoes and once more attempted to take away the buoys, this put us to the necessity of firing a few Musketoon shot over them which had the desired effect and altho none were hurt they were afterwards afraid to come near them and at last retired to the Shore and we were suffered to set down to dinner undisturbed. During these transactions a friendly old man in a small Canoe made several trips between us and the shore, bringing with him 2 or 3 Cocoa nutts or a yam each time and took in exchange what ever we gave him: another was on the gang way when the great gun was fired, but he was not to be prevailed upon to stay long after.

SATURDAY 6*th*. Wind at South a fresh breeze and fair weather. In the PM after the Ship was moor'd I landed with a strong party of Men at the head of the harbour without any opposition being made by a great number of the islanders assembled in two parties the one on our right and the other on our left, all arm'd with darts, clubs, slings, bows and arrows: after our men were drawn up upon the beach I distributed to the old people presents of pieces of Cloth, Medals &c^a and ordered two Casks of Water to be fill'd out of a Pond which we found conveniently situated behind the beach, giving the Natives to understand it was what we wanted. We got from them a few Cocoa-nuts which seem'd to be in plenty on the trees, but they would not on any account part with any of their Arms which they held in constant readiness and press'd so much upon us that little was wanting to make them attack us, however no attempt was made, our early embarqueing probably disconcerted their scheme and after that they all retired.

I now found it was practical to lay the Ship nearer to the landing place, and as we wanted to take in a large quantity of both wood and Water it would greatly facilitate that work as well as over-awe the Natives and be more ready to assist our people on Shore in case of an attack, we therefore in the morning went to work to transport her: while this was doing we observed the Natives assembling from all parts to the landing or Watering place where they form'd themselves into two parties one on each side the landing place, we judged there were not less than a thousand people arm'd in the same manner as in the evening. A Canoe conducted some times by one and at other times by 2 or 3 Men would now and then come off from them, invite us to go a Shore and bring us a few Cocoa-nuts or Plantains which they gave without asking for any thing in return but I took care they always had some thing. One of those who came off was the old man whose beheavour had attracted our attention yesterday. I gave him to under-stand by Signs (for we could not understand one another) that they were to lay a side their Arms, took those which were in his Canoe and threw them over board, there was no doubt but he understood me and I believe made it known to his country men on shore for as soon as he landed he went first to the one party and then to the other, and as to himself he was never after seen with any thing like a weapon in his hand. Three fellows coming under the Stern in a Canoe offered a Club for a String of beads and some other trifles all of which I sent down to them, but the Moment they were in their possession they padled off in all haste without makeing any return, this was what I expected and what I was not sorry for as I wanted a pretence to shew the Multitude on shore the effect of our fire arms without materially hurting any of them, having a Musquet ready load[ed] with Small Shott, (N° 3) I gave one of the fellows the Contents into the bargin and when they were above Musquet shott off, order'd 3 or 4 Musketoons or Wall pieces to be fired at them which made them quit the Canoe and keep under her off side and swim with her to the shore, this transaction seem'd to have little or no effect on the two divisions on shore, on the contrary they seem'd to think it sport.

After mooring the Ship by four anchors with her broad side to the landing place, from which she was hardly Musquet Shott, and placeing our Artillery in such a manner as to command the whole harbour, we embarked the Marines and a party of Seamen in three boats and rowed in for the Shore; I have already observed that the two divisions of the Natives were drawn up on each side the landing place, the space between was 30 or 40 yards, here were laid to the most advantage a few bunches of plantains, a yam and two Tara roots, between them and the shore were stuck in the sand four small reeds about 2 feet from each other in a line at right angles to the sea shore, for what purpose they were put there I never could learn; the old man before mentioned and two more stood by these things and by Signs invited us a Shore, but we were not in a hurry to land, I had not forgot the trap I had like to have been caught in at the last isle and this looked some thing like it; we answered the old men by makeing signs that the two divisions must retire farther back and give us more room, the old men seem'd to desire them so to do but as little regard was paid to them as us. More were continually joining them, and except the 3 old men, not one was without arms: In short every thing conspired to make us believe they intended to attack us as soon as we were on shore. The consequence of such a step was easily seen, many of them must have been kill'd and wounded and we should hardly have escaped unhurt. Sence therefore they would not give us the room we required I thought it was best to frighten them away rather than oblige them by the deadly effect of our fire Arms and accordingly order a Musquet to be fired over the heads of the party on our right for this was by far the Strongest body, the alarm it gave them was only momentary, in an instant they recovered themselves and began to display their weapons, one fellow shewed us his back side ın such a manner that it was not necessary to have an interpreter to explain his meaning; after this I ordered three or four more to be fired, this was the Signal for the Ship to fire a few four pound Shott over them which presently dispersed them and then we landed and marked out the limits on the right and [left] by a line. Our old friend stood his ground all the time, tho' diserted by his two companions, the moment we landed I made him a present of Cloth and other things I had taken with me for the purpose. Insencibly the Natives came to us seemingly in a more friendly manner, some even came without arms, but by far the greatest part brought them and when we made signs to them to lay them down, they told us to lay down ours first; they climed the Cocoa trees and threw us down the Nutts, without requiring any thing for their trouble, but we took care they were always paid. After filling half a doz^n Small Casks with Water and obtaining leave of the old man whose name was [Paowang] to cut wood for fireing, just to let the people see what we wanted we return'd on board to dinner after which they to a man retired. I never learnt that any one of them was hurt by our Shott.

SUNDAY 7*th*. . . . In the night the Volcano threw up vast quantities of fire and Smoak, the flames were seen to ascend above the hill between us and it, the night before it did the same and made a noise like that [of] thunder or the blowing up of mines at every eruption which happened every four or five Minutes; a heavy shower of rain which fell at this time seem'd to increase it: the wind blew from that quarter and brought such vast quantities of fine Sand or ashes that every thing was covered with it, and was also exceeding troublesom to the eyes. . . .

*   *   *

WEDNESDAY 10*th*. . . . Yesterday Mr Forster obtained from these people the Name of the Island (Tanna)[46] and to day I got from them the names of those in the nieghbourhood. They gave us to understand in such a manner which admited of no doubt that they eat human flesh, they began the subject themselves by asking us if we did: they like wise gave us to understand that Circumcision was practised amongest them. While the Launch was takeing in ballast on the West side of the harbour, one man employed on this work scalded his fingers in takeing up a stone out of some water, this circumstance produced the discovery of

46. The word *tanna* means ground or earth; Forster had pointed to the ground when asking what the island was called. The proper name for the island is Ipari, but Forster's misapprehension provided a name that has endured.

several hot springs at the foot of the clift rather below high-water mark. In the AM Mr F. and his party made an excursion into the country, he met with civil treatment from the Natives and saw several fine Plantations of Plantains, Sugar Cane, roots &c^a. The people now, especially those in our neighbourhood are so well reconciled to us that they take no notice of our going a Shooting in the woods.

THURSDAY 11*th*. Wind at South with some heavy showers of rain in the night. In the pm two or three boy's got behind some thickets and threw 2 or 3 stones at our people, who were cuting wood, for which they were fired at by the petty officers present. I was much displeased at such an abuse of our fire Arms and took measures to prevent it for the future. During the night and all the next day the Volcano made a terrible noise throwing up prodigeous colums of Smoak and fire at every erruption; at one time great stones were seen high in the air. In the AM beside the necessary work of Wooding and Watering, we struck the main-top-mast in order to fix new Tristle-trees and a pair of new back stays. Mr F. made a little excursion up the hill on the west side the harbour where he found three places from whence assended Smoak or Steam of a Sulpherous smell, they seem'd to keep pace with the Volcano, for at every erruption the quantity of smoak or steam was greatly increased and forced out of the ground in such quantities as to be seen at a great distance which we had before taken for the smoak of common fire; it is at the foot of this hill the hot springs before mentioned are.

FRIDAY 12*th*. In the After-noon Mr F. carried his botanical excursions to the other side of the harbour and fell in with Paowang's house where he saw most of the articles I had given him hanging on the adjoining bushes, probably they were in his eyes of so little Value as not to be worth house room. Some of the gentlemen accompanied Mr F. to the hot places he was at yesterday. [A thermometer] placed in a little hole made in one of them rose from 80 to 170. Several other parts of the hill emited Smoak or Steam all the day, the Volcano was unusaly furious and filled all the circumjacent air with its ashes so that the drops of rain which fell was mixed with its ashes, it mattered not which way the wind blew we were sure to be troubled with them. The Natives gave us now very little trouble and we made little excursions inland with safety, they would however have been better pleased if we had confined our selves to the Shore, as a proof of this, some of them undertook to conduct the gentlemen to a place where they might see the mouth of the Volcano, they very readily embraced the offer and were conducted down to the harbour before they preceived the cheat.

* * *

SUNDAY 14*th*. Wind northerly, weather as yesterday. After breakfast we made up a party consisting of 9 or 10 and set out in order to see if we could not have a nearer and better View of the Volcano, we first went to one of those burning or hot places before mentioned, having a Thermometer with us we made a hole in the ground where the greatest heat seem'd to be into which we put it; in the open air the mercury stood at   but here it presently rose to and stood at [210] which is only two below boiling Water. The Earth in this place was a kind of Pipe clay or whitish marl which had a sulpherous smell and was soft and wet, the upper surface only excepted which was crusted over with a thin dry crust, on which was Sulpher and a Vitriolick substance which tasted like Alumn: the whole space was no more than eight or ten yards square, near to which were some fig-trees who spread their branches over a part of it. . . . Happening to turn out of the common path we came into a plantation where there was a Man at work, he either out of good Nature or to get us the sooner out of his territories, undertook to be our guide, we had not gone with him far before we met a nother fellow standing at the junction of two roads with a Sling and a Stone in his hand, both of which he thought proper to lay aside when a Musquet was pointed at him, the Attitude we found him in and the ferosity which appear'd in his looks and his behaviour after, led us to think he meant to defend the path he stood in; he pointed to the other along which he and our guide led us, he counted us several times over and kept calling for assistance and was presently joined by two or three more one of which was a young Woman with a Club in her hand; they presently conducted us to the brow of a hill and pointed to a road which led down to the harbour and wanted us to go that way, we refused to comply and returned to the one we had left which we pursued alone our guide refusing to go with us; after assending a nother ridge as closely covered with Wood as those we had come over, we saw still other hills between us and the Volcano which discouraged us from proceeding farther especially as we could get no one to be our guide and therefore came to a resolution to return, we had but just put this into execution when we met twenty or thirty of the Natives collicted together and were close at our heels, we judged their design was to oppose our advancing into the Country but now they saw us returning they suffered us to pass unmolested and some of them put us into the right road and accompanied us down the hill, made us to stop in one place where they brought us Cocoa nutts, Plantains and Sugar Canes and [what] we did not eat on the spot, brought down the hill for us; thus we found these people Civil and good Natured when not prompted by jealousy to a contrary conduct, a conduct one cannot blame them for when one considers the light in which they must look upon us in, its impossible for them to know our real design, we enter their Ports without their daring to make opposition, we attempt to land in a peaceable manner, if this succeeds its well, if not we land nevertheless and mentain the footing we thus got by the Superiority of our fire arms, in what other light can they than at first look upon us but as invaders of their Country; time and some acquaintance with us can only convince them of their mistake.

MONDAY 15*th*. In the PM I made an excursion in company with Mr Wales on the other side of the harbour, where we met from the Natives very different treatment [from what] we had done in the morning, these people, in whose neighbourhood lived our friend Paowang, being better acquainted with us than those we had seen in the morning, shewed a readiness to oblige us in every thing in their power: here was a little Stragling Village consisting of a few house which need no other discription than to compare them to the roof of a thatched house taken of the walls and placed on the ground, the figure was oblong and open at both ends, some indeed had a little fence or wall of reeds at each end about 3 feet high, some seem'd to be intended for more families than one as they had a fire place near each end, there [were] other mean and small hovels which I understood were only to Sleep in, in one of these which with some others stood in a Plantation but separated from them by a fence, I understood was a dead Corps, they made Signs that he slipt or was dead, circumstances sufficiently pointed out the latter. Curious however to see all I could I prevailed on an elderly man to go with me within the fence which surrounded it, one end of the hut was closed up the same as the sides the other end had been open but now shut up with Matts which he would not suffer me to remove, he also seem'd unwilling I should look into a Matted bag or basket which hung to the end of the hutt, in which was a piece of roasted yam and some kind of leaves all quite fresh: thus I was led to believe that these people dispose of the dead some thing in the same manner as at Otahiete. The Man had about his neck fastned to a String two or three locks of human hair and a Woman present had several; I offered some thing in exchange for them but they gave me to understand this could not be done as they belonged to the person who laid in the hutt. A similar custom to this is observed by the New Zealanders. Near most of their larger houses are placed upright in the ground in a square position about 3 feet from each other the Stems of four Cocoa-nut trees, some of our gentlemen who first saw these seem'd to think they had a Religious tendancy, but I was now fully satisfied they were to hang cocoa upon to dry. Thier houses are generally built in an open Area where the air has a free circulation, in some are a large tree or two whose spreading branches afford an agreeable shade and retreat from the Scorching Sun. . . .

TUESDAY 16*th*. Winds northerly fair Weather. In the PM Mr F. and I took a Walk to the Eastern Sea shore in order to have a sight of an Island to the SE which these People called Annattom; the high table Island we discovered the Morning we anchored here is called Irromang or Foottoona and the flat isle lying off the harbour Immer. I observed that in their Sugar Plantations were dug holes or Pitts about 4 feet deep and 5 or six in diameter, we were made to understand that these Pitts were to catch Ratts which when once in they could not get out and so were easy killed, these animals which are distructive to the

Canes are here in plenty. In the Morning after having got every thing in readiness to put to Sea and waited for nothing but a wind we found the Tiler sprung and other ways deffective in the Rudder head and by some strange neglect we had never a spare one on board and this was not known till now we wanted it. While the Carpenter was unshiping the old tiler I went ashore to cut down a tree to make a new one, but as we knew but of one fit for the purpose which stood near the watering place and this Paowang had disired might not be cut down and I had promised it should not proper application was therefore necessary in order not to give umbrage to the Natives. Therefore as soon as I landed I sent for old Paowang and as soon as he came made him a present of a Dog and a large piece of Cloth and then made known to him that our great steering Paddle was broke and that I wanted that tree to make a new one, he presently gave his consent as well as several others present and we set people to work to cut it down. It was easy to see that this Method which I took to Obtain the tree was very agreeable to all the people present. After this I returned on board with Paowang who stayed dinner. After the tiler was unshiped we found that by scarfing a piece to the inner end and liting it farther into the rudder head it would still perform its office and the Carpenters and smiths were set about this work. . . .

*   *   *

THURSDAY 18th. In the PM Mr F. and I went to the west side of the Harbour to try the degree of heat of the hot Springs, in one of which the mercury in the Thermometer rose to 191 from 78 which it stood at in the open air. At this time it was high-water and within two or three feet of the spring which we judged might be in some degree cooled by it but the next morning we found just the contrary for repeting the experiment when the tide was out the Mercury rose no higher than 187, but at a nother Spring which bubbles out in large quantities from under a steep rock at the SW corner of the harbour, the Mercury rose to 202½ which is only 9½ below boiling water; I have already said that these Springs are at the foot of the same hill on the side of which we saw the hot places and Smokes ascend before mentioned: this hill belongs to the Same Ridge in which the Volcano is: the Ridge is of no great height nor is the Volcano at the highest part of it but on the SE side and contrary to the Opinion of Philosophers, which is that all Volcanos must be at the summits of the highest hills, here are hills in this island more than double the height of the ridge I have been speaking of. Nor was the Volcano on the isle of Ambrrym (which I now have not the least doubt of there being one if not two) on the highest part of the Island but seem'd to us to be in a Vally between the hills: to these remarks must be added [a] nother which is that during wet or moist weather the Volcano was most vehement. Here seems to be [a] feild open for some Philosophical reasoning on these extraordinary Phenomenon's of nature, but as I have no tallant that way I must content my self with stateing facts as I found and leave the causes to men of more abilities.

FRIDAY 19*th*. Winds northerly a gentle gale. In [the PM] the Tiller was finished and Shiped, so that we only waited for a fair Wind to put to sea. In the AM as the wind would not admit of our geting to sea I sent the guard on [shore] with Mr Wales as usual and at the same time a party to cut up and bring off the remainder of the tree we had cut a spare tiller of. A good many of the Natives were, as usual, assembled near the landing place and unfortunately one of them was Shott by one of our Centinals;[47] I who was present and on the Spot saw not the least cause for the commiting of such an outrage and was astonished beyond Measure at the inhumanity of the act, the rascal who perpetrated this crime pretended that one of the Natives laid his arrow across his bow and held it in the Attitude of Shooting so that he apprehen[d]ed himself in danger, but this was no more than what was done hourly and I beleive with no other View than to let us see they were Armed as well as us: what made this affair the more unfortunate it not appearing to be the man who bent the Bow but a nother who was near him.[48] After this unhappy affair most of the

47. The marine, William Wedgeborough. He had earlier been punished for drunkenness and for 'easing himself betwixt decks'. He fell overboard and was drowned off Tierra del Fuego.

48. Cook had Wedgeborough brought to the gangway to be flogged, but he was dissuaded by the officers on the grounds that the marine had been acting on the orders of his lieutenant, John Edgecumbe.

Natives fled and when we imbarked to go on board they retired to a man and only a few appeared in the afternoon. . . . During the night the Wind Veered round to SE. At 4 AM began to unmoor and at 8 got under sail and Stood out to Sea, leaving the Launch behind to take up a Kedge Anchor and hawser we had out to cast by and was obliged to Slip. As soon as were clear of the harbour we brought-to to wait for the Launch and to hoist her and the other boats in which was employment till Noon, when we made Sail and Stretched to the Eastward with our Starboard tacks on board in order to take a nearer View of the Island of Erronan the same as we discover'd in the morning of the 5th.

*   *   *

[*Cook went south round Tanna then north, spending the rest of August exploring the New Hebrides archipelago, circumnavigating the northern island which Quirós had named Austrialia del Espiritu Santo in 1606. On 1 September he began the voyage south towards New Zealand. On 5 September James Colnett saw land, a new land which Cook later took possession of under the name of New Caledonia. The people 'spoke a language quite new to us', but were very cooperative in the matter of fresh water. 'No people could behave with more civility than they did.' Cook thought that the island, with its mountains, streams, plantations, 'little Stragling Villages', woods and beaches, 'might afford a Picture for romance'. Exploration of the coastline on the eastern side was particularly difficult because of reefs and shoals. At the south-eastern extremity tall objects on a number of islands caused great puzzlement. On closer inspection 'every one were now satisfied they were trees, except our Philosophers [the Forsters], who still maintained they were Stone Pillars'. They had discovered the great* Araucaria columnaris *– or Cook pine, which Cook and his carpenter thought ideal for ships' masts. On 10 October, as they made their way towards New Zealand, they discovered an uninhabited island which Cook named Norfolk Isle. Cook noted again a source for masts in its magnificent trees. Then for Queen Charlotte Sound, 'there to refresh my people and to put the Ship in a condition to cross this great ocean in a high Latitude once more'.*]

[OCTOBER 1774]

MONDAY 17*th*. PM Fresh gales Northerly and Cloudy weather. At 4 Sound^d no ground with a line of 140 fathoms. Middnight heavy Squalls with rain, Thunder and Lightning. Wind shifted to sw, remain'd unsetled: Split the Jibb to pieces, lost great part of it, remains good for little, being much worn. Day-break saw Mount Egmont (covered with everlasting snow) bearing SE½E; sounded 70 fathoms, muddy bottom, distance off shore 3 Leagues. Wind Westerly a fresh gale, Steer'd SSE for Queen Charlottes Sound. Noon Cape Egmont ENE distant 3½ or 4 leagues, the Mount hid in the Clouds, judged it to be in one with the Cape. Lat Ob^d 39°24' Long^{de} in [Watch 173°1'].

TUESDAY 18*th*. Very strong gales at Westerly and Cloudy. Steered SSE for Queen Charlottes Sound. At 7 Close reefed the Fore & Main Top-sails and handed the Mizen Top-sail, got down Top g^t yards and hauled the wind close. At 11 Stephens's Isle SEBE. At middnight Tacked and made a trip to the North till 3 AM then bore up for the Sound under double reef'd Top-sails and Courses. At 9 hauled round point Jackson through a Sea which looked Terrible, occasioned by the Tide, Wind & Sea, but as we knew the Cause it did not alarm us; At 11 Anchored before Ship Cove the strong fluries from the land not permiting us to get in.

WEDNESDAY 19*th*. PM As we could not move the Ship I went into the Cove to try to catch some fish with the Sein. As soon as I landed I looked for the bottle I had left behind in which was the Memd^m it was gone, but by whom it did not appear. Two hauls with the Sein procured us only four small fish, after shooting a few old Shags and robing the Nests of some young ones we returned aboard. AM being little wind, weighed and Warped into the Cove and there moored a Cable each way, Intending to wait here to refresh the Crew, refit the Ship in the best manner we could and compleat her with Wood and Water. We unbent the Sails to repair several having been much damage'd in the late gale, the Main and Fore Course, already worn to the utmost, was condemned as useless. Struck and unriged the Fore and Main Topmasts to fix moveable Cheeks to them for want of which the

Trestle trees were Continually breaking. Set up the Forge to make bolts for the above use and repair what was wanting in the Iron way. Set up the Astronomers Observatory on shore in the bottom of the Cove and Tents for the reception of a Guard, Sail-makers, Coopers &c^a. Ordered Vegetable, of which here were plenty, to be boiled with Oatmeal & Portable Soup every Morning for breakfast and with Pease and Portable Soup every day to dinner for all hands. We now found that some Ship had been here sence we last left it not only by the bottle being gone as mentioned above, but by several trees having been Cut down with Saws and Axes which were standing when we sailed. This Ship could be no other than the Adventure Captain Furneaux.

THURSDAY 20*th*. PM Fresh gales at NW and fair weather. Sent all the Sails wanting repairs a Shore to the Tent and in the AM several empty Casks. Carpenters employed fixing Cheeks to the Top-masts, Caulkers caulking the sides and Seamen overhauling the rigging. Winds Southerly Hazey Cloudy weather.

FRIDAY 21*st*. Wind Southerly with continual rain.

SATURDAY 22*nd*. First part D° Weather, remainder Clear pleasent weather, which admited us to go on with our works and for my self and the Botanists to viset several parts of the Sound and a mongest others our gardens on Motouara which we found allmost in a state of Nature and had been wholy neglected by the Inhabitants, nevertheless many Articles were in a florishing state. None of the Natives having as yet made their appearence we made a fire on the isle, judgeing the smoke would draw their attention towards us.

SUNDAY 23*rd*. Variable light airs and pleasent weather. Every one who chused were at liberty to go a shore.

MONDAY 24*th*. Pleasent weather. AM went on with the various works in hand. Two Canoes were seen coming down the Sound but retired behind a point on the west side upon discovering us as was supposed. After breakfast I went in a Boat to look for them accompani'd by the Botanists. As we proceeded a long shore we shott sever^l birds, the report of our guns gave notice of our approach and the Natives discovered them selves by hollaing to us but when we came before their habitations only two men appeared on a rising ground, the rest had taken to the Woods and hills, but the moment we landed they knew us again, joy took place of fear, they hurried out of the woods, embraced us over and over and skiped about like Mad men. I made them presents of Hatchets, Knives, Cloth & Medals and in return they gave us a quantity of fish. There were only one or two amongst them whose faces we could well recolect, the account they gave us of our other friends whom we inquir'd after by name were variously understood concequently ended in nothing. After a short Stay we took leave and returned aboard, they promiseing to come to the Ship in the Morning and bring with them fish which was all I wished for by the intercourse.

TUESDAY 25*th*. Winds SW pleasant Weather. Early in the Morning our friends paid us a Viset and brought with them a quantity of fish which they exchanged for Otaheite cloth &c^a and then returned to their habitations.

WEDNESDAY 26*th*. PM fresh gales Southerly with rain. AM Variable light Airs and fair Weather. The Carpenters had no sooner finished the Cheeks to the Top-masts than we found one of the fore Cross-trees broke, set them to work to make a new one out of the Spare Anchor Stock. Got into the after hold four Launch Load of Shingle ballast and struck down Six guns from off the Deck, keeping no more than Six Mounted. Our good friends the Natives stick by us and supply us plentifully with fish.

THURSDAY 27*th*. Variable gentle breezes and pleasant weather, favourable for the carrying on of our works which increase upon us the more we examine and look into things.

FRIDAY 28*th*. PM Wind and Weather as before. AM fresh gale Westerly fair weather. Rigged and fidded the Topg^t Masts. Went on a Shooting party to the west bay, Viseted the place where I left the Hogs and fowls, saw no vestige's of them or of any people being there sence. Viseted some of the Natives who gave us some fish in return for some trifles I gave them. Soon after we left them Mr F. thought he heard the squeaking of a Pig in the woods hard by their habitations, probably they may yet have those they had when we were last here. Returned on board with about a Doz^n and a half of Wild fowl, Shaggs and Sea Pies. Sence the Natives have been with us a report has risen said to come first from them, that a ship has lately been lost, some where in the Strait, and all the crew Killed by them, when I examined them on this head they not only denied it but seem'd wholy ignorant of the matter.[49]

*   *   *

SUNDAY 30*th*. Wind Southerly a fresh gale with showers of rain. Natives a board most of the day tradeing with green talk, hatchets &c^a. One of the officers found in the Woods not far from our tents a fresh hens egg, a proof that the Poultry that we left here are living, the Natives tell us that they lost those I gave them in the Woods.

MONDAY 31*st*. AM Wind at NE fine pleasent weather. Our Botanists went to Long Island where some of the party saw a Hog, a boar as they judged, so wild that it took to the woods as soon as it saw them. It is probably one of those Captain Furneaux left behind and brought to this isle by the Natives. Sence the Natives did not distroy these Hogs when in their posession, we cannot suppose they will attempt it now, so that there is little fear but that this Country will soon be stocked with these Animals, both in a wild and domistick state. I am in doubt that the goats I put ashore are killed, for if they killed the goats why should they not the hogs also.

*   *   *

[NOVEMBER 1774]

THURSDAY 3*rd*. Variable light breezes and pleasent weather. Fided the Main Top-mast and set up the Main & Top-mast rigging. Compleated the Ship with Wood and Water and nearly finished all our other works except Caulking which goes on slowly, as having only two Caulkers

49. In the later MS, 'B', Cook wrote: 'These stories made me very uneasy about the Adventure.'

and a great deal to do and which must absolutely be done before we can put to sea.

FRIDAY 4*th*. Fine pleasent Weather. Most of the Natives retired up the Sound to their habitations there. Went over to Long Island to look for the Hog which had been seen there, found it to be one of the Sows Captain Furneaux left behind the same as was in the posession of the Natives when we were last here. From a Supposion of its being a boar I had carri'd over a Sow to leave with him but brought her back when I found the Contrary.

SATURDAY 5*th*. Light breeze Westerly and pleasent Weather. Early in the morning our old friend[s] paid us a second Viset and brought us a supply of fish. At 8 o'Clock went in the Pinnace up the Sound accompanied by Mr F. and his party. I had some thoughts of finding the termination of it or to see if it communicated with the sea, in our way we met with several people out fishing of whom we made the necessary enquiries, they all agree'd that there was no passage to Sea by the head of the Sound. After proceeding five Leagues up, which was farther than I had ever been before, we met a Canoe conducted by four or five men who confirm'd what the others had told us; we then enquired if their was any passage to the East and understood them there was, this was what I suspected for from the Hill I first discovered the Strait I saw a Bason into which the tide had access & recess, but I did not know whether it was an Arm of the Sound or an inlet of the Sea; to determine this point I laid aside the scheme of proceeding to the head of the Sound and went to this Inlet, which is on the SE side of the Sound four or five leagues above Ship Cove, here we found a large settlement of the Natives who received us with great courtesy; our stay with them was short as we found incourage-ment to persue the object we had in view and accordingly proceeded ENE down the Inlet which we at last found to open into the Sea by a Channell about a mile wide in which ran a very strong tide. It was four o'Clock in the after noon before we had made this discovery which opens a new passage into the Sound and as we came to a resolution to return aboard that same evening we were obliged to defer viseting a large Hippa or strong hold built on a rising ground on the North side a little within the entrance whose inhabitants seem'd to invite us to them and without makeing any stop proceeded for the Ship which [we reached] by 10 o'Clock bring[ing] with us some fish we had got from the Natives and a few birds we had shott, amongest which were some of the same sort of Ducks we got in Duskey Bay and we have reason to think they are all to be found here as the Inhabitants of this place have a particular [name] to each.

SUNDAY 6*th*. Wind NE, Gloomy weather with some rain. Had a present from one of the Natives whose name was *Pedero* of a Staff of honour, in return I dress'd him in an old suit of Clothes with which he was not a little proud: having got him and a nother in a communicative mood we began to enquire of them if the Adventure had been here and they gave us to understand in a manner which admited of no doubt that soon after we were gone she arrived and Stayed here about   Days, and farther asserted that neither her or any other Ship had been Stranded on the Coast as had been reported. After breakfast I took a number of men over to Long Island to endeavour to catch the Sow but we returned without being able to see her. [Pedero] dined with us, eat of every thing at table and drank more Wine than any of us.

MONDAY 7*th*. A fresh gale at NE attended with rain which put a stop to Calking.

TUESDAY 8*th*. First part rain remainder fair weather which enabled us to go on with Calking, the Seams we are obliged to pay with a kind of putty made of Cooks fat and Chalk, for as to Pitch and Tarr we have had none for some Monthes Past and a Cask of Varnish of Pine which served as a substitute for all purposses is now expended. Put two Piggs, a Boar and a sow a Shore in the Cove next without Cannibal Cove, its hardly possible for all the methods I have taken to stock this Country with these animals to fail.

WEDNESDAY 9*th*. Winds Westerly or NW, Squally with rain, got every thing off from the Shore, unmoor'd and hove short on the best bower, waiting for the Calkers to finish their work. Our friends the Natives brought us a seasonable and large supply of fish. I made my friend

[Pedero] a present of an Oyle Jarr which made him as happy as a prince.

THURSDAY 10*th*. Fresh gales at NW and fair weather. PM hove up the anchor and drop'd out of the Cove and then anchored in a clear place for the more readier geting under-sail in the morning. After this a party of us spent the afternoon a shore, we land where were two families of the Natives, variously employed, some sleeping, others makeing Matts, dressing Victuals &c^a. One little girl I observed was heating stones at a fire, curious to know what they were for I remained by her, for I thought they were to dress some sort of Victuals but I was misstaken for as soon as the stones were made hot, the girl took them hout of the fire and gave them to an hold Women who was siting in the hut, she put them in [a] heap and then laid over them a large handfull of green Sellery, over it a coarse Mat and then squated herself down upon her heels over all, thus she made what one may call a Dutch Warming-Pan on which she sit as close as a hare to her seat.

At Daylight AM weighed and stood out of the Sound with a gentle breeze at WNW. At 8 hauled round the two brothers and steered for Cape Campbel which is at the SE entrance of the Strait.[50]

FRIDAY 11*th*. In the morning the wind veered round by the west to South and forced us more to the East than I intended. At 7 o'Clock in the evening the Snowey Mountains bore WBS and Cape Palliser North ½ west dist^t 16 or 17 leagues. From this Cape I shall, for the third time, take my departure. After a few hours calm a breeze sprung up at North with which we steered SBE all sails Set, with a view of geting into the Latitude of 54° or 55°. My intention was to cross this vast Ocean nearly in these Parallels, and so as to pass over those parts which were left unexplored last summer.

*   *   *

50. The manuscript which Beaglehole has been using for this second voyage ends at this point. From now on Beaglehole uses the manuscript designated 'B', which is also in Cook's own hand, supplemented by some entries from manuscript 'A' (in the Public Record Office). 'B' uses civil time for each day's entry.

[*For two weeks the* Resolution *sailed south-east and then east without incident.*]

SATURDAY 26*th* and SUNDAY 27*th*. Had a steady fresh gale at NNW with which Steered East and at Noon on the latter we were in the Latitude of 55°6', Longitude 138°56' west. I now gave up all hopes of finding any more land in this Ocean and came to a Resolution to steer directly for the West entrance of the Straits of Magelhanes, with a View of coasting the out, or South side of Terra del Fuego round Cape Horn to Strait La Maire. As the world has but a very imperfect knowlidge of this Coast, I thought the Coasting it would be of more advantage to both Navigation and Geography than any thing I could expect to find in a higher latitude. In the after-noon of this day the Wind blew in squalls and occasioned the Main Topg^t mast to be carried away.

MONDAY 28*th*. A very strong gale Northerly, hazy rainy weather which obliged us to double reef the Fore and Main Top-sails, hand the Mizen Top-sail and get down the Fore Top-g^t yard. In the morn^g the bolt rope of the Main Top-sail broke and occasioned the Sail to be split. I have observed that the ropes to all our sails, the Square Sails especially, are not of a Size and strength sufficient to wear out the canvas. At Noon Latitude in 55°20', Longitude 134°16' west. A great swell from NW. Albatrosses and Blue Peterels seen.

*   *   *

[DECEMBER 1774]

FRIDAY 16*th*. In the Latitude of 53°25', Longitude 78°40' it was 17°38' East. About this time saw a Penguin and a piece of weed and the next morn a Seal and some diving Peterels. For the three preceeding days the wind has been at west a steady fresh gale, attended now and then with showers of rain or hail.

SATURDAY 17*th*. At 6 o'Clock in the Morning, being nearly in the same latitude as above and in the Longitude of 77°10' w the Variation was 18°33' E, and in the after-noon it was 21°38', Latitude in at that time 53°16' s, Longitude 75°9' West. In the Morning as well as in the after-noon I took some observations to determine the Longitude by the Watch, the results reduced to noon gave 76°18′30″ West Longitude: at the same time the Longitude by my reckoning was 76°17′ w, but I have reason to think that we were about half a degree more to the West than either the one or the other: our Latitude at the same time was 53°21′ s. We steered EBN and E½N all this day under all the sail we could carry with a fine fresh gale at NWBW in expectation of seeing the land before night but not making it before 10 o'Clock we took in the Studding sails, Topg^t Sails, and a reef in each Top-sail and steered ENE in order to make sure of falling in with Cape Deseado. Two hours after made the land, extending from NEBN to EBS about 6 Leagues dist^t. Upon this discovery we wore and brought to with the ships head to the South and then sounded and found 75 fathoms water, the bottom stones and shells. The land now before us can be no other than the west Coast of Terra del Fuego and near the West entrance to the Straits of Magelhanes. As this was the first run that had been made directly a Cross this ocean in a high Sothern Latitude.[51] I have been a little particular in noteing every circumstance that appeared attall Intresting and after all I must observe that I never was makeing a passage any where of such length, or even much shorter, where so few intresting circumstance[s] occrued, for if I except the Variation of the Compass I know of nothing else worth notice. The weather has neither been unusually Stormy nor cold, before we arrived in the Latitude of 50° the Mercury in the Thermometer fell gradually from 60 to 50 and after we arrived in the Latitude of 55° it was generally between 47 and 45, once or twice it fell to 43°; these observations were made at Noon. I have now done with the SOUTHERN PACIFIC OCEAN, and flatter my self that no one will think that I have left it unexplor'd, or that more could have been done in one voyage towards obtaining that end than has been done in this.

Soon after we left New Zealand, Mr Wales contrived and fixed up an Instrument which very accurately measured the Angle the Ship rolled when sailing large & in a great sea and lay down when sailing upon a wind. The greatest Angle he observed her to Roll was 38°,

---

51. Cook here inserted a conscientious footnote: 'It is not to be supposed that I could know at that time that the Adventure had made the Passage before me.'

this was on the 6th Inst. when the Sea was not unusually high, so that it cannot be reckoned the greatest Roll she had made. The most he observed her to heel or lay down when sailing upon a wind was 18°, this was under Double reef'd Topsails & Courses.

*   *   *

MONDAY 19*th*. At 2 o'Clock in the morning made sail and steered SEBE along the coast and soon passed the SE point of the bay of S' Barbara which I called *Cape Desolation*, because near it commenced the most desolate and barren Country I ever saw. . . . It seems to be intirely composed of Rocky Mountains without the least appearence of Vegetation, these Mountains terminate in horroable precipices whose craggy summits spire up to a vast hieght, so that hardly any thing in nature can appear with a more barren and savage aspect than the whole of this coast. The inland mountains were covered with Snow but those on the Sea Coast were not; we judged the former to belong to the Main of Terra del Fuego and the latter to be islands so ranged as apparently to form a Coast. After 3 hours Calm we got a breeze at SEBE and after makeing a short trip to the South, stood in for the land, the most advanced point of which we had in sight bore East, distant 10 leagues; this is a lofty Promontory lying ESE 10 leag⁵ from Gilbert isle and situated in Latitude 55°26′ S, Longitude 70°25′ west. From the situation we now saw it, it terminated in two high towers and within them a hill shaped like a Sugar Loafe. This Wild rock obtained the name of *York Minster*. . . .

TUESDAY 20*th*. . . . At 1 o'Clock a breeze sprung up at EBS. I took the oppertunity to stand in for the land with a view to going into one of the many Ports which seemed open to receive us, in order to take a view of the Country and recrute our stock of Wood and Water. In standing in for an opening which appeared on the East side of York Minster we had 40, 37, 50 and 60 fᵐˢ Water a bottom of small stones and shells; when we had the last Soundings we were nearly in the middle between the two points which forms the entrance to the Inlet, which we observed to branch in to two Arms, both of them lying in nearly north and disjoined by a high rocky point. We stood for the Eastern branch as being clear of islots, and after passing a black rocky islot, lying without the point just mentioned, we sounded and found no bottom with a line of 170 fathoms. This was altogether unexpected and a circumstance that would not have been regarded if the breeze had continued, but at this time it fell Calm, so that it was not possible to extricate our selves from this disagreeable situation. Two Boats were hoisted out and sent a head to tow, they would have availed but little if a breeze of wind had not, about 8 o'clock, sprung up at sw which put it in my power either to stand out to Sea, or up the inlet, prudence seemed to point out the former, but the desire of finding a good Port and learning something of the Country got the better of every other consideration and I resolved to stand in, but as night was approaching our safety depended on geting to an Anchor. With this view we continued to Sound but always in an unfathomable depth. Hauling up under the East side of the land which divided the two Arms and seeing a small Cove a head I sent a boat to Sound for anchorage and we kept as near the shore as the flurries from the land would admit in order to be able to get into this place if there was anchorage. The Boat soon returned and informed us that there was 30 and 25 fathom Water a full Cables length from the shore, here we Anchored in 30 fathom (the bottom Sand and broken shells) and carried out a Kedge and hawser to steady the Ship for the night.

[*Next day they made their way into Adventure Cove in Christmas Sound.*]

WEDNESDAY 21*st.* . . . Our distance from the shore was about one third of a mile. Thus situated we went to work to clear a place to fill Water, cut wood and set up a Tent for the reception of a guard, which was thought necessary as we had already discovered that barren as this country is it was not without people, altho' we had as yet seen none. Mr Wales also got his observatory and Instruments on shore, but it was with the greatest difficulty he could find a place of sufficient stability and clear of the Mountains which every were surrounded us, to set them up in, and at last was obliged to content himself with the top of a rock, not more than 9 feet over.

THURSDAY 22*nd.* Sent Lieutenants Clerke and Pickersgill, accompanied by some of the other officers, to examine and draw a sketch of the

Channel on the other side of the island and I went my self in a nother boat accompanied by the Botanists, to survey the Northern parts of the Sound. In my way I landed on the point of a low isle which was covered with herbage, part of which had been lately burnt, we likewise saw a hut, signs sufficient that people were in the neighbourhood. After I had taken the necessary bearings, we proceeded round the East end of Burnt Island and over to what we judged to be the Main of Terra del Fuego, where we found a very fine harbour, incompassed by steep rocks of vast height down which ran many limpid streams of Water. At the foot of the rock are some tufts of trees fit for little else but fuel. This Harbour, which I shall distinguish by the [name of] *Devil's Bason*, is divided as it were into two, an inner and outer one, the communication between them is by a narrow channell of 5 fathoms deep. In the outer Bason I found 13 and 17 fathom water and in the inner 17 & 23 fathom. This last is the most secure place that can be, but nothing can be more gloomy than it is, the vast hieght of the Savage rocks which incompass it deprived a great part of it, even on this day, of the meridion Sun; the outer harbour is not quite free of this illconveniency, but far less so than the other and is rather more commodious and equally safe. It lies in the direction of North 1½ miles dist^t from the East end of Burnt island, I likewise found a good anchoring place a little to the West of this harbour, before a stream of Water which comes out of a lake or large reservoir which is continually supplied by a Cascade falling into it. Leaving this place we proceeded a long the shore to the Westward and found other harbours which I had no time to look into. In all of them is fresh Water and wood for fuel, but except these little tufts of Shrubery, the whole Country was a barren Rock, doomed by Nature to everlasting sterility. The low islands and even some of the higher which lie scatered up and down the Sound are indeed mostly covered with shrubs & Herbage; the Soil a black rotten Turf evidently composed by length of time of decayed Vegetables. I had an oppertunity to verify what we had observed at Sea, viz. that the Sea Coast is composed of a number of large and small Islands and that the numerous inlets are formed by the junction of several channels, at least so it is here. On one of the low islands we found several huts which had lately been inhabited, near them was a good deal of celery with which we loaded our boat and returned on board at 7 o'Clock in the evening. In this expedition we met with little game, one duck, three or four shags and about the same number of Rails or Sea Pies was all we got. The other boat had been aboard some hours before; they had found two Harbours on the West side of the other Channel, the one large and the other small, but both safe and commodious, but by the sketch which Mr Pickersgill had taken the access to them appeared rather intricate. I was now told of a Melancholy circumstance which had happened to one of our Marines, he had not been seen sence 11 or 12 o'Clock the preceding night, it was supposed that he had fallen over board out of the head where he was last seen and was drownded.[52]

*   *   *

[*In fine pleasant weather, there were shooting expeditions. On Christmas Eve Cook's party shot sixty-two geese and Pickersgill's party fourteen. When they returned to the ship they found that nine canoes had visited the ship, and that the natives 'seem'd to be well enough acquainted with Europeans'.*]

SUNDAY 25*th* they made us another visit; I found them to be of the same Nation as I had formerly seen in Success Bay,[53] and the same which M. de Bougainville distinguishes by the name of Pecheras – a word which these had on every occasion in their mouths. They are a little ugly half starved beardless Race; I saw not a tall person amongst them. They were almost Naked; their cloathing was a Seal skin; some had two or three sew'd together, so as to make a cloak which reach'd to the knee, but the most of them had only one skin hardly large enough to cover their shoulders, and all their lower parts were quite naked. The Women, I was told, cover their privities with a flap of Seal skin, but in other respects were cloathed as the Men; they as well as the Children remain'd in the Canoes. I saw two young Children at the breast, as naked as they were born; thus they are inured from their infancy to Cold and hardships. They had with them bows & Arrows & darts, or rather harpoons made of bone and fitted to a staff.

52. This was William Wedgeborough. It was assumed that once again he was drunk. See 19 August 1774.
53. On the first voyage.

I suppose they were intended to kill Seals and fish; they may also kill Whales with them in the same manner as the Esquimaux's do; I know not if they are so fond of train Oyle but they and every thing they have about them smell most intolerable of it. I order'd them some Bisket; but I did not observe that they were so fond of it as I have heard said; they were much better pleas'd when I gave them some Medals, Knives &c^a. The Women & Children, as I have before observ'd, remain'd in the Canoes, which were made of Bark, and in each was a fire, over which the poor Creatures huddled themselves; I cannot suppose that they carry a fire in their Canoes for this purpose only, but rather that it may be allways ready to remove a shore wherever they land; for let their method of obtaining fire be what it will, they cannot be allways sure of finding dry fuel that will take fire from a spark. They likewise carry in their Canoes large Seal hides, which I judged was to shelter them when in the Canoes and to serve as covering to their hutts ashore, and may occasionally serve them for Sails. They all retir'd before dinner and did not wait to pertake of our Christmas Cheer, indeed I beleive no one invited them, and for good reasons, for their dirty persons and the stench they carried about them was enough to spoil any mans appetite, and that would have been a real disapointment, for we had not experienced such fare for some time, Roast and boiled Geese, Goose pies &c^a was victuals little known to us, and we had yet some Madeira Wine left, which was the only Article of our provisions that was mended by keeping; so that our friends in England did not perhaps, celebrate Christmas more cheerfully than we did.

MONDAY 26*th*. Little wind next to a Calm and fair weather, except in the morning when we had some showers of rain. In the evening the natives made us another viset; it was a Cold evening and distressing to see them stand trembling and naked on the deck and I could do no less than give them some Baize and old Canvas to cover themselves.

TUESDAY 27*th*. Fine pleas^t weather. Having already compleated our water, I order'd the Wood, Tent and observatory to be got onboard and as this was work for the day, a party of us went away in two boats to shoot Geese. We proceeded round by the South side of Goose

Island and pick'd up in all thirty one. On the East side of Goose island, to the North of the East point, is good Anchorage in 17 fathom water, where it is intirely land-lock'd. This is a good place for Ships to lay in who are bound to the West; on the North side of this isle I observ'd three fine Coves, in which were both wood and Water, but it being near night I had no time to sound them, but I have no doubt but there is Anchorage; the way to come at them is by the West end of the isle. When I got aboard I found every thing was got off from the shore, the launch in, so that we now only waited for a Wind to put to Sea. The Festival which we celebrated at this place occasion'd my giving it the name of *Christmas Sound*.

* * *

[*The* Resolution *rounded Cape Horn on 29 December, and headed north-east for Staten Island, pausing at Success Bay, visited on the first voyage (16 January 1769). On Staten Island they killed sea-lions and seals, the old ones 'cheifly for the sake of their Blubber or fat to make oil of', the young ones to eat ('very Palatable'). Gulls were in such numbers 'as to darken the air when disturbed and almost suffocated our people with their dung, which they seemed to void by way of defence'. Cook is able to extend and improve on his first-voyage chart, and he goes into detail on longitude, tides and currents with an authority which he himself contrasts with his observations on the flora and fauna, 'written more with a view to assist my own memory than to give information to others; I am neither a botanist nor a Naturalist and have not words to describe the productions of Nature either in the one Science or the other'. On 3 January 1775 they put to sea again.*]

[JANUARY 1775]

WEDNESDAY 4*th*. Having left the land the preceeding evening as already mentioned we saw it again this morning at 3 o'Clock bearing West. Wind continued to blow a steady fresh breeze till 6 in the PM when it shifted in a heavy squal to SW; it came so suddenly upon us that we had not time to take in the Sails and was the occasion of carrying away a topg^r mast, a Studding sail boom and the loss of a Fore studding sail. The Squall ended in a heavy shower of rain, but the wind remained at SW; our Course was SE with a view of discovering that extensive coast which Mr Dalrymple lies down in his Chart in which is the

Gulph of St Sebastian. I designed to make the Western point of that Gulph in order to have all the other parts before me. Indeed I had some doubts about the existence of such a Coast and this appeared to me to be the best rout to clear it up and to explore the Southern part of this ocean.

THURSDAY 5*th*. Fresh gales at West and Cloudy weather. At Noon observed in 57°09', Longitude made from Cape St John 5°2' East. At 6 o'Clock in the PM being in the Latitude 57°21' and in the Longitude of 57°45' W the Variation was 21°28' East.

FRIDAY 6*th*. At 8 o'Clock in the evening, being then in the Latitude of 58°9' S, Longitude 53°14' West, we close reefed our Top-sails and hauled to the North with a very strong gale at West attended with a thick haze and sleet. The situation just mentioned is nearly the same as Mr Dalrymple assigns for the SW point of the Gulph of St Sebastian, but as we saw neither land nor signs of any, I was the more doubtfull of its existence and was fearfull that by keeping to the South I might miss the land said to be discovered by La Roch in 1675 and by the Ship Lion in 1756, which Mr Dalrymple places in 54°30' Latitude and 45° of Longitude; but on looking over D'anvill's Chart I found it laid down 9° or 10° more to the West, this difference of situation was to me a Sign of the uncertainty of both and determined me to get into the Parallel as soon as possible and this was the reason of my hauling to the north at this time.

*   *   *

THURSDAY 12*th* at day-break bore away and steered East northerly with a fine fresh breeze at WSW. At Noon Observed in Latitude 54°28' S, Longitude in 42°08' West, which is near 3° E of the Situation in which Mr Dalrymple places the NE point of the Gulph of St Sebastian, but we had no other signs of land than seeing a Seal and a few Penguins; on the Contrary we had a Swell from ESE, which could hardly have been if any extensive tract of land laid in that direction. In the evening the gale abated and at Middnight it fell Calm.

FRIDAY 13*th*. The Calm attended by a thick Fogg continued till 6 o'Clock in the Morning, when we got a Wind at East but the Fogg still continued. We stood to the South till noon when being in the Latitude of 55°07° Tacked and stretched to the North with a fresh breeze at EBS and ESE. Cloudy wea^r. Saw several Penguins and a Snow Peterel which we looked upon to be signs of the vicinity of ice, the air too was much colder than we had felt it sence we left New Zealand. In the afternoon the Wind veered to SE and in the night to SSE and blew fresh with which we stood to the NE.

At 9 o'Clock the next morning saw an Island of ice, as we then thought, but at noon we were doubtfull whether it was ice or land; at this time it bore E¾s distant 13 Leagues, our Latitude was 53°56½', Longitude 39°24' West. Several Penguins, small divers, a snow Peterel and a vast number of blue Peterels about the Ship. We had but little wind all the morning and at 2 PM it fell Calm. It was now no longer doubted but that it was land and not ice which we had in sight: it was however in a manner wholy covered with snow. We were farther confirmed of its being land by finding Soundings at 175 fathoms, a muddy bottom, the land at this time bore EBS about 12 leagues distant. At 6 o'Clock the Calm was succeeded by a breeze at NE with which we stood to SE. At first it blew a gentle gale, but afterwards increased, so as to bring us under double reefed Top-sails and was attended with Snow and Sleet.

SUNDAY 15*th*. We continued to stand to the SE till 7 in the morn^g when the Wind veering to the SE tacked and stood to the North. A little before we tacked we saw the land bearing EBN. At Noon the mercury in the Thermometer was at 35¼°. The Wind blew in Squals attended with Snow and Sleet and we had a great sea to encounter. At a Lee Lurch which the ship took Mr Wales observed her to lay down 42°. At half an hour past 4 PM we took in the Top-sails, got down topg^t yards, wore the Ship and stood to the SW under two Courses. At Middnight the storm abated so that we could carry the Top-sails double reefed.

MONDAY 16*th*. At 4 in the Morning wore and stood to the East with the Wind at SSE a moderate breeze and fair. At 8 o'Clock saw the land extending from EBN to NEBN. Loosed a reef out of each Top-sail, got Topg^t yards across and set the Sails. At Noon observed in Latitude

54°25½′, Longitude in 38°18′ West, the land extending from N½W to East Six or eight leagues distant. It appeared to be very mountainous and rocky and was allmost wholy covered with Snow. In this Situation we had 110 fathom water. The Northern extreme was the land which we first saw and proved to be an Island which obtained the name of *Willis's Island* after the person who first saw it. At this time we had a swell from the South which made it probable no land was near us in that direction: but the Cold air which we felt and the vast quantity of Snow on the land in sight induced us to think that it was extensive and I chose to begin with exploring the Northern Coast. With this view we bore up for Willis's Island all sails set, having a fine gale at ssw. As we advanced to the North we preceived a nother isle lying East of Willis's island and between it and the Main. Seeing that there was a clear passage between the two isles, we steered for it and at 5 o'Clock we were in the Middle of it and found it to be about two miles broad. Willis's isle is a high rock of no great extent, near to which are some rocky islots. It is situated in the Latitude of 54°00′ S, Longitude 38°23′ W. The other isle which obtained the name of *Bird isle*, on accou^t of the vast number that were upon it, is not so high but of greater extent and lies close to the NE point of the Main land which I called *Cape North*. So much as we saw of the SE Coast of this land it lies in the direction of S 50° East and N 50° W, it seemed to form several Bays or inlets and we observed huge masses of snow or ice in the bottoms of them, especially in one which lies 10 miles to the SSE of Bird isle. After geting through the Passage we found the North Coast to trend EBN for about 9 miles and then East and East Southerly to *Cape Buller* which is a 11 miles more. We coasted or ranged the Coast at one league distance till near 10 o'Clock when we brought to for the night and on Sounding found 55 fathoms a muddy bottom.

TUESDAY 17*th*. At 2 o'Clock in the morning made sail in for the land with a fine breeze at sw. At 4 Willis Island bore WBS distant 32 Miles, Cape Buller to the west of which lies some rocky islots, bore SWBW and the most advanced point of land to the East S 63° E. We now steered along shore at the distance of 4 or 5 miles off till 7 o'Clock, when seeing the appearence of an Inlet we hauled in for it and as soon as we drew near the shore, hoisted out a Boat in which I (accompanied by Mr Forster and his party) imbarked with a View of reconoitring the Bay before we ventured in with the Ship. When we put off from the Ship which was about 4 Miles from land we had 40 fathom water. I continued to sound in going in for the shore, but could find no bottom with a line of 34 fathoms, which was the length of the one I had in the boat, and which also proved too short to sound the Bay, so far as I went up it. I found it to lie in SWBS about two leagues and to be about two miles broad and well sheltered from all Winds, and I judged there might be good Anchorage before some sandy beaches which appeared on each side, and likewise near a low flat isle near the head of the Bay. As I had come to a resolution not to bring the Ship in, I did not think it worth my while to go and examine these places where it did not seem probable that any one would ever be benifited by the descovery.

The head of the Bay, as well as two places on each side, was terminated by a huge Mass of Snow and ice of vast extent, it shewed a perpendicular clift of considerable height, just like the side or face of an ice isle; pieces were continually breaking from them and floating out to sea. A great fall happened while we were in the Bay; it made a noise like Cannon. The inner parts of the Country was not less savage and horrible: the Wild rocks raised their lofty summits till they were lost in the Clouds and the Vallies laid buried in everlasting Snow. Not a tree or shrub was to be seen, no not even big enough to make a tooth-pick. I landed in three different places, displayed our Colours and took possession of the Country in his Majestys name under a descharge of small Arms. . . .

We set out for the Ship and got on board a little after 12 o'Clock with a quantity of Seals and Penguins, an exceptable present to the Crew. It must however not be understood that we were in want of Provisions, we had yet plenty of every kind, and sence we had been on this Coast I had ordered, in addition to the common allowance, Wheat to be boiled every morning for breakfast, but any kind of fresh meat was prefered by most on board to Salt; for my own part, I was now, for the first time heartily tired of salt meat of every kind and prefer'd the Penguins, whose flesh eat nearly as well as bullocks liver, it was however fresh and that was sufficient to make it go down. I called the Bay we had been in *Possession Bay*, it is situated in the Latitude of 54°5′ s, Longitude 37°18′ West and a 11 Leagues to the East of Cape North. . . .

*   *   *

FRIDAY 20*th*. At 2 o'Clock in the morning made sail to sw round Coopers Island, it is a rock of considerable height about 5 miles in circuit and lies one from the main. At this isle the Coast takes a sw direction for the space of 4 or 5 leagues to a point which I called *Cape Disappointment* off which lie three small isles, the Southermost of which is green low and flat & lies one league from the Cape. As we advanced to sw land opened of this point in the direction of N 60° West and 9 leagues beyond it. It proved an Island quite detatched from the Main and obtained the name of *Pickersgill Island* after my third officers. Soon after a point of the main beyond this Island came in sight in the direction of N 55° West which exactly united the Coast at the very point we had seen and set the day we first came in with it and proved to a demonstration that this land which we had taken to be part of a great Continent was no more than an Island of 70 leagues in Circuit. Who would have thought that an Island of no greater extent than this is, situated between the Latitude of 54° and 55°, should in the very height of Summer be in a manner wholy covered many fathoms deep with frozen Snow, but more especially the sw Coast, the very sides and craggy summits of the lofty Mountains were cased with snow and ice, but the quantity which lay in the Vallies is incredable, before all of them the Coast was terminated by a wall of Ice of considerable height. It can hardly be doubted but that a great deal of ice is formed here in the Winter which in the Spring is broke off and dispersed over the Sea: but this isle cannot produce the ten thousand part of what we have seen, either there must be more land or else ice is formed without it. These reflections led me to think that the land we had seen the preceeding day might belong to an extensive tract and I still had hopes of discovering a continent. I must Confess the disapointment I now met with did not affect me much, for to judge of the bulk by the sample it would not be worth the discovery. This land I called the *Isle of Georgia* in honor of H. Majesty.

* * *

[*Satisfied that South Georgia was an island, Cook persevered to the south-east in very foggy weather until, reckoning he was in latitude 60° s, he decided to give up further search after Dalrymple's visions of a southern continent.*]

FRIDAY 27*th*. . . . I was now tired of these high Southern Latitudes where nothing was to be found but ice and thick fogs. We had now a long hollow swell from the West, a strong indication that there was no land in that direction. I think I may now venture to assert that that extensive coast, laid down in Mr Dalrymple's Chart of the Ocean between Africa and America, and the Gulph of St Sebastian does not exist. I too doubt if either Le Roche or the Ship Lion ever saw the Isle of Georgia, but this is a point I will not dispute as I neither know where they were bound or from whence they came, when they made the discovery; if it should be the same, Mr Dalrymple has placed it half a degree of Latitude too far South and 7° of Longitude too far West, and M. D'Anville 15 or 16 degrees, the only two Charts I have seen it inserted in; but be it how it will, I will allow them the merit of leading me to the discovery, for if it had not been on these maps, it is very probable I had passed to the South of it. . . .

* * *

[*Moving to the north, Cook encountered the rocky and inhospitable group now known as the South Sandwich Islands. He was unable to explore them thoroughly, but as he moved away he made some shrewd deductions about their significance.*]

[FEBRUARY 1775]

MONDAY 6*th*. We continued to steer to the South and SE till noon at which time we were in the Latitude of 58°15′ s, Longitude 21°34′ West and seeing neither land nor signs of any, I concluded that what we had seen, which I named *Sandwich Land* was either a group of Islands or else a point of the Continent, for I firmly beleive that there is a tract of land near the Pole, which is the Source of most of the ice which is spread over this vast Southern Ocean: and I think it also probable that it extends farthest to the North opposite the Southern Atlantick and Indian Oceans, because ice has always been found farther to the north in these Oceans than any where else which, I think, could not be if there was no land to the South, I mean a land of some considerable extent; for if we suppose there is not, and that ice may be formed without, it will follow of Course that the cold ought to be every where nearly equal round the Pole, as far as 70° or 60° of Latitude, or so far as to be out of the influence of any of the known Continents, consequently we ought to see ice every where under the same Parallel or near it, but the Contrary has been found. It is but few ships which have met with ice going round Cape Horn and we saw but little below the sixtieth degree of Latitude in the *Southern Pacifick Ocean*. Whereas in this ocean between the Meridion of 40° West and 50° or 60° East we have found Ice as far north as 51°. Bouvet found some in 48° and others have seen it in a much lower Latitude. It is however true that the greatest part of this Southern Continent (supposeing there is one) must lay within the Polar Circile where the Sea is so pestered with ice, that the land is thereby inacessible. The risk one runs in exploreing a coast in these unknown and Icy Seas, is so very great, that I can be bold to say, that no man will ever venture farther than I have done and that the lands which may lie to the South will never be explored. Thick fogs, Snow storms, Intense Cold and every other thing that can render Navigation dangerous one has to encounter and these difficulties are greatly heightned by the enexpressable horrid aspect of the Country, a Country doomed by Nature never once to feel the warmth of the Suns rays, but to lie for ever buried under everlasting snow and ice. The Ports which may be on the Coast are in a manner wholy filled up with frozen Snow of a vast thickness, but if any should so far be open as to admit a ship in, it is even dangerous to go in, for she runs a risk of being fixed there for ever, or coming out in an ice island. The islands and floats of ice on the Coast, the great falls from the ice clifts in the Port, or a heavy snow storm attended with a sharp frost, would prove equally fatal. After such an explanation as this the reader must not expect to find me much farther to the South. It is however not for want of inclination but other reasons. It would have been rashness in me to have risked all which had been done in the Voyage, in finding out and exploaring a Coast which when done would have answerd no end whatever, or been of the least use either to Navigation or Geography or indeed any other Science; Bouvets Discovery was yet before us, the existence of which was to be cleared up and lastly we were now not in a condition to undertake great things, nor indeed was there time had we been ever so well provided. These reasons induced me to alter the Course to East, with a very strong gale at North attended with an exceeding heavy fall of Snow, the quantity which fell into our sails was so great that we were obliged every now and then to throw the Ship up in the Wind to shake it out of the Sails, otherways neither them nor the Ship could have supported the wieght. In the evening it ceased to snow, the weather cleared up, the Wind backed to the West and we spent the night makeing two short boards under close reefed Top-sails and fore-sail.

* * *

[*Cook took the* Resolution *east for two weeks, searching for Cape Circumcision discovered by Bouvet in 1738, but failed to find it.*]

TUESDAY 21*st*. At Day-break made sail and bore away East and at Noon we observed in Latitude 54°16′ s, Longitude 16°13′ E which was 5° to the East of the Longitude Cape Circumcision was said to lie in, so that we began to think that no such land ever existed. I however continued to steer East inclining a little to the South till 4 o'Clock in the after noon of the next day, when we were in the Latitude of 54°24′ s, Longitude 19°18′ E. We had now run down 13° degrees of Longitude in the very Latitude Bouvets land was said to lie in, I was therefore well assured that what he had taken for land could be nothing but an Island of Ice, for if it was land, it is hardly possible we could have miss'd it, was it ever so small, besides sence we left the Southern lands, we had not met with the least signs of any, but even suppose we had, it would have been no proof of the existence of this land, for I am well assured that neither Seals, Penguins or any of the Oceanic birds are indubitable signs of the Vicinity of land. I will allow that they are found on the Coasts of all these Southern lands, but are they not allso to be found in all parts of this Southern Ocean. There are however some Oceanic or aquatic birds which point out the Vicinity of land, especially shags which seldom go out of sight of it, and Gannets, Boobies and Men of War birds I believe seldom go very far out to Sea. As we were now no more than two degrees of Longitude from our rout to the South after leaving the Cape of Good Hope, it was to no purpose to proceed any farther to the East under this parallel, knowing no land could be there; but as an oppertunity now offered of clearing up some doubts of our having seen land farther to the South, I steered SE to get into the Situation in which it was supposed to lie. We continued this Course till 4 o'Clock the next morning and then SEBE and ESE till eight in the evening, at which time we were in the Latitude of 55°25′ s, Longitude 23°22′ E, both deduced from observations made the same day, for in the Morning the sky was clear at intervals and afforded an oppertunity to observe several distances of the Sun and Moon which we had not been able to do for some time past, having had a constant succession of bad weather. Having now run over the place where the land was supposed to lie without seeing the least signs of any it was no longer to be doubted but that the Ice hills had decieved us as well as Mr Bouvet. The Wind by this time had veered to the North and increased to a perfect storm attended, as usual, with snow and sleet, we handed the Top-sails and hauled up ENE under the Courses. During the night the Wind abated and veered to NW which inabled us to steer more to the North having no business farther South.

I had now made the circuit of the Southern Ocean in a high Latitude and traversed it in such a manner as to leave not the least room for the Possibility of there being a continent, unless near the Pole and out of the reach of Navigation; by twice visiting the Pacific Tropical Sea, I had not only settled the situation of some old discoveries but made there many new ones and left, I conceive, very little more to be done even in that part. Thus I flater my self that the intention of the Voyage has in every respect been fully Answered, the Southern Hemisphere sufficiently explored and a final end put to the searching after a Southern Continent, which has at times ingrossed the attention of some of the Maritime Powers for near two Centuries past and the Geographers of all ages. That there may be a Continent or large tract of land near the Pole, I will not deny, on the contrary I am of opinion there is, and it is probable that we have seen a part of it. The excessive cold, the many islands and vast floats of ice all tend to prove that there must be land to the South and that this Southern land must lie or extend farthest to the North opposite the Southern Atlantick and Indian Oceans, I have already assigned some reasons, to which I may add the greater degree of cold which we have found in these Seas, than in the Southern Pacific Ocean under the same parallels of Latitude. In this last Ocean the Mercury in the Thermometer seldom fell so low as the freezing point, till we were in Sixty and upwards, whereas in the others it fell frequently as low in the Latitude of fifty four: this was certainly owing to there being a greater quantity of Ice and extending farther to the North in these two Seas than in the other, and if Ice is first formed at or near land, of which I have no doubt, it will follow that the land also extends farther North. . . .

I had at this time some thoughts of revisiting the place where the French discovery was said to lie,[54] but when I considered that if they had realy made this discovery, the end would be as fully answered as if I had done it my self, we know it can only be an island and if we may judge from the degree of cold we found in that Latitude it cannot be a fertile one. Besides this would have kept me two Months longer at sea and in a tempestious Latitude which we were not in a condition to support, our sails and rigging were so much worn that some thing was giving way every hour and we had nothing left either to repair or replace them.

We had been a long time without refreshments, our Provisions were in a state of decay and little more nourishment remained in them than just to keep life and Soul together. My people were yet healthy and would cheerfully have gone wherever I had thought proper to lead them, but I dreaded the Scurvy laying hold of them at a time when we had nothing left to remove it. Besides it would have been cruel in me to have continued the Fatigues and hardships they were continually exposed to longer than absolutely necessary, their behaviour throughout the whole voyage merited every indulgence which was in

54. Kerguelen Island, 49° 30′ s, 69° 30′ e (see map 5).

my power to give them. Animated by the conduct of the officers, they shewed themselves capable of surmounting every difficulty and danger which came in their way and never once looked upon either the one or the other to be a bit heightned by being seperated from our companion the Adventure. All these considerations induced me to lay a side looking for the French discoveries and to steer for the Cape of Good Hope, with a resolution however of looking for the isles of Denia and Marseveen, which are laid down in Dr Halley's Variation Chart, in the Latitude of [41½] s and about [4] of Longitude to the East of the Meridian of the Cape of Good Hope. With this view I steered NE with a hard gale at NW and thick weather and on

SATURDAY 26*th* at Noon we saw the last Ice island, we were at this time in the Latitude of 52°52' s, Longitude 26°31' East. The next day our Latitude at Noon was 50°34' s, Longitude 28°37' E, the Mercury in the Thermometer was no higher than 41. Continued to steer NE till

[MARCH 1775]

WEDNESDAY March 1*st* when the wind abated and veered to the South with which we steered West in order to get farther from Mr Bouvets track which was but a few degrees to the East of us. We were at this time in the Latitude of 46°44' s, Longitude 33°20' E and found the Variation to be 23°36' W.

*   *   *

THURSDAY 16*th*. At Day light saw two Sail in the NW quarter, standing to the westward, one of them shewed Dutch Colours. At 10 o'Clock we Tacked and stood to the west also, being at this time in the Latitude of 35°09' s, Longitude 22°38' E. I now in persuance to my Instructions demanded from the Officers and Petty officers the Log Books and Journals they had kept, which were delivered to me accordingly and Sealed up for the Inspection of the Admiralty. I also enjoined them and the whole crew not to devulge where we had been till they had their Lordships permission so to do. In the after noon the Wind veered to the west and increased to a hard gale which was of short duration for the next day it fell and at Noon veered to SE. At this time we were in the Latitude of 34°49′ s, Longitude 22°00′ E and on sounding found 56 fathoms water. In the evening Saw the land in the direction of ENE about Six leagues distant and during all the fore part of the night there was a great fire or light upon it.

SATURDAY 18*th*. Day break saw the land again bearing NNW Six or seven Leagues distant, depth of Water 48f^{ms}. At 9 o'Clock, having little or no wind, hoisted out a boat and sent on board one of the two ships before mentioned, which were about two leagues from us, but we were too impatient after News to regard the distance. Soon after a breeze sprung at West with which we stood to the South and presently three Sail more appeared in sight to windward, one of which shewed English Colours. At 1 PM the boat returned from on board the Bownkerke Polder, Captain Cornelis Bosch, a Dutch Indiaman from Bengal; Captain Bosch very obligingly offered us sugar, Arrack and whatever he had to spare. Our people were told by some English Seamen on board this Ship that the Adventure arrived at the Cape of Good Hope Twelve Months ago and that one of her boats crew had been Murdered and eat by the People of New Zealand, so that the story which we heard in Queen Charlottes Sound was now no longer to be doubted, it was to this effect: that a ship or boat had been dashed to pieces on the Coast, but that the crew got safe on shore; on the Natives who were present stealing some of the strangers clothes, they were fired upon till all their ammunition was spent, or as the Natives express'd, till they could fire no longer, after which the Natives fell upon them, knocked them all on the head and treated them as above mentioned; this was the substance of what our people understood from them; when I examined them about it they denied their knowing any thing about the matter or that any thing of the kind had happened and never after would mention it to any one, consequently I thought our people had missunderstood them. I shall make no ref[l]ections on this Melancholy affair untill I hear more about it. I must however observe in favour of the New Zealand[er]s that I have allways found them of a Brave, Noble, Open and benevolent disposition, but they are a people that will never put up with an insult if they have an oppertunity to resent it.

We had light airs next to a calm till 10 o'clock the next Morning when a breeze sprung up at West and the English Ship which was to windward bore down to us, she proved to be the True Briton, Captain Broadly from China. As he did not intend to touch at the Cape, I put a letter on board him for the Secretary of the Admiralty. The account which we had heard of the Adventure was confirmed to us by this ship; we also got from them a parcel of old News papers, which were new to us and gave us some amusement in reading; but these were the least favours which we received from Captain Broadly, he with a Generosity peculiar to the Commanders of the India Companies Ships, sent us fresh provisions, Tea and other articles, which were very acceptable and deserves from me this publick acknowlidgement. In the after noon we parted Company, the True Britton stood out to Sea and we in for the land, having a very fresh gale at West which split our Fore Top sail in such a manner that we were obliged to bring another to the Yard. At 6 o'Clock we tacked within 4 or 5 Miles of the shore and as we judged about 5 or 6 leagues to the East of Cape Auguilas. We stood off till Middnight, when the wind having veered round to the South, we Tacked and stood a long shore to the west. The Wind kept veering more and more in our favour and at last fixed at ESE and blew for some hours a perfect huricane, as soon as the Storm began to subside we made sail and hauled in for the land. On

TUESDAY 21*st* at Noon the Table Mountain over the Cape Town bore NEBE distant 9 or 10 Leagues. By makeing use of this bearing and distance to reduce the Longitude shewn by the watch to the Cape Town, the error was found to be no more than 18′ in Longitude which she was too far to the East, and the greatest difference we have found between it and the Lunar observations sence we left New Zealand has seldom exceeded half a degree and allways the same way. The next Morning, being with us Wednesday 22nd but with the people here Tuesday 21st we anchored in Table Bay, where we found several Dutch Ships, some French and the Ceres Captain Newte, an English East India Company Ship from China bound directly to England, by whom I sent a Copy of this Journal, Charts and other Drawings to the Admiralty which Captain Newte was so obliging as to take charge of and as he intended to make but a very short stay at St Helena will probably be the first that carries the news of our arrival to England. Before we had well got to an anchor, I dispatched an officer to acquaint the Governor with our arrival and to request the necessary stores and refreshments, which were readily granted. As soon as the officer returned we saluted the Garrison with 13 Guns which Compliment was immediately returned with an equal number. I found here a letter from Captain Furneaux acquainting me with the loss of Ten of his best men together with a boat in Queen Charlottes Sound. This together with a great part of his Bread being damaged was the reason he could not follow me in the rout I had proposed to take. He also informed me that he had sailed over the place where Cape Circumcision was said to lie, so that here is another proof that it must have been Ice and not Land which Bouvet saw.

The next day I went on shore and waited on the Governor Baron Plettenberg and other Principal officers who Received and treated us during our whole stay with the greatest politeness, and contributed all in their power to make it agreeable. And as there are few people who are more obligeing to strangers than the Dutch in general at this place, and no place where refreshments of all kinds are to be got in such abundance we enjoyed some real repose after the fatigues of so long a voyage.

*   *   *

[*Cook left the Cape on 27 April 1775. While he was there he saw for the first time Hawkesworth's narrative of the first voyage. He was incensed by what he considered its misrepresentations of his journals, particularly as regards St Helena, which caused embarrassment on his stay there from from 15 to 21 May. There was a stop for fresh turtle at Ascension from 28 to 31 May.*]

On WEDNESDAY 31*st* of May we left Ascension and steered to the Northward with a fine gale at SEBE. I had a great desire to visit the Island of St Mathew in order to settle its situation, but as I found the winds would not allow me to fetch it, I steered for the Island of Fernando de Norono on the Coast of Brazil, in order to determine its Longitude, as I could not find this had yet been done. Perhaps I should have done a more exceptable service to Navigation if I had gone in search of the Isle of St Paul and those Shoals which are said to lie near the Equator and about the Meridian of [20°] west, as neither their situation nor existance are well known. The truth is I was unwilling to prolong the passage in searching for what I was not sure to find, nor was I willing to give up every object which might tend to the improvement of Navigation and Geography for the sake of geting home a Week or a fortnight sooner. It is but seldom that oppertunities of this kind offer and when they do they are but too often neglected. In our Passage to Fernando de Norono, we had steady fresh gales between the SE and ESE attended with fair and Clear weather, and as we had the advantage of the Moon a day nor night did not pass without making Lunar observations for the determining our Longitude. In this run the Variation of the Compass gradually decreased from 11°   ′ w which it was at Ascinsion to 1°00′ w which is what we found it off Fernando de Norono, this was the Mean result of two Compasses one of which gave 1°37′ and the other 0°23′ West.

FRIDAY June 9*th* at Noon, we made the Island of Fernando de Norona bearing SWBW½W distance Six or 7 Leagues as we afterwards found by the Log, it appeared in ditatched and peaked hills, the largest of which looked like a Church Tower or steeple. As we drew near the SE end, or part of the isle, we preceived several detatched sunken rocks, lying near a league from the Shore on which the Sea broke in a great surf. After standing very near these rocks we hoisted our Colours and then bore up round the North end of the isle, or rather a group of little islots, for we could see that the land was divided by narrow Channels. On the one next the Main island is a strong fort, besides several others on this last mentioned island, all of which seem'd to have every advantage that Nature can give them, and so disposed as wholy to command all the Anchoring and landing places about the island. We continued to Steer round the Northern point, till the Sandy beaches (befor which is the Road for Shipping) began to appear and untill all the forts and the Peaked hill were open to the westward of the said point. At this time, and on a gun being fired at one of the forts, the Portuguese Colours were displayed and the example followed by all the other forts. As the purpose for which I made the island was now answered I had no intention to anchor and therefore after firing a gun to leeward we made sail and stood away to the Northward with a fine fresh gale at ESE, the Peaked hill or Church Tower bore s 27° w distant about 4 or 5 miles and from this point of view it leans or over hangs to the East. . . .

By reducing the Observed Latitude at Noon to the Peaked hill, its Latitude will be 3°53' s, and its Longitude by the Watch, carried on from St Helena is 32°34' West and by Observations of the Sun and Moon, made before and after we made the isle and reduced to it by the Watch 32°44'30" w. This was the mean result of my observations, the results of those made by Mr Wales, which were more numerous, gave about a quarter of a degree less. The mean of the two will be pretty near the Watch and probably nearest the truth. By knowing the Longitude of this isle we are able to determine that of the adjacent East Coast of Brazil which according to the Modern Charts lies about [sixty or seventy leagues] more to the west. We might very safely have trusted to these Charts, especially the Variation Chart for 1744 and Mr Dalrymples of the Southern Atlantic Ocean.

SUNDAY 11*th* at 3 o'Clock in the after-noon we crossed the Equator in the Longitude of 32°14' w: we had a fresh gale at ESE which blew in Squals attend by showers of rain which continued at certain intervals till Noon the next day, after which we had 24 hours fair Weather.

*   *   *

WEDNESDAY 21*st*. I ordered the Still to be fitted to the largest Copper, which held about Sixty-four gallons.[55] The fire was lighted at 4 o'Clock in the Morning and at Six the Still began to run, it was continued till Six o'Clock in the evening in which time we obtained 32 gallons of fresh Water, at the expence of one bushel and a half of Coals, which was about three quarters of a bushel more than what was necessary to have boiled the Ships Companies Victuals only, but the expence of fuel was no object with me. At this time the Victuals was dressed in the small Copper and the other applyed wholy to the Still and every

55. Both the *Resolution* and *Adventure* carried an experimental 'apparatus for distillation', invented by Dr Charles Irving in 1771.

method made use of to obtain from it the greatest quantity of fresh Water possible, as this was my sole Montive for seting it to work. The Mercury in the Thermometer at Noon was at 84½, and higher it is seldom found at Sea, had it been lower more Water, under the same circumstances, would undoubtedly have been produced, for the colder the air is, the cooler you can keep the still, which will condence the Steam the faster. Upon the whole this is a usefull invention; but I would advise no man to trust wholy to it, for altho' you may, provided you have plenty of fuel and good Coppers, obtain as much water as will support life, you cannot, with all your efforts, obtain Sufficient to support health, in hot climates especially, where it is the most wanting, for I am well convinced that nothing contributes more to the health of Seamen than having plenty of Water.

The Wind now remained invariably fixed at NE and ENE and blew fresh with Squalls attended with Showers of Rain and the Sky for the Most part Clouded.

* * *

[*After five days on the Island of Fayal in the Azores, 14–19 July, Cook headed for home.*]

[JULY 1775]

SATURDAY 22nd. . . . After two hours Calm, in the Latitude of 39°38′ N we got the wind at West, the next day it fixed at WNW and increased to a fresh [gale] with which we Steered directly for the Lizard and on

SATURDAY 29th we made the Land about Plymouth; Maker Church, at 5 o'Clock in the after-noon, bore N 10° west distant 7 Leagues, this bearing and distance shew that the error of Mr Kendals Watch in Longitude was only 7′45″, which was too far to the west. [The next morning anchored at Spit-head. Having been absent from England Three Years and Eighteen Days, in which time I lost but four men and one only of them by sickness.][56]

56. These concluding lines are taken from a revised version of the closing pages of journal 'B'.

THE THIRD VOYAGE
1776–1780

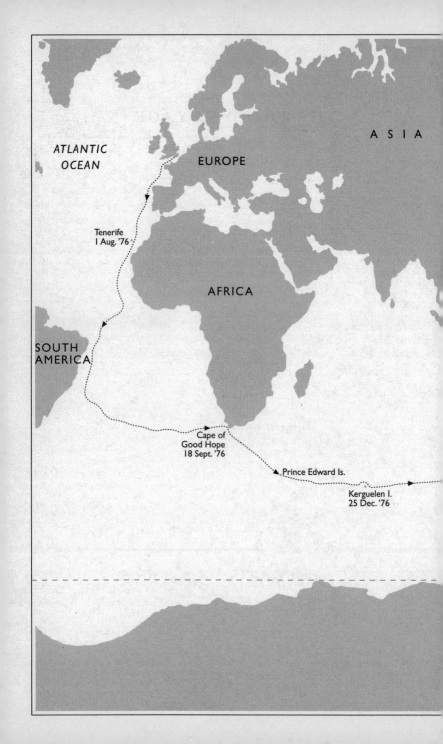

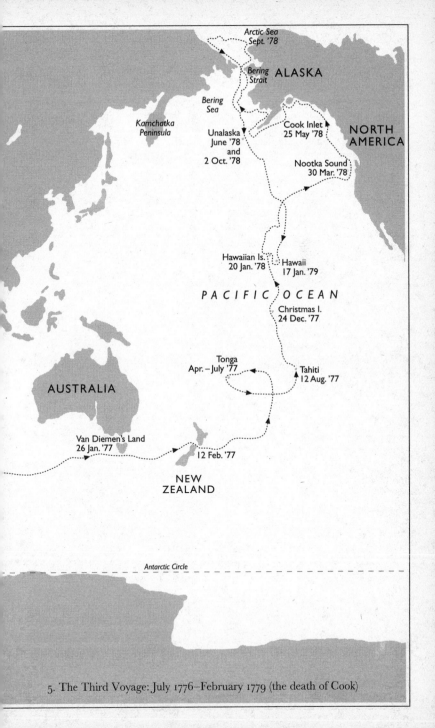

Arctic Sea
Sept. '78

Bering
Strait

ALASKA

Kamchatka
Peninsula

Bering
Sea

Cook Inlet
25 May '78

NORTH
AMERICA

Unalaska
June '78
and
2 Oct. '78

Nootka Sound
30 Mar. '78

Hawaiian Is.
20 Jan. '78

Hawaii
17 Jan. '79

PACIFIC OCEAN

Christmas I.
24 Dec. '77

Tonga
Apr. – July '77

Tahiti
12 Aug. '77

AUSTRALIA

Van Diemen's Land
26 Jan. '77

12 Feb. '77

NEW
ZEALAND

Antarctic Circle

5. The Third Voyage: July 1776–February 1779 (the death of Cook)

INTRODUCTION

In August 1775 Cook was promoted to post-captain and offered a place and a pension at Greenwich Hospital. He was not eager to retire, and accepted on condition that he could return to active service if he were needed. Meanwhile, the *Resolution* was being refitted for a further voyage – one task being the return of Omai to the Society Islands. Early in the new year the Earl of Sandwich and the Admiralty heard what they had no doubt hoped to hear – that Cook was willing to lead the new expedition. It was to be yet another attempt to make real that ancient dream of a navigable northern route connecting the Atlantic with the Pacific – the North-West Passage, to be explored from the western side. The project had been entrusted to John Byron in 1764, but once he got into the Pacific he had had better ideas. The critical area between Siberia and Alaska had been explored by Vitus Bering (1681–1741), the Danish navigator in the service of Peter the Great, in expeditions of 1728 and 1741. Bering's discoveries were described by G. F. Müller (English translation 1761) and J. Stählin (1774). The maps in both volumes were inadequate, the one in Stählin being positively treacherous in suggesting that Alaska was a huge island with a passage between it and the American coast heading for Baffin Bay.

The refitting of *Resolution* was not supervised by Cook and was very badly carried out, as the recurring serious problems with the masts and with leaks were to show. Another Whitby boat, eighteen months old, was bought and named *Discovery*. Cook was ashore for just less than a year between his second and third voyages. Too much of the time was taken up with the sad squabble with the Forsters, his scientists on the second voyage, over the rights to publish the official history of the voyage. Cook of course won, and he left his manuscript (and the young Forster's beautiful drawings) with Canon John Douglas to be prepared for publication. He never saw the published volumes.

Charles Clerke was in command of *Discovery*. In *Resolution*, Cook had John Gore as his first lieutenant, James King as second, John Williamson as third, and William Bligh as master. William Anderson, who died on the voyage, was surgeon; he was a brilliant naturalist and observer; his mate was David Samwell, who wrote the most important of the unofficial accounts of the voyage. Molesworth Phillips was lieutenant of marines, and John Webber was the expedition's artist. Clerke's officers were James Burney and John Rickman. Thomas Edgar was master, and William Bayley the expedition's astronomer.

The instructions to Cook from the Admiralty were to make an attempt 'to find out a Northern passage by Sea from the Pacific to the Atlantic Ocean'. He was to proceed south from the Cape of Good Hope 'in search of some Islands said to have been lately seen by the French', then proceed to Tahiti, touching at New Zealand if necessary, leaving in February 1777 for the coast of New Albion (north-western America) at latitude 45° and travel north to be in latitude 65° in June. He was to be careful not to touch upon any Spanish dominion, and if that was unavoidable he should give no 'umbrage or offence' to the subjects of His Catholic Majesty. If necessary he should winter in Kamchatka and make a second attempt in the following summer. He should give 'every kind of Civility and Regard' to the inhabitants of countries he visited, and take possession in the name of the king of 'convenient Situations' in such countries not claimed by other European powers.

The *Resolution* sailed from Plymouth on 12 July 1776. The *Discovery* was delayed for the extraordinary reason that Clerke was in a debtors' prison – or at least under legal restraint – having guaranteed debts incurred by his brother. If he was in prison, he may there have contracted the tuberculosis which weakened and then destroyed him when in command of the expedition after Cook's death. The two ships came together at the Cape of Good Hope, proceeded south-east to Prince Edward and Kerguelen Islands, then to Tasmania (Van

Diemen's Land), still thought to be part of the mainland of New Holland, and on to New Zealand, where relations with the Maoris were uncomfortable because of the massacre of the *Adventure*'s boat crew in December 1773. They were now much behind schedule, but, leaving New Zealand on 27 February 1777, they might possibly have made the New Albion coast in June if it had not been for adverse winds which forced Cook to abandon Tahiti and North America for that season. He was in serious difficulties about provisions for the many cattle they were carrying with them to be introduced into new territories, and found supplies first at Palmerston Island and then in the Tonga group, where the ships stayed for eleven weeks.

Cook's account of his relationships with the Tongan chiefs, of the elaborate entertainments and exchanges of gifts, of participation in ceremonies culminating in a great festival (*'inasi*) just before the ships left, is ample and fascinating. The impression Cook gives of the friendliness of the islanders is belied, however, by the increasing severity with which he punished the growing problem of theft, and by the plot on his life, involving Finau, the chief with whom he had the closest relationship.

The ships left Tonga in mid-July and reached Tahiti on 12 August 1777. On Eimeo, towards the end of October, Cook's reprisals for the theft of a goat were further signs of his increasing exasperation in his dealings with the peoples he was visiting. Omai was left on Huahine with the two boys he had brought from New Zealand.

Christmas was spent on the uninhabited Kiritimati, one of the Line Islands, which Cook named Christmas Island, and on 18 January 1778 they came across the Hawaiian archipelago, unknown to the western world, which Cook named the Sandwich Islands. Landings were made on the two northern islands, Kauai and Niihau; the islanders were able to understand the sailors' Tahitian. Cook was desperate to prevent 'venereal complaints . . . being communicated to these people', but he was not successful

The North American coast was sighted on 7 March, and on 30 March the ships anchored in an inlet, which they named Nootka Sound, on Vancouver Island (which was not known to be an island). The *Resolution's* foremast was repaired and the mizen replaced, and there was much contact with the Indians, who knew Europeans and were skilled in trafficking skins and in removing what they wanted from the ships. As they moved first north, then west along the Alaskan coast, it was found that the *Resolution* was leaking and some repairs were made in Prince William Sound. Eventually, a perilous passage was made through the Aleutian Islands into the Bering Sea via Unalaska island. After three months they were back, defeated by the Arctic ice. Cook withdrew, purposing to try again next summer

At Unalaska again Cook met Russian traders and the Russian factor, and left with them an account of his discoveries to be sent back to London. After three weeks the ships sailed south and on 26 November sighted the Hawaiian islands – this time the eastern island of Maui. As the canoes came off Cook issued injunctions to control trading and sexual contact. Unusually, he made no attempt to find a harbour but cruised slowly off the coast first of Maui and then of Hawaii, the largest and most southerly island. This tantalizing manoeuvring exasperated the crew of *Resolution*, who were on short rations; they refused to drink the sugar cane beer supplied and petitioned Cook, who wrote of them as 'mutinous' and 'turbulent', and withdrew their grog while the strike against the beer continued. King wrote that 'we were jaded and very heartily tir'd with Cruising off these Islands for near two months . . . The Disappointment in not trying for a place of Anchorage had a bad effect on the Spirits of our Ships Company.'

The last entry in Cook's journal is on 6 January 1779. There exists, however, a fragment of his log which takes us up to 17 January, when they had (at last) come to anchor in Kealakekua Bay on the western side of the island of Hawaii. What then followed, with the circumstances of Cook's death at the hands of the islanders on 14 February, is recounted in the Postscript.

On Cook's death Clerke, now seriously ill, was in command of *Resolution* and the expedition, and Gore was given the command of *Discovery*. Clerke got the fatal mast on board, and set about recovering the bodies of Cook and those who were killed with him. The bodies of the marines were never recovered. Cook's body had been dismembered and divided among chiefs: this was normal reverential treatment of the body of a great chief. However, some parts of the corpse were slowly brought back – with the bewildering inquiry as to when Lono would return and what would he do to them when he did. The remains were committed to the waters of the bay. Clerke did not want retaliation or vengeance, but not all were of the same mind. When a watering party was stoned there was a violent reaction; the houses of a whole village were burned to the ground and those who could not get away were bayoneted or shot, and two heads were severed and placed on poles.

Clerke wished to carry on as Cook had intended, and he went north to attempt the North-West Passage again. At Kamchatka he gave the Russians Cook's journal and other material, and an account of his death; the Admiralty received this seven months later. Clerke had no better fortune than Cook in penetrating the ice and on his way back south, within sight of Kamchatka, he died. Gore took over the *Resolution*, and King the *Discovery*. The ships left Kamchatka on 10 October; they came back via the Kurile Islands, putting in at Macao in China and the Cape of Good Hope, reaching the Orkneys in August 1780. On 4 October the ships were in the Thames.

There was no problem for Beaglehole in choosing the manuscript of Cook's journal for the third voyage, since any earlier version or versions of the existing journal have disappeared. The extant manuscript, in Cook's hand, is in the British Library (Egerton 2177A). It is evident that this time, as Beaglehole says, Cook had set out to write a book. The narrative sweeps away the daily records of conditions and distance sailed, and spreads itself as a continuous story over several days at a time. The printed version, supplemented by King and (once again) edited by Canon Douglas, appeared in 1784. The invaluable accounts of the voyage by Anderson and Samwell, supplemented by extracts from (among others) Edgar, Burney and Ledyard, may be found in Beaglehole's full edition.

JOURNAL OF THE
THIRD VOYAGE
1776–1780

1776

SATURDAY February 10*th*.[1] I received a Commission to Command His Majestys Sloop the Resolution, went on board hoisted the Pendant and began to enter men, her Complement being the same as on her late Voyage. At the same time the Discovery a Ship of 300 Tons burden just purchased into the Service, was Commissioned and the command given to Captain Clerke who was my second Lieut[t] in the Resolution last Voyage. These two Ships were at this time both in the Dock at Deptford under the hands of the Shipwrights.

SUNDAY March 10*th*. The Resolution was hauled out of Dock into the River where we compleated her Rigging and took on board the necessary Stores and Provisions for the Voyage which was as much as we could stow and the best of every kind that could be got.

MONDAY May 6*th*. A Pilot came on board to carry the Ship to Long reach, but it was the 29th before the wind would permit us to sail and the 30th before we reached that place. At Long reach we took on board our artillery, Powder Shot and other Ordnance stores.

SATURDAY June 8*th*. The Earl of Sandwich, S[r] Hugh Palliser JUNE and others of the Board of Admiralty, paid us the last mark of the extraordinary attention they had alalong paid to this equipment, by coming on board to see that every thing was compleated to their desire and to the satisfaction of all who where to embark in the voyage. They

1. Entries are in civil time until 7 January 1779.

and several other Noblemen and gentlemen honoured me with their Company at dinner and were saluted with 17 guns and 3 cheers at their coming on board and also on going a shore.

MONDAY 10*th*. Took on board a Bull, 2 Cows with their Calves & some sheep to carry to Otaheite with a quantity of Hay and Corn for thier subsistance. These Cattle were put on board at His Majestys Command and expence with a view of stocking Otahiete and the Neighbouring Islands with these usefull animals – nor was this the only attention paid to them; I was furnished by the Admiralty with many other useful articles for those Islands, and both Ships were provided with a proper assortment of Iron tools, trinquets &c^a to traffick and cultivate a friendship and an alliance with the Inhabitants of such new Countrys as we might meet with. Some additional cloathing adapted to a cold climate was put on board for the Crews and nothing was wanting that was thought condusive to either conveniency or health, such was the extraordinary care taken by those at the head of the Naval department.

TUESDAY 11*th*. Received on board several Astronomical & Nautical Instruments which the Board of Longitude intrusted to me and Mr King my second Lieutenant, we having engaged to that board to make all the necessary Astronomical and Nautical observations that should accrue and to supply the place of an Astronomer which was intended to be sent out in the Ship. They also put on board the same Watch Machine that was out with me last voyage: it was too slow for mean time at Greenwich this day at Noon by 3′31″,890 and its rate of going was loseing on mean time 1″..209 per day. Another Watch Machine and the same number and sort of Instruments were put on board the Discovery under the care of Mr Wm Baily who was the late voyage[2] with Captain Furneaux, and whom the Board of Longitude engage to go this.

Having Recieved an order to proceed to Plymouth and to take under my command the Discovery, I accordingly gave Captain Clerke

2. This unusual idiom is repeated in the entry for 11 October 1778.

an order to put himself under my Command and another to proceed to Plymouth.

SATURDAY 15*th*. The Resolution Sailed from Long reach with the Discovery in Company, and the same evening anch^d at the Nore.

SUNDAY 16*th*. The Discovery Sailed for Plymouth, but the Resolution was ordered to remain at the Nore till I joined her, being at this time in London.

MONDAY 24*th*. At 6 o'clock in the Morning I set out from London in company with Omai, we got to Chatham between 10 & 11 and after dining with Commissioner Proby he very obligingly ordered his yacht to convey us to Sheerness where my boat was waiting to carry us on board.

I observed that Omai left London with a Mixture of regret and joy: in speaking of England and such persons as had honoured him [with] their protection and friendship he would be very low spirited and with difficulty refrain from tears; but turn the conversation to his Native Country and his eyes would sparkle with joy. His behavour on this occasion seemed truely Natural; he was fully sencible of the good treatment he had met with in England and entertained the highest ideas of the Country and people but the prospect he now had of returning home to his native isle loaded with what they esteem riches, got the better of every other consideration and he seemed quite happy when on board the ship. He was furnished by the King with every thing that was thought usefull or Ornamental in his Country, besides many presents of the same Nature which he received from My Lord Sandwich, Mr Banks and several other gentlemen and Ladies of his acquaintance. In short every method had been taken both during his aboad in England and at his departure to make him convey to his Countrymen the highest opinion of the greatness and generosity of the British Nation.

*   *   *

SUNDAY 30*th*. At 3 PM Anchored in Plymouth Sound where the Discovery had arrived three days before.

*   *   *

[JULY]

MONDAY 8*th*. Received by express my Instructions for the Voyage and an order to proceed to the Cape of Good Hope with the Resolution, and to leave an order for Captain Clerk to follow as soon as he joined his Ship, he being at this time in London.

TUESDAY 9*th*. Received on board the party of Marines, consisting of a Lieut' Serjeant 2 Corporals one Drum and 15 private; Col. Bell who Command[ed] the Division gave me such Men as I had reason to be satisfied with. The overplus men which this reinforcement occasioned were discharged into the Ocean.[3]

WEDNESDAY 10*th*. The Commissioner and Pay Clerks came on board and paid the Officers and Crew up to the 30th of last Month and the Petty officers and Seamen two Months wages in advance: the latter is no more than is customary in the Navy, but the former was an indulgence ordered by the Admiralty in consideration of the Voyage, the better to inable them to provide necessaries for it.

*   *   *

FRIDAY 12*th*. At 8 PM Wieghed and stood out of the Sound with a gentle breeze at NWBW. We had not been long out before the Wind came more Westerly and blew fresh so that we had to ply down Channel. On the 14th at 8 PM we were off the Lizard, and on the 16th at Noon S' Agness Light house on the isles of scilly bore NWBW distant 7 or 8 Miles; our Latitude by observation was 49°53′30″ N and Longitude by the Watch 6°11′ W hence I reckon S' Agnes light house to be in Latitude 49°57′30″ N and Longitude 6°20′ West.

*   *   *

[*The* Resolution *called in at Tenerife for water, wine and provisions at the beginning of August. They touched in at the Cape Verde Islands but finding that the* Discovery *had not arrived continued southwards (16 August).*]

3. The *Ocean* was a 90-gun ship.

[AUGUST]

Between the Lat. of 12° and 7° N the weather was generally dark and gloomy, with frequent rains of which we saved as much Water as filled the most of our empty water casks. These rains and the close sultry weather they accompany but too often bring on sickness in this passage, one has at least every thing to fear from them, and cannot be too much on ones guard, by obliging the people to dry their cloathes and airing the Ship with fires and smoke at every oppertunity. This was constantly practised on board the Resolution & Discovery and we certainly profited by it, for we had fewer sick than on either of my former Voyages. We had however the Mortification to find the Ship exceeding leaky in all her upper works, the hot and dry weather we had just past through had opened her Seams, which had been badly Caulked at first, so wide that they admited the rain Water through as it fell and there was hardly a Man that could lie dry in his bed; the officers in the gunroom were all driven out of their cabbins by the Water that came thro' the sides. The sails in the Sail rooms got wet and before we had weather to dry them, many of them were quite ruined and occasioned a great expence of Canvas & time to make them in some degree serviceable. This complaint of our sail rooms we experienced on my late Voyage and was represented to the yard officers who undertook to remove it, but it did not appear to me that any thing had been done that could answer that end. To repair these defects the Caulkers were set to work as soon as we got into fair settled Weather, to caulk the Decks and inside Weather works of the Ship, for I would not trust them over the side while at sea.

On Sund September the first we cross'd the Equator in the Longitude of 27°38′ W with a fine gentle gale at SEbS and notwithstanding my apprehensions of falling in with the Coast of Brazil in stretching to the SW I kept the Ship a full point from the wind. I however found my fears were ill grounded for on drawing near that coast we found the Wind more and more Easterly, so that by the time we were in the Lat. of 10° South we could make a South Easterly course good.

*   *   *

[OCTOBER]

Thurs. 17   On the 17th we had sight of the Cape of Good Hope and
Frid. 18   the next day anchored in Table Bay in 4 fathom Water with
the Church bearing sw¼s and green point nw¼w. As soon as we
had received the usual Visit from the Master attendant & the Surgeon,
I sent an officer to wait on the governor Baron Plettenburg, and on
his return saluted the garrison with 13 guns, which complement was
returned with the same number. . . .

As soon as we had saluted I went on shore accompaned by some
of my officers and waited on the governor, Mr Hemmy the Second
governor, Mr   the fiscall and Major Prhen the Commander
of the troops; these gentlemen received me with the greatest civility
and the Governor on his part promised me every assistance that the
place afforded. At the same time I obtained leave to set up our
observatory wherever I thought proper, tents for the Sailmakers and
Coopers and to bring the Cattle on shore to graze near our tents, and
before I returned on board order'd soft bread, fresh meat and Greens
to be provided every day for the ships company.

*   *   *

[NOVEMBER]

SUNDAY 10th. In the Morning of the 10th the Discovery arrived in the
bay, Captain Clerke informed me that he sailed from Plymouth on
the 1st of August and should have arrived a Week sooner but for the
late gale of Wind which blew him off the Coast.

MONDAY 11th. Captain Clerke having reported the Discovery in want
of caulking, and as this service was performed to the Resolution I sent
all my Caulkers on board her and gave him every other assistance he
wanted to get on board his provisions and Water; having given him
an order to take on board as much of both articles as he could
conveniently stow. I now found that the Bakers had failed in bakeing
the bread I had ordered for the Discovery; they pretended they wanted
flour, but the truth was they were doubtfull of her coming and did
not care to begin till they saw her at Anchor in the Bay.

I have before made mention of our geting our cattle on shore, the Bull and two Cows with their Calves were sent to graze along with some other Cattle, but the sheep sixteen in Number I was advised to keep by our tents, where they were pen'd up every night. The night preceding the 14th some person or persons put some dogs in a mongst them which forced them out of the Pen kill'd four and dispersed the rest; six were found the next day but the two Rams and   Thurs. 14 two of the finest ewes in the whole flock were amongst those missing. This was sufficient to confirm the general opinion that the Dogs were put in to disperse them with a view of having an oppertunity to carry off these very sheep. . . .

SATURDAY 23rd. Got on board the observatory, Clock &cᵃ. By a mean of the several results of the equal altitudes of the Sun taken with the astronomical Quadᵗ the astronomical Clock was found to lose on Siderial time 1'8",368 per day: the Pendulum was kept at the same length as at Greenwich where the clock lost 4"   on siderial time per day. The Watch by the mean of the results of fifteen days observations was found to be losing 2",261 on mean time per day, 1".052 more than at Greenwich, and on the 21st at Noon she was too slow for mean time by 1ʰ20'57",66 from which 6'38",956 is to be substracted for what she was too slow on June the 11th and her daily rate sence and the remainder viz. 1ʰ14'08",704 or 18°32'10" will be the Longitude of the Cape Town by Watch. Its true Longitude as found by Messʳˢ Mason and Dixon is 18°23'15". As our observations were made about half a mile to the East of thiers, consequently the error of the Watch in longitude is no more than 8'25"; hence we have reason to conclude that she had gone well all the way from England and that the longitude given by it may be nearer the truth that any other. If this is admited it will in a great measure inable me to find the direction and strength of the Currents we met with on this passage, for by comparing the Latitude and longitude by dead reckoning with those by observation and the Watch, we shall have very accurately from time to time the error of the Ships reckoning, be the cause what it will; but as all imagineable care was taken in heaving and keeping the log and every necessary allowance made for lee way, heave of the Sea &cᵃ I cannot attribute those errors that did happen to anything else but currents. But more particularly when the error was constantly the same way for several days successively; if on the Contrary we find the Ship ahead of the reckoning on one day and a stern of it on another we have reason to believe that such errors are owing to accidental causes and not to currents. . . .

After the disaster which happened to our sheep, it may well be supposed I did not let those that remained stay long on shore, but got them and the other Cattle on board imidiately. To which I added two young Bulls, two Heifers, two young stone Horses, two Mares, two Rams, several Ewes and Goats and some Rabbits and Poultry, all of them intended for New Zealand, Otaheite and the neighbouring islands, or any other place we might meet, where there was a prospect that the leaving of some of them might prove usefull to posterity.

Towards the latter end of the Month the Discovery was caulked and had got on board all her Provisions and Water, of the former we had for two years and upwards and every other necessary thing we could think of for such a Voyage, neither knowing when nor where we should come to a place where we could supply our selves so well.

SATURDAY 30*th*. Having given Captain Clerke a Copy of my Instructions and an order how to proceed in case of separation, we in the Morning of the 30th repaired on board and at 5 in the afternoon a breeze sprung up at SE with which we weighed and stood out of the bay. . . .

[DECEMBER]

THURSDAY 12*th*. On the 12th at Noon we saw land extending from SEbS to SEbE which upon a nearer approach we found to be two Islands. . . . The distance from the one to the other is about 5 leagues, we pass'd through this Channel at equal distance from both, and could not discover with the assistance of our best glasses either tree or shrub on either of them. They seem'd to have a rocky and bold shore and excepting the SE parts where the land is rather low and flat, a surface composed of barren mountains which rise to a considerable hieght, and whose sumits and sides were covered with snow. . . . These islands as also four others which lie from 9° to 12 degrees of longitude more to the East and nearly in the same latitude, were discovered by Captains Morion & Crozet Frenchman in Jan^ry 1772, on their passage from the Cape of Good Hope to Manila. . . . As thise islands have no name in the French Chart, I shall distinguish the two we have seen by the name of *Prince Edward Islands* after His Majestys 4th Son and the others *Morion* and *Crozets* Islands. After leaving Prince Edward Islands I shaped my Course to pass to the Southward of the others and to get into the Latitude of the land discovered by M. *Kerguelen.* We had for the Most part Strong gales between the North and West and but very indifferent weather, not better than we generally have in England in the very depth of Winter. . . .

We had now much foggy weather, and as we expected to fall in with the land every hour, our Navigation became both tedious and dangerous. At length on the 24th as we were Steering to the Eastward, the fog clearing away a little, we saw land bearing sse which upon a nearer approach we found to be an Island of considerable height and about 3 leagues in circuit. Soon after we saw a nother of the same Magnitude one league to the Eastward, and between them in the direction of se some smaller ones and in the direction of sbe½e from the East end of the first Island a third high island was seen and at times, as the fog broke away, we thought we saw land over the small islands which I had thoughts of steering for by runing in between the islands.[4] But on drawing near them, I found this would be a dangerous attempt while the Weather continued foggy, for if there was no passage or we should meet with any sudden danger, we should not be able to get off, as the wind was right on and there run a prodigious sea that broke on all the shores in a frightfull surf; and seeing a nother island in the ne direction and not knowing but there might be more I thought proper to haul off and wait for clearer weather least we should get intangled amongst the islands in a thick fog. We did but just weather the island last mentioned; it is a high round rock which was named Bligh's Cap, perhaps it is the same as M. de Kerguelen calls the isle of Rendez-vouz, but I know nothing

Tues. 24

4. The islets to the north-west of the main Kerguelen Island.

that can Rendezvouz at it but fowls of the air, for it is certainly inaccessible to every other animal. . . .

We had no sooner get off the Cape[5] than we observed the Coast to the Southward to be much indented by projecting points and bays so that we made sure of soon finding a good harbour, and did not run a mile farther before we discovered one behind the Cape into which we began to ply; but after makeing one board it fell Calm and we anchored at the entrance in 45 fathom water the bottom black sand, as did the Discovery also soon after. I immidiately dispatched Mr Bligh the Master in a boat to Sound the Harbour, who on his return reported it to be safe and commodious with good anchorage in every part, and great plenty of fresh Water, Seals, Penguins and other birds on the shore but not a stick of Wood. While we lay at Anchor we observed the flood tide came from the SE and to run 2 knots an hour at least.

WEDNESDAY 25*th*. At day break in the Morning of the 25th we weighed and with a gentle breeze at west worked into the harbour to within a quarter of a mile of the sandy beach at the head, where we anchored in 8 fathom water, the bottom a fine dark sand. The Discovery did not get in till 2 o'clock in the after-noon. . . .

As soon as we had anchored I ordered all the boats to be hoisted out, the Ship to be moored with a Kedge anchor and the water casks to be got ready to send on shore. In the Mean time I went a shore to look for the most convenient place to fill them and to see what else the place afforded. I found the shore in a manner covered with Penguins and other birds and Seals, but these were not numerous, but so fearless that we killed as ma[n]y as we chose for the sake of their fat or blubber to make Oil for our lamps and other uses. Fresh water was in no less plenty than birds for every gully afforded a large Stream, but I found not a single tree or shrub nor the least signs of any, and very little herbage of any sort; tho appearences had flattered us with meeting with something considerable, by observing the sides of many of the hills to be of a lively green, but this was occasioned by a single plant which with the other natural productions shall be mentiond in a nother place. Before I came on board I ascended the

5. Cap Français.

first ridge of rocks, which rise in a kind of amphitheatre one above another, in order to have a View of the Country, but before I got up there came on so thick a fog that I could hardly find my way down again. . . .

THURSDAY 26*th*. The Morning proved foggy with rain, we nevertheless went to work to fill Water and to cut grass for our Cattle which we found in small spots near the head of the harbour. The rain which fell to day swelled all the Rivulets to that degree, that the sides of the hills bounding the harbour seemed to be covered with a sheet of Water; for the interior parts being nothing but a bare rock, the rain as it fell run into the fissures and crags of the rocks and was precipitated down the hills in prodigious turrents.

FRIDAY 27*th*. The people having worked hard the preceding day and nearly compleated our Water, I gave them this to celibrate Christmas. Many of them went on shore and made excursions in different directions into the Country which they found barren and desolate in the highest degree. In the evening one of them brought me a bottle he had found hanging to a rock on the north side of the harbour, in which was the following inscription written on parchment (viz)

> *Ludovico XV galliarum*
> *rege. et d. de Boynes*
> *regi a Secretis ad res*
> *maritimas annis 1772 et*
> *1773*

This Inscription must have been left here by M de Bougueneuc who landed on this land the 13th of Feb. 1772, the same day that M de Kerguelen discover'd it as appears by a note in the French Chart of the Southern Hemisphere published the following year. After causing the following Inscription to be written on the other side viz

> *Naves Resolution*
> *& Discovery*
> *de Rege Magnæ Brittaniæ*
> *Decembris 1776.*

I put it again into a bottle together with a Silver 2 penny piece of 1772 covered the mouth of the bottle with a leaden cap and the next morning placed it in a pile of stones errected for the purpose on a little eminence on the north shore of the harbour and near to the place where it was first found, and where it cannot escape the Notice of any European who either chance or disign may bring into this port. Here I display'd the British flag and named the harbour Chrismas harbour as we entered it on that Festival.[6]

* * *

[*Cook spent several days exploring the northern coast of the island, 'which from its stirility I shall call the Island of Desolation' – not knowing apparently that that was precisely what Kerguélen had named it. He took leave of it on 30 December.*]

After leaving the Island of Desolation I steer'd EBN intend to touch next at New Zealand, to recrute our Water, take in Wood and make hay for the Cattle. Their number by this time were considerably reduced, the two young bulls and one of the heifers were dead; as also the two rams and most of the goats.

TUESDAY 31*st*. The 31st in the Morning, being the day after we left the land, we had several observations of the Sun and Moon: thier results gave the Longitude 72°33′36″ E: the Timekeeper at the same time gave 72°38′15″ E. These observations were the more usefull as we had not had any for some time before, and served to assure us that no material error had crept into the Timekeeper.

* * *

1777
[JANUARY]

We continued our Course to the Eastward without meeting with any
Sun. 19   thing worthy of note till 4 oclock in the Morning of the 19th when in a sudden squal of wind the Fore Topmast went by the board and carried the Main Topg^t mast with it: this occasioned some delay, as it took us up the whole day to clear the wreck fit and get up another

6. It was Kerguélen's Baie de l'Oiseau.

topmast. The former was accomplished without losing any part of it except a few fathoms of sm¹ rope. The Main-top gallant we could not replace, as we had neither a spare one on board nor a spar to make one. The Wind continued Westerly blew a fresh gale and was attended with clear weather, so that scarce a day passed without our get[ting] observations for the Longitude and Variation of the Compass. The latter decreased in such a manner that in the Latitude of 44°18′ s, long. 132°2′ E it was no more than 5°34′18″ w and in the lat. of 43°27′ s, long. 141°50′ E it was 1°24′15″ East; so that we had crossed the line where the Compass has no variation.

FRIDAY 24*th*. On the 24ᵗʰ at 3 AM we made the Coast of Van Diemen land, bearing N½w: at 4 the sw Cape bore NNW½w and the Mewstone NEBE three leagues distant. . . .

At 6 PM sounded and found 60 fathˢ over a bottom of broken Coral & shells; the SE Cape bore N 75° W 2 or 3 leagues distant, Tasmans head NE and Swilly rock SBW½w. About a league to the Eastward of Swilly isle or rock, is a nother elevated rock that is not taken notice of by Captain Furneaux; I called it the Eddystone from its very great resemblence to that light house. Nature seems to have left these two rocks here for the same purpose that the Eddystone light house was built by man, viz to give navigators notice of the dangers about them, for they are the elevated summits of a ledge of rocks under water on which the sea in many places breakes very high: their surface is white with the dung of Sea fowl, so that they may be seen some distance even in the night. . . .

Soon after we made the land, the westerly winds left us and were succeeded by Variable light airs and Calms by turns till the 26ᵗʰ at Noon, when a breeze Sprung up and freshened at SE   Sun. 26 and put it [in] my power to carry into execution a design I had formed of puting into Adventure Bay to get a little Wood and some grass for our Cattle both of which we were in great want of. We therefore stood for the Bay, in which we anchored at 4 in the afternoon in 12 fathom Water over a bottom of Sand and owse. . . .

As soon as we had anchored I ordered the boats to be hoisted out, in one of which I went to looke for the most convenient place to supply our selves with what we wanted and Capt. Clerke went in his boat on the same service. Wood and Water we found in plenty and Convenient enough, especially the first, but grass, which we most wanted, was scarce and not good; necessity however obliged us to take such as we could get.

MONDAY 27th. Early in the Morning I sent Lieutenant King to the East side of the bay with two parties, one to cut wood and the other grass, under the protection of the Marines whom I sent as a guard, for altho' we had as yet seen none of the Inhabitants we however saw their smoaks but a little way up in the woods: I also sent the Launch for a turn of Water, and afterwards visited all the parties my self. In the evening we drew the Seine at the head of the bay and at one haul caught a great number of fish, and should have got many more had not the net broke in drawing it a shore by which accedent many were lost; the most of them were of that sort known to Seamen by the name of Elephant fish. After this every one repaired on board with what Wood & grass we had cut, so that we might be ready to sail whenever the wind served. This not happening the next Morning the people were sent on shore again on the same duty as the day before; I also sent the Carpenter with part of his crew to cut some Spars for the use of the Ship, and Mr Roberts, one of the Mates, in a small boat to survey the Bay.

Tues. 28 the wind served.

In the afternoon we were agreeably surprised at the place where we were cuting Wood, with a Visit from some of the Natives, Eight men and a boy: they came out of the Woods to us without shewing the least mark of fear and with the greatest confidence immaginable, for none of them had any weapons, except one who had in his hand a stick about 2 feet long and pointed at one end. They were quite naked & wore no ornaments, except the large punctures or ridges raised on the skin, some in straight and others in curved lines, might be reckoned as such: they were of the common stature but rather slender; their skin was black and also their hair, which was as woolly as any Native of Guinea, but they were not distinguished by remarkable thick lips nor flat noses, on the contrary their features were far from disagreeable; they had pretty good eyes and their teeth were tolerable

even but very dirty; most of them had their hair and beards anointed
with red ointment and some had their faces painted with the same
composition. They differ in many respects from the Inhabitants of the
more northern parts of this Country, nor do they seem to be that
miserable people Dampier mentions to have seen on the western coast.
They received every thing we gave them without the least appearence
of satisfaction; some bread was given them but as soon as they understood it was to eat, they either return'd it or threw it away without so
much as tasting it; and the same by fish either dress'd or undressed,
but birds they kept & gave us to understand they would eat them. I
shew'd them two Pigs I had brought a shore to leave in the woods,
the instant they saw them they seized [them] by the ears like a dog
and were for carrying them off immidiatily, with no other view as we
could perceive but to kill them. As I wanted to know the use of the
stick which one of them carried in his hand I made signs to them to
shew me, and so far succeeded that one of them set up a mark at
about 20 yards distance and threw at it, but did not seem to be a good
marks man: Omai to shew them how much superior our weapons were
to theirs, fired his musket at the Mark, on which they instantly
ran into the woods not withstanding all we could do or say to prevent
them: one of them was so frightened that he let drop an ax and two
knives that were given him. From us they went to the Watering place
where the Discoverys boat was taking in Water, the officer not knowing
they had been with us nor what thier intent might be fired a musket
in the air which sent them off as fast as their heels could carry them.

After they were gone I tooke the two Pigs a boar and a Sow, and
carried them about a mile within the woods at the head of the bay
and there left them by the side of a fresh Water brook. I did intend
to have left also a young Bull & Cow, some sheep and Goats, and
should have done it had I not been fully satisfied that the Natives
would distroy them, as I am persuaided they will do the Pigs if ever
they meet with them; but as this is an animal that soon becomes wild
and is fond of the thickest part of the woods, there is a great probability
of their escaping, whereas the other Cattle must have been left in an
open place where it would have been impossible for them to remain
concealed many days.

WEDNESDAY 29*th*. The Morning was ushered in with a dead Calm which continued all the day and effectually prevented our sailing; I therefore sent the grass Cutters over to the East point of the bay, where I was told there was some good grass, and the Wooding party to the usual place: with this party I went my self, as several of the Natives were at this time stroling along the shore. We had not be[en] long landed before about twenty of them men and boys joined us without expressing the least fear or distrust, some of them were the same as had been with us the day before, but the greatest part were strangers. There was one who was much deformed, being hump-backed, he was not less distinguishable by his wit and humour, which he shewed on all occasions and we regreted much that we could not understand him for their language was wholy unintilligible to us: it is different from that spoken by the inhabitants of the more Northern parts of this Country, which is not extraordinary sence they differ in many other respects. Some of these men wore loose round the neck 3 or 4 folds of small Cord which was made of the fur of some animal, and others wore a narrow slip of the Kanguroo skin tied round the ankle; these were all the ornaments I saw any of them wear.

I gave each of them a string of Beads and a Medal, which I thought they received with some satisfaction. They seem'd to set no value on Iron or Iron tools nor did they seem to know the use of fish hooks; yet we cannot suppose but that people who inhabit a Sea Coast must have ways and means to catch fish, altho we did not see it, nor did we see a Canoe or any Vessel in which they could go upon the water. Either fish is plenty with them or they do not eat it for they absolutely rejected all we offered them, but I think the first the most probable: it was evedent that shel fish made a part of their food by the many heaps of Muscle shels we saw in different parts near the shore and about some deserted habitations near the head of the bay. These were little Shades or hovels built of sticks and covered with bark; we also saw evedent signs of them some times takeing up their aboad in the trunks of large trees, which had been hollowed out by fire most probable for this very purpose. In or near all these habitations, and where ever there was a heap of shells there remained the marks of fire, an indubitable sign that they do not eat their food raw.

After staying about an hour with the Wooding party and the Natives and finding that the latter was not likely to give the former any disturbance, I left them and went over to the party that were cuting grass and found they had met with a fine patch. After lading the boats I left that party and return'd on board to dinner, where Mr King arrived soon after; from whom I learnt that soon after I had left him several Women and Children made there appearance, and were interduced to him by some of the Men; he made them all presents of such trifles as he had about him, and the Men gave them the most of what they had got from me. The Women wore a Kanguroo skin in the same shape as it came from the animal, tied over the shoulder and round the waist, but it was evidently intended for no other purpose than for the conveniency of carrying the child, for in all other respects they [are] as naked as the men, and as black, with hair of the same Colour & texture. Some had their heads wholy shaved, some only on one side, while others again shaved all the upper part and leaving a circle of hair round the head as is the custom with some Fryers. Many of the Children had fine features and were thought pretty, but the Women, especially those advanced in years, were thought otherways; Some of the Gentlemen belonging to the Discovery I was told, paid their addresses and made them large offers which were rejected with great disdain whether from a sence of Verture or for fear of displeasing the Men I shall not pretend to determine. This thing was certainly not very agreeable to the latter, for an elderly man as soon as he observed it, ordered all the Women & Children away, which they obeyed, but not without some of them shewing a little reluctancy. This conduct to Indian Women is highly blameable, as it creates a jealousy in the men that may be attended with fatal consequences, without answering any one purpose whatever, not even that of the lover obtaining the object of his wishes. I believe it has generally been found amongst uncivilized people that where the Women are easy of access, the Men are the first who offer them to strangers, and where this is not the case they are not easily come at, neither large presents nor privacy will induce them to violate the laws of chastity or custom. This observation I am sure will hold good throughout all parts of the South

Sea where I have been, why then should men risk their own safety where nothing is to be obtained? . . .

Van diemen Land has been twice visited before, first by Captain Tasman who discovered it in November 1642, and by Captain Furneaux in Mar. 1773, I hardly need say it is the Southern point of New Holland, which if not a Continent is one of the largest islands in the World. The land is for the most part of a good height, diversified with hill and Vally and every where of a greenish hue, it is well wooded and if one may judge from appearences and what we met with in Adventure Bay, not badly watered. . . .

THURSDAY 30*th*. At eight o'clock in the Morning of the 30th, a light breeze springing up at West we weighed and put to sea. Soon after the wind veered to the Southward and increased to a perfect storm; in the evening its fury abated and it veer'd to the East & NE. This gale was indicated by the fall of the Barometer, but the Wind no sooner began to blow than the marcury in the tube began to fall: a nother remarkable thing attended the coming on of this wind which was very faint at first, it brought with it a degree of heat that was almost intolerable, the Mercury in the Thermometer rose almost in an Instant from about 70° to near 90°: this heat was of so short a continuance that it seemed to be wafted away before the breeze that brought it, so that some on board did not perceive it.

FEB^ry   We persued our course to the Eastward without meeting with any thing worthy of note, till the night between the 6th & 7th of Feb^ry, when a Marine belong^g to the Discovery fell over board and was never seen afterwards: this was the second Marine Captain Clerke had had the Missfortune to lose sence he left England.

MONDAY 10*th*. On the tenth at 4 PM we discovered the land of New Zealand, it proved to be Rocks point[7] and bore SEBS about 8 or 9 leagues distant. . . .

TUESDAY 11*th*. After makeing the land I steered for Cape Farewell, which at day break the next Morning bore SBW distant about four leagues, at 8 o'clock it bore SWBS about five leagues distant and in

7. On the west coast of South Island, some 45 miles south of Cape Farewell.

this situation we had 45 fathom water over a sandy bottom; in rounding the Cape we had 50 fathom, the same sort of bottom.

I now steered for Stephens's island which we came up with at 9 PM and at 10 the next Morning anchored in our old station Wed. 12 in Queen Charlottes Sound. In the after noon we got a number of empty Water Casks on shore, cleared a place to set up the two observatories, and tents for the reception of a guard and such people whose business made it necessary for them to remain on shore.

We had not been long at anchor before several Canoes filled with natives came along side the Ships, but very few of them would venture on board; which appeared the more extraordinary, as I was well known to them all. There was one man amongst them, that I had treated with remarkable kindness during the whole of my stay when I was last here yet now neither professions of friendship nor presents would induce him to come into the ship. It appeared to me that they were apprehensive we were come to revenge the death of Captain Furneux's people: seing Omai on board whose first conversation with them generally turned on that subject; they must be well assured that I was no longer a stranger to that unhappy affair, and I did all in my power to assure them of the continuance of my friendship, and that I should not disturb them on that account. I do not know whether or no this had any weight with them, but certain it is that they very soon laid a side almanner of restraint and distrust.

THURSDAY 13*th*. . . . For the protection of the party on shore I appointed a guard of ten Marines and ordered arms for all the workmen, and Mr King and two or three petty officers remained constantly with them. A boat was never sent any considerable distance from the Ships without being armed, and under the direction of such officers as I could depend upon and who were well acquainted with the Natives. Some of these were precautions I had never taken before in this place, nor were they, I firmly beleive, more necessary now, but after the sacrifice which the Natives made of the boats crew belonging to the Adventure in this place, and the French in the Bay of islands[8]

---

8. Marion du Fresne and his men, in June 1772.

it was impossible, totally, to divest our selves of apprehinsions of the same Nature.

If the Natives had any suspicion of our revenging these acts of Barbarity, they very soon laid it aside, for during the course of this day a great many Families came from different parts and took up their residence by us; so that their was not a place in the Cove where a Hut could be built that was not occupied by some or another: the place where we had fixed our little incampment they left us in quiet possession of, but they came and took away the remains of old huts that were there. . . .

Besides the people who took up their aboad by us, we were occasionally visited by others whose residence was not far off, and other who lived more remote. Their articles of commerce were Curiosities, Fish and Women the two first always came to a good market, which the latter did not: the Seamen had taken a kind of dislike to these people and were either unwilling or affraid to associate with them; it had a good effect as I never knew a man quit his station to go to their habitations. A connection with Women I allow because I cannot prevent it, but never encourage tho many Men are of opinion it is one of the greatest securities amongst Indians, and it may hold good when you intend to settle amongst them; but with travelers and strangers, it is generally otherwise and more men are betrayed than saved by having connection with their women, and how can it be otherwise sence all their View are selfish without the least mixture of regard or attatchment whatever; at least my observations which have been pretty general, have not pointed out to me one instance to the contrary.

Amongst those occasional Visiters was a Chief named *Kahoura* who headed the party that cut off Captain Furneux's boat and who himself killed the officer that commanded. To judge of the character of this man by what some of his Country said of him, he seemed to be a man more feared than beloved by them: many of them said he was a very bad man and importuned me to kill him, and I beleive they were not a little surprised that I did not, for accord[ing] to their ideas of equity this ought to have been done. But if I had followed the advice of all our pretended friends, I might have extirpated the whole race, for the people of each Hamlet or village by turns applyed to me to distroy the other, a very striking proof of the divided state in which they live. We could not misunderstand them as Omai who understood their language perfectly well was our interpreter.

*　　*　　*

SUNDAY 16*th*. The 16th at day break, I set out with a party of Men in five boats, accompaned by two of the Natives, Omai, Captain Clerke and several of the officers, to collect grass, we proceeded about three leagues up the Sound and then landed on the East side, at a place I had formerly been, and where we cut as much as laded the two launches. We next proceeded down to Grass Cove, remarkable for being the place where the Natives cut off Captain Furneaux's boat; here I met with my old friend Pedro who was almost continually with me the last time I was in this Sound; he and a nother man received us on the beach armed with the Pat-too and spear, whether out of courtesy or causion I cannot say, but I thought they shewed manifest signs of fear. However if they had any a few presents soon removed them and brought down two or three more of the family but the greatest part of them remained out of sight.

Whilst we were at this place our curiosity prompt[ed] us to enquire the reason why our country men were killed, and Omai put several questions to Pedro and those about him on that head, all of which they answered without reserve, and like people who are under no apprehenson of punishment for a crime they are not guilty of, for we already k[n]ew that none of these people had any hand in this unhappy affair. They told us that while our people were at victuals with several of the natives about them some of the latter stole or snatched from them some bread, & fish for which they were beat this being resented a quarrel insued, in which two of the Natives were shot dead, by the only two Muskets that were fired, for before they had time to discharge a third or load those that were fired they were all seized and knocked on the head. They pointed to the place of the Sun when this happened, and according to it it must have been late in the afternoon: they also shewed us the spot where the boats crew sat at Victuals, and the place where the boat laid which was about two hundred yards from them with Captain Furneaux's black servant in her. We were afterwards told that he was the cause of the quarrel, which happened thus; one of the Natives stealing some thing out of the boat, he struck him a heavy blow with a stick on which the fellow called out to his country men that he was killed, on this they all rose and fell upon the unhappy suffer[er]s who before they had time to recover the boat or arm themselves against the impending danger, fell a sacrifice to savage fury. The first of these accounts was confirm'd by the testimony of many people who I think, could have no intrest in deceiving us, the second we had from a young man who went away with us and therefore could certainly have none. As all agree that the quarrel happen'd while the boats crew were at Victuals, it is highly probable that both accounts are true, for nothing is more likely, than whilst some were stealing from the Man in the boat others were doing the same thing from those on shore. Be this as it will, all agree that the quarrel first took its rise from some thefts which they (the Natives) commited, all agree also, that the thing was not premeditated, and that if these thefts had not, unfortunately, been too hastily resented no ill consequence had attended, for Kahoura's greatest enemies, those who solicited his distruction the most, owned that he had no intention to quarrel, much less to kill till the quarrel was actually commenced. It also appears that the unhappy Victims were under no sort of apprehensions of their impending fate otherwise they never would have sat down to a repast so far from thier boat amongst people who the next Moment were to be their butcherer's. . . .

* * *

FRIDAY 21*st*. . . . By this time more than two thirds of the inhabitants of the Sound were settled about us, and great numbers daily frequented the Ships, and the incampment on shore, what partly induced them to resort to the latter more than usual, was some Seal blubber we were melting down. No Greenlander can be fonder of train oil than these people, the very dregs of the casks and skimings of the kettle they eat, but a little pure oil was a feast they seemed not often to enjoy.

Sun. 23   Having got on board as much hay and grass as was thought sufficient to serve the Cattle to Otaheite, and compleated the wood and water of both ships, we struck the tents and got every thing off from the shore, and the next morning weighed and stood   Mon. 24 out of the Cove. But as the wind was not very favourable, and finding that the Tide of Ebb would be spent before we could get out of the Sound, I came to an anchor a little without the island Motuara to wait for a more favourable oppertunity to put into the Strait. . . .

We had not been long at anchor before three or four Canoes filled with Indians came off to us from the SE side of the Sound and traded away divers curiositys. In one of the Canoes was Kahourah, the Chief who headed the party that cut of Captain Furneaux's people. This was the third visit he had paid us without shewing the least mark of fear, I was a shore when he came but got on board just as he was going away; Omai, who was with me, presently pointed him out, and wanted me to shoot him, he even threatened to do it himself if ever he came again. The chief paid so little regard to these threats that he returned the next Morning with his whole Family, Men   Tues. 25 Women and Children to the number of twenty and upwards. Omai was the first who acquainted me with his coming and desired to know if he should ask him on board. I told him he might and accordingly he interduced him into the Cabbin, saying 'there is Kahourah kill him' but as if he would have no hand in it himself, retired immidiately, but returned again in a short time and seeing the chief unhurt, said 'why do not you kill him, you till me if a man kills an other in England he is hanged for it, this Man has killed ten and yet you will not kill him, tho a great many of his countrymen desire it and it would be very good'. Omais arguments, tho reasonable enough, having no weight with me, I desired him to ask the cheif why he killed Captain Furneaux's people, at this Question he folded his arms hung down his head and looked like one caught in a trap; And I firmly believe expected every moment to be his last, but was no sooner assured of his safety than he became cheerfull, yet did not seem willing to answer the question that had been put to him, till I had again and again assured him he should not be hurt. Then he ventured to till us, that on offering a stone hatchet for sale to one of the people, he kept it and would give nothing in return, on which they snatched from them some bread while they were at victuals. The remainder of his account of this unhappy affair differed very little from what we had been told by other people, but the story of the Hatchet was certainly invented by Kahourah to make the English appear the first agressors.

This man would have been one of those that were shot dead, but hiding himself behind the boat was not seen, so that a nother man was killed who stood behind him; as soon as the musket was discharged, he instantly seized the oppertunity to attack Mr Rowe, who commanded the party and who defended himself with his Hanger (with which he wounded Kahourah in the Arm) till over powered by numbers. What became of the boat I never could learn, some said she was pulled to pieces and burnt, others said she was carri'd they knew not where by a party of strangers. Thus I have related the whole I was able to learn of this Melancholy affair, and for which the perpretrators have escaped unpunished for they received no hurt from the party which Captain Furneaux sent the next day to look for his people, under the Command of Lieut^t Burney, for according to the account of the Indian's not one of the Shot which they fired took effect.

It was evident that most of the Inhabitants, after seeing Omai on board and therefore could no longer doubt of my being fully acquainted with the whole subject, expected I should revenge it with the death of Kahourah at least, and many of them seemed not only to wish it but surprized I did not. As he could not be ignorant of this it was a matter of wonder to me that he put himself so often in my power; in the visits he made us in Ship Cove he might [have] confided in the number of his friends that accompaned him, but this could not possibly have any weight with him in the two last visits he made us; we were then at anchor in the entra[n]ce of the Sound some distance from any shore, so that he neither could escape nor have any assista[n]ce from thence, had I thought proper to [have] detained him. But after his first fears were over he was so far from shewing any uneasiness, that on seeing a Portrait of one of his countrymen hanging up in the Cabbin, he desired to be drawn, and sat till Mr Webber had finished without the least restraint. I must confess I admired his courage and was not a little pleased at the confidence he put in me. Perhaps in this he placed his whole safety, for I had always declared to those who solicited his death that I had always been a friend to them all and would continue so unless they gave me cause to act otherwise; as to what was past, I should think no more of it as it was some time sence and done when I was not there, but if ever they made a Second attempt of that kind, they might rest assured of feeling the weight of my resentment.

For some time before we arrived at New Zealand Omai had express'd a desire to take one of the Natives with him to his own Country. We had not been there many days before he had an oppertunity to gratify his desire, by a youth about 17 or 18 years of age, named *Tiarooa* offering to accompany him and took up his residence on board. At first I thought little of it, thinking he would leave us when we were about to depart and after he had got what he could from Omai. At length seeing he was fixed on going, and finding he was the only Son of a Chief who some years before had fallen a sacrifice to their Savage Custom and that his Mother, still living, was a Woman much respected amongst them, I was apprehensive Omai had deceived both him and his friends by a promise of returning back: I therefore caused it to be made known to all of them that if he went away with us he would never return, but this seemed to make no sort of impression on either him or his freinds. The after noon before we left the Cove *Tiratoutou* his Mother came on board to receive her last present from Omai; the same evening she and Tiarooa parted with all the Marks of tender affection that might be expected between a Mother and her Son who were never to meet again. But she said she would cry no more, and sure enough she kept her word, for when she came the next morning to take her last farewell of him, she remained all the time she was on board quite cheerfull and went away wholy unconcerned. That Tiarooa might be sent away in a manner becoming his birth, a nother youth was to have gone with him as his servant and with this view, as we supposed, he remained on board till we were about to sail when his friends took him a shore. His place was however supplyed by a nother the next Morning, a boy about 9 or 10 years of age named *Coaa*, he was presented to me by his own Father with far less[9] indifference than he would have parted with his dog; the very little cloathing the boy

---

9. The word 'less' is presumably a slip for 'more'.

had he took from him and left him as naked as he was born. It was to no purpose my endeavouring to convince these people of the improbability or rather impossibility of these youths ever returning, Not one, even their nearest relations seemed to trouble themselves about what became of them. Sence this was the case I was well satisfied the boys would not be losers by exchange of place, and therefore the more readily gave my consent to their going.

*   *   *

On Tuesday the 25th at 10 AM a light breeze springing up at NWBN, we weighed, stood out of the Sound and made sail through the Strait with the Discovery in Company. We had hardly got the length of Cape Tierawhitte, before the Wind took us aback at SE; where it continued till two oclock the next Morning when we had a few hours Calm, after which we had a breeze at North: but it continued not long before it veered to the East and after that to South. At length Thur. 27   on the 27th at 8 AM we took our departure from Cape Palliser which at this time bore West 7 or 8 leagues distant, we had a fine gale and I steered EBN.

We had no sooner lost sight of the land than our two Adventurers, what from Sea sickness and reflection, repented heartily of the step they had taken, all the soothing incouragement we could think of availed but little; they wept both in publick, and in private and made their lamentations in a kind of song, which so far as we could understand of it was in praze of their Country and people they should never see more. Thus they continued for many days, till their Sea sickness wore of, and the tumult of their minds began to subside, these fits of lamentation became less and less frequent and at length quite went of, so that their friends nor their Native country were no more thought of and were as firmly attatched to us as if they had been born amongst us.

*   *   *

[*Because of unhelpful winds, progress to the north was very slow. 'My proceeding to the North depended entirely on my making a quick passage to Otaihete or the Society islands,' Cook wrote on 17 March. New islands were discovered in the group later known as the Cook Islands – first Mangaia, then Atiu. At Atiu a strong landing party spent an extremely uncomfortable day, imprisoned by the curious crowd. In neither place did Cook manage to get the replenishments he urgently needed – especially provision for the animals. Scurvy-grass and coconuts gathered further north, on Takutea, did not alter the situation. Cook now headed for the Hervey Islands, seen on the second voyage, which they wrongly believed to be uninhabited. They reached Manuae on 6 April, and King was sent to find an anchorage. He reported that there was none, and that the ships would have to lie outside the reef.]*

[APRIL]

Having received this report, I considered that as the Ships could not be brought to an anchor the procuring grass here would be very tedious as well as attended with some danger; besides we were equally in want of Water, and the inhabitants had told us there was water on the island yet we neither knew in what quantity nor how far we might have to fetch it and after all we should find it both difficult and tedious to get over the reef. Being thus disapointed at all these islands, and the summer in the northern Hemisphere already too far advanced for me to think of doing any thing there this year, It was therefore absolutely necessary to persue such methods as was most likely to preser[v]e the Cattle we had on board in the first place, and save the Ships stores and Provisions in the second the better to enable us to procecute the Discoverys in the high northern latitudes the ensuing summer. I intended to have stood back to the south till I had met with a westerly wind, provided I had got a supply of Water and grass at any of these islands; but the consequence of doing this without, would have been the loss of all the Cattle without gaining any one advantage. I therefore determined to bear away for the Friendly Isl^ds where I was sure of being supplied with every thing I wanted; and as it was necessary to run in the night as well as in the day, I ordered Capt. Clerke to keep about a league ahead of the Resolution, as his Ship could better claw of a lee shore than mine.

The Longitude of Harveys island (when first discover'd) deduced from Otaheite by the Time keeper, was found to be 201°06′ E and now by the same Time-keeper deduced from Queen Charlotte's Sound

200°56′ E, hence I concluded that the error of the time-keeper at this time did not exceed 12′ in longitude.

In order to save our Water I ordered the still to be kept at work from 6 in the Morning to four in the after noon, during which time we procured from 13 to 16 gallons of fresh Water: There has been lately made some improvement as they are pleased to call it, to this Machine, which in my opinion is much for the worse.

When we bore away I steered WBS with a fine breeze Easterly, intending to proceed first to Middleburg,[10] thinking if the wind continued we had food enough on board for the Cattle to last till we got there. But about Noon the next day we had again those faint breezes that had attended us so long, and I found it necessary to haul more to the North to get into the latitude of Palmerstone and Savage islands; that if necessity required it we might have recourse to them. These light breezes continued till the 10th when we had for some hours the Wind from the North and NNW a fresh breeze being then in the latitude of 18°38′, Longitude 198°24′ E. In the afternoon we had some Thunder squals from the South attend[ed] with heavy rain, five Puncheons of which water we collected. After these Squals had blown over, the wind came round to the NE and NW being very unsetled both in strength [and] position. At length about Noon the next day it fixed at NW & WNW and blew a fresh breeze with fair weather, thus we were persecuted with a Wind in our teeth which ever way we directed our course, and the farther Mortification to find here those very winds we had reason to expect 8° or 10° farther South. They came now too late for I durst not trust to their continuance and the event proved that I judged right.

Sun. 13   At length at day break in the Morning of the 13th we descried Palmerstone islands bearing WBS distant about five leagues.

Mon. 14   But it was eight oclock the next morning before we got up with it, when I sent four boats, three from the Resolution and one from the Discovery, with an Officer in each, to search the Coast for the most convenient landing place, for now we were under an absolute necessity of procuring from this island some food for the Cattle

10. Eua, in the Tongatapu group, southern Tonga.

otherwise we must lose them. The Boats first examined the S. Eastermost isle which compose this Group, and then ran down to the second where we had the satisfaction to see them land. I then bore down with the Ships, till abreast of the place, where we kept standing off and on, for no bottom was to be found to anchor upon; nor was this of much consequence as we were the only human beings upon the island. About 1 PM one of the boats came aboard, laden with scurvey grass and young Cocoanut trees which at this time was a feast for the cattle, the same boat brought a message from Mr Gore, who commanded the party, informing me that there was plenty of this on the island, as also of the Wharra tree and some Cocoanuts; this determined me to get a good supply of these articles before I quited the island. In the evening I went ashore in a small boat accompaned by Captain Clerke; we found every body hard at work, and the landing place to be in a small creek, formed by the reef, of something more than a boats length in every direction, and covered from the force of the Sea by rocks projecting out on each side of it. After the boats were laden I returned on board leaving Mr Gore with a party on shore, in order to be ready to go to work early the next morning, Tues. 15 being the 15th and which was spent in collecting and bringing on board food for the Cattle, consisting chiefly, of Palm Cabbage, young Cocoanut trees, and the tender branches of the Wharra tree, there not being a blade of common grass on the island. Having got a sufficient Supply, by sunset I ordered every body on board; but having little or no Wind, I determined to wait till the next day and endeavour to get some Cocoanuts from the next island, to leeward, where the trees appeared to be numerous. With this view I kept stand[ing] off and on all night, and in the Morning I went with the boats Wed. 16 to the West side of the isle, landed with little difficulty and set the people with me to gather Cocoa[nu]ts which we found in great abundance; but the worst was we had to carry them a full half mile over the reef up to the middle in Water to the boats, which took up a great deal of our time. Omai who was with me, caught with a scoop net in a very short time as much fish as served the whole party for dinner, beside sending some to both ships; here were also great abundance of birds particularly Men of War and Tropic birds, so that we on shore fared sumptuously. The boats made two trips before night, with the last I returned on board, leaving Mr Williamson with a party on shore.

THURSDAY 17*th*. At 7 AM sent the boats again a Shore and they returned laden by noon, when they were again despatched a second time with orders for every body to be on board by sunset, which being complied with we hoisted in the boats and made sail to the Westward with a light air of wind from the northward. At this last isle we got about 1200 cocoanuts which were equally divided amongst the whole Crew and proved of no small use to them. What is comprehended under the name of *Palmerstone Island*, is a group of small Isles of which there are in the whole nine or ten, laying in circular direction and connected together by a reef of Coral rock, of which they may be reckoned the heads or summits, covered only with a thin Coat of Sand, yet cloathed with trees and Plants of which there are in the whole about

and the most of them such as are found on the low ground of the high islands. The only animals we saw were Sea birds Land crabs, Lizards and a few rats. We found on the shore some pieces of a Canoe and broken paddles, but saw no traces of inhabitants or any human being having been there before us. . . .

After leaving Palmerstone Island I steered west with a view of making the best of my way to Annamocka. We still continued to have variable Winds, frequently between the North and West, with Squals, thunder and much rain. During these Showers which were generally very copious we saved a good quantity of water; and finding we could get more by the rain in an hour than by the still in a Month, I laid it aside as a thing attended with more trouble than profit.

Thur. 24   In the night between the 24th and 25th we pass'd Savage
Fri. 25   island, and on the 28th at 10 AM we made the islands which
Mon. 28   lay to the Eastward of Anamocka, bearing WBN about 4 or 5 leagues distant. I steered to the South of these islands and then hauled up for Anamocka, which at 4 PM bore NWbN, Tellefages SWBS and Comango NBW distant about five miles.[11] The Weather being

11. Annamocka (Tasman's Rotterdam) is Nomuka, Tellefages is Kelefesia, Comango is Mango, all in the central Tongan group.

Squally with rain, I anchored at the approach of night in 15 fathom water over a bottom of Coral sand and Shells, Comango bearing NW about 2 leagues distant. Soon after we had Anchored, we caught with hook and line a good quantity of fish and the inhabitants of the island brought off a few Cocoanuts and bread fruit which they exchanged for nails.

TUESDAY 29*th*. At 4 AM sent Lieutenant King with two boats to Comango to procure refreshments, and at 5 made the Signal weighed in order to ply up to Anamocka, the wind being at NW.

*   *   *

[MAY]

I came to an anchor in the very same place as I did when last here, viz, in 18 fathom Water, the bottom Coarse Coral sand; the island extending from E to SW and the West point of the Westermost Cove SE about ¾ of a mile dist[t]. The next morning while preparation Fri. 2 were making for Watering, I went ashore accompaned by Captain Clerke and some of the officers, to fix on a place to set up the observatories and to keep a guard, leave being soon obtained of the Natives who accomodated us with a boat house and shewed us every other Mark of civility. *Toobow* the Cheif of the island took me and Omai to his house, situated in a pleasent spot in the midst of his plantation, a fine grass plat lay round the [door?] which he gave us to understand was to clean their feet upon, a mark of cleanness I had no where observed in this sea before, but afterwards found it was very common at these islands. The floor of the house was laid with Mats and no carpet could be kept cleaner. While we were a shore we bartered for a few hogs and some fruit, and before we got on board the Ships were filled with the natives and as few came empty we found no want of anything. In the after noon I went ashore again with a party of Marines and such of the Cattle as were weak, I remained there till sunset when every thing be[ing] settled to my satisfaction I returned on board leaving the Command on shore to M[r] King. Tapa who was now become our fast friend and seemed to be the only active man about us, had a house brought on Mens shoulders a full quarter of a mile and placed by the one we occupied, in order to be near us as well in the night as day.

SATURDAY 3rd. Began to Water, cut wood, and make hay for the catle. We at first began to cut wood abreast of the Ship it being there in the greatest plenty and the most convenient to get on board, but it proved to be of the Mancheneel kind, yeilding a juice of a Milky colour & of so corrosive a nature that it raised blisters on the Skin and injured the eys of such of the workmen as it happened to fly upon; so that the wooding party were obliged to remove to the Cove where wee took off Water and kept guard, where the natives furnished us with other wood. Mr King and Mr Bailey began to observe equal altitudes of the sun in order to get the rate of the time keepers. . . .

Sun. 4   The Discoveries Small bower Cable parted, being cut in
Mon. 5   two by the rocks, this occasioned us to look at ours which
Tues. 6   were found unhurt. On the 6th we were Visited by a great Chief of Tongatabu, whose name was *Feenough*, and whom Tapah was pleased to interduce to us as King of all the friendly isles.[12] I was told that on my arrival a Canoe was despatched to that island with the news, which brought this Chief here. The Officer on shore told me, that when he first appeared all the natives were ordered out to meet him and paid their obeisance by bowing their heads to his feet, so that there was no room to suspect him being any thing less than the King.

In the after noon I went to pay this great man a visit, having first received a present of two fish from him sent me by one of his servants. As soon as I landed he came up to me and when the first salutation was over, I asked if he was the King, for seeing he was not the man I had seen before[13] I rather suspected it. Tapah answer'd for him, and enumerated one hundred and fi[f]ty three islands of which he said Feenough was the King. He and five or six of his attendants accompaned me on board where I made them all presents and entertained them in such a manner as I thought would be most agreeable, and in the evening attended them a shore in my boat, in to which the cheif ordered three hogs as a return for the presents I had made him. . . .

12. A formidable chief, but not king. [B]
13. On the second voyage.

The Discovery having recovered her small bower anchor Wed. 7
Shifted her birth, but not before the best bour Cable shared the same
fate as the other. Had the Company of Feenough to dinner, and also
the next day when he was attended by Tapah, Toobow and Thur. 8
some other Chiefs, none but Tapah was allowed to sit at table with
him or to eat in the same place; before his arrival I had generally,
what with men and Women a larger company than I could find room
for. It is not here as at Otaheite, for the women to be denied the
previledge of eating with the men. The first day of our arrival the
Indians stole out of the Ship a larg[e] Junk ax, I applied to Feenough
to have it again and it was brought on board while we were at dinner.
These people very frequently took oppertunities to shew us what expert
thieves they were, even some of the Cheifs did not think this profession
beneath them; one was caught carrying out of the Ship concealed
under his cloathes the bolt belonging to ye Spun yarn wench, for which
I ordered him a dozen lashes and made him pay a hog for his liberty,
after this we were not troubled with thieves of rank, their servants or
slaves were employed in this dirty work, on which a floging made no
more impression than it would have done upon the Main-mast; their
masters so far from making intrest for them when they were caught
would very often advise us to kill them, and as this was a punishment
we did not chouse to inflect they generally escaped unpunished,
because we could inflict nothing which they thought a punishment.
Capt. Clerke hit upon a method which had some effect, this was by
shaving their heads for though it is not a very uncommon thing to see
both men and women with their heads shaved, yet its being done on
this occasion was looked upon as a mark of infamy and marked out
the man. On the 10th Feenough dined on board as indeed he Sat. 10
did every day, after we had dined some of his servants brought on
board a mess for him, it consisted of fish soup and yams; the fish and
soup was brought off in a Plantain leafe. Instead of common water to
make the soup they had made use of Cocoanut water in which the
fish had been boiled or stewed; this was probably done in a wooden
vessel with hot stones. I tasted of it and found it so good that I had
afterwards fish dress'd the same way and found it very good though
my Cook did not come up to theres.

SUNDAY 11*th*. Finding that we had quite exhausted the island of all most every thing it produced I this day got every thing off from the shore, intending as soon as the Discovery had recovered her best bower anchor, to proceed to an island called Happi, laying to the NE where Feenough told me I should meet with every thing I wanted and strongly importuned me to go thither before I visited Tongatabu.

Mon. 12   The 12th and 13th was spent in recovering the Discoveries
Tues. 13   Anchor which was at last accomplished and on the 14th in
Wed. 14   the Morning we weighed anchor and steered for Aghao, with a view of passing to the NW of the small islands that lay to the North and NE of Anamocka, as I could not be assured of a passage amongst them. . . .

*   *   *

[*Cook sailed north round the Ha'apai group, with Finau in attendance — sometimes on board* Resolution, *sometimes in his canoe. The ships came to anchor at the northern end of Lifuka island.*]

SATURDAY 17*th*. . . . . By the time we had anchored the Ships were filled with the Natives and surrounded by a multitude of Canoes, filled also with them. They brought with them hogs, Fowls, fruit and roots which they exchanged for Hatchets, Knives, Nails, beads, Cloth &c[a]. Fenough and Omai having come on board soon after it was light in order to interduce me to the people ashore I now accompaned them to the isle for that purpose; The Chief conducted me to a house situated close to the Sea beach which I had seen brought thether but a few minutes before. In this we were seated that is The Chief, Omai and my self, the other chiefs, and the Multitude seated themselves in a circle without before us. I was then asked how long I intended to stay, on my saying five days, Tapah was order[ed] to come and sit by me and proclaime it to the people. He then Harangu'd them in a set speach mostly dictated by Feenough. The purport of this speach as I lear[n]t by Omai, was that all the people both young and old were to look upon me as a friend who was come to remain with them a few days, that they were not to steal or molest me in any thing, that they were to bring hogs, fowls, fruit &c[a] to the ships where they would receive in exchange such and such things. Soon after Tapah had done haranguing the people, Fenough left us and Tapah gave me to understand it necessary I should make a present to the Chief of the island whose name was *Earoupa*, I was not unprepared and made him a present that far exceeded his expectation, this brought upon me two Cheifs of other isles and lastly Tapah himself. When Feenough returned which was immidiately after I had made the last present, he pretended to be angry with Tapah for suffering me to give away so much, but I looked upon this to be all a feness. The Cheif again took his seat and ordered Earoupa to set by him and to harangue the people as Tapah had done, the subject was chiefly dictated by Feenough and was to the same effect as the other. . . .

SUNDAY 18*th*. Early in the Morning Omai, who generally slept ashore, and Feenough came on board. After some time I accompanied them ashore and was conducted to the same place as I was at the day before, where a large concourse of people were assembled, I guess'd some thing or another was going to be done but could not till what nor could Omai inform me. I had not sit long before near a hundred people came laden with Yams, Bread fruit, Plantain Cocoanuts and Sugar Cane which were laid in two heaps or piles on our left, being the side they came from. Soon after came a number of others from the right, laden with the same kind of articles which were laid in two piles on our right; to these were tied two Pigs and six Fowls, and to those on the left six Pigs and two turtle. Earoupa sat before the several arti[c]les on the left and a nother Chief before those on the right they being, as I judged, the two Chiefs who had collected them and being a kind of Tax Feenough had laid upon them for the present occasion. As soon as every thing was laid in order and to shew to the most advantage, those who had brought in the things joined the Multitude who formed a large circle round the whole. Presently after a number of men entered the Circle or Area before us, armed with Clubs made of the green branches of the Cocoanut tree, these paraded about for a few minutes and then retired the one half to one side and the other half to the other, and seated themselves before the spectators: but soon after went to single Combat, one or two steping forward from the one side and challenging those on the other which was done more by actions than words; if the Challenge was excepted, which was generally the case, each put himself in a proper atitude and began to engage and continued till one or the other gave out or their weapons were broke. When the contest was over, the Victor squated himself down facing the cheif then rose up and retired, at the same time some old men, who seemed to sit as judges, gave their plaudit in a few words and the multitude, especially those on the side to which the victor belonged, celebrated it in two or three huzzas. This entertainment was now and then suspended for a few minutes, at these intervals there were Wristling and Boxing matches; the first were performed in the same m[an]ner as at Otahiete, and the second very little different from the method practiced in England. But what struck us with the most surprise was to see a couple of lusty wenches step forth and without the least ceremony fall to boxing, and with a[s] much art as the men. The contest did not last above half a minute before one gave it up; the Victor received the aplause of the spectors in the same manner as the men. We expressed some dislike at this part of the entertainment, this however did not prevent two others from entering the list, who seemed to be girls of spirit and would certainly have given each other a good drubing had not two old Women got up and parted them. These several contests were carried on in the midst of at least three thousand people and with the greatest good humour on all sides, though some, Women as well as men must have received blows they must feel some time after. . . .

TUESDAY 20th. Fenough havi[ng] expressed a desire to see the Marines go through their exercize and being willing to gratify him, I ordered them all ashore from both ships in the Morning of the 20th. After they had gone through their exercize and fired several Volleys, the Cheif entertained us again in his turn with a sight intirely new. It was a kind of dance, performed by men and youths of the first rank; but so much unlike any thing I know of in any other part of the World, that no discription I can give will convey even a tolerable Idea of it. Any number may perform it, there were in this one hundred and five, each having in his hand an Instrument shaped something like a paddle of $2\frac{1}{2}$ feet in length, with a small handle and thin blade so that they were very light and the most of them neatly made. With these Instruments, they made many and various flourishes each of which was attended with a different attitude of the body and some different movement or a nother. They at first ranged themselves in three lines, and by different movements and motions each man changed his station in such a manner that those who were in the rear came in front. Nor did they remain long in the same form, but these changes were made by pretty quick movements; they at one time extended themselves in one line then formed into a semicircle and lastly into two square Columns, while this last was performing, one of them came and danced a harlequin dance before me with which the whole ended. The musick was two drums or rather two hollow logs of wood on each of which they beat with two sticks. It did not appear to me that the dance was much assisted or directed by this Musick, but by a Song in which every one joined as with one voice; it was musical and harmonious and all their motions were performed with such justness that the whole party moved and acted as one man. It was the opinion of every one of us that such a performance whould have met with universal applause on a European Theatre, and so far exceeded any thing we had done to amuse them that they seemed to pique themselves in the superiority they had over us. Not one of our musical instruments, except the drum did they hold in the least esteem, and even the Drum they did not think superiour to their own; as to the French horns they very seldom would attend to them attall either here or at any of the other islands.

In order to give them a better opinion of English amusements, I ordered a set of Fire works to be got ready and after it was dark played them off before the Chief and a great concourse of people; some of the works were spoiled, but there were enough good to answer the end I intended, particular some sky and Water Rockets which astonished and pleased them beyond measure and intirely turned the scale in our favour.

By such time as the fire works were over Fenough had got ready a nother entertainment, this consisted of musick, singing and dancing. A number of men seated themselves in a circle before us and began a Song not one word of which we understood; the musick was in the middle of the circle and consisted simply of two large pieces of bamboo with which they struck the ground endways and produced a dead hollow sound, each was managed by one man, who held it nearly in a Virtical position, the upper end was open but the other was closed by one of the joints. In a short time a number of Women, dressed better than Common, came and encircled the men in a kind of dance and joined in the Song; thus they continued for a full half hour, when two elderly women (one on each side, and who seemed to have the management of the whole) brough[t] the others up, dancing, two by two and ranged them before the chief, which ended the dance and the assembly broke up. Both men and Women accompaned the Song with a variety of motions of the hands and snaping of the fingers, which seems to be an essential part of their singing; their voices are however extreemly musical and their actions gracefull and decent, if we except some few which in a English assemb[l]y would be thought otherwise. But these indecent actions few as they are, do not arrise from any wanton ideas, but merely to increase the variety, for it is as[t]onishing to see the number of actions they observe in their dances and songs.

WEDNESDAY 21st. The next morning I took a walk into the island, which I found to be finely laid out into Plantations that were extreemly well Cultivated and planted with such roots and fruits as are common to the island, and I made some addition by sowing the seeds of Indian Corn, Millons Pumpkins &c[a]. All the Plantations were finced round and publick roads lay between them. When I went on board to dinner I found a large sailing Canoe fast to the Ships stern; in this Canoe was *Latouliboula* who, we understood, was King of Tongatabu when I visited the island last Voyage.[14] He sat in the Canoe with all that gravity by which he was distinguished at that time, nor could I by any means prevail upon [him] to come into the Ship. The people called him *Arekee* which signifies King, a title I had never heard one of them give Feenough which made me suspect he was not the King. Latouliboula remained under the stern till the evening when he retired to one of the isles. Feenough was on board at the same time but neither took any notice of the other.

14. See 6 October 1773.

*   *   *

[Finau and Omai set out for Vavaʻu, 60 miles to the north, to get red-feathered caps to take to Tahiti. Cook took the ships to the south coast of Lifuka.]

TUESDAY 27*th*. At day break the next Morning I made the Signal to wiegh, and as I intended to attempt a passage to Anamocka by the sw in amongst the islands, I sent the Master away in a boat to Sound before the Ships. But before we could get under sail, the wind became unsettled and made it unsafe to attempt a passage this way till we were better acquainted with it or had a steady wind. I therefore lay fast and made the sign for the Master to return, and afterwards sent him and the Master of the Discovery, each in a boat to examine the Channels as far as they could allowing time to return on board before dark. The wind was unsettled all day and blew in squals with some Showers of rain. About Noon a large sailing Canoe came under our Stern in which the Indians on board told us was *Fattafee Polaho* King of all the Isles; we had reason to doubt this, but they stood to it and now for the first time told us that Feenough was not the King. As it was my intrest as well as inclination to pay my Court to all these great men, without enquiring into the legality of their titles, I sent a boat to bring him on board as I understood he wanted to come. He brought with him as a present to me two good fat hogs, though not so fat as himself, for he was the most corperate plump fellow we had met with. I found him to be a Sedate sensible man, he viewed the Ship and the several new objects with uncommon attention, and asked several pertinent questions one of which was 'what brought us to these islands'. After he had satisfied his curiosity in looking at the Cattle &cᵃ on deck, I asked him down into the Cabbin, some of his attendants objected to this, saying if he went there people would walk over his head and this was never done. I desired Omai to till them I would remove that objection by giving orders that no one should walk on that part of the deck which was over the Cabbin, but this probably would not have done if the cheif had not waved the ceremony and walked down with me without any more to do. Both he and his attendants took some pains to convince us he was King and not Feenough, for he soon perceived we had some doubts about it, and particularly Omai who was a good deal chagrined at finding there was a greater man than his friend Feenough, or Omai as he was now called for they had from the first chang'd names. The Chief sat down with us to dinner, he eat but little and drank less. After dinner he asked Omai and me to accompany him ashore, Omai excused himself but I attended upon him in my own boat, having first presented him with such things as I knew would secure his friendship and what he most Valued and but little expected. As soon as we landed and before he went out of the boat he ordered two hogs to be brought and put into her; he was then carried a shore by some of his own people on a board like unto a hand barrow, and went and seated himself in a small neat house near the shore, which seemed to have been built for to accomodate traveling Chiefs. He desired me to sit by him, his attendance, which were not numerous, seated themselves in a semicircle before us without the house; an old woman sat behind or rather on one side the Cheif with a fan in her hand to fan away the flies that came near him. The several articles his people had got by truck aboard the Ships were now displayed before him, he looked over them all and enquired what they had given in exchange and seemed pleased with the bargins they had made. At length he ordered every thing to be returned except a glass bowl which he kept to himself. The persons who brought these things to him first squated themselves down before him, then laid down the things and rose up and retired, the same order was observed in taking them away and I observed no one spoke to him standing. I stayed till several of his attendants left him, first paying him Obseisance by bowing the head to the sole of his foot, and touching or taping the same with the upper and under sides of the fingers of both hands. Others who were not in the circle came as it seemed on purpose and paid him this mark of respect and then retired without speaking one word. I was quite charmed with the decorum that was observed, I had no where seen the like, no not even amongst more civilized nations.

When I got on board I found the Master returned, he informed me that so far as he had been, there was anchorage and a passage for the Ships, but that towards the South and SE he saw a number of small isles, shoals and breakers. Fore seeing that to go this way would be attended with some risk, I thought it better to return by the same rout as we came and should have sailed the next morning, Wed. 28 had not the wind been too far Southerly and very unsettled withal. Fattafee Polaho the King as I shall now call him came on board betimes and brought me one of their Caps made or at least covered with red feathers: these Caps were much sought after by us from knowing they would be highly valued at Otaheite. But though very large prices were offered not one was ever brought for sale, which shewed they were no less valuable to the people here, nor was there a person in either Ship that got one but my self Capt Clerke and Omai. . . .

The Cheif stayed on board till the evening when he left us but his Brother, whose name was also Fattafee, and one or two more remained on board all night.

THURSDAY 29*th*. At day-break the next Morning I weighed with a fine breeze a[t] ENE and stood to the westward, intending to return by the same rout as I came. We were followed by several sailing Canoes in one of which was Fattafee the King, as soon as he got on board he enquired for his Brother and the others who had been on board all night; it now appeared that they had stayed without his leave, for he gave them in very few words such a reprimand as brought tears from their eyes, and yet they were men not less than thirty years of age. He was however soon reconciled to their making a longer stay, for he left his brother and five of his attendants on board. And we had also the Company of a Chief just then arrived from Tongatabu whose name was *Tooboweitoa*; he no sooner got on board than he sent his Canoe away and declared that he and five more who came with him would sleep on board, so that I had now my Cabbin filled with them, and this was all the ilconveniency they gave me, for they brought plenty of provisions with them, but this I always looked upon as a present to me and made a return accordingly. About 1 PM the easterly wind was succeeded by a fresh breeze at SSE. Our Course now being SSW or more Southerly we had to ply to windward and did but just fetch the North side of Fodua by 8 oclock, where we spent the night making short boards. The next Morning we plyed up to Callafanga Frid. 30

where our friends told us was anchorage. It was 1 PM before we got soundings under the lee or NW side, in 40 fath. near half a mile from the shore; but the bank was steep and the bottom rocky and there lay a chain of breakers to leward. All these circumstances being against us I stretched away for Ogodoo with the expectation of finding better anchorage under that island, but so much time had been spent in plying up to Callafanga, that it was dark before we reached the other, and finding no place to anchor the night was spent as the preceding one.[15]

SATURDAY 31st. The 31st at day-break I stood for the Channel, which is between Ogodoo and the reef of rocks that lay to the westward of it, but on drawing near, I found the wind too scant to lead us through, and therefore bore up without the reef and stretched to the sw till 11 oclock when finding we got nothing to windward and being apprehinsive of losing the islands with so many of the Natives on board, I tacked and stood back intending to wait till some more favourable oppertunity. We did but just fetch in with Fodua, between which and Ogodoo we spent the night under reefed Topsails and Fore sail, the Wind blew fresh and by squals with rain and we were not without apprehensions of danger. I kept the deck till 12 oclock when I left it to the Master, with such direction as I thought would keep the Ships clear of the dangers that lay round us; but after making a trip to the north and standing back again to the south the Ship, by a small shift

JUNE   of the wind fetched farther to windward than was expected;
Sun. 1   by this means she was very near runing plump upon a low Sandy isle surrounded by breakers. It happened very fortunately that the people had just been turned up to put the Ship about and the most of them at their stations, so that the necessary movements were not only executed with judgement but with alertness and this alone saved the Ship. The Discovery being a stern was out of danger. Such resks as thise are the unavoidable Companions of the Man who goes on Discoveries. This circumstance frigh[t]ened our passengers so much that they express'd a stong desire to get a shore, as soon as it was light

15. Fodua is Fotuha'a, Callafanga is Lofanga, Ogodoo is Kotu; all in the north-western part of the Ha'apai group.

I hoisted out a boat and sent them to Ogodoo, and ordered the officer in the boat, after landing them to Sound along the reef which spits off from that island, for Anchorage, for I was as tired with beating about amongst the islands and shoals as they were and determined to get to an anchor some where or a nother if possible. . . .

On the 4th at 7 AM we wieghed with a fresh gale at ESE   Wed. 4 and stood away for Anamocka where we anchored the next   Thur. 5 Morning nearly in the same place where we lay before. I landed soon after and found the Inhabitants very busy in their plantations diging up yams to bring to Market, they were now in the greatest perfection and we procured a good quantity for pieces of iron. Before I returned on board I visited the several places where Mellon seeds & plants had been planted and had the Mortification to find that the most of them were distroyed by a small ant, but [the] Pine-aple plants I had planted were in a flourishing state. About noon the next day Feenough   Frid. 6 arrived from Vaughwaugh he told us that several Canoes laden with hogs &c^a that sailed with him from the island were lost in the late blowing weather and every soul in them perished; but as this melancholy tale seemed not to affect any one of the Indians, I did not beleive it; yet it might be, for it had blown hard for these parts, in so much that the King and others at Ogodoo durst not venture to Sea when we did, but desired I would wait for them at Anamocka which was the reason of my anchoring there the second time. The following Morning the King and all those who had been wind bound   Sat. 7 with him arrived, I was at this time a shore with Feenough and left him to visit the other; who I found seting with a few people before him, but as several came to pay their court to him the circle increased pretty fast. At length Feenough came and took his seat amongst the rest, some little conversation passed between these two Cheifs which none of us understood, nor was we satisfied with Omai's interpretation of it, we were however by this time fully satisfied who was the greater man of the two. I took them both aboard to dinner but only Fattafee sat at table, Feenough made his Obiesance in the usual way and retired out of the Cabbin; this confirmed what the King had before told us, that Feenough could neither eat nor drink in his presence.

SUNDAY 8*th*. At 8 oclock the next Morning we wieghed and steered for Tongataba having a gentle breeze at NE and about fourteen or fifteen sailing vessels in company every one of which considerably out run us. Feenough was to have taken a passage with us in the Ship but prefered his own Canoe and put two men on board to conduct us to the best anchorage. We steered SBW by compass the Course the Canoes steered; at 5 oclock in the evening we saw two small islands bearing west about 4 leagues distant. Our pilots called the one Hunga happi and the other Hunga Tonga; they lay in the Latitude of 20°36' and 10 or 11 leagues from the west point of Anamocka in the direction of [s 46° West]. We continued the same Course till 2 AM the next morning, when seeing some lights ahead and not knowing whither they were on shore or on board the Canoes, we hauled the Wind and Mon. 9   made a short trip each way till day-break, when we resumed our course to the SBW. And presently after saw several small islands a head and Middleburg and Tongatabu beyond them; the depth of water at this time was 25 fathom over a bottom of broken coral and sand. The depth of water gradually decreased as we drew near the isles which lie ranged along the NE side of Tongatabu. By the direction of our Pilots we steered for the middle of the island and for the widest space between the small islands with our boats ahead sounding. Insencibly were we drawn upon a large flat on which lay innumerable coral rocks of different depths below the surface of the water. It was not possible to keep the ship clear of them, all our care and attention did not prevent her from striking on one of them, nor did the Discovery who followed us escape any better, fortunately neither of them stuck fast nor received any damage. We could not return without increasing the danger, as we had come in before the wind, nor could we anchor but with the certainty of having our cables instantly cut in two by the rocks. We had no other resourse but to proceed, to which we were incouraged not only by being told, but seeing deep water between us and the shore; but to be better informed the moment we found a spot where we could drop the anchor clear of rocks we came to and sent away the Masters with the boats to sound. Soon after we had anchored which was about noon several of the Inhabitants came off in their canoes to the Ships. These as also our two Pilots assured us we should

find deep water farther in and a bottom free from rocks, and so it
proved for about 4 PM the boats made the signal for having found
good anchorage – upon which we weighed and stood in till dark, then
anchored in 9 fathom a fine clear sandy bottom. During the night
had some showers of rain, but towards the morning the wind shifted
to the South & SE and brought on fair weather. At day break   Tues. 10
weighed and worked in for the shore, meeting with no obstruction
but what was vissible and easily avoided. While we were plying up to
the harbour the Natives directed us to, the King kept sailing round
us in his Canoe, there were at the same time a great many small
Canoes about the Ships; two who could not get out of his way he run
quite over with as little concern as if they had been bits of wood.
Amongst many others who came on board the Ship was Otaga who
was so usefull to me when I was here last voyage, and one Toobough
who at the same time was the Friend of Captain Furneaux. They
brought each of them a hog and some yams as a testimony of their
friendship and I was not wanting on my part in making them a sutable
return.

At length about 2 PM we arrived at our intended Station, being a
very snug place formed by the shore of Tongatabu on the SE and two
small islands on the East and NE: here we anchored in 10 fathom
Water over a bottom of owsey sand, distant from the shore one third
of a mile. Soon after we had Anchored, I landed accompanied by
Omai and some of the Officers, we found the King waiting for us on
the beach, ready to conduct us to a small neat house, situated a little
within the skirts of the woods with a fine large area before it; this
house the Cheif told me was at my service during my stay and a better
situation we could not wish for. We had not been long in the house
before a pretty large circle of people were assembled before us and
seated on the Area. A root of the Cava plant was brought and laid
down before the King, he ordered it to be split into pieces and given
to several people, men and women, to chew and a bowl of liquer was
presently prepared. In the mean time a baked hog and two baskets of
baked yams were brought and afterwards divided into ten portions,
each of these portions were given to certain people present but how
many each was intend[ed] for I could not tell, one was sent to the

Kings brother and one remained which I judged was for himself as it was a choise bit. The liquor was next served out, but the King seemed to give no directions about it; the first cup was brought to him, he ordered it to be give[n] to one who sat near him, the second was brought him which he kept, the third was brought me, I gave it to Omai for their manner of brewing had quenched my thirst; the rest was served out to different people by direction of the man who had the management of it. A Cup was carri'd to the Kings Brother, with which and his victuals he retired, as did some others also, and the reason was they could neither eat nor drink before the King; but there were others of a much inferior rank who did both. Soon after the most of them retired, each carrying with them what victuals he or she had not eat. It is necessary to observe that not one 4th part of the Company had either Victuals or drink and some had one and not the other: those who had the Victuals I took to be of the Kings household. The Servants who served out the Victuals and Cava always delivered it out of their hand siting, not only to the King but to every other person. And altho this was the first time of our landing, and a great many people present who had never seen us before yet no one was troublesome, but the greatest good order was Observed throughout the whole. Before I went on board I was shewed some pools or holes of fresh Water as they were pleased to call it; the Water in one was indeed tolerable but it was some distance in land and but little of it. The next morning I went over to the island of *Pangymaudoo*, near which we lay, to look for Water being told there was some there; I was conducted to a small Pool that was tolerable and had it cleaned out and here it was we watered the Ships. As I intended to make some stay here I got all the Cattle a shore, a party of Marines with the officer for a guard, set up the observatory and Mr King resided a shore to attend the observations and superintend the several works carrying on there, for I had the sails a shore to repair and a party cuting wood for fuel and Plank for the use of the Ship. The gunners of both Ships were ordered a shore to traffick with the natives, who thronged from all parts with Hogs, yams, & cocoanuts &c^a so that our little post was like a fair and the Ships so thronged that we had hardly room to stir on the decks.

Wed. 11

*   *   *

[The ships stopped at Tongatapu for a whole month, and Cook gives a long and detailed account of the mutual exchange of courtesies, which were sometimes complicated by the perplexities of the Europeans over the relative status of their hosts. Even the great chief, or king, Fatafehi, made obeisance to an unknown woman (a sacred person). The English participated in many elaborate ceremonies and entertainments ashore, and Cook did his best to reciprocate with shipboard hospitality, firework displays and exercises by the marines. They suffered much from thieving, and Cook's punishments, which he does not himself describe, greatly surprised witnesses for their severity – mutilation of arms and ears as well as heavy floggings. In early July they were making preparations to leave.]

[JULY]

We were now ready to sail, but as the wind was easterly we   Sun. 6
had not day light to turn through the narrows with neither the Morning
nor evening flood, the one falling out too early and the other   Mon. 7
too late; so that without a leading wind we were under a necessity of
waiting two or three days. I took the oppertunity of this delay to be
present at a public ceremony, which was to be on the 8th and to which
the King had invited us. He and all the people of note left us on the
7th and repaired to M[oa] where it was to be performed. A party of
us in two boats followed them the next morning and got to   Tues. 8
the place about 8 oclock. We found the King with a large Circle before
him within a small dirty inclosure, such a one as I thought had not
been in the whole place. They were as usual making a large bowl of
Cava, and as this was no liquer for us, we walked out to visit some of
our Friends and to see what was going forward without. About 10
oclock the people began to assemble in a large Area which is before
the great house we were conducted to the first time we visited this
Village. At the end of a lane opening into this place were some Men
with Spears & Clubs in their hands, some of them stood up and
continued to sing short sentances, while a number of other men were
coming in with Yams, each tied to the middle of a pole. In the mean
time the King and the Prince came and seated themselves on the area,
and we were desired to sit down by them, to pull of our hats and untie

our hair that we might appear the more decent. The men with the yams being all come in, each pole with the yam was taken up between two men who carried it over their shoulders; and after forming themselves into companies of ten or twelve they marched a cross the place with a quick pace each company headed by a man bearing a club or spear and guarded on the right by several others armed with different Weapons. A man carrying a live Pigeon on a pearch Closed the rear. Omai was desired to ask the Cheif where the yams were going to be carried to, he answered to be baked. This appeared probable enough as we had been told that the occasion of this ceremony was him and his Son eating together, a thing that had never yet been done. However as he seemed unwilling to give us the information we wanted two or three of us followed them contrary to his inclination. We found they had stoped before a Morai or Affiatouca, which was hardly a quarter of a Mile from the place where they first assembled; here they were making up the yams in bundles but for what purpose could not learn, and as our presence seemed to give them uneasiness we left them and returned to the Cheif, who told us we might amuse our selves by walking about awhile for that nothing would be done for some time; the fear of loseing part of this Ceremony made us not be long absent. When we returned to the King he desired me to order the boats crew not to stir from the boat, for as every thing would very soon be *Tabu*, who ever was found walking about would be *Mated*, that is killed or beat. He also informed us that we could not be present at the Ceremony, but that we should be conducted to a place where we might see every thing that passed; objection were made to our dress, to be present it was necessary we should be naked as low as the breast with our hats off and hair untied. Omai offered to conform to this Custom and began to strip, other objections were then started so that he could not be present no more than us. I did not much like this restriction and stole out to see what was now going forward, I found very few people stiring, except those dressed to attend the ceremony, some of whom had in their hands a small stick about four feet long and to them were tied two or three others not biger than ones finger. These men were going towards the Morai before mentioned, I took the same road, and was several times stoped by them all crying out *Tabu*. I however went

forward without much regarding them till I came in sight of the Morai
and the people who were seting before it; I was no[w] urged very
strongly to go back and not knowing what might be the consequence
of a refusal, I complyed. I had observed that those people with the
sticks passed this Morai or what I may as well call church, and thinking
something was going forward beyond it, which by taken a turn round
I might get a sight of, but I was so clos[e]ly watched by three men
that I could not put this in execution. In order to shake these fellows
off I returned to the Kings and from thence stole out a second time,
but I was no sooner out than I met with the same three men, so that
it seemed as if they had been set on purpose to watch me. I paid no
regard to what the[y] did or said till I came in sight of the Kings
affiatouca or Morai before which a great number of men were seting
and were those I had seen pass the other Morai from which this was
but a little distant. Oberving that I could watch the motions of this
company from the Kings Plantation I returned, very much to the
satisfaction of those who attended me. As soon as I got in I accquainted
my companions with what I had seen and we took our Stations to
watch their Motions. Several afterwards joined them and at length
they all got up and Marched off in Procession one after a nother,
every two carrying one of those small sticks over their shoulders. The
small pieces of sticks that were tyed to the others we were told were
yams, so that probably they were to represent this root emblametically.
The hindmost Man of each couple for the most part placed one of
his hands to the midd[l]e of the stick as if it alone was not sufficient
to support the weight that hung to it, and under which they all seemed
to bend as they walked. This procession consisted of one hundred and
eight couple, and all or most of them men of rank; they passed close
by the fence behind which we stood so that we had a full view of them.
As soon as they were passed we repaired to the Chiefs house and saw
him going out, we were not allowed to follow but was forthwith
conducted to the place alotted us, which was behind a fence that
fronted the first Morai in which we took the liberty to cut small holes
to peep through the better to see what passed on the other side. As
we were not the only people who were excluded from being publickly
present at this ceremony, but allowed to peep from behind the Curten,

we had a good deal of Company, and I observed that all the other inclosures adjoining to the place were filled with people. But notwithstanding they admit this, all imaginable care seemed to be taken that they should see as little as possible, for the fences had not only been repaired that Morning but in many places raised higher than common so that the tallest man could not look over them.

On our arrival at our stations we found several men seated on our right or on the left of the Area before the Morai and on each side of the road which crossed it; others were continually joining them. At length some appeared carr[y]ing small poles or sticks, and branches or leaves of the Cocoanut tree plated into each other as when used for covering of Sheds &c^a. On these appearing a man seated himself in the road and with his face towards them made a set oraision and then retired back and the others passed on to the middle of the Area where they built a small shed of the Materials above mentioned; when done they all squated down for a Moment before it then rose up and retired to the other company. Soon after came the Prince, preceeded by four or five men and seated themselves on one side the Shed and rather behind it. Then came twelve or fourteen Women of the first rank following each other, two and two carrying between them a stripe of Cloth of about two or three yards in length; these marched up to the Prince, squated down before him, wraped some of the Cloth round him and those with him, then rose up and retired in the same order a little to his left and there seated themselves. Next came the King, preceded by four men two and two a breast, he seated himself on the Princes left hand, rather behind and about twenty paces from him; this was no sooner done then three parties of ten or a dozen men in each Started up and ran a Cross the Area, squated down on the other side for a Moment, then rose and returned in the same manner to their former stations. The Procession before mentioned now came in; to judge of the circuit they had made from the time they had been absent, it must have been pretty large. But before the procession appeared the Prince and those with him seated themselves under the Shed, the Prince sat facing us or rather the people and with his back to the Morai. As the Procession came in they March up to the right of the Prince, squated down on the grass, laid down their burdens (being the sticks before mentioned) faced round to the Prince, then rose up and retired in the same order and seated themselves along the front of the Area. Three men who sat with the Prince continued to make an Oraision consisting of seperate sentences all the time the Procession was coming in. After this a man who sat in the front began an Oraision and at the several times during it, went and broke one of those Sticks brought in in the procession. As soon as this man had ended his Oraision the assembly broke up and we were at liberty to go where we pleased; some repaired on board but I and two or three more remain'd to see the end of the Ceremony, which was not to be till the next day. The shed was left standing and the small sticks or poles brought in by the Procession were left lying on the ground; after the assembly broke up I went and examined them and found that to the middle of each was tied two or three small sticks as has been related, yet we had been repeatedly told by those about us that they were young yams, insomuch that some [of] our gentlemen beleived them rather than their own eyes, whereas it is clear we ought to have understood them that they were only the representation of these roots.

Our supper was got ready about 7 o'clock it consisted of fish and Yams, we might have had Pork also, but we did not chuse to kill a large hog the King had given us for the same purpose. The King supped with us and drank pretty freely of Brandy and Water so that he went to bed grogish; he and several of his attendants slept in the same house with us. About one or two o'clock they waked   Wed. 9 and chated for about an hour then went to sleep again. All but the Chief rose at day break and went I knew not where. Soon after a Woman, one of those who generally attended upon him, came in and asked where he was, I shewed her him laying fast a sleep; she immediately sat down by him and began to beat a kind of Tattoo on his breech with her clinched fists, which in stead of keeping asleep as it was intended it waked him, however he continued to ly down. This is a nother odd custom which they have, whenever the King lies down to sleep or rist two or three Women for the most part attend him, one of them beats or taps gently with her fists on his breech or thighs and as she is tired a nother takes her place, thus they continue some times a whole night. One would at first think this would produce the Contrary effect to what is intended but it is not so, for it creates a very agreeable and pleasing sensation. Omai and I now went to visit the Prince who parted from us early in the evening, for he did not lodge with the King but in apartments of his own, or such as had been alloted him some distance from his Fathers; we found him with a Circle of Boys or youths like himself before him, and an old Woman and an old man who seemed to have the care of him siting behind; there were others both men and Women who seemed to make a part of his household, that were employed about their necessary affairs in different apartments. From the Prince we returned to the King, by this time he was up and had a crowded Circle before him, composed chiefly of old men; while a large bowl of Cava was preparing a Baked hog and yams Smoaking hot was brought in, the greatest part of which fell to our share, that is to the boats crew, for these people eat very little in a Morning and especially the Cava drinkers. I afterward walked out and visited several other Chiefs and found that all of them either were or had been taking their morning draughts. Returning to the King I found him a Sleep in a small retired hut with two Women taping his breech. About 11 oclock he got up, some fish and yam, which tasted as it had been stewed in Cocoanut milk, was brought him of which he eat a large portion and then laid down to sleep again, when I left him to visit the Prince and to make him a present of Cloth, Beads &c[a] I had brought with me for the purpose; there was sufficient to make him a compleat suit of Clothing, in which he was immediately dress'd. He first went and shewed himself to his Father, and then carried me to his Mother, with whom was ten or a dozen other respectable looking Women. Here the Prince changed his apparel and made me a present of two peices of their Cloth. By this time it was pass'd Noon, when every one of us according to appointment repaired to the Palace to dine and presently after dinner was served up consisting of two Pigs and yams, I rouse'd the King up to pertake of what he had provided for us. In the mean time two Mullet and some shell fish was brought him as I supposed for his dinner; he joined it to ours, sat down with us and made a hearty meal.

Soon after dinner was over, we were told that the ceremony would soon begin and desired not to walk out, I however had resolved to peep no longer from behind the Curtin, but to make one of the number in the Ceremony if possible; with this View I stole out of the Plantation and walked to wards the Morai; I was several times applied to to go back by people who were passing to and fro, but I paid no regard to them and they suffered me to pass on. When I got to the Morai, I found a number of men seated on one side of the Area on each side of the road which led up to it; a few were seting on the other side the area and two in the Middle of it facing the Morai. When I got into the midst of the first company I was desired to sit down which I accordingly did. Where I sat down were a number of small bundles or parcels made up of Cocoanut leaves, and tied to sticks made into the form of hand barrows, all the information I could get of them was that they were *Tabu*. Our number kept continually increasing, every one coming from the same quarter; every now and then, one or another of the Company would turn himself to those that were coming and make a short spea[c]h in which the word *Arekee*, that is King was generally mentioned. One made a speach which made them all laugh heartily, others met with publick applause. I was several times desired to go away, and at last when the[y] found I would not stir, they, after some seeming consultation, desired I would bare my shoulders as they were, with this I complied after which they seemed no longer uneasy at my presence. I sat here a full hour without any thing more going forward than what I have mentioned. At length the Prince, the Women and the King all came in as they did the day before and as soon as the King was seated three Companies ran forward and backward a cross the Area as they did then. Soon after the two men who sat in the Middle of the Area, made a short speach or prayer, then all of us started up and ran and seated our selves before the shed under which the Prince and three or four men were siting. I was now partly under the management of a man who seemed very assiduous to serve me and placed me in such a situation, that if I had been allowed to make use of my eyes, I might very well have seen every thing that passed, but it was necessary to sit with down cast eyes and as demure as Maids. Soon after the Procession came in as the day before, with a Cocoanut leafe plated round the Middle of the pole or stick which they bore on their Shoulders, and which they laid down with the same ceremony as they did those the preceding day. This first Procession was followed by a second, the Men who composed it brought Baskets such as are usually used to carry provisions in and made of Palm leaves. These were followed by a third Procession who brought in different kinds of small fish stuck to the end of a forked stick.

The Baskets were brought up to an old man whom I took to be the Chief Priest and who sat on the Princes right just without the Shed. He held each in his hand till he made a short speach or prayer, then laid it down and called for a nother and repeated the same words as before and thus he went through the whole. The fish were presented one by one on the forked Sticks as they came in to two Men who sat on the left and who till now held green branches in their hands. The first fish they laid down on their right and the second on the left; when the third was presented, a stout man who sat behind the other two, reached his arm over between them and made a snatch at it, as also did the other two at the very same time, thus they seemed to contend for every fish that was presented, but as there were two hands against one with the advantage of situation the Man behind got nothing but pieces, for he never quited his hold till the fish was torn out of his hand and what remained in it he shook out behind him and the others laid what they got on the right and left alternatly. At length either by accedent or design, the man behind got a whole fish without either of the other two so much as touching it, at this the word *Ma rēē ai* which signifies very go[o]d or well done, was uttered in a low voice throughout the whole crowd. It seemed that he had now performed all that was expected of him, for the few fish that came after he made no attempt upon. These fish as also the Baskets were all delivered by the persons who brought them in seting, and in the same order and manner the small sticks had been brought in and laid on the ground. After the last procession were all come in there was some speaking or praying by different persons, then on some signal being given we all started up and ran several paces to the left and sat down with our backs to the Prince and the few who remained with him and I was desired not to looke behind me, Niether this commandment nor the remembrance of Lots wife, discouraged me from facing about, when I saw the Prince had turned his face to the Morai; but this last Movement had brought so many people between him and me that I could not see well what was doing; but was afterward told that the King and Prince were each presented with a piece of roasted yam, this was the more probable as all the people turned their backs to them at this time. After some little time we all faced about and formed a large semicircle before the Prince, leaving a large open place between us. Presently there appeared some men coming to wards us, two and two bearing large sticks or poles on their Shoulders making a noise like singing and waving their hands as they came. As soon as they got close up to us they made shew of walking very fast without advancing a single step; presently three or four men started up from the crowd with large sticks in their hands and ran to those new comers who instantly threw down the poles from their shoulders and ran off, and the others fell on these poles and beat them most unmercifully and then returned to their places. As the men ran off they gave the challenge usual in wristling, and not long after a number of stout fellows came from the same quarter, giving the Challenge as they advanced, these were opposed by a party who came from the opposite side almost at the same instant; these two parties paraded the Area for a few minutes and then retired each to his own side. After this there was wrestling and boxing Matches for about half an hour, then two men seated themselves before the Prince and made a speach address'd I thought wholy to him, with this the ceremony ended and the whole assembly broke up. I now went and examined the several Baskets which had been brought in, a thing I was not allowed to do before because every thing was then *Tabu*, but the ceremony being over they became simply what they realy were, viz. empty baskets, so that whatever they were supposed to Contain was emblematically represented, and so indeed was every other thing they brought in except the fish.

We endeavoured in vain to find out the meaning not only of the whole but the different parts of this ceremony, we seldom got any other answers to our enquir[i]es than *Tabu*, a word which as I have before observed is applied to many other things. But as the Prince was the principal person concerned in it, and we had been told by the King ten days before it happened, that the people would bring in yams for them two to eat and even described some part of the ceremony, we concluded from this and what we saw, that it was an Oath of Alligiancy or solemn promise which they made the Prince as the immediate successor to the Regale Dignity, to stand by him and to furnish him with the several articles that were here emblematically represented. But be this as it will the whole was conducted with a great deal of Ceremonious solemnity, and that it was mixed with a great deal of Religion is evident not only from the place where it was performed, but from the manner of performing it. Our dress and deportment had never been called in question on any account whatever before. Now it was expected that we should be uncove[re]d as low as the waist, that our hair should be loose and flowing over our shoulders; that we should like them sit cross leged and at times in the most humble posture with downcast eyes and hands locked together, all of which they themselves observed; lastly every one was excluded but the Principle people and those who acted a part. These to me were a sufficient testimony that they looked upon themselves to be acting under the immediate eye of a Supreme Being. We were told that a far greater or grandeur ceremony than this would be performed on the same account in about three months time in which ten Men were to be Sacrificed; this is sufficient for us to beleive that Human Sacrifices here as well as at Otaheite are considered as necessary.

Before the Ceremony was over the day was far spent and as we were some distance from the Ships and had an intricate Navigation to go through, we made haste to be gone.

* * *

[*With regret, Cook turned down an invitation to witness a funeral ceremony – which would last five days – and on Thursday 10 July took advantage of wind and tide to begin making his way to Eua (Tasman's Middleburg) where the ships arrived on Saturday 12 July.*]

We had no sooner anchored than Taoofa the Chief and several other made us a visit and seemed to rejoice much at our coming: this Taoofa was my Tayo when I was here last voyage, consequently we were no strangers to each other. Soon after I went a shore with him to look for fresh water, the Chief object that brought me to the island, for I had been told here was a stream running from the hills into the Sea, but this was not the case now. The first I was conducted to was a brackish spring between low and high water mark, amongst rocks in the Cove where we landed and where no one would ever have thought of looking for fresh Water, and yet I beleive the Water might be good was it possible to take it up before the Sea Water mixes with it. Finding we did not like this Water they took us a little way into the island, where in a deep chasm was some very good Water which at the expence of some time and trouble might be conveyed down to the Sea by means of Spouts or troughs that might be made with Plantain leaves and the stem of the tree, but rather than be at that trouble I resol[v]ed to make what we had got serve. Before I returned on board I set on foot a trade for Hogs and Yams, of the first we got but few but of the latter plenty. I put a shore at this island the Sheep I gave to Mariwaggy,[16] viz a Ram and two Ewes of the Cape breed; they were intrusted to the care of Ta-oo-fa who seemed to be proud of his charge. As the Dogs had not yet got to this island I looked upon it to be the properest place for sheep.

SUNDAY 13*th*. The 13th in the after noon a party of us traveled to the top of the highest hill in order to have a View of the interior parts of the island. . . . From this hill we had a full View of the whole island except a part of the south point; the SE side from which the hills are not far distant, rises with very great inequalities directly from the Sea, so that the plains and Medows, of which here are some of great extent, lay all on the NW side; and as they are adorned with tufts of trees and here and there plantations, make a very beautiful Landskip from whatever point they are viewed. Whilst I was viewing these delightfull spots, I could not help flatering my self with the idea that some future Navigator may from the very same station behould these Medows stocked with Cattle, the English have planted at these islands. Our guides informed us that all or most of the land on this island belonged to the great Lords of Tongatabu and that the Inhabitants were only tenants or rather Vassals to them; indeed it seemed to be the same at

16. This is Maealiuaki, a principal chief on Tongatapu, with whom Cook had much to do. But he had shown no interest in a Cape ram and two ewes presented to him by Cook.

all the other isles except Anamocka, where there were some chiefs who seemed to act with some kind of independency. Omai who was a great favourate with Feenough and these people in general, was offered to be made Chief of this island if he would stay amongst them, and it is not clear to me but Omai would have stayed if I had approved of it, but altho I disapproved of it, it was not because I thought he

Mon. 14   would do better in his own Native isle. The next Morning I planted a pine apple and sowed the seeds of Millons &c^a in the Cheifs Planatation, and had a dish of Turnips to dinner, being the produce of the seeds I left last Voyage.

Tues. 15   The 15th I had fixed upon for Sailing, till Taoofa press'd me to stay a day or two longer to receive his present of yams &c^a this and the daily expectation of seeing some of our friends from

Wed. 16   Tongatabu made me comply. Accordingly the next day I received the Cheifs present consisting of two small heaps of yams and some fruit. On this occasion most of the people of the island had assembled at the place, and as usual gave us not a little trouble to prevent them from pelfering whatever they could lay their hands upon. We were entertained with Cudgeling, Wristling and Boxing Matches, the latter both by Men and Women. And in the evening we were to have had singing and dancing, but an accident either put a total stop to it or at least prevented any of us from staying a shore to see it. This was a party of the Indians knocking down one of my people and striping him of every thing he had on his back. On hearing of this I immediately seized on two Canoes and a large hog and insisted on Taoofa causing the things to be restored and the offenders to be delivered up to me; he seemed much concerned at what had happened and forthwith took the necessary steps to satisfy me. This affair, so alarmed the people that most of them fled, however when they found I took no other measures to revenge the insult they returned. It was not long before one of the offenders, with a shirt and a pair of Trowsers were delivered up to me, the remainder not coming before dark I was under a necessity of leaving them to go a board as there run so high a sea that it was with great difficulty the boats could get out of the

Thur. 17   Creek with day light much less in the dark. The next Morning I landed again, provided with a present for the Chief in return for what he had given me. As it was early, there were but few people at the landing place and these few not without their fears, but on being assured by Omai we meant them no harm, they resumed their usual gaiety and presently a large circile was formed in which was the Chief and all the principal men in the island. The remainder of the Clothes were brought me, but as they had been torn off the Mans back by pieces they were not worth carrying on board. I now made the Chief a present which he divided amongst three or four other Chiefs, keeping only a small part for himse[l]f: this present so much exceeded their expectation that an ancient and venerable Chief told me that they did not deserve it, considering the little they had given me and the ill treatment one of my people had met with. I remained with them till they had finished their bowl of Cava, then paid for the hog I tooke the day before (the Canoes were before given up) set the offender at liberty without punishment and returned on board with Taoofa and one of Fattafee Polaho's servants, by whom I sent as a mark of my esteem and regard for that Chief, a piece of bar Iron, being as valuable a present as any I could make him. Soon after I got on board we weighed and with a light breeze at SE stood out to sea, and then Taoofa and a few others that were on board left us. On heaving up the Anchor we found that the Cable had suffered considerably by the rocks so that the bottom in this road is not to be depended upon and we experienced that there some times rolls in a prodigious swell from the SW. . . .

Thus we we took leave of the *Friendly Islands* and their Inhabitants after a stay of between two and three Months, during which time we lived together in the most cordial friendship, some accidental differences its true now and then happened owing to their great propensity to thieving, but too often incouraged by the negligence of our own people. But these differences were never attended with any fatal consequences, to prevent which all my measures were directed. Also during this time we expended very little of our Sea Provisions but lived upon the produce of the islands; and beside the oppertunity of leaving the Cattle before mentioned amongst them, those designed for Otaheite received fresh strength; so that upon the whole the advantages we received by touching here was very great, when it is considered that the Season for proceeding to the North was lost before I steered for these islands.

*   *   *

I continued to Stretch to the ESE with the wind at NE and North, without meeting with any thing worthy of note till 7 oclock in the

Tues. 29   evening of the 29th when we had a sudden and very heavy squal of wind from the North, at this time we were under single reef'd Topsails, Courses and stay-sails, two of the latter were blown to pieces, and it was with difficulty we saved the other sails. After this Squal we observed several lights moving about on board the Discovery by which we concluded that some thing had given way, and the next

Wed. 30   Morning we Saw her Main topmast was gone. Both wind and weather continued very unsittled till noon the next day, when the latter cleared up and the former settled in the sw quarter. At this time we were in the latitude of 28°06′ s, longitude [198°23′] East. Here we saw some Pintadoe birds, being the first sence we left the land. The 31st at Noon Captain Clerke made the signal to speak with me, by the return of the boat which I sent on board, he informed me they had just descovered that the head of the Mainmast was sprung in such a manner as to render the rigging a nother topmast very dangerous and that he must rig something lighter in its place. He also informed me that he had lost his Main Topgallant yard and had never a nother nor a spar to make one; the Resolutions Sprit sail topsail yard which

AUG^t [1]   I sent him supplyed this want. The next day he got up a Jury topmast on which he set a Mizon topsail and this inabled him to keep way with the Resolution. The Wind now fixed in the Western board that is from the North round by the West to South, and I Steered ENE an[d] NE without meeting with any thing remarkable till 11 oclock

Frid. 8   in the Morning of 8th of August when land was seen bearing NNE½E 9 or 10 leagues distant. At first it appeared in detatched hills like so many islands but as we drew nearer we found they were all on one and the same island. I steered directly for it with a fine gale at SEbS and at half past 6 PM it extended from NBE to NNE¾E destant 3 or 4 leagues. The night was spent standing off and on, and at day

Sat. 9   break the next Morning I steered for the NW, or lee side of the island, which we soon perceived to be guarded on every side by a reef of Coral rock which in some places extend[ed] a full mile from the land. Some thought they saw land to the Southward of this island but as this was to windward it was left undetermined. As we drew near we saw people on several parts of the Coast and as soon as we were under the lee side of the island they launched two Canoes, into which ten or a dozen men got and paddled towards us: I shortned sail as well to give them time to come up with us as to sound for anchorage. We found from 40 to 35^{fms} water over a bottom of fine sand at the distance of half a mile from the reef; nearer in the bottom was strewed with Coral rocks. The Canoes stoped at about a pistol shot from the Ship, all that Omai could say or do did not prevail on the men in them to come nearer, they kept pointing to the shore and told us to go there. This we could very well have done as there was good anchorage without the reef and a break or opening in it, in which if there was not water for the Ships, there was more than sufficient for the boats, but I did not think proper to risk lossing the advantage of a fair wind for the sake of examining an island that appeared of little consequence. Therefore after makeing several unsuccessfull attempts to get these people a long side, I made sail to the North and left them, first geting from them the name of the island which they call *Toobouai.*[17] It is situated in the Latitude of 23°25′ s, Longitude [210°37′] East; its greatest extent in any direction, exclusive of the reef, is not above 5 or 6 miles and yet there are hills in it of a considerable elevation. The hills are not barren and the Vallies and low land which border on the sea, is covered with fruit trees. We learnt from the Men in the Canoes, that they had Hogs, Fowls, and the several fruits and roots that are found at the other islands. These men spoke the Otahiete language consequently must be of the same nation, they had nothing on but the Maro – but there were some a shore clothed in white. One man in the Canoes continued to blow a Conch most part of the time they were near us, what this might mean I cannot say, but I never found it the messinger of Peace. These Canoes were single with out-riggers, but broader than usual, something like those of New Zealand; both

17. Tubuai.

both head and stern was raised and the latter was ornamented with Carved work. After leaving this island I steered to the North with a
Tues. 12   fresh gale at EBS and at day break in the Morning of the 12th we made the island of Maitea and soon after Otaheite, which at Noon extended from SWBW to WNW, and the point of Oaitepeha bay bore West about 4 leagues distant. I steered for this bay intending to anchor there in order to draw what refreshments I could from the SE part of the island before I went down to Matavai. We had a fresh gale Easterly till 2 PM when being about a league from the bay, the wind suddenly died away and was succeeded by bafling light airs from every direction and Calms by turns. This lasted about two hours, then we had sudden squals with rain from the East, these carried us before the bay where we got a breeze from the land and attempted in vain to work in, so that at last we were obliged to stand out and spend the night at Sea.

When we first drew near the island, several Canoes came off to the Ships each conducted by two or three men, but as they were only common fellows Omai took no notice of them nor they of him, they did not even seem to perceive he was one of their Countrymen although they conversed with him for some time. At length a Chief whom I had known before named Ootie and Omai's Brother in law, who chanced to be here, came on board, and three or four more, all of whom knew Omai before he imbarked with Captain Furneaux; yet there was nothing either tender or striking in their meeting. On the contrary there seemed to be a perfect indifference on both sides, till Omai asked his Brother down into the Cabbin, opened the drawer where he kept his red feathers and gave him a few. This being presently known to those on deck, the face of affairs were intirely turned and Ootie who would hardly speak to Omai before, now beged they might be Tyo's and change names. Omai axcepted of the honour and confirm'd it with a present of red feathers, and Ootie by way of return sent a shore for a hog but it was evident to every one that it was not the Man but his property they were in love with, for had he not shewed them his red feathers, which is the most Valuable thing that can be carried to the island, I question if they had given him a Cocoanut. Such was Omai's first reception amongst his Countrymen and such as I always expected, but I expected, that with the property he was master of he would [have] had prudence enough to [have] made himself respected and even courted by the first persons in the island, but in stead of that he rejected the advice of those who wished him well and suffered himself to be duped by every designing knave.

From these people we learnt that two Ships had been twice at Oaitepeha bay sence I was last at the island and that they had left cattle such as we had on board, but on further inquiry we found they were only Hogs, Dogs, Goats, one Bull and the Male of some other animal that we could not make out and which was gone to Ulietea. They told us these ships came from a Country called *Rema* which undoubtedly must be Lima the Capital of *Peru*; that the first time they came they built a house and left four men behind them viz. two Priests, a boy or a servant and one *Mateama*, who was much spoke of at this time, that after a stay of ten Months the same two Ships returned and took them away, but the house was left standing and near it a Cross (as they described it) at the foot of which the Commodore of the first two Ships, who died while they lay in the bay, was buried. They call him Oreddee.[18]

The news of red feathers being on board the Ships having reached the shore by Omai's friends, day no sooner broke the next   Wed. 13 Morning than we were surrounded by a Multitude of Canoes filled with people with hogs and fruit to barter; not more feathers than might be got from a Tom tit would purch[ase] a hog of 40 or 50 pound weight, but as every one in the Ships had some they fell in their value above five hundred per cent before night but even than the ballance of trade was much in our favour and they never lessened in their value afterwards. Some however would not part with a hog without an ax, but Nails and beads, which formerly had so great a run at this island, they would not now so much as look at. As there was but little wind all the Morning it was 9 oclock before we got to an Anchor in the bay where we Moored with the two bowers and then sent all the Cattle ashore. While we lay here we inspected into all the Provisions that was in the Main and Forehold, got the Casks

18. Don Domingo de Boenechea had first visited Tahiti in the *Aguila* in 1772. He came again in 1774 (plus a storeship) but died on the island. The ships departed but made a brief return in November 1775. 'So ended the hopes of a Spanish Tahiti.'[B]

of Beef and Pork up out of the ground tier, the Coals and took in some ballast. The Caulkers were set to work to caulk the Ship, a thing that was much wanting, for she had at times made much water on our passage from the Friendly Islands. Soon after we had anchored Omai's sister came on board to see him, their meeting was extreamly moving and better concieved than discribed.

After the Ship was Moored Omai and I went a Shore to pay a visit to a man which he said was the God of Bolabola: we found him seated under one of those small Awnings they carry in their traveling Canoes; he was an elderly man and had lost the use of his legs so that he was carried from place to place on a ha[n]d barrow. Some call'd him Olla, the same name as the God of Bolabola, but his proper name was Etary. From Omai's account of this Man I expected to have seen him adored as a God, but excepting some young Plantain trees laying before him and upon the Awning, I saw nothing by which he might be distinguished from other Chiefs. Omai presented him with a small tuft of red feathers tied to the end of a small stick and after a little conversation on indifferent matters, Omais attention was drawn to an old Woman the Sister of his Mother; she was already at his feet and had bedewed them plentifully with tears of joy. I left him with the old Lady in the midst of a number of people who gathered round him, and went to take a View of the house, said to be built by the Spaniards; the Materials which was boards, had been brought out for the purpose as every part was numbered; it consisted of two small rooms, in them was a Table a Bench a bedstead and a few other trifles. A shed was built over it to guard it from the Sun; this seemed to have been done by the Natives. At a little distance from it stood the cross on which was cut out the following inscription, viz. *Christus Vincit Car[o]lus III imperat* 1774. On the other side of the Post which supported the Cross I had cut out, *Georgius tertius Rex Annis* 1767, 69, 73, 74 & 77. I saw some very fine large hogs of the Spanish breed, two goats and Dogs of two or three sorts, all of them either brought here by the Spaniards or bread from those they did bring. I met with no Chief of any note, Waheatua, the Chief of this Distr[i]ct was absent, and as I afterwards found was not the same as was Chief when I was at the island last Voyage but his brother, who had succeeded at the death of the other about twenty months before we arrived. We were also told that the celebrated Oberea was dead but Otoo and all our other friends were living. When I returned to Omai I found him holding forth to a large company and it was with some difficulty he could get away to accompany me on board.

Foreseeing that Cocoa-nuts would be got at the island in great plenty and thinking it a good time to save our Spirit[s], I called all hands together and acquainted them with what further was expected to be done in the Voyage. I pointed out to them the improbability of our geting any supplies of Provisions after leaving the Society isles and the hardship they would feel in being at short allowance in a Cold Clemate, and that rather than run this risk it was better for them to be without grog now, but that I left it intirely to their own choice. I had the satisfaction to find that it remained not under a moments consideration but was consented to immidiately. The next day I ordered Captain Clerke to make the same proposal to his people, which they also consented to and we stoped serving grog except on Saturday nights when they had full allowance to drink to their feemale friends in England, lest amongst the pretty girls of Otaheite they should be wholy forgoten.

*   *   *

[*Cook and Omai made a formal visit to the young Vehiatua, who was attended by his mother and step-father ('Etary'). Cook was told that the Spaniards had urged them to keep him out as the island belonged to them. He understood that the assembled chiefs now made him 'a formal surender of the Province and every thing in it'. On Saturday 23 August the ships got ready to leave.*]

As soon as I got on board a light breeze spring^g up at East we got under sail and steered for Matavai bay where the Resolution Anchored the same evening, but the Discovery did not get in till the next Morning. . . . About 9 oclock, Otoo the King, attended   Sun. 24 by a great many Canoes full of people came from Oparre and landed on Matavai point and sent word on board that he should be glad to see me there. Accordingly I went, accompaned by Omai and some of the officers; on this occasion a prodigious number of people had assembled together in the midst of them we found the King with his

Father, his two Brothers and three Sisters. I first went up and saluted him, Omai follow'd kneeled and embraced his legs. Omai was dress'd in his very best suit of clothes and conducted himself with a great deal of respect and Modesty, nevertheless very little notice was taken of him, perhaps envy had some share in it. He made the Chief a present of a large piece of red feathers and about two or three yards of gold cloth, and I gave him a Suit of fine linnen a gold laced hat, some tools and what was of more Value than all the others, a large piece of red feathers and one of the Friendly islands bonnets. After the hurry of this visit was over the King and the whole royal family accompaned me on board the Ship, followed by several Canoes laden with all kinds of Provisions, sufficient to have served the Companies of both Ships for a Week, would it have kept good so long. Each of the family owned or pretended to own a part, so that I had a present from every one of them and I made them all such returns I thought was most exceptable. Soon after the Kings Mother, who was not present at the first interview, came on board with a quantity of Provisions and cloth which she divided between me and Omai. For altho he was but little noticed at first, they no sooner gained the knowlidge of his riches than they began to Court his friendship; this I incouraged all I could, for it was my wish to fix him with Otoo, as I inten[d]ed to leave the Cattle Poultry &cᵃ at this island, I thought he would be able to give some instruction about the Management of them and of their use, beside I knew, and saw, that the farther he was from his native island the better he would be respected. But Omai rejected my advice, and conducted himself in such a manner as not only to lose the friendship of Otoo but that of every other person of note in the island. He associated with none but refugees and strangers whose sole Views were to plunder him and if I had not interfered they would not have left him a single thing worthe the carrying from the island, this was what got him the ill will of the principal chiefs, for many of these low people got from him such things as no one in the Ships could give to them. But to return to my visiters, as soon as we had dined, a party of us accompaned Otoo to Oparre, taking with us the Poultry viz. a Peacock and Hen which my Lord Besborough was so kind as [to] send me for this purpose a few days before I left London, a Turkey-cock and Hen, one

Gander and three Geese, a Drake and four Ducks, all of which I left at Oparre in the possession of Otoo. We found here the Gander which the Natives told us was the same that Captain Wallis gave to Obarea ten years ago, several Goats and the Spanish Bull, and a finer beast than he was I hardly ever saw; he belonged to Etary and had been brought from Oaitepehu to this place in order to be shiped for Bolobolo, but how they intended to carry him in one of their Canoes I cannot say. I wondered to find this Bull the property of a Stranger and the more so as we were told he purchased him of the Spaniards for a Mat. Indeed it was of little consequence who had him, as without a Cow he could be of no use, for none were left with him, we may reasonably suppose that they died on the passage, though the Natives told us there were some on board, but that they took them away with them, but this I cannot beleive. The next day I sent the three Cows   Mon. 25 I had on board to this Bull, the Bull, the Horse and Mare and Sheep I put a shore at Matavai. And now found my self lightened of a very heavy burden, the trouble and vexation that attended the bringing these Animals thus far is hardly to be conceived. But the satisfaction I felt in having been so fortunate as to fulfill His Majestys design in sending such usefull Animals to two worthy Nations sufficiently recompenced me for the many anxious hours I had on their account.

As I intended to make some stay here, we set up the two observatorys on Matavai point, erected two tents for the reception of a guard and such people as was necessary to have a Shore, and Mr King was intrusted with the Command, who at the same time attended the observations for assertaining the going of the Time keeper and other purposes. . . .

*   *   *

[*The ships were visited by 'all our old friends'. Cook also came across Odiddy, who had been on board for much of the second voyage. Unsettled weather hampered the repairs to the ships.*]

The next morning some messengers arrived from Eimeo with   Sat. 30 an acco^t that the people in that island were in arms and that Otoos friends had been obliged to fly to the Mountains. The difference which subsisted between the two islands in 1774 as mentioned in my last

Voyage has partly subsisted ever sence; the Armoment I saw at that time actually went against the Malecontents of Eimeo but returned without effecting much. On the arrival of these messengers all the Chiefs that were at Matavai assembled at Otoo's house where I happened to be at the time. One of the messengers opened the assembly in a long and set speach, but little of which I understood any further than the general purport, he explained the situation of affairs in Eimeo and endevoured to excite the assembly to arm on this occasion. After this there was great debates on both sides which were carried on with great order, no more than one man speaking at a time but at last they became very noisy and I expected it would have ended like a Polish Diet, but I found they cooled as fast as they heated and soon returned to order, at length it was resolved to send a strong force to assist their friends at Eimeo: but this resolution was not obtained without some opposition. Otoo was silent all the time except now and then speaking a word or two to the speakers. Those who were for procecuting the War asked for my assistance and all of them wanted to know what part I would take. Omai was sent for to be my interpreter, but as he was not to be found I was obliged to speak for my self and told them as well as I could that as I was not throughly acquainted with the dispute and the people of Eimeo having never offended me I could take no part in it, with this declaration they either were or seemed satisfied. After this the assembly broke up, but before I left them Otoo desired I would come to him in the afternoon and bring Omai with me. Accordingly a party of us went, he carried us to his Father when the dispute with Eimeo was renewed. I wanted to have found out some method to have made up this breach and sounded the old gentleman on that head, but we found him deaf to any thing of that kind and fully determined to procecute the war and wanted very much to prevail on me to give them my assistance. On our enquiring into the cause of the War, we were told that some years ago a Brother of Waheatua of Tierraboo, (a boy), was sent to Eimeo at the request of Maheine, a popular Cheif of that island, to be their King, but he had not been their a Week before Maheine caused him to be killed and set up for himself, in opposition to Tieratabunue his sisters Son who became the lawfull heir or else was set up by Otaheite upon the death of the other. T'towha one of the Chiefs of Attahourou and a man of much weight in the island happened not to be at Matavai at this time consequently not present at any of these consultation, it however appeared that he was no stranger to what had happened and entered with more spirit into the affair than any other chief, for early in the Morning of the 1st of Sepr he sent to acquaint Otoo that he SEPr had killed a Man to be sacrificed to the Eatua, to implore the Mon. 1 assistance of the God against Eimeo. This was to be done at the great Morai at Attahourou, where on this occasion Otoo's presence was absolutely necessary. I thought this a good oppertunity to see something of this extraordinary and Barbarous custom and proposed to Otoo to accompany him to which he readily consented, accordingly we set out in my boat with Potattow, Dr Anderson and Mr Webber and Omai followed in a Canoe. In our way we landed on a little island which lays off Tettaha where we found T'towha and his retinue, after some little conversation had pass'd between the two cheifs on the subject of the War Towha asked me to assist them and when I excused my self he seemed angry, and thought it strange that I who had always declared my self to be their friend would not now go and fight against their enimies. Before we parted he gave to Otoo two or three red feathers tied up in a tuft and a lean half sturved dog was put into a Canoe that was to accompany us. We then embarked and proceeded to the Morai at Attahourou, take[ing] on board in our way a Priest who was to assist at the Ceremony. As soon as we landed Otoo desired I would order the Seamen to remain in the boat and that I, Mr Anderson and Mr Webber would take of our hats as soon as we came to the Morai, to which we immediately proceeded, attended by a great many Men and some boys, but not one Woman. When we got to the Morai we found the Priests, four in Number and their attendants, or assistants waiting for us, the Corps or Sacrifice laid in a small Canoe before the Morai and partly in the wash of the Sea; two of the Priests with some of their attendants seting by it, the others at the Morai. The whole company stoped about twenty or thirty paces from the Priests, indeed the bulk of the people were further off, this being Otoo's station and we and a few others were with him. One of the Priests attendants brought a young Plantain tree and laid [it] down before Otoo, a nother

came with a small tuft of red feathers with which he touched one of
his feet and then retired with it to his companions, who now went to
some small Morais hard by and sat down facing those on the beach.
One of the Priests began a long prayer, and at set times sent down a
small plantain tree and laid it on the Sacrifice. During this prayer a
man who stood by the Priest held in his hands two small bundles
seemingly of Cloth, in one as we afterwards found, was the Royal
Maro and the other, if I may be allowed the expression, was the ark
of the Eatua. As soon as this prayer was ended the Priests at the Morais
with their attendants went and sat down by those on the beach,
carrying with them the two bundles. Here they renewed their prayers
during which the Plantain trees were taken one by one at different
times from off the Sacrifice and laid down before the Priests, and lastly
the Sacrifice, which was partly wraped up in leaves and small branches.
It was laid on the beach with the feet next the Sea round which the
Priests place'd themselves, some seting and others standing, and one
or more of them prayed Continually, holding in their hands small
tufts of red feathers. After some time the Sacrifice was striped of the
leaves &cᵃ and laid in a parallel direction with the Sea shore, one of
the Priests stood at the feet and pronounced a long prayer, in which
he was at times joined by the others, each holding in his hand a tuft
of red feathers. In the Course of this prayer some hair was pulled off
the head of the Sacrifice one of the eyes taken out and present[ed]
wraped in a green leafe, to Otoo, who however did not touch it, but
gave it to the Man who presented it the tuft of feathers he got from
T'towha, which with the hair and eye was carred back to the priests.
Soon after Otoo sent a nother piece of feathers he had given me in
the Morning to keep in my pocket. During some part of this last
ceremony a Kings fisher made a noise in the trees, Otoo turned to
me and said 'thats the Eatua' and seem'd to look upon it to be a good
omen.

The Sacrifice was now carried to the foot of one of the small Morais
before mentioned and laid down with the head towards it; the bundles
of cloth were laid on the Morai and the tufts of red feathers were
placed at the feet of the Sacrifice, round which the Priests placed
themselves and we were now allowed to go as near as we pleased.

The Cheif priest made a set speach or prayer, than addressed the Sacrifice (into whom they supposed the Spirit of the Eatua was entered) in a nother, the subject of this Speach or rather prayer, was to implore the distruction of their Enim[i]es whom he mentioned serveral times by name. After this they all prayed in a kind of song in which Potattow and some others joined; in the Course of this prayer a nother piece of hair was pulled of and laid on the Morai. After this the Chief Priest p[r]ayed alone holding in his hand the feathers which came from T'towha; when he had done he gave them to a nother who p[r]ayed in like manner, then all the tufts of feathers were laid on the bundles of Cloth which ended the ceremony at this place. They now took the bundles the feathers and the Sacrifice to the great Morai, the two first were laid against the pile of Stones, and at the foot of them the latter was placed round which the Priests Seated themselves and began again their prayers, while some of their attendants dug a hole at the foot of the Morai in which they burryed the Victim. As it was puting into the Grave a boy squeaked out aloud, Omai said it was the Eatua. In the Mean time a fire was made, the Dog before mentioned produced and killèd, the hair was got off by holding over the fire, the entrails taken out and thrown into the fire where they were left to consume; the hart liver kidnies &c^a were laid on the hot stones for a few Minutes and the blood was collected into a Cocoanut shell and afterward rubed over the dog which was held over the fire for about a Minute, then it together with the heart kidnies &c^a were carried and laid down before the Priests who were seting round the foot of the grave praying, and which they continued over the dog for some time, while two men beat at times on two drums very loud, and a boy squeeked out as before in a long shrill voice thrice, this as we were told was to call the Eatua to eat of what they had prepared for him. As soon as the Priests had ended their prayers, the dog with what belonged to it was laid on a Whatta or alter close by, where lay the remains of two others and three pigs not yet consumed, so that they stunk most intolerably and kept us at a greater distance than otherways we need to have been, for after the Victim was removed from the sea side we were allowed to be as near as we pleased; indeed after that neither solemnity nor attention was observ'd by the spectators.

The Ceremony being thus ended and with it the day we repaired to a house of Potattows where we were entertained and lodged for the night, being told that the Ceremony would be renewed again the next Morning. Being unwilling to lose any part of it, some of us repaired thither pretty early, but found nothing going forward, however soon after a pig was sacrificed and laid on the same alter with the others. About 8 o'clock Otoo took us again to the Morai where the Priests and a great number of men were assembled. The two bundles were lying in the same place they were in the evening before, the two drums stood in the front of the Morai but something nearer it than before and the Priests were without them. Otoo placed himself between the two drums and desired me to stand by him. The Ceremony began as usual with bring[ing] a young Plantain tree and laying down at the Kings feet, after which the Priests began to repeat their prayers, holding in their hands several tufts of red feathers and also a plume of Oysterage feathers I gave to Otoo on my first arrival and had been consecrated to this use. When the Priests had made an end of this prayer, they removed to between us and the Morai and there repeated a prayer, during which the tufts of feathers were one by one carryed and laid on the Ark of the Eatua; some little time after four pigs were produced and one was immediately killed, the others were taken to a sty hard by, probably for some future occasion. One of the bundles was now untied and it was found, as I have before observed, to contain the Maro with which they invest their Kings with Royalty. It was carefully taken out and spread out at full length on the ground before the Priests, it was about five yards long and fifteen inches broad, and composed of red and yellow feathers but mostly of the latter; the one end was bordered with eight pieces, each about the size and shape of [a] horse shoe, with their edges fringed with black pigeon feathers; the other end was forked and the ends not of the same length. The feathers were in square compartments ranged in two rows and otherways so desposed as to have a good effect being first paisted or fixed to thier Country cloth and then the whole sewed to the upper end of the English Pendant, Captain Wallis desplayed, and left flying a shore the first time he landed at Matavai, so at least we were told and we had no reason to doubt it as it was part of an

Tues. 2

English pend'. About six or eight inches square of the Maro was not compleat, that is there were no feathers upon it except a few that were sent by Waheatua as before mentioned. The Priests made a long Prayer over the Maro in different forms which, if I misstake not, they called the prayer of the Maro. When it was finished, the Maro was carefully foulded up put into the Cloth and laid upon the Morai. One end of the other bundle, which I call the ark, was next opened but we were not allowed to go near enough to examine its contents, but was told the Eatua was concealed in it, or rather what is supposed to represent him. This is a thing made of the twisted fibres of the husk of the coca-nut, shaped something like a large fid, that is roundish with one end much thicker than the other. We have very often got small ones from different people, but never knew their use before. By this time the pig was cleaned, the entrails taken out and laid before the Priests, who prayed over them for some time, during which one of them kept turning them gently with a stick and from their appearences some favourable Omens were conceived. After the Priest had done with them they were thrown into the fire and left to consume, the pig and the remainder of the entrails were treated and desposed of as the dog was the day before, and then all the feathers except the plume were put up with the Eatua that is into the Ark which ended the ceremony. Four double Canoes lay on the beach before the Morai all the Morning, on the fore part of each was what they called a Morai made or covered with palm leaves like some of their alters, on each lay some Cocoanuts Plantains and pieces of Bread fruit; they told us that they belonged to the Eatua and were to go with the fleet designed to go against Eimeo.

The unhappy sufferer seemed to be a Middle aged man, and as we were told a *Tou tou* but I never understood he had done any crime so as to merit death; it is however certain that they make choise of such for these sacrifices, or else common low fellows who strol about from place to place and island to island without any vesible way of geting an honist livelyhood, of such sort here are enough at these islands. This man was bloody about the head and face, which we attributed to the manner he was killed having been privatly knocked on the head with a Stone, for those who fall a sacrifice to this barbarous custom are never apprised of their fate till the Moment that puts an end to their existence. Whenever any of the Great cheifs thinks a human Sacrifice necessary on any particular occasion, he pitches upon the Victim, sends some of his trusty Servants who fall upon him and kill him; the King is then acquainted with it, whose presence at the Ceremony, as I was told is absolutely necessary, indeed except the Priests he was the only man that had any thing to do in it. From what we could learn these Sacrifices are not very uncommon, there were in the face of the Morai where this man was buried forty nine Sculls, every one of which were those of men who had been sacrificed at this place; and I have seen Sculls at many of the other great Morais, so that it is not confined to this place alone. This is not the only barbarous custom we find amongst these people, we have great reason to beleive there was a time when they were Canibals; however I will not insist upon this but confine my self to such as we have unquestionable authority for. Besides the cuting out the jaw-bones of the enemy that is slain in battle, they in some Measure offer their bodies as a Sacrifice to the Eatua the day after when the Victors collect all the dead that have fallen into their hands and bring them to the Morai, where with a great deal of ceremony they dig a hole and bury them all in it as an offering to the Gods. But the great cheifs who fall in battle and into the hands of their enimies are treated in a different manner. We were told that the late King Tootaha, Tebourai Tamaida, and a nother Chief who fell with them were brought to this Morai, their bowels cut out by the Priests before the great alter, and the bodies afterwards buried in three different places, which were pointed out to us in the great pile of stones which compose the most conspicious part of this Morai. And the Common Men who fell also in this battle were all burried in one hole at the foot of the pile. This Omai, who was present, told me was done the day after the Battle, with much Pomp and ceremony, and in the midst of a great Concourse of people, as a thanksgiving offering to the Eatua for the Victory they had obtained, while the vanquished had taken refuge in the Mountains, where they remain'd about a week or ten days till the fury of the Victors was over and a treaty set on foot that concluded with Otoo being invested with the Maro and made King which was done with great ceremony at the same Morai in the presence of all the principal men in the island.

About Noon we embarked in order to return to Matavai and visited Towha in our way, who had remained on the little island, some conversation pass'd between Otoo and him on the present posture of affairs and then the Chief asked me again to assist them; by my refusal I intirely lost the good will of this Chief. Before we parted he asked us how we liked the Ceremony we had seen, what our opinion was of it and if we observed such Customs in our own Country. During the Ceremony we were silent but as soon as it was over we made no scruple in giving our sent[i]ments very freely upon it and of Course condemned it. I told the Chief that this Sacrifice was so far from pleasing the Eatua as they intended that he would be angry with them for it and that they would not succeed against Maheine. This was venturing a good deal upon conjecture, but I thought their was little danger of being misstaken; for I found there was three parties in the island, one extremely Violent, one perfectly indifferent about the Matter and the third openly declaring themselves friends to Maheine and his party. Under these circumstances it was not likely such a plan of opperation would be settled as would insure even a probability of success. Omai was our spokesman and entered into our arguments with so much Spirit that he put the Cheif out of all manner of patience, especially when he was told that if he a Cheif in England had put a Man to death as he had done this he would be hanged for it; on this he balled out 'Maeno maeno' (Vile vile) and would not here a nother word; so that we left him with as great a contempt of our customs as we could possibly have of theirs. During this debate most of the people on the spot were present, which were chiefly the Attendants and servants of the Chief, and when Omai began to explaine the punishment that would be inflicted upon even the greatest man in England if he killed his Servant, they seemed to listen with attention and were probably of a different opinion with their master.

*   *   *

In the evening of the the 14th Captain Clerke and I took a   Sun. 14
ride round the plain of Matavai to the Very great surprise and astonishment of a great train of people who attended us; for tho Omai

had been once or twice on horseback he had been as often thrown off before he got himself seated, so that this was the first time they had seen any body ride a horse. It was afterwards continued every day by one or a nother so long as we stayed and yet their curiosity was not then satisfied; they were exceedingly delighted with these Animals after they had seen the use that was made of them. And I think they gave them a better idea of the greatness of other Nations than all the other things put together that had been carried amongst them. Both the horse and Mare was in good case and looked extreamly well.

* * *

Having got all our Water on board the Ships Caulked the rigging overhauled and every thing put in order I began to think about leaving the island, that I might have sufficient time to spare to visit the others. With this view we got on board the observatories, the Instruments Sun. 21 and bent the sails. Early the next Morning Otoo came aboard to acquaint me that all the war Canoes of Matavai were going to Oparre to join those of that place where there would be a general review. Soon after all those of Matavai were in Motion and after parading awhile about the bay they assembled ashore near the middle of it. I now went in my boat to take a view of them and to go with them to Oparre but soon after a resolution was taken by the Cheifs not to go there till the next day. I looked upon this to be a good oppertunity to get some insight into their Manner of fighting and desired Otoo to order some of them to go through the necessary manouvres. Two were accordingly ordered off, in one of them Otoo Mr King and my self went and Omai in the other. After we were out in the bay, we faced, and advanced upon each other and retreated by turns, as quick as the paddlers could move them; during this the wariors on the Stages flourished their weapons and played a hundred Antick tricks which could answer no other end that I could see than to work up their passions for fighting. Otoo stood by the side of the Stage and gave the necessary orders when to advance and when to retreat, in this great judgement and a quick eye combined together seemed necessary to seize every advantage that might offer and to avoide giving advantage. At last after advancing and retreating, to and from each other at least a dozen times, the two canoes closed, head to head, or stage to stage and after a short conflict, the troops on our Stage were supposed to be killed and we were board[ed] by Omai and his associates, and that very instant Otoo and all the paddlers leaped over board to save their lives by swiming. If Omai's information is to be depended upon their Naval engagements are not always conducted in this Manner, he tills me that they some times lash the two Vessels together head to head and then fall too and fight till all the wariors are killed in either one or the other of the Canoes. But this way of fighting I apprehend, is never practised but when they are determined to conquer or die, indeed one or the other must happen for all agree that they never give quarter, unless it be to reserve them for a more cruel death the next day. The power and strength of these islands lies intirely in their Navies, I never heard of a general engagement on land, so that all their desitive battles are fought on the Water. . . .

As soon as this Mock fight was over, Omai put on his Suit of Armour, mounted a stage in one of the Canoes and was paddled all along the shore of the bay, so that every one had a full View of him but it did not draw their attention so much as might be expected.

MONDAY 22nd. Early in the Morning of the 22nd Otoo and his Father came aboard to know when I intended to sail, for having been told that there was a very good harbour at Eimeo, I intended visiting that island in my way to Huaheine, and they were desireous of takeing a passage with me and going with their fleet at the same time. As I was ready I left it to them to name the day and the Wednesday following was fixed upon, when I was to take on board Otoo, his Father, Mother and in short the whole family. These points being settled I got ready to go to Oparre to see the review, for there all the Vessels were to rendezvouse. I had but just got into my boat when news arrived that Towha had concluded a Peace with Maheine and was returned to Attahourou; this made all further proceeding unnecessary and the Canoes all returned from whence they came, it did not however hinder me from following Otoo to Oparre, accompanied by Mr King and

Omai. Soon after we got their a Messenger arrived from Eimeo and related the terms of the Peace or rather a Truce for it was for a limited time. The terms were disadvantagious and all the blame fell upon Otoo for not going to assist Towha in time. The current report was now, that Towha assisted by the forces of Waheatua would, as soon as I was gone, come and fall upon Otoo; this called upon me to support my friend by threatening to retaliate it upon all who came against him when I returned again to the island, if there was any truth in the report at first this had the desired effect, for we heard no more of it. Happi, Otoo's Father, highly desaproved of the Peace and blamed Towha very much for concluding it. This sencible old Man no doubt foresaw that my going down with them must have added great weight to their cause without my takeing any other part whatever in the quarrel, and it was on this it was he built all his arguments and excused Otoo for not giving Towha assistance so soon as he expected. These debates were hardly ended before a Messenger arrived from Towha desireing Otoos attendance the next day at the Morai at Attahourou, to give thanks to the gods for the Peace he had concluded. I was asked to go but being much out of order was obliged to decline it, but Mʳ King and Omai went and I returned on board with Otoo's Mother, his three Sisters and eight more Women. At first I thought they came into my boat with no other view than to get a passage to Matavai, but when they got to the Ship they told me they were come to sleep on board and to cure me of the desorder that I complained of, which was a sort of Rheumatick pain in one side from my hip to the foot. This kind offer I excepted of, made them up a bed in the Cabbin floor and submited myself to their direction, I was desired to lay down in the Midst of them, then as many as could get round me began to squeeze me with both hands from head to foot, but more especially the parts where the pain was, till they made my bones crack and a perfect Mummy of my flesh – in short after being under their hands about a quarter of an hour I was glad to get away from them. How[ev]er I found immediate relief from the operation, they gave me a nother rubing down before I went to bed and I found my self pretty easy all Tues. 23   the night after. They repeated the operation the next Morning before they went a shore, and again in the evening when they came on board, after which I found the pains intirely removed and the next Morning they left me. This they call *Romy* an operation   Wed. 24 which in my opi[ni]on far exceed[s] the flesh brush, or any thing we make use of of the kind. It is universally practiced among them, it is some times performed by the men but more generally by the Woman. If at any time one appear languid or tired and sit down by any of them they immeditely begin with Romy upon your legs, which I have always found to have an exceeding good effect. The 25th in   Thur. 25 the Morning Otoo, Mr King and Omai returned from Attahourou, when Mr King gave me the following account of what he had seen. . . .

[*James King described the elaborate ceremony of reconciliation between Tu (Otoo), and Towha and Potatau.*]

FRIDAY 26*th*. The War with Eimeo and the Ceremonies it occasioned being over, all our friends paid us a visit on the 26th and as they knew we were upon the point of sailing they brought with them more hogs than we could take of their hands, for having no salt left to salt any we wanted no more than for present expence.

SATURDAY 27*th*. . . . Our friend Omai got one good thing here for the many good things he gave away, this was a very fine double Sailing Canoe, compleatly equiped Man'd and fit for the Sea. I had made him up a suit of English Colours[19] some time before, but he thought them too good or too Valuable to wear at this time and made up a parcel of Colours, such as flags and pendants to the Number of ten or a dozen which he spread on different parts of his Vessel at the same time and drew together as many people to look at her as a Man of War would dressed in a European port. These Streamers of Omais were a Mixture of English, French, Spanish and Dutch which were all the European colours he had seen. When I was last at this island I gave Otoo an English Jack and Pendant and to Towha a Pendant, which they still preserve with great care.

    Omai had also provided himself with a good stock of Cloth and Cocoanut Oil which is not only in greater plenty but much better at Otaheite than at any of the other Society islands, in so much that they

19. i.e., an ensign, a jack and a pennant.

are articles of trade. Omai would not have acted so inconsistant and so much unlike himself as he did but for his Sister and Brother in law, who together with a few more of thier acquaintance ingross'd him intirely to themselves with no other view than to strip him of every thing he had got, and they would have succeeded if I had not put a stop to it in time by taking the most usefull things into my possission. But this would not have done if I had suffered them to have gone with, or followed us to Huaheine as they intended, in this they were disapointed for I forbid their coming while I was at the islands and they knew me too well not to comply.

SUNDAY 28th. The 28th Otoo came on board and informed me that he had got a Canoe which he desired I would take on board and carry home as a present from him to the Earee rahie no Pretane;[20] it being the only thing he said he could send worth His Majestys acceptance. I was not a little pleased with Otoo for this mark of his gratitude, it was a thought intirely his own without any of us mentioning a word about it and shewed that he fully understood to whom he was indebted for the most Valuable presents he had received. At first I thought this Canoe had been a Model of one of their Vessels of war, but I found it was a small Ivahah about sixteen feet long; it was double and seemed to have been built for the purpose, and was decorated with all those pieces of Carved work they usually fix upon their Canoes. As it was too large for me to take on board I could only thank him for his good intention, but it would have pleased him much better to have taken it. We were detained here some days longer than I expected by light breezes from the West and Calms by turns, so that we could not get out of the bay. During this time the Ships were crowded by our friends and surrounded every day by a Multitude of Canoes, for not one would leave the place till we were gone. At length at 3 oclock in the Mon. 29 after noon of the 29th the wind came at East and we weighed anchor; as soon as the Ships were under sail, I, at the request of Otoo fired Seven Guns after which all our friends except him and two or three more, left us with such marks of affection and grief as sufficiently shewed how much they regreted our departure. Otoo being desireous

20. *Arii rahi no Pretane*: the great chief of Britain.

of seeing the Ship sail, I made a stretch out to sea and then in again when he also bid us fare well.

The commands which I had from Otoo was to desire the Earee rahie no Pretane to send him by the next Ships, red feathers and the birds that produce them, axes, half a dozen muskets with powder and shot, and by no means to forget horses. . . .

TUESDAY 30*th*. As I did not give up the design of touching at Eimeo, at day-break in the Morning after leaving Otaheate I stood for the North side of the island where we were told the harbour lay; Omai had got there long before us and had taken the most necessary measures to shew us the place, we were however not without Pilots, having several men of Otahiete on board and not a few women. Not caring to trust intirely to these guides I sent two boats to examine the harbour and on their making the Signal for safe Anchorage, we stood in with the Ships and anchored close up to the head of it in 10 fathom water over a bottom of soft mud and Moored with a hawser fast to the shore. This harbour is called *Talough* it is situated on the North side of the island in the district of *Oboonohou*; it extends in south or SBE between the hills above two miles, for security and the goodness of its bottom it is not inferior to any harbour I have met with in any of the islands, and has this advantage over the most of them, that a Ship can sail both in and out with the reigning trade wind, so that the access and recess are equally easy. . . .

We had no sooner anchored than the ships were crowded with the Inhabitents whom curiosity alone brought on board, for they brought nothing with them to exchange. But the next morning they came in Canoes from more destant parts, and brought with them Bread fruit, Cocoanuts and a few hogs which they exchanged for hatchets, Nails and beads, red feathers not being so much sought after as at Otaheite. The Ship being a good [deal] pestered with rats, I hauled her within thirty yards of the Shore, being as near as the depth of water would allow, and made conveniences for them to go a Shore, being in hopes some would be induced to it, but I beleive we got clear of very few if any. In the Morning of the 2nd *Maheine* the Cheif made me a visit, he approached the Ship with great caution and

OCT^r
Wed. 1

Thur. 2

it required some persuasion to get him on board; he was accompaned by his Wife or Mistress, she was Sister to Oamo of Otahiete who died while we were at this island. I made both Maheine and his Mistress presents of such things as they most Valued and after a stay of about half an hour they went away, but not long after returned with a large hog, which they meant as a return for my present but I made them another present to the full value of it, after this they paid Captain Clerke a visit. This Cheif who with a few people has made himself in a manner independant of Otaheite, is between 40 and 50 years of age, he is bald headed, a thing rather uncommon in these islands at that age, he wore a kind of Turban and seem'd ashamed to shew his head, but whether a bald head is a Mark of desgrace with them or they thought it was so with us I cannot say; we judged it was the latter, as we had shaved the head of a Indian we had caught Stealing. . . .

MONDAY 6*th*. On the 6th in the Morning hauled the Ship off into the Stream, intending to put to Sea the next day, but a circumstance happened that prevented it and gave me a good deal of trouble, this was some of the Natives in the evening stealing one of our Goats, that we had ashore in the day time grazeing, with two men to look after them. The loss of this Goat would have been nothing if it had not interfered with my views of Stocking other islands with these Animals but as it did it was necessary to get it again if possible. The next Morning we got intillengence that it was carried to Maheine the Chief, who was at this time at Parowroah harbour;[21] two old men offered to conduct any of my people I might think proper to send to him to bring back the goat. Accordingly I sent a boat with them and a threatening message to Maheine if the goat was not immediately delivered up and also the thief. It was but the day before that this cheif asked me for two, but as I could not spare any but at the expence of other islands that might never have another oppertunity to get any and had heard there were already two on this, I did not gratify him. I however desired Tidooah an Otaheite chief, who was present, to beg of Otoo to send him two, and by way of ensuring it, sent Otoo

Tues. 7

21. It is not known what places Cook is referring to by Parowroah here and Watea below.

by the same Chief a large piece of red feathers equal to the Value of the two goats. This I expected would have satisfied, not only Maheine, but all the other chiefs in the island, but the event proved that I was misstaken. Not thinking that any one would dare to take a nother at the very time I was taking measures to recover the first, the Goats were again put ashore this Morning and in the evening a boat was sent to bring them on board for good; as they were geting them into the boat one was carried off undiscovered, As it was immediately missed I made no doubt of geting it again without much troble, as it could not be gone far. Ten or twelve of the Natives set out at different times to bring it back, or to look for it, for not one would own it was stolen but that it was stray'd into the woods and indeed I thought so my self. But was convinced to the Contrary, when I found that not one of those who whent after it returned, so that their only view was to amuse me till it was out of my reach and night put a stop to all further search. About this time the boat returned with the other and one of the Men who had Stolen it, the first instance of the kind I had met with amongst these islands.

WEDNESDAY 8*th.* The next morning I found that most of the Inhabitents in the neighbour hood was, according to custom, moved off and that Maheine was gone to the very further part of the island. I was now convinced that a plan had been laid to Steal what I had refused to give, and that altho they had given up one they were resolved to keep the other, which was a she goat and big with kid, and I was determined they should not. I therefore applyed to the two old men who had been in[s]trumental in geting back the other; they told me it was carried to *Wate-a,* a district on the South side of the island, by Hamoah the cheif of that place, but that if I would send any body for it it would be delivered up. They offered to conduct some of my people a Cross the island, but on my learning from them, that a boat might go and return the same day, I sent one with two petty officers, Mr Roberts and Mr Shuttleworth, one to remain with the boat in case she could not get to the place while the other went with the guides and one or two of our people. Late in the evening the boat returned, and the officers enformed me, that after proceeding as far in the boat as rocks and

shoals would allow them, Mr Shuttleworth, with two marines and one
of the guides, landed and traveled to Watea to the house of Hamoah
where the people of the place amused them for some time, by teling
them the Goat would soon be brought them and pretending they had
sent for it, it however never came and the approach of night obliged
Mr Shuttleworth to return to the boat without it. I was now very sorry
I had proceeded so far, as I could not retreat with any tolerable credet,
and without giving incouragement to the people of the other islands
we had yet to visit to rob us with impunity. I asked Omai and the two
old men what methods I should next take, they without hesitation,
advised me to go with a party of men into the Country, and shoot
every Soul I met with. This bloody advice I could not follow, but I
resolved to march a party of men a[c]ross the island, and at day break
Thur. 9   the next Morning set out with thirty five accompanied by
one of the old men, Omai and three or four of his people; at the same
time, I ordered Lieutenant Williamson with three Armed boats round
the western part of the island to meet us. I no sooner landed with my
party than the few Natives that had remained fled before us, the first
man Omai saw, he asked me if he should shoot him, so fully was he
persuaded I was going to carry his advice into execution. I immediately
ordered both him and our guide to make it known, that I did not
intend to hurt, much less kill a single endividial. These glad tidings
flew before us like lightning and stoped the flight of the Inhabitants;
so that no one quited either his house or imployment afterward. As
we began to ascend the ridge of hills over which we had to pass, we
got intellengence that the Goat was gone before us, and as we understood not yet gone over the hills, so that we marched up in great
silence in hopes of surprising the party that had her; but whin we got
to the uppermost plantation on the side of the ridge the people there
told us, she was kept there the first night and the next Morning carri'd
to Watea by Hamoah. We then crossed the ridge, without making
any further enquiry, till we came in sight of Watea, when some people
shew'd us Hamoah's house and told us the Goat was there so that I
made myself sure of geting it immediately, and was not a little surprised
to find on my geting to the place, the few people we met with deny
having ever seen her, even Hamoah himself. On my first coming to

the place I observed several Men runing to and from in the woods with Clubs and bundles of darts in their hands, and Omai who followed them had some stones thrown at him, so that it seemed as tho' they had intended to oppose any step I should take by force, but seeing my party too strong droped the design: a nother thing which made me think so, was all their houses being empty. After geting a few of the people of the place together I desired Omai to expostulate with them on the conduct they were persuing, and to tell them, that from the testimony of so many people, I was well assured they had the Goat and therefore insisted upon its being deliv[er]ed up, if not I would burn their houses and boats. But notwithstanding all I, or Omai could say, they continued to deny having any knowledge of it; the consequence was, my seting fire to six or eight houses, which were presently consumed, together with two or three War Canoes that lay [in] some of them. This done I marched off to join the boats, which lay about seven or eight miles from us, and in our way burnt six more War Canoes, without any one attempting to oppose us, on the contrary many assisted but this was probably done more out of fear than good will. In one place Omai who was in a canoe a little before us, cauld and told us, a great many men were getting together to attack us, we made ready to receive them, but instead of offensive weapons, they were headed by ten or twelve men with plantain trees in their hands, which they laid down at my feet and beg'd I would spare a Canoe that lay close by, which I did. At length about 4 PM we got to the boats, that were waiting at *Whararade* the District of *Tieratabunue*, but this Cheif as well as all the principal people of the place were fled to the hills, although I touched not a single thing belonging to them, as they were the friends of Otoo. After resting ourselves at this place about an hour, we set out for the Ships were we arrived about eight oclock and were no account of the Goat had been received, so that all I had yet done had not had the desired effect.

FRIDAY 10*th*. Early in the Morning of the 10th I despatched One of Omais men to Maheine to till him if he did not send the goat I would not leave him a Canoe on the island and that I would continue destroying till it came. And that the Messenger might see I was in earnest, I sent the Carpenters to break up three or four Canoes that lay a shore at the head of the harbour; the plank we took on board to build Omai a house at Huaheine, or where he intended to sittle. I after ward went to the next harbour, broke up three or four more and burnt as many and then returned on board about seven in the evening, where about half a hour before, the goat was brought from the very place I had been the day before, in consequence of the Message I sent to the Cheif in the Morning. Thus this troublesome, and rather unfortunate affair ended, which could not be more regreted on the part of the Natives than it was on mine.[22]

SATURDAY 11th. The next Morning we were again all good friends the people bring[ing] to the Ships fruit &c^a to ba[r]ter with the same confidence as at first. About 9 AM we weig[h]ed with a breeze down the harbour, but it prov'd so fai[n]t and Variable, that it was Noon before we got out to Sea, when I steer'd for Huaheine with Omai in his Canoe in company, he did not depend intirely upon his own judgment, but had got on board a Pilot, I observed that they shaped as direct a Course for the island as I could do. . . .

SUNDAY 12th. The 12th at Noon we Anchored at the North entrance of *O Wharre* harbour, which is on the West side of the island; the whole after-noon was spent in warping the Ships into a proper birth and Mooring. Omai entered the harbour with his canoe just before us, but did not land nor did he take much Notice of any of his Country men, though many crowded to see him, but far more came off to the Ships, in so much that we could hardly work for them. Our passengers presently acquainted them with what we had done at Eimeo and multiplyed the number of Canoes and houses we had distroyed by ten at least which I was not sorry for, as I saw it had great effect upon all who heard it, so that I had hopes they would behave a little better than they usually had done at this island.

While I was at Otaheite, I was told that my old friend *Oree* was no longer the chief and that at this time he was at Ulietea, he indeed was

22. George Gilbert, in his narrative of the voyage, wrote: 'I can't well account for Capt Cook's proceedings on this occasion; as they were so very different from his conduct in like cases in his former voyages.'

never more than Regent during the Minority of *Tareederria* the present Earee rahie, but he did not give up the Regency till he was forced. His two Sons, Opoony and Towha were the first who made me a visit and a present, they came aboard before the Ship was well in the harbour. Our arrival brought the next Morning being the   Mon. 13 13th all the principal people in the island together, this was just what I wished, as I wanted to sittle Omai in the best manner I could, he now seem'd inclinable to go to Ulietea and I was not against it, as there is a piece of land at that island which the Bolabola men despossess'd his Father of and I thought I could get it restored to the Son, but we could not agree upon the conditions, I wanted to reconcile him to the Bolabola men, and he was too great a Patriot to listen to any such thing. Huaheine was therefore the island to leave him at and no other. After the hurry of the morning was over, we got ready to pay a formal visit to the young chief, Omai dress'd himself very properly on the occasion and prepared a very handsome present for the chief and a nother for his Eatua, indeed after he got clear of the gang that surrounded him at Otahiete, he behaved with such prudence as to gain respect. Our landing drew most of the company from the Ship, they as well as those a shore assembled in a large house. We waited some time for the Chief as I would do nothing till he came, but I found his presence quite unnecessary, as he was not above eight or ten years of age. Omai who stood at a little distance from the company, began with making his offering to the Gods, consisting of red feathers cloth &c^a then followed a nother for the Chief to give to the Gods and after it several other small pieces and tufts of red feathers, one after another. Every thing was laid before one of the company, who I understood was a priest, each was delivered with a set speach or prayer, spoken by one of Omais friends who sat by him but mostly digtated by him self. In these prayers, he did not forget his friends in England, nor those that had brought him out. Earee rahie no Pretane, Lord Sandwich, Tootee, Tatee were mentioned in every one of them. When Omai had done, the Priest took each Article in the same order as it was given him, and after repeating a prayer, sent it to the Morai, which Omai told us was a great distance off, otherwise this ceremony would have been performed at it. The Religious part of the Ceremony being over, Omai sat down by me, I made the you[n]g Chief a present and received his in return, which was pretty considerable. After pointing out to them how I wished the intercourse to be carried on betwixt us, and the consequences that would attend there robing us as they had formerly done, Omai acquainted them that he had been in England where he was well received and treated, and sent back with many articles that would be very usefull in the island. He then asked them in my name for a piece of land to build a house upon and to Mentain himself and servants, that if this was not complyed with, neither by gift nor purchas, I should carry him to Ulietea and fix him there. This last proposal, they all seemed to like, but as I was apprized of their views, which was to go with Omai to Ulietea and with my assistance (which Omai without any reason whatever had made them believe they were to expect) to drive all the Bolabola men from the island, I told them that I neither would assist them in such a design nor suffer them to put it into execution while I was there, that if Omai went there he must be a friend not an Enemy to the Bolabola men. This gave a new turn to the affair, a Man rose up and told me that the whole island of Huaheine and every thing in it was mine and therefore I might give what part I pleased of it to Omai. Omai, who like the rest of his Country men seldom sees things beyond the present moment, was greatly pleased with this declaration, thinking no doubt that I should be very liberal and give him enough; but it was by far too general for me; and therefore desired they would not only point out the place, but the quantity of land he was to have. On this some Chiefs who had left the assembly were sent for, and after a short consultation amongst themselves my request was granted by general consent and the ground immediately pointed out, adjoining to the house in which we were assembled. The extent along the shore of the harbour was about two hundred yards and its depth to the foot of the hill something more, but a proportional part of the hill was included in the grant. This point being settled to the satisfaction of all parties, I set up a tent a shore, established a post, there Set up the observatorys to make the necessary Observations and the Carpenters of both Ships were set to work to build a small house for Omai to secure his property in; in the mean time some hands were employed making a Garden,

Planting Shaddocks, Vines, Pine apples, Millons and several other articles, all of which were in a flourishing state before we left the island. Omai now began seriously to attend to his own affairs and repented of his prodigality at Otaheite, he found here a Brother, a Sister and Brother in law, the Sister being married but these did not plunder him like those at Otaheite, but they had neither weight nor influance to protect either him or his property, and I saw that he was liable to loss every thing he had got as soon as we were gone. To prevent which, I advised him to give a good part of his Moveables, usefull as well as Ornamental, to two or three of the principal Chiefs, by which means he would both satisfy them, and secure them in his favour and then he need not mind the rest; he promised to follow my advice and I was afterward told he did. It is here as in many other Countries, a man that is richer than his Neighbour is sure to be invied, this was Omais fate, and there were numbers who wished to see him upon a level with themselves; from these he had every thing to fear, as many of them were far more powerfull than himself. In order to intimidate these, I gave out that I should return to the island again after being absent the usual time, and that if I did not find Omai in the same state as I left him all those who had been his enemy would feel the weight of my resentment, this will certainly have some effect as they have not a doubt but that I shall return again to the island.

While we lay here we got the Bread remaining in the bread room ashore to clear it of Vermin, the number of Cock roaches that were in the Ship at this time is incredable, the damage they did us was very considerable and every method we took to distroy them proved ineffectual.

Every thing was carried on between us and the Natives without being disturbed by any one accedent till the evening of the   Wed. 22 22nd when a man found means to get into Mr Baileys Observatory and carry off a Sextant unobserved; as soon as I was made acquinted with the theft I went a shore and got Omai to apply to the Chiefs to have it returned, he did so but they took no steps towards it being more attentive to a play that was then acting, till I ordered the performers to desist, they were then convinced I was in earnest and began to make some enquiry after the thief, who was siting in the midst of them quite unconcerned; in so much that I was in great doubt of his being the man as he denied it. But as Omai assured me he was I sent him aboard the Ship and there confined him, this spread a general alarm and every one fled in spite of all I could do to stop them. Omai went aboard and with some difficulty got out of the fellow where he had hid the sextant, but as it was dark we could not find it till day light the next morning when it was got again unhurt. After this the Natives recovered from their fright and began to gather about us as usual, and as to the thief, he appearing to be a hardened Scounderal I punished him with greater severity than I had ever done any one before and then dismiss'd him.[23] This however did not deter him from giving us farther trouble, for in the night between the 24th and

Sat. 25   25th a general Alarm was spread occasioned as was said by one of our Goats being Stolen by this very man, it proved not so, probably he found them too well guarded to put his disign in execution, but we found he had destroyed and carri'd off several Vines and Cabbage plants in Omais plantation, and he publickly threatened to kill him and burn his house as soon as we were gone. To prevent his giving me and Omai any further trouble I had him Siezed and confined on board the Ship with a view of carrying him off the island, this seemed to give general satisfaction. He was from Bolabola nevertheless he had a strong party in this island that were ready to assist him in any of his designs whenever there was an oppertunity. I had always met with more troublesome people at this island than any of the others, and it was only fear and the want of oppertunities that made them behave better now. Anarchy seemed to prevail more here than at any other place, the Earee rahie as I have before observed was but a Child and I did not find there was any one man or set of Men who managed the Goverment for him, so that when ever any missunderstanding happened between us I never knew whom to apply to to settle matters. The you[n]g Chiefs Mother would some times exert her self but I did not see she had greater authority than many others.

SUNDAY 26th. On the 26th Omais house being nearly finished many of his Moveables were got a shore; amongst many other useless things,

23. His ears were cut off.

was a box of Toys which when exposed to publick view seemed to please the gazing Multitude very much; but as to his Pots, Kettles, Dishes, plates, drinking mugs, glasses &c^a &c^a &c^a hardly any one so much as looked at. Omai himself now found that they were of no manner of use to him, that a baked hog eat better than a boiled one, that a plantain leafe made as good a dish or plate as pewter and that a Cocoanut shell was as good to drink out of as a black-jack; and therefore he very wisely disposed of as many of these things as he could to the people of the Ships for hatchets and other usefull articles. In the evening of the 28th we exhibited some of Omais fire-   Tues. 28 works, before a great concourse of people who beheld them with a mixture of pleasure and fear, what remained were put in order and left with him, agreeable to the intintion for which they were put on board, but by far the greatest part were either already expended or rendered useless by keeping so long.

THURSDAY 30*th*. Between 12 and 4 in the Morning of the 30th the Man, I had in confinement, found means to make his escape, he carried with him the shakle of the bilboo-bolt that was about his leg, which was taken from him as soon as he got a shore by one of the Chiefs and given to Omai who came on board very early in the Morning to acquaint me that his Mortal enimy was again let loose upon him. It appeared, on enquiry, that not only the sentry that was over the man but the whole watch on the quarter deck where he was confined, laid down to sleep, he seized this oppertunity to take the Key of the irons out of the bittacle drawer, where he had seen it put, and let himself at liberty. This affair convinced me that a very bad, or rather no lookout, was kept in the night, which made it necessary to punish those that were in fault and make some new regulations to prevent the like for the future.[24]

As soon as Omai was settled in his new habitation, I began to think of leaving the island and with that view get every thing off from the shore, except the horse and Mare and a goat big with kid, which were

24. The punishments were extensive: the mate was disrated and sent to the *Discovery*; the midshipman turned before the mast, two marines flogged – one of them on three successive days.

left in the possession of Omai. I also gave him a boar and two sows of the English breed and he had got a sow or two of his own. The Horse covered the Mare while we were at Otahiete so that there is little fear but they will in time have a breed of Horses. Omai had picked up at Otaheite four or five Toutous, the two New Zealand youths remained with him and his Brother and some others joined him here, so that his family already consisted of eight or ten without ever a woman among them, nor did Omai seem attall desposed to take unto himself a Wife. The House which we built him was [24] feet by [18] and [10] feet high, it was built of boards and with as few nails as possible, that there might be no inducement to pull it down. As soon as we were gone he was with the assistance of some of the chiefs, to build after the Country fashion a large house over it; if it cover the grou[n]d which he marked out it will be as large as most on the island. His armour consi[s]ted of a Musket, bayonet and cartouch-box; a Fowling piece, two pair of pistols and two or three Swords and cutlasses. And I left him about twenty pound of powder, a few Musket Cartridges, Musket and pistol balls; these made him quite happy, which was my only view for giving him them, for I was always of Opinion he would have been better without fire Arms than with them. After Omai had got his things a shore he had most of the officers of both Ships two or three times to dinner, his table was always well covered with the very best the island afforded. Before I left the island I had the following Inscription cut out upon the one end of his house viz.

Georgius tertius Rex 2 *Novembris* 1777

Naves $\begin{cases} \textit{Resolution Fac. Cook P}^r \\ \textit{Discovery Car. Clerke P}^r \end{cases}$ [25]

NOVEM^r SUNDAY 2*nd*. On the 2nd of November at 4 PM I took the advantage of a breeze which then sprung up at East and sailed out of the harbour. Most of our friends remained on board till the Ships were under sail, when to gratify them, I ordered five guns to be fired and then they all took leave, except Omai who remained till we were

25. *Pr: praefectus*, captain of a ship.

at Sea. We had come to sail by a hawser we had fast to the shore, in casting the Ship it parted (being cut by the rocks) and the outer end left behind, as those who cast it off did not perceive it was broke; so that we had a boat to send for it. In this boat Omai went ashore, after taking a very affectionate farewell of all the Officers; he sustained himself with a manly resolution till he came to me then his utmost eforts to conceal his tears failed, and Mr King, who went in the boat, told me he wept all the time in going ashore. Whatever faults this Indian had they were more than over ballanced by his great good Nature and docile disposition, during the whole time he was with me I very seldom had reason to find fault with his conduct. His gratifull heart always retained the highest sence of the favours he received in England nor will he ever forget those who honoured him with their protection and friendship during his stay there. He had a tolerable share of understanding, but wanted application and perseverance to exert it, so that his knowledge of things was very general and in many instances imperfect. He was not a man of much observation, there were many little arts as well as amusements amongst the people of the Friendly islands which he might have conveyed to his own, where they probably would have been adopted, as being so much in their own way, but I never found that he used the least endeavours to make himself master of any one. This kind of indifferency is the true Character of his Nation, Europeans have visited them at times for these ten years past, yet we find neither new arts nor improvements in the old, nor have they copied after us in any one thing. We are therefore not to expect that Omai will be able to interduce many of our arts and customs amongst them or much improve those they have got, I think however he will endeavour to bring to perfection the fruits &c^a we planted which will be no small acquisition. But the greatest benifit these islands will receive from Omais travels will be in the Animals that have been left upon them, which probably they never would have got had he not come to England; when these multiplies of which I think there is little doubt, they will equal, if not exceed any place in the known World for provisions. Omais return occasioned a number of volunteers to go to Pretane, and he was so ambitious of being the only great traveler that he frequently put me in mind that

Lord Sandwich told him no more were [to] come. If there had been the most distant probability of any Ship being sent again to New Zealand I would have brought the two youths of that Country home with me, as they were both desireous of coming; Tiarooa the eldest, was an exceeding well disposed young man with strong natural parts and capable of receiving any instructions. He seemed to be fully sencible of the difference between his own Country and these islands and resigned himself very contentedly to end his days upon them; but the other was so strongly attatched to us that he was taken out of the Ship and carried a shore by force; he was a witty smart boy and on that account much noticed in the Ship.[26]

*   *   *

[*The ships now proceeded to Raiatea (Ulietea), where Cook foiled a plot to take himself and Clerke prisoner. Cook now gave Clerke his instructions in case of separation on their long voyage north. The contrast between where they now were and where they were heading produced a foreseeable reaction – desertion. Marine John Harrison deserted, taking his musket and equipment with him. Efforts to get him back failing, Cook himself took an armed party in two boats and discovered him in a house with two women. The other desertion, from the* Discovery, *was more serious in that one of the two men was the sixteen-year-old midshipman Alexander Mouat, son of the naval captain who had circumnavigated with Byron. Concerned to 'save the Son of a brother officer from being lost to the World', and conscious that there were others 'who wanted to end their days at these islands', Cook again led the search, with two armed boats. He returned when told that the fugitives had left the island, and took hostages instead: the chief Orio, his son and son-in-law, and his daughter, the beautiful Poetua (whom Webber painted). Cook let the chief go on the understanding that he would produce the offenders – who were soon brought back from the island of Tupai and put in irons.*

Cook called at Bora-Bora on 8 December and recovered an anchor lost by Bougainville at Tahiti.]

After leaving Bolabola I steered to the Northward close hauled with the wind between the NE and East, hardly ever once having it to the southward of East till after we had [c]ross'd the line and got into North

---

26. Omai and both the New Zealand boys died within three to four years.

latitude; so that our course made good was always to the west of North and some time no better than NW.

As I had examined into the state of our Provisions at the last islands, I now had a survey taken of all the Boatswain and Carpenters Stores that were in the Ship, that I might be fully informed of the quantity, state and condition of every article, and by that means know how to use them to the most advantage.

Before I left the Society isles I enquired of the inhabitents if there were any islands in a North, or NW direction from them, but I did not find that they knew of any. Nor did we meet with any thing to indicate the vecinity of land till we came to about the latitude of 8° s where we began to see birds; such as boobies, Tropick and Men of War birds, Tern and some other sorts. At this time our Longitude was 205 E. *Mendana*, in his first Voyage in 1568, descovered an island that he named *Isla de Jesus*, in latitude 6°45's and 1450 leagues from Callao, which is 200° East longitude from Greenwich. We crossed this latitude near a hundred leagues to the Eastward of this longitude and saw there many of the above mentioned birds which are seldom known to go very far from land. In the night between the 22nd and 23rd we crossed the line in the Longitude of 20[3°15'] E; here the variation of the Compass was 6°30' E nea[r]ly.   Mon. 22   Tues. 23

WEDNESDAY 24*th.* On the 24th about half an hour after day breake, land was discovered bearing NEBE½E; which upon a nearer approach was found to be one of those low islands so common in this sea; that is a narrow bank of land incloseing the sea within; a few Cocoa nut trees were seen in two or three places, but in general the land had a very barren appearences. At Noon it extended from NEBE to SBE½E about four miles distant. The wind was at ESE so that we had to make a few boards to get up to the lee, or west side, where we found from 40 to 20 and 14 fathom water over a bottom of fine sand, the least depth about ½ a mile from the breakers and the greatest about one mile. The meeting with Soundings determined me to anchor to try to get some turtle, as the island seemed to be a good place for them and to be without inhabitents. Accordingly we droped anchor in 30 fathoms, and then sent a boat to see if there was any landing, for the Sea broke in a dreadfull surf all along the shore. When the boat returned the officer who was in her reported that he could see no place where a boat could land, but that there was great abundance of fish in the shoal water without the breakers.

THURSDAY 25*th*. At day-break the next Morning, I sent two boats, one from each Ship to looke for a landing place, and at the same time other two afishing; these last returned by 8 oclock with upwards of two hundred weight of fish. After breakfast they were sent again and I went in another to take a view of the coast and try to land, but this I found wholy impracticable. Towards noon the two boats I had sent to examine the coast returned; the Master, who was in the Resolutions boat reported that about a league and a half to the North was a break in the land and a Channell into the lagoon, consequently there was landing and he had found the same soundings off it as where we lay. In consequence of this report, we weighed, and after making two or three trips, came to again in 20 fathom water over a bottom of fine dark sand; about a mile from the breakers and before the channel leading into the lagoon. Here are two channels, divided from each other by a small island, but they are only fit for boats because it is all shallow water in the lagoon.

* * *

[*During the next few days boat-parties took a considerable number of turtles. Cook, King and Bailey observed an eclipse of the sun from the small island at the entrance to the lagoon.*]

TUESDAY 30*th*. . . . In the after noon the boats and turtling party at the SE part of the island all returned on board, except a seaman belonging to the Discovery, who had been missing two days. There were two of them at first, but disagreeing about which way they should go, they seperated and one joined the party after being absent twenty four hours, and very much distressed for want of water; in order to allay his thirst, he killed a turtle and drank of the blood, which gave him great reliefe, the other man could not drink of it and was of course in still greater distress, for not a drop of fresh water was found on the whole island nor were there any cocoanuts in that part. It was a matter of surprise to every one how these men contrived to loss themselves, the land, over which they had to travel from the sea coast to the lagoon where the boats lay, was not more than three miles a cross, and a plain with here and there a few shrubs upon it and from many parts of which the Ships masts were to be seen; but this was a thing they never once thought of looking for, nor did they know in what direction the ships were from them, nor which way to go to find either them or the party no more than if they had but just droped from the clouds. Considering what a strange set of beings, the generality of seamen are when on shore, instead of being surprised at these men lossing themselves we ought rather to have been surprised there were no more of them; indeed one of my people lost himself in the same place, but happening to have sagasity enough to know that the ships were to leeward, he got on board almost as soon as it was known he was missing. As soon as Captain Clerke knew the man was left behind, he sent a party in search of him. The next morning seeing   Wed. 31 neither the man nor the party, I ordered two boats into the lagoon to go different ways to look for him. Not long after the party returned with the man and I called the boats back by signal. Having some Cocoanuts and Yams on board in a state of vegetation, I ordered them to be planted on the island where we made the observation and some Millon seeds were sowen in another place. I also left on the little island a bottle containing this inscription,

Georgius tertius Rex 31 *Decembris* 1777

Naves { *Resolution Iac. Cook P^r*
Discovery Car. Clerke P^r

1778

On the 1st of Jan^{ry} 1778, I sent boats to bring all the parties   JAN^{ry} we had ashore on board and the turtle they had caught. Thurs. 1 Before this was done it was late in the after noon, so that I did not think proper to sail till the next morning. . . .

As we kept our Christmas here I called it *Christmas Island*, I judge it to be about fifteen or twenty leagues in circuit, it seemed to be of a simicircular form, or like the Moon in the last quarter, the two horns

being the north and south points and bear from each other, nearly
NBE and SBW four or five leagues distant. . . .

FRIDAY 2nd. On the 2nd at day-break we weighed anchor and resumed
our Course to the North, having fine weather and a gentle breeze at
East and ESE till we got into the latitude of 7°45′ N, Longitude 205 E
where we had one calm day. This was succeeded by a NEBE and ENE
wind, at first it blew faint but freshened as we advanced to the north.
We continued to see birds every day, of the sorts last mentioned,
sometimes in greater numbers than at others: and between the latitude
of 10 and a 11 we saw several turtle. All these are looked upon as signs
of the vecinity of land; we however saw none till day break in the
Sun. 18   Morning of the 18th when an island was descovered bearing
NEBE and soon after we saw more land bearing North and intirely
ditatched from the first; both had the appearence of being high
land.²⁷ . . .

MONDAY 19th. On the 19th at Sun rise the island first seen bore East
        leagues distant at least; this being directly to windward there
was no geting nearer it so that I stood for the other, and not long after
discovered a third island in the direction of WNW and as far distant
as an island could be seen. We had now a fine breeze at EBN and I
stood for the East end of the second island, which at noon extended
from N¹/2E to WNW¹/4W, the nearest part about two leagues distant. At
this time we were in some doubt whether or no the land before [us]
was inhabited, this doubt was soon cleared up, by seeing some Canoes
coming off from the shore towards the Ships, I immediately brought
to to give them time to come up, there were three and four men in
each and we were agreeably surprised to find them of the same Nation
as the people of Otahiete and the other islands we had lately visited.
It required but very little address to get them to come along side, but
we could not prevail upon any one to come on board; they exchanged
a few fish they had in the Canoes for any thing we offered them, but
valued nails, or iron above every other thing; the only weapons they

27. The ships were approaching the western islands of the Hawaiian group. The
first landing was on Kauai.

had were a few stones in some of the Canoes and these they threw overboard when they found they were not wanted. Seeing no signs of an anchoring place at this part of the island, I boar up for the lee side, and ranged the SE side at the distance of half a league from the shore. As soon as we made sail the Canoes left us, but others came off from the shore and brought with them roasting pigs and some very fine Potatoes, which they exchanged, as the others had done, for whatever was offered them; several small pigs were got for a sixpeny nail or two apiece, so that we again found our selves in the land of plenty, just as the turtle we had taken on board at the last island was nearly expended. We passed several villages, some seated upon the sea shore and other up in the Country; the inhabitants of all of them crowded to the shore and on the elevated places to view the Ships. The land on this side of the island rises in a gentle slope from the sea shore to the foot of the Mountions that are in the middle of the island, except in one place, near the east end where they rise directly from the sea; here they seemed to be formed of nothing but stone which lay in horizontal stratas; we saw no wood but what was up in the interior part of the island and a few trees about the villages; we observed several plantations of Plantains and sugar canes, and places that seemed to be planted with roots. . . .

The next morning we stood in for the land and were met   Tues. 20 by several Canoes filled with people, some of them took courage and ventured on board. I never saw Indians so much astonished at the entering a ship before, their eyes were continually flying from object to object, the wildness of thier looks and actions fully express'd their surprise and astonishment at the several new o[b]jects before them and evinced that they never had been on board of a ship before. However the first man that came on board did not with all his surprise, forget his own intrest, the first moveable thing that came in his way was the lead and line, which he without asking any questions took to put into his Canoe and when we stoped him said 'I am only going to put it into my boat' nor would he quit it till some of his countrymen spoke to him. At 9 o'clock being pretty near the shore, I sent three armed boats under the command of Lieutenant Williamson, to look for a landing place and fresh water. I ordered him, that if he found it necessary to land to look for the latter not to suffer more than one man to go out of the boat. As the boats put off an Indian stole the Butcher['s] cleaver, leaped over board with it, got into his canoe and made for the shore, the boats pursued him but to no effect.

As there were some venereal complaints on board both the Ships, in order to prevent its being communicated to these people, I gave orders that no Women, on any account whatever were to be admited on board the Ships, I also forbid all manner of connection with them, and ordered that none who had the veneral upon them should go out of the ships. But whether these regulations had the desired effect or no time can only discover. It is no more than what I did when I first visited the Friendly Islands yet I afterwards found it did not succeed, and I am much afraid this will always be the case where it is necessary to have a number of people on shore; the oppertunities and induce-ments to an intercourse between the sex, are there too many to be guarded against. It is also a doubt with me, that the most skilfull of the Faculty can tell whether every man who has had the veneral is so far cured as not to communicate it further, I think I could mention some instances to the contrary. It is likewise well known that amongst a number of men, there will be found some who will endeavour to conceal this desorder, and there are some again who care not to whom they communicate it, of this last we had an instance at Tongatabu in the Gunner of the Discovery, who remained a shore to manage the trade for Captain Clerke. After he knew he had contracted this disease he continued to sleep with different women who were supposed not to have contracted it; his companions expostulated with him without effect; till it came to Captain Clerke's knowlidge who ordered him on board.

While the boats were in shore examining the coast we stood on and off with the Ships, waiting their return, at length, about noon Mr Williamson came on board and reported that he had seen a large pond behind a beach near one of the Villages, which the natives told him was fresh water and that there was anchorage before it. He also reported that he attempted to land in a nother place but was prevented by the Indians coming down to the boat in great numbers, and were for taking away the oars, muskets and in short every thing they could lay hold upon and pressed so thick upon him that he was obliged to fire, by which one man was killed. But this unhappy circumstance I did not know till after we left the islands, so that all my measures were directed as if nothing of the kind had happened. Mr Williamson told me that after the man fell they took him up, [c]arried him off, and then retired from the boat and made signs for them to land, but this he declined. It did not appear to Mr Williamson that they had any design to kill or even hurt any of the people in the boat but were excited by mere curiosity to get what they had from them, and were at the same time, ready to give in return any thing they had.

After the boats were on board I sent away one of them to lay in the best anchoring ground, and as soon as she got to her station I bore down with the ships and anchored in 25 fathom water, the bottom a fine grey owsey sand. The East point of the road, which was the low point before mentioned, bore s [51]° E, the west point N[65°]w and the Village where the water was said to be, NEBE distant one mile, but there were breakers little more than a quarter of a mile which I did not see till after we had anchored; The Discovery anchored to the Eastward of us and farther from the shore. As soon as the Ships was anchored I went a shore with three boats, to look at the water and try the desposition of the inhabitants, several hundreds of whom were assembled on a sandy beach before the village. The very instant I leaped ashore, they all fell flat on their faces, and remained in that humble posture till I made signs to them to rise. They then brought a great many small pigs and gave us without regarding whether they got any thing in return or no indeed the most of them were present[ed] to me with plantain trees, in a ceremonious way as is usual on such like occasions, and I ratified these marks of friendship by presenting them with such things as I had with me. After things were a little settled I left a guard upon the beach and got some of the Indians to shew me the water, which proved to be very good and convenient to come at. Being satisfied with the conveniency of Watering and that we had nothing to fear from the Natives, I returned on board and gave orders for every thing to be in readiness for Watering in the Morning, when I went ashore with the people employed on   Wed. 21 this service my self, having a party of Marines for a guard which were stationed on the beach. We no sooner landed, that a trade was set on foot for hogs and potatoes, which the people gave us in exchange for nails and pieces of iron formed into some thing like chisels. We met with no obstruction in watering on the contrary the Natives assisted our people to roll the Casks to and from the pond. As soon as every thing was settled to my saitisfaction, I left the command to Mr Williamson who was with me and took a walk up the Vally, accompaned by Dr Anderson and Mr Webber; conducted by one of the Natives and attended by a tolerable train. Our guide proclamed our approach and every one whom we met fell on their faces and remained in that position till we had passed. This, as I afterwards understood, is done to their great chiefs. Our road lay in among the Plantations, which were chiefly of Tara, and sunk a little below the common level so as to contain the water necessary to nourish the roots. As we ranged down the coast from the East in the Ships, we observed at every Village one or more elevated objects, like Pyramids and we had seen one in this vally that we were desireous of going to see. Our guide understood us, but as this was on the other side of the river, he conducted us to one on the same side we were upon; it proved to be in a Morai which in many respects was like those of Otaheite. . . .

After having seen every thing that was to be seen about this Morai and Mr Webber had taken a drawing of it, we returned to the beach by a different rout to the one we came. . . .

At the beach I found a great crowd and a brisk trade for pigs, fowls and roots which was carried on with the greatest good order, though I did not see a man that appeared of more consequince than a nother, if there was they did not shew themselves to us. . . . No people could trade with more honisty than these people, never once attempting to cheat us, either ashore or along side the ships. Some indeed at first betrayed a thievish disposition, or rather they thought they had a right to any thing they could lay their hands upon but this conduct they soon laid aside.

*   *   *

[*Bad weather drove the ships from their anchorage and after a few days Cook found a convenient anchorage off the island of Niihau, to the west.*]

FRIDAY 30*th*. On the 30th I sent Mr Gore ashore again with a guard of Marines and a party to trade with the Natives for refreshments; I intended to have followed soon after and went from the Ship with that design, but the surf had increased so much, that I was fearfull if I got ashore I should not get off again as realy happened to the party that was ashore, the communication by our own boats being soon stoped. In the evening the party a shore made the Signal for the boats, sent them accordingly. Not long after they returned with a few yams and salt, a tolerable quantity of both was procured during the day but the greatest part was lost in geting into the boats. The officer with about twenty men were left a shore; thus the very thing happened that I had above all others wished to prevent. Most of what we got to day was brought off by the Natives and purchased along side the ship in exchange for Nails and pieces of iron hopes. About 10 or 11 oclock the wind veered to the South and the sky seemed to foreboad a storm; thinking we were rather too near the shore, took up the anchor and shoot into 42 fathom and there came to again. This precausion was unnecessary as the wind soon veered to NNE where it blew a fresh gale with Squals attended with very heavy showers of rain. This weather continued all the next day, and the sea run so high that we had no manner of communication with the people on shore; even the Natives durst not venture out in their canoes. In the evening I sent the master in a boat up to the SE head, or point, to see if a boat could land under it, he returned with a favourable report, but too late to send for the party till the next mor[n]ing when I sent an order to Mr Gore, that if he could not imbark the people where he was to march them up to the point. As the boat could not land a person swam a shore with the order; on the return of the boat I went my self with the Pinnace and Launch up to the point to bring the party on board, taking with me a Ram goat and two Ewes, a Boar and Sow pig of the English breed, the seeds of Millons, Pumpkins and onions. I landed with great ease under the west side of the point, and found the party already there, with a few of the Natives among them. There was one man whom Mr Gore had observed to have some command over the others, to him I gave the Goats, Pigs and seeds. I should have left these things at the other island, had we not been so

Sat. 31

FEB^{ry}

Sun. 1

unexpectedly driven from it. While the people were filling four water casks from a small stream occasioned by the late rain, I took a little walk into the island attended by the man above mentioned, and followed by two others carrying the two pigs. As soon as we got upon a rising ground I stoped to look round me, a woman on the other side of the vally where I landed, called to the men with me, on which the Chief began to mutter something like a prayer and the two men with the pigs continued to walk round me all the time, not less than ten or a dozen times before the other had finished. This ceremony being ended, we proceeded and presently met people coming from all parts, who, on the men with me calling to them laid down till I was out of sight. The ground over which I walked was in a state of nature, very stony and the soil seemed poor; it was however covered with shrubs and plants, some of which sent forth the most fragrant smell I had any were met with in this sea. After the water casks were filled and got into the boat, and purchasing from the Natives a few roots, a little salt and salted fish, I returned on board with all the people, intending to visit the island again the next day. But about 7 oclock in the evening, the anchor started and the Ship drove off the bank. As we had a whole cable out it was some time before the anchor was at the bows, and then we had the Launch to hoist up along side before we could make sail, so that at day-break the next morning we were three leagues to leeward of our last station. And foreseeing that it would require some time to recover it, more at least than I chused to spend, I made the signal for the Discovery to weigh and join us which was done about Noon when we stood away to the Northward. Thus after spending more time about these islands than was necessary to have answered all our purposes, we were obliged to leave them before we had compleated our Water, and got from them such a quantity of refreshments as the inhabitents were able and willing to supply us with. But as it was we procured from them full three weeks provisions and Captain Clerke got roots sufficient for two months or upwards.

These five Islands, *Atoui*, *Enēēhēēōū*, *Orrehoua*, *Otaoora* and *Wouahoo*, names by which they are known to the Natives,[28] I named *Sandwich*

28. Kauai, Niihau, Lehua, Kaula, Oahu.

Islands, in honour of the Earl of Sandwich. They are situated between the Latitude of 21°30′ and 22°15′ N and between the Longitude of 199°20′ and 201°30′ East. *Wouahoo*, which is the Eastermost and lies in the Latitude of 21°36′ we knew no more of than that it is high land and inhabited. . . .

I have already observed that these people are of the same nation as the people of Otaheite and many others of the South sea islands, consequently they differ but little from them in their persons. These have a darker hue than the generality of the Otahietians, which may be owing to their being more exposed to the Sun and wearing less cloathing. How shall we account for this Nation spreading it self so far over this Vast ocean? We find them from New Zealand to the South, to these islands to the North and from Easter Island to the Hebrides; an extent of 60° of latitude or twelve hundred leagues north and south and 83° of longitude or sixteen hundred and sixty leagues east and west, how much farther is not known, but we may safly conclude that they extend to the west beyond the Hebrides.

* * *

[*Cook now gives the best account he can of these new islands and their people, but he can only guess about social organization and religion. He describes the canoes and the houses ('not unlike oblong corn stacks'). He wonders about the source of the iron of some of their tools, and, because of the astonishment at the appearance of the ships, thinks it must have come from Spanish wrecks rather than from visits. Spain, he thinks, is most likely to derive benefit from the discovery of the islands.*]

After the Discovery had joined us I stood away to the North-   Mon. 2
ward close hauled with a gentle gale Easterly. On the 7ᵗʰ   Sat. 7
being in the Latitude of 29 N Longit. 200 E, the wind veered to SE and enabled us to steer NE & East which courses were continued till the 12ᵗʰ when the wind had veered round by the South and   Thurs. 12
west to NE and ENE. I then tacked and stood to the Northward: at this time our latitude was 30° N, Longit. 206°15′ E.

On the 19ᵗʰ in the latitude of 37° N, longitude 206° E the wind veered to SE and I again steered to the East inclining to the North. In the Latitude of 42°30′, longit. 219° we began to see of the rock weed mentioned by Walters under the name of sea leek and now   Wed. 25

and then a piece of wood. But if we had not known that the continent of America was not far distant, from the few signs we had met with of the vicinity of land we might have concluded that there was none within some thousand leagues of us, for we had hardly seen a bird or any other Oceanic animal sence we left Sandwich islands.

MARCH   On Sunday the 1ˢᵗ of March being in the latitude of
Sun. 1   44°49′ N longitude 228° E, we had one Calm day: this was succeeded by a wind from the North, with which I stood to the East in order to make the land, which according to the Charts, ought not to have been far from us.

Fri. 6   On the 6ᵗʰ at Noon being in the latitude of 44°10, longit. 234½, we saw two Seals and several whales, and at day break the
Sat. 7   next Morning, the long looked for Coast of new Albion was seen extending from NE to SE distant 10 or 12 leagues. At Noon our latitude was 44°33′ N, longitude 235°20′ E and the land extended from NE½N to SEbS about 8 leagues distant. In this situation we had 73 fathoms water over a muddy bottom and about a league farthour off, had 90 fathoms. The land appeared to be of a moderate height, deversifed with hill and Vally and almost every where covered with wood. There was nothing remarkable about it, except one hill, whose elevated summit was flat, it bore from us east at Noon. At the northern extreme, the land formed a point, which I called *Cape Foul Weather* from the very bad weather we soon after met with: I judge it to lie in the latitude of 44°55′ N, longitude 235°54′ East.²⁹

*   *   *

[*Cook moved north along the coast in bad weather. He found the cape which he named Cape Flattery, but as for 'the pretended Strait of Juan de Fuca . . . we saw nothing like it, nor is there the least probability that iver any such thing exhisted'. So they moved up the coast of Vancouver Island without realizing it was an island. On 29 March they were nearing Nootka Sound.*]

As we drew nearer the Coast we perceived the appearence of two inlets one in the NW and the other in the NE corner of the bay. As I could not fetch the first I bore up for the latter and pass'd some

---

29. The coast of northern Oregon, north of Newport.

breakers, or sunken rocks, that lay a league or more from the shore. We had 19 and 20f^m water without them, a rocky bottom; as soon as past them 30, 40 and 50f^m a sandy bottom and then no ground with the last length of line. We had got pretty near the inlet before we were sure there was one; but as we were in a bay I had resolved to anchor to endeavour to get some Water, of which were in great want. At length the inlet was no longer doubtfull, at 5 oclock we reached the west point where we were becalmed for some time, during which hoisted out all the boats to tow the Ship in. This was hardly done before a fresh breeze sprung up again at NW, with it stretched up into an Arm of the Inlet we observed runing into the NE where we were again Calm'd, and was obliged to anchor in 85f^m water and so near the shore as to reach it with a hawser. The wind failed the Discovery without the Arm where she anchor[ed] in 70 fathoms. .

We no sooner drew near the inlet than we found the coast to be inhabited and the people came off to the Ships in Canoes without shewing the least mark of fear or distrust. We had at one time thirty two Canoes filled with people about us, and a groupe of ten or a dozen remained along side the Resolution most part of the night. They seemed to be a mild inoffensive people, shewed great readiness to part with any thing they had and took whatever was offered them in exchange, but were more desireous of iron than any thing else, the use of which they very well knew and had several tools and instruments that were made of it.

MONDAY 30*th*. In the Morning I sent three armed boats under the command of Mr King to look for a harbour for the Ships and soon after I went my self in a small boat on the same service. On the NW side of the Arm we were in and not far from the Ship, I found a pretty snug Cove, and Mr King who returned about Noon found one still better on the NW side of the Sound; but as it would have required more time to get to it than the other, it was resolved to make the nearest serve. But being too late in the day to transport the Ships thither before night, I ordered the sails to be unbent, the Topmast to be struck and the Foremast to be unrig'd, in order to fix a new bib, one of the old ones being decayed. A great many Canoes filled with the Natives were about the Ships all day, and a trade commenced betwixt us and them, which was carried on with the Strictest honisty on boath sides. Their articles were the Skins of various animals, such as Bears, Wolfs, Foxes, Dear, Rackoons, Polecats, Martins and in particular the Sea Beaver, the same as is found on the coast of Kamtchatka. Cloathing made of these skins and a nother sort made, either of the bark of a tree or some plant like hemp; Weapons, such as Bows and Arrows, Spears &c.ª Fish hooks and Instruments of various kinds, pieces of carved work and even human sculs and hands, and a variety of little articles too tedious to mention. For these things they took in exchange, Knives, chissels, pieces of iron & Tin, Nails, Buttons, or any kind of metal. Beads they were not fond of and cloth of all kinds they rejected.

TUESDAY 31st. The next day the Ships were got into the Cove and their moored head and stern most of the Moorings being fast to the shore. We found on heaving up the anchor that notwithstanding the great depth of water it was let go in, there were rocks at the bottom which had done some considerable damage to the Cable, and the hawsers that were carried out to warp the Ship into the cove got also foul of rocks, so that it appeared that the whole bottom was strewed with them. As we found the Ship again very leaky in her upper works, the Caulkers were set to work to caulk her and repair such other defects as were wanting.

We had the company of the natives all the day, who now laid aside all manner of restraint, if they ever had any, and came on board the Ships and mixed with our people with the greatest freedom. And we soon found that they were as light fingered as any people we had before met with, and were far more dangerous for with their knives and other cut[ting] instruments of iron, they would cut a hook from a tackle or any other piece of iron from a rope, the instant our backs was turned. We lost the Fish-hook, a large hook between 20 and 30 pound weight, several lesser hooks and other articles of iron in this manner, and as to our boats they striped them of every article of iron about them worth carrying away, though we had always men in them to guard them, but one fellow would amuse the boat keeper at one end of the boat while another was puling her to pieces at the other. If we missed a thing immediately after it was Stolen, we found no difficulty in finding out the thief, as they were ready enough to impeach one another, but the thief generally relinquished his prize with reluctancy and sometimes not without force. As soon as the Ships were securely Moored, other business was taken in ha[n]d; the observatorys and Instruments for making observations were set up on a elevated rock on one side of the Cove close to the Resolution; a party of men with an officer was sent ashore to cut wood and clear a place and make conveniences for watering and the Forge was set up to make the iron work wanting about the foremast, for bisides one of the bibs being defective the larboard Trestle-tree and one of the cross-trees was sprung. AP[1] Wed. 1

A considerable number of the Natives visited us daily and we every now and then saw new faces. On their first coming they generally went through a singular ceremony; they would paddle with all thier strength quite round both Ships, A Chief or other principal person standing up with a Spear, or some other Weapon in his hand and speaking, or rather holloaing all the time, sometimes this person would have his face cover[ed] with a mask, either that of the human face or some animal, and some times instead of a weapon would hold in his hand a rattle. After making the Circuit of the ships they would come along side and begin to trade without further ceremony. Very often indeed they would first give us a song in which all joined with a very agreable harmony.

*   *   *

[*There were serious problems with rot in both the foremast and the mizen-mast of the* Resolution. *There was no lack of wood, both standing timber and driftwood, for repairs. There were visits from new groups of Indians, who seemed to be kept at a distance by the original group.*]

In the after noon of the next day, I went into the woods with a party of men and cut down a tree for a Mizen Mast and the next morning it was got to the place where the Carpenters were at work upon the Fore-mast. In the evening the wind, which had been for some time westerly, veered to SE and increased to a very hard gale Mon. 13

Wed. 15   with rain which continued till 8 oclock the next morning
when it abated and veered again to the West. On the Morning of the
15th the Foremast being finished got it along side and set the Carpenters
to work to make a new Mizen Mast, but the weather was so bad that
the Foremast could not be got in till the after noon. At this time several
Indians were about the Ship who looked on with more silent attention
than is usual with Indians.

The Foremast being in we set about rigging it with all immaginable
haste, while the Carpenters were employed making a Mizenmast;
Thurs. 16   which was more than half done when they descovered that
the Stick they were making [it] of was sprung or wounded, supposed
to have been done when it was cut down; so that their labour was lost
and we had a nother tree to get out of the wood which employed all
hands half a day.

SATURDAY 18*th.* On the 18th a party of Strangers in Six or eight Canoes
came into the Cove where they remained looking at us for some time,
then retired without coming along side either ship. We supposed our
old friends would not suffer them, who were more numerous at this
time about us than the strangers. It was evident that they engrossed
us intirely to themselves, or if at any time they allowed Strangers to
trade with us it was always managed the trade for them in such a
manner that the price of their articles was always kept up while the
Value of ours was lessening daily. We also found that many of the
principals of those about us carried on a trade with their neighbours
with the articles they got from us; as they would frequintly be gone
from us four or five days at a time and then return with a fresh cargo
of skins curiosities &c^a and such was the passion for these things among
our people that they always came to a good Market whether they
were of any value or no. But such of them as visited us daily we reaped
the most benifit from, these, after disposing of all their little trifles,
employed a part of their time in fishing and we always got at least a
part of the fruits of their labour. We also got from these people a
quantity of very good Animal oil which they had reserved in bladers;
in this traffick some would attempt to cheat us by mixing Water with
the oil, once or twice they had the address to impose upon us whole

bladers of water wi[t]hout a drop of Oil in them. It was always better to put up with these tricks than to quarrel with them, as our articles of trafick consisted for the most part in trifles, and yet we were put to our shifts to find these trifles, for beads and such things of which I had yet some left, were in little esteem. Nothing would go down with them but metal and brass was now become their favourate, So that before we left the place, hardly a bit of brass was left in the Ship, except what was in the necessary instruments. Whole Suits of cloaths were striped of every button, Bureaus &c^a of their furniture and Copper kettle[s], Tin canesters, Candle sticks, &c^a all went to wreck; so that these people got a greater middly and variety of things from us than any other people we had visited.

The next day, being the first fair day we had had for a fortnight past, we got up the Topmasts and yards and set up the rigging. And having now got the most of our heavy work out of hand, I set out early the next morning with [2] boats to take a view of the Sound. I first went to the West point where I found a large Indian Village and before it a very Snug harbour in which was from 9 to 4 fathom water and a bottom of fine Sand. The people of this Village who were numerous and to most of whom I was known, received me very curtiously, every one pressing me to go in to his house, or rather appartment for several families live under the same roof, and there spread a mat for me to sit down upon and shewed me every other mark of civility. Sun. 19 Mon. 20

In most of the houses there were Women at work making dresses of the bark or plant before mentioned which they performed in every respect in the same manner as the New Zealanders. Others were at work opening and Smoke drying Sardins, a large quantity of these fish were landed while I was there, divided by Measure amongst several people who carried them up to the house to be cured. They hang them on small rods at first about a foot from the fire, afterwards they remove them higher and higher to make room for others till they get to the roof of the house; when dryed they are made up into bales and covered with Mats; thus they are kept till wanting and eat very well, but there is but little meat upon them. In the same manner they cure Cod and other large fish, and some are cured in the air without fire.

From this place I proceeded up the West side of the Sound, for about three miles I found the shore covered with small islands, which are the means of forming several Snug harbours, in which are various depths of water from 30 to 7 fathoms with a good bottom. Two leagues within the Sound on the West side there runs in an Arm in the direction of NNW and two miles farther a nother nearly in the same direction, with a pretty large island in the entrance. I had no time to examine ether of them but beleive they do not extend far inland as the water was no more than brackish at their entrances. A mile above the second arm was the remains of a Village the logs or framing of the houses were standing, but the boards that had composed the sides and roof were wanting. Before this Village were some large fishing weares, but I saw no one attending them. These weares were composed of pieces of wicker work made of small rods some closer than others according to the size of the fish intended to be caught in them. These pieces of wickerwork (some of whose superficies are twenty feet by twelve at least) they fix up edgeways, in 3 or 4 feet water at low water, by strong poles or pickets fixed firm in the ground. Behind this ruined Village is a plane of a few acres covered with some of the largest pine trees I ever saw, whereas the elevated ground on most parts of this side the Sound was rather naked. From this place I crossed over to the other side of the Sound passing an Arm of it extending in NNE to appearence not far. I now found what I had before conjectured, that the land under which the ships laid was an island and that there were many small ones laying scatered in the Sound on the West side of it. Opposite the North end of the large island on the Continent was an Indian Village at which I landed, the inhabitants were not so polite as those of the other I had visited; but this seemed in a great measure if not wholy owing to one Surly chief, who would not let me enter their houses, following me where ever I went and several times made signs for me to be gone; the presents I made him did not induce him to alter his behaviour. Some young women, more polite than their surly Lord, dress'd themselves in a hurry in their best cloaths, got together and sung us a song which was far from being harsh or disagreeable.

The day being now far spent, I proceeded for the Ships round the North end of the large island, meeting in my way several Canoes laden with Sardins which they had caught some where in the East corner of the Sound.

The 21st the New Mizen mast being finished, got it in and rigged and set the Carpenters to work to make a new Fore topmast to replace the one carried away some time before.　Tues. 21

WEDNESDAY 22nd. The next Morning we were Visited by a number of Strangers in twelve or fourteen Canoes; they lay drawn up in a body a full half hour about two or three hundred yards from the ships. At first we thought they were afraid to advance nearer, in this we were misstaken, it was rather to entertain us with a Song or dance which was perform'd in concert, while two of the Canoes kept parading between the others and us. After they had finished their Songs which we heard with admiration, they came along side the Ships, and then we found that several of our old friends were among them, who took upon them the intire management of the trade between us and them very much to the advantage of the others. Having a few Goats and two or three sheep left I went in a boat accompanied by Captain Clerke in a nother, to the Village at the west point of the Sound to get some grass for them, having seen some at that place. The Inhabitants of this village received us in the same friendly manner they had d[o]ne before, and the Moment we landed I sent some to cut grass not thinking that the Natives could or would have the least objection, but it proved otherways for the Moment our people began to cut they stoped them and told them they must *Makook* for it, that is first buy it. As soon as I heard of this I went to the place and found about a dozen men who all laid cla[i]m to some part of the grass which I purchased of them and as I thought liberty to cut where ever I pleased, but here again I was misstaken, for the liberal manner I had paid the first pretended pr[o]prietors brought more upon me and there was not a blade of grass that had not a seperated owner, so that I very soon emptied my pockets with purchasing, and when they found I had nothing more to give they let us cut where ever we pleased.

Here I must observe that I have no were met with Indians who had such high notions of every thing the Country produced being their exclusive property as these; the very wood and water we took on board they at first wanted us to pay for, and we had certainly done it, had I been upon the spot when the demands were made; but as I never happened to be there the workmen took but little notice of their importunities and at last they ceased applying. But made a Merit on necessity and frequently afterwards told us they had given us Wood and Water out of friendship. . . .

Thurs. 23   The next day bent the Sails, tooke down the Observatorys, got them and the Instruments on board.

Fri. 24   The 24th and 25th were spent in clearing and puting the
Sat. 25   Ship in a condition for sea; geting on board some small spars for different uses and some pieces of timber to saw into boards for the use of the Ship.

SUNDAY 26th. The 26th in the Morning every thing being ready, I intended to have sailed, but both wind and Tide being against us was obliged to wait till noon, when the sw Wind was succeeded by a Calm and the tide turning in our favour, we cast off the Moorings and with our boats towed the Ships out of the Cove: after which we had variable light airs and calms till 4 PM when a breeze sprung up Northerly with very thick hazey weather. The Marcury in the Barometer fell unusually low and we had every other token of an approaching storm which we had reason to expect would be from the Southward, so that I was in some doubt as night was at hand, whether I should venture to put to sea or not, till the next Morning. But the anxiety I was under of geting to Sea and the fear of loseing this oppertunity got the better of every other consideration and determined me to put to sea at all events.

Our Friends the Indians attended upon us till we were almost out of the Sound, some on board the Ships and others in Canoes a Chief named   who had some time before attatched himself to me was one of the last who left us, before he went I made him up a small present and in return he present[ed] me with a Beaver skin of greater value, this occasioned me to make some addition to my present, on which he gave me the Beaver skin Cloak he had on, that I knew he set a value upon. And as I was desireous he should be no suffer[er] by his friendship and generosity to me, I made him a present of a New Broad Sword with a brass hilt which made him as happy as a prince. He as also many others importuned us much to return to them again and by way of incouragement promised to lay in a good stock of skins for us, and I have not the least doubt but they will.

*   *   *

[*Cook now enters on a long description of the inhabitants of the inlet which 'I honoured with the name of King Georges Sound', though 'its name with the Natives is Nookka'. (Elsewhere he writes 'Nootka'.)*]

Having put to Sea on the evening of the 26th as before related, with strong signs of an aproaching Storm; these signs did not diceive us: we were hardly out of the Sound before the Wind in a instant shifted from NE to SEBE and increased to a Strong gale with Squals and rain and so dark that we could not see the length of the Ship. Being apprehensive of the wind veering more to the South, as usual, and puting us in danger of a lee shore, got the tacks on board and stretched off to the SW under all the sail the Ships could bear. Fortunaly the Wind veered no farther Southerly than SSE so that at day light the next Morning we were quite clear of the Coast. The Discovery   Mon. 27 being some distance astern, I brought to till she came up and then bore away and steered NW the direction I supposed the Coast to take. The Wind was at SE blew very hard and in squals with rain and thick hazey weather. At half past one PM it blew a perfect hurricane, so that I Judged it highly dangerous to run any longer before it, and therefore brought the Ships to with their heads to the Southward under the fore sails and Mizen staysails. At this time the Resolution Sprung a leak which at first alarmed us not a little; it was found to be under the Starboard buttock, where from the bread room we could both hear and see the Water rush in, and as we then thought, two feet under water but in this were happily misstaken, for it was afterward found to be even, if not above the water-line when the Ship was upright. It was no sooner discovered than the fish room was found to be full of water and the Casks in it afloat, but this was owing in a great measure to the water not finding its way through the Coals that lay in the bottom of the room, to the pumps. For after the water was bailed out which employed us till midnight and the water found its way directly from the leak to the pumps, one pump kept it under, which gave us no small satisfaction. In the evening the wind veered to the South and abated some thing of its fury, on which set the Main sail, two topsails close reefed and stretched to the westward. But at a 11 the gale again increased and obliged us to take in the topsails till Tues. 28   5 OClock the next morning when the storm began to abate, so that we could bear to set them again. The Weather now began to clear up, so that we could see several leagues round us and I steered more to the Northward. At Noon the Latitude by observation was 50°01′ N, Longitude 229°26′ E. I now steered NWBN with a fresh gale at SSE and fair weather, but at 9 PM it began again to blow hard, and in squals with rain. With such weather and the wind between SSE and Thurs. 30   SW I continued the same course till the 30th at 4 AM when I steered NBW in order to make the land, regreting very much that I could not do it sooner, especially as we were passing the place where Geographers have placed the pretended Strait of Admiral de Fonte. For my own part, I give no credet to such vague and improbable stories, that carry their own confutation along with them nevertheless I was very desirous of keeping the Coast aboard in order to clear up this point beyond dispute; but it would have been highly imprudent in me to have ingaged with the land in such exceeding tempestious weather, or to have lost the advantage of a fair wind by waiting for better weather. This same day at Noon we were in the Latitude of 53°22′ N, longitude 225°14′ E.

*   *   *

[*Cook proceeded north and then west along the Alaskan coast until in early May he was roughly 60° N, 144° W.*]

[MAY]

SUNDAY 10*th.* The 10th at Noon we were in the latitude of 59°51′, longitude 215°56′ E and no more than 3 leagues from the coast of the continent, which extended from E½N to NW½W as far as the eye could reach. To the westward of this last direction was an island that extended from N 52° W to S 85° W distant 6 leagues; a point shoots out from the Main towards the NE end of this island which at this time bore N 30 W 5 or 6 leagues distant. This point I named *Cape Suckling* the point of the Cape is low, but within it is a tolerable high hill which is disjoined from the Mountains by low land, so that at a distance the Cape looks like an island. On the North side of Cape Suckling there is a bay that appeared to be of some extent and to be covered from most winds; to this bay I had some thoughts of going to stop our leak as all our endeavours to do it at sea had proved ineffectual. With this view I steered for the Cape, but as we had but variable light breezes we approached it but slowly. However before night we were near inough to see some low-land spiting out from the Cape to the NW so as to cover the East part of the bay from the South wind; we also saw some small islands in the bay and elevated rocks between the Cape and the NE end of the island: there however appeared to be a passage on both sides of these rocks and I continued steering for them all night, having from 43 to 27 fathom water over a muddy bottom.

MONDAY 11*th.* The 11th at 4 AM the wind which had been mostly at NE shifted to North, this being against us I gave up the design of going within the island or into the bay as neither could be done without loss of time. I therefore bore up for the west end of the island; the wind blew faint and at 10 oclock it fell Calm. Being not far from the island I went in a boat and landed upon it a with view of seeing what lay on the other side, but finding it farther to the hills than I expected and the way steep and woody, I was obliged to drop the design. At the foot of a tree on a little eminency not far from the Shore, I left a bottle in which was an Inscription seting forth the Ships Names, date &c[a] and two Silver two penny pieces (date 1772) which with many others were furnished me by the Rev[d] D[r] Kaye. And as a mark of my esteem and regard for that Gentleman I named the island after him.[30] *Keyes Island* is 11 or 12 leagues in length in the direction of NE and SW but its breadth is not above a league or a league and a half in any part of it. The SW point, which lies in the latitude of 59°49′ N, longitude 216°58′ E, is very remarkable, being a naked rock elevated considerably

30. Now Kayak Island, the St Elias island of Bering.

above the land within it; there is also an elevated rock laying of it which from some points of View appears like a runed Castle. . . .

[*Beyond a cape which Cook named Cape Hinchinbrook there was an inlet, and then the land seemed to incline to the southward. Cook thought he might have found a passage to the north, but he was in fact at the entrance to what he later named Sandwich Sound, afterwards Prince William Sound. He urgently needed 'to get into some place to stop the leak', and steered into the inlet. With thick fog descending, he anchored in a small cove just within the cape.*]

Tues. 12   The boats were then hoisted out, some to Sound and others to fish &c^a, the Seine was drawn in the Cove but it was torn so that no fish were caught. At some short intervals the fog cleared away and gave us a sight of the lands around us; the Cape bore SBW½W one league distant, the West point of the inlet SWBW distant 5 leagues and the land on that side extended as far as WBN. Between this point and NWBW we could see no land, and what was in the last direction seemed to be at a great distance. The Westermost we had in sight on the North shore NNW½W 2 leagues distant; between this point and the shore we were at anchor under is a bay of about 3 leagues deep, on the SE side of which, there are two or three Coves such as we had anchored before and in the Middle some rocky islands. To these island[s] Mr Gore went in a boat in hopes of shooting something for the pot or spit. But he had hardly got there before about twenty Indians made their appearence in two large Canoes, on which he thought proper to return to the Ships and they followed him. They would not venture along side but kept talking to us at a distance, not one word of which we understood; they were cloathed in skins made into a dress like a shirt, or rather more like a wagonners frock, it reached nearly as low as the knee and their was no slit either behind or before. The Canoes were not built of wood like those of King Georges Sound; the frame only was of wood or slender laths and the out side sealskin, or the skin of some suchlike animal. When these people first came to the Ships, they displayed a white dress and unfolded their arms to the utmost extent, this we understood to be a sign of friendship and answered them in the same manner, but for all this they would not trust themselves along side; but after remain[in]g near us for about an hour and receiving some presents that were thrown them they retired from whence they came; giving us to understand by signs they would visit us again the next morn[g], but two of them each in a small Canoe paid us a visit in the night probably with a design to plunder us thinking we should be all a sleep, for they retired as soon as they found themselves discovered. During the night the Wind was at SSE blew hard and in Squals with rain and very thick weather; at 10 oclock the next Morning the wind became   Wed. 13 more moderate, the weather some thing clearer and we got under sail in order to look for some snuger place to search for and Stop the leak, as the place where we lay was too much exposed for this purpose. At first I intended to have gone up the bay before which we had anchored, but the weather clearing up tempted me to steer to the northward up the inlet as being all in our way. . . . At length, at 8 oclock, the Violance of the squals obliged us to anchor in 13 f[m] water, before we had got so far into the bay as I intended, but thought our selves well of, in having got into a secure port before dark for the night proved exceeding stormy. The weather bad as it was did not however hinder three of the Natives from paying us a visit they came off in two Canoes, two men in one and one in the other, being the number each would carry, for they were built and constructed in the same manner as the Esquimauxs, only in the one was two holes for two men to sit in and in the other but one. Each of these men had a stick about 3 feet long with the large feathers or wings of birds tied to it: these they frequently held up to shew us, with a view, as we guessed, to express their peacable sentiments.

THURSDAY 14*th*. The treatment these men met with induced many more to visit us between one and two the next morning in both great and small Canoes; Some ventured on board the Ship, but not before some of our people went into their boats. Amongst those that came on board was a good looking middle aged man who we afterward found to be the Chief; he was cloathed in a dress made of the Sea beaver skin and on his head such a Cap as is worn by the people of King Georges Sound, Ornamented with sky blue glass beads about the size of a large pea; these he seemed to set ten times more Value upon than our white glass beads which they probably thought was only crystal which they have among them. They however essteemed beads of all sorts and gave whatever they had in exchange for them, even their fine Sea beaver skins. But here I must observe that they set no more value upon these skins than others, neither here nor at King Georges Sound, till our people put a Value upon them, and even then at the last place they would sooner part with a dress made of these than one made of the skins of wild Cats or Martins. These people were also desirous of iron, but it must be peices eight or ten inches long at least, and three or four fingers broad for small peices they absolutly rejected; consequently they got but little from us, as it was now become rather a scarce article. The points of some of their spears or lances, were of Iron shaped into the form of a Bear spear, others were of Copper and a few of bone which the points of their darts, arrows &c^a were made of. I could not prevail on the cheif to trust himself below the upper deck, nor did he and his companions remain long on board; but while they were it was necessary to look after them as they soon betrayed a thevesh dispossission. At length, after being 3 or 4 hours along side the Resolution, they all to a man left her and went to the Discovery, none having been there before except one man, who at this time came from her and immidiately returned with the others with him. When I saw this I thought this Man had seen some thing there that pleased them better than any thing we had offered them, but in this I was misstaken as will soon appear.

As soon as they were gone I sent a boat to sound the head of the bay, for as the wind was now moderate I had thoughts of laying the Ship a shore, if I found a convenient place, to stop the leak. It was not long before all the Indians returned to us again, but instead of coming to the Ship they went towards the boat, the officer in her seeing this, returned to the Ship and was followed by all the Canoes. The crew were no sooner out of the boat, all but two to look after her, than Some of the Indians steped into her, some held spears before the two men, others cast loose the rope she was fast to, while others attempted to tow her away. But the instant they saw us preparing to oppose them they let her go steped out of her into their canoes and made signs to us to lay down our arms, and not only seemed but were as perfictly unconcerned as if they had done nothing amiss. This though rather a more daring attempt was hardly equal to what they attempted on board the Discovery. The man who came and carri'd them all from the Resolution to the Discovery, had first been on board of her, where, after looking down all the hatchways, and seeing no body but the officer of the watch and one or two more he no doubt thought they might plunder her with ease, especially as she lay some distance from us: and it was unquestionable with this View they all went to her. Several without any ceremony went on board, drew their knives, made signs to the officer and people on deck to keep off and began to look about them to see what they could find; the first thing they met with was the Rudder of one of the boats which they threw over board to those who remained in the Canoes. Before they had time to through a Second thing over board the Crew were alarmed and began to come on deck armed with cutlasses on which the others sneaked off into their Canoes. . . .

Just as we were going to wiegh the anchor to go farther up the bay it came on to blow and rain as hard as before, so that we were obliged to bear away the Cable again and lay fast. Towards the evening finding the gale did not moderate and that it might be some time before an oppertunity offered to get higher up, I came to a resolution to heel the Ship where we were, and with this view Moored her with a kedge Anchor and hawser; in heaving the Anchor out of the boat, one of the Seamen, either through egnorance or carelessness or both, was carried out of the boat by the buoy rope and to the bottom with the anchor. In this very cretical situation he had presence of mind to disingage him self and come up to the surface of the water where he was taken up with one of his legs fractured in a dangerous manner.

FRIDAY 15*th*. Early the next morning we gave the ship a good heel to port, in order to come at and stop the leak, on riping off the Sheathing, it was found to be in the Seams which both in and under the wale, were very open and in several places not a bit of Oakam in them. While the Carpenters were making good these defects we filled all our empty water Casks at a stream hard by the Ship. The wind was now moderate but the weather was thick and hazey with rain.

The Natives who left us yesterday when the bad weather came on, paid us a nother Visit this Morning; the first came in small Canoes others afterwards came in large boats, in one were twenty women and one man besides children. I attentively examined these boats with Crantz discription of the Womens boat in greenland before me and found these were built and constructed in the same manner, parts like parts with no other difference than the form of the head and stern; particularly in the first, which bears some resemblance to the head of a Whale. The framing is of slender pieces of Wood and the out side is seal skin or perhaps the skins of some larger sea animal. The small Canoes were also made nearly of the same form and of the same materials as those used by the Greenlanders and Esquemaux's, at least the difference is not material; some of these as I have before observed carry two men; they are considerable broader in proportion to their length than those used by the Esquimauxs, and the head or fore part curves up some thing like the head of a fiddle.

Men Women and Children were all Cloathed alike, in a kind of frocks made of the Skins of different animals, such as the Sea-beaver, Racoons, Martins Hares squerrels &c^a all of which they wore with the fur side out. Some of the Women wore a bear skin over this dress and most of the men wore what Crantz calls a leather pelt, or rather a shirt made of the skin of large guts, probably those of the whale, they are made to draw tight round the neck, the sleeves reach as low as the wrist round which they are tied with a string and the skirts are drawn over the rim of the hole in which they sit in the Canoe, so that no water can enter, and at the same time it keeps the man intirely dry, for no water can penetrate through them no more than through a bladder; they must be kept continually wet or moist otherways they Crack and break.

The Men had Mittins made of the skins of bears paws, and high-crowned conical straw caps; also others made of wood resembling a seals head. But I saw not a woman with a head dress of any kind, they had all long black hair a part of which was tied up in a bunch over the forehead. The men had beards though not large to which they hang beads, or peices of bone and the women in some measure endeavoured to imitate them by tattowing or staining the chin with black that comes to a point on each cheek, something of this kind is mentioned by Crantz to be the Custom in greenland. Some both men and women have the under lip slit quite through horizontally, and so large as to admit the tongue which I have seen them thrust through, which happened to be the case when it was first discovered by one of the Seamen, who called out there was a man with two mouths and indeed it does not look unlike it. Though the lips of all were not slit, yet all were bored, espicially the women and even the young girls; to these holes and slits they fix pieces of bone of this size ( ) and shape, placed side by side in the inside of the lip; a thread is run through them to keep them together, and some goes quite through the lip and fastens, or fore-locks on the out side to which they hang other pieces of bones or beads. This Ornament is a very great impediment to the Speach and makes them look as if they had a double row of teeth in the under jaw. Besides these lip-jewels which they seemed to value above all others, they wear a bone, or some bugle beads strung on a stif string or Cord 3 or 4 inch long, run through the cartilage that divides the nostrils from each other. Their ears are bored all round to which they hang beads or pieces of bone; they wear braclets and some other oraments and to crown all they use both black and red paint so that I have nowhere seen Indians that take more pains to ornament, or rather disfigure themselves, than these people.

Their Weapons, or rather their Instruments for fishing and hunting, are the very same as are made use of by the Esquemaux and Greenlanders and are all of them very accuratly discribed by Crantz; I did not see one with these people that he has not mentioned, nor has he mentioned one that they have not. For defensive armour they have a kind of Jacket made of thin laths bound together with Sinews. As none of these people lived in the bay where we had Anchored, we saw none of their hab[i]tations and I had no time to look after them.

These people are not of the same Nation as those who Inhabit King Georges Sound, both their language and features are wid[e]ly different: These are small of stature, but thick set good looking people and from Crantz discription of the Greenlander, seem to bear some affinity to them. But as I never saw either a Greenlander or an Esquemaus, who are said to be of the same nation, I cannot be a sufficient judge and as we may very probably see more of them I shall reserve the discussion of this point to some other time.

SATURDAY 16*th*. The 16th in the evening the weather cleared up when we found our selves surrounded on every side by land; our station was on the East side of the Sound in a place which in the Chart is distinguished by the name of *Snug Corner bay*, and a very snug place it is. I went accompanied by some of the officers to view the head of it and found it to be sheltered from all winds and to have in it from 7 to 3 fath. water a Muddy bottom. The land near the shoar is low, part clear and part wooded, the clear ground was covered two or three feet thick with Snow, but very little lay in the woods. The trees were all of the Spruce or fir kind and some were tolerable large. The very summits of the neighbouring hills were covered with wood, but those farther inland seemed to be naked rocks burried in snow. Here were a good many Ducks, geese and a few other birds but all of them so fearfull that it was hardly possible to get a shot at them.

SUNDAY 17*th*. The leak being stoped and the Sheathing made good over it, at 4 oclock in the Morning of the 17th we weighed and Steered to the NW with a light breeze at ENE: thinking if their was any passage to the North through this inlet it would be in that direction.

*   *   *

[*There was no passage through. Cook turned back into the open sea and proceeded south-west along the coast, struggling in vain to make some correspondence between what lay before him and the printed acounts and charts of Bering's voyages. Soon 'a very large and deep bay' gave promise of being the looked-for northern passage. Their painstaking investigation of the inlet for over 100 miles ended in the mouth of 'a great River', which Cook named River Turnagain. (They were near the site of modern Anchorage.)*]

JUNE   MONDAY 1*st*. . . . . If the discovery of this River should prove of use, either to the present or future ages, the time spent in exploring it ought to be the less regreted, but to us who had a much greater object in View it was an essential loss; the season was advancing apace, we knew not how far we might have to proceed to the South and we were now convinced that the Continent extended farther to the west than from the Modern Charts we had reason to expect and made a passage into Baffin or Hudson bays far less probable, or at least made it of greater extent. But if I had not examined this place it would have been concluded, nay asserted that it communicated with the Sea to the North, or with one of these bays to the East. In the after noon I sent Mr King again with two armed boats, with orders to land on the northern point of the low land on the SE side of the River, there to desplay the flag, take possession of the Country and River in his Majestys name and to bury in the ground a bottle containing t[w]o pieces of English coin (date 1772) and a paper on which was in[s]cribed the Ships names date &c^a. In the mean time the Ships were got under sail in order to proceed down the River, the wind still blowing fresh Easterly, but died away soon after we were under way and meeting the flood tide off point possession obliged us to drop anchor in 5 fathom water with the point bearing South 2 Miles distant. When Mr King returned he informed me that as he approached the Shore, several of the Natives made their appearence with their arms extended, probably to express their peacable intentions and to shew they were without weapons. On Mr King and the Gentlemen with him landing with Muskets in their hand they seemed alarmed, and made signs to lay them down which was accordingly done, then they suffered the gentlemen to walk up to them and appeared cheerfull and sociable. They had with them a few pieces of fresh Salmon and several dogs, Mr Law Surgeon of the Discovery, who was one of the party bought one of the latter took it down to the boat and shot it dead in their sight which seemed to surprise them very much, and as if they thought themselves not safe in such company walked away and then it was discover'd that their Spears and other weapons, were hid in the bushes close behind them. Mr King also informed me that the ground was swampy, the Soil poor light and black; it produced a few trees and shrubs, such as spruce, birch, willow, Rose and Current bushes and a little grass; but they saw not a single plant in flower.

TUESDAY 2*nd*. At high water wieghed and with a faint breeze Southerly

Stood over to the West shore where the return of the flood obliged us to anchor. Soon after several of the Natives paid us a visit, and brought with them a few skins some pieces of Salmon and Holibut, which they exchan[g]ed with our people for old cloaths or whatever they could get. At half past 10 AM wieghed with the first of the Ebb and with a gentle breeze at South plyed down the River, in the doing of which, by the inattention and neglect of the Man at the lead, the Ship struck and stuck fast on a bank that lies nearly in the Middle of the River and about two miles above the two projecting bluf points before mentioned, and was the occasion of that very strong ripling or agitation of the stream mentioned in turning up the River. There was not less than 12 feet water about the Ship at low-water but some part of the bank was dry. As soon as the Resolution came a ground I made the Signal for the Discovery to Anchor, she, as I afterwards understood, was near being a shore on the West side of the bank. As the flood tide made the Ship floated off without receiving the least damage or giving us the least trouble and after standing over to the West shore into deep water anchored to wait for the Ebb for the Wind was still contrary.

WEDNESDAY 3rd. Weighed with the Ebb and got about two miles below the bluf point on the West shore where we stoped tide in 19 fathom water. A good many of the Indians attended upon us all the Morning, their company was very exceptable, as they brought with them a large quantity of very fine Salmon which they exchanged for such trifles as we had to give them: the most of it was Split ready for drying. In the after noon the Mountains for the first time sence we arrived in the River were clear of Clouds and we discovered a Volcano in one of these on the West side, it is in the lat. of 60°[23′ N] and the first high Mou[n]tain to the North of Mount St Augustine: the Volcano is on that side of the hill next the River and not far from the Summit;
Thur. 4   it is not considerable emitting a white smoke but no fire which made some think it was no more than a white thick cloud such as we have frequently seen on the Coast, for the most part appearing on the sides of the hills and often extends along a whole range and at different times falls or rises, expands or contracts it self and has a resemblance to Clouds of white smoke. But this besides being too

small for one of those clouds, remained as it were fixed in the same spot for the whole time the Mountain was clear which was above 48 hours.

The Wind remaining Southerly we continued to Tide it down the River and on the 5th in the Morning coming to the place   Frid. 5 where we had lost our Kedge Anchor, made an attempt to find it which miscarried. Before we left this place Six Canoes came of from the East shore, some conducted by one and others by two men; they remained at a small distance from the Ships, viewing them with a kind of silent surprise a full half hour, without exchanging a single word with us, or with one another. At length they took Courage and came along side, began to barter with our people and did not leave us till they had parted with all or most of what they brought with them, consisting of a few firs and a little Salmon. All the people we have met with in this River are of the same Nation as those who Inhabit *Sandwich Sound*, but differ essentially from those of *Nootka* or *King Georges Sound*, both in their persons and Language. The language of these is rather more Gutaral, but like the others they speak slowly and distinct, in words which seem sentences. I have before observed that they were in possession of iron, that is they had Spears and knives of this metal and they had also of the former made of Copper. Thier spears are like a Spontoon and their knives, which they kept in sheaths, are of a considerable length, these with a few glass beads were the only things we saw amongst them that were not of their own Manufacture. It is probable they may get them from some of their Neighbours with whome the Russians may have a trade, for I will be bold to say that the Russians were never amongst these people, nor carry on any commerce with them, for if they did they would hardly be cloathed in such valuable skins as those of the Sea beaver; the Russians would find some means or other to get them all from them.

There is no doubt but a very benificial fur trade might be carried on with the Inhabitants of this vast coast, but unless a northern passage is found it seems rather too remote for Great Britain to receive any emolument from it. It must however be observed that the most, nay the only valuable skins, I saw amongst them was the Sea beaver, or the Sea otter as some call it; all the other skins that I saw were of an inferior kind the foxes and Martins in particular. It must also be observed that the most of the skins we got, which were not many, were made up in dresses, some were however very good other old and ragged enough, and all of them very lousey. But as they make no other use of skins than cloathing it cannot be supposed they are at the trouble to dress more than what is necessary for this purpose and perhaps this is the cheif use for which they kill the animal for the Sea and Rivers seems to supply them with food. Whereas a trade with Foreigners would increase their wants by introducing new luxuries amongst them, in order to purchas which they would be the more assiduous in procuring skins, for I think it is pretty evident they are not a scarce article in the Country, and to judge from the skins we saw amongst the Inhabitants, here are all the Animals that are found in the Northern parts of the world whose skins are sought after, though they may not be all of that high perfection.

*　　*　　*

[*The ships left what is now Cook Inlet, and sailed outside the Kodiak Island complex before rejoining the Alaskan peninsula proper. They then made their way through the Shumagin Islands.*]

Frid. 19　Soon after we were through this Channell in which we found 40f^{ms} water, we were a good deal alarmed at the Discovery, who was about two miles a stern, firing three guns, bringing to and making the signal to speak with us; as no apparent danger appeared in the passage, it was concluded some sudden accident as springing a leak must have happened. A boat was immidiately se[n]t to her and returned in a short time with Captain Clerke, who informed me that some Indians in three or four Canoes, who had been following the Ship for some time, at length got under his stern. An Indian in one of them made many signs, took of his cap and bowed after the manner of Europeans, which induced them to throw him a rope, to which he fastened a small thin wood case or box and then, after speaking somthing and making some more signs droped astern and left them. No one had any suspicion of the box containing any thing till after the Canoes were gone when it was accidentally opened and found to contain a piece of paper folded up and carefully laid in on which were some writing in the Russian language, as was supposed, with the date 1778 prefixed to it, and in the body of the note was something that refer'd to the year 1776, which was all that could be understood of it, as no one on board either ship could read it. Captain Clerke was at first of opinion that some Russians had been shipwrecked here, and seeing us pass had taken this method to inform us of their situation. No such idea occur'd to me, for if this had been the case and they were desireous of being reliev'd from their distress, it was very extra-ordinary that no one of them came of in the Canoes to secure to themselves and their fellows what they must long have wished for. I rather thought it to be a note of information left by some Russian trader who had lat[e]ly been in these parts, to be deliverd to the next that came, and that the Indians seeing us pass by and supposeing us to be Russians were determined to give us the note thinking it might make us stop: and therefore I did not stay to enquire any farther into the matter, but made sail and stood away to the Westward along the coast, or islands, for we could not till whether the nearest land within was continent or islands.[31] If not the latter than the coast forms some tolerable large and deep bays. We continued to run all night with a gentle breeze at NE and at two oclock the next Morning some breakers were seen within us at 2 Miles distance; two hours after others were seen ahead and on our larboard bow and between us and the land they were innumerable, and we did but just clear them with a south course. These breakers were occasioned by rocks some of which are above and others under water; they extend 7 leagues from the land and are very dangerous especially in thick weather, which this coast seems subject to. . . .

Sat. 20

SUNDAY 21*st*. . . . The rock and breakers before mentioned, forced us so far from the Continent, that we had but a distant View of the Coast between Rocks Point and Halibut isles.[32] Over these islands we could see the main land covered with snow; but particularly some hills whose elevated summits were seen towering above the clouds to a most stupendious height. The most South westerly was discovered to be a

31. It turned out to be a receipt for tribute paid to the Russians.
32. Halibut Island is Sanak.

Volcano which continually threw out a vast column of black smoke; it stands not far from the coast, and in the latitude of 54°48′ N, longitude 195°45′ E. It is also remarkable from its figure, which is a compleat cone and the Volcano is at the very summit. We seldom saw this or any of the other mountains wholy clear of clouds, at times both base and summit would be clear, when a narrow cloud, sometimes two or three one above the other, would embrace the middle like a girdle, which with the Column of smoke rising perpendicular to a great height out of it[s] summit and spreading before the wind into a tail of vast length, made a very picturesque appearences. It may be worth remarking, that the Wind at the height the smoke of this Volcano reached moved sometimes in a contrary direction to what it did at sea even when it blew a fresh gale. In the after noon having three or four hours calm our people caught upward of a hundred Halibut, some of which weighed 100 lb and none less than 20, which proved a very great refreshing to us. In the height of our fishery, which was in [35] fathom water & 3 or 4 miles from the shore, a small Canoe, conducted by one man, came to us from the large island. On his approaching the Ship he took off his cap and bowed in the same manner as those who visited the Discovery on the 19th. It was evident that the Russians must have a communication and trafic with these people, not only from their acquired politness which has doubtless been borrowed from them but from the note before mentioned, and this man having a pair of green cloth breeches and a Jacket of black cloth or stuff under his own gut shirt or frock. He had nothing to barter, except a grey fox skin and fishing implements or harpoons, the heads of the shafts of which for the length of a foot or more were neatly made of bone as thick as a walking cane and carved. He had with him a bladder full of something which we supposed to be oil, as he opened it took a Mouthfull and than fastened it again. The Canoe was of the same make as those we had seen before, but rather smaller; he used the double bladed paddle as did also those who vis[i]ted the Discovery. In his size and features he exactly resembled those we saw in Sandwich Sound and the other places but was quite free from paint of any kind; and had the perforation of his lip made in an oblique direction without any ornament in it. He did not seem to understand any of the common words used by the people of Sandwich Sound when repeated to him, but perhaps this might be owing to our not pronu[n]cing them properly. . . .

*   *   *

THURSDAY 25*th*. The next Morning we got a breeze Easterly, and what was uncommon with this wind, clear weather, so that we not only saw the Volcano, but other Mountains both to the East and West of it, and all the coast of the Mainland under them much plainer than at any time before. It extended from NEBN, to NW½W where it seemed to terminate. Between this point and the islands without it, there appeared a large opening for which I steered,[33] till we raised land beyond it; which land, altho we did not see it join to the Continent, made a passage through the opening rather doubtfull; it also made it doubtfull whether the land we saw to the SW were Islands or Continent, and if the latter than the opening would be a deep bay or inlet into which, if we entered with an Easterly wind we could not so easily get out. Not caring therefore, to trust too much to appearences, I steered to the Southward with a view of going without all and then steered West the direction the islands laid, for such we found this land to be. By 8 oclock we had pass'd three of them all of a good hieght and saw more to the westward; the swermost part of them bore WNW. The Weather in the after noon became gloomy and at length turned to a mist and the wind blew fresh at East. At 10 oclock hauled the Wind to the Southward till day break then resumed our course to the West. Day light availed us little as the Weather was so thick that   Frid. 26 we could not see a hundred yards before us, but as the wind was now very moderate I ventured to run. At half past 4 we were alarmed at hearing the Sound of breakers on our larboard bow; on heaving the lead found 28 fathom water and the next cast 25; I immideately brought the ship to with her head to the Northward and anchored in this last depth over a bottom of Coarse Sand, and called to the

---

33. Cook has now passed the extremity of the Alaskan peninsula and the most easterly of the Aleutian Islands, Unimak. The opening for which he steered, until caution made him hold back, was in fact the Unimak Pass, quite the best passage through the islands.

Discovery who was close by us to anchor also. A few hours after, the fog cleared away a little and it was percieved we had scaped very emminant danger; we found our selves three quarters of a mile from the NE side of an island which extended from sBw½w to NBE½E, each extreme about a league distant, two elevated rocks the one bearing sBE and the other EBs each half a league distant and about the same distance from each other. There were several breakers about them and yet Providence had conducted us through between these rocks where I should not have ventured in a clear day, and to such an anchoring place that I could not have chosen a better.[34] After finding our selves so near land and before a Cove where landing appeared easy, I sent a boat to sea what the shore produced. In the after noon she returned and the officer who commanded her, reported that it produced some tolerable good grass and several other small plants, one of which was like Parsley and eat very well either in soups or as a Sallad; there was no appearence of shrubs or trees, but on the beach were a few pieces of drift wood. It was judged to be low water between 10 and 11 oclock and we found where we lay at Anchor that the Flood tide came from the East or SE.

SATURDAY 27th. In the Night the Wind blew fresh at South, but moderated towards the Morning and the fog partly despersed. At 7 AM wieghed and steered to the North between the island we had anchored under and a small one near it and about 4 miles from this last station. Before we were through the Channell which is not more than a mile broad, the wind faild and obliged us to Anchor in 34 fathoms water. We had now land in every direction, that to the South extended to the sw in a ridge of Mountains beyond our sight, but could not till whether it composed one or more islands. It was after-wards found to be only one island and known by the Name of *Oonalaschka*; between it and the land to the North, which had the appeerence of being a group of islands, there seemed to be a Channell in the direction of NWBN.[35] On a Point which bore West from the Ship

34. They are just off Sedanka Island, off the north-east coast of the island Unalaska.
35. This is the Unalga Pass, between Unalaska and the small Unalga island to the north-east. It is about 1¾ miles wide at its narrowest.

³/₄ of a mile distant, were several Indians and their habitations; to this place we saw them tow in two Whales which we supposed they had killed that Morning. A few now and then came off to the Ships and bartered a few trifling things with our people, but never remained above a quarter of an hour at one time on the contrary they rather seemed shy, and yet seemed to be no strangers to Vessels in some degree like ours, and had acquired a degree of politeness uncommon to Indians. At 1 PM wieghed and with a light breeze at NE and the Tide of flood in our favour steered for the Channell above mentioned in hopes after we were through of finding the land trend away to the Northward, or at least find a passage to the West or SW out to Sea, for we supposed our selves, as it realy happened, to be amongst islands and not in an inlet of the Continent. We had not been long under sail before the Wind veered to the North so that we had to ply, the Soundings were from 40 to 27 fathoms over a bottom of Sand and Mud. At 8 oclock the Tide of Ebb making against us Anchored in 35 fathom Water about 3 leagues from our last station with the Passage bearing NW. Where we lay at Anchor the Tide was trifling, but about ¹/₂ a mile NE of us there was a race that looked frightfull.

SUNDAY 28*th*. At Day break the next Morning weigh'd with a light breeze at South which carried us the length of the Passage, when it was succeeded by variable light airs from all directions but as there run a rappid Tide in our favour, the Resolution got through before the Ebb made, but the Discovery did not, she was carried back got into the race and had some trouble to get clear of it. As soon as we were through we found the land on one side to trend West and SW and on the other North so that we were in great hopes the Continent here took a remarkable turn in our favour. Being in want of Water and perceiving we ran some risk in driving about in a rappid Tide without Wind to govern the Ships I stood for a harbour we had passed lying on the South side of the passage, but we were very soon driven past it and to prevent being driven back through the passage, came to an anchor in 28 fathom water, pretty near the South shore out of the strength of the Tide and yet we found it to run full five knots and a half. . . .

At low water which happened between a 11 & 12 oclock, wieghed and towed the Ship into the Bay[36] and there Anchored in 9 fathom water over a bottom of sand and mud. The Discovery got in not long after. As soon as we had anchored the Launch was sent for Water and a boat to draw the Seine, in which was caugh[t] only four Trout and a few other small fish.

An Indian brought on board such another note as was given to Captain Clerke which he presented to me; it was written in the Russian Language which as I have before observed none of us could read. As it was of no use to me and for any thin[g] I then knew might be of consequince to the bearer I returned it him again and then dismissed him with a few presents, for which he expressed his thanks by making several low bows as he retired.

* * *

[*The ships now proceeded east-north-east along the northern coast of the Alaskan peninsula until they reached the Kvichak River, which they named the River Bristol. Then they sailed westward until they reached a promontory where John Williamson landed and took possession of the country in His Majesty's name; the promontory was named Cape Newenham after a friend of Williamson's. Some fruitless days were spent among the shoals of Kuskokwim Bay, with the masters of both ships (Bligh and Edgar) out in boats ahead taking soundings. They were visited by twenty-seven men in canoes. Cook turned west and on 29 July was off Point Upright, the eastern end of St Matthew Island, where there was 'an incredable Number of birds all of the Auk kind'.*]

THURSDAY 30*th*. The 30th at 4 AM Point upright bore NWBN 6 leagues distant. About this time a light breeze sprung up at NNW attended with a thick fog with now and then a clear interval. We stood NE till 4 AM when the Wind veering to the Eastward we tacked and Stood to the NW. Soon after the Wind came to SE and we steered NEBN having foggy and clear weather by turns. We continued this Course
AUG^t   till Noon on Saturday 1st of Aug, our Soundings were from
Sat. 1   35 to 20 fathoms. At this time we were in the latitude of

36. This is Samgoonoodha (or Samgunuda) Harbour on Unalaska, later called English Bay.

60°58′ N, longitude 191° 00′ E, the Wind veering to NE and increased to a fresh breeze with Cloudy gloomy weather. I first made a stretch of about 10 leagues to the NW but seeing no land in that direction, I stood back to the Eastward about 15 leagues and met with nothing but pieces of drift wood. The Soundings were from 22 to 19 fathoms.

   The 2ⁿᵈ We had Variable light Winds with Showers of   Sun. 2
rain. The 3ʳᵈ in the Morning the Wind fixed in the SE quarter   Mon. 3
and we resumed our Course to the Northward. At Noon we were by observation in the latitude of 62°34′ N, Longitude 192°30′ E and the depth of Water 16 fathoms. Mʳ Anderson my Surgeon who had been lingering under a consumption for more than twelve Months, expired between 3 and 4 this after noon. He was a Sensible Young Man, an agreeable companion, well skilld in his profession, and had acquired much knowlidge in other Sciences, that had it pleased God to have spar'd his life might have been usefull in the Course of the Voyage. Soon after land was Seen to the Westward, 12 leagues distant, it was supposed to be an Island and to perpetuate the Memory of the deseased for whom I had a very great regard, I named [it] *Andersons Island*.³⁷ The next day I removed Mʳ Law the Surgeon of the Discovery   Tues. 4
into the Resolution and appointed Mʳ Samuel the Surgeons first mate of the Resolution to be surgeon of the Discovery.

*   *   *

[*The ships advanced slowly up the American coast past 'Sledge Island' (after an 'admirably well constructed' sledge which they found) and King Island. Land now began to be visible in the north-west.*]

SATURDAY 8*th*. The 8ᵗʰ between 4 and 5 in the Morning we had again a sight of the NW land. Soon after we had a Calm, and finding that the Ships were carried by a Tide or Current fast in towards the land, we droped Anchor in 12 fathoms water, about two miles from the Coast which extended from NNW to NWBW. Over the Western extreme is an elevated peaked hill situated in the Latitude of 65°[42]′ N, long. 19[2°50′] E. At 8 oClock a breeze sprunging up at NE we weighed and

---

37. St Lawrence Island, 63° 18′ N, 168° 42′ W, discovered and named by Bering, August 1728.

stood to the SE in hopes of finding a passage between the Coast we had anchored under on the 6th in the evening and this NW land. But we did not steer long upon this Course before we got in to seven fathoms water, the weather clearing we saw low land connecting the two Coasts and high land behind it. Being now satisfied that the whole was a continued Coast, I tacked and stood away for its NW part, and after making a few boards came to an anchor under it in 17 fathoms water where we found a strong current seting to the NE or in the same direction as the Coast. The weather at this time was very thick with

Sun. 9   rain; but at 4 the next Morning it cleared so that we could see the lands about us. A high steep rock or island descovered the preceding evening, bore WBS a Nother island to the North of it and much larger bore WBN, the peaked hill above mentioned SEBE and the point under it S 32° E. Under this hill lies some low land stretching out towards the NW the extreme point of which bore NEBE about 3 Miles distant, over and beyond it some high land was seen supposed to be a continuation of the continent. This Point of land which I named *Cape Prince of Wales*, is the more remarkable by being the Western extremity of all America hitherto known; it is situated in the Latitude of 65°46' N, Longitude 191°[45]' E: the observations by which both were determined, altho made in sight of it, were liable to some small error on account of the haziness of the weather. . . .

MONDAY 10*th*. At day break in the Morning of the 10th resumed our Course to the West for the land we had seen the preceding evening, which at 7^h11' when the Longitude by the Time keeper was 189°24' E extended from S 72° West to N 41° E. Between the SW extreme and a point which bore West 2 leagues distant, the shore forms a large bay in which we anchored at 10 AM about 2 miles from the North shore in 10 fathoms Water over a gravely bottom; the South point of the bay bore S 58° W the North point N 43° E, the bottom of the bay N 60° W two or three leagues distant and the two islands we past the preceding day N 72° E distant 14 leagues.[38] As we were standing into this place we perceived on the North shore an Indian Village, and some people whom the sight of the Ships seemed to have thrown into

38. The ships had now crossed Bering Strait, and were on the Asian shore.

some confufion or fear, as we could see some runing inland with burdthens on their backs. To this place I went with three Armed boats, accompanied by some of the Offi[c]ers, and found 40 or 50 Men each armed with a Spontoon Bow and Arrows drawn up on a rising ground on which the village stood. As we drew near three of them came down towards the shore and were so polite as to take of their Caps and make us a low bow: we returned the Compliment but this did not inspire them with sufficient confidence to wait our landing, for the Moment we put the boats a shore they retired. I followed them alone without any thing in my hand, and by signs and actions got them to stop and receive some trifles I presented them with and in return they gave me two fox skins and a couple of Sea horse teeth. I cannot say whether they or I made the first present, for these things they brought down with them for this very purpose and would have given me them without my making any return. They seemed very fearfull and causious, making signs for no more of our people to come up, and on my laying my hand on one mans Shoulder he started back several paces. In proportion as I advanced they retreated backwards always in the attitude of being ready to make use of their Spears, while those on the hill behind them stood ready to support them with thier arrows. Insensibly my self and two or three more got in amongst them, a few beads distributed to those about us brought on a kind of confidence so that two or three more of our people joining us did not Alarm them, and by degrees a sort of traffick between us commenced. They gave us in exchange for Knives, Beads, Tobacco &c^a some of their cloathing and a few Arrows, but nothing we had to offer them would induce them to part with a Spear or a Bow, which they held in constant readiness never once quiting them, excepting one time, four or five laid them down while they gave us a Song and a Dance, and then they placed them in such a manner as they could lay hold of them in an instant and for greater security desired us to sit down. The Arrows were pointed with either bone or Stone, but very few were barbed and some had a round blunt point of bone, I cannot say what use these were for unless to kill small animals without hurting the Skin. The Bow[s] were such as we had seen on the America Coast and like those used by the Esqumaux's; the Spears or Spontoons were of Iron or steel and of European or

Asiatic workmanship in which no little pains had been taken to ornament them with carving and inlayings of brass and a white Metal. Those who stood ready with Bow and arrows in hand had the Spear slung over their Shoulder by a leather strap. The Arrows they carried in a lather quiver slung over the left Shoulder; some of the quivers were extremely beautifull, being made of red leather on which was very neat embroidery and other ornaments. Several other things and in particular, their cloathing shewed them possessed of a degree of ingenuty far surpassing any thing one could expect amongst so Northern a people. All the Americans we had seen before were rather low of Stature with round chubby faces and high cheek bones, whereas these are long visaged Stout made men and appeared to be a quite different Nation.[39] We saw neither Women nor Children, Boys nor girls nor aged except one man, who was bald headed, and he was the only one who had not a spear as well as a bow and arrows; the others seemed to be picked men and rather under than above the middle age. The old man had a black mark a cross his face which I did not see in any others, all of them had their ears bored and some had glass beads hanging to them which were the only fixed Ornaments we saw about them, for they wear none to the lips, which is another thing in which the[y] differ from the Americans. Thier cloathing consisted of a Cap, a Frock a pair of Breeches, a pair of Boots and a pair of gloves, all made of leather or the Skins of Dear, Dogs, Seals &cᵃ all extremely well dress'd some with the fur or hair on and other with it off. The caps were made to fit the head very close, and besides these caps which most of them had on, we got from them some hoods made of dog skins that were large enough to cover both head and Shoulders. Their hair seemed to be black, but their heads were either shaved or the hair cut close off and none wore any beard. Of the few articles they got from us knives and Tobacco were what they most Valued.

Here were both their Winter and summer habitations, the former are exactly like a Vault the floor of which is sunk a little below the surface of the earth. The one I examined was of an oval form the

39. They were the Chuchki, a Mongoloid people, who had beaten back Russian attempts to control them.

length where of was about twenty four feet and the height 12 or more; the framing was composed of Wood and the ribs of Whales, disposed in a judicious manner and bound together with smaller matterrials of the same sort. Over this framing is laid a covering of strong coarse grass and over it a covering of earth; so that on the out side it looks like a little hillock, supported by a wall of Stone about 3 or 4 feet high which is built round the two sides and one end; at the other end the earth is raised sloaping to walk up to the entrance which is by a hole in the top of the roof over that end. The floor was boarded and under it was a kind of cellar, in which I saw nothing but Water, and at the end of each house was a Vaulted room which I took to be a store room; it communicated with the other by a dark passage and with the open air by a hole in the roof which was even with the ground one Walked upon, but one cannot say they were wholy under ground as one end reached to the edge of the hill along which they were made and was built up of Stone, over which was built a kind of Sentry box or tower of the large bones of large fish.

The Summer huts were pretty large, and circular and brought to a point at the top; the framing was of slight poles and bones, covered with the skins of Sea animals. I examined the inside of one; there was a fire place just within the door or entrance where lay a few wooden vessels all very dirty; thier bed places were close to the side and took up about half the circuit; some privecy seemd to be observed as there were several partitions made with skins, the bed and beding were of dear skins and the most of them were dry and clean. About the habitations were erected several stages ten or twelve feet high, such as we had observed on some part of the America coast; they were built wholy of bones and seemed to be intended to dry skins, fish &c[a] upon, out of the reach of their dogs, of which they had a great many; they were of the fox kind rather large and of different Colours with long soft hair like wool. These Dogs are probably of no other use than to draw their sledges in Winter, for sledges they have as I saw a good many laid up in one of the Winter huts; It is also not improbable but dogs may make a part of their food; several laid dead about them that had been killed that Morning, but why they were then killed or why they let them lay there I cannot say.

They have the same sort of Canoes as the Americans, we saw some of both sorts in a little creek under the Village. By the large fish bones and the Skins of other Sea Animals, it appeared that the sea supply'd them with the greatest part of their subsistance. The Country appeared to be exceeding barren, yeilding neither Tree nor shrub that we could see, some distance in land to the westward was seen a ridge of Mountains covered with snow that had lately fell.

This land we supposed to be a part of the island of *Alaschka* laid down in Mr Staehlins Map[40] before q[u]oted though from the figure of the Coast, the situation of the opposite coast of America and the longitude it appeared rather more probable to be the Country of the Tchuktschians explored by Behring in 1728. But to have admitted this at first sight I must have concluded Mr Staehlins Map and account to be either exceeding erronious even in latitude or else a mere fiction, a Sentance I had no right to pass upon it without farther proof.

After a Stay of between two or three hours with these people we returned to the Ships; soon after the Wind veered to the South, with it we weighed stood out of the bay and steered to the NE between the Coast and the Two islands. . . .

* * *

[*During the next five days Cook took the ships north-east towards the Alaskan shore then north past Cape Lisburne.*]

Mon. 17   From the Noon of this day to 6 oclock in the Morning of the following I steered EBN which Course brought us into 16 fathoms Water. The Weather was now tolerable clear in every direction, except to the Eastward, where lay a fog bank, which was the reason of our not seeing the land. I now steered NEBE thinking by this Course we could deepen our Water, but in the space of Six leagues it shoaled to 11 fathom; on which I thought proper to haul close to the wind which was at West this Course brought us into 19 fathoms. Towards Noon both the Sun and Moon shone out at intervals and we got some flying observations for the longitude, which reduced to Noon when the Latitude was 70°33′ N gave 197°41′ E, the Time keeper for the same

40. See introduction to this voyage.

time gave 198°00 E and the Variation was 35°1'22" E. We had afterwards reason to beleive that the observed longitude was within a
very few miles of the truth. Some time before Noon we percieved a
brigh[t]ness in the Northern horizon like that reflected from ice,
commonly called the blink; it was little noticed from a supposition
that it was improbable we should meet with ice so soon, and yet the
sharpness of the air and Gloomyness of the Weather for two or three
days past seemed to indicate some sudden change. At 1 PM the sight
of a large field of ice left us in no longer doubt about the cause of the
brightness of the Horizon we had observed. At ½ past 2 we tacked
close to the edge of it in 22 fathoms Water being then in the latitude
of 70°41', not being able to stand any fa[r]ther, for the ice was quite
impenetrable and extend[ed] from WBS to EBN as far as the eye could
reach. Here were abundance of Sea Horses, some in the Water but
far more upon the Ice; I had thoughts of hoisting the boats out to kill
some, but the Wind freshning I gave up the design and continued to
ply to the southward, or rather to the Westward for the Wind was
from that quarter; but we gained nothing, For on the 18th at   Tues. 18
Noon our latitude was 70°44' and the Timekeeper shewed that we
were near five leagues farther to the Eastward. We were at this time
in 20 fathoms Water, close to the edge of the ice which was as compact
as a Wall and seemed to be ten or twelve feet high at least, but farther
North it appeared much higher, its surface was extremely rugged and
here and there were pools of Water.

We now stood to the Southward and after runing Six leagues
shoaled the Water to 7 fathoms, which depth continued for near half
a mile and then it deepened to 8 and 9 fathom. At this time the
weather which had been very hazey cleared a little and we saw low
land extending from South to SEBE about 3 or 4 miles distant. The
East extreme form[s] a point which was much incumbered with ice
for which Reason it obtained the name of *Icey Cape*, Lat. 70°29' N,
long. 198°20' E but the other extreme was lost in the horizon, so that
there can be no doubt but it was a continuation of the Amirica
cont[i]nent. The Discovery being about a mile astern and to leeward
found less water than we did and was obliged to tack for it, which
obliged me to tack also for fear of being Separated. Our situation was

now more and more critical, we were in shoald water upon a lee shore and the main body of the ice in sight to windward driving down upon us. It was evident, if we remained much longer between it and the land it would force us ashore unless it should happen to take the ground before us; it seemed nearly if not quite to join to the land to leeward and the only direction that was open was to the sw. After making a short board to the Northward I made the Signal for the Discovery to tack and tacked my self at the same time. The Wind proved rather favourable so that we laid up sw and swbw having never less than 10 fathom water, but generally 12 and 13.

WEDNESDAY 19*th*. The 19th at 8 AM the Wind veering back to West I tacked to the Northward and at Noon the Latitude was 70°06′ N, Longitude 196°42′ E. In this situation we had a good deal of drift ice about us and the main ice was about two leagues to the North.

At ½ past 1 PM we got close in with the edge of the main ice, it was not so compact as that which we had seen more to the Northward, but it was too close and in too large pieces to force the ships through it. On the ice lay a prodigious number of Sea horses and as we were in want of fresh provisions the boats from each ship were sent to get some. By 7 oclock in the evening we had got on board the Resolution Nine of these Animals which till now we had supposed to be Sea Cows, so that we were not a little disapointed, especially some of the Seamen who for the Novelty of the thing, had been feasting their eyes for some days past, nor would they have been disapointed now, or known the difference, if we had not happened to have one or two on board who had been in Greenland and declared what animals these were, and that no one ever eat of them. But not withstanding this we lived upon them so long as they lasted and there were few on board who did not prefer it to salt meat. The fat at first is as sweet as Marrow but in a few days it grows ransid onless it is salted, then it will keep good much longer, the lean is coarse, black and rather a strong taste, the heart is nearly as well tasted as that of a bullock. The fat when Melted yeilds a good deal of Oil which burns very well in lamps, and their hides, which are very thick, were very usefull about our rigging. The teeth or tusks of most of them were at this time very small, even some of the largest and oldest had them not passing six inches long, from which we conclude that they had lately shed their old teeth. They lay in herds of many hundred upon the ice, huddling one over the other like swine, and roar or bray very loud, so that in the night or foggy weather they gave us notice of the ice long before we could see it. We never found the Whole herd a sleep, some were always upon the watch, these, on the approach of the boat, would wake those next to them and these the others, so that the whole herd would be awake presently. But they were seldom in a hurry to get away till after they had been once fire[d] at, then they would tumble one over the other into the sea in the utmost confusion, and if we did not at the first discharge kill those we fired at out right we generally lost them tho' mortally wounded. They did not appear to us to be that dangerous animal some Authors have discribed, not even when attacked, they are rather more so to appearence than reality; Vast numbers of them would follow and come close up to the boats, but the flash of a Musket in the pan, or even pointing one at them would send them down in an instant. The feemale will defend the young one to the very last and at the expence of her life whether in the Water or on the ice; nor will the young quit the dam though she be dead so that if you kill one you are sure of the other. The Dam when in the Water holds the young one between her fore fins. . . .

By such time as we had done with the Sea horses we were in a manner surrounded by the ice and had no way left to clear it but by standing to the Southward which was done till 3 AM of the 20th with a gentle breeze Westerly and for the most part thick foggy weather. The Sounding[s] were from twelve to 15 fathoms. At 2 AM we tacked and stood to the North till 10 when the Wind veering to the Northward we stood West South West and West. At 2 PM we fell in with the Main ice, along the edge of which we kept, being partly directed by the roaring of the Sea Horses, for we had a very thick fog. Thus we continued sailing till ½ past a 11 when we got in amongst the loose ice and heard the surge of the Sea upon the main ice. The fog being very thick and the Wind easterly I haul'd to the southward, and at 10 o'clock the next Morning, the fog clearing away we saw the Continent of America extending from SBE to EBS and at

Thurs. 20

Frid. 21

Noon from sw½s to East, the nearest part five leagues distant. At this time we were in the latitude of 69°32′ N, Longitude 195°48′ E and as the Main ice was at no great distance from us, it is evedent that it now covered a part of the sea which but a few days before was clear and that it extended farther to the South than where we first fell in with it. It must not be understood that I supposed any part of the ice we had seen fixed, on the contrary I am well assured that the whole was a moveable Mass. . . .

* * *

[*Cook spent eight days traversing the ice-shelf and looking for a passage through, going himself by boat to examine the ice to try to deduce what its nature was ('frozen Snow . . . all formed at sea', the produce of a great many winters). By 28 August he had come to the western edge, on the Asian shore.*]

SATURDAY 29*th*. The 29ᵗʰ in the Morning we saw the Main ice to the Northward and not long after land bearing SWBW; presently after this more land was seen bearing West, it made in two hills like islands, but afterwards the whole appeared to be connected. As we approached the land the depth of Water decreased very fast, so that at Noon, when we tacked, we had only 8 fathoms, being 3 Miles from the Coast which extended from S 30° E to N 60° W, this last extreme terminated in a bluf point being one of the hills above mentioned. The Weather at this time was very hazey with drizling rain, but soon after it cleared, especially to the Southward, Westward and Northward, so that we had a pretty good View of the Coast which in every respect is like that of America, that is low land next the Sea with elevated land farther back. It was perfectly distitude of Wood and even Snow, but was probably covered with a Mossy substance that gave it a brownish cast, in the low ground lying between the high land and the Sea was a lake extending to the SE fa[r]ther than we could see. As we stood off, the Westermost of the two hills before mentioned came open of the bluf point in the direction of NW, it had the appearence of being an island, but it might be joined to the other by low land without our seeing it, and if so there is a two fold point with a bay between them. This point which is steep and rocky was named [Cape

North][41] its situation is nearly in the latitude of 68°56′ N, longitude 180°51′ E. The Coast beyond it must take a very westerly direction, as we could see no land to the Northward of it though the horizon was there pretty clear. Being desirouse of seeing more of the Coast to the westward, we tacked again at 2 PM thinking we could weather the [Cape North] but finding we could not, the Wind freshening, a thick fog coming on with much snow, and being fearfull of the ice coming down upon us, I gave up the design I had formed of plying to the Westward and stood off shore again after standing into 10 fathoms water.

The season was now so very far advanced and the time when the frost is expected to set in so near at hand, that I did not think it consistant with prudence to make any farther attempts to find a passage this year in any direction so little was the prospect of succeeding. My attention was now directed towards finding out some place where we could Wood and Water, and in the considering how I should spend the Winter, so as to make some improvement to Geography and Navigation and at the same time be in a condition to return to the North in further search of a Passage the ensuing summer.

* * *

[*Cook now took the ships south-east, following the Asian coast, with the weather getting colder, with thick snow showers, the water vessels on deck being covered with a sheet of ice. He made his way back through the Bering Strait, still vexed by the problem of making sense of the descriptions and charts available concerning Russian exploration. In particular, it was necessary to verify the evidence of Stählin's map that Alaska was an island separated from the American continent, for the channel between might be their salvation. The huge inlet of Norton Sound seemed a possible entrance to such a channel, and on 11 September Cook anchored just south of Cape Denbigh.*]

41. Left blank by Cook; filled in by King.

[SEPTEMBER]

After dinner Lieutenant Gore was sent to the Peninsula to see if Wood and Water was to be got or rather Water, for the whole beach round the bay seemed to be covered with drift wood. At the same time a boat from each Ship was sent to Sound round the Bay, and at 3 PM the Wind freshening at NE weighed in order to work farther in, but it was very little farther we could go, for Shoald ground which extending quite round the bay to two or three miles from the Shore as the officers who had been sent to Sound reported. We therefore kept standing to and again with the Ships waiting for M[r] Gore who returned about 8 with the Launch laden with wood. He reported that there was but little fresh water and the Wood difficult to come at, by reason of the boats grounding some distance from the shore. Finding it would require much time and trouble to Wood here, I stood back to the

Sat. 12   other shore and at 8 oclock the next Morning, sent all the boats and a party of Men with an Officer to get wood from the place where I had landed two days before. We continued to stand on and off with the Ships for a while, but at length came to an Anchor in a ¼ less 5 fathom water, half a league from the coast, the South point whereof bore s 26° w and bald head N 60° E 9 leagues distant: Cape Denbigh bore s 72° E 26 miles distant and the Island under the East shore to the Southward of Cape Denbigh named *Besborough isle* s 72° E distant 15 leagues. As this was but a very open road for this season of the year or indeed any other, I resolved not to wait to compleat our Water, as that would require some time, but only fill the Ships with Wood and then go in search of a more convenient place to Water. We took of the drift wood that lay upon the beach and as the Wind blew a long shore the boats could sail both ways, so that we made great dispatch.

In the after noon I went ashore and walked a little into the Country, which where there was no wood was covered with heath and other plants some of which produced berries in abundance; all the berries were ripe the hurtle berries too much so and hardly a single plant was in flower. It was bad traveling in the Woods for under wood such as birch, willows, Alder and other shrubbery, the trees were all spruce, and none of them above six or eight inches in diameter, but there were some thrown upon the beach more than twice this size. All the drift wood in these parts was fir, I saw not a stick of any other sort.

SUNDAY 13*th*. The 13th In the afternoon a family of the Natives came near to the place where we were taking off wood; I know not how many there were at first, I saw no more than a Man, his wife and child, and a nother man who bore the human shape and that was all, for he was the most deformed cripple I either ever saw or heard of, so much so that I could not even bear to look at him: this state he seemed to have been in from his birth. The other man was almost blind and neither he or his wife were such good looking people as some we had seen; the under lips of both were bored and they had in their possession some such glass beads as I have before noticed, but iron was their beloved Metal, for four knives made out of an old iron hoop I got from them near 400 pound of fish they had caught the same day or the day before, some were trout and the rest a fish in size and taste between a Mullet and a Harren. I gave the Child, which was a girl, a few beads, on which the Mother fell a crying, then the Father, then the other man and at last to compleat the consort the child but this Musick continued not long.

By night we had got the Ships filled with wood and about twelve Tons of Water to each.

MONDAY 14*th*. The 14th a party of Men were sent a shore to cut brooms which we were in want of, and the branches of the spruce trees for brewing of beer. Towards Noon every body were taken on board, for the wind freshening made such a surf on the beach that it was with great difficulty the boats could land.

Being in doubt whether the coast we were now upon belonged to an island or the America Continent, and as this could not be determined with the Ships, I sent two boats under the Command of Lieutenant King to make the discovery. And the next day   Tues. 15 removed the Ships over to the Bay which is on the SE side of Cape Denbigh where, in the after noon, we anchored in a ¼ less 5 fathom water, with the Cape bearing N 60° W 2 or 3 Miles distant. A few of the Natives came off in their small Canoes and bartered a little dryed Salmon for such trifles as our people had to give them.

WEDNESDAY 16*th*. The 16th at day break Nine Men each in his Canoe paid us a Visit, they approached the Ship with some causion and evidently came with no other view than to satify their curiosity. They drew up a breast of each other under the Ships stern and gave us a Song, while one Man beat upon a kind of drum and a Nother made a thousand antic Motions with his hands and body; there was however nothing Savage either in the Song or the Actions that accompaned it. None of us could perceive any difference either in the shape or features of these people and those we had met with on every other part of the coast King Georges Sound excepted. Their cloathing which were mostly of Dear skins were made after the same fashion and they observed the custom of boring and fixing O[r]naments to the under lip. The Dwellings of these people are seated upon the Sea coast close to the beach, I had no oppertunity to examine any but those that were uninhabited. They are simply a sloaping roof without any side wall, composed of logs and covered with grass and earth. The floor is also laid with logs, the entrance is at one end, the fire place just within it and a small hole is made near the door to let out the smoke. After breakfast a party of Men was sent to the Peninsula for Brooms and Spruce, there being a few of these trees upon it and some Shrubbery hardly convertable to any other use but brooms. At the same time half the remainder of the people in each Ship had leave to go and pick berries, these returned on board at Noon when the other half went. The berries to be got here were Wild Current berries, hurtle-berries, Partridg berries and Heath berries. I also went a shore myself and walked over part of the Peninsula, I found in several places a good deal of very good grass and of a considerable length; and there was hardly a spot but what produced some vegetable or another. The low land which joins this Peninsula to the Continent is full of narrow creeks and small ponds of Water some of which were already frozen over. Here were a great Many geese and Bustards, but as they were very shy and no sort of Cover it was not possible to get within gun shot of them. We also met with some snipes and on the high ground were Partridges of two sorts and where we wooded plenty of Musketoes. Some of the Officers who traveled farther than I did met with a few of the Natives of both sex who treated them with civility. It appeared to me that this Peninsula must have been an island in remote times as there was marks of the Sea having been over the Isthmus and it was even kept out now by a bank of Sand, Stones and Wood thrown up by the waves. By this bank it was very evident that the land was incroaching upon the sea and one could see the progress it had made from time to time.

About 7 oclock in the evening I got on board, at the same time Mr King returned from his expedition and reported that he proceeded with the boats about 3 or 4 leagues farther then we did with the [ships] where landing on the West side from the heights saw the two coast[s] join and the inlet to terminate in a small River or Creek, before which were banks of Sand or Mud and every where Shoald Water. The land too was low and Swampy for some distance to the Northward, then it swelled into hills and united those which are on the East & West sides of the inlet. This inlet was Named *Norton Sound*, in honour of Sr Fletcher, speaker of the House of Commons; it extends to the North-ward as far as the Latitude of 64°55 N, the bay in which we were now at Anchor, lies on the SE side of it and is called by the Natives *Chachtoole*. It is but an indifferent place, being exposed to Southerly and SW winds, nor is there a harbour in all this Sound. . . .

Haveing now fully satisfied myself that Mr Stæhlin's Map must be erroneous and not mine it was high time to think of leaving these Northern parts, and to retire to some place to spend the Winter where I could procure refreshments for the people and a small supply of Provisions. *Petropaulowska* in *Kamtschatka*, did not appear to me a place where I could procure either the one or the other for so large a number of men, and besides I had other reasons for not going there at this time, the first and on which all the others depended was the great dislike I had to lay inactive for Six or Seven Months, which must have been the case had I wintered in any of these Northern parts. No place was so conveniently within our reach where we could expect to meet with these necessary articles, as *Sandwich Islands*, to these islands, therefore, I intended to proceed, but before this could be carried into execution it was necessary to have a supply of Water. With this View I resolved to search the America coast for a harbour, by proceeding along it to the Southward and endeavour to connect the Survey of this coast with that to the North of Cape Newenham. If I failed of finding a harb. then to proceed to *Samgoonoodha* which was fixed upon for a Rendezvouse in case of Separ[a]tion.

* * *

[*On 2 October they reached Unalaska. A considerable leak had been discovered under the starboard buttock of the* Resolution *on 25 September.*]

[OCTOBER]

SATURDAY 3*rd.* The 3rd at 1 PM we Anchored in Samgoonoodha and the next Morning the Carpenters belonging to both Ships were set to work to rip off the Sheathing of and under the Wale on the Starboard side abaft, where many of the Seams were found quite open so that it was no wonder that so much water found its way into the Ship. While we lay here we cleared the Fish room, Spirit room and after hold, desposed things in such a manner that if we should happen to have any more leaks of the same Nature the Water might find its way to the pumps. And besides this work [and] compleating our Water we cleared the Fore hold to the very bottom and took in a quantity of ballast.

The Vegetables we met with when first at this place were now mostly in a state of decay, so that we benifited but little by them; but this loss was more than made up by the great quantity of berries every where found a Shore, and in order that we might benifit as much as possible by them one third of the people by turns, had leave to go and pick them and besides a good quantity were procured from the Natives; so that if there was any seeds of the S[c]urvey in either Ship, these berries and Spruce beer which they had to drink every other day, effectually removed it. We also got plenty of fish, at first from the Inhabitants, mostly Salmon both fresh and dryed; some of the fresh salmon was in high perfection, but there was one sort which we called hook nosed from the figure of its head, that was but indifferent. We drew the Seine several times at the head of the bay, caught a good many Salmon trout and once a Halibut that weighed 254 lb. This fishery failing we had recourse to hooks and lines, sending a boat out every Morning, who seldom returned without eight or ten Halibut which was more than sufficient to serve all hands. The Halibut were excellent and there were few that did not prefer them to Salmon. Thus we not only procured a supply of fish for present consumption but had some to carry to sea with us, and was some saving to our Provisions, which was an object of no small importance.

THURSDAY 8*th*. On the 8th I received by the hand of an Indian named *Derramoushk* a very singular present considering the place, it was a rye loaf or rather a pie made in the form of a loaf, for some salmon highly seasoned with peper &c[a] was in it. He had the like present for Captain Clerke and a Note to each of us written in a language none of us could read. We however had no doubt but this present was from some Russians in our Neighbourhood and sent to these our unknown friends by the same ha[n]d a few bottles of Rum, Wine and Porter which we thought would be as acceptable as any thing we had besides, and the event prove[d] we were not misstaken. I also sent along with Derramoushk and his party Corp[l] Ledyard of the Marines, an inteligent man in order to gain some further information, with orders, if he met with any Russians, or others, to endeavour to make them understand that we were English, Friends and Allies.

The 10th he returned with three Russian Seamen or   Sat. 10 Furriers, who with some others resided in *Egoochshac* where they had a dweling house some store houses and a Sloop of about thirty Tons burden. One of these Men was either Master or Mate of this Vessel, a nother wrote a very good hand and understood figures; they were all three well behaved intellingent men, and very ready to give me all the information I could disire, but for want of an interpretor we had some difficulty to understand each other. They seemed to have a thorough knowlidge of the attempts that had been made by   Sun. 11 their Country men to Navigate the Frozen Sea, and the discoveries which had been made in this by *Behring Tchirekoff* and *Spanburg*, but seemed to know no more of Lieutenant *Sindo* or *Sind* than his name: Nor had they the least idea of what part of the World Mr *Stæhlins* Map refered to when leaid before them; and when I pointed out *Kamtschatka* and some other known places, they asked if I had seen the islands laid down [on] the Chart and on my answering in the negative, one of them laid his finger upon the Chart where a number of islands are laid down and said he had been cruzing there for land and could never find any. I laid before them my Chart, and found they were strangers to every part of the America Coast except what lies opposite to them. One of these Men said he was the America Voyage with *Behring*, he must however been very young for he had not now the appearence of an old man. The Memory of few men is held in greater esteem than these Men do *Behrings*, probably from his being the occation of thier fur trade being extended to the Eastward, which was the consequence of that able Navigators missfortunes, for had not chance and his distresses carried him to the island which bears his name, and where he died, its probable the Russians would never have thought of making further discover[ie]s on the America Coast, as indeed Goverment did not for what has been sence done, has been by traders. But to turn from this degression to these three men, they

Mon. 12   remained with me all night, Visited Captain Clerke the next Morning and then went away very well satisfied with the reception they had met with, promising to return in a few days and to bring me a Chart of the Islands lying between this place and Kamtschatka. The

Wed. 14   14th in the evening, as Mr Webber and I was at an Indian Village a little way from Samgoonoodha, a Russian landed there who I found was the principal person amongst the Russians in this and the neighbouring islands. His name was *Erasim Gregorioff Sin Ismyloff*, he came in a Canoe carrying three people, attended by twenty or thirty other Canoes each conducted by one man; I took notice that the first thing they did after landing was to make a small tent for Ismyloff of materials which they brought with them, and then they made others for themselves of their Canoes paddles &c^a which they covered with grass, so that the people of the Village were at no trouble to find them lodging. Ismyloff invited us into his tent, set before us some dryed Salmon and berries which I was satisfied was the best cheer he had; he was a sencible intelligent man, and I felt no small Mortification in not being able to converse with him any other way then by signs assisted by figures and other Characters which however was a very great help. I desired to see him on board the next day and accordingly he came with all his attendants; indeed this was what   Thurs. 15 brought him this way. I was in hopes to have had by him the Chart which the others had promised, but I was disapointed, he however renued the promise of it and was as good as his word. I found he was very well acquainted with the Geography of these parts and with all the discoveries the Russians had made and at once pointed out the errors of the Modern Maps. . . .

[Ismailov told of his travels with Sind in the Bering Sea, and of a remarkable expedition to Japan, China – and France.]

FRIDAY 16*th*. The next Morning he would fain have made me a present of a Sea Beaver, or otter skin which he said was worth eighty Rubles at Kamtschatka, I however thought proper to decline it, but I excepted of some dryed fish and several baskets of the Lilly or Saranne root which is discribed by Muller in the history of Kamtschatka page 83 & 84.

In the after noon Mr Ismyloff, after dining with Captain Clerke left us with all his retinue promising to return again in a few days. Accordingly on the 19th he made us a nother visit and brought with him the Charts Afore mentioned which he allowed me to Copy. There were two of them both Manuscripts and had every mark of being Authentick. The first comprehended the *Penschinskian Sea*, the coast of *Tartary* as low as the latitude of 41°, the Kurilian Islands and the *Peninsula of Kamtschatka*. . . .

The Second Chart was to me the most intresting as it comprehended all the discoveries made by the Russians to the Eastward of Kamtschatka towards America, which if we exclude the Voyage of *Behring* and *Tcherikoff*, will amount to little or nothing. . . .

[A good deal about the geography of the Aleutians and the other islands he has been among becomes clearer to Cook, but the most important realization is that Alaska is part of the American continent.]

This is all the information I got from these people relating to the geography of those parts, and which I have reason to beleive is all they were able to give; for they assured me over and over again that they k[n]ew of no other islands but what were laid down on this chart and that no Russian had ever seen any part of the Continent to the northward, excepting that part lying opposite the Country of the Tchuktschis.

If Mr *Stæhlin* was not greatly imposed upon what could induce him to publish so erroneous a Map? in which many of these islands are jumbled in in regular confusion, without the least regard to truth and yet he is pleased to call it a very accurate little Map? A Map that the most illiterate of his illiterate Sea-faring men would have been ashamed to put his name to.

Wed. 21 Mr *Ismyloff* remained with us till the 21st in the evening when he took his final leave. To his care I intrusted a letter to the Admiralty in which was inclosed a chart of all the Northern coasts I had Visited, he said their would be an oppertunity to send it to *Kamtschatka* or *Okhotsk* the ensuing Spring and that it would be at Petersburg the following [winter].

He was so obliging as to give me a letter to Major *Bairme* Governor of *Kamtschatka*, who resides at *Bolscheretskoi*, and a nother to the Commanding Officer at *Petropaulowska*.

This Mr *Ismyloff* seemed to have abilities to intitle him to a higher station in life than that in which he was employed, he was tolerably well versed in Astronomy and other necessary parts of the Mathematicks. I complemented him with an Hadlys Octant and altho it was the first he had perhaps ever seen, yet he made himself acquainted with most of the uses that Instrument is capable of in a very short time.

Thurs. 22   In the Morning of the 22nd we made an attempt to get to Sea with the Wind at SE, which misscarried.

The following after noon we were visited by one *Jacob Iwanawitch*, a Russian Chief who Commanded a boat or small Vessel at Oomanak. This man seemed to be the very reverse of all the other Russians, he had a great share of Modesty and would drink no strong liquor, which all the other were immoderatly fond of. He knew better what was to be got at the harbour of Petropaulowska and the price of the different articles than Mr Ismyloff, but by all accounts every thing we should want was there very scarce and bore a high price. Flour, for instance he said was from 3 to 5 Rubles the poud (36 lb) and Deer from 3 to 5 Rubles a piece. This Man told us he was to be at Petropaulowska in May next and was as I understood to have the charge of my letter; he seemed exceedingly desirous of some token frome me to carry to Major *Bairme* and to gratify him I sent a small spy glass.

After we became acquainted with these Russians some of our gentlemen at different times visited there settlement where they always met with a hearty welcome. This settlement consisted of a dwelling house & two store houses; and besides the Russians, there were a number of Kamtschatkadales and Natives, as servants or slaves to the former, some others of the Natives, that seemed independent of the Russians lived at the same place. Such of the Natives as belong to the Russians were all Males and are taken, perhaps purchased, from thier Parents when young and brought up by the Russians; they had at this time about twenty that could be looked upon in no other light than Children. They all live in the same house, the Russians at the upper end, the Kamtschatkdales, in the Middle and the Natives at the lower end, where is fixed a large boiler, for boiling their Victuals consisting chiefly of what the Sea produceth, with the addition of Wild roots and berries. There is little more difference between the first and last table than what is produced by Cookery, in which the Russians have the art to make indifferent things palatable. I have eat whales flesh of their Cooking that I thought very good, and they made a kind of Pan-pudding of Salmon roe beat up fine and fryed that is no bad succedaneum for bread. The Russians may now and then taste bread, or have a dish in which flour is a part of the ingredience, but this can be done but seldom as may be very well supposed. If we except the juice of berries which they sip at their Meals, they have no other liquor than pure Water and it seems very happy for them they have nothing stronger.

As the place supplies them with Victuals, so it does in a great Measure with cloathing, which are made chiefly of skins, and is perhaps the best they could have. The upper garment is made like a Waggoners frock and reaches as low as the knee and besides it they wear a waistcoat or two, a pair of Breeches, a fur Cap, and a pair of boots the Soals and upper leathers of which are of Russia leather but the legs are of some kind of strong gut. The two cheifs wore each a blue calico frock and they as well as some others had Shirts which were of silk, these were perhaps the only part of their dress that were not made amongst themselves.

There are Russians on all the principal Islands between this and *Kamtschatka*, for the sole purpose of furing, and the first and great object is the Sea Beaver or Otter; I never heard them enquire after any other Animal, not that they let any other furs slip through their fingers whin they can get them. I never thought to ask how long it was sence they got a footing upon *Oonalaska* and the neighbouring isles, but to judge from the great subjection the Natives are under, it must have been some time. All these Furriers are releived from time to time by others, those we met with came here from *Okhotsk* in 1776 and are to return in 1781, so that there stay at the island will be four years at least.

It is now time to give some account of the Native Inhabitants, who (to all appearence) are the most peaceable inoffensive people I ever met with, and as to honisty they might serve as a pattern to the most civilized nation upon earth. . . .

These people are rather low of Stature, but plump and well shaped, with rather short necks, swarthy chubby faces, black eyes, small beards, and streight long black hair, which the Men wear loose behind and cut before, but the women tie it up in a bunch behind. . . . They make use of no paint but the Women punctulate their faces slitely and both men and Women bore the under lip to which they fix pieces of bone, but it is as uncommon at Onalaska to see a man with this ornament as a women without it. . . .

As these people use no paint they are not so dirty in their persons as Indians who do, but they are full as lousy and filthy in their *Houses*   houses; this last is in some measure unavoidable from their method of building which is thus. They dig an oblong square hole in the earth about two feet deep, in some not so much, the breadth and length of which seldom exceeds fifty feet by twenty, but in general they are not so large. Over this hole they form the roof of wood the Sea throws ashore; this they cover with grass and lastly with earth, so that the outward appearence is like a dung hill. In the middle of the roof, towards each end is left a square hole, by which the light is admited; one of the holes being for this purpose only and the other to go in and out by, by means of a ladder or rather a post with steps cut in it. In some houses there is a nother entrance below but this is not common. Round the sides and ends of the hut each family have their separate appartments, where they sleep and sit at work, not on benches but in a kind of a Concave trench, which is dug all round inside of the house and covered with Mats, so that these places are tolerable decent. But the middle of the house, which is common to all, is just the reverse for altho it is covered with dry grass it is a receptacle for all the dirt in the house and the place for the Urine trough, the stench of which is not a bit mended by raw hides or leather being almost continually steeping in it. Behind, and over the trench, are placed the little effects they are Master of, such as their cloathing, Mats, Skins &c^a. . . .

There are few if any that do not both smoke and chew Tobacco and take snuf, a luxury that bids fair to keep them always poor. They did not even seem to wish fore more iron or want any other instruments, except sewing needles, their own being made of bone, with which they not only sew their Canoes and make their cloaths, but make also very curious embroidery. Instead of thread they make use of the fibres of sinews, which they split to the thickness they require: all sewing is performed by the Women, they are the Taylors, shoe makers and boat builders, or coverers, for the men most probably *Arts and* make the frame. They make Mats and baskets of grass, *Manufacture* that are both beautifull and strong; indeed there is a neatness and perfection in most of their work that shows they neither want for engenuity nor perseverence.

I saw not a fire place in any one of their houses, they are lighted as well as heated by lamps which are simple and yet answer the purpose very well. They are made of a flat stone hollowed on one side like a plate, and about the same size or rather larger, in these they put the oil mixed with a little dry grass which serve as wicks; both men and Women frequently warm their bodies over one of these lamps, by placing it between their legs under their garments and so sit over it for a few minutes. They produce fire both by Collision and attrition, the first by striking two stones one against the other, first rubing a good deal of brimstone upon one of them, for tinder they use dry grass and powdered brimstone. The second method is with two pieces of Wood, one is a stick about eightteen inches long, the other a flat piece: the pointed end of the stick thy press upon the other, whirl it nimbly round in the same manner as a drill and thus produce fire in a few minutes. This method of produceing fire is common in many part[s] of the World, it is practised by the Kamtschatkadales, by these people, by the greenlanders, by the Brazilians, by the Otahei-tians, by the New Hollanders and probably by many other nations. . . .

What their notions are of the deity and a future state, I know not; nor do I know any thing of their deversions; nothing was seen that could give us an inssight into either.

They are remarkably cheerfull and friendly amongst each other and always behaved with great civility to our people. The Women grant the last favour without the least scruple; young or old, Married or Single, I have been told, never hisitate a Moment. The Russians told us they never had any connections with the Indian Women, because they were not Christians; our people were not so scruplus, and some were taken in, for the Venereal distemper is not unknown to these people; they are also subject to the cancer or a disease like it, which those who have it are very careful to conceal. . . .

*   *   *

In the Morning of Monday the 26th, we put to sea and as the Wind was Southerly stood away to the Westward.

My intention was now to proceed to *Sandwich Islands* to spend a few of the Winter Months provided we met with the necessary refreshments there, and then proceed to *Kamtschatka*, endeavouring to be there by the Middle of May next. In consequence of this resolution I gave Captain Clerke orders how to proceed in case of separation, appointing Sandwich islands for the first place of Rendezvouze and the harbour of *Petropaulowska* in Kamtschatka the second. . . .

*   *   *

At 3 PM after geting a sight of Oonalaska, shortned sail and hauled the Wind, not having time to get through the passage before dark. At

day break the next morning bore away under Courses and   Frid. 30
close reefed top sails having a very hard gale at WNW with heavy
squals attended with snow. At Noon we were in the Middle of the
strait between Oonalaska and Oonalla, the harbour of Samgoonoodha
bore SSE one league distant. At 3 PM being through the strait and clear
of the isles, Cape Providence bearing WSW two or three leagues distant,
Steer'd to the Southward under double reefed topsails and courses
with the wind at WNW a strong gale and fair weather.

On Monday the second of November the Wind Veered   NOVEM^r
to the Southward and before night blew a Violent storm,   Mon. 2
which oblig'd us to bring to. The [Discovery] fired several guns, which
we answered, but without knowing on what occasion they were fired.
At 8 oClock we lost sight of her and did not see her again till 8 the
next Morning. At 10 she joined us, and as the height of the gale was
now over, and the Wind had veer'd back to WNW we made sail and
resumed our course to the Southward.

The 6th in the evening being in the latitude of 42°12′, longitude
201°26′, the Variation was 17°15′ E. The next Morning, in the   Sat. 7
latitude of 41°20′, longitude 202° E, a shag, or Cormorant flew several
times round the Ship: as these birds are seldom, if ever, known to fly
far out of sight of land, I judged some was not far distant, we however
could see none. In the after Noon, there being but little wind, Captain
Clerke came on board and informed me of a melancholy accident
that happened on board his Ship the second night after we left
Samgoonoodha; the Main tack gave way, killed one man out right
and wounded the Boatswain and two or three more; that on the
evening of the 3rd his sails and rigging received considerable damage
and that the Guns which he fired was the Signal to bring to.

The 8th the Wind was at North, a gentle breeze with clear   Sun. 8
weather. The 9th in the latitude of 39½° we had eight hours   Mon. 9
Calm, this was succeeded by the Wind from the South attended with
fair Weather. As many people as could handle a sail Needle were set
to work to repair the sails and the Carpenters to put the boats in
order. The 12th at Noon, being then in the latitude of   Thurs. 12
38°14′ N, longitude 206°17′ E the Wind returned back to the Northward and on the 15th in the latitude of 33°30′ it veered to East.   Sun. 15

At this time we saw a Tropic bird and a Dolphin, the first we had seen on the passage.

Tues. 17   The 17th the Wind veered to the Southward, where it
Thur. 19   continued till the after noon of the 19th when a Squall of wind and rain brought it at once round by the West to the North. This was in the latitude of 32°26′, longitude 20[7°30]′ E. The Wind presently increased to a very strong gale attended with rain, so as to bring us under double reefed top-sail. In lowering down the Main topsail to reef it was torn by the wind quite out of the foot rope and split in Several other parts; it had only been brought to the Yard the day before after having had a repair. The next Morning we got a nother topsail to the yard. This Wind proved to be the forerunner of the trade, which in 25° veer'd to East and ESE. I continued to steer
Wed. 25   to the Southward till daylight in the Morning of the 25th, at which time we were in the latitude of 20°55′ N, longitude   , I spread the Ships and steered to the west. In the evening we joined
Thur. 26   and at Midnight brought to. The 26th at day-break saw land extending from SSE to West. Made sail and stood for [it]. At 8 it extended from SE½S to West, the nearest part two leagues distant. It was supposed we saw the extent of the land to the East but not to the West. In the country was an elevated saddle hill whose summit appear'd above the Clouds,[42] from this hill the land fell in a gentle sloap and terminated in a steep rocky coast against which the sea broke in a dreadfull surf. Finding we could not weather the island I bore up and ranged along the coast to the westward. It was not long before we saw people on several parts of the coast, some houses and plantations, and the Country seemed to be both well wooded and Watered, the latter was seen falling into the Sea in several places.

As it was of the last importance to procure a supply of provisions at these islands, and knowing from experience this could not be done if a free trade was allowed, that is every man allowed to trade for what he pleased and as he pleased, I therefore published an order prohibiting all persons from trading but such as should be appoint'd by me or

42. They were coming in to the southern Hawaiian islands from the east; the land they now see is Maui, the second largest island.

Captain Clerke and these only for provisions and refreshments. Women were also forbid to be admited into the Ships, but under certain restrictions, but the evil I meant to prevent by this I found had already got amongst them.

At Noon the coast extended from s 81° E to N 56° West, a low flat like an isthmus bore s 42° w the nearest shore 3 or 4 Miles distant. Lat. 20°57′, longi. 203° [28′] E. Seeing some Canoes coming off to us I brought to; as soon as they got a long side many of the people who conducted them came into the Ships without the least hisitation. They were of the same Nation as those of the leeward islands, and if we did not misstake them they knew of our being there. Indeed it appeared rather too evident as these people had got amongst [them] the Veneral distemper, and I as yet knew of no other way they could come by it. We got from these people in exchange for Nails and pieces of iron a quantity of Cuttle fish: fruit and roots they brought very little, but told us the[y] had plenty ashore, as also hogs and fowls. In the evening the horizon being clear to the Westward, we judged the westermost land to be an island separated from the one we were off. Having no doubt but these people would come off with the produce of the island the next day, I kept plying off all night and in the Morning   Frid. 27 stood close in shore. At first but a few people visited us, but towards noon we had the company of a good many who brought with them bread fruit, Potatoes, Tarra or eddy roots, a few plantains and small pigs, all of which they exchanged for Nails and iron tools; indeed we had nothing else to give them. We continued trading with them till 4 o'clock in the after noon, when having disposed of all they had and not seemingly disposed to fetch more, we made Sail and stood off shore.

While we were laying to, tho the wind blew fresh, I observed that the Ships drifted to windward; consequently there must have been a current seting in that direction. This incouraged me to ply to windward with a view of geting round the East end of the island and so have the whole lee side before us.

MONDAY 30*th.* In the after noon of the 30th being off the NE end of the island, several Canoes came off to the Ships, the most of them belonged to a Chief named Terryaboo who came in one; he made me a present of two or three small pigs and we got by barter from the other people a little fruit. After a stay of about two hours they all left us except six or eight who chused to remain, a double sailing canoe came soon after to attend upon them which we towed a stern all night. In the evening we discovered another island to windward which the Natives call [O'why'he] the name of the one we had been off we now learnt was [Mow'ēē].[43]

DECEM^r   The 1st of December at 8 AM [O'why'he] extended from
Tues. 1   s 22° E to s 12° w and [Mow'ēē] from N 41° to N 83° w. Finding we could fetch [O'why'he] I stood for it; our Indian friends not chusing to accompany us, imbarked in their canoe and left us.

At 7 PM we were close up with the North side of [O'why'he] where we spent the night standing off and on.

WEDNESDAY 2*nd*. The 2nd in the Morning we were surprised to see the summits of the highest [mountains] cover[ed] with snow; they did not appear to be of any extraordinary height and yet in some places the snow seemed to be of a considerable depth and to have laid there some time. As we drew near the shore, some of the Natives came off to us; they were a little shy at first, but we soon inticed some on board and at length prevailed upon them to go a shore and bring off what we wanted. Soon after these reached the shore we had company enough, and as few came empty, we got a tolerable supply of small pigs, fruit and roots. We continued tradeing with them till Six in the evening when we made sail and stood off, with a view of plying to windward round the island.

*   *   *

[*On Friday 4 December Cook and James King observed an eclipse of the moon.*]

Sun. 6   On the 6th in the evening, being about [five] leagues farther up the coast and near the shore, had some traffick with the Natives
Mon. 7   but as it proved but trifling, I stood in again the next Morning, when a good many Visited us, and we lay to tradeing with them till 2 PM by which time we had procured pork, fruit and roots sufficient

43. These names were inserted by Canon Douglas (see Index of Persons).

for four or five days. We then made sail and Continued to ply to windward.

Having procured a quantity of Sugar Cane and had upon trial made but a few days before, found that a strong decoction of it made a very palatable beer, which was esteemed by every one on board, I ordered some more to be brewed, but when the Cask came to be broached not one of my Mutinous crew would even so much as taste it. As I had no montive for doing it but to save our spirit for a Colder climate, I gave my self no trouble either to oblige or persuaid them to drink it, knowing there was no danger of the Scurvy so long as we had plenty of other Vegetables; but that I might not be disapointed in my views I gave orders that no grog should be served in either Ship. My self and the Officers continued to make use of this beer whenever we could get cane to make it; a few hops, of which we had on board, was a great addition to it: it has the taste of new malt beer, and I beleive no one will d[o]ubt but it must be very wholesom, though my turbulent crew alleged it was injurious to their healths. They had no better reason to support a resolution they took on our first arrival in King Georges Sound, not to drink the spruce beer we made there, but whether from a consideration that this was no new thing or any other reason they did not attempt to carry their risolution into execution and I never heard of it till now. Every innovation whatever tho ever so much to their advantage is sure to meet with the highest disapprobation from Seamen, Portable Soup and Sour Krout were at first both condemned by them as stuff not fit for human being[s] to eat. Few men have introduced into their Ships more novelties in the way of victuals and drink than I have done; indeed few men have had the same oppertunity or been driven to the same necessity. It has however in a great measure been owing to such little innovations that I have always kept my people generally speaking free from that dreadful distemper the Scurvy.

SUNDAY 13*th*. I kept at some distance from the Coast, till the 13th when I stood in again Six leagues farther to wind ward than we had yet been; and after having some trade with the Natives who visited us, stood out to sea. I should have stood in again on the 15th to   Tues. 15

procure a supply of fruit or roots, but the wind hapening to be at SEBS and SSE I thought [it] a good time to stretch to the Eastward in order to get round, or at least a sight of the SE end of the island. The Wind

Wed. 16 continued at SEBS most part of the 16th. The 17th was variable
Thurs. 17 between South and E. And on the 18th it was continually
Frid. 18 varying from one quarter to a nother: blowing sometimes in hard squals and at other times Calm with thunder lightning and rain. In the after noon we had the wind Westerly for a few hours, but in the evening it shifted to EBS and we stood to the Southward close hauled, under an easy sail as the Discovery was some distance a stern. At this time the SE point of the island bore SWBS about 5 leagues distant and I had not a doubt but we should weather it. But at

Sat. 19 one oclock in the morning it fell Calm and left us to the Mercy of a North easterly swell which hove us fast towards the land, so that long before day light we saw lights upon the Shore which was not more than a league distant. The night was dark with thunder, lightning and rain. At 3 the calm was succeeded by a breeze from the SEBE blowing in squals with rain; we stood to NE thinking it the best tack to clear the coast but had it been day-light we should have made choice of the other. At day-break the coast was seen extending from NBW to SWBW, a dreadfull surf broke upon the shore which was not more than half a league distant, it was evident we had been in the most eminent danger, nor were we yet out of danger; the wind veering more easterly so that for some time we did but just keep our distance from the coast. What made our situation more alarming was the leach rope of the Main topsail giving way, which was the occasion of the sail being rent in two and the two topgallant sails gave way in the same manner tho not half worn, by takeing a favourable oppertunity we soon got others to the yards and then we left the land a stern. The Discovery by being some distance to the North was never near the land, nor did we see her till 8 oclock.

On this occasion I cannot hilp observing, that I have always found that the bolt-ropes to our sails have not been of sufficient strength, or substance, to even half wear out the Canvas: this at different times has been the occasion of much expence of canvas and infinate trouble and vexation. Nor are the cordage and canvas or indeed hardly any other stores made use of in the Navy, of equal goodness with those in general used in the Merchant service, of this I had incontestable proof last voyage. When the Resolution was purchased for the King her standing rigging, some runing rigging, blocks and sails were also purchased along with her, and altho the most of these things had been in wear fourteen Months yet they wore longer than any of those of the same kind put on board new out of the Kings stores. The fore rigging are yet over the mast head, the brace blocks and some others in equal use still in their places and as good as ever. And yet on my return home last voyage these very blocks were condemned by the yard officers and thrown amongst other decayed blocks from which they permited my Boatswain to select them when the ship was again fited out. These evils are likely never to be redressed, for besides the difficulty of procuring stores for the Crown of equal goodness with [those] purchased by private people for their own use, it is a general received opinion amongst Naval officers of all ranks that no stores are equal in goodness to those of the Crown and that no ships are found like those of the Navy. In the latter they are right but it is in the quantity and not in the quallity of the stores, this last is seldom tried, for things are generally Condemned or converted to some other use by such time as they are half wore out. It is only on such Voyages as these we have an oppertunity to make the trial where every thing is obliged to be worn to the very utmost.[44]

As soon as day light appeared the Natives a shore displayed a white flag understood by us as a signal of peace and friendship; some ventured out after us but the wind freshening and we could not wait they were soon left astern.

In the after noon after makeing a nother attempt to weather the island which faild I gave it up and run down to the Discovery. Indeed it was of no consequence to get round the island sence we had seen its extent to the SE which was the thing I aimed at, and according to the information we had got from the natives this is the Windward island. However as we were so near the SE end of the island that the

44. Much of this paragraph was cut out in the printed account on the orders of Palliser, who was Comptroller of the Navy.

least shift of wind in our favour must have carried us round, I did not wholy give up the idea of weathering it and therefore continued to ply.

SUNDAY 20*th*. The 20th at Noon this SE point bore South 3 leagues distant the Snow hills WNW and the nearest shore distant four miles. In the after noon some of the Natives came off in their canoes, bringing with them a few pigs and plantains; the latter was very acceptable as we had had neither fruit nor roots for some days. But what they brought now were trifling and not sufficient for one day; so that I stood in again the next Morning to within about three or four miles of the shore, where we were met by a number of Canoes laden with provisions. We brought to [to] trade with the people in them till 4 PM when having got a pretty good supply we made sail and stretched off to the Northward.

Mon. 21

These people trade with the least suspicion of any Indians I ever met with, it is very common for them to send up into the Ship every thing they bring off to despose of: afterwards come in themselves and make their bargins on the quarter deck. This is more than the people of Otahiete will do even at this day, which shews that these people are more faithfull in their dealings one with another than they are; for if little faith was observed among themselves they would not be so ready to trust strangers. It is also remarkable that they have never once attempted to cheat us in exchanges or once to commit a thieft. They understand tradeing as well as most people and seem to have discovered what we are plying upon the coast for, for tho they bring off things in great plenty, particularly pigs, yet they keep up their price and rather than despose of them for less than they demand will take them a shore again.

TUESDAY 22*nd*. The 22nd at 8 AM tacked to the Southward with the wind at EBN a fresh breeze. At Noon the lat. was 20°28′30″ and the Snow peak bore SW½S. The preciding day we had a good view of it on which there seemed to be more snow than before and to extend lower down the hill.

WEDNESDAY 23*rd*. I stood to the SE till midnight, then tacked to the

North till 4 AM when we returned to the SE tack, and as the Wind was at NEBE we had hopes of weathering the island and should have succeeded had not the Wind died away and left us to the Mercy of a great swell which hove us fast towards the land which was not two leagues distant. At length we got our head off and some light puffs of Wind which came with the Showers of rain put us out of danger. While we lay as it were becalmed, several of the islanders came off with Hogs, fowls, fruit and roots to exchange. We got out of one Canoe a goose, which was about the Size of a Muscovey duck, its plumage was dark grey and the bill and legs black.

At 4 PM after purchasing every thing the Natives brought off, which was full as much as we could dispence with, made sail and stretched to the North with the Wind at ENE. At Midnight tacked and stood to the SE. From a supposition that the Discovery would see us tack the signal was omited to be made, but it after appeared she did not and continued standing to the North, for at daylight in the   Thurs. 24 Morning she was not to be seen. At this time the Weather was hazey so that we could not see far and being past the NE part of the Island, I was tempted to stand on, till, by the Wind veering to NE we could not weather the land upon [the] other tack, consequently could not stand to the North to join or look for the Discovery. At Noon we were by observation in the Latitude of 19°55′N, Longitude 20[4°36′] E, the SE point of the island bore SBE¼E Six leagues distant, the other extreme N 60° W and the nearest shore two leagues. At 6 in the evening the Souther. extreme of the island bore SW¾W, the nearest shore 7 or 8 Miles distance; so that we had now got to windward of the island and had accomplished what we had been so long aiming at. The Discovery was however not yet to be seen, but as the wind, as we had it was favourable for her to follow us I concluded it would not be long before she joined us. I therefore kept cruzing off this SE point of the island which lies in the Latitude of 19° [34]′, Longit. 20[5°6′] E till I was satisfied Captain Clerke could not join me here. I guessed it had not been able to weather the Northeast part of the island and had gone to leeward in order to meet me that way. As I generally kept from five to ten leagues from the land, no Canoes except one came off to us till the 28th when we were visited by a dozen or fourteen; the people who conducted them, brought as usual the produce of the island. I was sorry they had taken the trouble to come so far as we could not trade with them, our old stock not being yet consumed, and we had found that the hogs would not live, nor the roots keep many days. I however intended not to leave this part of the island before I got a supply, as it would not be easy to return to it again, in case it should be found necessary.

WEDNESDAY 30*th*. The 30th we began to be in want and I would have Stood in near the shore, but was prevented by a Calm. At Midnight the Calm was succeed[ed] by a breeze from South and sw with which at day break I stood in for the land. At 10 clock we were met by the islanders with fruit and roots tho in no great quantity and amongst them all no more than three small pigs; our not buying those they brought before we supposed to be the reason of their bringing so few now. We now brought to to trade, but as it soon after came on to rain very hard we had but a scanty Market, and besides we were rather too far from the Shore, as I could not depend upon the wind remaining where it was a moment I durst not go nearer, the swell being high and seting obliquely upon the shore against which it broak in a dreadfull surf. In the evening the Weather cleared up, the night was clear and we spent it makeing short boards.

1779

JANUARY   Before day break the Atmosphere was again loaded with
Frid. 1   heavy Clouds, and the new year was ushered in with very hard rain, which continued at intervals till past 10 oclock; the Wind was southerly a light breeze with some calms. When the rain ceased, the sky cleared and the breeze freshened. Being at this time about five miles from the land, several Canoes came off with fruit and roots and at last with hogs, tho' not many. We lay to, tradeing with them till 3 oclock in the after noon, when having got fruit &c[a] for four or five days and pigs for two, we made sail, with a view of proceeding to the sw or lee side of the island to look for the Discovery. But as the Wind was at South it was necessary to stretch first to the Eastward till midnight when the wind came more favourable and we went upon

the other tack. For several days past both Wind and weather was exceedingly unsittled and there fell a great deal of rain.

The Three following days were spent in runing down the   Sat. 2
SE side [of the] island, for the night[s] were spent in plying   Sun. 3
and a part of each day laying to trading with the Natives   Mon. 4
who some times came to us five leagues off to sea. But whether from a fear of lossing their goods in the Sea or the uncertainty of a Market, they never brought much with them, the Cheif article we got was salt, which was extremely good.

TUESDAY 5*th*. The 5th in the Morning we passed the South point of the island which lies in the latitude of [18°54′] and from which we found the coast to trend N 60 W. On this point stands a pritty large Village, the inhabitants of which thronged off to the Ship with hogs and women. It was not possible to keep the latter out of the Ship and no women I ever met with were more ready to bestow their favours, indeed it appeared to me that they came with no other view. As we had now got a quantity of salt I purchased no hogs but what were fit for salting, refuseing all that were under size, in general they bring no other at first, but when they found we took none but large ones, several went a shore and returned with some, however we could seldom get one above 50 or 60 lb weight. As to fruit and roots we did not want and it was well we did not for it was very little of either they brought with them, indeed the Country did not seem capable of producing many of either having been distroyed by a Volcano, though as yet we had seen nothing like one upon the island, but the devastation it had made was visible to the naked eye. This part of the Coast is sheltered from the reigning winds but we could find no bottom to Anchor upon, a line of 160 fathoms did not reach it at the distance of half a mile from the shore. Towards the evening all the islanders leaving us, we ran a few miles down the coast and there spent the night standing off and on.

WEDNESDAY 6*th*. The next Morning the people viseted [us] again bringing with them the same articles as before. Being near the shore I sent Mr Bligh the Master in a boat to Sound the Coast with orders to land and look for fresh Water. On his return he reported that at two cables lengths from the shore he had no soundings with a 160 fathom of line; that where he landed he found no fresh water, but rain water lying in holes in the rocks and that brackish with the spray of the sea, and that the surface of the Country was wholy composed of large slags and ashes here and there partly covered with plants. Between 10 and 11 oclock we saw the Discovery coming round the South point of the island and at 1 PM she joined us when Captain Clerke came on board and informed me that he cruzed four or five days where we were separated and than plyed round the East part of the island, but meeting with unfavourable winds was carri'd some distance from the coast. He had one of the islanders on board all the time, it was his own choice nor did no[t] leave them the first oppertunity that offered.[45]

THURSDAY 7th. At 1 PM the Discovery joined us, Captain Clerke came on board and informed me that he Cruzed five days where we parted, afterwards plyed round the East point of the island. He had one of the islanders aboard all the time, he came and remained on board by choise, nor did he take the first oppertunity to go ashore, but remained till he met with a friend with whom he wint. At 6 Made sail and spint the night standing off and on: in the morning stood in again, at 9 being a league from the shore, brought to to trade with the Natives many of whome came off to the ships. During the night the wind blew very fresh at ENE, in the morning it abated, and during the day we had light airs from all directions, especially near the land. At Noon Lat. observed 19°1′15″ N, Long. p^r T.K.[46] 203°26½′ E, the island extending from s 74 E to N 13 W the nearest part 2 Leagues distant.

FRIDAY 8th. Wind from EBS to NEBE a fresh breeze and fine weather. At 6 AM made sail and spent the night plying. At day break, found that the Currents had carried us considerably to Windward so that we were now of the SW point of the island and where we brought to to trade with the Natives. At Noon Latitude observed 19°1′15″, Long. p^r T.K. 203°39′, the SW point of the island N 30° E 2 Miles distant.

45. At this point, Cook's MS journal ends. What follows is a fragment of Cook's log, also preserved in the British Library. Civil time now changes to ship time.
46. i.e., time-keeper (the chronometer).

SATURDAY 9*th*. Wind Easterly a fresh breeze, the fore and Middle part clear weather, latter Cloudy with rain. As soon as the Natives retired ashore we made sail and spent our time standing off and on. It happened that four Men and ten women were left on board, as I did not like the company of the latter, I stood in shore towards noon with no other View than to get clear of them.

SUNDAY 10*th*. At 2 PM drawing near the shore a few Canoes Came off and in them we sent away our guests. At 6 the wind Veered to the westward and not long after the weather cleared up. We had light airs from NW and SW and Calms till a 11 AM when the Wind freshened at WNW and brought with it rain. At $7^h38'$ Long. p^r Time keeper $203°48'$ the South point of the island N $10\frac{1}{2}°$ W 4 leagues distant, and the South Snow Hill N $1\frac{1}{2}$ E. A Strong Current Seting to S.

MONDAY 11*th*. PM Wind at WSW, NW and NE Cloudy rainy weather. AM Wind Westerly a fresh breeze and Clear weather. At 4 AM when the wind fixed at West I stood in for the land in order to get some refreshments. As we drew near the shore the Natives began to come off, we lay to, or stood on and off trading with them all the day and got but very little at last. Many Canoes came off with not a single thing to barter, so that it appeared that this part of the island must be very poor and that we had already got all they could spare. At the South point of the island bore WBS 3 or 4 leagues distant; Lat. observed $18°55'30''$ N.

TUESDAY 12*th*. Plying on and off with the Wind at West a fresh gale. A Mile from the shore and to the NE of the South point of the island, tryed Soundings and found ground at 55 fathoms, the bottom a fine sand. At 5 PM Stood to SW, wind at WNW which before Midnight veered to NBW and soon after we had a Calm. At Noon the South point of the island bore North 20 Miles distant. Lat. ob. $18°35'45''$ N, Long. p^r T.K. 20 ° . Inclination of the diping Needle $38°30'$.

WEDNESDAY 13*th*. First part light airs at SE next to a Calm, in the night a small breeze at SW & SSW which at 8 AM Veered to SSE. Steering to the NNW in for the land. At 9 a few Canoes came along side with a few hogs, but neither fruit nor roots, articles we most wanted. At Noon the South point of the island bore N 86½′ E, the sw point N 13° E, the South Snow hill N 19° E and the north extreme N 13° w; nearest shore 2 leagues distant, latitude Observed 18°56′34″, long. pʳ T.K. 203° [40′].

THURSDAY 14*th*. PM with a small breeze at sw we got the length of the NW point of the island, where the Wind veered to the Westward and Northward, so that before the Morning we lost all that we had gained. In the Morning being off the sw point of the island, some Canoes came off, but they brought nothing we were in want of. We had now neither fruit or roots and were under a necessity of makeing use of some of our sea Provisions. At length Some Canoes from the Northward brought us a small supply of both hogs and roots. At Noon the South point of the island bore E¾s and the sw point NBE one league distant, latitude Observed 19°

FRIDAY 15*th*. Variable light airs next to a Calm till 5 PM when a small breeze sprung up at ENE and with it steered along shore to the Northward. At Noon the sw point of the island s 65 w 3 leagues distant, the NW point N 68° E one league distant, the Extremes of the island to the North N 6° w and the high land of Mowwee N 16° w: Latitude observed 19°7′30″ N. As it was a fine pleasent day we had plenty of Company and abundence of every thing. We had the Company of several all night and their Canoes towing a stern.

SATURDAY 16*th*. First and middle parts had variable Winds with some showers of rain, the latter part the Wind was Easterly and attended with fair weather. Plying to the Northward. At day break seeing the appearence of a bay, sent Mʳ Bligh with a boat from each Ship to examine it, being at this time 3 leagues off. Canoes now began to come off from all parts, so that before 10 oclock there were not less than a thousand about the two Ships, the most of them filled with people, hogs and other productions of the Island. Not a man had with him a Weapon of any sort, Trade and curiosity alone brought them off. Among such numbers as we had at times on board, it is no wonder that some betrayed a thievish disposition, one man took out of the Ship a boats ruther, he was discovered but too late to recover it. I thought this a good oppertunity to shew them the use of fire arms, two or three muskets and as many four pound shot were fired over the Canoe which carried off the ruther. As it was not intended that any of the Shot should take effect, the Indians seemed rather more surprised than frightened.

SUNDAY 17*th*. Fine pleasent Weather and variable faint breezes of Wind. In the Evening Mr Bligh returned and reported that he had found a bay in which was good anchorage and fresh water tolerable easy to come at, into this bay I resolved to go to refit the Ships and take in water. As the night approached the Indians retired to the shore, a good [many] however desired to Sleep on board, curiosity was not their only Montive, at least not with some of them, for the next Morning several things were Missing which determined me not to entertain so many another night. At 11 AM anchored in the bay (which is called by the Natives [Karakakooa]^47) in 13 fathom water over a Sandy bottom and a quarter of a mile from the NE shore. In this situation the South point of the bay bore s¼w and the North point w¼s. Moored with the Stream Anchor and Cable to the Northward, Unbent the sails and struck yards and topmasts. The Ships very much Crouded with Indians and surrounded by a multitude of Canoes. I have no where in this Sea seen such a number of people assembled at one place, besides those in the Canoes all the Shore of the bay was covered with people and hundreds were swiming about the Ships like shoals of fish. We should have found it difficult to have kept them in order had not a Chief or Servant of *Terrioboos* named *Parea* now and then [exerted] his authority by turning or rather driving them all out of the Ships. Among our numerous Visiters was a man named *Tou-ah-ah*, who we soon found belonged to the Church, he intorduced himself with much ceremony, in the Course of which he presented me with a small pig, two Cocoanuts and a piece of red cloth which he wraped round me: in this manner all or most of the chiefs or people of Note interduce them selves, but this man went farther, he brought with him a large hog and a quant[it]y of fruits and roots all of which

47. The name looks as if inserted by King. It was Kealakekua, the best anchorage on the western side of the island.

he included in the present. In the after noon I went a shore to view the place, accompanied by Touahah, Parea, Mr King and others; as soon as we landed Touahah took me by the hand and conducted me to a large Morai, the other gentlemen with Parea and four or five more of the Natives followed.

POSTSCRIPT:
THE DEATH OF COOK

Whatever else Cook wrote has not survived. His log breaks off at a moment of considerable importance, the ceremony at the 'morai', or *heiau*, or temple, called Hikiau, on the eastern side of the bay, a substantial raised platform on the beach, surrounded by a fence, containing images of gods, especially of the primal god Ku. Lieutenant King, whose journal provides the fullest evidence of this period, noted that the islanders prostrated themselves as Cook and the priest Koah with his train passed, and that the priest and his acolytes repeated the word 'Erono' – 'the name by which the Capn has for some time been distinguish'd by the Natives'. That is Lono, the name of the god of fertility, whose annual return was customarily celebrated at this time of year. There was a long and elaborate ceremony, during which Cook allowed himself to be led round the images and followed Koah in prostrating himself before and kissing the image of Ku. Two days later Cook was the centre of a second ceremony, also involving the sacrifice of pigs and the drinking of kava.

Meanwhile, observatories and tents had been set up near the *heiau*, and the caulking of the ships went forward. 'Remarkable homage', including prostration, continued to be paid to Cook, and to a lesser extent to Clerke (who didn't like it), while the islanders awaited the return of the king, Kalaniʻopuʻu, and his chief priest, Kao, from neighbouring Maui. When he came, King says they were surprised to find him 'the same immaciated infirm man' they had met at Maui (whose name they made out as Terryaboo or Terrioboo). The king came on board, and he and Cook exchanged names. Next day there was a magnificent procession of canoes; the king did honour to Cook and there was a formal exchange of presents.

All this time there was constant trading from canoes with the ships – foodstuff in exchange for anything of iron, especially spikes or bars beaten into daggers. It had all along been impossible to keep women from the ships, but Cook had men flogged who had connections with women in spite of having venereal disease. The 'gentlemen' made expeditions into the interior, and there were exhibitions of boxing and wrestling. David Samwell wrote that 'these people behave to us . . . with the utmost kindness and Hospitality'.

On 1 February Cook asked King 'to treat with the Natives' to let them have the palings round the *heiau*, Hikiau, for firewood. This strange request was, says King, readily granted. In pulling up the fence, however, the sailors also took the wooden images, which not surprisingly caused resentment. King went in alarm to the chief priest, Kao, who, he wrote, 'desir'd only that we would return the little Image' (of Ku) and two others. A second event on this day was the death of William Watman, an old sailor who had also been on the second voyage, and in whom Cook took a special interest. Once again, the *heiau* was central, for Watman was buried within its confine. King says the chiefs themselves requested it. It seems more likely that in spite of pulling up its fence for firewood the officers thought the temple the nearest thing to consecrated ground. There was a very strange burial service, an amalgam of Anglican and Hawaiian rites.

Next day Kalani'opu'u and his chiefs 'became inquisitive as to the time of our departing & seemd well pleas'd that it was to be soon'. On 4 February the ships took their departure. They sailed north, in the direction of Maui, keeping to the coast, and in continuous contact with the Hawaiians by canoe. On the third day the weather became squally, and worsened, and on the morning of 9 February, it was found that the head of the *Resolution*'s foremast was 'badly sprung', i.e., split. The problem lay in the fishes, or splints, made of driftwood, which had been put on the mast to strengthen it in Nootka Bay. It was 'absolutely necessary to replace them with others', and to do that the whole foremast had to be got out. No sheltered anchorage was available where they were, and there was no help for it but to head back to Kealakekua Bay, 'all hands much chagrin'd & damning the Foremast' (King). They anchored at daylight on the 12th.

They were surprised that in contrast to the previous welcoming crowds, 'very few of the Natives came to us'. It was understood that this was a temporary taboo. The foremast was got out on the 13th and sent ashore to the area to the east previously used, near the Hikiau shrine. Kalani'opu'u arrived in the morning, came aboard with his chiefs and 'was very inquisitive' to know why the ships had returned. When given the reason, he 'appeared very much dissatisfied with it' (Burney). From then on there was nothing but trouble. A Hawaiian stole the armourer's tongs in the *Discovery*, was flogged with forty lashes and tied up to the main shrouds. King, ashore on the eastern beach, was told that a watering party was being hindered and that 'the Indians had now arm'd themselves with Stones'. This row was quietened, but Cook, who was on hand ashore, told King to be prepared to fire ball instead of shot, and the sentries' muskets were accordingly reloaded. Just after this they heard firing from the *Discovery*, and saw a canoe being chased by one of her boats. The armourer's tongs had again been stolen, and the master, Edgar, was in pursuit of the offenders. Both King and Cook went in chase of the thief when he landed; 'we kept running on till dark' – being misdirected by bystanders. While they were away, there was a fracas over the canoe. Edgar tried to impound it; in the row that followed, Palea, a consistently friendly chief, was struck on the head with an oar by a seaman, the crews of two boats were stoned, and Edgar and the midshipman Vancouver were assaulted with stones, broken oars and staves. The whole episode was a frightening defeat and humiliation.

Back on board, Cook told King 'that the behaviour of the Indians would at last oblige him to use force, for that they must not he said imagine they have gaind an advantage over us'. At daybreak, the *Discovery*'s Officer of the Watch realized that the ship's cutter, moored to a buoy, had been taken away. Clerke immediately went aboard *Resolution* to inform Cook, who ordered boats from both ships to blockade the bay on either side to prevent the escape of any canoe. He himself went ashore in his pinnace with an armed party of marines under their lieutenant, Molesworth Phillips. He had made the fatal decision to take Kalaniʻopuʻu hostage. The king's house was in the village of Kaawaloa, at the north-western end of the bay – the opposite end from Hikiau. They found Kalaniʻopuʻu asleep, and Cook sent in Molesworth Phillips to bring him out. He willingly accompanied them as far as the shore, and was ready to go aboard with them, but 'an immense Mob . . . of at least 2 or 3 thousand People' had gathered (said Phillips). The king's wife was in tears and appeared to be pleading with her husband. Two chiefs took hold of him, made him sit down, and said he should not go aboard. 'The old man now appear'd dejected and frighten'd' (Phillips). The marines were drawn up on the shore facing the crowd. Cook told Phillips that it would be impossible to get Kalaniʻopuʻu aboard 'without killing a number of these People', and seemed to be about to abandon the scheme. But the crowd was now very hostile. It is impossible to work out from the reports of eyewitnesses exactly what happened. It would seem that someone threatened Cook with a stone and a dagger. Cook fired at him with small shot, which had no effect against the mat worn as armour. He then fired his other barrel, loaded with ball, and killed another man. Phillips and his marines were firing into the crowd, and so were the seamen in the boats. But Cook was stabbed from behind with an iron dagger, and he fell face down into the water. He was set upon and killed by a number of assailants with daggers and stones. Four marines were also killed. The pinnace took in Phillips and the rest of the marines. The cutter, lying off, came up and joined in the firing. Incomprehensibly, the launch, under Lieutenant Williamson, pulled further out and made no attempt to assist. The guns of the *Resolution* fired, but had little effect. The boats pulled back to the ships, leaving the bodies to be dragged off the beach.

The underlying reason why Cook was killed will never be known. But I think one must take with great caution the view that he was killed *because* he had been taken for the powerful fertility god Lono. Lono's return from the sky was celebrated every year in the *makahiki* festival, and Cook's ships appeared from over the horizon at the right time, and they departed at the right time, seeming to set out on Lono's expected clockwise circuit of the island. Cook was greeted as and constantly called 'Lono', and not only the homage and reverence and honour shown by everyone, king, chiefs, priests, common people, but also the elaborate religious ceremonies of which he was made the centre, seem to demonstrate that he was assumed to be a god. The theory was given immense impetus by the work of the distinguished anthropologist Marshall Sahlins in a number of works from 1978 to 1995. Sahlins not only provided a formidable context in Polynesian myth and ritual for the identification of Cook as Lono, but an explanation of why he was killed. For kingship involves contest; power is gained by violent usurpation. The god of Kalani'opu'u was the warlike Ku. During *makahiki* Lono is in the ascendant, but the climax of the celebration is the *kali'i*, the ritual mock battle in which Lono cedes to Ku and the reinvigorated king wins back his sovereignty. But Cook was a dying god with a difference. He left at the right time but he came back, and he tried to take Ku's protégé away over the water. Cook-Lono, now *hors-cadre*, had to be killed in earnest.

Sahlins' views were attacked by Gananath Obeyesekere in *The Apotheosis of Captain Cook* in 1992. Obeyesekere believes that the long-lived view that the Hawaiians thought Cook was a god is an illustration of the arrogance of western imperialist culture. The Hawaiians were not such fools. They thought Cook was an extremely powerful chief, they honoured him as they honoured many others with the appellation 'Lono'. They wanted to recruit him in Kalani'opu'u's war against Maui. They installed him as a chief and in the Hikiau ceremony he was dedicated to Ku. He was killed because he tried to kidnap the king, whose god Ku he had insulted by desecrating his shrine (taking the palings for firewood). But after his death, when his remains had been treated with the honour due to a great chief, he was deified.

One does not need to share Obeyesekere's *casus belli*, or accept his reconstruction of the Hawaiian reception of Cook, to feel that his abrasive scepticism has done irretrievable damage to Sahlins' hypothesis. It simply does not seem necessary to make the assumption that Cook was believed to be a god to account either for the Hawaiians' homage or for his death. That he was revered as a person of unique power and importance, that he brought a tincture of the divine with him and was given honour 'that seemd to approach to Adoration'

(King) – all this may be agreed without accepting that the Hawaiians thought he was one of their gods, and it certainly does not need the theory of divine status to explain why he was killed.

It is often held that it was the news that Lieutenant Rickman, carrying out the blockade in the bay, had shot and killed a chief that inflamed the crowd on the shore and triggered the anger that led to the assault on Cook. It may be that this news *had* arrived, and it may have increased the anger of the crowd assembled and armed to protect their king. But the situation, as Gavin Kennedy holds in his book *The Death of Captain Cook* (1978), was one of war. And Cook lost the battle, because of his belief that ultimately Pacific islanders would not be able to withstand European firepower. In all his dealings with 'natives', he was humane, tolerant, patient, anxious for peaceful relations, deeply interested in their customs and manner of life. But there was a strict and firm boundary to his tolerance and patience. It was peaceful coexistence that he wanted, but it *was* coexistence. His presence had to be accepted, and – *nemo me impune lacessit*. It was a constant refrain throughout the three voyages that natives should never be allowed to think that they had defeated him, outwitted him, or got the better of him in any way. His prime sanctions against injury were confiscation and destruction of property (canoes in particular), taking the most powerful person available as hostage, and (if all else failed) firepower.[48]

It is remarked by every commentator that, for whatever reason, Cook was less patient and tolerant, more given to anger, more severe in his punishments, both in regard to his own men and the people they encountered, during this last voyage. His measures to secure the relationship with indigenous people which he required had never really failed, but there probably had to be a point when they would be resisted. The Hawaiians on this second visit to Kealakekua Bay were the first to meet his challenge and repudiate his conditions for coexistence. They would not allow their king to be taken into custody, and they were not deterred by musketry. They won the skirmish, and Cook paid the price of his high-risk strategy with his own life.

48. Cook had known well enough of the danger of relying on fire-power. On the second voyage he wrote (concerning his own people) of the 'Vain opinion that fire Arms rendred them invincible' (see 23 May 1774).

The very marked change in the attitude of the Hawaiians to Cook on this second visit is not really difficult to explain. They had given him everything, and he had gone away. Their foodstuff and livestock were seriously depleted. They did not want him back. Their repudiation of his conditions was a repudiation of his presence, or rather of the western presence. He brought them iron, and they used it to kill him. But they won themselves only a short respite.

GLOSSARY

aboard: to keep the land aboard, or on board, is to keep close to it.
affiatouka: *see fa'itoka*
amplitude: the angle between the sun's rising and due east, or setting and
    due west. Used in calculating the magnetic variation of the compass.
amuse: distract, divert attention.
anchor: the main anchors are the best bower on the starboard bow, and the
    small bower on the port bow. Smaller spare anchors, not having their own
    permanent cables, were the sheet, the kedge, and the stream anchors (the
    last being generally used astern). *See also* coasting anchor.
arii rahi, arii nui: high chief (Society Is.).
arioi: privileged sect or society performing religious and dramatic rituals,
    understood to practise infanticide (Society Is.).
azimuth compass: compass designed to ascertain magnetic variation.

backstays: standing rigging running aft from the top of each mast.
banyan days: meatless days – Monday, Wednesday, Friday (from the name
    for vegetarian Hindu traders).
bear up: to run before the wind by putting the tiller to windward.
bend: knot or hitch to make fast a rope.
bends: the heaviest of the planks or timbers forming a ship's side.
bib: piece of timber helping to support the trestle-trees (q.v.).
bilbo-bolt: the bar of iron on which slide the shackles which fetter those who
    are 'put in irons', fastened with a padlock.
bit: to secure (cable) to the bitts, two posts fastened to the deck.
bittacle: binnacle, the wooden housing of the compass.
black-jack: large tar-coated leather jug.
board: (1) to make boards is to move in zig-zag fashion by tacking; (2) by the
    board is overboard; (3) on board *see* aboard.
boats: ship's boats referred to are, in order of size: the launch or longboat,

equipped with masts and sails; the cutter and the pinnace, for rowing or sailing; the jolly-boat (rounded, tub-like shape); the yawl with four to six oars; and the light skiff.

bolt-rope: rope sewn round the edge of a sail to prevent fraying.

boot-topping: scraping the upper part of the ship's bottom and daubing it with tallow, sulphur and resin.

borrow: approach closely.

bour: (bower) *see* anchor

brail: rope attached to leech or edge of sail to truss it up closely when furling.

brow: gangway.

buttock: the broadest area of a hull's convexity at the stern.

cable: a large rope, normally used with the bower anchors. Also, a length of cable (100–120 fathoms, i.e., 600–720 feet); or the length of a cable, as a measure of distance.

careen: to heave the ship down on one side, e.g., by means of a strong purchase on the masts.

cast: to pull (a ship's head) round.

chains: platforms either side of the ship where the shrouds were secured, and from which the lead was cast in taking soundings.

change: (of the moon) appearance of the new moon.

channel: ('chain-wale') plank forming part of the chains (q.v.).

clew up: to draw the lower corners (clews) of the sails up to the yards.

coasting anchor: anchor on seaward side of moored or anchored ship to prevent her being driven on to the shore.

cod: recess of a bay; literally, bag.

couch: (coach) captain's cabin.

courses: the main lower sails of a square-rigged ship.

crank: top-heavy; unable to carry sail without danger of capsizing.

cutter: *see* boats

'Deping Needle': dipping needle lent to Cook on the first voyage by the Royal Society to assist in investigating terrestrial magnetism.

dridge: dredge (for fish, especially shell-fish).

eatua: (properly *atua*) a god (Tahiti).

emersion: (astron.) reappearance after eclipse or occultation.

ephemeris: astronomical almanac, giving predicted times (GMT) of the positions of celestial bodies. Nevil Maskelyne's *Nautical Almanac and Astronomical Ephemeris* was first produced in 1766.

fascines: (fascines) bundles of sticks used in making fortifications.

fa'itoka: tomb, *marae* (Tonga).

fall: the rope which is the handling end of a tackle.

false fire: combustible compound used as a signalling flare.

fearnought jacket: jacket of heavy woollen cloth.

feness: (finesse) device or stratagem.

fetch: reach, arrive at.

fid: (1) to provide a fid, the square bar of wood used to secure a topmast to a lower mast; (2) a tapered pin of hard wood used to open the strands of a rope during splicing.

fish-hook: iron hook used to secure the flukes of an anchor when it is catted (i.e., hauled up to the cat-head at the bow).

floor: the inner side of a ship's bottom, either side of the keel.

floor-head: that part of the floor (q.v.) nearest the bow.

flux: dysentery.

fly of a jack: flywheel of a mechanical device (such as a turnspit or a spun-yarn winch).

fore-foot: piece of timber which terminates the keel at the fore end, attaching the keel to the stem of the ship.

fother: stop a leak by bandaging the ship with a sail filled with oakum etc.

fusee: spindle in the winding mechanism of a watch.

gerbua: (jerboa) small rodent, using long hind legs for jumping.

gig: fish-spear.

green-talk: (green-talc) nephrite, a form of jade.

guanaco: kind of llama.

gum-dragon: gum from the shrub tragacanth.

gum-lac: dark-red gum used as a dye, and for shellac.

haāhow: (*kakahu*) a woven cloak (Tahiti and New Zealand).

hand: to take in or furl (a square sail).

hanger: short sword.

harren: herring.

haul the wind: to bring the ship closer to the wind.

hawser: a large rope, but smaller than a cable.

heel (verb): to lay a ship on its side, to careen (q.v.).

heppa: (*hippa*) i.e., *he pa* = it is a *pa*, *see pa*.

jolly-boat: *see* boats

junk axe: axe for chopping old cable.
jury mast: makeshift temporary mast.

kava: (cava) the root of the plant *Piper methysticum*, chewed and spat out to make an intoxicating liquor.

larboard: port side of ship.
large: a ship is sailing large when the wind is abaft the beam.
launch: *see* boats
leach: (leech) (naut.) the vertical side of a sail.
leager: (leaguer) large water cask.
league: three miles.
letting: (also liting) inserting a piece of wood into another to make a joint.
log: device for measuring a ship's speed through the water, and so of calculating the distance sailed in a given period. A weighted piece of wood was hove astern; to this was attached the log-line, which had knots every 50 feet; a sand-glass measured the number of knots running past in 30 seconds. This gave the speed in knots (taking a nautical mile as 6000 feet).
longboat: *see* boats
loof: *see* luff
lorryqueet: (lorikeet) brightly coloured parrot from the Malay archipelago.
luff: to bring a ship's head towards the wind by putting the tiller to leeward.

marae: (*morai* etc.) religious centre, temple site (Society Is.).
maro: royal girdle (Tahiti).
matte: beat, punish (Society Is., Tonga).
meridian: (1) noon, or relating to noon; (2) line of longitude.
Mother Cary's chickens: stormy petrels.
musketoon: (also known as wall-piece) large-bore musket mounted on a swivel.

neap: (neep) to lay a ship ashore on a high spring tide so that she will not refloat with the lesser neap tide.

ockam: (oakum) shredded fibres of old rope used for caulking.
offing: the part of the visible sea from the shore or beyond the anchoring ground; also, a position clear of the shore.
open: to bring into view, as when rounding a headland.
open hawse: said of a ship when lying at two anchors the cables of which are not crossing.

pa: (*heppa, hippa*) fortified Maori village.

patu: Maori club or truncheon.

pay: to daub a surface with a mixture of tallow, resin, tar etc. for waterproofing and anti-fouling.

pickets: sharp stakes used for palisades etc.

pinnace: *see* boats

ply: to work to windward by tacking.

portable soup: congealed and dried meat-stock, to be mixed with oatmeal or peas and boiling water, usually issued on banyan days (q.v.).

proe: (*proa*) East Indies sailing boat.

puncheon: very large cask for liquids.

puttock plates: iron bands securing the puttock shrouds, by which the topmast shrouds are connected with the lower shrouds (later known as futtock shrouds).

road: sheltered water near the shore suitable for anchorage.

rob: syrup made from fruit.

ruther: rudder.

salleting: vegetables, green-stuff.

scarfing: a method of joining two pieces of wood end to end by means of slanting cuts. The scarf of the stem is where it is jointed to the keel.

scuttle: opening in the deck or bulkhead; the cover for such an opening.

scuttle cask: open cask (with a hole at its widest point to prevent over-filling) lashed to the quarterdeck for daily use.

sea-cow: the manatee.

sea-horse: the walrus, frequently called morse by sailors.

sea-pie: oyster-catcher, *Haematopus ostralegus*.

seine: net for taking fish near to the surface.

set up: overhaul (shrouds), especially to make taut.

shabander: master of the port (originally a Persian word).

shaddock: citrus fruit resembling a grapefruit.

shade: shelter.

sheathing: a skin of thin boards nailed to the outside of a ship's bottom to protect against worm etc. (Copper sheathing was rejected because of possible corrosion and the difficulty of repairs on a distant voyage.)

sheer-hulk: hulk or body of disused ship fitted with sheers (shears), or lifting gear.

shivers: sheaves (the wheels within blocks).

shoalden: to become shallow, or to find shallow water.

simples: medicinal herbs.

skiff: *see* boats.

sloop: as a naval term, indicates ships of varying rigs used for auxiliary duties.

snow: two-masted ship.

souse: (souce) suddenly and heavily, without warning.

spar-deck: lightweight upper deck.

spontoon: spear.

spritsail: small sail set on a yard below the bowsprit.

spun-yarn winch: small winch with a flywheel for making ropes and spun-yarn.

start: to discharge, pour out.

stays, to miss: when, during tacking, a ship comes head to wind but falls back on the former tack, she is said to miss stays.

staysail: triangular fore-and-aft sail.

stearing: Arctic tern (Beaglehole); there is no other record of this word.

strake: line of planking.

stream anchor: *see* anchor

strike: (of yards, topmasts) to lower or bring down.

studding sail: (stunsail) extra sail, projecting outside the standard sails, laced to extended yards.

sweeps: large oars to assist manoeuvring a ship.

swivel: (swivel-gun) a smaller gun fixed to a swivel, capable of being used in a ship's boat (*compare* musketoon).

tackle: assembly of ropes and blocks, or pulleys, to increase power in lifting or heaving.

tacks: ropes attached to the lower weather corner of the main sails, which are hauled close to the ship's side when sailing close to the wind ('getting the tacks on board').

tara: edible fern, resembling bracken.

tayo, tiyo, tyo: friend (Tahiti and Tonga).

timbers: the curved ribs of a ship, branching vertically up from the keel.

toutou: servant (Tahiti).

trade wind: any regular and constant wind.

train-oil: oil from the blubber of whales etc.

trestle-trees: short pieces of timber placed fore and aft on each side of the masthead to support the topmast.

turn: (of water) as much as can be obtained (from ashore) in a single operation.

waist: middle part of upper deck.

wale: protective rib of wood running along a ship's side.

warp: to move a ship by hauling in a cable attached to an anchor, jetty or stout tree.

watch: when the ship's company is divided into two watches, they work 'watch and watch', four hours on and four hours off; when divided into three watches, it is four hours on and eight hours off.

wear: to put a ship about, on to the other tack, by bringing the stern through the wind (i.e. the reverse of tacking).

whenooa: (*fenua*) ? estate (Raiatea).

windlass: lifting-machine placed forward, differing from the capstan in that its drum was rotated horizontally.

without: on the outside of.

wort: infusion of malt, unfermented.

yard: (1) horizontal spar from which the sails are set; (2) (obs.) penis.

yaw: temporary swing or deviation, intended or unintended, from ship's chosen course.

yawl: *see* boats

INDEX OF PERSONS

Russia. Explored east from Kamchatka in 1728 and 1741. Died of scurvy after wreck on Bering I, 427, 549, 556, 567, 584–5

Bessborough, William Ponsonby (1704–93): Lord of the Admiralty, 1746–56, 498

Bird, John (1709–76): scientific instrument-maker, renowned for 8-foot radius quadrant for the Royal Observatory, 1750. Made the astronomical quadrant used by Cook in Newfoundland, 49

Bligh, William (1754–1817): master *Resolution* 3rd voyage; commander of the *Bounty* 1787-9; Governor of NSW 1806–8, 428, 441–2, 471–2, 474, 528, 566, 601, 604

Boba: *arii rahi* of Taahi, Society Is., 363

Boenechea, Don Domingo de: Spanish navigator, sailed in *Aguila* from Lima and visited Tahiti in 1772 and 1774; died there, 279, 495

Bootie, John: midshipman *Endeavour* 1st voyage; died at sea 4 February 1771, 193

Bougainville, Louis-Antoine de (1729–1811): French soldier, mathematician and navigator. Circumnavigation 1766–69, 9, 55, 279, 283, 333, 374, 403, 526

Bouguenec, M. de (properly Boisguehenneuc): officer with Kerguélen (q.v.), 443

Bouvet de Lozier, Jean-Baptiste-Charles (1705–86): French East India Company captain; discovered Cape Circumcision (Bouvet I.) in 1738, thought of as possible tip of southern continent, 221, 244, 332, 412–13, 416

Boynes, Pierre Étienne Bourgeois de: Secretary of the Marine, France, 443

Buchan, Alexander: artist engaged by Banks, *Endeavour* 1st voyage. An epileptic with gastric problems; died Tahiti 17 April 1769, 44

Burney, Charles (1726–1814): musicologist, 220

Burney, James (1750–1821): son of Dr Charles Burney and brother of Fanny Burney. A B *Resolution* 2nd voyage, transferred to *Adventure* as 2nd lieutenant; 1st lieutenant *Discovery* 3rd voyage. *History of the Discoveries in the South Sea* (1803–17). FRS 1809, 220, 232, 428, 431, 456, 609

Byron, Hon. John, Admiral (1723–86): circumnavigated in *Dolphin* 1764–6, x, 8, 10, 204, 427

Campbell, Vice-Admiral John: introduced Cook to the Council of the Royal Society in May 1768. Cape Campbell (NZ) named after him, 109

Carteret, Philip (d. 1796): commander of *Swallow*, which became separated from *Dolphin* on Wallis's expedition. Discovered Pitcairn and other islands, x, 8, 178, 278

Dozey, John: from 'the Brazils'. AB *Endeavour* 1st voyage; died 7 April 1771, 203

Drake, Sir Francis (*c.* 1540–96): English seaman and circumnavigator, 7

Dunster, Thomas: private of marines *Endeavour* 1st voyage; died 25 January 1771, 16

Earoupa: chief on Lifuka I., Tonga, 467

Edgar, Thomas: master *Discovery* 3rd voyage, 428, 431, 566, 609

Edgcumbe, John : sergeant of marines *Endeavour* 1st voyage; lieutenant of marines, *Resolution* 2nd voyage, 11, 263, 285, 308, 336–7, 347, 376, 389

Egmont, John Perceval, Earl of (1711–70): First Lord of the Admiralty 1763–6, who sponsored the series of Pacific voyages immediately preceding Cook's, 8, 99

Elliott, John (1759–1834): midshipman *Resolution* 2nd voyage, 220, 328

Ereti (Oretti): chief of 'Ohidea', Tahiti, 55, 286

'Etary': stepfather of Vehiatua, 497, 499

Evans, Samuel: quartermaster, boatswain's mate and coxswain of the pinnace, then boatswain, *Endeavour* 1st voyage, 194

Fannin, Peter: master *Adventure* 2nd voyage, 272

Fatafehi Paulaho: 'King of all the Isles', Tonga, 3rd voyage, 471–5, 479, 491

Feenough *see* Finau

Fernandez, Juan (*c.* 1536–*c.*1604): Spanish navigator who discovered the islands in the eastern Pacific named after him, reputed to have discovered other lands, 333–4

Ferrara, Manuel *see* Pereira

Finau ('Feenough'): chief in Tongatupu group, 3rd voyage, 429, 464–72, 475, 490

Fishburn, Mr: shipbuilder of Whitby, 223

Flinders, Matthew (1774–1814): naval officer, hydrographer and explorer, responsible for charting NSW, Tasmania etc., 7

Flower, Peter: seaman *Endeavour* 1st voyage; drowned Rio de Janeiro, 2 December 1768, 23

Forster, George (1754–94): assistant scientist to his father, J. R. Forster, *Resolution* 2nd voyage. Wrote in collaboration with him *A Voyage Round the World* (1777), 220, 228, 264, 346, 390, 427

Forster, Johann Reinhold (1729–98): scientist *Resolution* 2nd voyage. Journal published 1982, 220, 228, 232, 236, 247, 252, 262–74 *passim*, 288–303 *passim*, 307, 317, 336, 346–95 *passim*, 409, 427

Kendall, Larcum: watchmaker. 'K-1', his copy of Harrison's chronometer 'H-4', was aboard *Resolution* 2nd and 3rd voyages, 219, 224, 232

Kennedy, Gavin: author, 612

Kerguélen-Trémarec, Yves-Joseph de: French naval commander, who discovered Kerguelen I., 49° 30's, 69° 30'E, in February 1772, 244, 441, 443–4

King, James (1750–84): 2nd lieutenant *Resolution* 3rd voyage; commander *Discovery* after Cook's death. FRS 1782, 428, 430–31, 434, 446, 449, 451, 463, 509–11, 525, 528, 539, 557, 579, 581, 594, 607–9, 612

Knight, Dr Gowin: inventor of ship's compass designed to show magnetic variation (see also Gregory), 247

Knowel, John *see* Nowell

Koa (Coaa): boy companion of Tiarooa aboard *Resolution* 3rd voyage, 457

Koah (Tou-ah-ah): priest, Hawaii, 605–7

Latouliboula *see* Latunipulu

Latunipulu: 'King' of Tongatapu, 2nd and 3rd voyages, 470

Law, John: surgeon *Discovery* 3rd voyage, then *Resolution* 5 August 1778, 557, 567

Ledyard, John (1751–89): from Connecticut. Corporal of marines *Resolution* 3rd voyage. Published journal of 3rd voyage. Later attempted a walk across America and Russia, 431, 583

Le Maire, Jakob: Dutch navigator who with Schouten went round Cape Horn and far into the Pacific 1615–16, 373

Lind, James (1716–94): Scottish naval surgeon and pioneer of shipboard hygiene. *Treatise of the Scurvy* (1753), 220

Lind, James: Scottish physician and scientist proposed for 2nd voyage, 220, 224, 227

Lindsay, Alexander: AB joining *Endeavour* at Batavia, 1st voyage; died at sea 14 February 1771, 195

Lono: fertility god, Hawaii, 431, 607, 610–11

Lorrain, John: AB *Endeavour* 1st voyage; died 4 April 1771, 203

'Lycurgus' *see* Toobouratomita

Maealiuaki ('Mariwaggy'): principal chief at Tongatapu, 3rd voyage, 489

Magellan, Ferdinand (*c.* 1480–1521): Portuguese navigator. Expedition to the Pacific 1519–21, 7

Magra, James M.: from New York. AB, midshipman 27 May 1771, *Endeavour* 1st voyage. Later served in British consular service (as J. M. Matra), 131–2

Mahine: chief of Moorea, Society Is., 500, 507, 509, 513–15, 517

Mahine (another name for Odiddy, q.v.)

Marion du Fresne, Marc Joseph: French navigator, at first in company with Kerguélen. Killed in New Zealand 1772, 441, 451

Maritata: Tahitian chief, 2nd voyage, 284

Mariwaggy *see* Maealiuaki

Marra, John: gunner's mate *Resolution* 2nd voyage. Several times flogged for insubordination; twice tried to desert (Tahiti and NZ). Author of clandestine journal of the voyage, 355

Mason, Charles: appointed with Jeremiah Dixon by the Royal Society to observe transit of Venus at Bencoolen, but being delayed, they made their observation at Cape Town, 198, 439

Mateamo: Tahitian name for Máximo Rodriguez, Spanish marine left at Tahiti 1775, 495

Mendaña, Álvaro de: Spanish navigator, led expedition to Solomon Is. 1567–9; discovered Marquesas on a 2nd voyage 1595–6, 7, 339, 527

Molyneux, Robert: master *Endeavour* 1st voyage; died 16 April 1771, 10, 106, 134, 150–51, 205

Monkhouse, Jonathan: Brother of the surgeon. Midshipman *Endeavour* 1st voyage; died at sea, 6 February 1771, 11, 43, 62, 142, 194

Monkhouse, William Brougham: from Penrith, Cumberland. Surgeon *Endeavour* 1st voyage; died Batavia 5 November 1770, 11, 38, 41, 54, 66–7, 70–71, 108, 126–8, 185

Monte Negro y Velasca, Don Antonio: captain of Spanish packet at Rio de Janeiro, 23

Moody, Samuel: AB, carpenter's crew *Endeavour* 1st voyage; died at sea 30 January 1771, 193

Morgan, Peter: AB *Endeavour* 1st voyage, joining at Batavia; died at sea 27 February 1771, 195

Morion *see* Marion du Fresne

Mouat, Alexander: midshipman *Discovery* 3rd voyage; disrated for desertion at Raiatea December 1777; reinstated April 1780, 526

Müller, Gerhard Friedrich: historian. *Voyages from Asia to America* (1761, 1764), 428, 585

Narborough, Sir John (1640–88): English naval captain, explorer of the South Sea, 8

Nicholson, James: AB *Endeavour* 1st voyage; died at sea 31 January 1771, 57, 193

Norton, Sir Fletcher (1716–89): Attorney-General 1763–5. Speaker of the House of Commons 1778–80, 581

Simpson, Alexander: AB *Endeavour* 1st voyage; died at sea 21 February 1771, 195

Sind, Ivan: Russian navigator, 1764, 1767, 583, 585

Smock, Henry: AB, carpenter's mate *Resolution* 2nd voyage; died 29 October 1772, 231

Solander, Daniel Carl (1732–82): Swedish pupil of Linnaeus. Naturalist *Endeavour* 1st voyage. FRS 1764. Keeper of Natural History Department, British Museum 1773, 11, 14, 22, 27, 41–105 *passim*, 122–37 *passim*, 154, 170, 174–5, 220, 224, 227

Spanberg, Martin: companion of Bering, 583

Sparrman, Anders: Swedish naturalist. Joined *Resolution* at Cape of Good Hope as Forster's assistant 2nd voyage. *Voyage to the Cape of Good Hope* (1783; English translation 1785), 220, 232, 291–4, 366

Spöring, Hermann Diedrich: Swedish. Assistant naturalist *Endeavour* 1st voyage; died 25 January 1771, 11, 54, 175, 192

Stählin, Jacob von: historian of Russian exploration, published (with map) 1774, 427, 572, 577, 581, 583, 586

Stephens, Henry: AB *Endeavour* 1st voyage, 16, 95

Stephens, Philip (1725–1809): Secretary to the Admiralty 1763–95. FRS 1771, 48, 118, 182

Suckling, Maurice (1725–78): uncle of Nelson. Comptroller of the Navy from 1775, 549

Sutherland, Forby ('Torby'): AB *Endeavour* 1st voyage; died Botany Bay 1 May 1770, 125

Ta'ata-uraura: chief of Outer Teva, Tahiti, 2nd voyage, 284

Taiata: servant to Tupaia, 1st voyage, 65, 77

Tairatutu: mother of Tiaraooa, q.v., 457

Taoofa: (?same as Tioona, 2nd voyage) chief on Eua, Tonga, 3rd voyage, 488, 490–91

Tapa: chief on Nomuka, Tonga, 3rd voyage, 463–7

Tareederria *see* Teri'itari'a.

Tasman, Abel Janszoon (1603–c. 1659): Dutch navigator. In December 1642, sailing east from Van Diemen's Land, he sighted NZ and anchored in 'Murderer's Bay' in Cook Strait, where four men were killed, 8, 97, 101, 118, 120, 126, 254, 269, 299, 307, 372, 450

Tchirekoff *see* Chirikov

Tee *see* Ti'i

Teeratu: supposed by Cook to be the name of a king or high chief in NZ, probably through a misunderstanding, 91

Tunley, James: AB *Endeavour* 1st voyage, 58

Tupaia: *arii* and priest from Raiatea. Taken aboard *Endeavour* at Tahiti with his servant Taiata 1st voyage; both died Batavia 1770, 65–110 *passim*, 122–3, 133, 152, 177, 182, 189–90, 274–5, 283, 285, 295, 321, 363

Tupia *see* Tupaia

Tupoulangi (Toobow): chief of Nomuka, Tonga, 3rd voyage, 463, 465

Tupouto'a (Tooboweitoa): chief of Tongatapu, 3rd voyage, 473

Tuteha (Tootaha, Toutaha): Tahitian chief, nicknamed Hercules, 1st voyage; killed 1773, 41, 47–62 *passim*, 283, 285–6, 364, 506

Uru (Oo ooru): titular *arii rahi* of Raiatea, Society Is., 2nd voyage, 363–4

Vancouver, George (1757–98): AB *Resolution* 2nd voyage; AB then midshipman *Discovery* 3rd voyage. Surveyed NW American coast 1791–5. Captain 1794, 7, 221, 609

Van Diemen, Antony (1593–1645): Governor-General, Dutch East Indies, 1631–45, 8

Vehiatua (Oheatua, Waheatua): a titular name. *Arii rahi* of Teva in Taiarapu, southern Tahiti, 2nd and 3rd voyages, 284, 349, 496–7, 500, 505, 510

Wafer, Lionel: ship's surgeon and companion of Dampier, 8

Waheatua *see* Vehiatua

Wales, William (*c.* 1734–98): astronomer *Resolution* 2nd voyage, 220, 228, 232, 255, 263, 285, 345, 386, 389, 399, 401, 407, 421

Walker, John: shipowner of Whitby, 10, 219

Wallis, Samuel (1728–95): in command of *Dolphin* in her circumnavigation of 1766–8, during which Tahiti was discovered (and named King George's Island), x, 8, 10, 11, 32, 41, 66, 178, 221, 334, 373, 499, 504

Walter, Richard: chaplain of *Centurion*, Anson's flagship in his voyage round the world 1740–44. Gave his name to the official narrative of the voyage, 32, 537

Watman, William: AB *Resolution* 2nd and 3rd voyages; died Hawaii 1 February 1779, 608

Watt, Sir James (b. 1914): Surgeon Vice-Admiral and medical Director-General of the Navy 1972–7, xii

Webb, Clement: private of marines *Endeavour* 1st voyage, 61–4

Webber, John (1752–93): of Swiss descent. Landscape painter *Resolution* 3rd voyage, 428, 456, 501, 526, 534, 584

Wedgeborough, William: private of marines *Resolution* 2nd voyage; drowned 22 December 1774, 389, 403

INDEX OF PLACES

Note. Many places have more than one name. Normally, the main entry is the name as given in the text, with cross references from variant forms or alternative names. When, however, the text gives Cook's transcription of a native name (e.g., Annamocka), and Beaglehole provides a more correct version (Nomuka), the main entry is under Beaglehole's corrected version with cross-references from all other versions. Names given by a previous navigator, which Cook sometimes uses (in this case, Rotterdam) are also indexed. Sometimes it is also desirable to index and cross-reference a modern name, when different.

In indicating regions, Cook's appellations are used for the eastern coast of Australia (New South Wales = NSW), the Hawaiian Islands (Sandwich Islands), and Tasmania (Van Diemen's Land).

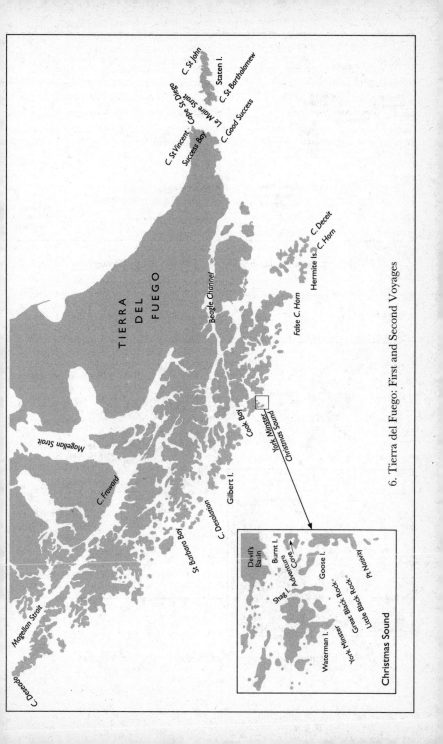

6. Tierra del Fuego: First and Second Voyages

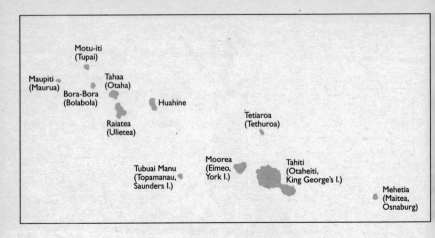

7. Society Islands: First, Second and Third Voyages

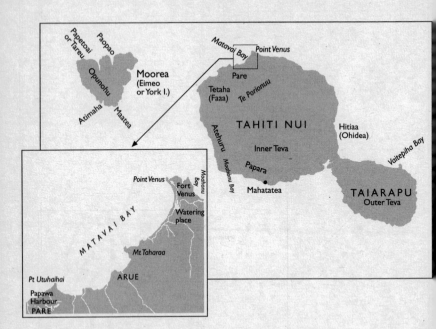

8. Tahiti and Moorea: First, Second and Third Voyages

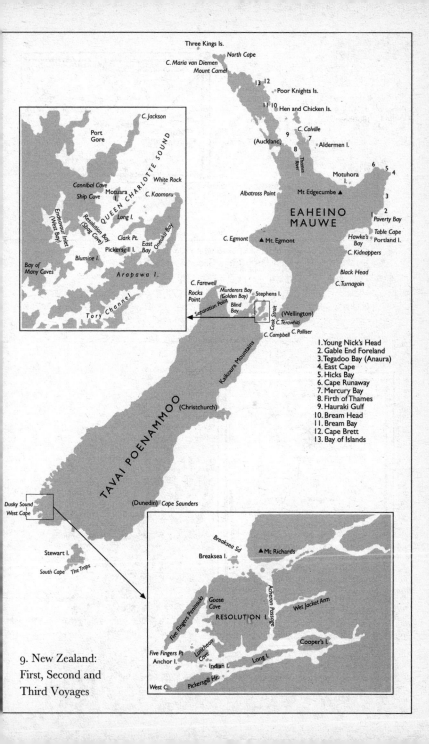

9. New Zealand:
First, Second and
Third Voyages

1. Young Nick's Head
2. Gable End Foreland
3. Tegadoo Bay (Anaura)
4. East Cape
5. Hicks Bay
6. Cape Runaway
7. Mercury Bay
8. Firth of Thames
9. Hauraki Gulf
10. Bream Head
11. Bream Bay
12. Cape Brett
13. Bay of Islands

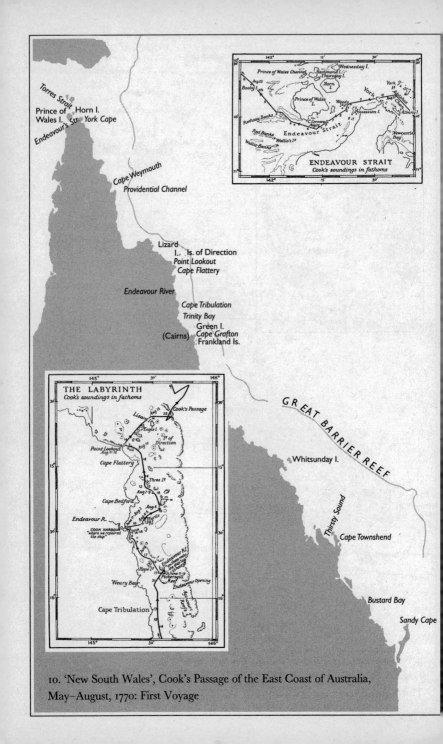

10. 'New South Wales', Cook's Passage of the East Coast of Australia, May–August, 1770: First Voyage

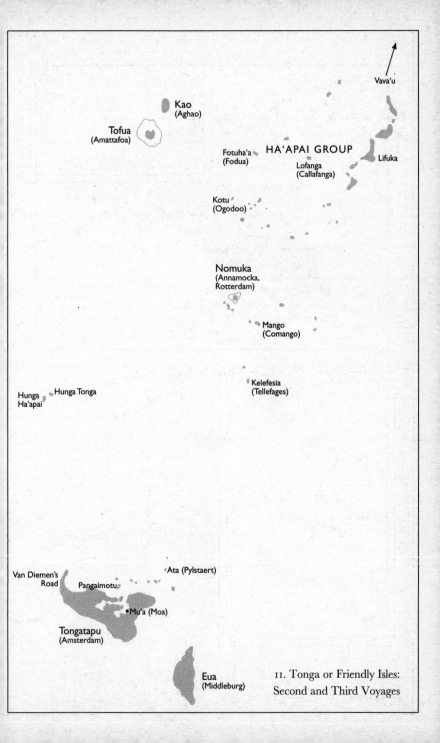

Kao
(Aghao)

Tofua
(Amattafoa)

Fotuha'a
(Fodua)

HA'APAI GROUP

Lofanga
(Callafanga)

Vava'u

Lifuka

Kotu
(Ogodoo)

Nomuka
(Annamocka,
Rotterdam)

Mango
(Comango)

Kelefesia
(Tellefages)

Hunga
Ha'apai

Hunga Tonga

Ata (Pylstaert)

Van Diemen's
Road

Pangaimotu

Mu'a (Moa)

Tongatapu
(Amsterdam)

Eua
(Middleburg)

11. Tonga or Friendly Isles:
Second and Third Voyages

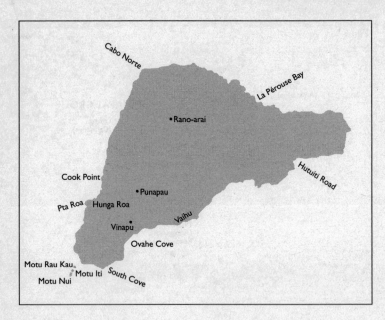

12. Easter Island: Second Voyage

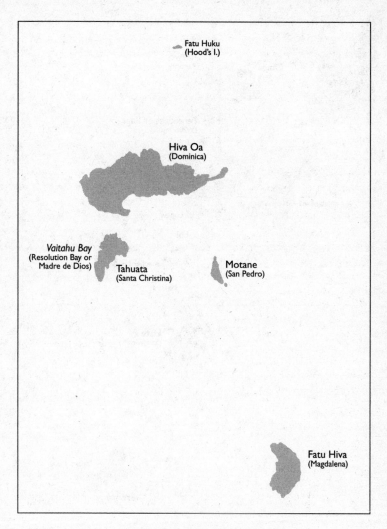

Fatu Huku
(Hood's I.)

Hiva Oa
(Dominica)

Vaitahu Bay
(Resolution Bay or
Madre de Dios)

Tahuata
(Santa Christina)

Motane
(San Pedro)

Fatu Hiva
(Magdalena)

13. Marquesas Islands: Second Voyage

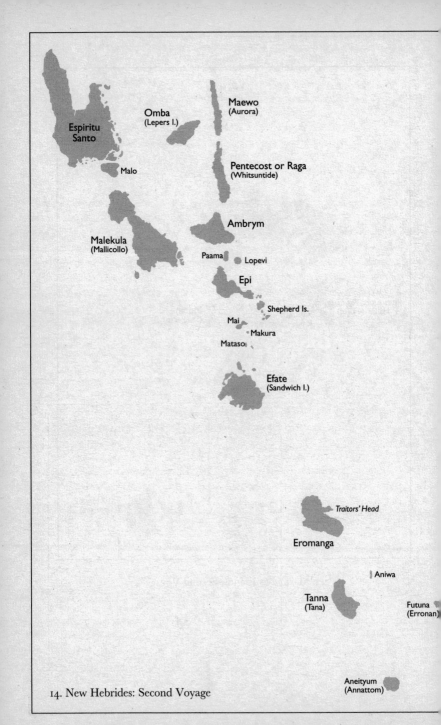

Espiritu
Santo

Omba
(Lepers I.)

Maewo
(Aurora)

Malo

Pentecost or Raga
(Whitsuntide)

Ambrym

Malekula
(Mallicollo)

Paama   Lopevi

Epi

Shepherd Is.

Mai

Makura

Mataso

Efate
(Sandwich I.)

Traitors' Head

Eromanga

Aniwa

Tanna
(Tana)

Futuna
(Erronan)

Aneityum
(Annattom)

14. New Hebrides: Second Voyage

15. Sandwich Islands (Hawaiian Islands): Third Voyage

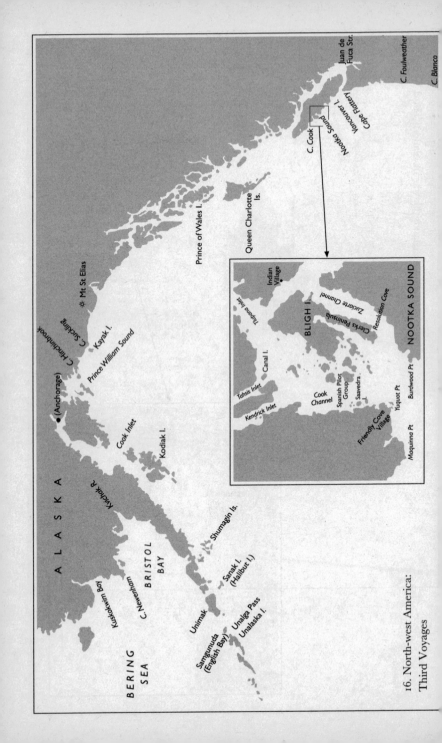

16. North-west America: Third Voyages

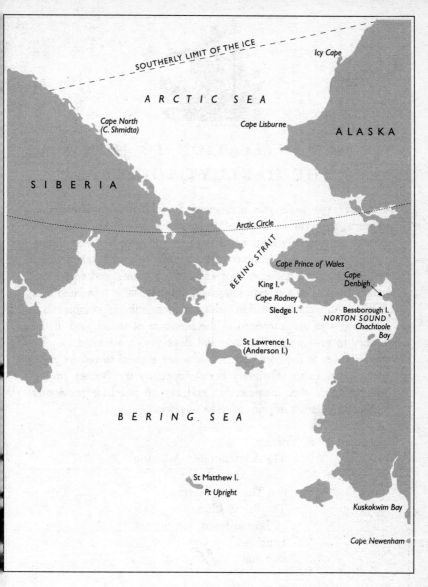

17. The Bering Sea and Arctic Sea: Third Voyage

AN INVITATION TO JOIN
THE HAKLUYT SOCIETY

For over 150 years this prestigious Society, whose membership exceeds 2,300 in over sixty-five countries worldwide, has been publishing scholarly editions of voyages and travels. Texts dating from the seventh to the nineteenth centuries are used, taken either from manuscript documents or early rare editions, and where the original text is in a foreign language, the material is translated into English. All texts are provided with a modern editorial commentary.

Those who are interested in the literature of travel, and in the history of geographical science and discovery, are invited to join. No proposer is required and members are entitled to receive *free*, all volumes in the Ordinary Series issued by the Society during the period of their membership and also to purchase previously published volumes in print at reduced prices.

For more details, contact:

> The Administrative Assistant
> The Hakluyt Society
> c/o The Map Library
> The British Library
> 96 Euston Road
> London
> NW1 2DB

> Tel: 01986 788359
> Fax: 01986 788181
> E-mail: office@hakluyt.com
> Website: www.hakluyt.com